Second International Conference on Dependency Linguistics

(DepLing 2013)

Prague, Czech Republic
27-30 August 2013

Editors:

Eva Hajičová
Kim Gerdes
Leo Wanner

ISBN: 978-1-62993-538-6

Printed from e-media with permission by:

Curran Associates, Inc.
57 Morehouse Lane
Red Hook, NY 12571

Some format issues inherent in the e-media version may also appear in this print version.

Printed by Curran Associates, Inc. (2014)

Association for Computational Linguistics
209 N. Eighth Street
Stroudsburg, Pennsylvania 18360

Phone: 1-570-476-8006
Fax: 1-570-476-0860

acl@aclweb.org

Additional copies of this publication are available from:

Curran Associates, Inc.
57 Morehouse Lane
Red Hook, NY 12571 USA
Phone: 845-758-0400
Fax: 845-758-2634
Email: curran@proceedings.com
Web: www.proceedings.com

DepLing 2013

Proceedings of the Second International Conference on Dependency Linguistics

August 27 – 30, 2013, Prague, Czech Republic

edited by

Eva Hajičová, Kim Gerdes, Leo Wanner

ÚFAL

LINDAT CLARIN

META-NET

Vilém Mathesius Foundation Prague

ČSKI

khresmoi
MEDICAL INFORMATION ANALYSIS & RETRIEVAL

CLARIN ERIC
Common Language Resources and Technology Infrastructure

Editors and program committee co-chairs

Kim Gerdes, Université Sorbonne Nouvelle (co-chair, editor)
Eva Hajičová, Charles University in Prague (co-chair, editor)
Leo Wanner, Universitat Pompeu Fabra (co-chair, editor)
Jiří Mírovský (technical editor)
Eduard Bejček (technical editor)

Reviewers

Margarita Alonso-Ramos, Universidade da Coruña
David Beck, University of Alberta
Xavier Blanco, UAB
Igor Boguslavsky, Universidad Politécnica de Madrid
Bernd Bohnet, University Stuttgart
Marie Candito, Université Paris 7 / INRIA
Silvie Cinková, Charles University in Prague
Benoit Crabbé, Paris 7 et INRIA
Eric De La Clergerie, INRIA
Denys Duchier, Université d'Orléans
Dina El Kassas, Minya University
Koldo Gojenola, University of the Basque Country UPV/EHU
Thomas Gross, Aichi University
Barbora Hladká, Charles University in Prague
Richard Hudson, UCL
Leonid Iomdin, Russian Academy of Sciences
Sylvain Kahane Modyco, Université Paris Ouest & CNRS / Alpage, INRIA
Marco Kuhlmann, Uppsala University
François Lareau, Macquarie University
Alessandro Lenci, University of Pisa
Haitao Liu, Zhejiang University
Henning Lobin, Justus-Liebig-University Giessen
Markéta Lopatková, Charles University in Prague
Christopher Manning, Stanford University
Jasmina Milićević, Dalhousie University
Henrik Høeg Müller, Copenhagen Business School (CBS)
Alexis Nasr, Université de la Méditerranée Laboratoire d'Informatique Fondamentale
Joakim Nivre, Uppsala University
Kemal Oflazer, Carnegie Mellon University in Qatar
Martha Palmer, University of Colorado
Jarmila Panevová, Charles University in Prague
Alain Polguère, Université Nancy 2
Prokopis Prokopidis, Institute for Language and Speech Processing, Athena Research and Innovation Center
Ines Rehbein, Potsdam University
Dipti Sharma, IIIT
Pavel Straňák, Charles University in Prague
Gertjan van Noord, University of Groningen
Daniel Zeman, Charles University in Prague
Zdeněk Žabokrtský, Charles University in Prague

Published by

MATFYZPRESS Publishing House
of the Faculty of Mathematics and Physics
Charles University in Prague
Sokolovská 83, 186 75 Praha 8, Czech Republic
as the 434th publication

Designed and printed by Reprostředisko UK MFF
Sokolovská 83, 186 75 Praha 8, Czech Republic

First edition, Praha 2013

Organized by the Charles University in Prague, Faculty of Mathematics and Physics, Institute of Formal and Applied Linguistics (ÚFAL MFF UK).

Foreword

The DepLing 2013 conference is the second meeting in the newly established series of international conferences on dependency linguistics started in 2011 by the first DepLing in Barcelona. The response to the initiative to organize special meetings devoted to the dependency linguistic theory (which nowadays seems to be in the forefront of interests among both theoretical and computational linguists) was quite supportive. We do hope that the present conference will manage to keep pace with the high standards set at the Barcelona meeting.

To make all the accepted contributions available to the linguistic community and beyond, we have decided to publish a full volume of Proceedings of both oral papers and poster presentations. The coverage is rather broad: from the formal point of view, the papers present different theoretical dependency models or compare the dependency approach with the phrase structure based one. Issues pertaining to different language layers range from morphology and morphosyntax to syntax proper and even discourse, and language material is supplied for 10 languages both modern and old or ancient. Several papers describe the application of dependency analysis to the build-up of monolingual and multilingual treebanks.

We are proud that the invitation to give a plenary speech was accepted by two prominent scholars, Richard Hudson as one of the main figures in dependency linguistics and father of the Word Grammar, and Aravind Joshi, a prominent representative of formal description of language and the original proponent of the tree-adjoining grammar formalism.

Our sincere thanks go to the members of the Scientific Committee, who have undertaken the task to read three papers each and have sent in – at least in majority – detailed comments and suggestions.

We are also most grateful to our young colleagues from the Institute of Formal and Applied Linguistics (ÚFAL), Charles University in Prague, who took care of the conference management system (through EasyChair) and prepared the Proceedings volume, first of all Filip Jurčíček, Jiří Mírovský, and Eduard Bejček. Our thanks also go to Mrs. Anna Kotěšovcová, who was our link to the MatfyzPress Publishers.

Last but not least, we gratefully acknowledge the financial and moral support given by the ÚFAL Management, by the LINDAT/CLARIN infrastructural project funded by the Ministry of Education, Youth and Sports of the Czech Republic, by the 7th framework EC-funded META-NET network and the Khresmoi integrated project, and by the two Czech Grant Agency projects, namely P406/12/0658 (Coreference, discourse relations and information structure in a contrastive perspective) and P406/2010/0875 (Computational Linguistics: Explicit description of language and annotated data focused on Czech).

Welcome to DepLing 2013 in Prague and have a good and rewarding time there!

Kim Gerdes Eva Hajičová Leo Wanner

DepLing 2013

the Second International Conference on Dependency Linguistics
August 27 - 30, 2013, Prague, Czech Republic

Organized by

Institute of Formal and Applied Linguistics (ÚFAL)
Faculty of Mathematics and Physics
Charles University in Prague
Czech Republic
(http://ufal.mff.cuni.cz)

and

CONFORG, s.r.o.
Czech Republic
(http://www.conforg.cz)

in the historic building at

Malostranské nám. 25
118 00 Prague 1
Czech Republic

Table of Contents

Dependency Structure and Cognition

Invited talk

Richard Hudson
emeritus professor in the Department of Phonetics and Linguistics
University College London
Great Britain
r.hudson@ucl.ac.uk

1 Language and cognition

We probably all share an interest in syntax, so we would dearly love a clear and certain answer to the question: what is syntactic structure like? Is it based on dependencies between words, or on phrases? What kinds of relation are there? And so on. But before we can answer relatively specific questions like these, we must first answer a much more general question: What kind of thing do we think language is? Or maybe: Where do we think language is – nowhere, in society, in our minds? Our answer will decide what basic assumptions we make, and how our discipline, linguistics, relates to other disciplines.

Is language a set of abstract patterns like those of mathematics, without any particular location? This is a popular answer, and makes a good deal of sense. After all, what is language if not abstract patterning? The patterns made by words in a sentence, or by segments in a syllable, are certainly abstract and regular, and can be studied as a branch of mathematics – as indeed they have been studied and still are studied in linguistics. For some researchers who take this approach, the aim is elegance and consistency; so in a competition between alternative analyses, the prize goes to the simplest one. For others, though, the goal is a working computational system, so the criterion is some kind of efficiency. One problem for this approach is that the material in which these patterns are embedded is inescapably human activity; in contrast with mathematical patterns, linguistic patterns only exist because humans create them. And another problem with the mathematical approach is that it provides few explanations for why language is as it is. If language patterns always turned out to be the most elegant possible patterns, the mathematical approach would indeed explain why; but they don't, and as we all know, language can be frustratingly messy.

Another possible answer is that language is a set of conventions that exist in society. For some linguists the social character of language is fundamental (Halliday and Matthiessen 2006), and they like to focus on the role of language in 'construing' experience. Language exists 'out there'in the community, as well as being shared by all its members; so the methods of sociology and cultural anthropology should apply. Similarly, some sociolinguists see the social patterning of variation as belonging to the community, though not to any of its members (Labov 1972). The trouble with this approach is that communities are much harder to define, and much less homogeneous, than we might expect; and once again, the basic data are irreducibly individual products – individuals speaking and listening to each other.

The third answer – and this is my preferred option – is that language is an example of individual knowledge. As in the first answer, the knowledge involves mathematically expressible patterning; and as in the second, it has a strong social dimension – after all, we learn the knowledge from others in our community, and we reveal our knowledge through our own social behaviour as speakers and listeners. But ultimately language is a matter of individual psychology. We learn it as individuals, we use it as individuals, and others know us, as individuals, through it. Who could deny this? And yet the other views of language have been very influential, and still are.

As an important example of its influence, take the criterion of elegance or simplicity. This is very widely accepted in linguistics, and those of us who support dependency structure might argue that one of the attractions of our approach, in contrast with phrase structure, is its simplicity. Just count the nodes! We have precisely one node per word, whereas a phrase-structure analysis contains all these word nodes, plus extra nodes for the phrases. But is this criterion really relevant? If we were physicists, it certainly

Proceedings of the Second International Conference on Dependency Linguistics (DepLing 2013), pages 1–11,
Prague, August 27–30, 2013.

would be; but we aren't. We're studying a part of the human mind, and any human mind is the product of a long and complicated experience; so why should we believe that any mind is simple? As cognitive linguists argue, we learn our language from 'usage' (Barlow and Kemmer 2000) – from the millions of examples of language that we hear, each embedded in a very specific social context. And we interpret each example in terms of the examples that went before, using a growing system of concepts. Nothing there is simple: for any given language, thousands or millions of speakers all follow different routes to a slightly different adult grammar, with numerous false starts and detours on the way. It's easy to understand why linguists welcome the idea of a simple, perfect and uniform language as a way to escape from this buzz of confusion and complexity. But, like the drunk looking for the keys that he has dropped, we have a choice: we can look under the street lamp, where the light is good; or we can look over in the dark corner, where we know that we actually dropped the keys – a choice between esthetics and truth.

In short, I believe we have to accept that language is part of cognition. And with that acceptance comes the principle that our theories of language structure should be compatible with cognitive science – in fact, our theories are part of cognitive science, and arguably a particularly important part of cognitive science, given the relative clarity and detail of the data found in language. The reality that we are trying to capture in our theories is what is often called 'psychological reality'.

But, you may object, how can we know what is psychologically real? It's true that I can't even look inside my own mind, let alone inside someone else's mind; but then, psychology has moved a long way from the bad old days of introspection, and has findings which are supported by very robust experimental methods. The rest of this paper is an attempt to develop some of the consequences of taking these findings seriously when building models of language. I shall pay special attention to their consequences for my own theory, Word Grammar (**WG**, Hudson 1984, Hudson 1990, Hudson 2007, Hudson 2010, Gisborne 2010, Eppler 2010).

But before I go on to consider some of these findings, I must admit that there is a way to avoid my arguments. This is to claim that although language is part of cognition, it is actually different from everything else – a unique 'module' of the mind (Chomsky 1986, Fodor 1983). Our generative colleagues are free to invent principles, parameters and structures at will, unconstrained by anything but their basic formal assumptions and the purely 'linguistic' facts. As you can guess, I don't think this is a good way to study language because I believe that language is, in fact, just like the rest of cognition in spite of all the attempts to show the contrary.

2 Some things we know about cognition

We start with four very elementary findings which can be found in introductory textbooks on cognitive psychology such as Reisberg (2007), concerning networks, mental relations, complexity and classification.

Knowledge is a **network** of concepts in which each concept is associated with a number of other concepts. These 'associations' explain why experiences evoke neighbouring memories – memories that share links (in the network) to the same concepts; why we make mistakes (including speech errors) when we choose a neighbouring concept in place of the intended target; and why an object in a psychological laboratory 'primes' objects that are its neighbours (as when hearing the word *doctor* makes the word *nurse* easier to retrieve than it would otherwise be). The notion of networks explains all these familiar facts about cognition. But if knowledge in general is a network, and if language is part of knowledge, then language itself must be a network. And that includes not only the whole of language – the grammar and phonology as well as the lexicon – but also the utterances that we interpret in terms of this network of knowledge.

But even though the notion of 'association' is important, we can be sure that the links in our mental network are not merely associations, but **relations** of many different kinds. Just think of all the words you know for kinship relations – words such as *father*, *aunt* and *ancestor*, each of which names a relationship. Then think of all the other person-to-person relationships you can name, including 'father-in-law', 'neighbour' and 'boss'? And then think of the prepositions and nouns you know for non-human relationships, such as *beneath*, *opposite* and *consequence*. The point is that we seem to be able to freely create and learn relational concepts, just as we do non-relational concepts such as 'bird' and 'Londoner'. This conclusion takes us a long way from theories in which our minds recognise only a small, innate set of inbuilt relations called 'syntactic functions' or 'semantic roles'.

However, alongside these learnable relations there is at least one fundamental relation which may well be innate: what AI researchers often call 'is-a', as in 'penguin is-a bird', relating a subcategory to its 'supercategory'. This is the relation that allows all generalisations, so it is bound to play an important part in any theory of cognition. Mental networks seem to be built round taxonomies of concepts related in this way, but with multiple other inter-relations as well. Since this is such an important relation, it has its own special notation in WG: a small triangle whose (large) base rests on the (large) supercategory and whose apex points at the subcategory. This notation is illustrated in the taxonomy of my family members in Figure 1.

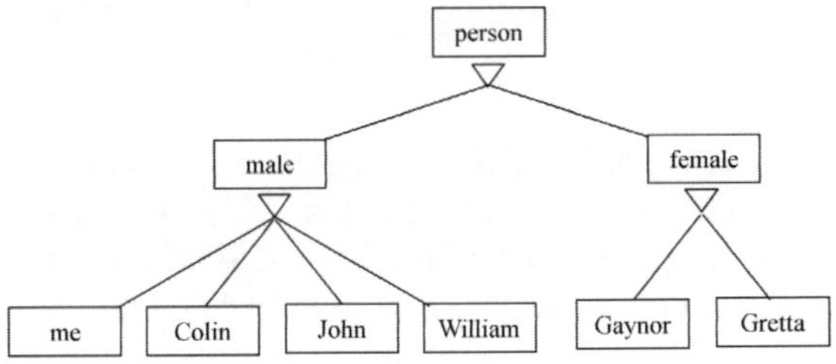

Figure 1: A taxonomy of people

The third relevant claim of elementary psychology is that these knowledge networks can be very **complex**. This is clearly true of language, but other areas of knowledge also turn out to be astonishingly complex. Take once again the example of kinship, as illustrated in Figure 2 by the male members of my immediate family.

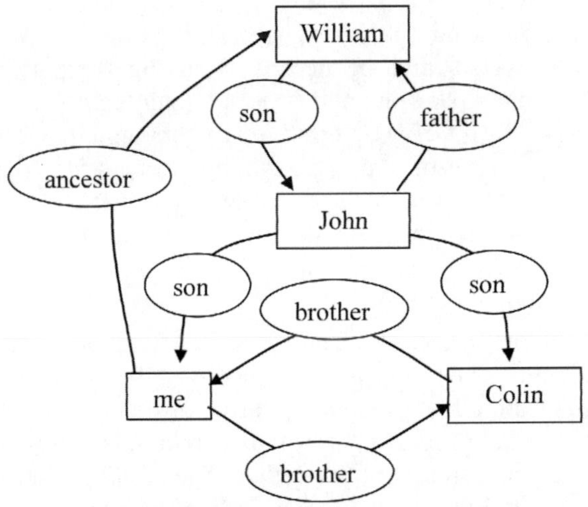

Figure 2: My family

The structure in Figure 2 is part of the same network as that in Figure 1, and like this, it must be part of my cognition because every bit of it is something I know. I know all the people named in the square boxes, and I know how they are (or were) related to each other. Even this tiny fragment of my total knowledge illustrates some important formal properties of the human cognitive network:

- Relations aren't merely 'associations', but are classified (as 'father', 'son' and so on).
- Relations are asymmetrical, in the sense that each one consists of an 'argument' and a 'value' (so the 'son' relation near the top of the diagram has William as its argument and John as its value, showing that John is William's son). In the notation that I use in this diagram (and indeed in later ones), the arrow points towards the value.
- Mutual relations are possible: if John is William's son, then William is John's father; and two individuals may even each have the same relation to the other, as where Colin and I are each other's brother.
- Relations may be recursive. The relevant example here is 'ancestor', which has a recursive definition (A is the ancestor of B either if A is a parent of B, or if A is a parent of an ancestor of B).

These formal properties can be described mathematically, but the one thing they don't do is to limit the space of possibilities: almost anything seems to be possible. This is a very different approach to formal structures compared with the familiar aim of explaining grammars by limiting their formal properties.

The fourth important fact about cognition is that classification ('categorization') is based on **prototypes** – typical cases where a bundle of properties (such as beaks, two legs, flying, feathers and laying eggs which define the typical bird) coincide – with other cases (such as non-flying birds) arranged round these typical ones as more or less exceptional or unclear examples. This way of organising knowledge requires a special kind of logic, called '**default inheritance**', in which generalisations apply 'by default', but can be overridden.

It seems reasonable to assume, therefore, that our minds are capable of handling complex networks in which there are at least two kinds of relations between nodes: the basic 'is-a' relation of categorization and default inheritance, and an open-ended list of relational concepts which are created as needed and learned in the same way as other concepts. This is the mental machinery that we can, and indeed must, assume when building our theories of how language is organised – again, a very different starting point from the rather simple and sparse assumptions behind most of the familiar theories in either the PS or DS families.

3 Dependencies and phrases

These assumption are directly relevant to the debate between PS and DS. The question is how we represent the words in a sentence to ourselves: do we represent them as parts to larger wholes (phrases), or do our mental representations link them directly to one another? For example, is *cows* in (1) related only to the phrase *cows moo*, or is it related directly to *moo*?

(1) Cows moo.

The PS answer evolved out of Wundt's rather impoverished theory of cognition which concentrated on the relation between a whole 'idea' and its immediate parts – the origins of Bloomfield's Immediate-constituent analysis, which in turn led to Chomsky's Phrase structure (Percival 1976). PS analysis rests crucially on the assumption that the whole-part relation between a phrase and its parts is the only possible relation (although of course even PS users talk informally about dependencies such as 'long-distance dependencies').

But the evidence from section 2 shows that the human mind, which creates sentence structure, can handle much, much more complicated structures than whole-part relations. Just think of my family. If we assume, as surely we must, that the full power of the human mind is available for language, and if we can handle direct relations between people then surely we can also handle direct DS relations between words. Moreover, this conclusion confirms what grammarians have been saying for two thousand years about valency links between words. In the fourth century BC, Panini showed the need for semantic relations between verbs and their arguments, and in the second century AD Apollonius pointed out how verbs and prepositions required their objects to have different case inflections (Robins 1967:37). Since then, and through the Arabic grammarians and our Middle Ages up to recent times, these semantic and syntactic links between words have been a regular part of a grammarian's work. It seems very clear, therefore, that our minds are not only capable of recognising word-word dependencies, but actually do recognise them. And in our example, we can be sure that *cows* and *moo* are held together by a direct bond which explains why *moo* has no {s} (in contrast with *the cow moos*).

But where does that leave the notion of phrase? Evidence in favour of word-word relations is not in itself evidence against whole-part relations. By recognising a dependency between *cows* and *moo*, are we also recognising a larger unit, *cows moo*? Here the answer is much less clear, at least to me even after nearly forty years of thinking about it. But I am sure of three things.

- The larger unit, if it exists, is no more than the sum of its parts, because all of its properties – its meaning, its syntactic classification and so on – are the properties of its head word. (I explain in section 8 how the head word carries the meaning of the whole phrase.)
- The larger unit does have boundaries, which certainly are relevant at least for punctuation which marks phrase boundaries: *Cows moo.* No doubt the same is true of intonation. And in phonology and morphology, it is widely accepted that some phenomena are limited to the 'edges' of constituents (Hyman 2008). But maybe that's all there is to a phrase: just its boundaries.
- Unary branching – where a phrase has just one constituent – is where PS is most vulnerable. If we say that *cows* is a noun phrase consisting of a single word, then we are stretching the notion of 'part' beyond its limit. The fact is, or seems to me to be, that we don't normally allow objects to have just one part. For instance, if a box normally has a lid, but we lose the lid, we don't think of the box as having one part. What would that part be, other than the box itself? But if we forbid unary branching, we lose one of the main supposed benefits of phrases, which is to allow generalisations across complex phrases and single words (so that *cows*, *brown cows* and even *they* count as 'noun phrases').

In short, we can be much more sure about the mental existence of word-word dependencies than about that of phrases; but we're certainly capable of recognising whole-part relations, so we can't rule them out altogether. The result is that we certainly need an analysis like the righthand one in Figure 3, but we may also need to include the lefthand structure. (I discuss the unorthodox DS notation below.)

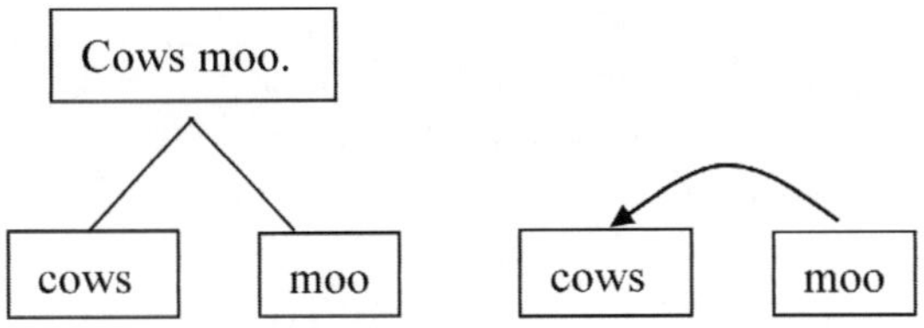

Figure 3: PS or DS?

4 Bundles or levels?

Dependencies do many different jobs, from carrying 'deep' information such as semantic roles to carrying more 'surface' information such as word order and inflectional categories. Moreover, dependency relations can be classified in terms of familiar syntactic functions such as 'subject', whose definitions typically span a range of different kinds of information from deep to surface (Keenan 1976). One major theoretical question for DS analysis is what to do with this diversity of information 'carried' by dependencies. As so often in theoretical questions, we find 'splitters' and 'lumpers' – those who split dependencies into different types according to the information they carry, and those who lump the different relations together. Once again, our cognitive assumptions throw important light on the question.

Remember that relational concepts (such as dependencies) are concepts, so like other concepts, their main function is to bring together properties that tend to combine. For instance, the relation 'father' brings together biological properties (procreation) with social properties (parental rights and responsibilities), just as the closely related concept 'male' does. Splitters might argue that the biological and social are importantly different, so they should be separated to give 'b-father', carrying the biological properties, and 's-father' with the social ones. But lumpers would argue – rightly, in my opinion – that this misses the point. After all, the two property-sets tend to coincide, so even if you distinguish two kinds of father, you also need some mechanism to show the special connection between them. So why not simply call them both 'father', and allow the 'father' prototype to have both sets of properties? The existence of exceptional cases (men who father children without looking after them, or vice versa) is easily accommodated thanks to the logic of default inheritance.

Exactly the same argument supports the lumpers in syntax against those who favour separating 'deep' dependents from more 'surface' ones, as in the separation of semantic, syntactic and morphological dependencies in Meaning-Text Theory (Mel'cuk 2003). So for instance between *cows* and *moo*, we can recognise a single dependency which is classified as 'subject' and carries a wide assortment of information about the two words and their relationship. Of course this is not to deny that a word is different both from its meaning and from its realization in morphology; even lumpers should not be tempted to blur these distinctions. But these other levels of structure are among the typical properties that can be predicted from the syntactic dependency: one dependency, many properties. The kind of analysis I have in mind can be seen in Figure 4, where once again I use a non-standard notation for DS which I justify below. The main point about this diagram is that the relation labelled 'subject' allows the prediction ('inheritance') of at least three very different properties:

- the semantic relation labelled 'actor'
- the word order
- the number-agreement.

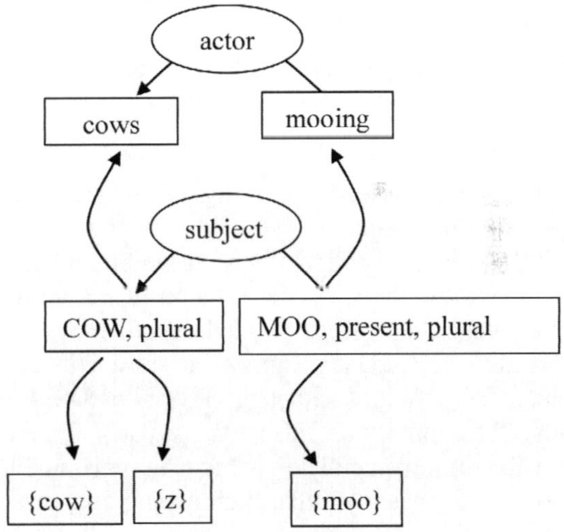

Figure 4: Syntax, semantics and morphology

5 Mutual dependency

Another question for DS theory is how rich DS is; and the answer that I shall suggest will also explain why I use non-standard notation. The standard answer is that DS is about as rich as very elementary PS – in short, very poor. This is the assumption behind the early arguments that DS and PS are equivalent (Gaifman 1965), but of course there is no reason to accept the assumption; indeed, what we know about cognition suggests just the opposite. If our minds are capable of representing complex social structures, then why should the same not be true of syntactic structures?

Take the case of mutual relations such as the relations between me and my father (whereby he is my father and I am his son). All the standard assumptions about syntax rule out the possibility of mutual dependency, but as Mel'cuk comments, mutual government clearly does exist in some languages (Mel'cuk 2003). For example, a Russian numeral such as *dva,* 'two', requires a singular genitive noun, but its gender is determined by the noun; so in *dva stola*, 'two tables', *stola* is genitive singular because of *dva*, but *dva* is masculine because of *stola*. More familiar data confirms this conclusion. Consider (2).

(2) Who came?

Who clearly depends, as subject, on *came*, in just the same way that *cows* depends on *moo* in (1). But the reverse is also true: *came* depends on *who* by virtue of the latter being an interrogative pronoun. This is what allows *who came* to depend on a verb such as *wonder*:

(3) I wonder who came. (compare: *I wonder cows moo)

Moreover, English interrogative pronouns allow ellipsis of the rest of the clause, as in

(4) Apparently someone came; I wonder who.

Facts such as these show strongly that interrogative pronouns (such as *who*) take a finite verb (such as *came*) as an optional complement. But we also know that *who* depends on *came*, so we have a very clear case of mutual dependency.

Mutual dependency cannot be shown in any standard notation, whether for PS or for DS, because these notations all use the vertical dimension for dominance. The problem is that mutual dependency means mutual dominance, and verticality does not allow two objects each to be higher than the other. This is why I prefer in WG to use arrows, where the direction of dominance is shown by the arrow-head (which more generally distinguishes values from arguments). In this notation, then, the structure of (2) is shown in Figure 5.

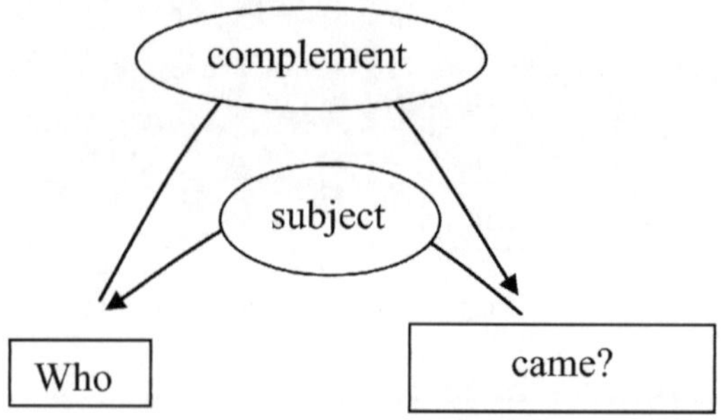

Figure 5: Mutual dependencies

6 More about cognition: logic and tokens

We now return to consider another feature of general cognition: **node-creation**. This is the idea that we create mental nodes to represent the tokens of ongoing experience (which psychologists call 'exemplars'). For example, when I see an object in the sky, I first create a token node for that object and then try to enrich it by linking it to some stored node (what linguists call a 'type'), such as the 'bird' node from which it can inherit further properties. The token needs a node to itself, most obviously at the point in processing where it hasn't yet been assigned to a type. Moreover the token has properties of its own, such as its unique position in space and time. Because no single node can carry two different sets of properties, we must create a token node which will eventually be classified by an is-a link to some type which effectively integrates the token temporarily into the total network.

This system for handling tokens by creating temporary nodes may seem rather obvious and trivial, but it has important ramifications for my argument below so it is worth pursuing a little.

- The main consequence is that one token may act as supercategory for another; for instance, suppose I see a small yellow bird, for which I create node A1, and then I see another one, and create node A2. The very act of recognising A2 as 'another one' means that I register its similarities to A1, with A1 as the supercategory for A2, and I can recognise this link even if I don't know how to classify A1. The same is true whenever we create one token as a copy of another (as in games such as 'Follow my leader', where everyone does the same as the leader). Thus two distinct objects or events may be linked by is-a even though they are both only temporary tokens.
- But multiple tokens are possible even for single objects or events. For example, suppose I create node B for a rather nondescript brown bird which I can't classify, and then, minutes later, I see another bird of similar size hopping around near the first bird, for which I create node C. From its colour I know that C is a blackbird, so I assume that B is its mate, and is

also a blackbird; but I can also remember my original failure to classify B, so I need a separate node for the newly classified B, which we may call B*. We might say that blackbird C has 'modified' B into B* – an example of one concept's properties being affected by those of a related concept.

- Another possibility is where we predict one token as part of the enrichment for another token. For example, suppose I see a duck swimming in a pond, and wonder where its nest is. This mental operation presupposes two nodes, D1 for the duck and N1 for its nest. Now suppose I think the typical relation between a duck and its nest is for the duck to be sitting on the nest; thanks to default inheritance, I expect D1 to be sitting on N1. But of course this is wrong, because D1 is actually swimming in the pond. I then spot a nest N2 with another duck D2 sitting on it, and, putting two and two together, I work out that D1 is D2's mate, and N2 is their shared nest. In other words, the expected N1 (the nest I expect D1 to be sitting on) is actually D2, which is in the expected relation to D2 but not to D1. Once again, default inheritance provides precisely the right analysis if we recognise N2 as a 'subcategory' of N1 – the actual nest that N1 was meant to anticipate.

All these examples are brought together in Figure 6, where the greyed boxes indicate permanent types and the others are temporary tokens. The main point of this figure is to show that an is-a relation is possible between one token and another, as in A1-A2, B-B* and N1-N2.

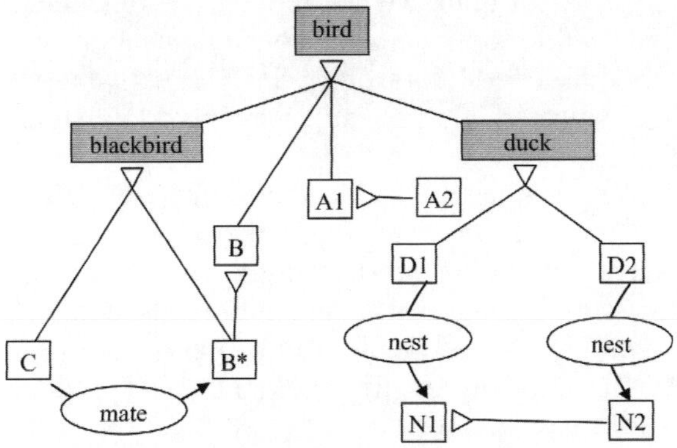

Figure 6: Tokens as supercategories

7 Structure sharing, raising and lowering

Returning to syntax, let's assume that the mental resources we can apply to birds are also available for words. Let's also assume, with Tree Adjoining Grammar, that a dependency grammar consists of 'elementary dependency trees anchored on lexical items' (Joshi and Rambow 2003). For example, by default inheritance the word token *moo* has a subject, in just the same way that a duck has a nest, and in processing this bit of experience we have to identify the expected subject or nest with some other token. And of course in both cases the expected token has a 'valency' of its own: the nest needs an owner, and the noun needs a 'parent' word to depend on. In fact, just the same process lies behind the classification of the tokens: so each token starts with an unknown supercategory which has to be identified with a known type. The little grammar in Figure 7 shows these identifications by the '=' linking the expected but unknown '?' to its target.

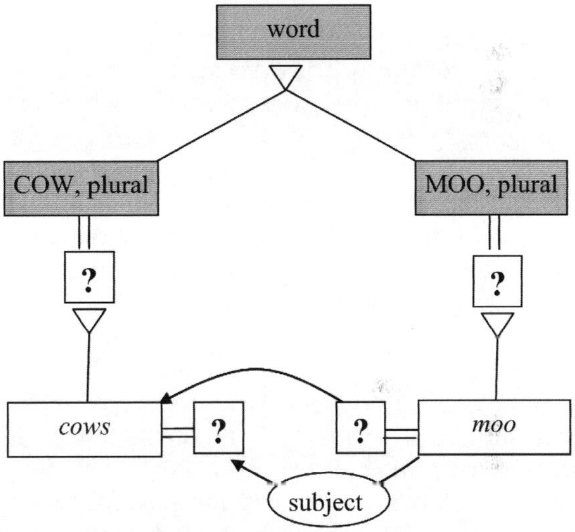

Figure 7: A grammar for Cows moo

This much is probably common ground among DS grammarians. But an important question arises for DS theory: how many parents can one word have? Once again, the standard answer is very simple: one – just the same answer as in PS theory, where the 'single mother condition' is widely accepted (Anderson 1979, Zwicky 1985). But syntactic research over the last few decades has produced very clear evidence that a word may in fact depend on more than one other word. For example, 'raising' structures such as (5) contain a word which is the subject of two verbs at the same time.

(5) It keeps raining.

In this example, *it* must be the subject of *keeps* – for example, this is the word that *keeps* agrees with. But equally clearly, *it* is the subject of *raining*, as required by the restriction that the subject of the verb RAIN must be *it*. Some PS theories (such as HPSG) allow 'structure sharing', which is equivalent to recognising two 'mothers' (Pollard and Sag 1994:4); and this has always been possible in WG. Once again, the arrow notation helps, as in Figure 8 (which I am about to revise):

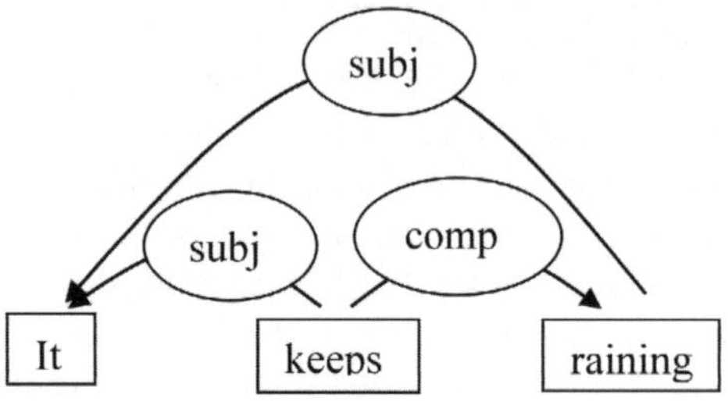

Figure 8: Raising

DS provides a very good framework for discussing structure sharing because it reveals a very general 'triangle' of dependencies which recurs in every example of structure sharing: three words connected by dependencies so that one of the sharing parents depends on the other. In this example, *it* depends both on *keeps* and on *raining,* but *raining* also depends on *is*. We might call these words the 'shared' (*it*), the 'higher parent' (*keeps*) and the 'lower parent' (*raining*).

But the existence of two parents in structure sharing raises a problem. What happens if their parental 'rights' conflict? For example, since *it* depends on *raining*, these two words ought to be next to each other, or at least not separated by a word such as *keeps* which does not depend on either of them; but putting *it* next to *raining* would produce **Keeps it raining*, which is ungrammatical. The general principle that governs almost every case of structure sharing is that the higher parent wins; we might call this the 'raising' principle. But how can we build this principle into the grammar so that raising is automatic?

The answer I shall offer now is new to WG, and builds on the earlier discussion of tokens in cognition, where I argued that one token may take another token as its supercategory. It also develops the idea that each token inherits a 'typical' underlying structure such as the 'tectogrammatical' representations of Functional Generative Description (Sgall and others 1986). Suppose that both the verbs in *It keeps raining* inherit a normal subject, which by default should be next to them: *it keeps* and *it raining*. But suppose also that the two *it*'s are distinct tokens linked by is-a, so that *it,* the subject of *keeps*, is-a *it*,* the subject of *raining*. Formally, this would be just like the relation between nest N2 and nest N1 in Figure 6, and the logic of default inheritance would explain why *it1* wins in the conflict over position in just the same way that it explains why N2 is under a duck but N1 isn't.

This answer requires a change in the analysis of Figure 8, which follows the tradition of WG (and also of other theories such as HPSG). In fact, if anything it is more similar to a Chomskyan analysis with 'traces', where the trace shows the expected position. But unlike the Chomskyan analysis, this does not involve any notion of 'movement'; all it involves is the ordinary logic of default inheritance. The structure I am now suggesting is shown in Figure 9.

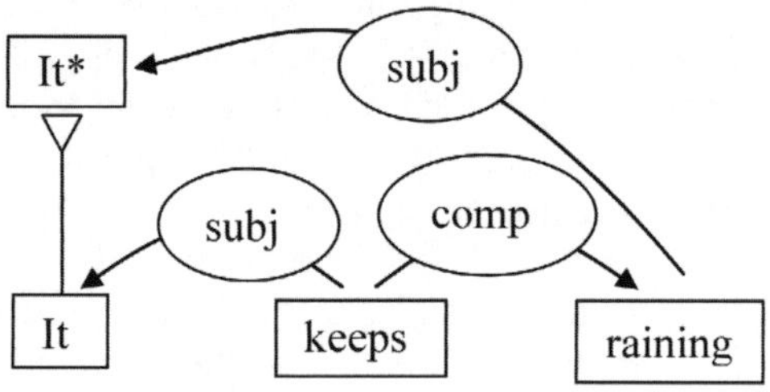

Figure 9: Raising and the raising principle

Why do languages and their speakers prefer raising to its opposite, lowering? I believe there is an easy functional explanation if we think of grammatical dependencies as tools for providing each word with an 'anchor' in the sentence which is in some sense already more integrated than the dependent. Clearly, from this point of view the higher parent must be more integrated than the lower parent, so it provides a better anchor for the shared. I think we can rely on this functional explanation to explain why our linguistic ancestors developed the raising principle and why we so easily learned it; so there is no need to assume that it is innate.

Which is just as well, because there are clear exceptions to the raising principle. In some languages, there are constructions where it is the lower parent that wins – in other words, cases of 'lowering'. For example, German allows 'partial VP fronting' as in (6) (Uszkoreit 1987, Haider 1990).

(6) Eine Concorde gelandet ist hier noch nie.
'A Concorde hasn't yet landed here.'

There is overwhelming evidence that *eine Concorde* is the subject of both *gelandet* and *ist*, but it is equally clear that it takes its position from the non-finite, and dependent, *gelandet* rather than from the finite *ist*. In this case, then, the expected raising relation is reversed, so that the subject of the lower parent is-a that of the higher parent, and the lower parent (*gelandet*) wins.

Moreover, German isn't the only language with lowering. Sylvain Kahane has drawn my attention to apparently lowered examples in French such as (7), which are easy to find on the internet.

(7) Avez-vous lu la lettre qu'a écrite Gilles à Pauline? 'Have you read the letter which Gilles wrote to Pauline?'

The important thing here is that *Gilles* is the subject of both the auxiliary *a* ('has') and its complement, the verb *écrite* (written), but it takes its position among the dependents of the latter, which is the lower parent.

It would seem, then, that sharing usually involves raising, but can involve lowering; and if raising has functional benefits, then presumably lowering also has benefits, even if the attractions of raising generally win out. And of course the two patterns can coexist in the same language, so we may assume that learners of German and French can induce the generalisation shown in Figure 10, with the general raising pattern shown as the A-B-C-A* configuration, and the exceptional lowering one as D-E-F-D*.

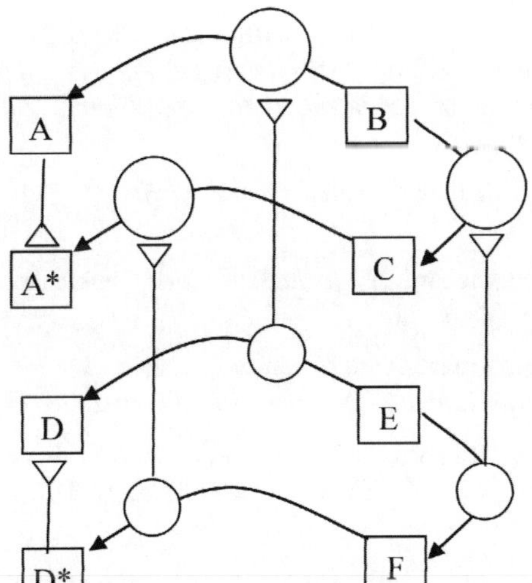

Figure 10: Raising and lowering

Once again, the main point is that we can analyse, and perhaps even explain, the most abstract of syntactic patterns if we assume that the full apparatus of human cognition is available for learning language.

One of the challenges for the very 'flat' structures of DS is to explain examples like (8) (Dahl 1980).

(8) typical French house

The problem here is that a DS analysis treats both *typical* and *French* as dependents of *house*, so there is no syntactic unit which contains *French house* but not *typical*; but the meaning does involve a unit 'French house', because this is needed to determine typicality: the house in question is not just French and typical (i.e. a typical house), but it is a French house which is like most other French houses. This phenomenon is what I have called 'semantic phrasing' (Hudson 1990:146-151), but I can now offer a better analysis which builds, once again, on the possibility of multiple tokens for one word.

This problem is actually a particular case of a more general problem: how to allow dependents to modify the meaning of the 'parent' word (the word on which they depend) – for example, how to show that *French house* doesn't just mean 'house', but means 'French house'. In PS analysis, the answer is easy because the node for the phrase *French house* is different from that for *house*, so it can carry a different meaning. I anticipated the solution to this problem in section 6 when I was discussing the case of the unclassifiable bird turning out to be a blackbird. In that discussion I said that the male bird 'modified' the classification of the other bird, deliberately using the linguistic term for the effect of a dependent on the meaning of its parent.

Suppose we assign the word token *house* not one node but two, just as I suggested we might do with the female blackbird. One node carries the properties inherited directly from the type HOUSE, including the meaning 'house', and the other, which of course is-a the first, shows the modifying effect of the dependent *French*, giving the meaning 'French house'. My suggestion is that modification works cumulatively by creating a new word token for each dependent. If this is right, then we have an explanation for *typical French house*, because 'French house' is the meaning which *typical* modifies. One challenge for this analysis is to find suitable names for the word tokens, but there is a simple solution: to name each token by a combination of the head word and the dependent concerned: *house – house+French – house+typical*.

This multiplication of word tokens would also explain many other things, such as why the anaphoric ONE can copy either meaning of a phrase such as *French house* as in (9) and (10).

(9) He bought a French house last year and she bought a German one [= house] this year.

(10) He bought a French house last year and she bought one [= French house] this year.

Once again the challenge for DS is how a single word token (*house*) can simultaneously mean either 'house' or 'French house'. But if *house* and *house+French* are actually different tokens, the problem disappears. Moreover, this example also reminds us that anaphora essentially involves the copying of one word token's properties onto another – in other words, an is-a relation between two word tokens, further evidence that one token may act as a supercategory for another. The relations in (9) and (10) are displayed in Figure 11.

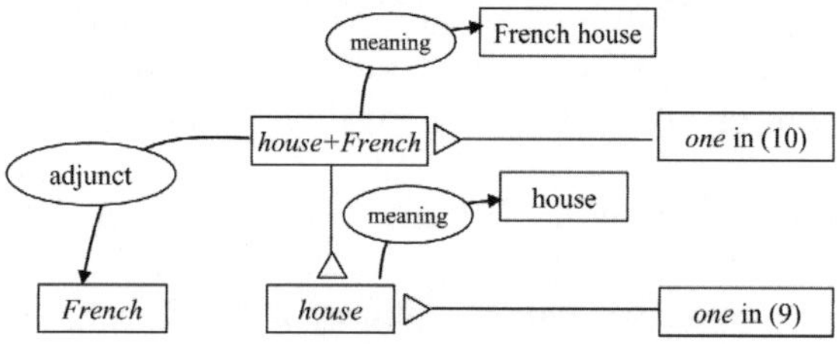

Figure 11: Anaphora between word tokens

This general principle has the interesting consequence of greatly reducing the difference between DS and PS. Both analyses assign an extra node to any word for each dependent that that word has, and assign to that node the modified meaning as affected by the dependent. The similarities are illustrated in Figure 12.

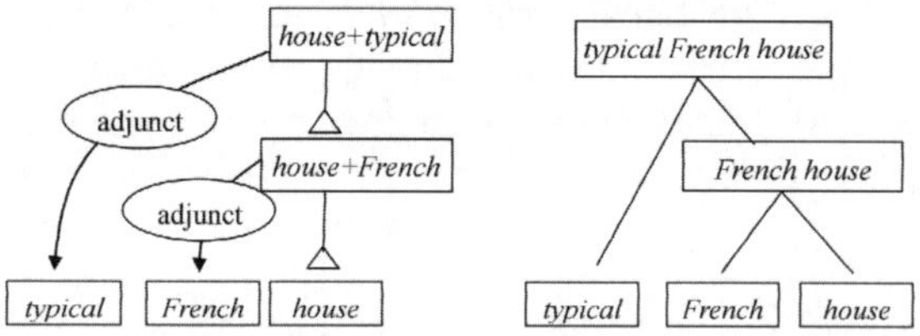

Figure 12: DS (WG style) and PS

Nevertheless, important differences remain: DS allows structures that are impossible in PS, including mutual dependencies, and conversely, PS allows structures that are impossible in DS, including not only unary branching but also exocentric constructions (even if these are excluded by the X-bar principle – Jackendoff 1977). And most importantly, the relevant relations are logically very different: the whole-part relation in PS, and the supercategory-subcategory relation in DS.

References

Anderson, John 1979. 'Syntax and the single mother', *Journal of Linguistics* 15: 267-287.

Barlow, Michael and Kemmer, Suzanne 2000. *Usage based models of language*. Stanford: CSLI.

Chomsky, Noam 1986. Knowledge of Language. Its nature, origin and use. New York: Praeger.

Dahl, Östen 1980. 'Some arguments for higher nodes in syntax: A reply to Hudson's 'Constituency and dependency'.', *Linguistics* 18: 485-488.

Eppler, Eva 2010. *Emigranto: the syntax of German-English code-switching.* Vienna: Braumueller Verlag.

Fodor, Jerry 1983. *The Modularity of the Mind.* Cambridge, MA: MIT Press.

Gaifman, Haim 1965. 'Dependency systems and phrase-structure systems.', *Information and Control* 8: 304-337.

Gisborne, Nikolas 2010. *The event structure of perception verbs.* Oxford: Oxford University Press.

Haider, Hubert 1990. 'Topicalization and other puzzles of German syntax.', in Gunther Grewendorf & Wolfgang Sternefeld (eds.) *Scrambling and Barriers*. Amsterdam: Benjamins, pp. 93-112.

Halliday, Michael and Matthiessen, Christian 2006. *Construing Experience Through Meaning: A Language-based Approach to Cognition.* London: Continuum.

Hudson, Richard 1984. *Word Grammar.* Oxford: Blackwell.

Hudson, Richard 1990. *English Word Grammar.* Oxford: Blackwell.

Hudson, Richard 2007. *Language networks: the new Word Grammar*. Oxford: Oxford University Press

Hudson, Richard 2010. *An Introduction to Word Grammar*. Cambridge: Cambridge University Press.

Hyman, Larry 2008. 'Directional Asymmetries in the Morphology and Phonology of Words, with Special Reference to Bantu.', *Linguistics* 46: 309-350.

Jackendoff, Ray 1977. *X-bar Syntax: A Study of Phrase Structure.* Cambridge, MA: MIT Press.

Joshi, Aravind and Rambow, Owen 2003. 'A Formalism for Dependency Grammar Based on Tree Adjoining Grammar.', in Sylvain Kahane & Alexis Nasr (eds.) *Proceedings of the First International Conference on Meaning-Text Theory*. Paris: Ecole Normale Supérieure.

Keenan, Edward 1976. 'Towards a universal definition of 'subject'.', in Charles Li (ed.) *Subject and Topic*. New York: Academic Press, pp. 303-333.

Labov, William 1972. *Sociolinguistic Patterns*. Oxford: Blackwell.

Mel'cuk, Igor 2003. 'Levels of Dependency in Linguistic Description: Concepts and Problems', in V Agel, Ludwig Eichinger, Hans-Werner Eroms, Peter Hellwig, Hans Jürgen Heringer, & Henning Lobin (eds.) *Dependency and Valency. An International Handbook of Contemporary Research, vol. 1*. Berlin: de Gruyter, pp. 188-229.

Percival, Keith 1976. 'On the historical source of immediate constituent analysis.', in James McCawley (ed.) *Notes from the Linguistic Underground*. London: Academic Press, pp. 229-242.

Pollard, Carl and Sag, Ivan 1994. *Head-Driven Phrase Structure Grammar*. Chicago: Chicago University Press.

Reisberg, Daniel 2007. Cognition. Exploring the Science of the Mind. Third media edition. New York: Norton.

Robins, Robert 1967. *A Short History of Linguistics*. London: Longman.

Sgall, Petr, Hajicová, Eva, and Panevova, Jarmila 1986. *The Meaning of the Sentence in its Semantic and Pragmatic Aspects*. Prague: Academia.

Uszkoreit, Hans 1987. 'Linear precedence in discontinuous constituents: complex fronting in German.', in Geoffrey Huck & Almerindo Ojeda (eds.) *Discontinuous Constituents (Syntax and Semantics 20)*. San Diego: Academic Press, pp. 405-425.

Zwicky, Arnold 1985. 'The case against plain vanilla syntax', *Studies in the Linguistic Sciences* 15: 1-21.

Dependency Representations, Grammars, Folded Structures, among Other Things![*]

Abstract of invited talk

Aravind K. Joshi
Department of Computer and Information Science
and Institute for Research in Cognitive Science
University of Pennsylvania
Philadelphia PA USA
joshi@seas.upenn.edu

In a dependency grammar (DG) dependency representations (trees) directly express the dependency relations between words. The hierarchical structure emerges out of the representation. There are no labels other than the words themselves. In a phrase structure type of representation words are associated with some category labels and then the dependencies between the words emerge indirectly in terms of the phrase structure, the non-terminal labels, and possibly some indices associated with the labels. Behind the scene there is a phrase structure grammar (PSG) that builds the hierarchical structure. In a categorical type of grammar (CG), words are associated with labels that encode the combinatory potential of each word. Then the hierarchical structure (tree structure) emerges out of a set of operations such as application, function composition, type raising, among others. In a tree-adjoining grammar (TAG), each word is associated with an elementary tree that encodes both the hierarchical and the dependency structure associated with the lexical anchor and the tree(s) associated with a word. The elementary trees are then composed with the operations of substitution and adjoining. In a way, the dependency potential of a word is localized within the elementary tree (trees) associated with a word. Already TAG and TAG like grammars are able to represent dependencies that go beyond those that can be represented by context-free grammars, but in a controlled way. With this perspective and with the availability of larger dependency annotated corpora (e.g. the Prague Dependency Treebank) one is able to assess how far one can cover the dependencies that actually appear in the corpora. This approach has the potential of carrying out an 'empirical' investigation of the power of representations and the associated grammars. Here by 'empirical' we do not mean 'statistical or distributional' but rather in the sense of covering as much as possible the actual data in annotated corpora!

If time permits, I will talk about how dependencies are represented in nature. For example, grammars have been used to describe the folded structure of RNA biomolecules. The folded structure here describes the dependencies between the amino acids as they appear in an RNA biomolecule. One can then ask the question: Can we represent a sentence structure as a folded structure, where the fold captures both the dependencies and the structure, without any additional labels?

[*] Part of this work is in cooperation with Joan Chen Main, University of Pennsylvania, Philadelphia PA and Johns Hopkins University Baltimore, MD.

Proceedings of the Second International Conference on Dependency Linguistics (DepLing 2013), page 12,
Prague, August 27–30, 2013.

Exploring Morphosyntactic Annotation Over a Spanish Corpus for Dependency Parsing

Miguel Ballesteros Simon Mille Alicia Burga
Natural Language Processing Group
Pompeu Fabra University
Barcelona, Spain
{firstname.lastname}@upf.edu

Abstract

It has been observed that the inclusion of morphosyntactic information in dependency treebanks is crucial to obtain high results in dependency parsing for some languages. In this paper we explore in depth to what extent it is useful to include morphological features, and the impact of diverse morphosyntactic annotations on statistical dependency parsing of Spanish. For this, we give a detailed analysis of the results of over 80 experiments performed with MaltParser through the application of MaltOptimizer. Our goal is to isolate configurations of morphosyntactic features which would allow for optimizing the parsing of Spanish texts, and to evaluate the impact that each feature has, independently and in combination with others.

1 Introduction

As shown in natural language processing (NLP) research, a careful selection of the linguistic information is relevant in order to produce an impact on the results. In this paper, we want to look into different sets of morphosyntactic features in order to test their effect on the quality of parsing for Spanish. To this end, we apply MaltParser (Nivre et al., 2007b), and MaltOptimizer (Ballesteros and Nivre, 2012b; Ballesteros and Nivre, 2012a), which is a system capable of exploring and exploiting the different feature sets that can be extracted from the data and used over the models generated for MaltParser.

Starting from a corpus annotated with fine-grained language-specific information, we can use all, or a part of the morphosyntactic features to build different models and see the impact of each feature set on the Labeled Attachment Score (henceforth LAS) of the parser.

We decided to use MaltOptimizer in order to answer the following questions: (i) is the inclusion of all morphological features found in an annotation useful for Spanish parsing?; (ii) what are the optimal configurations of morphological features?; (iii) can we explain why different features are more or less important for the parser?

For this purpose, we used the UPF version of a subsection of the AnCora corpus (Mille et al., 2013) (see also Section 3.2), which includes features such as number, gender, person, mood, tense, finiteness, and coarse- and fine-grained part-of-speech (PoS). The impact of each feature or combination of features on subsets of dependency relations is also analyzed; for this, a fine-grained annotation of the syntactic layer is preferred since it allows for a more detailed analysis. The version of the AnCora-UPF corpus that we use contains 41 language-specific syntactic tags and thus is perfectly suitable for our task.

In the rest of the paper, we situate our goals within the state-of-the-art (Section 2), we describe the experimental setup, i.e. MaltParser, MaltOptimizer, the corpus used and the experiments that we carried out (Section 3), we report and discuss the results of the experiments (Section 4), and finally present the conclusions and some suggestions for further work (Section 5).

2 Motivation and Related Work

Other researchers have already applied MaltOptimizer to their datasets, with different objectives in mind. Thus, the work of Seraji et al. (2012) shows that, for Persian, the parser results improve when following the model suggested by the optimizer. Tsarfaty et al. (2012a) work with Hebrew –a morphologically rich language- and incorporate the optimization offered by MaltOptimizer for presenting novel metrics that allow for jointly evaluating syntactic parsing and morphological segmentation. Mambrini and Passarotti (2012) use the op-

Proceedings of the Second International Conference on Dependency Linguistics (DepLing 2013), pages 13–22,
Prague, August 27–30, 2013.

timizer not only to capture the feature model that fits best Ancient Greek, but also to evaluate how the genre used in the training set affects the parsing results. A step further is taken by Atutxa et al. (2012) for Basque: they want not only a good performance of the parser, but also a better disambiguation of those nominal phrases that can be either subjects or objects. In order to do that, they use the optimizer to detect the features (including morphosyntactic ones) in the annotation that are useful for this task.

Even though the state-of-the-art results of parsing are very good when working with English, the results notoriously worsen when working with morphologically rich languages (MRLs). In this way, Tsarfaty et al. (2012b) present three different parsing challenges, broadly described as: (i) the architectural challenge, which focuses on how and when to introduce morphological segmentation; (ii) the modeling challenge, focused on how and where the morphological information should be encoded; and (iii) the lexical challenge, which faces the question of how to deal with morphological variants of a word that are not included in the corpus. Our work is directly related to the modeling challenge, given that we analyze in depth whether it is useful to incorporate morphological information as independent features.

Eryigit et al. (2008) have already contributed to this topic by testing different morphosyntactic combinations and their effect on MaltParser when applied to Turkish: they point out that some features do not make the dependency parser improve (in their case, number and person), and that Labeled and Unlabeled Attachment Scores (LAS/UAS) are unequally impacted by the feature variation (inflectional features affect more the labeled than the unlabeled accuracy). We also find interesting the work of Bengoetxea and Gojenola (2009) and Atutxa et al. (2012), which have respectively tried to include semantic classes and feature propagation between different parsing models, with the intention of improving the parsing results for Basque. However, none of these works made use of MaltOptimizer in their experiments, for the simple reason that it was not available at the time.

Spanish may not be as morphologically rich as other languages such as Hebrew, Turkish or Basque, but it involves enough morphological interactions to allow our research to contribute to such important discussion (Tsarfaty et al., 2010). For instance, determiners and adjectives agree in number and gender with the governing noun, finite verbs in number and person with their subjects; more complex types of agreement are (i) sibling interactions, such as copulative with subject, adjectival or past-participial with subject or object, (ii) dependents of siblings in the compound passive analytical construction, (iii) agreement of pronouns with their antecedent, (ii) and (iii) involving gender, number and sometimes person sharing; furthermore, some features are required on some verbs by their syntactic governor, such as a certain type of finiteness (gerund, participle, infinitive, finite) or mood. All those properties are encoded in the tagset used for the annotation of the AnCora-UPF corpus (see (Burga et al., 2011; Mille et al., 2013) for details about how the tagset was designed), so we expect that the presence or absence of one or more of these features in the training corpus will have a clear impact on the quality of the parsing.

In this way, the work of (Cowan and Collins, 2005) makes a step exploring how specific morphologic features (encoded as different PoS) affect the parsing results in Spanish. Even though the authors use a constituent-based treebank and not a dependency-based one, they find that *number* and *mood* (verbal feature that overlaps our *mood* and *finiteness*) are the features that most affect the parser's behaviour.

3 Experimental Setup

Here are the five steps we followed:

1. The corpus was divided into a training set (3263 sentences, 93803 tokens, 28.7 tokens/sentence) and a test set (250 sentences, 7089 tokens, 28.4 tokens/sentence);

2. 82 different versions of the training and test sets were created, based on different combinations of morphosyntactic features;

3. MaltParser was trained on a baseline model that does not include morphological features but uses the default feature models and parameters set in MaltOptimizer Phase 2, which provides general parameters and the best parsing algorithm for the data set.

4. We applied MaltOptimizer Phase 3, on each of the 82 training sets, and each configured model output was applied to the test set in order to obtain an evaluation;

5. We retained from the evaluation file LAS, UAS and LA (Labeled Accuracy) over all relations, as well as the recall of [*dependency relation + attachment*] for each of the 41 edge types.[1]

In the rest of this section, we give more details about MaltParser and MaltOptimizer, before explaining the annotation that is used as the basis of this experiment.

3.1 MaltParser, MalOptimizer and the CoNLL Data Format

MaltParser (Nivre et al., 2007b) is a transition-based dependency parser generator that requires as an input a training set annotated in CoNLL-X data format,[2] and provides models capable of producing the dependency parsing of new sentences. MaltParser implements four different transition-based parsers families and provides high and stable performance (see, e.g., (Mille et al., 2012)). In the CoNLL Shared Tasks in 2006 and 2007 (Buchholz and Marsi, 2006; Nivre et al., 2007a), it was one of the best parsers, achieving either the first or the second place for most of the languages.

A transition-based parser is based on a state machine over mainly two data structures: (i) a buffer that stores the words to be processed and (ii) a stack that stores the ones that are being processed (see Figure 1 for details). The different transitions are shown in Figure 2; as can be observed, the state machine transitions manage the input words in order to assign dependencies between them. The transition-based parsers implemented in MaltParser use a model learned over a training corpus by using a classifier with the intention of selecting the best action (transition) in each state of the state-machine. The classifiers make their decisions according to the linguistic annotation included in the data, shown in Figure 3. This basically means that the better the linguistic annotation is, the better the results are expected to be.

The CoNLL data format is now a standard for dependency parsers; the following attributes are the ones included in the CoNLL-X format that are used as features by the parser:

1. FORM: Word form.
2. LEMMA: Stemmed version of the word.

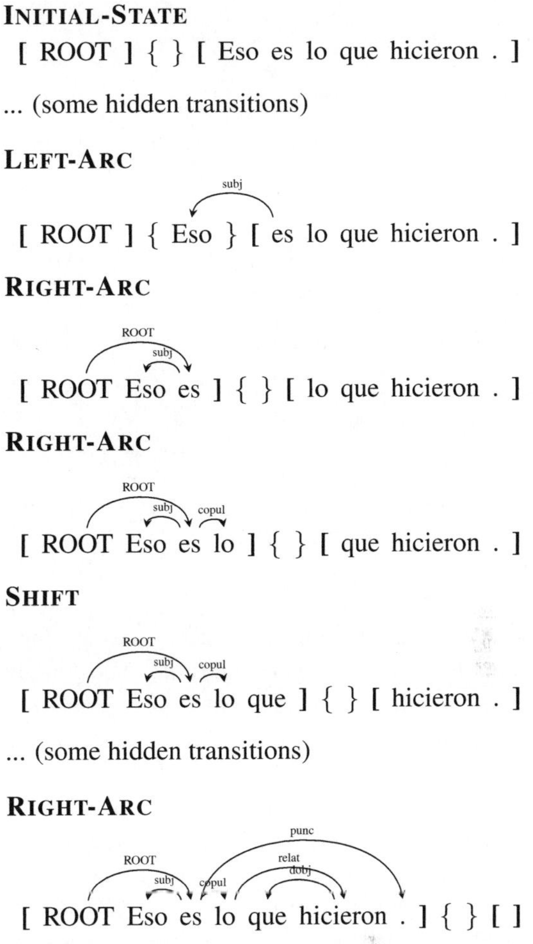

Figure 1: Some of the parsing transitions of the sentence included in the AnCora-UPF corpus: *Eso es lo que hicieron - That's what they did*. The buffer is the structure that is represented to the right of the picture between '[' and ']', and the stack is the one to the left. Between each parsing state we show the transitions selected by the parser considering the features over the stack and the buffer.

3. CPOSTAG: Coarse-grained part-of-speech tag.
4. POSTAG: Fine-grained part-of-speech tag.
5. **FEATS**: List of morphosyntactic features (such as number, gender, person, case, finiteness, tense, mood, etc.)
6. DEPREL: Dependency relation to head.[3]

A feature model is an option file in a MaltParser specific language based on XML that provides the linguistic annotation that the parser must take into account in order to produce the transitions. In each parsing state, the parser only knows the linguistic annotation included in the

[1]Because each training set contains different features, the test sets are obviously parsed differently and, in some cases, not all of the 41 dependency relations were predicted by the parser.

[2]http://ilk.uvt.nl/conll/#dataformat

[3]These six attributes are located in columns 2, 3, 4, 5, 6, 8 respectively in Figure 3.

Nivre's transition system:

$$Initial = \langle [], [w_1 \ldots w_n], \emptyset, \emptyset \rangle \rightarrow Final = \{\langle \Pi, [], H, \Delta \rangle \in C\}$$

Transitions:

Shift	$\langle \Pi, w_i \vert \beta, H, \Delta \rangle \Rightarrow \langle \Pi \vert w_i, \beta, H, \Delta \rangle$
Reduce	$\langle \Pi \vert w_i, \beta, H, \Delta \rangle \Rightarrow \langle \Pi, \beta, H, \Delta \rangle$
Left-Arc (dr)	$\langle \Pi \vert w_i, w_j \vert \beta, H, \Delta \rangle \Rightarrow \langle \Pi, w_j \vert \beta, H[w_i \rightarrow w_j], \Delta[w_i(dr)]\} \rangle$ if $h(w_i) \neq 0$.
Right-Arc (dr)	$\langle \Pi \vert w_i, w_j \vert \beta, H, \Delta \rangle \Rightarrow \langle \Pi \vert w_i \vert w_j, \beta, H[w_j \rightarrow w_i], \Delta[w_j(dr)]\} \rangle$ if $h(w_j) = 0$

Figure 2: Transition System for Nivre's algorithms with *reduce* transition (Nivre et al., 2007b).

```
1    Los      el       A    DT   gender=MASC|number=PL|spos=determiner                          2  det   _  _
2    Mbitis   mbitis   N    NN   gender=MASC|number=PL|spos=noun                                4  subj  _  _
3    también también  Adv  RB   spos=adverb                                                    4  adv   _  _
4    mueren   morir    V    VV   finiteness=FIN|mood=IND|number=PL|person=3|spos=verb|tense=PRES 0  ROOT  _  _
5    .        .        SYM  SYM  spos=punctuation                                               4  punc  _  _
```

Figure 3: Sample AnCora-UPF annotated sentence in the 10-column CoNLL format: *Los Mbitis también mueren* (*lit.* 'the Mbitis also die').

feature model. MaltParser includes a default feature model for each parsing algorithm. The default feature models, as we can see in Figure 4, only include features based on part-of-speech (POSTAG), the word form (FORM) and the partially built dependency structure (the output column, DEPREL) over the first positions of the stack and the buffer. Therefore, in order to let the parser know about the rest of the annotation (LEMMA, CPOSTAG and FEATS), if it exists, we need to perform a search of the different possible features.

```
<?xml version="1.0" encoding="UTF-8"?>
<featuremodels>
	<featuremodel name="nivreeager">
		<feature>InputColumn(POSTAG, Stack[0])</feature>
		<feature>InputColumn(POSTAG, Input[0])</feature>
		<feature>InputColumn(POSTAG, Input[1])</feature>
		<feature>InputColumn(POSTAG, Input[2])</feature>
		<feature>InputColumn(POSTAG, Input[3])</feature>
		<feature>InputColumn(POSTAG, Stack[1])</feature>
		<feature>OutputColumn(DEPREL, Stack[0])</feature>
		<feature>OutputColumn(DEPREL, ldep(Stack[0]))</feature>
		<feature>OutputColumn(DEPREL, rdep(Stack[0]))</feature>
		<feature>OutputColumn(DEPREL, ldep(Input[0]))</feature>
		<feature>InputColumn(FORM, Stack[0])</feature>
		<feature>InputColumn(FORM, Input[0])</feature>
		<feature>InputColumn(FORM, Input[1])</feature>
		<feature>InputColumn(FORM, head(Stack[0]))</feature>
	</featuremodel>
</featuremodels>
```

Figure 4: Default feature model for the Nivre arc-eager parsing algorithm.

To this end, we used *MaltOptimizer* (Ballesteros and Nivre, 2012b; Ballesteros and Nivre, 2012a) which is a system that not only implements a search of an optimal feature model, but also provides an optimal configuration based on the data set, exploring the parsing algorithms and the parameters within by performing a deep analysis of the data set. Thus, MaltOptimizer takes as input a training set and it returns an options file and an optimal feature model. MaltOptimizer uses LAS as default evaluation measure and a threshold (>0.05) in order to select either the parameters, parsing algorithms or features. Due to the size of the training corpus, we run MaltOptimizer with 5 fold cross-validation in order to ensure the reliability of the produced outcome, and following the recommended settings of the system. Note also that MaltOptimizer sets a held-out development set during the optimization process (actually, 5 different development sets, one for each fold cross-validation), thus the evaluation results provided over the test set are actually using unseen data during the optimization process.

We are aware of the interactions between the features that are included in the feature model –the ones included in the default feature model- and the ones selected or rejected by MaltOptimizer. However, our intention is to study the effect of the features included in the FEATS column, and the interaction with the other features is actually the real case scenario. By performing an automatic search of the linguistic annotation with MaltOptimizer, we are sure that all the morphosyntactic annotation included in the FEATS column is studied and tested by MaltOptimizer.

After running MaltOptimizer for Phase 1 and Phase 2, the best parser for (all) our data sets is Nivre arc-eager (Nivre, 2003), which behaves as shown in Figure 1; we were therefore ready to run the feature selection implemented in the Phase 3 of MaltOptimizer. Furthermore, the experiments performed by MaltOptimizer ensure that our features are tested in the last steps of the optimization process (Ballesteros and Nivre, 2012a).

3.2 The AnCora-UPF dependency corpus

This corpus, presented by Mille et al. (2013), consists of a small section (3513 sentences, 100892 tokens) of the Spanish dependency corpus AnCora (Taulé et al., 2008). Mille et al. (2009) explain the partially automatic mapping between the two corpora, and Burga et al. (2011) detail what kind of information is encoded in the syntactic tags.[4] The annotation is theoretically based on the Meaning-Text Theory (MTT, (Mel'čuk, 1988)), according to which the set of surface syntactic (SSynt) relations is unique to each language, and should cover as many syntactic idiosyncracies of the given language. Lexical and morphologic features are not directly encoded into the syntactic relations, but rather into attribute/value pairs associated to each node. The authors manually revised the syntactic annotation, but no manual revision was performed on the morphosyntactic features.

The AnCora-UPF corpus is released in the CoNLL'08 format[5]; hence, it contains all the information that a CoNLL file as described in Section 3.1 can contain. We took a close look at the annotation, and in particular at the FEAT column, in which there are **7 features**: *finiteness*, *gender*, *mood*, *number*, *person*, *spos*, *tense*. Unlike in the source AnCora corpus, the authors did not annotate cases. One explanation could be that there are no very clear case markers in Spanish apart from on personal pronouns. However, there is a new feature, *spos*, which is another feature for part-of-speech. The possible values for this attribute are very similar to those of the POSTAG column[6], but the few differences between the two tagsets have noticeable consequences on the results of the evaluation, as discussed in Section 4.3. Table 1 shows these discrepancies: four POSTAGs have been split into two (*IN*, *SYM*, *VB*, *WP*), while two *spos* tags (in bold) correspond to twice as many POSTAGs.

Table 2 shows the possible values that the remaining six features can take, and Table 3 how these morphosyntactic features are distributed through the corpus with respect to generic part-of-speech. We can see that *gender* and *number* are the most frequent attributes, and that they are annotated on elements of different parts-of-speech. The 2.02% of verbs that include *gender* are actually past participles. *gender=C* is not common; it stands for elements that do not express masculine or feminine gender, e.g. the dative pronoun "le". The other four attributes, (*finiteness*, *mood*, *person* and *tense*) are exclusively verbal features (except for the annotation errors).

POSTAG	spos
CC	**conjunction**
CD	cardinal number
DT	determiner
IN	**conjunction** preposition
JJ	adjective
NN	common noun
NP	proper noun
PP	personal pronoun
RB	adverb
SYM	punctuation percentage
UH	interjection
VB	**auxiliary** copula
VH	**auxiliary**
VV	verb
WP	interrogative pronoun relative pronoun
Formula	formula
-	foreign word

Table 1: Correspondences between PoS and *spos* tagsets.

FEAT	Possible Values	#Occurrences
fin	finite, gerund, infinitive, past participle	11776
gen	neutral, femenine, masculine	41735
moo	imperative, indicative, subjunctive	8116
num	plural, singular	53608
per	1st, 2nd, 3rd	8132
ten	future, past, present	8070

Table 2: Possible values and total number of occurrences of the 6 features.

3.3 Versions of the corpus

We prepared 82 different versions of the corpus in our experiments. The total number of possible combinations of the 7 features is 128 (0 features:1 combination; 1:7; 2:21; 3:35; 4:35; 5:21; 6:7; 7:1). However, after looking at figures with 1, 5, 6 and 7

[4]For downloading the corpus, see http://www.taln.upf.edu/content/resources/495.

[5]We transformed it into the 10-column CoNLL-X format for our experiments.

[6]This column contains a subset of the Tree Tagger PoS tagset, widely used in corpus annotation nowadays.

FEAT	V	N	Adj	Det	Pro	Other
fin	99.91	0.01	0.06	0	0	0.02
gen	2.02	46.72	14.31	32.33	4.37	0.25
moo	99.95	0.01	0	0	0	0.04
num	16.74	36.57	15.15	27.1	4.25	0.19
per	99.98	0.01	0	0	0	0.01
ten	99.98	0	0	0	0	0.02

Table 3: Distribution of features over elements of different generic part-of-speech (%).

features, we noticed that the combinations that excluded the *spos* feature were systematically making the parser unable to reach a certain score. As a result, for the rest of the experiments, we focused on combinations that do include *spos*.

The 82 combinations are: 7 features (1 combination); 6 features (7); 5 features (21); 4 features, only those including *spos* (20); 3 features, only those including *spos* (15); 2 features, only those including *spos* (6); 1 feature (7); 0 features (baseline, 1); 4 extra combinations in order to test the PoS/*spos* impact.

4 Results and Discussion

First, we discuss the results of the first 78 experiments. In the last subsection, we will discuss the part-of-speech issues related to the other 4 experiments.

4.1 Feature combinations and general labeled accuracy

The LAS recall provided by the baseline model (no features) is 82.25%.[7] From a general perspective, 25 out of the 78 feature combinations make the baseline LAS rise by at least 0.9 points; 14 of them make the LAS rise by more than 1 point. The biggest improvement, 1.33 points, is obtained with four features, namely [*finiteness gender number spos*]. Some similar improvements, between 1.28 and 1.3 points, have been obtained with the following combinations: [*finiteness number person spos*], [*gender number spos tense*], [*finiteness gender number spos tense*]. Three out of the four biggest enhancements have been obtained with only 4 features.This goes along the lines of Eryigit et al. (2008), who report for Turkish the best results with only a subset of the morphological features present in the annotation.

What makes some features inefficient? In order to answer that question, we looked at the results from another perspective. For a given set of features, we wondered (1) if adding one particular feature makes the LAS better or worse; and (2) which of the remaining features triggers the best LAS improvement. For instance, for the combination [*finiteness gender spos*]: (1) what happens to the LAS when we add one of the four remaining features? is it getting better or worse? and (2) which of these four features improves the most the LAS obtained while using only [*finiteness gender spos*]?

[7]The full set of results can be checked at http://www.taln.upf.edu/system/files/resources_files/table.pdf

	spo	num	fin	gen	per	ten	moo
14	14	14	10	10	8	6	5
25	25	22	17	15	13	11	12

Table 4: Occurrences of features in the 14 and 25 best scoring feature combinations.

FEAT	#Comb.	#better	#worse	#Best/Worst
spo	6	6	0	6/0
num	31	30	1	22/3
fin	31	25	4	16/6
gen	31	21	10	9/11
per	31	16	15	7/9
moo	31	13	17	1/14
ten	31	12	19	1/22

Table 5: Contribution of each feature when enlarging the number of elements in a combination.

Thus, based on the comparison between combinations that contain X elements and combinations that contain X+1 elements, we counted how many times each added feature made the LAS better, and how many times it made it worse. We also counted how many times each feature was involved in the best-scoring feature combination. The results obtained according to those lines are presented in Table 5. In the following, the detailed analysis for each feature is provided:

- ***spos*** was measured just when comparing the groups of five and six features (6 cases in total). It always improves the results (half of the times with a percentage higher than 0.3 points). It never worsens and never belongs to the worst feature combination. See Section 4.3 for more details about this feature.
- ***number*** makes the LAS improve 30 out of 31 times (17 times the improvement is higher than 0.3 points), and is involved 22 times in the best scoring combination. It only worsens the results once (from 5 to 6 features, when combined with [*finiteness gender mood person tense*].[8] This feature is very useful

[8]All the feature combinations improve the baseline; how-

in our experiments, and this could be explained by the following: (i) as shown in Table 2, this feature appears more frequently than any other feature (except *spos*), and it is distributed over elements of a great variety of PoS (see Table 3); (ii) many dependency relations in the AnCora-UPF corpus use *number* directly or indirectly, on the head and/or the dependent: most verbal argumental relations (subjects, copulatives, direct objects, completives, clitic objects), verbal non-argumental relations (passive analytical, copredicatives); nominal relations (determinative, modificative); etc.

- ***finiteness*** makes the LAS improve 25 times out of 31 (8 times the change is superior to 0.3 points). This feature is included in the optimal combination 16 times. On the other hand, it only worsens the results 4 times (and only once by more than 0.3 points, when combined with [*gender mood number person tense*], and it belongs to the worst combination 6 times. This feature often participates in improving the LAS, which could be due to the fact that it is the most important verbal feature, since it determines the presence or absence of other verbal features (e.g. it is only when *finiteness* has as value *finite* that other features such as *number*, *tense* or *person* can also be associated to the verb in question). In addition, this feature has a direct correlation with very frequent dependency relations as annotated in the corpus: only finite verbs can have a subject or be the head of a relative clause; only non-finite verbs can be governed by a preposition; in all analytical constructions (perfect, progressive, passive, future) the finiteness of the verb that depends on the auxiliary is always the same; etc.
- ***gender*** improves the results 21 times out of 31 (7 times the change is higher than 0.3 points), and belongs to the best combination 9 times. However, it makes the LAS worsen 10 times (although just once –in combination with [*finiteness mood number person tense*] the variation is higher than 0.3 points), and belongs to the worst combination 11 times. Even though there are numerous relations that directly use this feature, most of the time it co-occurs with *number*, which possibly overshadows it. As a result, only in certain cases *gender* can bring new information that actually helps the parser.
- ***person*** improves the results 16 times out of 31 (4 times the change is higher than 0.3 points), and belongs to the best combination 7 times. On the other hand, it worsens the results 17 times (two times the change is higher than 0.3 points) and belongs to the worst combinations 14 times.
- ***mood*** improves the results 13 times out of 31 (only 2 times the variation is higher than 0.3 points), and belongs to the best combination just 1 time (with [*finiteness gender number person spos*]). It worsens the results 17 times (two times by more than 0.3 points) and belongs to the worst combination 14 times.
- ***tense*** is, according to this perspective, the "less useful" feature, in the sense that it improves the results just 12 times (and 2 times with a variation higher than 0.3 points). At the same time, *tense* makes the LAS drop 19 times out of 31, and it belongs to the worst combination 22 times. The only time that it belongs to the best combination (even if the results worsen) is with [*finiteness gender number spos*] (the "strongest" features).

We believe that *mood*, *tense*, and *person* are more redundant than informative for the parser, because (1) their presence on a node also indicates that a verb is finite, overlapping with the *finiteness* feature, and (2) no dependency relation uses the tense in the tagset, very few use the mood of a verb (only a subclass of the *conj* relation), and the person is only used in order to differentiate a subject from an object, since only the subject has to have the same *person* value as the verb. However, being Spanish an SVO (subject-verb-object) language, it is possible that the linear order –which is also taken into account by the parser- is sufficient to decide who is the subject and who is not; in addition, most nouns are 3rd person, thus, it is not surprising that this feature does not help much. This redundancy is reflected in McNemar's test for $p<0.05$, which indicates that there is a statistically significant difference between the best model with 4 features and another model that has the same number of features, but includes, for instance, *mood* instead of *gender*.[9]

The first conclusion is that the observations of

ever, some of them do it in a more significant way.

[9]McNemar's test shows no statistically significant differ-

this section coincide almost exactly with the ones made in Table 4: the features that individually tend to improve the LAS when added to other features are more likely to be in the best scoring combinations, while the features that often contribute to make the LAS drop are not. Interestingly, the four most frequent features in the 14 and 25 best combinations are also the four features that combine the best together, resulting in an increase of the baseline LAS of 1.33 points. This is not really a surprise, but it was a little less expected that this best scoring feature combination –[*finiteness gender number spos*]- comprises all (and only) the features that have a largely positive ratio of times they improve the LAS to times they make the LAS drop: respectively 25/4, 21/10, 30/1 and 6/0, as opposed the remaining three features that have 16/15, 13/17 and 12/19.

Second, the four best features according to our experiments are also the four most frequent in the corpus (see Table 2). The fact that a feature is productive in an annotation makes it obviously more likely to help a parser. However, it is not that straightforward: for instance, *finiteness* is four times less frequent than *gender*, but it triggers LAS improvements more often.

Third, it is not possible to get the best feature combination by simply looking at how each feature improves the LAS when being on its own: for instance, *number* and *gender* do not increase the LAS a lot by themselves (respectively ranks 77 and 78 out of 78 combinations), but they do very well when they are combined to other attributes.

4.2 UAS, LA and specific dependency relations

We look first at general LAS figures, because we are primarily interested in the general quality of the labeled parsing. However, depending on the type of application one is interested in, one may not be interested in labels, or may want to parse better some dependency relations in particular.

For this, we first compared the UAS and LA scores to the LAS, and as expected, they are behaving very similarly to the LAS results in that the same feature combinations work the best for all metrics. However, two differences can be pointed out: (1) the best LAS and LA are obtained with four features, while the best UAS is obtained with 5 features; (2) the LAS improves by up to 1.33 points (from 82.25% to 83.58%), while the LA and UAS rise up to 1.04 and 1.06 points respectively (from 86.38% to 87.42% and from 87.99% to 89.05%), corresponding to a reduction of errors of respectively 7.49%, 7.64% and 8.83%.

Then, we tried to find direct correlations between the presence or absence of a feature in the annotation and the improvement (or not) of the LAS figures for some relations in particular. The task was maybe too ambitious: it appears to be very hard to find such correlations by simply looking at the figures. For example, relations like subjects and different kind of objects are systematically parsed better with the introduction of any (combination of) feature(s), but some similar improvements are obtained with very different sets, which makes it hard to interpret. As pointed out recently by Schwartz et al. (2012) in a work about how to annotate some key dependencies in order to optimize parser results, annotating one dependency in a particular way will not only influence the parsing of this dependency, but also that of the surrounding dependencies. We believe that we failed in our task because one of the reasons is that there are a lot of indirect correlations that the human eye cannot see.

However, we wondered which feature combinations were the most efficient for specific applications, in particular, for the identification of verbal arguments and of the root of the sentences, and for the analysis of nominal groups and coordinated structures; interestingly, even if performing very well, the best general combination is never the best for any of those cases. For instance, for the identification of verbal arguments and sentence root, the best set is [*finiteness number person spos*]; for the internal NP structure, one should prefer [*gender mood number person spos tense*]; finally, for coordinated structures, one of [*finiteness gender number spos tense*], [*finiteness gender number person spos*] or [*gender number spos tense*].

4.3 Some comments on Part-of-Speech

In this section, we detail shortly the last four experiments, that aim at finding out more about the importance of part-of-speech. In two feature combinations that did not include *spos*, we filled the POSTAG column –which normally contains the Tree Tagger PoS tags- with the *spos* tags from the

ence between the best 14 feature combinations, but we consider that the differences can be interpreted anyway; in the rest of the section we look at the results taking into account both perspectives.

AnCora-UPF corpus. Both times, the LAS was 0.5 points better. We also inverted PoS and *spos* in two other experiments, putting the latter in the POSTAG column of the CoNLL file, and the former in the FEATS column.[10] Again, the parser's LAS dropped half a point in both cases. It is obviously due to the tagsets differences between *PoS* and *spos* pointed out in Section 3.2, and we believe that in particular to the fact that the *spos* tagset splits the *IN* tag into *conjunction* and *preposition*, since this tag is way more frequent than the other mismatching tags.

Therefore, when the more fine-grained tagset *spos* is in the FEATS column, it specifies the POSTAG column and can be used in order to improve the parsing; however, it does not work the other way around: the Tree Tagger PoS tags in the FEATS column do not bring any new information to that one already introduced in the POSTAG column, and thus are ignored by MaltOptimizer. Also, MaltOptimizer follows a stepwise procedure, under this scenario it starts with a higher baseline and it is therefore difficult to get improvements during the optimization steps by testing new features, and thus the features are not selected. There is therefore less room for improvement.

Klein and Manning (2003) present similar improvements when splitting the *IN* tag during their experiments on constituency parsing with a PCFG; we can see now that it is probably the case for dependency parsing too.

5 Conclusions and Future Work

The best configuration for MaltParser and AnCora-UPF corpus is [*finiteness gender number spos*]. For parsing purposes, then, it seems enough to enrich the morphosyntactic annotation just with these features, at least in the case of Spanish. These features not only work well together, but also very often improve the results when are individually added to any combination of features.

On the one hand, there is an almost perfect correlation between feature frequency and performance: those features that appear most frequently are the ones that provide best performance (see Section 4.1). On the other hand, we have observed that the interaction between features also influences significantly the results. So, in order to get the highest performance, frequency and linguistic knowledge should be both taken into account. However, it is important to see how features combine in practice, because when we look at how each feature makes the LAS improve individually (1FEAT), there is no way to say which combination is going to work the best. Another interesting conclusion is that it seems like separating the part-of-speech of prepositions and conjunctions has an important impact on the dependency parsing results, at least in the conditions of our experiments.

We believe that this paper opens many perspectives for further experiments. The next step will be to study whether different levels of dependency relation granularity are affected by the combination of several features and the analysis of the results presented in this paper, following the same idea as presented by Mille et al. (2012). It will also be interesting to study in depth the effect of different feature combinations for specific dependency relations, taking into account that the results for a specific dependency relation are deeply affected by the others that are interacting at the same time. For this, an automatic analysis of the results could allow for reaching conclusions that seem out of reach for the human eye.

A question that remains open is how to compare the effect of different morphological features on dependency parsing of different languages. Moreover, another interesting experiment would be to make use of an automatic morphological-analyzer/tagger that could show the accuracy provided by the parser when it does not use gold morphosyntactic tags coming from the treebank.

We could create new CoNLL columns in the data format, one for each feature, and generate new feature models; we are actually doing a similar thing with the *split* MaltParser feature specification of the FEATS column, but we think that the features could be explored by the parser in a different way.[11] Finally, we could also try other parsers that use different parsing strategies, such as graph-based parsing (e.g.(McDonald et al., 2005)), other transition-based parsers (e.g. (Zhang and Clark, 2008; Zhang and Nivre, 2011; Bohnet and Nivre, 2012)), joint systems (e.g (Bohnet and Kuhn, 2012)) or even study the effect of the features in different algorithms included in MaltParser.

[10] Note that the default feature models include several feature specifications for the POSTAG column and the deepest experiments performed by MaltOptimizer are indeed in this feature window.

[11] We did not do it for these experiments because this would make the use of the current version of MaltOptimizer impossible; however, we are planning to modify the MaltOptimizer source code in order to make it possible.

References

A. Atutxa, E. Agirre, and K. Sarasola. 2012. Contribution of Complex Lexical Information to Solve Syntactic Ambiguity in Basque. In *Proceedings of COLING*, pages 97–114.

M. Ballesteros and J. Nivre. 2012a. MaltOptimizer: A System for MaltParser Optimization. In *Proceedings of the 8th LREC*, pages 2757–2763.

M. Ballesteros and J. Nivre. 2012b. MaltOptimizer: An Optimization Tool for MaltParser. In *Proceedings of the System Demonstration Session of the 13th EACL*, pages 58–62.

K. Bengoetxea and K. Gojenola. 2009. Application of feature propagation to dependency parsing. In *Proceedings of IWPT*, pages 142–145.

B. Bohnet and J. Kuhn. 2012. The Best of Both Worlds - A Graph-based Completion Model for transition-based parsers. In *Proceedings of EACL*, pages 77–87.

B. Bohnet and J. Nivre. 2012. A Transition-Based System for Joint Part-of-Speech Tagging and Labeled Non-Projective Dependency Parsing. In *Proceedings of EMNLP-CoNLL*, pages 1455–1465.

S. Buchholz and E. Marsi. 2006. CoNLL-X Shared Task on Multilingual Dependency Parsing. In *Proceedings of CoNLL-06*, pages 149–164.

A. Burga, S. Mille, and L. Wanner. 2011. Looking Behind the Scenes of Syntactic Dependency Corpus Annotation: Towards a Motivated Annotation Schema of Surface-Syntax in Spanish. In *Proceedings of DepLing '11*, pages 104–114.

B. Cowan and M. Collins. 2005. Morphology and reranking for the statistical parsing of Spanish. In *Proceedings of EMNLP*, pages 795–802.

G. Eryigit, J. Nivre, and K. Oflazer. 2008. Dependency parsing of Turkish. *Computational Linguistics*, 34(3):357–389.

D. Klein and Ch. Manning. 2003. Accurate Unlexicalized Parsing. In *Proceedings of ACL-03*, pages 423–430.

F. Mambrini and M.C. Passarotti. 2012. Will a Parser Overtake Achilles? First experiments on parsing the Ancient Greek Dependency Treebank. In *Proceedings of the 11th TLT*, pages 133–144.

R. McDonald, F. Pereira, K. Ribarov, and J. Hajič. 2005. Non-Projective Dependency Parsing using Spanning Tree Algorithms. In *HLT-EMNLP*, pages 523–530.

I.A. Mel'čuk. 1988. *Dependency Syntax: Theory and Practice*. State University of New York Press, Albany.

S. Mille, L. Wanner, V. Vidal, and A. Burga. 2009. Towards a rich dependency annotation of Spanish corpora. *Procesamiento del Lenguaje Natural*, 1(43):325–333.

S. Mille, A. Burga, G. Ferraro, and L. Wanner. 2012. How Does the Granularity of an Annotation Scheme Influence Dependency Parsing Performance? In *Proceedings of COLING 2012*, pages 839–852.

S. Mille, A. Burga, and L. Wanner. 2013. Ancora-UPF: A Multi-Level Annotation of Spanish. In *Proceedings of DepLing*.

J. Nivre, J. Hall, S. Kübler, R. McDonald, J. Nilsson, S. Riedel, and D. Yuret. 2007a. The CoNLL 2007 Shared Task on Dependency Parsing. In *Proceedings of CoNLL-ST-07*, pages 915–932.

J. Nivre, J. Hall, J. Nilsson, A. Chanev, G. Eryiğit, S. Kübler, S. Marinov, and E. Marsi. 2007b. Maltparser: A Language-Independent System for Data-Driven Dependency Parsing. *Natural Language Engineering*, 13:95–135.

J. Nivre. 2003. An Efficient Algorithm for Projective Dependency Parsing. In *Proceedings of IWPT-03*, pages 149–160.

R. Schwartz, O. Abend, and A. Rappoport. 2012. Learnability-based Syntactic Annotation Design. In *Proceedings of COLING 2012*, pages 2405–2422.

M. Seraji, B. Megyesi, and J. Nivre. 2012. Dependency parsers for Persian. In *Proceedings of 10th Workshop on Asian Language Resources, COLING 2012*, pages 35–44.

M. Taulé, M. A. Martí, and M. Recasens. 2008. Ancora: Multilevel Annotated Corpora for Catalan and Spanish. In *Proceedings of the 6th LREC*, pages 96–101.

R. Tsarfaty, D. Seddah, Y. Goldberg, S. Kübler, M. Candito, J. Foster, Y. Versley, I. Rehbein, and L. Tounsi. 2010. Statistical Parsing of Morphologically Rich Languages (SPMRL): What, How and Whither. In *Proceedings of the NAACL HLT 2010 First Workshop on SPMRL*, pages 1–12.

R. Tsarfaty, J. Nivre, and E. Andersson. 2012a. Cross-Framework Evaluation for Statistical Parsing. In *Proceedings of EACL*, pages 44–54.

R. Tsarfaty, D. Seddah, S. Kübler, and J. Nivre. 2012b. Parsing Morphologically Rich Languages: Introduction to the Special Issue. *Computational Linguistics*, 39(1):15–22.

Y. Zhang and S. Clark. 2008. A Tale of Two Parsers: Investigating and Combining Graph-based and Transition-based Dependency Parsing. In *Proceedings of EMNLP*, pages 562–571.

Y. Zhang and J. Nivre. 2011. Transition-Based Parsing with Rich Non-Local Features. In *Proceedings of ACL*, pages 188–193.

Towards Joint Morphological Analysis and Dependency Parsing of Turkish

Özlem Çetinoğlu and **Jonas Kuhn**
IMS, University of Stuttgart
Germany
{ozlem,jonas}@ims.uni-stuttgart.de

Abstract

Turkish is an agglutinative language with rich morphology-syntax interactions. As an extension of this property, the Turkish Treebank is designed to represent sublexical dependencies, which brings extra challenges to parsing raw text. In this work, we use a joint POS tagging and parsing approach to parse Turkish raw text, and we show it outperforms a pipeline approach. Then we experiment with incorporating morphological feature prediction into the joint system. Our results show statistically significant improvements with the joint systems and achieve the state-of-the-art accuracy for Turkish dependency parsing.

1 Introduction

Turkish is a morphologically rich language (MRL) that has been known to pose interesting research questions to linguists and computational linguists, including architectural issues at the morphology-syntax interface. Today, good quality tools for morphological analysis are available for analysing Turkish raw text input at the word level, and in work on the Turkish Dependency Treebank (Oflazer et al., 2003), a representation scheme has been developed that captures the peculiarities at the morphology-syntax interface in a dependency format that is formally compatible with the standard CoNLL dependency format.

So, it might seem as if all Turkish-specific challenges have been resolved, and only language-independent data-driven methods are required from now on (after all, the Turkish Dependency Treebank was included in the CoNLL 2006 and 2007 Shared Tasks (Buchholz and Marsi, 2006; Nivre et al., 2007), and several researchers working on language-independent methods have reported scores on the available data).

However, Turkish still causes a considerable architectural challenge for the standard pipeline architecture used in data-driven dependency parsing: the dependency treebank scheme for Turkish is based on segments that are not identical to the words from the raw text input, but are often sublexical units that form parts of morphological derivations.

While it is straightforward to train data-driven parsers on the gold standard segmentation from the treebank (which is what happened in the shared tasks), any realistic application starting out with raw text has to involve morphological disambiguation in the preprocessing which means it is not guaranteed that treebank-compatible segment boundaries will be produced. For instance, when training a dependency parser on predicted POS and morphology features, the treebank is of course used to provide the gold standard dependency arcs, but with an automatic (and hence imperfect) morphological disambiguator, there will be cases where the gold standard assumes two segments for a word, but morphological prediction assumes only one. So any standard learning algorithm will break down because the node sets for the dependency graphs are incompatible.

For many languages, realistic parsing scenarios assume gold tokens and use predicted POS (and morphological features). For Turkish, keeping the gold segmentation and assigning predicted POS and morphology would converge to using an oracle because gold segmentation would sometimes disambiguate morphology. Instead, realistic scenarios include segmentation, and a statistical morphological disambiguator picks the most probable analysis among all possibilities a morphological analyser produces. It is the morphological analysis that determines the lemma, POS, morphological features, and segmentation of a word is based on the number of its word-internal derivations.

For instance, in (1), the middle word *bende* has

Proceedings of the Second International Conference on Dependency Linguistics (DepLing 2013), pages 23–32,
Prague, August 27–30, 2013.

four morphological analyses with different lemma and POS combinations, meaning 'at me', 'on the mole', 'to the dam', and 'servant' respectively.[1] Hence, unlike many other languages, the segmentation, POS tagging, and morphological analysis are tightly connected for Turkish.

Eryiğit et al. (2008) is the first work that addresses the segmentation problem in parsing predicted text. They set up a pipeline architecture of a morphological analyser and disambiguator but leave out handling the multiword expressions.[2] A recent work from Eryiğit (2012) solely focuses on the impact of the morphological analysis and disambiguation of the Turkish treebank. Again, it follows the standard pipeline but this time with a treebank version that represents multiwords as detached segments, which allows avoiding to use a multiword extractor.

The major drawback of a pipeline system is to propagate the disambiguator's mistakes to the parsing step. Moreover, the disambiguator cannot take advantage of syntactic information that could help disambiguate certain morphological analyses.

In (1), the first word *kahveleri* means 'the coffees (Acc)', 'his/her coffees', 'their (one) coffee', 'their coffees' from (1a) to (1d). When the first two words come together, they make a sentence meaning 'His/her/their coffees are at my place'. *kahveleri* is still ambiguous but its dependency relation is clear; *bende*, with morphological analysis (1e), behaves as a copular predicate with no overt marker and *kahveleri* is dependent on *bende* as a subject.

When the third word *içelim* 'let's drink' follows the former two, the meaning of the sentence changes to 'Let's drink the coffees at my place', which also changes the morphological analysis of *kahveleri* to (1a). It now behaves as the object of the main predicate *içelim*. A pipeline system cannot benefit from such a disambiguation advantage.

An alternative approach to pipeline architectures is making joint decisions on morphological disambiguation and parsing. It has been shown that such an architecture improves constituency parsing accuracy both for Arabic (Green and Manning, 2010) and for Hebrew (Goldberg and Tsarfaty, 2008). On the dependency parsing front, Lee et al. (2011) introduces a joint morphological disambiguation and dependency parsing architecture which proves to outperform their pipeline architecture for Latin, Ancient Greek, Czech, and Hungarian. However it is limited to unlabelled dependency parsing and initial scores are below the state-of-the-art. On the other hand, parsers that can jointly POS tag become more common in the last years (Bohnet and Nivre, 2012; Hatori et al., 2011; Li et al., 2011). Bohnet and Nivre (2012) propose a joint POS tagger and labelled dependency parser that outperforms the pipeline results and also improves the state-of-the-art accuracy for German, Czech, English, and Chinese.

Joint POS tagger and dependency parsers are not originally designed for predicting morphological features, but they provide a flexible field (POS) where the parser is not dependent on the morphological disambiguator decisions. So the use of this field can actually be extended to accommodating morphological features instead of or in addition to POS tags, which gives parsers an opportunity to override fixed disambiguator mistakes. Hence, those parsers approximate to a joint morphological disambiguation and dependency parsing architecture, which provides us with a testbed until genuinely full-fledged joint parsers are developed.

In this paper we use Bohnet and Nivre's (2012) system to apply their approach to Turkish and later to explore ways to include morphological feature prediction into parsing. Experimental results show that even a partial flexibility in predicting the morphological features helps improve the parsing accuracy statistically significantly.

The paper is structured as follows: Section 2 gives an overview on how morphological features are used in parsing MRLs. Section 3 explains the morphological analysis representation and its relation with segmentation. Section 4 describes the use of morphological features in joint parsing experiments. The setup for experiments are given in Section 5 and results are discussed in Section 6. We conclude with Section 7.

2 Use of Morphological Features

Using morphological information as features in parsing has been a commonly used method for MRLs (Tsarfaty et al., 2010). The effect is controversial: in some cases gold morphology clearly

[1] A3pl: 3rd personal plural agreement, A3sg: 3rd personal singular agreement, Pnon: no possessives, P3sg: 3rd personal singular possessive, P3pl: 3rd personal plural possessive, Nom: Nominative, Acc: Accusative, Loc: Locative, Dat: Dative, Zero: No overt derivation, Pos: Positive, Opt: Optative mood

[2] because of the lack of a multiword extractor. Hence the experiments are not in a fully predicted setting.

	Kahveleri	bende	içelim
(1)	a.kahve+Noun+A3pl+Pnon+Acc	e.ben+PersP+A1sg+Pnon+Loc	iç+Verb+Pos+Opt+A1pl
	b.kahve+Noun+A3pl+P3sg+Nom	f.ben+Noun+A3sg+Pnon+Loc	
	c.kahve+Noun+A3sg+P3pl+Nom	g.bent+Noun+A3sg+Pnon+Dat	
	d.kahve+Noun+A3pl+P3pl+Nom	h.bende+Noun+A3sg+Pnon+Nom	

helps, in others its impact is little. For some settings predicted information causes a drop, for some settings a partial set of morphological features improves parsing accuracy.

Ambati et al. (2010) explore ways of integrating local morphosyntactic features into Hindi dependency parsing. They experiment with different sets of features both on a graph-based and a transition-based dependency parser. Both with gold and predicted settings using morphological features root, case, and suffix outperform using POS as the only feature.

Bengoetxea and Gojenola (2010) utilise the CoNLL-X format and MaltParser's feature configuration file to take advantage of morphological features in parsing Basque with gold data. Their experiments show that case and subordination type increase parsing accuracy.

Marton et al. (2010) explore which morphological features could be useful in dependency parsing of Arabic. They observe the effect of features by adding them one at a time separately and comparing the outcomes. Experiments show that when gold morphology is provided, case markers help the most, whereas when the morphology is automatically predicted the outcome is the opposite: using case harms the results the most. When features are combined in a greedy heuristic, using definiteness, person, number, and gender information improves accuracy.

To overcome the exhaustive feature space problem of Arabic, Dehdari et al. (2011) use heuristic search algorithms for the optimal feature combination. Similar to Marton et al. (2010) they run experiments by including one feature at a time to their no-feature baseline, and also conduct a second set of experiments where they remove one feature at a time from the whole feature set. They also conclude that leaving out the predicted case improved the parsing most among the possible candidates to remove, this time for constituency parsing. In the single feature experiments, genitive clitics help the most. The optimal combination they achieve consists of the features determiner, proper noun, genitive clitics, and negation.

Another Semitic language that is studied within the MRLs is Hebrew. Initial results on Hebrew dependency parsing (Goldberg and Elhadad, 2009) show predicted morphological features help in a transition-based parser with a tailored feature configuration file, although scores drop in a graph-based parser. The same authors later prove both gold and predicted agreement features improve accuracy for an easy-first, non-directional dependency parser (Goldberg and Elhadad, 2010). Tsarfaty and Sima'an (2010) report agreement features are useful also for constituency parsing when they extend the Relational Realisational (Tsarfaty and Sima'an, 2008) models with this information.

Seeker and Kuhn (2011) focus on the internal structures and grammatical functions of German noun phrases. Their experiments show grammatical functions are predicted with higher accuracy when a graph-based dependency parser is provided with both gold and predicted case markers.

They further explore the effects of using case in dependency parsing, this time for Czech and Hungarian as well as for German (Seeker and Kuhn, 2013). On a graph-based parser German does not benefit much from using predicted morphology but Czech and Hungarian clearly profit. They also use case as a constraint on integer linear programming (ILP) parsing models to filter out ungrammatical case-function mappings. For all three languages, the constrained models outperform the unconstrained models and graph-based parser in predicting core grammatical functions.

The research discussed in this section show case and agreement are among the most investigated features, and most of the time they are among the most beneficial ones. These are the features we also look into. But first, we describe the interaction between the morphology and syntax in Turkish in Section 3.

3 The Morphology-Syntax Interface in Turkish

The motivation behind using sublexical units in the Turkish treebank comes from its agglutinative nature. Many linguistic phenomena that are syntactic in other languages are represented with derivational morphology in Turkish (Sulger et al., 2013). For instance *çekti* is a one-word sentence in Turkish meaning 'It was a cheque'. The word *çek* 'cheque' is derived into a verb (with no overt suffix) and then the past tense suffix *-ti* is attached. (2) is the morphological representation of this word where `^DB` denotes the derivational boundary:

(2) `çek+Noun+A3sg+Pnon+Nom^DB+Verb+Zero +Past+A3sg`

Each sequence of inflectional features divided by a derivational boundary is called an *inflectional group* (IG hereafter). The word in (2) has two IGs. A further example clarifies why inflectional groups are chosen as the unit of the treebank. Figure 1 gives the dependency representation of the sentence *açık çekti* 'It was a blank cheque'. The adjective *açık* 'blank' modifies the noun *çek* only, not the derived verb *çekti*. A word based representation would disregard this distinction.

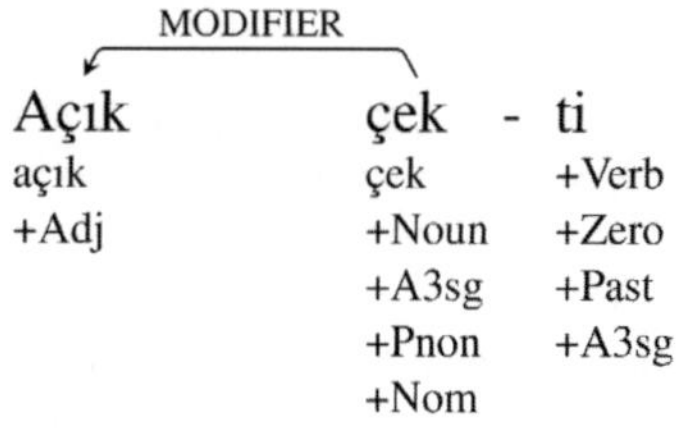

Figure 1: The dependency representation for *açık çekti*

The Turkish Treebank follows this IG notation. A word is segmented into segments from its derivational boundaries. If it is derived n times, it is represented as n+1 segments. The first segment has the lemma, and the last segment has the whole word as the surface form. The surface forms of non-final segments are underscores. (3) gives the treebank representation of the sentence in Figure 1 in the CoNLL format. The derived verb *çekti* is represented as two segments.

The possible segmentation problem arises when words have ambiguous morphological analyses with different number of IGs. For instance, the word *çekti* has a second interpretation with the meaning 's/he pulled' which is the past tense of the verb *çek* 'to pull' in 3rd person singular. The morphological representation of this sense is given in (4).

(4) `çek+Verb+Pos+Past+A3sg`

Note that in this analysis, there are no derivational boundaries, hence it only has a single IG. When the gold standard is the first interpretation of the word *çekti* and a morphological prediction suggests the second interpretation, the number of segments do not match any more.

4 Morphological Feature Prediction

Like many other free-word-order languages, Turkish has overt case markers. It is the case marker that determines the function of a word in a sentence rather than the POS of that word. For instance, an accusative nominal is an object no matter if it is a noun, proper noun, or pronoun.

However, the case-function mapping is not completely unambiguous. Nominative case is associated with subjects and indefinite direct objects. Subjects of sentential complements are genitive. Dative, ablative, genitive, and instrumental can be non-canonical objects (Çetinoğlu and Butt, 2008), although their primary function is adjunct. In copular sentences, the nominal predicate, with or without an overt copular suffix, can bear any case marker except accusative.

Another morphological feature that parsing algorithms can benefit from is agreement. In Turkish, subjects and verbs must agree in number and person. There is an exception to this rule: a third person plural subject might agree with a verb in third person singular as well as a verb in third person plural.

To explore the question whether we can benefit from case and agreement features in parsing Turkish, we employ two different representation methods. First, we append case markers to nominal POS tags[3] to see if a more informative POS field could facilitate parsing (*Pos+Case*). Then, with the intuition that case markers alone could determine the function, we categorise nominals according to CASE instead of their POS (*Case*).

In the implementation, in order to represent case markers as categories we move them to the POS field. POS tags are moved to the morphological features field. For instance, In the CoNLL format[4], *çeki* 'cheque.Acc' has normally the representation in (5a). Appending CASE to POS results in (5b). When CASE replaces POS, the representation is as in (5c).

[3]These are namely nouns, proper nouns, pronouns, nominal participals, and infinitives.

[4]The columns are Form, Lemma, POS, Morphological Features respectively.

	ID	Form	Lemma	POS	Morph. Feat.	Head	Dep. Rel.
(3)	1	açık	açık	Adj	_	2	MODIFIER
	2	_	çek	Noun	A3sg|Pnon|Nom	3	DERIV
	3	çekti	_	Verb	Zero|Past|A3sg	0	ROOT

(5)	a.	çeki	çek	Noun	A3sg|Pnon|Acc
	b.	çeki	çek	Noun|Acc	A3sg|Pnon
	c.	çeki	çek	Acc	A3sg|Pnon|Noun

This representation has two benefits. We can still use the POS tags as features for the parser, and after parsing, it is possible to restore the POS tags by switching them back. This allows us to evaluate our system against the standard gold data.

When combined with a joint parsing system, both approaches extend the use of the parser and practically carry it to a level between POS tagging and morphological analysis. We applied the CASE-POS replacement technique to agreement markers (*Agr*) hoping that the parser can learn and predict the relation between subjects and verbs better. We also collected the finite verbs under the `VFin` umbrella instead of `Verb` to distinguish verbs with an agreement marker from non-finite ones (*VFin*). We discuss the effects of those changes in Section 6.2.

5 Experimental Setup

5.1 Data Set

We use the METU-Sabancı Turkish Treebank (Oflazer et al., 2003) for training and ITU validation set (Eryiğit, 2007) for testing. The training and test sets consist of 5635 and 300 sentences respectively. There are no separate development sets. The original version of the treebank contains multiword expressions[5] where words that construct the multiword are attached together with an underscore. The POS and morphological features of a MWE are that of the last word of the MWE. Eryiğit et al. (2011) have created a detached version of the original treebank. In the detached version, multiword expressions are splitted into words, and POS and morphological features are assigned to the new words. They are dependent on the final word of the multiword with the relation MWE. (6a) and (6b) give the original and detached versions of *söz vermiştim* 'I have promised', respectively. Note that if a MWE consists derived words they will also be represented with multiple IGs. In our experiments we use the detached version of the treebank.

5.2 Tools

In order to parse data with predicted segmentation, POS and morphological features, the raw data is first passed through a morphological analyser (Oflazer, 1994) and then through a morphological disambiguator (Sak et al., 2008). Heuristic rules are used for some unknown types[6] and the rest of unknowns are considered to be nominative proper nouns. We adopt Bohnet's (2010) state-of-the-art graph-based parser as our *Pipeline* parser[7] and Bohnet and Nivre's (2012) transition-based parser as our *Joint* parser that can jointly handle POS tagging and dependency parsing.

5.3 Evaluation

The standard evaluation metrics labelled and unlabelled attachement scores (LAS and UAS) (Buchholz and Marsi, 2006) are not applicable to compare a predicted file to a gold file if the segment sizes are different. We handle this problem by using an evaluation tool based on IGs (Eryiğit et al., 2008). The unlabelled attachement score UAS_{IG} gives the ratio of IGs that are attached to the correct head, and the labelled attachement score LAS_{IG} gives the ratio of IGs attached to the correct head with the correct label. In cases where the morphology (segmentation, POS, and morphological features) of the head word is different from the gold one, an attachement is correct only if the dependent is attached to the correct word *and* the head IG has the gold main POS. Note that when gold segmentation and POS are used LAS_{IG} and UAS_{IG} are identical to the standard LAS an UAS respectively. We omit punctuation in evaluation.

[5]E.g., named entities, collocations, date-time expressions, noun-verb compounds as in (6).

[6]E.g. if a word ends with an apostrophe followed by the surface form of a case marker, the string before the apostrophe is the root of a proper noun and the case is determined from the surface form.

[7]We also ran baseline experiments with Bohnet's transition-based parser. The graph-based parser clearly outperforms it in the gold setting. When the parsers are provided with predicted POS tags and morphological features, the scores are comparable.

		ID	Form	Lemma	POS	Morph. Feat.	Head	Dep. Rel.
(6)	a.	4	söz_vermiştim	söz_ver	Verb	Pos|Narr|Past|A1sg	5	SENTENCE
	b.	4	söz	söz	Noun	A3sg|Pnon|Nom	5	MWE
		5	vermiştim	ver	Verb	Pos|Narr|Past|A1sg	6	SENTENCE

6 Experiments and Analyses

We conduct 10-fold cross validation experiments on the training data and report the average scores for pipeline and joint parsers. Gold settings use gold segmentation, POS, and morphological features, whereas in predicted settings, all this information is predicted (either by the morphological analyser+disambiguator or by the joint parser). For systems we observe improvements on 10-fold cross validation experiments, we also give the test set results.[8]

6.1 Pipeline Experiments

In the first set of experiments, we examine the effect of using morphological features in parsing. Table 1 gives the average 10-fold cross validation scores on the training data. As discussed in Section 2, there are controversial results of using morphological features in parsing MRLs: although gold features help, predicted features might harm the accuracy. For Turkish, Eryiğit et al. (2008) have already shown that adding gold morphological features to Malt parser trained on the original treebank improves accuracy. Our findings are in line with theirs.

The first row of Table 1 gives the graph-based parser results when both the training and parsing data have morphological information. The predicted LAS_{IG} is 4.5% lower than the gold one. When the graph-based parser is trained on gold data with morphological features, but the features are not provided during parsing, there are 12.4% and 10.7% LAS_{IG} drops in the gold and predicted settings respectively. A drop in such a scenario is of course expected, but the impact of no morphology in parsing is huge as compared to many other MRLs (e.g., Seeker and Kuhn (2013) report 6.3%, 2.4%, and only 0.4% absolute drops in LAS for Hungarian, Czech, and German respectively). When the morphological information is not used in training at all, the parser can cope with the lack of morphological information better during parsing. Still, the gold and predicted LAS_{IG} scores are absolute 5-6% lower than a setting that uses morphology both in training and parsing.

	Gold		Predicted	
System	**LAS_{IG}**	**UAS_{IG}**	**LAS_{IG}**	**UAS_{IG}**
GB +T,+P	66.29	77.51	61.79	73.89
GB +T,-P	53.88	71.49	51.02	69.71
GB -T,-P	60.62	75.36	56.31	71.42

Table 1: The effect of using morphological features on the graph-based parser. Morphological features are used in neither training nor parsing (-T,-P), used in training but not provided in parsing (+T,-P), used both in training and parsing (+T,+P). Results given are the average 10-fold cross-validation scores on the training data.

6.2 Joint Parsing Experiments

Table 2 gives the training set 10-fold cross validation average scores for systems we experimented in this paper, as well as for previous work. It is observed that moving CASE to the POS field helps with a 0.3% absolute increase in the gold pipeline settings. Joint parsing results with gold features, are 1-1.5% absolute lower than the pipeline scores. This is expected; the gold setting for joint parsing is not exactly gold, as by definition the parser predicts POS tags during parsing instead of gold ones although the segmentation and morphological features are gold. As a result, they cannot beat purely gold settings.

If we have a closer look at the joint systems, we witness that only $Joint_{Case}$ outperforms *Joint*. $Joint_{Pos+Case}$ increases the tagset to be learned and predicted from 35 to 107 which is probably too fine-grained for the parser. Agreement markers, which are not directly related to grammatical functions like CASE, have a negative impact in the gold settings when used instead of `Verb`. Still, when agreement markers are used only to introduce an extra category, namely `VFin`, the scores come closer to the baseline of joint parsing with gold information, and even improves over the baseline LAS_{IG} in the predicted setting.

In the pipeline approach with predicted morphology, using CASE instead of nominal POS im-

[8]For replicability, experimental settings are available at `http://www.ims.uni-stuttgart.de/~ozlem/cetinogluDepling13.html`

	Gold		Predicted	
System	**LAS_{IG}**	**UAS_{IG}**	**LAS_{IG}**	**UAS_{IG}**
Pipeline	66.29	77.51	61.79	73.89
$Pipeline_{Case}$	**66.60**	**77.60**	62.07	74.00
Joint	64.61	75.83	62.21	73.86
$Joint_{Case}$	64.92	76.27	**62.58**	**74.35**
$Joint_{Pos+Case}$	63.99	75.45	62.02	73.76
$Joint_{Agr}$	63.65	74.95	61.32	73.17
$Joint_{VFin}$	64.44	75.68	62.34	72.59
Ery11-Ery12	65.90	76.00	58.3/61.1	70.70

Table 2: **Training set 10-fold cross validation average scores.** Gold scores Ery11 are taken from Eryiğit et al. (2011) and predicted scores Ery12 are taken from Eryiğit (2012). Ery12 (Eryiğit, 2012) gives an interval LAS_{IG} corresponding 0% and 100% accuracy for MWE relations

	Gold		Predicted	
System	**LAS_{IG}**	**UAS_{IG}**	**LAS_{IG}**	**UAS_{IG}**
Pipeline	**68.92**	78.85	64.59	76.32
$Pipeline_{Case}$	68.86	**78.98**	65.00	76.35
Joint	66.14	76.86	63.77	75.06
$Joint_{Case}$	67.25	78.50	**65.19**	**77.05**
Ery11-Ery12	-	-	64.2/66.2	75.53

Table 3: **Testset scores.** Ery11 (Eryiğit et al., 2011) does not provide gold scores for testset. Ery12 (Eryiğit, 2012) gives an interval LAS_{IG} corresponding 0% and 100% accuracy for MWE relations.

proves the labelled accuracy by 0.3% absolute for the training set. Letting the parser predict POS in the joint system adds 0.14 points more. The best score is achieved with *Joint*$_{Case}$ which has a 0.3% absolute increase as compared to *Joint*. The difference between pipeline systems and joint systems are statistically significant both for LAS_{IG} and UAS_{IG}, in the gold setting. When predicted data is used, *Pipeline*$_{Case}$, *Joint*, *Joint*$_{Case}$ LAS_{IG} scores are statistically significantly better than *Pipeline* ($p<0.05$, paired *t*-test).

The testset scores are given in Table 3. They follow the training set trend, except for the *Joint* system to our surprise. This is perhaps due to the different characteristics of test and training data. When we look at the breakdown of dependencies from 10-fold cross validation results in Section 6.3, we discuss a recall drop in some labels when they are parsed with the *Joint* parser. We do not look at the dependency distribution of the test data but if it is different from the training data then a possibly similar drop in the same labels might impact the overall score more. In parsing the test data with gold features, pipeline systems statistically significantly outperform joint systems. In the predicted setting, only *Joint* vs. *JointCase* UAS_{IG} difference is statistically significant.

Both in Tables 2 and 3, predicted LAS_{IG} scores from Eryiğit (2012) are given as an interval. In her experiments, the parser is trained on the original treebank (that is, no MWE relations are present in the training data) and tested on the detached version. She reports lower and upper bounds corresponding 0% and 100% accuracy for MWE relations. To compare our results to those of Eryiğit's, we also calculate the upper bounds with 100% MWE accuracy in our best performing system. When we accept all MWE labels correct[9] we achieve **64.49%** LAS_{IG} on the average score of 10-fold cross validation on the training set and **66.46%** LAS_{IG} on the testset for the *Joint*$_{Case}$ system. For both the predicted and gold systems our parsers outperform previous work.

For comparability with other existing results, we also trained the *Pipeline* parser on the original version of the treebank which is used in the CoNLL 2007 Shared Task. Nivre et al. (2007) report **71.6%** LAS on the testset (excluding punctuation) for the best system (Titov and Henderson, 2007). Eryiğit (2012) increases the LAS to **71.98%** and the *Pipeline* parser outperform both systems with **72.53%** LAS .

6.3 Error Analysis

For a detailed error analysis we take into account the *Pipeline*, *Pipeline*$_{Case}$, *Joint*, and *Joint*$_{Case}$ 10-fold cross validation results on the training set. In the predicted setting, scores from these four parsers are in ascending order (Table 2, predicted LAS_{IG} column, first four rows). When we look at the dependency breakdown of pipeline and joint systems, we observe subjects and objects follow this trend, together with question particles, negative particles, and modifiers.

The dependencies that benefit from joint parsing the most are determiners. This is due to the fact that some frequently occuring determiners are ambiguous. For instance, *O* has the determiner ('that') and personal pronoun ('he/she/it') readings, and similarly *bu* 'this' is both a determiner and a demonstrative pronoun. Joint parsing lets the parser assign the correct POS to those words where the morphological disambiguator fails. Let-

[9]through a parameter in the evaluation script

Dependency	Precision	Recall
ABLATIVE.ADJUNCT	41.9	50.3
APPOSITION	48.3	15.0
CLASSIFIER	59.1	68.1
COORDINATION	53.0	48.4
DATIVE.ADJUNCT	40.5	45.8
DETERMINER	73.5	81.3
INSTRUMENTAL.ADJUNCT	24.6	21.0
INTENSIFIER	70.7	70.7
LOCATIVE.ADJUNCT	40.4	46.0
MODIFIER	60.3	58.3
MWE	63.5	58.1
NEGATIVE.PARTICLE	67.0	45.6
OBJECT	59.9	58.2
POSSESSOR	70.9	74.5
QUESTION.PARTICLE	71.5	62.8
SENTENCE	86.6	88.0
S.MODIFIER	49.4	46.1
SUBJECT	48.9	51.0
VOCATIVE	29.6	19.5

Table 4: The dependency breakdown of the 10-fold cross validation scores for $Joint_{Case}$ with predicted morphological information. Precision and recall are given in percent. Dependencies with less than 100 occurrences are omitted.

ting the parser predict CASE instead of POS causes some drop, but both precision and recall are still higher than both pipeline systems.

Another dependency with *Joint* as the most accurate system is coordination. CASE helps in $Pipeline_{Case}$ as compared to *Pipeline*, but causes an accuracy decrease when going from *Joint* to $Joint_{Case}$. The COORDINATION label attaches conjunctions to their conjunct to the right. The most frequent conjunctions comma and *ve* 'and' can be predicted with very high accuracy. When the *Joint* parser is used, there are slight improvements on attachements to head conjuncts with various POS tags and a systematic improvement on attaching conjunctions to head copulars and conditionals.

The precision of possessors does not change much with different systems, but the recall drops in *Joint*. That drop is recovered when $Joint_{Case}$ is applied. Intensifiers (e.g., particles *de* 'also, too', *bile* 'even') also have a similar trend. Precision, on the other hand increases with *Joint*.

A large subset of dependencies that suffers from the same drop is adjuncts. Dative, ablative, locative, and instrumental adjuncts commonly have drops in the *Joint* recall as compared to pipeline systems. Their precision, however, increases. When we look into the parser output, we see that the *Joint* system has systematically mistaken by assigning `Adj` to the `Verb` root of participles. Then all arguments attached to this incorrectly POS-tagged root are penalised by the evaluation script although most of the time attachements are correct.

The incorrect POS assignment problem disappears when the joint parser is trained on the CASE feature of nominals instead of their POS. This explains why the precision of adjuncts improves a bit more and their recall has a jump. The only exception is the precision drop in instrumental adjuncts. The reason could be nouns in instrumental case that behave as adverbs, such as *hızla* (`speed+Ins`, 'quickly'). The parser cannot learn to distinguish an instrumental adjunct from an adverbial modifier when `+Ins` is used as POS in $Joint_{Case}$.

The advantage of $Joint_{Case}$ over *Pipeline* is exemplified with a comparison in Figure 2. The *Pipeline* and $Joint_{Case}$ parse trees, together with POS tags and case markers are given in (a) and (b) respectively. The *Pipeline* parser relies on the morphological disambiguator output which incorrectly assigns the analyses (1b) to *kahveleri* and (1h) to *bende*. As a result, the parser assigns the incorrect labels to both dependencies.

On the other hand, the $Joint_{Case}$ parser replaces the case `Nom` with its prediction `Acc` in *kahveleri* and `Nom` replaces `Loc` in *bende*. These corrections result in predicting dependencies identical to gold ones. Note that the lemma of *bende* is still incorrect, but it does not affect the attachements.

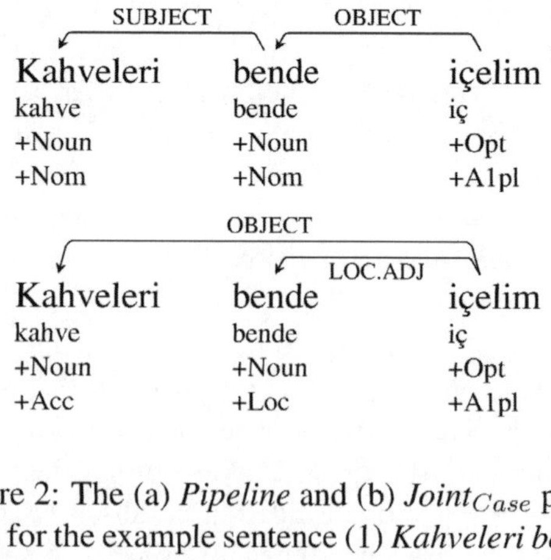

Figure 2: The (a) *Pipeline* and (b) $Joint_{Case}$ parse trees for the example sentence (1) *Kahveleri bende içelim* 'Let's drink coffee at my place.'

The dependency breakdown of the 10-fold cross validation parses for $Joint_{Case}$ with predicted morphological information is given in Table 4. In the

Turkish treebank representation, the root of a tree is the sentence-final punctuation. The main predicate of the sentence is attached to the sentence-final punctuation with the SENTENCE label. By far, this label is the easiest to predict with our systems. It is followed by determiners, intersifiers, possessors, and question particles, which are all local dependencies. Then come classifiers, coordination, modifiers, multiword expressions within a range of 50-65% precision and recall.

Despite getting improvements with the $Joint_{Case}$ system, grammatical functions are still quite low in accuracy. Except for objects, all such labels are below 50% precision and recall. This is due to both the free-word-order nature of Turkish and the ambiguous case-function mapping mentioned in Section 4.

And finally, appositions, vocatives, and instumental adjuncts are at the bottom of the accuracy ranking with scores going down to 20-30%. Their frequencies are also low and they have different POS and morphological features within the same class, which complicates parsers' learning.

7 Conclusion and Future Work

We have presented a set of experiments on parsing raw Turkish text. We argue the ideal method for parsing Turkish would be joint segmentation, POS tagging, morphological analysis, and dependency parsing. In this work we keep the segmentation fixed and first show using a joint POS tagging and parsing approach outperforms a pipeline approach in a realistic scenario. Then we come one step closer to the ideal case and attemp to incorporate some morphological features into joint prediction. As a second outcome, we show categorising nominals according to CASE instead of their POS improves parsing at all settings (gold vs. predicted, pipeline vs. joint). With the combination of joint parsing and CASE incorporation we not only show statistically significant improvements but also achieve the state-of-the-art parsing accuracy.

We believe these positive results prove there is room for improvement in predicting morphological features with a joint POS tagging and dependency parsing system. Even for the joint parsing experiments below the *Joint* baseline, more clever ways of integration into joint prediction might help achieve higher scores. Past research on MRLs present such cases. Bengoetxea and Gojenola (2010) show a simple integration of morphological features does not improve Basque parsing results on the first attemp, but taking advantage of the data representation and parser configuration changes the impact. Similarly, Tsarfaty and Sima'an (2010) has negative results initially for the impact of using agreement markers on Hebrew parsing. After they modify the way they use the morphological information, it actually helps.

In future work, we intend to explore ways to make more use of the joint parser and to apply the same or similar techniques to other MRLs such as German, Czech, and Hungarian.

We also want to add TedEval (Tsarfaty et al., 2012), which also supports mismatching system-gold segmentation, to our evaluation tools to verify our scores and to use a language-independent metric in a multilingual setting.

Acknowledgments

We thank Bernd Bohnet for his help on using the joint parser and Gülşen Eryiğit for providing us with the IG evaluation script. This work is funded by the Collaborative Research Centre (SFB 732) at the University of Stuttgart.

References

Bharat Ram Ambati, Samar Husain, Sambhav Jain, Dipti Misra Sharma, and Rajeev Sangal. 2010. Two methods to incorporate 'local morphosyntactic' features in Hindi dependency parsing. In *Proc. of the SPMRL Workshop of NAACL-HLT*, pages 22–30, Los Angeles, CA, USA.

Kepa Bengoetxea and Koldo Gojenola. 2010. Application of different techniques to dependency parsing of Basque. In *Proc. of the SPMRL Workshop of NAACL-HLT*, pages 31–39, Los Angeles, CA, USA.

Bernd Bohnet and Joakim Nivre. 2012. A transition-based system for joint part-of-speech tagging and labeled non-projective dependency parsing. In *Proc. of the EMNLP-CoNLL*, pages 1455–1465, Jeju, Korea.

Bernd Bohnet. 2010. Top accuracy and fast dependency parsing is not a contradiction. In *Proc. of COLING*, pages 89–97, Beijing, China.

Sabine Buchholz and Erwin Marsi. 2006. CoNLL-X shared task on multilingual dependency parsing. In *Proc. of CoNLL-X*, pages 149–164, Stroudsburg, PA, USA.

Özlem Çetinoğlu and Miriam Butt. 2008. Turkish non-canonical objects. In *Proc. of LFG08 Conference*, Sydney, Australia. CSLI Publications.

Jon Dehdari, Lamia Tounsi, and Josef van Genabith. 2011. Morphological features for parsing morphologically-rich languages: A case of Arabic. In *Proc. of the SPMRL Workshop of IWPT*, pages 12–21, Dublin, Ireland.

Gülşen Eryiğit. 2007. ITU validation set for METU-Sabancı Turkish treebank.

Gülşen Eryiğit. 2012. The impact of automatic morphological analysis & disambiguation on dependency parsing of Turkish. In *Proc. of LREC*, Istanbul, Turkey.

Gülşen Eryiğit, Joakim Nivre, and Kemal Oflazer. 2008. Dependency parsing of Turkish. *Computational Linguistics*, 34(3):357–389.

Gülşen Eryiğit, Tugay Ilbay, and Ozan Arkan Can. 2011. Multiword expressions in statistical dependency parsing. In *Proc. of the SPMRL Workshop of IWPT*, pages 45–55, Dublin, Ireland.

Yoav Goldberg and Michael Elhadad. 2009. Hebrew dependency parsing: Initial results. In *Proc. of IWPT*, pages 129–133, Paris, France.

Yoav Goldberg and Michael Elhadad. 2010. Easy-first dependency parsing of modern Hebrew. In *Proc. of the SPMRL Workshop of NAACL-HLT*, pages 103–107, Los Angeles, CA, USA.

Yoav Goldberg and Reut Tsarfaty. 2008. A single generative model for joint morphological segmentation and syntactic parsing. In *Proc. of ACL-HLT*, pages 371–379, Columbus, Ohio.

Spence Green and Christopher D. Manning. 2010. Better Arabic parsing: baselines, evaluations, and analysis. In *Proc. of COLING*, pages 394–402, Stroudsburg, PA, USA.

Jun Hatori, Takuya Matsuzaki, Yusuke Miyao, and Jun'ichi Tsujii. 2011. Incremental joint POS tagging and dependency parsing in Chinese. In *Proc. of IJCNLP*, pages 1216–1224, Chiang Mai, Thailand.

John Lee, Jason Naradowsky, and David A. Smith. 2011. A discriminative model for joint morphological disambiguation and dependency parsing. In *Proc. of ACL-HLT*, Portland, Oregon, USA.

Zhenghua Li, Min Zhang, Wanxiang Che, Ting Liu, Wenliang Chen, and Haizhou Li. 2011. Joint models for Chinese POS tagging and dependency parsing. In *Proc. of EMNLP*, pages 1180–1191, Edinburgh, Scotland, UK.

Yuval Marton, Nizar Habash, and Owen Rambow. 2010. Improving Arabic dependency parsing with lexical and inflectional morphological features. In *Proc. of the SPMRL Workshop of NAACL-HLT*, pages 13–21, Los Angeles, CA, USA.

Joakim Nivre, Johan Hall, Sandra Kübler, Ryan Mac Donald, Jens Nilsson, Sebastian Riedel, and Deniz Yuret. 2007. The conll 2007 shared task on dependency parsing. In *Proc. of the CoNLL Shared Task Session of EMNLP-CoNLL*.

Kemal Oflazer, Bilge Say, Dilek Zeynep Hakkani-Tür, and Gökhan Tür. 2003. Building a Turkish treebank. In Anne Abeille, editor, *Building and Exploiting Syntactically-annotated Corpora*. Kluwer Academic Publishers, Dordrecht.

Kemal Oflazer. 1994. Two-level description of Turkish morphology. *Literary and Linguistic Computing*, 9(2):137–148.

Haşim Sak, Tunga Güngör, and Murat Saraçlar. 2008. Turkish language resources: Morphological parser, morphological disambiguator and web corpus. In *Proc. of GoTAL 2008*, pages 417–427.

Wolfgang Seeker and Jonas Kuhn. 2011. On the role of explicit morphological feature representation in syntactic dependency parsing for German. In *Proc. of IWPT*, pages 58–62, Dublin, Ireland.

Wolfgang Seeker and Jonas Kuhn. 2013. Morphological and syntactic case in statistical dependency parsing. *Computational Linguistics*, 39:23–55.

Sebastian Sulger, Miriam Butt, Tracy Holloway King, Paul Meurer, Tibor Laczkó, György Rákosi, Cheikh Bamba Dione, Helge Dyvik, Victoria Rosén, Koenraad De Smedt, Agnieszka Patejuk, Özlem Çetinoğlu, I Wayan Arka, and Meladel Mistica. 2013. Pargrambank: The pargram parallel treebank. In *Proc. of ACL*, Sofia, Bulgaria.

Ivan Titov and James Henderson. 2007. Fast and robust multilingual dependency parsing with a generative latent variable model. In *Proc. of the CoNLL Shared Task Session of EMNLP-CoNLL 2007*, pages 947–951.

Reut Tsarfaty and Khalil Sima'an. 2008. Relational-realizational parsing. In *Proc. of COLING*, pages 889–896, Manchester, UK.

Reut Tsarfaty and Khalil Sima'an. 2010. Modeling morphosyntactic agreement in constituency-based parsing of modern Hebrew. In *Proc. of the SPMRL Workshop of NAACL-HLT*, pages 40–48, Los Angeles, CA, USA.

Reut Tsarfaty, Djamé Seddah, Yoav Goldberg, Sandra Kuebler, Yannick Versley, Marie Candito, Jennifer Foster, Ines Rehbein, and Lamia Tounsi. 2010. Statistical parsing of morphologically rich languages (SPMRL) what, how and whither. In *Proc. of the SPMRL Workshop of NAACL-HLT*, pages 1–12, Los Angeles, CA, USA.

Reut Tsarfaty, Joakim Nivre, and Evelina Andersson. 2012. Joint evaluation for morphological segmentation and syntactic parsing. In *Proc. of ACL*, Jeju, Korea.

Divergences in English-Hindi Parallel Dependency Treebanks

Himani Chaudhry, Himanshu Sharma and **Dipti Misra Sharma**
Language Technologies Research Centre
International Institute of Information Technology-Hyderabad
India
{himani,himanshu.sharma}@research.iiit.ac.in
{dipti}@iiit.ac.in

Abstract

We present, here, our analysis of systematic divergences in parallel English-Hindi dependency treebanks based on the Computational Paninian Grammar (CPG) framework. Study of structural divergences in parallel treebanks not only helps in developing larger treebanks automatically, but can also be useful for many NLP applications such as data-driven machine translation (MT) systems. Given that the two treebanks are based on the same grammatical model, a study of divergences in them could be of advantage to such tasks, along with making it more interesting to study how and where they diverge. We consider two parallel trees divergent based on differences in constructions, relations marked, frequency of annotation labels and tree depth. Some interesting instances of structural divergences in the treebanks have been discussed in the course of this paper. We also present our task of alignment of the two treebanks, wherein we talk about our extraction of divergent structures in the trees, and discuss the results of this exercise.

1 Introduction

Treebanks play an increasingly important role in computational linguistics, and with the availability of a number of treebanks of various languages now, studies based on parallel treebanks are one of the directions application/use of treebanks has taken. "Such resources could be useful for many applications, e.g. as training or evaluation corpora for word and phrase alignment, as training material for data-driven MT systems and for the automatic induction of transfer rules" (Hearne et al., 2007) and so on. However, though recent years have seen an increasing interest in research based on parallel corpora, "surprisingly little work has been reported on parallel treebanks." opine Volk et al. (2004). "A parallel treebank comprises syntactically annotated aligned sentences in two or more languages. In addition to this, the trees are aligned on a sub-sentential level." (Tinsley et al., 2009)

In this paper we report our study on parallel English and Hindi dependency treebanks based on the CPG model. The annotation labels used to mark the relations in the example trees here (as also in the treebanks) conform to the dependency annotation scheme given by Begum et al. (2008). An adaptation of this scheme was subsequently used for the English treebank, as reported in (Chaudhry and Sharma, 2011)

We detail here, how we make use of the existing Hindi dependency treebank and its parallel English dependency treebank, to study systematic divergences in the treebank pair, given that both of these treebanks use the same dependency grammar formalism. We sought to find here, the types and reasons for these differences. We find that the two treebanks diverge mainly from two aspects:

- Stylistic
- Structural

A good example of stylistic variation or translator preference, from our data would be:

(1) kendrIya sarkAr-ke anek varishtha netA bhI mojUd the.

kendriiya	*sarkaar-ke*	*anek*	*varishtha*
ruling	party-of	many	senior
netaa	*bhii*	*mojuud*	*the*
leaders	also	in-attendance	were

'A number of senior leaders from the ruling party were also in attendance.'

Proceedings of the Second International Conference on Dependency Linguistics (DepLing 2013), pages 33–40,
Prague, August 27–30, 2013.

The Hindi sentence in example (1), has been translated as *'A number of senior leaders from the ruling party were also in attendance.'* in our corpus. While another possible (more regular/natural) translation of the sentence would be:

A number of senior leaders from the ruling party were also present.

Stylistic divergences can be due to preferred translations in the language or due to the lexical choice of the translator, (or even translator's preference for a specific type of constructions). This said, though study of stylistic divergence can help recognize preferred constructions in a given language, this would need copies of translations by multiple translators to perform exercises such as inter-translator agreement. Since our data has only one translator, analysis of stylistic divergences is beyond the scope of the work we report here.

Structural divergence, thus, is the focus of our study here, as it abounds in these treebanks and brings forth interesting examples of divergences between the two treebanks. We discuss some occurrences of it in our data. Further, we aim to see if some systematic patterns of divergence could be arrived at, in the treebanks, through a comparative study of the structures of their trees. However, since this is a work in progress, we are yet to sum up any such generalizations, and we do not include them here.

The remainder of this paper is organized as follows: Section 2 gives some background on the data, the annotation scheme and the methodology we used for our study. In Section 3 we take a look at the dissimilarities in the two treebanks, and discuss our investigations into the reasons behind them. Section 4 presents our observations. Section 5 presents the task of our alignment of the two treebanks, where in we talk about our extraction of divergent structures in the trees, and discusses the results of this exercise. And, in Sections 6, we conclude and sketch the possibilities for some future work in this direction.

2 Methodology

2.1 The Data

The data for this study comprises a set of parallel English and Hindi dependency treebanks. A small section (25000 words) of the Hindi dependency treebank (Bhatt et al., 2009) (being developed at IIIT-H, under the Hindi-Urdu Treebank (HUTB) project) was translated to English to form a parallel corpus. The English treebank used here (reported in (Chaudhry and Sharma, 2011)), has been developed on these translations and has 1143 sentences annotated using the dependency annotation scheme modeled on the CPG framework (Begum et al., 2008) (as also the Hindi treebank used here).

2.2 The Annotation Scheme

As mentioned earlier, the annotation scheme used for the creation of the two parallel dependency treebanks (English and Hindi) is based on CPG, a dependency grammar model proposed by Bharati et al. (1995). This annotation scheme, developed for Hindi and other Indian languages, by Begum et al. (2008) was later applied to English first by Vaidya et al. (2009) and then, by Chaudhry and Sharma (2011) to develop their English dependency treebank (used for this work). Paninian Grammar assigns 'karaka' (verb argument relations) to arguments in a sentence, based on the relationship they have with the verb. "karaka relations are syntactico-semantic (or semantico-syntactic) relations between the verbals and other related constituents in a sentence." (Bharati et al., 1995). There are six basic karakas, namely *adhikarana* 'location', *apaadaan* 'source', *sampradaan* 'recipient', *karana* 'instrument', *karma* 'theme', *karta* 'agent'. It must be noted, that though the first four karakas (as listed here) can be roughly mapped to their thematic role counterparts, *karma* and *karta* tend to be different from 'theme' and 'agent' respectively". (Begum et al., 2008) Further, the annotation directly represents the relations between a syntactic head and its arguments and adjuncts (that is, its dependents or modifiers) in a sentence/clause. It is noteworthy, that the main verb is taken to be the central and binding element of the sentence, and is therefore, the root node of a dependency tree, per the annotation scheme. However, there can be exceptions to this, such as in the cases of co-ordination, where a co-ordinating conjunct co-ordinates sentences/clauses that do not have dependencies over/with each other. For example:

'Ram ate an apple and Ravi drank milk.'

Here, the two verbs 'ate' and 'drank' are the root nodes for their respective sentences, and these two are then co-ordinated by the co-ordinating conjunct 'and', which is taken as the head of the entire co-ordinated structure.

Futher, two types of relations are marked under this scheme–karaka and others. (Bhatt et al., 2009). Relations other than karakas, such as purpose, reason, and possession (adjuncts) and also, non-dependency relations as in co-ordination and light verb constructions etc., too are therefore, taken care of, using the relational concepts prescribed by this annotation scheme. *Table 1* provides information about the relation labels (from the two treebanks) referred to, in this work.

The dependency relations are marked at interchunk level, instead of marking relations between words. So, function words are attached to (chunked with) their lexical heads. Per this scheme, a chunk (with boundaries marked), by definition, represents a group of adjacent words in a sentence, which are in dependency relation with each other, and where one of them is their head (Mannem et al., 2009).

2.3 Procedure

For the purpose of a detailed comparative study of the two treebanks, about 700 sentence pairs from the two treebanks were manually aligned at sentence level and the trees were then aligned automatically. "A *sentence pair* is a pair of sentences which are translations of each other, and the dependency trees for the two sentences in a sentence pair form a *tree pair*." (Georgi et al., 2012)

After this, various instances of the dependency relations in the parallel sentences were automatically extracted for the study. We then (manually) compared the tree pairs as regards their similarities and contrasts. The comparisons were made not just for their spans as complete trees, but also at the level of their subtrees. Given a sentence pair, we first observed the entire tree spans for potential divergences. And, if they were divergent, we looked further on, to find where they diverged, followed by how much they diverged, and why. This has been discussed in detail in section 5. We sought to find what type of divergences they were. We talk in detail of these aspects the two treebanks were compared on, in Section 3.

3 Divergence Types

The two treebanks were considered 'divergent' if the paralle trees fell under any of the following:

- Differences in the construction (structure)
- Difference in relations marked (on the parallel sentences)
- Difference in tree depth
- Difference in the frequency of annotation labels

3.1 Difference in construction

Changes in lexical category of a word of one language and its counterpart in the other, lead to Categorial divergence visible in the data. *'It suffices.'* would be translated in Hindi as *'yaha kAfI hE.'* (It sufficient is). While the word *'suffices'* is realized as the main verb in English it is an adjectival modifier *'kAfI'* (sufficient) in the phrase *'kAfI hE'*, in Hindi. *Figure 1* shows the divergent trees for the sentence pair.

(2) Hindi: 'yaha kAfI hE.'

yaha kaafii hE
It sufficient is
English: 'It suffices'

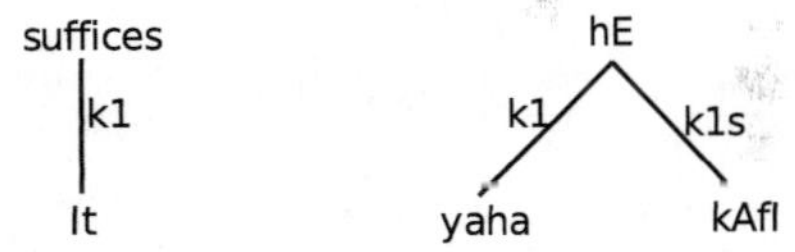

Figure 1: Example showing categorial divergence.

Event verbs of English such as *'flagged'* or *'flagged off'* may not have Hindi equivalents. In such cases they are substituted with description/descriptive phrases such as *'jhandI dikhA kar ravAnA kiyA'*, as seen in *figure 2*, for the sentence pair:

(3) Hindi: 'unhone tren ko jhandI dikhA kar ravAnA kiyA.'

unhone tren ko jhandii dikhaa kar
He train to flag show do
ravaanaa kiyaa.
send did
English: 'He flagged off the train.'

Label Name	Relation Name	Description
k1	karta	Doer/agent/subject.
k1s	karta samaanaadhikarana	Noun complement of karta.
k2	karma	Object/patient.
pof-phrv	Phrasal verb	Part of units in phrasal verb constructions.
vmod	Verb modifier	General verb modification.
k3	karana	Instrument that helps achieve the action/activity.
k4a	anubhava karta	Experiencer.
k7	vishayaadhikarana	Abstract location in time or place.
r6	shashthi	The genitive/possessive relation between nouns.
nmod__emph	emphatic marker	noun modifier of the type emphatic marker.
k7p	deshaadhikarana	Place/Location.
fragof	Fragment-of	Relation to link elements of a fragmented chunk.
k5	apaadaana	A point of separation/departure from source.
ccof	Conjunct-of	Co-ordination and sub-ordination.
k7t	samayaadhikarana	Location in time.
nmod	Noun modifier	General noun modification, including participles.
pof	Part-of relation	Part of units such as light-verb+noun.
r6-k1	karta of noun in 'part-of' relation	Karta of noun in light-verb+noun construction.
r6-k2	karma of noun in 'part-of' relation	Karma of noun in light-verb+noun construction.
rs	Relation samaanaadhikarana	Noun complement/elaboration.
sent-adv	Sentential Adverb	Adverbial expression with a sentence in its scope.

Table 1: Description of Dependency Relations.

Figure 2: Categorial divergence due to Event verbs (Example (3)).

3.2 Difference in relations marked

We see that the frequency of the core arguments (such as 'karta', 'karma' and thus, the labels pertaining to them) does not vary much, between the two languages, since these are mandatory arguments for both of the languages, and must be present. However, these relations (and their labels) may not always match for all of the trees, of the two treebanks, since there are instances where a word that is a mandatory argument in one language data may realize differently in the other. This happens in the case of other arguments too. For example, 'preposition-stranding' in English is another reason for difference in dependency relations marked on parallel trees. This is because preposition-stranding is specific to English, and is not found in Hindi, which has postpositions that are required to follow the noun they are associated with. Prepositions of English are different from Hindi postpositions which seldom occur discontiguous with the noun they relate with, and never due to movement. Occasional examples that one comes across, of a Hindi postposition separated from its noun, are due to translational choices or due to some additional information about the noun (in written texts). Thus, Hindi doesn't have the phenomena of 'stranding'. An example of this kind of divergence would be:

(4) Hindi: 'jUn kaun-sI dukAn mein gayI?'

juun kaun-sii dukaan mein gayii?
June which shop in go+PAST
English: 'Which shop did June go to?'

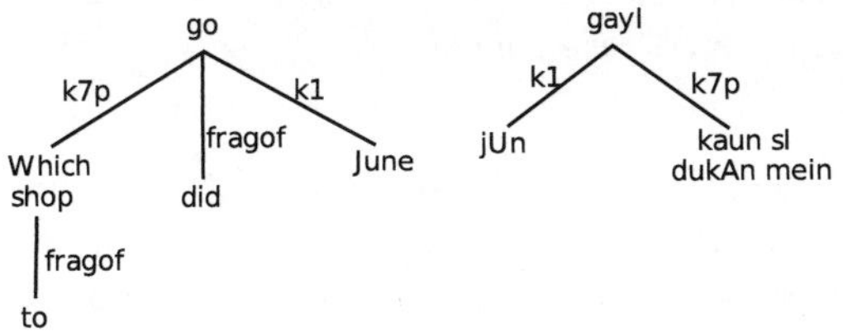

Figure 3: Divergence due to 'preposition-stranding' in English.

In example (4), while in English the preposition '*to*' will have the relation 'fragment-of' (annotated with the label 'fragof') with the noun phrase (NP) '*which shop*', to indicate that though separated from it, the preposition is related to the NP. It may be noted that noun within the NP of a Preposition Phrase (PP) is considered the head of the phrase, in our analysis. In its Hindi counterpart, the postposition '*mein*' will be part of the NP preceding it, and doesn't need to be annotated separately. Also, the auxiliary '*did*' will be a 'fragof' of the verb '*go*' because the auxilliary '*did*' and the verb '*go*' are discontiguous here. While in Hindi the verb is a single word expression. Thus, as seen in *figure 3*, the English tree has extra relations marked in it, making the two trees divergent.

Null subject divergence is another major aspect leading to divergences in the two treebanks. In Hindi the subject of a sentence is left to be implicit many times, since Hindi allows dropping of the subject where it is obvious. This is not so with English. Being a positional language English encodes much information in the subject (even object) position, hence the subject can't be dropped. For an insight into subject dropping in Hindi, let us look at example (5) in (*figure 4*)

(5) Hindi: '(tum) kyA kar rahe ho?'

(tum) kyaa kar-rahe-ho?
(you) what do+CONT+be+PRES
English: 'What are you doing?'

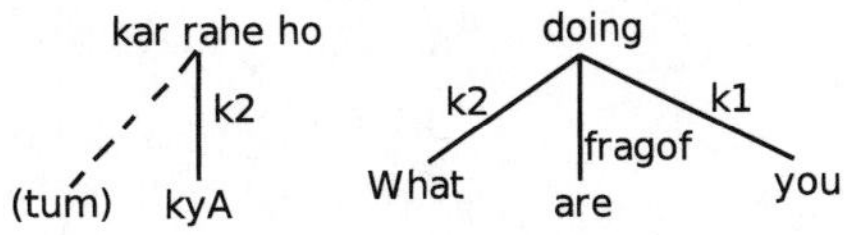

Figure 4: Example of null subject divergence.

Thus, while it is possible to ask someone '*kyA kar rahe ho?*' in Hindi, it is ungrammatical to ask '*what (are) doing?*' in English, dropping the subject, in such sentences. Divergence is bound to creep in, between the trees of two parallel sentences, in terms of dependency relations as well as labels, for such instances.

3.3 Difference in tree depth

Varying relations (not just their number, but their types too) affect the depth of trees from one language to the other. For instance, the presence of modifier-modified relations such as 'nmod' (noun modifier) or fragmented chunks (depicted with the label 'fragof' in our annotation), in the sentences of one language, and their absence in the parallel sentence in the other, can cause such divergences. This leads to a difference in the depths of the two trees, as is evident from the trees in *figure 3* of example (4).

3.4 Difference in the frequency of annotation labels

We also automatically extracted the relation labels from the parallel dependency treebanks, and studied their instances in the data, based on their high frequency or paucity in either of the language's treebank (The automatic extraction and its results are discussed in section 5). In cases where we found consistency in divergence patterns we investigated further to analyze what lay beneath their surfaces.

Tag/Label	Relation Name	English Count	Hindi Count
ccof	Conjunct-of	1161	730
k1	karta	1206	1032
k1s	karta samaanaadhikarana	153	160
k2	karma	873	1040
k7	vishayaadhikarana	460	282
k7p	deshaadhikarana	272	200
k7t	samayaadhikarana	396	297
nmod	Noun modier	256	296
pof	Part-of relation	781	63
r6	shashthi	935	284
r6-k1	karta of a noun in a lightverb+noun construction	53	04
r6-k2	karma of a noun in a lightverb+noun construction	151	14
r6v	Genetive relation with verb	04	0
rs	Relation samaanaadhikarana	45	0
sent-adv	Sentential Adverb	44	68
vmod	Verb modier	218	175

Table 2: A comparative Dependency Relations count.

For instance, the frequency of the 'part-of' relation label, 'pof', in Hindi and paucity of the same in English (as seen in *Table 2*) point to the fact that Hindi abounds in complex predicates, where as English has few instances of them. As mentioned earlier in the discussion, the noun components of conjunct verbs are annotated with the label 'pof' to convey that that noun has a 'part-of' relation with the verb it is attached to. Another relation label that needs mention here, is 'r6v'. While there are instances of this in the Hindi side of the data, there are none in English. The reason being, this is a relation that attaches to the verb, though not a karaka relation. It indicates a sense of possession, so it is given the tag 'r6v', where 'r6' indicates a possession relation, and 'v' indicates that this relation is marked with the verb. There are no instances of this relation in the English data as this type of realization wasn't encountered in English. The relation tag hasn't therefore, been included in the annotation scheme for English, as of now.

4 Observations

English and Hindi being significantly divergent, we came across varied instances of diversities in the two treebanks. The instances of English manner-motion verbs we came across in the data seemingly indicate regular divergence in that English has the tendency to pair up with satellite prepositions such as 'into' in the expression 'danced into', to form manner-motion verbs. Whereas, Hindi resorts to using separate verbs for manner and motion to represent the action as a whole. For example, 'He broke into the house.' would translate as 'vah zabardastI ghar main ghusA.' (he forcefully home-in enter). Another example for this would be, 'She danced into the room.' which translates as 'vah nAchte hue kamare main ghusI.' (she dance+cont+manner room-in enter).

Another divergence is that English induces *expletives* to fill the canonical subject position in a sentence, in the absence of a logical subject. However, Hindi can conveniently drop the subject as and when. An example for this would be:

(6) Hindi: 'bAhar bArish ho rahI hE.'

baahar baarish ho-rahii-hai.
outside rain be+PRES+CONT
English: 'It is raining outside.'

The examples show that the two sentences diverge syntactically, since the Hindi sentence has no equivalent for 'it', here. However, our annotation scheme licenses incorporation of semantic information along with syntactic analysis (being syntactico-semantic). This said, if we delve a little into their semantics, we see that the dissimilar-

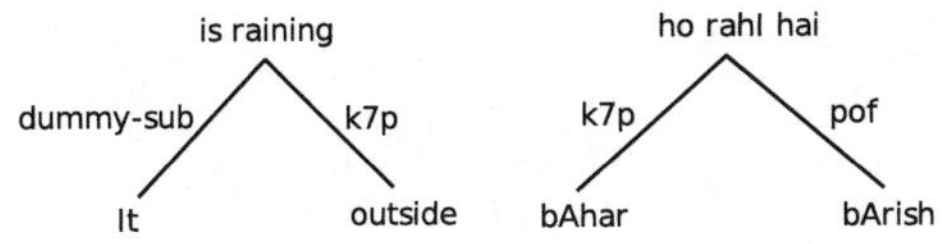

Figure 5: Observation: No 'karta'

ity isn't as pronounced. Expletive 'it', though in the subject position in the sentence, is annotated 'dummy-subject' of the verb. Thus there isn't a *karta* in the English sentence, as also is the case for its Hindi counterpart.

5 Automatic Tree Comparison and Results

In this section, we discuss the structural comparison between the two treebanks, and its results.

5.1 Comparison Criteria

The basis of this comparison is the divergence in the tree structures and in the labels. For any given pair of source (English) sentence, target (Hindi) sentence and the respective Source Sentence Dependency Tree (sTree) and Target Sentence Dependency Tree (tTree), the comparison criteria was:

- Full Structure Match
- Partial Structure Match

5.1.1 Full Structure Match

We consider it a full structure match if the full structure of the sTree matches the tTree. Starting with the ROOT Node, the child nodes in a sub-tree of an sTree are matched with the child nodes of the corresponding sub-tree in the tTree. This process is repeated recursively for each node. If there is a full structure match, then the number of chunk nodes in the sTree matches the number of chunk nodes in the tTree and the tree structure is exactly similar. There are 15 sentences where the structure of the sentences is similar in both the languages.

5.1.2 Partial Match

Partial match between sTree and tTree is calculated on the basis of:

1. Argument/Arc Match for a given node: To see if a particular node has a fixed number of arguments in both the languages.
2. Particular Label Match: If a particular node (event) demands an argument with a particular label, then the label is bound to occur in both of the languages. For Example, if an event X has a 'k1' in its demand-frame for an sTree, and the construction and the lexical choice of words imply that 'k1' should occur in the tTree as well, then there is a potential positive case for Label Match, regardless of the lexical items assigned to the label in the tree pair.
3. Both, Argument and Label Match

5.2 Results

In this section, we take a look at the results of Structural Comparison. For partial sub-tree matching, we calculated the number of sub-trees that have the same number of arguments from a set of possible subTrees.
In our data, 113 sub-trees (*Same Argument Count*) out of 215 (*Total Sub-trees*) were found satisfying the criteria.

In the calculation of Labelled Accuracy, three types of statistics were calculated. "*Common Labels*" gives the number of labels that were shared by the aligned node in both, the source (S) and the target (T) language (L). "*Source Unique Labels*" shows the number of labels owned only by the SL that were not present in the TL. While "*Target Unique Labels*" shows the number of labels present in the TL, but not present in the SL.
Their values for our data are:
$CommonLabels = 371$
$SourceUniqueLabels = 209$
$TargetUniqueLabels = 219$

6 Conclusion and Future Works

In this paper we looked at the divergences in the CPG based English and Hindi parallel treebanks. The English treebank varies from its Hindi counterpart in certain aspects, (in spite of being based on the same grammatical model, and using a quite similar annotation scheme) given the dissimilarities between the two languages. The treebank pair was compared and contrasted based on differences in constructions, relations marked, frequency of annotation labels and tree depth. The tree pairs were considered divergent if their differences fell under one of the criteria above.

Further, we investigated into the reasons behind these divergences. Though we have calculated the extent of divergences in the treebanks, at this point we do not make any generalizations about them. Our observations and their classifications regarding these treebanks can provide insights into improvement of algorithms used for NLP tasks, especially Machine Translation.

Also, as a future work, stylistic divergences between parallel treebanks can be an interesting subject of study, with the availability of data suited to the needs of this task.

Acknowledgments

We gratefully acknowledge the provision of the useful resource by way of the Hindi Treebank developed under HUTB, of which the Hindi treebank used for our research purpose is a part, and the work for which is supported by the NSF grant (Award Number: CNS 0751202; CFDA Number: 47.070). Also, any opinions, findings, and conclusions or recommendations expressed in this material are those of the author(s) and do not necessarily reflect the views of the National Science Foundation.

References

Rafiya Begum, Samar Husain, Arun Dhwaj, Dipti Misra Sharma, Lakshmi Bai, and Rajeev Sangal. 2008. Dependency annotation scheme for indian languages. In *Proceedings of IJCNLP*.

Akshar Bharati, Vineet Chaitanya, Rajeev Sangal, and KV Ramakrishnamacharyulu. 1995. *Natural language processing: a Paninian perspective*. Prentice-Hall of India New Delhi.

Rajesh Bhatt, Bhuvana Narasimhan, Martha Palmer, Owen Rambow, Dipti Misra Sharma, and Fei Xia. 2009. A multi-representational and multi-layered treebank for hindi/urdu. In *Proceedings of the Third Linguistic Annotation Workshop*, pages 186–189. Association for Computational Linguistics.

Himani Chaudhry and Dipti M Sharma. 2011. Annotation and issues in building an english dependency treebank.

Ryan Georgi, Fei Xia, and W Lewis. 2012. Measuring the divergence of dependency structures cross-linguistically to improve syntactic projection algorithms. In *Proceedings of the Eight International Conference on Language Resources and Evaluation (LREC12), Istanbul, Turkey. European Language Resources Association (ELRA)*.

Mary Hearne, John Tinsley, Ventsislav Zhechev, and Andy Way. 2007. Capturing translational divergences with a statistical tree-to-tree aligner.

Prashanth Mannem, Himani Chaudhry, and Akshar Bharati. 2009. Insights into non-projectivity in hindi. In *Proceedings of the ACL-IJCNLP 2009 Student Research Workshop*, pages 10–17. Association for Computational Linguistics.

John Tinsley, Mary Hearne, and Andy Way. 2009. Exploiting parallel treebanks to improve phrase-based statistical machine translation. In *Computational Linguistics and Intelligent Text Processing*, pages 318–331. Springer.

Ashwini Vaidya, Samar Husain, Prashanth Mannem, and Dipti Misra Sharma. 2009. A karaka based annotation scheme for english. In *Computational Linguistics and Intelligent Text Processing*, pages 41–52. Springer.

Martin Volk and Yvonne Samuelsson. 2004. Bootstrapping parallel treebanks. In *Proc. of Workshop on Linguistically Interpreted Corpora (LINC) at COLING*.

Dependency Network Syntax

From Dependency Treebanks to a Classification of Chinese Function Words

Xinying Chen
School of International Study
Xi'an Jiaotong University, China
chenxinying@mail.xjtu.edu.cn

Abstract

This article presents a new approach of using dependency treebanks in theoretical syntactic research: the view of dependency treebanks as combined networks. This allows the usage of advanced tools for network analysis that quite easily provide novel insight into the syntactic structure of language. As an example of this approach, we will show how the network approach can provide clear structural distinctions among the Chinese function words, which are very difficult to obtain directly from the original treebank. We hope to illustrate the enormous potential of the language network approach through a simple example.

1 Why treebanks?

Treebanks are the latest hype in linguistics. The interest in treebanks can roughly be explained by two main charms: the NLP push to data driven approaches and the linguist's fascination of creating a treebank following specific theoretical principles.

In greater detail, we can observe that Natural Language Processing requires treebanks for all kinds of data-driven approaches ranging from Machine Translation to text classification. Great efforts, monetary and personal, go into the creation of treebanks or the transformation of existing treebanks into new formats. In particular dependency treebanks offer interesting connections between texts and the representation of meaning, the ultimate goal of Computational Linguistics. This NLP interest in dependency treebanks has also enthused (and frequently financed) the community of "pure" linguists, who have discovered that the creation of coherent treebanks is linguistically challenging and fascinating. Work has been done on error detection (Dickinson & Meurers 2003), alignment of multilingual (Lopez et al. 2002) and of multi-stratal treebanks (Böhmová et al. 2003; Mille & Wanner 2010), on written and spoken data, just to name a few. The creation of a treebank can also have a unifying effect on a linguistic community by providing a reference analysis, other analysis have to be compared to (Penn Tree Bank, Marcus et al. 1993). But the creation of a treebank following a specific syntactic theory cannot in itself be considered as a confirmation of this theory (other than being a sociological proof of the existence of sufficient support for the theory to be able to create a treebank).

What is crucially missing in this picture is the usage of treebanks for linguistic discovery and theory confirmation or refutation that goes beyond searching for examples in the annotated data. Simple concordancers exist, some of them with sophisticated query languages (Zeldes et al. 2009) but it is up to the syntactician to go through the results and make conclusions. No generally accepted approach on how to interpret this type of data has been established.

The community of "corpus linguistics" is nearly exclusively busy with statistical analysis on pure text corpora, using tools like Wordsmith or Lexico3. At most, they use POS tagged corpora, often simply to disambiguate word usages. This domain of research has achieved impressive results in historical linguistics, sociolinguistics, and other domains where large amounts of data finally are systematically ploughed through (Baker 1993; Charteris-Black 2004). However, the mentioned tools and methods can not easily be applied to treebanks because first, the structure of the data is very different, and secondly, the limited size of treebanks compared to the vast amounts of unannotated text, makes a statistical approach less interesting.

Notable exceptions to this rule include work on usually small hand-coded treebanks like the ones used in Liu et al. (2009) for the study of dependency distance and in Liu (2009a) for the research of probability distribution of dependencies, where the traditional statistical approaches have shown their potential in theoretic syntactic research. As an emerging statistical method, the network approach brings a new angle to this type of research.

In this paper, we attempt to illuminate the network view of dependency treebanks. We will show how this approach reduces the diffi-

Proceedings of the Second International Conference on Dependency Linguistics (DepLing 2013), pages 41–50,
Prague, August 27–30, 2013.

culties in exploiting treebank data and how this approach can be successfully applied to small dependency treebanks, reducing the size limitations of existing dependency treebanks.

2 Language networks

The basic idea underlying dependency networks is very simple: instead of viewing the trees as linearly aligned on the sentences of the corpus, we fuse together each occurrence of the same word to a unique node, thus creating a unique and (commonly) connected network of words, in which the tokens are the vertices and dependency relations are the edges or arcs. This connected network is then ready to undergo common network analysis with tools like UCINET (Borgatti et al. 2002), PAJEK (Nooy et al. 2005), NETDRAW (Borgatti 2002), CYTOSCAPE (Shannon 2003), and so on.

In reality, extracting a network from a dependency treebank is slightly more complicated, as we have to use some heuristics to fuse together only the words that belong to the same lexeme (same category, near meaning). We refer to Liu (2008) for a description of multiple ways of network creation from dependency treebanks.

Linguistic research with using modern network analysis tools is an upcoming domain. The first conference on this subject, Modeling Linguistic Networks, was held in December 2012 in Frankfurt and united nearly 40 scholars from 14 countries. This community is guided by two assumptions: First, Language is physiognomicly a network and modeling of language should follow this guiding principle, and secondly, computational tools that have proven to be successful in sociology and computer science can be used for language networks, too.

The key interest of the network approach in linguistic research is that it provides a new way to analyze language systems. A central assumption of modern linguistic theories is that language is a system (Kretzschmar 2009). This widely accepted point of view, however, has remained on a purely theoretic level due to the absence of an operational methodology, until corpora and modern network analysis tools appeared. As language is a system, we expect there to be rules that cannot be predicted directly on the basis of the units. So looking at some specific words (or the relationship between them) may not be an efficient way for discovering the global features of a language system. Modeling language as a network provides an operational way for observing the macroscopic features of language system and the relationship between the units and the whole system. For example, it can be used for determining the function or status of some units, such as words, in the language system as a whole.

Some research has been done on the structure of syntactic dependency networks (Ferrer i Cancho 2005; Liu 2008; Chen & Liu 2011; Čech et al. 2011), the patterns in syntactic dependency networks (Ferrer i Cancho 2004; Chen et al. 2011), the language development or language evolution (Ke & Yao 2008; Mukherjee et al. 2013; Mehler et al. 2011), language clustering and linguistic categorization (Liu 2010; Liu & Cong 2013; Gong et al. 2012; Abramov & Mehler 2011), manual and machine translation (Amancio et al. 2008 &2011), word sense disambiguation (Christiano Silva & Raphael Amancio 2013), communication and interaction (Banisch et al. 2010; Mehler et al. 2010), the structure of semantic networks (Borge Holthoefer & Arenas 2010; Liu 2009b), phonetics (Arbesman et al. 2010; Yu et al. 2010), morphology (Čech & Mačutek 2009; Liu & Xu 2011), parts of speech (Ferrer i Cancho et al. 2007), Knowledge Networks (Allee 2000), cognitive networks (Mehler et al. 2012).

Works on Chinese include networks that use as nodes the Chinese characters (Li & Zhou 2007; Peng et al. 2008), words and phrases (Li et al. 2005), phoneme and syllables (Yu et al. 2011; Peng et al. 2008), syntactic structure (Liu 2008; Liu 2010; Chen & Liu 2011; Chen et al. 2011), semantic structure (Liu 2009b).

In general, the language network research, including that on Chinese language network, is developing rapidly in recent years. But the language network research inevitably has some aspects that need to be improved in order to establish this new domain. It seems that most of the language networks studies put a heavy emphasis on common features of various networks, such as 'small world' (Watts & Strogatz 1998) and 'scale-free' (Barabási & Bonabeau 2003) features, treating alike different levels of language and different concerns on which the networks are built. At the same time, many language networks were built without proper guide of a specific linguistic theory, such as words', characters', or phrases' co-occurrence networks (Li & Zhou 2007; Peng et al. 2008; Liu & Sun 2007; Li et al. 2005), resulting in research that lacks a strong connection to existing linguistic theories and research. But as more and more linguists get involved in the study of language networks, this situation is gradually changing.

3 The Chinese Dependency Network for this study

For the present work, we used the following treebank of Chinese: The treebank has 37,024 tokens and is composed of 2 sections of different styles:

- "新闻联播" *xin-wen-lian-bo* 'news feeds' (name of a famous Chinese TV news program), hereinafter referred to as XWLB, is a transcription of the program. The text is usually read and the style of the language is quite formal. The section contains 17,061 words.
- "实话实说" *shi-hua-shi-shuo* 'straight talk' (name of a famous Chinese talk show), hereinafter referred to as SHSS, is of more colloquial language type, containing spontaneous speech appearing in interviews of people of various social backgrounds, ranging from farmers to successful businessmen, The section contains 19, 963 words.

Both sections have been annotated manually as described by Liu (2006). Table 1 shows the file format of this Chinese dependency treebank, which is similar to the CoNLL dependency format, although a bit more redundant (double information on the governor's POS) to allow for easy exploitation of the data in a spreadsheet and converting to language networks. The data can be represented as a dependency graph as shown in Figure 1.

The POS and dependency annotation is done on the transcribed texts. As the treebank contains different styles, it allows for general conclusions about the language, in spite of the limited size of the corpus. Another benefit of the double nature of the data is that we can do comparative work based on these 2 sections.

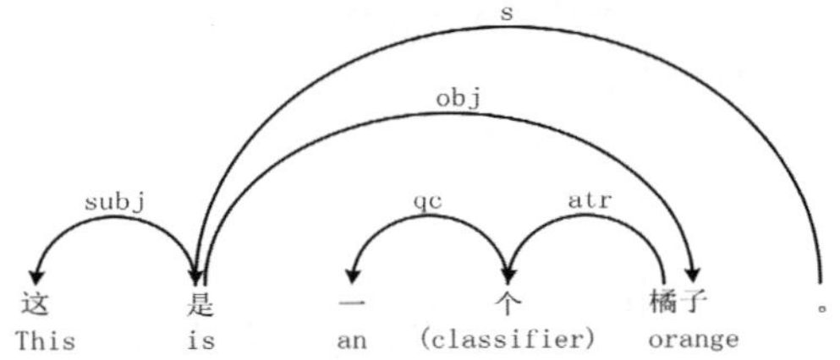

Figure 1. The graph of the dependency analysis of 这是一个橘子 *zhe-shi-yi-ge-ju-zi* 'this is an orange'

With words as nodes, dependencies as arcs, and the frequency of the dependencies as the value of arcs, we can build a network. For example, the sample shown in Figure 1 can be converted to a network as shown in Figure 2 (excluding punctuation).

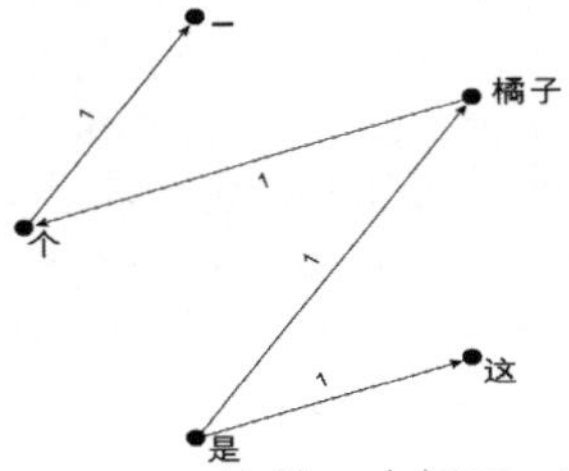

Figure 2. Network of 这是一个橘子 zhe-shi-yi-ge-ju-zi 'this is an orange'

Following the same principle, our Chinese treebank can be presented as Figure 3, an image that gives a broad overview of the global structure of the treebank.

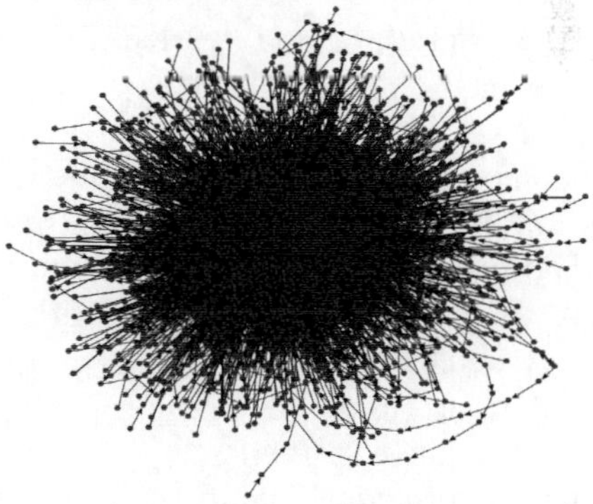

Figure 3. The network of our Chinese treebank

The resulting network has the following prop-

Sentence Order	Dependent			Governor			Dependency type
	Order	Character	POS	Order	Character	POS	
S1	1	*zhe*	pronoun	2	*shi*	verb	subject
S1	2	*shi*	verb	6	。	punctuation	main governor
S1	3	*yi*	numeral	4	*ge*	classifier	complement of classifier
S1	4	*ge*	classifier	5	*juzi*	noun	attributer
S1	5	*juzi*	noun	2	*shi*	verb	object
S1	6	。	punctuation				

Table 1. Annotation of a sample sentence in the Treebank. 这是一个橘子 *zhe-shi-yi-ge-ju-zi* 'this is an orange'

erties: it is fully connected and there are no isolated vertices, it is a 'small word' and has a 'scale-free' structure. As we mentioned before, there are not many language characteristics that we can deduce directly from this big picture. What we need to do is to looki into the structure of some specific words in this big network, which in our study has brought about some interesting findings. The first step is to decide on the words we wanted to look into: the function words.

4 Chinese Function Words

Chinese is an isolating language: syntactic structure relies primarily on function words and word order rather than on rich morphological information to encode functional relations between elements (Levy & Manning 2003). Function words are words that have little lexical meaning or have ambiguous meaning, but instead express grammatical relationships with other words within a sentence, or specify the attitude or mood of the speaker" (Klammer et al. 2000). In Chinese, function words include prepositions, conjunctions, and auxiliary and modal particles (Yu 1998).

As in any language, function words distinguish themselves not only by their syntactic properties, but also simply by their frequency. The words we are interested in are among the most common Chinese words: 在[1] *zai* '(to be located) in or at', 了 *le* 'perfective aspect marker or modal particle intensifying the preceding clause'.

We compared the frequent function words shown in XWLB, SHSS, and the *Modern Chinese Frequency Dictionary* and found that there are 3 function words that appear in all these 3 resources. They are: '的' *de* 'ablative cause suffix or possessive particle similar to the English genitive marker *'s*', *zai* and *le*. The frequency information of these 3 function words is shown in Table 2[2].

We will exclude *de* from this study because of its unique behavior[3]. We only chose *zai* and *le* as our research objects.

The differences in distribution between the two genres of texts are mostly based on the lexical poverty of spontaneous speech (SHSS) compared to written style, resulting in higher frequencies (of the smaller number of types) in the former genre. Moreover, the notably higher relative frequency of *le* in SHSS can be explained by the fact that one usage of *le* is an intensifier typical for the genre of spontaneous oral language. Inversely, *zai* can be omitted before locatives in oral Chinese.

XWLB			SHSS			MCFD		
R	F_1	W	R	F_1	W	R	F_2	W
1	930	*de*	1	1051	*de*	1	69080	*de*
3	223	*zai*	6	429	*le*	2	26342	*le*
4	202	*le*	21	124	*zai*	6	13438	*zai*

Table 2. The frequency information of 3 function words. *R-rank, F_1-frequency, W-word, F_2-frequency in 10000,*
MCFD-Modern Chinese Frequency Dictionary[4]

5 Chinese function words in treebanks

The traditional research on Chinese function words categorizes the linguistic units, describes which words function words can connect to, and defines the relationship between function words and other linguistic units by giving some examples. This type of research has achieved valuable results and contributed to the commonly accepted classification of Chinese function words. But due to the lack of tools for collecting and processing large data, the examples are limited and most of them are not drawn from real language data either. Recently, with the appearance of corpora in Chinese linguistic research, these points improved slightly. Simple text corpora or POS tagged corpora can supply giant amounts of examples. Treebanks, however, are able to provide much richer structural information, of syntactic or semantic nature, though their size is usually rather limited. For studies on syntactic structures, as the present work on function words, treebanks are the best choice.

---

1 In Chinese, *zai* may be a verb, adverb or preposition. Here we only refer to the preposition.

2 Considering the size of XWLB and SHSS, we only paid attention on the function words whose frequency is in the top 30 of all words that have shown in these transcriptions.

3 In Chinese, the function word '的' *de* ''s' is a very special word. It can pretty much follow any language unit and construct a so-called *de-structure*, *de* together with the preceding unit becoming an attribute or an expression referring to something or someone. Considering the complicated situations of the *de-structure*, they would require a special and extensive discussion, and are left for future research.

4 In Chinese, *le* and *zai* also can be content words even though these phenomena are not common. The Modern Chinese Frequency Dictionary doesn't distinguish these difference but we believe the deviation of the data won't change the fact that these 2 function words are among the most common Chinese words.

This paper focuses on the structural distribution of linguistic units (words, in this study), more specifically of the function words *zai* and *le*. There is similar research on Chinese with different concerns: Liu (2007) analyzed the distribution of dependency relations and dependency distance in a Chinese treebank, including but not centered on function words. Gao (2010) and Gao et al. (2010) described the syntactic functions of nouns and verbs in mandarin Chinese, dividing syntactic functions of nouns and verbs into typical ones and atypical ones for a quantitative analysis. Chen et al. (2011) tried to build a model of valency pattern from syntactic networks based on treebanks. All these works are done from the perspective of parts of speech instead of specific words. At the same time, there are several studies in Chinese concerned with specific words. For example, Liu and Liu (2011) have engaged in a study on the evolution process of the syntactic valency of the verb. They constructed three corpora of ancient classical Chinese, ancient vernacular and the modern vernacular, and selected ten verbs as the objects of their study to ascertain the diachronic behavior of these words. Even though they analyzed the complements and modifications of the words, they failed to give specific information about the complements and modifications, only distinguishing single word units from more complicated linguistic units. In contrast, our study provided more information of the words that can connect with *zai* and *le*.

We analyzed the distribution of the dependents and governors of *zai* and *le* in XWLB and SHSS. The results are shown in Table 3 and Table 4.

Note that the genre differences are visible for both words: The governors of *zai* are very similarly diversely distributed for both genres but in spontaneous speech, the dependents of *zai* are much more diverse than in written style. Compared to *zai*, *le* has simpler combinatory possibilities (and no dependents), and here, the governors are more diverse in spontaneous speech than in written style.

Comparing these two words, we can see that, in general, *zai* can relate to more types of part of speech than *le*. However, it is not easy to interpret these tables and we will see that when passing to a network representation, the differences become much more easily accessible.

XWLB			SHSS		
X ——> '在' *zai*					
Gov of *zai*	Freq	%	Gov of *zai*	Freq	%
verb	208	92.86	verb	115	92.74
auxiliary	9	4.02	auxiliary	5	4.03
conjunction	2	0.89	adjective	2	1.61
adjective	1	0.45	noun	1	0.81
noun	1	0.45			
preposition	1	0.45			
pronoun	1	0.45			
'在' *zai* ——> X					
Dep of *zai*	Freq	%	Dep of *zai*	Freq	%
noun	215	96.41	noun	106	78.52
pronoun	4	1.79	pronoun	12	8.89
classifier	2	0.90	verb	8	5.93
conjunction	1	0.45	adverb	6	4.44
verb	1	0.45	auxiliary	2	1.48
			conjunction	1	0.74

Table 3. The distribution of governors and dependents of function word *zai*. *Freq-frequency, Dep-dependent, Gov-governor*

XWLB			SHSS		
X ——> '了' *le*					
Gov of *le*	Freq	%	Gov of *le*	Freq	%
verb	198	98.02	verb	384	89.51
adjective	3	1.49	adjective	38	8.86
noun	1	0.50	noun	5	1.17
			adverb	1	0.23
			classifier	1	0.23

Table 4. The distribution of governors of function word *le*. *Freq-frequency, Dep-dependent, Gov-governor*

6 Network properties of Chinese function words

6.1 Properties of '在' *zai* and '了' *le*

With the XWLB and SHSS syntactic networks, we studied the most frequently used network parameter of the words, the *degree*: The *degree* of a vertex (a word) refers to the number of its neighbors. This variable actually describes the number of different word types which are connected with a specific word. The directions of the arcs distinguish between *indegree* and *outdegree*. The *indegree* of a word is the number of arcs it receives while the *outdegree* is the number of arcs it sends. Reformulated linguistically, the *indegree* reflects the number of governors of a word and the *outdegree*, the number of the word's dependents. In our network, these two function words have the following properties in Table 5.

Although the size of the original sections of XWLB and SHSS in the treebank is similar (in tokens), the size of the XWLB and SHSS networks is quite different due to the difference in the lexical richness. In order to make the data more comparable, we standardized the original data, also shown in Table 5. The table clearly shows that: *le* has a zero outdegree because it cannot govern other words in our analysis of Chinese while *zai* has both indegree and outdegree; Besides, *le*'s degree is higher in SHSS than XWLB which states that the combinatory possibilities of *le* is more diverse in spontaneous speech. On the contrary the distribution of word types that *zai* can connect with is more diverse in written style, especially obvious when it comes to the indegree.

Features	'了' *le*		'在' *zai*	
	XWLB	SHSS	XWLB	SHSS
Degree	133	234	222	131
SD	0.14	0.28	0.23	0.16
Outdegree	0	0	88	61
SOD	0	0	0.17	0.12
Indegree	133	234	134	70
SID	0.29	0.55	0.29	0.16

Table 5. The degree, indegree and outdegree of the function words *zai* and *le*. *SD-Standard degree, SOD-Standard outdegree, SID-Standard Indegree*

6.2 Network Manipulation

To see the role that these 2 words play in the whole language network system, we carry out the following manipulations on the network: Since we are only concerned with the vertices connected to these two words, we removed all the vertices and arcs that are not connected to them. Figure 4 illustrates the graph of the remaining vertices and arcs of *zai* in XWLB. Actually, we tried to do the same thing based on the original treebank. No doubt, the idea is workable but it is difficult to visualize the result. Since the words, which are either the governors or dependents of these function words, are numerous, it would take a very big table, more than 200 lines, to show all the detailed information. A more reasonable way to visualize the data, making it more readable, is making a graphical representation of the information, such as a scatter diagram or a network diagram as the one in Figure 4.

In this diagram, we managed to arrange the words by the value of their arcs connected with *zai*. The words between circle Ⓐ and Ⓑ labeled with smallest vertices, far away from the center vertex *zai*, only connected with *zai* once in the treebank. The lines between these words and *zai* are numbered by the frequency of the connection shown in the treebank. Following the same principle, the words between circle Ⓑ and Ⓒ connected with *zai* twice in the treebank, and so they are nearer to the center vertex. The words between circle Ⓒ and Ⓓ connected *zai* three times and the words in circle Ⓓ, except the word *zai* itself, connected with *zai* more than three times in the treebank. The more connections there are between the words and *zai*, the bigger the size of the vertices representing the words, the shorter the distance between the words and *zai*. In this way, the diagram 4 clearly shows that, even though *zai* has many neighbors, most of them seem to prefer visiting it just once or twice, in other

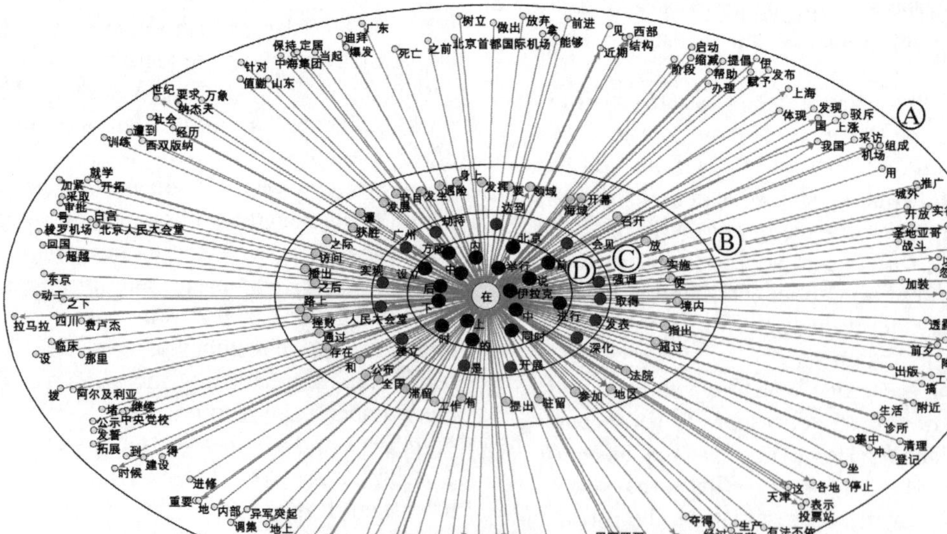

Figure 4. The sub-network of '在' *zai* and its neighbors in the XWLB network

words, the number of connection is distributed more evenly among its neighbors.

After removing the vertices, we combined all the words with the same part of speech except the two words we are studying. So we got a new "mixed language network". It mixes two types of vertices, one representing a word while the other one representing the part of speech. This new graph, as shown in Figure 5, also included the information of Table 3 and Table 4. The results we got from analyzing the treebank can also be extracted from the language networks.

rectly from the original treebank and that can be seen directly in the network? One of the advantages of the language network model is that it views the language as a connected whole system. Without the language network approach, describing the language system is more like talking about an unspecified abstract structure. The language network model gives a more specific structure model to the language system and also provides different computational tools that have proven to be successful in sociology and computer science, which are able to describe the different elements of a

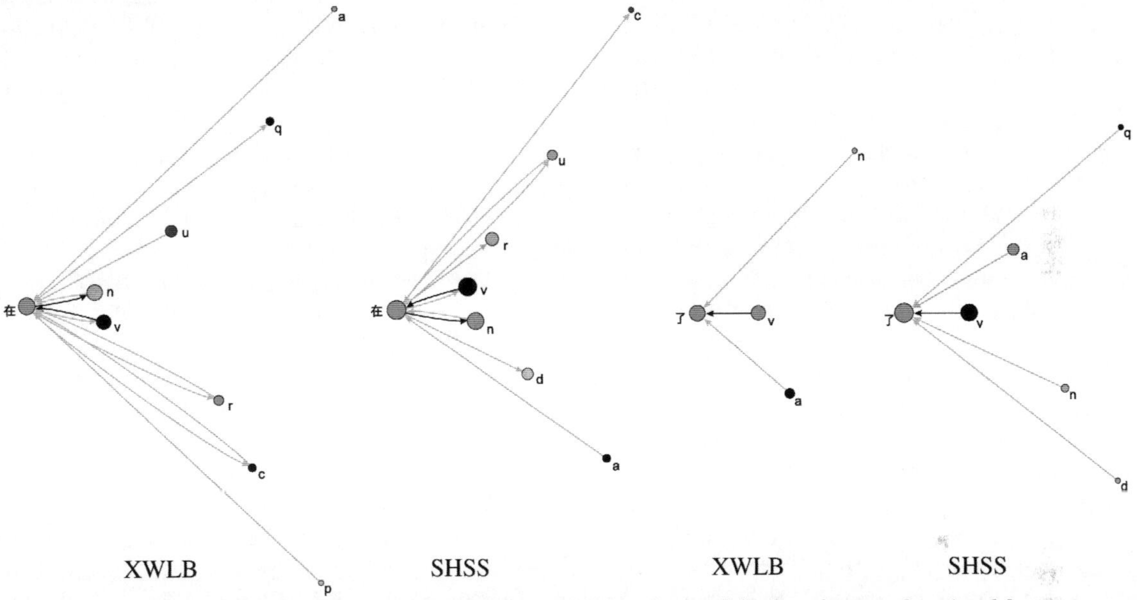

Figure 5. The distribution of governors and dependents of the function words *zai* and *le*

In this diagram, we put the arcs in different grayscales. The higher the value of an arc is, i.e. the frequency in Table 3 and Table 4, the darker their color, the bigger size of the vertices which represent the parts of speech. It is even easier to get the same conclusion than that drawn from Table 3 and Table 4: *le* can only be a dependent while *zai* can be a governor and a dependent; *zai* can relate to more types of part of speech than the *le*, *zai* can related to more words in XWLB than in SHSS while *le* can related to more words in SHSS than in XWLB.

Now, we can see that the main difference between analysing the original treebank and the language network is that the language network can provide an easier and direct access to a graphic output, especially when the data is too complex or too big to be included in a limited table.

So are there other facts about the language structure that are extremely difficult to see di-

network system, or, as in our case, a language system. So we tried to manipulate the XWLB and SHSS networks to find out the roles of these two function words in the language networks systems. The way we tried actually follows a very simple logic. If you want to know the function of one element in a system, the simplest way is to remove it from the system and then to see what the consequences are: We respectively removed the vertices representing *zai* and *le* from XWLB and SHSS language networks and compared several most common features of the networks, *the number of vertices, average degree, the number of isolated vertices*, before and after removing the vertex.

The numbers of vertices are actually the numbers of word types in the treebank. Although the sizes of XWLB and SHSS are similar, the numbers of vertices of XWLB and SHSS networks, or the size of the networks, are obviously different due to the difference of lexical richness.

Network		Num	IV	AD
XWLB	Original	4011	0	6.15
	le Removed	4010	0	6.09
	zai Removed	4010	17	6.04
SHSS	Original	2601	0	8.56
	le Removed	2600	0	8.38
	zai Removed	2600	5	8.46

Table 6. The network data before and after removing the function words. *Num: Numbers of vertices, IV: Isolated Vertices, AD: Average Degree*

The isolated vertices represent the vertices without any neighbors. This is the interesting part here. According to the data, there are no isolated vertices after removing *le*. All the remained vertices are still fully connected. So, if we believe the network somehow can be seen as the model of the syntactic structure of the language system drawn from this part of the treebank, then removing *le* seems to cause no significant trouble here. The whole structure didn't suffer from a systematic crisis, even though the *le* was a high frequency word with very high degrees. At the same time, removing *zai* caused isolated vertices in both XWLB and SHSS networks, especially in SHSS, even though the *zai* has lower frequency than *le* in the treebank and lower degrees in the network. In other words, removing this word created a much bigger systematic crisis. The reason is simple: *le* can only be a dependent. Take a picture like diagram 6: In the simple full connected network there is a vertex A that only has indegree and no outdegree. Because vertex A only attaches to other vertices and it doesn't convey any unique information between its neighbors, removing it from the network won't render any vertex isolated.

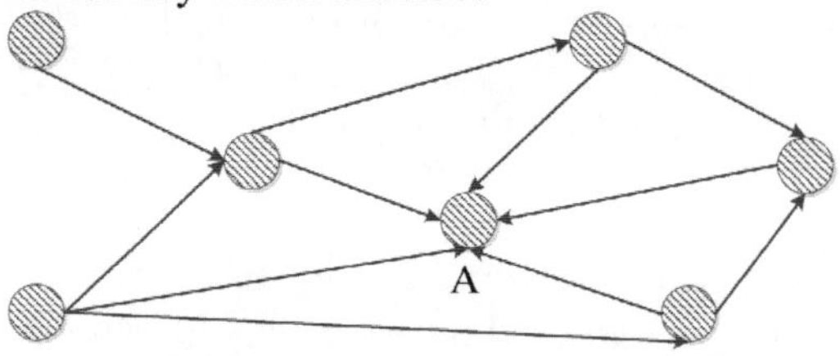

Figure 6. A simple network example

This result fits a common sense in syntax that the governors are somehow more important than dependents when it comes to the structural completion of sentences. But it is very difficult to quantify the syntactic importance, especially for the whole treebank, text or language systems. We see that the analyzed function words, which share high frequency and degrees, in fact play very different roles in the system model: As a result, it seems safe to claim that *zai* is more important than *le* for this model's structure. The syntactic importance of specific words can be quantified in this way. Developing a numeric scale of a well-defined notion of "syntactic importance" is left for future research.

This study shows that the language network approach can not only provide an easier and direct access to getting a graphic output but also can bring some fresh new angles for language analyzing.

7 Conclusion

This paper addresses the importance of developing techniques of treebank exploitation for syntactic research ranging from theorem verification to discovery of new relations invisible to the eye.

We advocate in particular the usage of network tools in this process and show how a treebank can, and, in our view, should be seen as a unique network.

We have shown in more detail, by opposing the function words *zai* and *le*, that the frequency of words is not equivalent to the word's importance in the syntactic structure, pointing to a notion that we may call the "centrality" of the word. The importance in the syntactic structure is still a vague notion that needs to be refined further, but simple network manipulations like removal of the words in question can reveal properties of the words that seem to be closely related to the words' structural roles. For example, a word A whose removal breaks the network in parts is clearly more important than a word B whose removal preserves the connectedness of the network (as the word only occupies exterior nodes). Since the results shown in this paper confirm well-known facts concerning these two function words, the same method can be applied to other function words as well content words. Ongoing research includes analyses of the Chinese equivalent of the following words: *de* 'ablative cause suffix or possessive particle similar to the English genitive marker 's', *wo* 'I, me, myself', *shi* 'are, am, yes', *ge* 'individual, entries', *yi* 'one, single', *zhe* 'this, it,these', *bu* 'do not, need not', *ta* 'he, him', *shuo* 'speak, talk, say', *ren* 'person, people, human being', and *dao* 'arrive, reach, get to'.

We leave it for further research to develop the notion of "centrality" into a numerical value that would allow comparing any pair of words.

Equally, the active field of network analysis will in time reveal new techniques that have in turn to be applied to new and bigger language networks based on treebanks of different types and languages. This could establish network syntax as one branch of the emerging field of data-driven linguistics.

References

Abramov O. and Mehler A. 2011. Automatic language classification by means of syntactic dependency networks. *Journal of Quantitative Linguistics*, 18(4), 291-336.

Allee V. 2000. Knowledge networks and communities of practice. *OD Practitioner Online*, 32(4), 1-15.

Amancio D. R., Antiqueira L., Pardo T. A. S., da F. Costa L., Oliveira Jr O. N. and Nunes M. G. V. 2008. Complex networks analysis of manual and machine translations. *International Journal of Modern Physics C*, 19(04), 583-598.

Amancio D. R., Nunes M. G. V., Oliveira Jr O. N., Pardo T. A. S., Antiqueira L. and da F Costa L. 2011. Using metrics from complex networks to evaluate machine translation. *Physica A*, 390(1), 131-142.

Arbesman S., Strogatz S. H. and Vitevitch M. S. 2010. The structure of phonological networks across multiple languages. *International Journal of Bifurcation and Chaos*, 20(03), 679-685.

Baker M. 1993. Corpus linguistics and translation studies: Implications and applications. *Text and technology: in honour of John Sinclair*, 233, 250.

Banisch S., Araújo T. and Louçã J. 2010. Opinion dynamics and communication networks. *Advances in Complex Systems*, 13(01), 95-111.

Barabási A. L. and Bonabeau E. 2003. Scale-free networks. *Scientific American*, 288(5), 50-9.

Böhmová A., Hajič J., Hajičová E., et al. 2003. *The Prague dependency treebank*. In *Treebanks*, 103-127. Springer, Netherlands.

Borgatti S. P., Everett M. G. and Freeman L. C. 2002. *Ucinet for Windows: Software for social network analysis*. Analytic Technologies, Harvard.

Borgatti S. P. 2002. *NetDraw: Graph visualization software*. Analytic Technologies, Harvard.

Borge-Holthoefer J. and Arenas A. 2010. Semantic Networks: Structure and Dynamics. *Entropy*, 12(5), 1264-1302.

Čech R. and Mačutek J. 2009. Word form and lemma syntactic dependency networks in Czech: A comparative study. *Glottometrics*, 19, 85-98.

Čech R., Mačutek J. and Žabokrtský Z. 2011. The role of syntax in complex networks: Local and global importance of verbs in a syntactic dependency network. *Physica A*, 390(20), 3614-3623.

Charteris-Black J. 2004. *Corpus approaches to critical metaphor analysis*. Palgrave-MacMillan.

Chen X. and Liu H. 2011. Central nodes of the Chinese syntactic networks. *Chinese Science Bulletin*, 56(1): 735-740.

Chen X., Xu C. and Li W. 2011. Extracting Valency Patterns of Word Classes from Syntactic Complex Networks. *Proceedings of Depling 2011, International Conference on Dependency Linguistics*. Barcelona, 165-172.

Christiano Silva T. and Raphael Amancio D. 2013. Network-based stochastic competitive learning approach to disambiguation in collaborative networks. *Chaos: An Interdisciplinary Journal of Nonlinear Science*, 23(1), 013139-013139.

Dickinson M. and Meurers W. D. 2003. Detecting inconsistencies in treebanks. *Proceedings of TLT*, 3, 45-56.

Ferrer i Cancho R. 2005. The structure of syntactic dependency networks: insights from recent advances in network theory. *Problems of quantitative linguistics*, 60-75.

Ferrer i Cancho R., Capocci A. and Caldarelli G. 2007. Spectral methods cluster words of the same class in a syntactic dependency network. *International Journal of Bifurcation and Chaos*, 17(07), 2453-2463.

Ferrer i Cancho R., Solé R. V. and Köhler R. 2004. Patterns in syntactic dependency networks. *Physical Review E*, 69(5), 051915.

Gao S. 2010. A Quantitative Study on Syntactic Functions of Nouns in Mandarin Chinese: Based on Chinese Dependency Treebank. *TCSOL Studies*, 2, 54-60.

Gao S., Yan W. & Liu H. 2010. A Quantitative Study on Syntactic Functions of Chinese Verbs Based on Dependency Treebank. *Chinese Language Learning*, 5, 105-112.

Gong T., Baronchelli A., Puglisi A. and Loreto V. 2012. Exploring the role of complex networks in linguistic categorization. Artificial Life, 18(1), 107.

Ke J. and Yao Y. A. O. 2008. Analysing Language Development from a Network Approach. *Journal of Quantitative Linguistics*, 15(1), 70-99.

Klammer T. P., Klammer T. P., Schulz M. R. and Della Volpe A. 2000. *Analyzing English Grammar*, 6^{ed}. Pearson Education India.

Kretzschmar W. A. 2009. The linguistics of speech. Cambridge University Press, New York.

Levy R. and Manning C. 2003. Is it harder to parse Chinese, or the Chinese Treebank?. *Proceedings of the 41st Annual Meeting on Association for Computational Linguistics*, 1, 439-446. Association for Computational Linguistics.

Li J. and Zhou J. 2007. Chinese character structure analysis based on complex networks. *Physica A*, 380, 629-638.

Li Y., Wei L., Li W., Niu, Y. and Luo S. 2005. Small-world patterns in Chinese phrase networks. *Chinese Science Bulletin*, 50(3), 287-289.

Liu B. & Liu H. 2011. A Study on the Evolution of the Verbal Syntactic Valence Based on Corpus. *Language Teaching and Linguistic Studies*, 6, 83-89.

Liu H. 2006. Syntactic Parsing Based on Dependency Relations. *Grkg/Humankybernetik*, 47:124-135.

Liu H. 2007. Probability distribution of dependency distance. *Glottometrics*, 15, 1-12.

Liu H. 2008. The complexity of Chinese dependency syntactic networks. *Physica A*, 387, 3048-3058.

Liu H. 2009a. Probability distribution of dependencies based on a Chinese dependency treebank. *Journal of Quantitative Linguistics*, 16(3), 256-273.

Liu H. 2009b. Statistical Properties of Chinese Semantic Networks. *Chinese Science Bulletin*, 54(16), 2781-2785.

Liu H. 2010. Language Clusters based on Linguistic Complex Networks. *Chinese Science Bulletin*, 55(30), 3458-3465.

Liu H. and Cong J. 2013. Language clustering with word cooccurrence networks based on parallel texts. *Chinese Science Bulletin*, 58(10), 1139-1144.

Liu H., Hudson R., and Feng Z. 2009. Using a Chinese treebank to measure dependency distance. *Corpus Linguistics and Linguistic Theory*, 5(2), 161-174.

Liu H. and Xu C. 2011. Can syntactic networks indicate morphological complexity of a language?. *EPL (Europhysics Letters)*, 93(2), 28005.

Liu Z. Y. and Sun M. S. 2007. Chinese word co-occurrence network: its small world effect and scale-free property. *Journal of Chinese Information Processing*, 21(6), 52-58.

Lopez A., Nossal M., Hwa R. and Resnik, P. 2002. *Word-level alignment for multilingual resource acquisition*. Maryland Univ College Park Inst For Advanced Computer Studies.

Marcus M. P., Marcinkiewicz M. A. and Santorini B. 1993. Building a large annotated corpus of English: The Penn Treebank. *Computational linguistics*, 19(2), 313-330.

Mehler A., Diewald N., Waltinger U., Gleim R., Esch D., Job B., ... and Blanchard, P. 2011. Evolution of Romance language in written communication: Network analysis of late Latin and early Romance corpora. *Leonardo*, 44(3), 244-245.

Mehler A., Lücking A. and Menke P. 2012. Assessing cognitive alignment in different types of dialog by means of a network model. *Neural Networks*, 32, 159-164.

Mehler A., Lücking A. and Weiß P. 2010. A network model of interpersonal alignment in dialog. *Entropy*, 12(6), 1440-1483.

Mille S. and Wanner L. 2010. Syntactic dependencies for multilingual and multilevel corpus annotation. *Proceedings of LREC 2010*. Malta.

Mukherjee A., Choudhury M., Ganguly N. and Basu A. 2013. Language Dynamics in the Framework of Complex Networks: A Case Study on Self-organization of the Consonant Inventories. In *Cognitive Aspects of Computational Language Acquisition*, Springer, Netherlands, 51-78.

Nooy W., Mrvar A. and Batagelj V. 2005. *Exploratory Network Analysis with Pajek*. Cambridge University Press, New York.

Peng G., Minett J. W. and Wang W. S. Y. 2008. The networks of syllables and characters in Chinese. *Journal of Quantitative Linguistics*, 15(3), 243-255.

Shannon P., Markiel A., Ozier O., Baliga N. S., Wang J. T., Ramage D., ... and Ideker T. 2003. Cytoscape: a software environment for integrated models of biomolecular interaction networks. *Genome research*, 13(11), 2498-2504.

Watts D. J. and Strogatz S. H. 1998. Collective dynamics of 'small-world' networks. *nature*, 393(6684), 440-442.

Yu S. 1998. *Modern Chinese grammatical information dictionary explanation*. Tsinghua university, Beijing.

Yu S., Liu H. and Xu C. 2011. Statistical properties of Chinese phonemic networks. *Physica A*, 390(7), 1370-1380.

Zeldes A., Ritz J., Lüdeling A. and Chiarcos C. 2009. ANNIS: A search tool for multi-layer annotated corpora. *Proceedings of corpus linguistics*, 9.

Verb Cluster, Non-Projectivity, and Syntax-Topology Interface in Korean

Jihye Chun
MoDyCo – UMR7114
University of Paris Ouest Nanterre La Défense
France
chunjihye@gmail.com

Abstract

This article proposes a simple modeling of Korean word order within the framework of the topological dependency grammar – the first topological modeling for this language – a system of formal rules accounting for the correspondence between the dependency tree of a sentence and an ordered constituent structure. We show that a fairly small number of linearization rules can account for the word order facts of Korean, considered to be a language with a relatively free order. These rules will be described, especially the non-projectivity phenomenon based of the notion of "verb cluster", a cohesive topological constituent, which appears in a syntax-topology interface.

1 Introduction

First of all, let us consider the following examples. The difference between these declarative sentences is the placement of the two verbs, *ta-ko* 'take' and *ka-ss-da* 'go', marked in bold:

(1) a. 영이가 엄마 차를 **타고**
Yeongi-ka eomma cha-leul **ta-ko**
Yeongi-NOM mother car-ACC take-VM
시골에 **갔다**
sigol-e **ka-ss-da**
country-LOC go-P-DEC[1]
'Yeongi went to the countryside taking her mother's car'

b. 영이가 시골에 엄마 차를
Yeongi-ka sigol-e eomma cha-leul
Yeongi-NOM country-LOC mother car-ACC
타고 **갔다**
ta-ko **ka-ss-da**
take-VM go-P-DEC
'Yeongi went to the countryside taking her mother's car'

These two sentences are acceptable and natural. On the other hand, when the nominal dependent of *ta-ko* 'take' is extracted, we remark that there are restrictions on the placement of verbs. Let us observe the following examples in which the nominal dependent of *ta-ko* 'take' is extracted:

(2) a. 영이가 시골에 **타고** **간**
Yeongi-ka sigol-e **ta-ko** **ka-n**
Yeongi-NOM country-LOC take-VM go-REL
엄마 차는 검은색이다
eomm cha-neun keomeunsaek-i-da
mother car-TOP black-C-DEC
'the mother's car that Yeongi took for going to the countryside is black'

b. ?* 영이가 **타고** 시골에 **간**
Yeongi-ka **ta-ko** sigol-e **ka-n**
Yeongi-NOM take-VM country-LOC go-REL
엄마 차는 검은색이다
eomm cha-neun keomeunsaek-i-da
mother car-TOP black-C-DEC

As illustrated above, when the dependent verb is separated from its governor (example 2b), it is not possible that the nominal dependent of this dependent verb is extracted. On the other hand, when the dependent verb is placed next to its governor (example 2a), it is possible that the nominal dependent is extracted. This fact leads us to think about the correlation between extraction and constraints on the placement of verbs.

In this paper, we are interested in this restriction of the linear position of verbs in the case of extraction, and we'd like to propose a simple modeling for this linguistic fact. To do this, we think that it is necessary to present a

[1] ACC: accusative, ADV: adverb, C: copula, DAT: dative, DEC: declarative, HON: honorification, LOC: locative, NEG: negation, NM: nominalization, NOM: nominative, P: past, PRES: present, REL: relative, TOP: topic, VM: verbal morpheme with which verb dependents are combined (note that Korean is an agglutinative language).

Proceedings of the Second International Conference on Dependency Linguistics (DepLing 2013), pages 51–59,
Prague, August 27–30, 2013.

general description of Korean word order. Then, we will discuss the selection of suitable framework for word order variation of this language (section 2). We will propose to be placed in a topological approach based on Gerdes & Kahane (2001). In section 3, we will define a topological structure for Korean, based on its word order property. We will also develop a topological dependency grammar. In section 4, we will show that our grammar is fully capable of establishing the correct linear order, with non-projectivity phenomena illustrated in the examples above. We will show the utility of the notion of the "verb cluster", a cohesive topological constituent which controls non-projectivity phenomena.

2 Word Order Variation of Korean

Korean is known as a language in which word order is relatively free (Chung 1998, Choi 1999, Kim & Lee 2001 etc). First of all, let us consider the following examples in which the verb *ju-* 'give' has three nominal dependents: *Yeongi-ka* 'Yeongi', *Cheolsu-eke* 'to Cheolsu', and *chaek-eul* 'a book'. The order variation of these constituents permits six possible orders:

(3) a. 영이가 철수에게 책을 주었다
Yeongi-ka Cheolsu-eke chaek-eul ju-eoss-da
Yeongi-NOM Cheolsu-DAT book-ACC give-P-DEC
'Yeongi gave a book to Cheolsu'

b. 영이가 책을 철수에게 주었다
Yeongi-ka chaek-eul Cheolsu-eke ju-eoss-da
Yeongi-NOM book-ACC Cheolsu-DAT give-P-DEC
'Yeongi gave a book to Cheolsu'

c. 철수에게 영이가 책을 주었다
Cheolsu-eke Yeongi-ka chaek-eul ju-eoss-da
Cheolsu-DAT Yeongi-NOM book-ACC give-P-DEC
'Yeongi gave a book to Cheolsu'

d. 철수에게 책을 영이가 주었다
Cheolsu-eke chaek-eul Yeongi-ka ju-eoss-da
Cheolsu-DAT book-ACC Yeongi-NOM give-P-DEC
'Yeongi gave a book to Cheolsu'

e. 책을 영이가 철수에게 주었다
chaek-eul Yeongi-ka Cheolsu-eke ju-eoss-da
book-ACC Yeongi-NOM Cheolsu-DAT give-P-DEC
'Yeongi gave a book to Cheolsu'

f. 책을 철수에게 영이가 주었다
chaek-eul Cheolsu-eke Yeongi-ka ju-eoss-da
book-ACC Cheolsu-DAT Yeongi-NOM give-P-DEC
'Yeongi gave a book to Cheolsu'

As illustrated in these examples, the verb occurs at the end of these sentences (i.e. Korean is a verb final language), while the nominal elements of the main verb are freely placed.
This linear behavior of nominal elements in the examples above brings about two questions: First, is the idea of *standard* word order SOV pertinent in the case of Korean? Second, how could we represent word order variation in a simple and elegant way?
Greenberg (1963) proposed classifying word order types of languages from a typological point of view in terms of their *basic order* such as SVO, SOV, VSO, VOS, OSV or OVS. This proposition implies a fixed or at least clearly dominant order, which does not apply to Korean word order variation as illustrated above.[2] Moreover, following Ross (1967), Korean word order variation has been discussed in terms of "scrambling" (Han 1998, Chung 1998, Choi 1999 etc.), which demands the concept of *movement*. We believe that this operation could make such a representation very complicated for Korean where the communicative structure plays an important role, unlike English or French where word order largely depends on the syntactic function.
According to Choi (1999) and Kim & Lee (2001), there are several factors intervening in Korean word order variation: grammatical morphemes, communicative structure, syntactic functions etc. From this point of view, in our study, we do not suppose a *standard* word order contrary to X-bar syntax in which syntactic function and constituency are represented in a same structure. We believe that it is more convincing to separate different levels of information, for representing word order variation in a simple way. We thus propose to use the framework of Dependency Grammar where syntactic function and constituency are separately represented (Tesnière 1959, Mel'čuk 1988). More precisely, we base ourselves on Gerdes & Kahane (2001), broadly inspired by the classical topological model first introduced in the description of German. They integrated this model into the framework of dependency grammar, elaborating a syntax-topology interface. Note that topology is an intermediate level between a dependency-based syntactic structure and a prosodic structure.[3] That is to say,

[2] Note that Korean also has an unmarked order which is communicatively neutral.
[3] We are based on the Meaning-Text model (Mel'čuk 1988) which posits multiple strata of representations

word groupings in topology are strongly related to prosodic units.

In this paper, keeping the issue raised in the introduction in mind, we describe the correspondence between unordered syntactic structures and ordered constituent structures on the basis of the Korean topological dependency grammar we propose. We will remark that linearization rules are simpler than we thought for a language considered as a relatively free order language. This will be described precisely in the section 4 with the case of non-projectivity phenomena. This description will be a solution of the question raised in the introduction.

3 Syntax-Topology Interface in Korean

In this section, we propose a topological model for Korean, based on its word order property. We also define the Korean topological dependency grammar, which accounts for all possible word order variations. This grammar will allow for describing the correspondence between a given dependency tree and an ordered topological structure.

3.1 Topological Structure for Korean

The basic idea of the topological model is to "consider that a sentence is a template-like sequence of different fields each being able to host different types of constituents" (Gerdes & Kahane 2007). These different types of constituents correspond to "domains". The internal structure of domains is a sequence of "fields".

Choi (1999) and Gerdes (2002) insist on the fact that constraints on word order in Korean resemble those of German. However, we do not follow the architecture of the topological structure of German, in which the superior domain directly contains five fields (Vorfeld, left bracket, Mittelfeld, right bracket, Nachfeld). Korean is often considered as a discourse-oriented language (Kim 2003), or a topic-prominent language (Li & Thompson 1976). In other words, the communicative structure plays an important role in the organization of sentences in Korean. Furthermore, all the elements are not obligatorily present. That is to say, it is not necessary to produce the elements that speakers understand in a given context (i.e. frequency of zero anaphora, cf. Kim 2003). This could make interpretation of the structure of sentences complicated, and we could have at least two interpretations: 1) elements in a sentence are under subcategorization of the main verb, and 2) they are simply repetition of elements of the antecedent sentences in a context.

Moreover, the topological behaviors of the *neun*-phrase are very interesting in that it can appear in different linear order depending on the communicative structure (cf. Chun 2013). Consider the following examples in which the two *neun*-phrases appear:

(4) a. 그 이야기는 저는 들었어요
keu iyaki-neun jeo-neun deul-eoss-eo-yo
this story-TOP me-TOP hear-P-DEC-HON
'for that story, it's me who heard that'

b. 저는 그 이야기는 들었어요
jeo-neun keu iyaki-neun deul-eoss-eo-yo
me-TOP this story-TOP hear-P-DEC-HON
'for me, it's that story that I heard'

As illustrated in the gloss of the examples above, their interpretation differs from the linear position of the *neun*-phrase: in (4a), *keu iyaki-neun* 'that story' is interpreted as a topic, while in (4b), this is interpreted as a focus contrastive. This means that there is a particular linear position of elements of a sentence. Furthermore, the first constituent containing the *neun* marker in each sentence tends to be separated from the following element with a high prominence in prosody (Seong & Song 1997, Hwang 2002).

These points we mentioned above lead us to introduce two syntactic modules: the macro-syntax and the micro-syntax following Blanche-Benveniste (1990). The latter is for elements in "proper" syntactic level, while the former contains detached elements which don't fall under subcategorization. We believe that the introduction of two syntactic modules (macro- and micro-syntax) allows us to better understand the overall organization of sentences on different levels: syntactic level, communicative level and prosodic level etc.

Let us now present our architecture of the Korean topological structure (cf. Figure 1). The two modules, the macro- and micro-syntax are integrated into our model as a macro-domain and a micro-domain respectively. Note that for a sequence of fields in the macro-domain, we introduce the term "kernel"[4] interpreted as

related by explicit interfaces. We are interested especially in an interface where linearization takes place.

[4] We borrow this term from Gerdes *et al.* (2005).

"noyau" in French following Blanche-Benveniste (1990). The macro-domain is composed of three fields: the pre-kernel field, the kernel field, and the post-kernel field. The kernel field "receives the other verbal dependents, especially all the elements that saturate the verbal valency" (Gerdes *et al.* 2005). The pre-kernel field and post-kernel field contain detached elements such as toplicalized or dislocated elements. In the example (5), there is one more element apart from the elements under subcategorization of the main verb, namely, *na-neun* 'me' interpreted as a topic. This means that this element is placed in another topological position than in the kernel field:

(5) **나는** 내가 많이 발전했지
na-neun nae-ka manhi baljeonha-eoss-ji
me-TOP me-NOM much progress-P-DEC
'for me, I have much progressed'

We thus propose the pre-kernel field before the kernel field.

Note that Korean nominal dependents can appear after the main verb. In the example (6), the subject is placed after the main verb *haneunde* marked in bold:

(6) 다시 생각을 해야 **하는데** 너는
dasi saengkak-eul ha-eoya ha-neunde neo-neun
again thought-ACC do-VM do-although you-TOP
'you have to think again'

Therefore, we need one more field behind the kernel field, i.e. the post-kernel field.

The micro-domain has two fields: the principal field and the head field. This domain hosts the elements governed by the principal verb. This principal verb is placed in the head field, and its dependents occupy the principal field.

In our architecture of the topological structure, there is a particular verbal grouping of words, namely, a verb cluster, in that this is not a simple verbal constituent, but a constituent which intervenes in the case of extraction. This is our main problem in this paper, and we will discuss that in detail in the section 4. The verb cluster is composed of four fields: the dependent verb (dep-V) field, the adverb (ADV) field, the negation (NEG) field and the verb (V) field.[5] The verb cluster forms a very rigid verbal constituent with great cohesion, which tends to form one prosodic unit.[6] The order of these four fields is fixed:

(7) 요즘 영이 공부 잘 안 해
yoseum Yeongi kongbu jal an ha-eo
these days Yeongi-TOP study well NEG do-DEC
'these days, Yeongi doesn't study well'

Note that certain constructions do not permit insertion of adverb or negation[7] between two verbs, contrary to the example (7):

(8) a. 영이가 철수를 **도와** **주었다**
Yeongi-ka Cheolsu-leul dou-a ju-eoss-da
Yeongi-NOM Cheolsu-ACC help-VM do a favor-P-DEC
'Yeongi hepled Cheolsu with favor'

b. * 영이가 철수를
Yeongi-ka Cheolsu-leul
Yeongi-NOM Cheolsu-ACC
도와 **안** 주었다
dou-a an ju-eoss-da
help-VM NEG do a favor-P-DEC
'Yeongi didn't help Cheolsu with favor'

We now propose the Korean topological structure with three embedded levels:

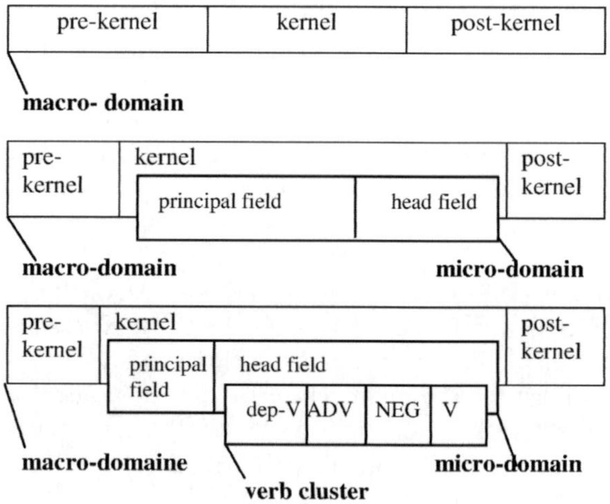

Figure1. Three embedded levels of the topological structure in Korean[8]

[5] Note that the verb cluster is not a domain such as macro- and micro-syntax.

[6] There is also a nominal cohesive constituent corresponding to the verb cluster, i.e. a noun cluster. The noun cluster is a topological unit with a strong cohesion among nouns.

[7] Korean has two negations: short negation such as *an* appearing in front of verbs, and long negation such as an auxiliary verb *anh-*.

[8] There is no such field proposed for the complementizer. This is related to the fact that Korean is an agglutinative language in which it is the morphemes that play a role of complementizer.

3.2 Topological Dependency Grammar

In this section, we develop a topological dependency grammar for Korean, based on Gerdes & Kahane (2001) in which the parameters of topological dependency grammar are defined as follows:

> ▸ Six components of a grammar
> - the vocabulary V
> - the set of (lexical) categories C
> - the set of syntactic relations R
> - the set of box names B
> - the set of field names F
> - the field of initialization i
>
> ▸ Order of permeability of the boxes (which is a partial ordering on B used for emancipation[9])
>
> ▸ Four sets of rules
> - box description rules
> - field description rules
> - correspondence rules
> - box creation rules

Note that in a topological approach, non-projectivity phenomena are related to the notion of "emancipation", which means that "the dependents of a verb do not have to be placed in their governor's domain" (Gerdes & Kahane 2007). We will give the order rules for linear placement of nominal dependents in terms of emancipation.
We now present the six components of the Korean grammar, and two of the four sets of rules, i.e. the box description rules and the field description rules, in a formalized manner. For clarity, the correspondence rules and the box creation rules are going to be described in natural language, and at the same time we will show the steps of the derivation of a declarative sentence.

▶ Six components of the Korean grammar

> V = the Korean words
> C = {V, V-*eo*, V-*ji*, V-*ko*, V-*myeonseo*, *neun*-phrase…Y}
> R = {subj, obj, obji, attr, mod, cv[10]}
> B = {macro-domain, micro-domain, verb cluster}
> F = {pre-kernel field, kernel field, post-kernel field, principal field, head field, dep-V field, lexical field}
> i is the field of initialization

▶ Permeability order

> micro-domain > verb cluster

This formula means that it is easier for the nominal dependent to be emancipated from the micro-domain than from the verb cluster.

▶ Box description rules

This rule indicates that such a box is composed of the list of fields.

> macro-domain → pre-kernel field, kernel field, post-kernel field
> micro-domain → principal field, head field
> verb cluster → dep-V field, ADV field, NEG field, V field

▶ Field description rules

Still following Gerdes & Kahane (2001), we present the field description in the form of pair (f,ε) in which f is a field and ε is a symbol among {!,?,+,*}. The pair means that the field f has to contain exactly one element (!), at most one element (?), at least one element (+) or any number of elements (*):

> (i, !), (lexical field, !), (pre-kernel field, *), (post-kernel field, *), (kernel field, !), (head field, !), (principal field, *), (dep-V field, ?)

▶ Correspondence rules and box creation rules

We have established the following correspondence rules and box creation rules for the linearization of verbs and their dependents.

1) The root of the dependency tree opens a macro-domain containing three fields, i.e. the pre-kernel field, the kernel field, and the post-kernel field. Then, the principal verb opens a micro-domain in the kernel field having two fields, the principal field and the head field. It finally opens a verb cluster in the head field:

[9] The definition of the notion of emancipation is going to be followed after this presentation of parameters.

[10] This means "verbal complement", for verbal dependents such as infinitive, completive.

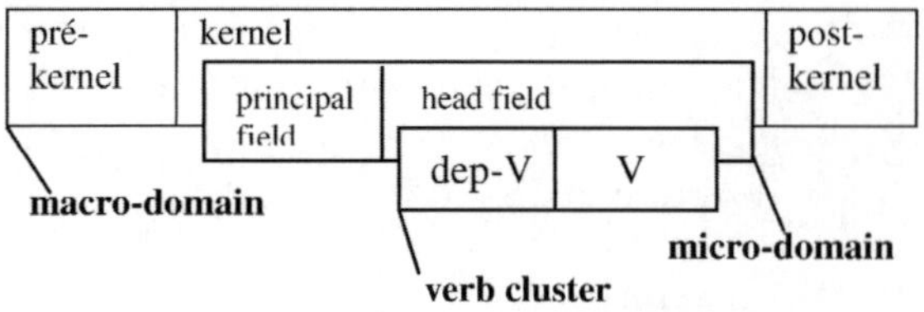

Figure2. Illustration of the topological structure of Korean

2) The principal verb opens a field for its dependent verb, after being placed in the verb cluster. The latter can occupy this dep-V field in the verb cluster, where it opens an embedded verb cluster:

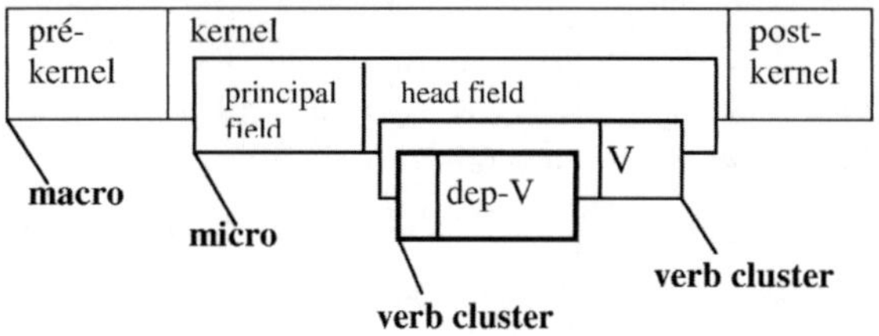

Figure3. Dependent verb in the verb cluster

If the dependent verb of the root has its dependent verb, the latter proposes anew a place for its possible dependent. This process is *recursive.*

3) The dependent verb is not obliged to stay with its governor in the verb cluster:

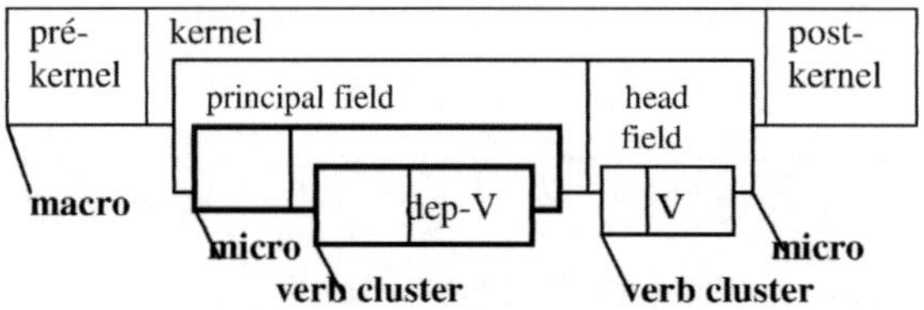

Figure4. Micro-domain of the dependent verb in the principal field

The place of the dependent verb largely depends on the type of verbal morphemes with which it is combined, and on the communicative structure:

- The V-*eo/ji* obligatorily goes into the verb cluster;
- The V-*ko* has two possibilities: to stay in the verb cluster or to create a micro-domain in terms of the communicative structure;
- The V-*myeonseo*[11] is obliged to create a micro-domain in one of the three major fields (the pre-kernel field, the principal field and the post-kernel field).

4) Other non-verbal predicative dependents such as the predicative noun can join the dep-V field in the verb cluster. In this case, it is preferable that the predicative noun does not bear any markers (cf. example 7)

5) All dependents of a verb can create a subdomain that should be placed in one of the three major fields in terms of the communicative constraints:

- Any dependent can go into the principal field without emancipation;
- Any dependent can go into the pre-kernel field with possibly emancipation from a verb cluster;
- Any dependent can go into the post-kernel field with possibly emancipation from a micro-domain.

6) The *neun*-phrase interpreted as a topic has to be emancipated from the micro-domain ; the *neun*-phrase interpreted as a contrastive focus should remain in the principal field without emancipation ;

7) In the case of extraction, the verbs belonging to the verbal nucleus (cf. section 4 for its definition) governing the extracted element must form a verb cluster.

We now try to solve our problem presented in the examples (1) and (2). In the following section, we will show how the correspondence rules and box creation rules are applied from a given dependency tree. In particular, we will see that the dependent verb should go into the verb cluster, created by its governor, in the case of extraction of its nominal dependent.

4 Non-projectivity and Verb Cluster

In this section, based on our topological dependency grammar, we will insist on the utility of the verb cluster in the syntax-topology interface for solving constraint on the relation between extraction and the placement of verbs in sentences with relatives. We will also show that in our analysis, unlike Ross (1967), it is

[11] This is considered as a morpheme which marks an adverbial clause.

not necessary to consider the concept of movement or "island constraint" phenomena. Throughout this section, we refer to the rule 7 which allows for describing non-projectivity phenomena in a simple way.
We have shown the relation between extraction and restriction on the placement of verbs contrary to the case of declarative sentences (The examples (2a) and (2b) are reproduced here as (9) for convenience of the reader):

(9) a. 영이가 시골에 **타고 간**
Yeongi-ka sigol-e **ta-ko ka-n**
Yeongi-NOM country-LOC take-VM go-REL
엄마 차는 검은색이다
eomm cha-neun keomeunsaek-i-da
mother car-TOP black-C-DEC
'the mother's car that Yeongi took for going to the countryside is black'

b. ?* 영이가 **타고** 시골에 **간**
Yeongi-ka **ta-ko** sigol-e **ka-n**
Yeongi-NOM take-VM country-LOC go-REL
엄마 차는 검은색이다
eomm cha-neun keomeunsaek-i-da
mother car-TOP black-C-DEC

The problem is whether two verbs form a constituent or not. How can we account for this phenomenon? We postulate the notion of "verbal nucleus", a syntactic position of a single verb, which can also receive a sequence of verbs, a notion introduced by Kahane (1997), for modeling of non-projectivity phenomena. This means that in the dependency tree, we postulate that the syntactic position of verbs or complex units containing a sequence of verbs corresponds to one verb. For example, verbal nuclei in English are auxiliary-participles (*be eating, have eaten*), verb-infinitives (*want to eat*), verb-conjunction-verbs (*think that...eat*), and verb-prepositions (*look for*) (cf. Kahane 1997). Our hypothesis is that in the case of extraction, the verbal nucleus tends to form a topological constituent, i.e. the verb cluster.
The following figure shows a dependency tree with a relative, and a topological constituent containing the two verbs is superimposed on this tree. The dotted oval represents the verbal nucleus:

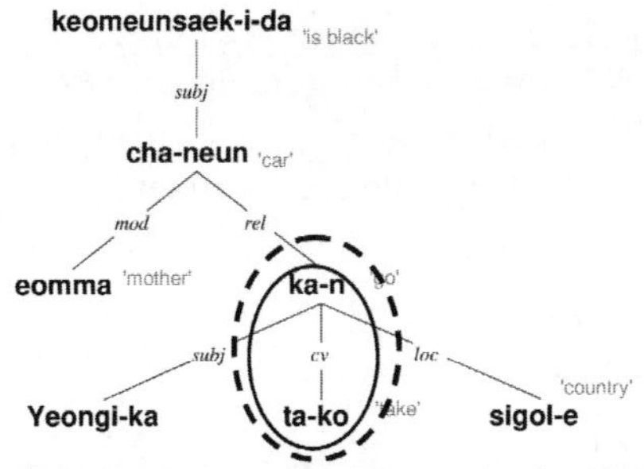

Figure5. Dependency tree of the examples (9a)

Let us show how the correspondence is established from this dependency tree of the example (9a), referring to our grammar. Recall our correspondence rules and box creation rules.

1) The root of this tree opens a verb cluster after creating a macro-domain and a micro-domain. And then it is placed in the head field:

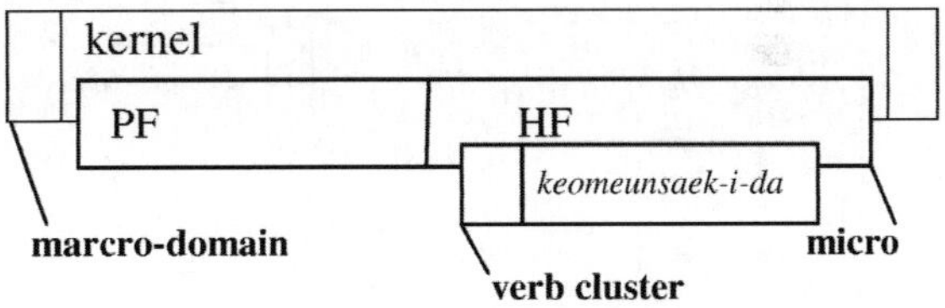

2) The nominal head of the relative opens a micro-domain in the principal field as a nominal dependent of the root. It is placed in the field proposed for nouns in the noun cluster. Its dependent *eomma* 'mother' rejoins the noun cluster:

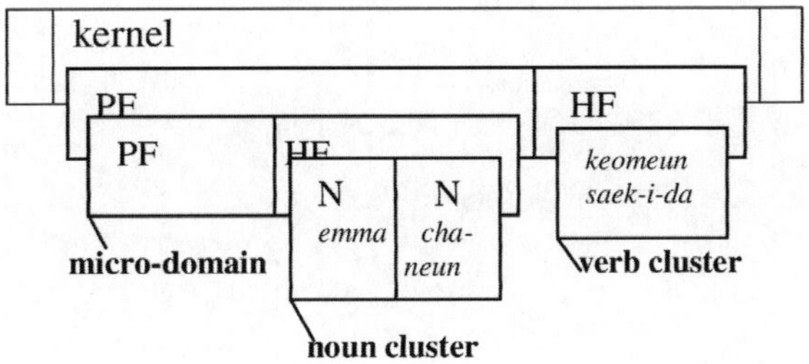

3) *ka-n* 'go' opens a verb cluster in the head field:

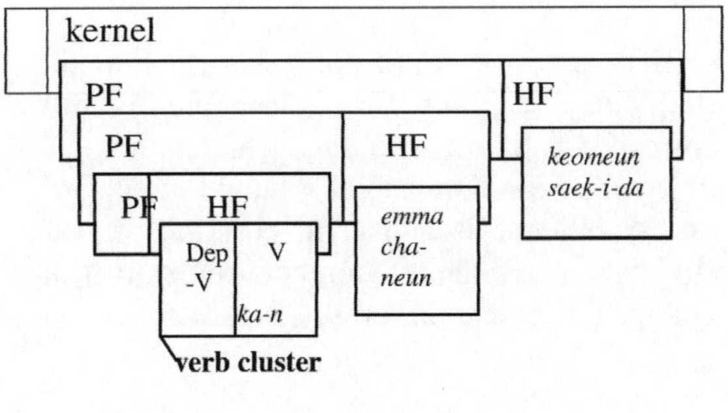

4) *ta-ko* 'take' ***has to*** be placed in the dep-V field of the verb cluster opened by its governor *ka-n* 'go', instead of creating an independent constituent:

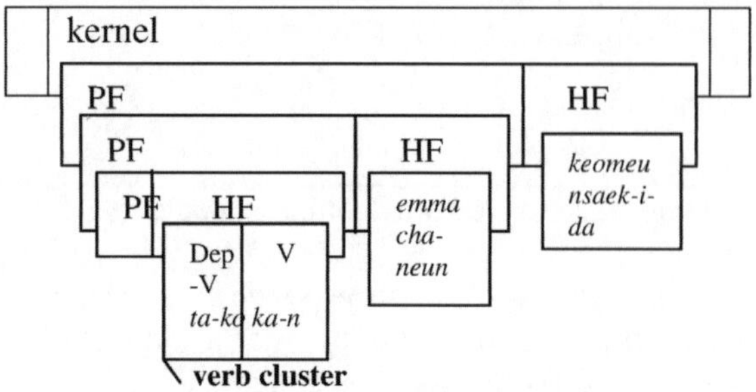

5) Finally, the nominal dependents of *ka-n* 'go' and those of *ta-ko* 'take' rejoin the principal field:

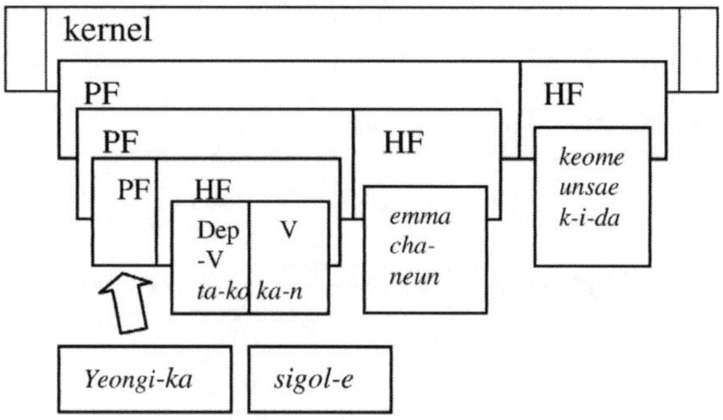

Figure6. Topological structure of the example (9a)

Let us consider other possible linearization if the two verbs in a verbal nucleus do not form a topological constituent, i.e. a verb cluster.

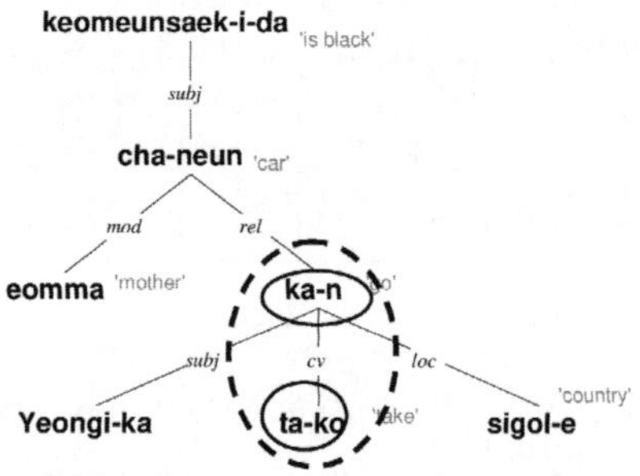

Figure7. Dependency tree of the examples (9b)

In this case, we could not have the example (9a). One of the word orders from the Figure 7 corresponds to example (9b), which is not natural, rather ungrammatical. This point enhances our hypothesis above. In corpora, we can find data where the relation between extraction and the placement of verbs is attested:

(10) a. 평소에 그거 <u>**입고 다니는**</u>
pyeongso-e keukeo ip-ko dani-neun
usually-LOC this wear-VM go-REL
아저씨 많이 봤어
ajeossi manhi bo-ass-eo
man much see-P-DEC
'I saw a man who was walking wearing this'

b. 사회자가 <u>**이끌어 가는**</u>
sahoija-ka ikkeul-eo ka-neun
announcer-NOM lead-VM go-REL
대화가 큰 비중을
daewha-ka keu-n bijung-eul
conversation-NOM be big-REL importance-ACC
차지한다
chajiha-nda
occupy-PRES.DEC
'the conversation that the announcer lead has a great importance'

We thereby believe that the notion of verb cluster is useful to describe non-projectivity phenomena.

5 Conclusion

We have discussed and proposed a simple solution of the description of extraction in terms of the verb cluster, in the framework of the topological dependency grammar, a simple modeling of Korean word order.
On the level of modeling word order variation, we have shown that our model allows us to determine the order of nominal and verbal dependents, with a small number of correspondence rules or box creation rules. Moreover, we have shown that we can describe the word order variation, postulating only three types of boxes: the macro-domain, the micro-domain, and the verb cluster. The internal structure of these boxes is much simpler than those of German, considered as a language with similar word order properties as Korean (Choi 1999, Gerdes 2002). For example, we have shown that in Korean, it is sufficient for the micro-domain to have only two fields (principal field and head field) for the relative, the completive and the nominal groups.
This paper is the early stage in a study of the topology for Korean. We should investigate further in various directions. Especially, we are aware of the importance to understand the communicative (or information) structure of sentences, which plays a crucial role in linearization. The word order rules should be further developed to include constraints on the communicative structure.

We have simply mentioned the topological behaviors of the *neun* marker, referring to Chun (2013). Korean is an agglutinative language. This means that in addition to this morpheme *neun*, further work will have to be done to study the topological behaviors of other morphemes such as *eul*, traditionally considered as an accusative marker, but more recently as a marker of communicative values (Han 1999) which, of course, is related to its linear position. In other words, understanding its syntactic behaviors and communicative values could allow for characterizing its topological position as being in the macro- or micro- domain.

References

Claire Blanche-Benveniste. 1990. *Le français parlé: etudes grammaticales*, CNRS Editions, Paris.

Hye-Won Choi. 1999. *Optimizing Structure in Context: Scrambling and Information Structure*, CSLI Publications, Stanford.

Jihye Chun. 2013. *Interface syntaxe-topologie et amas verbal en coréen et en français*, Ph.D. Dissertation, University of Paris Ouest Nanterre La Défense, Paris.

Chan Chung. 1998. Argument Composition and Long-distance Scrambling in Korean, in Erhard Hinrichs(ed.), *Complex predicates in Nonderivational Syntax : Syntax and Semantics*, 30:158-220, Academic Press, New York.

Kim Gerdes. 2002. *Topologie et grammaires formelles de l'allemand*, Ph.D.Dissertation, University of Denis Diderot, Paris.

Kim Gerdes and Sylvain Kahane. 2001. Word order in German: a Formal Dependency Grammar Using a Topological Hierarchy, *Proceedings Association for Computational Linguistic*, Toulouse.

Kim Gerdes and Sylvain Kahane. 2007. Phrasing it differently, in Leo Wanner (ed). *Selected lexical and grammatical issues in the Meaning-Text Theory*, 297-335.

Kim Gerdes, Sylvain Kahane and Hiyon Yoo. 2005. On the descriptive adequacy of topology, *Proceedings of MTT'05*, Moscou.

Joseph Greenberg. 1963. Universals of Language (2nd edition), MIT Press, Cambridge.

Chung-Hye Han. 1998. Asymmetry in the Interpretation of -(n)un in Korean, *Japanese and Korean Linguistics*, 7:1-15.

Jeonghan Han. 1999. *Morphosyntactic Coding of Information Structure in Korean*, Ph.D. Dissertation, State University of New York at Buffalo.

Son-Moon Hwang. 2002. Hankukeo hwaje kumuneui unyul-jeok kochal (Study on Prosody of the Korean topic construction), *Eumseong Kwahak*, 9(2):59-68.

Sylvain Kahane. 1997. Bubble trees and syntactic representations, in Tilman Becker and Hans-Ulrich Krieger(eds), *Proceedings of 5th Meeting the Mathematics of Language (MOL5)*, Saarbrücken.

Jong-Bok Kim and Minghaeng Lee. 2001. Realizations of Information Structure and Its Projection in Korean, *Harvard Studies in Korean Linguistics*, IX:463-494, Hanshin Publishing Company, Seoul.

Mi-Young Kim. 2003. *An Optimality Approach to the Referential Interpretation of Zero Anaphora in Korean*, Ph.D. Dissertation, Seoul National University, Seoul.

Charles Li and Sandra Thompson. 1976. Subject and Topics: A New Typology, in Charles Li (ed), *Subject and Topic*, Academic Press, New York.

Igor Mel'čuk. 1988. *Dependency Syntax: Theory and Practice*. The SUNY Press, Albany, N.Y.

John Ross. 1967. Constraints on Variables in Syntax, Ph.D. Dissertation, MIT.

Cheol-Jae Seong and YoonKyoung Song. 1997. Jueojali josa-eui unyoulpaeteon-e kwanhan siheomeumseonghak-jeok yeonku (Experimental study on particles in the subject position), *Malsoli*, 33/34:23-42.

Lucien Tesnière. 1959. *Éléments de syntaxe structurale*. Klincksieck, Paris.

Rule-based extraction of English verb collocates from a dependency-parsed corpus

Silvie Cinková, Martin Holub, Ema Krejčová, Lenka Smejkalová
Charles University in Prague, Faculty of Mathematics and Physics
Institute of Formal and Applied Linguistics
Malostranské nám. 25
118 00 Praha 1 Czech Republic
{cinkova,holub,krejcova}@ufal.mff.cuni.cz

Abstract

We report on a rule-based procedure of extracting and labeling English verb collocates from a dependency-parsed corpus. Instead of relying on the syntactic labels provided by the parser, we use a simple topological sequence that we fill with the extracted collocates in a prescribed order. A more accurate syntactic labeling will be obtained from the topological fields by comparison of corresponding collocate positions across the most common syntactic alternations. So far, we have extracted and labeled verb forms and predicate complements according to their morphosyntactic structure. In the next future, we will provide the syntactic labeling of the complements.

1 Introduction

We commonly perceive the verb as the center of the sentence. By using a verb to interconnect nouns that we want to refer to, we make them participants in an event. About one half of the entries in the Oxford English Dictionary are noun entries whereas only one seventh of the entries are verb entries 'OED Online. March 2013. Oxford University Press.' <http://www.oed.com/view/Entry/113184 (accessed April 11, 2013).>.. The percentage rates vary slightly in European languages, but there are always fewer verbs than nouns. Isn't it astonishing that we need relatively few verbs to describe all events we want to comment on? No wonder that verbs are used in a variety of different argument structure patterns and with very different collocates. Let us consider a common verb such as *give*:

```
(1) The wooden chair gave a frightened squeak.
(2) Mom gave me a cookie.
(3) The results gave them quite a shock.
(4) Joanna gave her a disgusted look.
(5) The audience gave him the raspberry.
(6) Eventually, they had to give up.
```

We intuitively perceive combinations of syntactic patterns and collocates as different word senses, but in fact there is no such thing as a universal set of senses for each verb: the number of word senses in a dictionary, as well as their definitions, is based on individual judgments of the lexicographer and regulated by the editorial policy of a particular dictionary. Thus, making a dictionary is by no means objective modeling of the meaning of a lexical item, and lexicographers have never even claimed that ambition: "I don't believe in word senses", goes a thought-provoking quote of Sue Atkins, a respectable practitioner and pioneer of modern lexicography. On the other hand, the concept of semantic grouping of some sort is deeply anchored in our linguistic intuition, and we can hardly think of a different starting point, should the lexical description be intelligible. The question remains what sort of grouping should be applied and what the perception of a meaning shift is based on, which is where the lexicographical policies differ with respect to the intended use of each particular lexicon.

Already in 1997, Adam Kilgarriff, a visionary of computational lexicography, used Atkins' remark for the title of his influential paper (Kilgarriff 1997) to argue that "the corpus citations, not the word senses, are the basic objects in the ontology. The corpus citations will be clustered into senses according to the purposes of whoever or

Proceedings of the Second International Conference on Dependency Linguistics (DepLing 2013), pages 60–67, Prague, August 27–30, 2013.

whatever does the clustering. In the absence of such purposes, word senses do not exist." (p. 91).

2 Related Work

Many important authors have elaborated the intuitive observation that what is perceived as lexical meaning arises from an interplay of syntactic and semantic features in the context of each actual use of the lexical unit under examination (e.g. Firth 1957; Sinclair 1991; Hoey 2005; Hanks 2013, Levin 1993, Gross 1994; Fillmore 2006; Palmer et al., 2005; Hudson 2006). They all describe, with a varying degree of formalization, the behavior of individual words; sometimes by their own or a collective introspection (Firth, Levin, Gross), sometimes based on the manual findings in a text corpus (Sinclair, Hanks, Fillmore and Palmer). However, their approach results again in man-made lexicons. These are necessarily biased towards the data on which they are based, and the word senses are hard-wired.

On the other hand, a number of collocation analysis tools are available; e.g. Sketch Engine (Ki lgarriff et al. 2004) and DeepDict (Bick 2009). While the Sketch Engine uses linear search, DeepDict extracts collocates from dependency trees.

3 Five-slot forms and Canonical Sequence

We have a working hypothesis regarding verbs that their selectional preferences can be modeled by a statistical analysis of the surface-syntax structures of their uses and the distributional similarity of the nouns that occur as their complements and perhaps in some other positions. Since we do not want to confine ourselves to verb arguments and adjuncts, we refer to them as *verb collocates.* Under *collocations* we do not only understand idiosyncratic combinations of content words, but, more broadly, significantly co-occuring combinations of a given lexical verb with other content words as well as with the grammatical patterns surrounding it. Our conception of collocation overlaps e.g. with Hoey's term *textual colligation* (Hoey 2005), p. 52).

Unlike Sketch Engine and DeepDict, we want to regard the significance of each collocate noun with respect to its syntactic function in a given *clause template (CLT).* We have therefore selected the most common clause structures and are recording them as conditions in dependency trees. We formulated the templates with the Prague Markup Query Language (Pajas and Štěpánek 2009). The clause templates are in fact corpus queries. They highlight the verb under examination (*target verb*) and the present collocates. The collocates are numbered according to the position in the linear order of a statement clause in active verb voice with a neutral word order (no topicalizations, no verb-subject inversions), to which we refer as *Canonical Sequence* (Fig 1). Besides, they are marked with a letter. For instance, number 3 in the label `a3` encodes the information that the particular node would occur in the third position in a regular statement clause. The letter `a` indicates that it occurred in the first position in the given template. That would be the case of the subject of a passive clause.

1	2	3	4	5
Agent	TV	OBJ1/SC	OBJ2/OC	Prep+NP/ADV /RP/NPquant

Figure 1: Canonical Sequence of sentence elements

We have introduced the character-digit pair to consider the similarity of the lexical population of positions across different clause templates. We hope to be able to e.g. densify our data by neglecting passivization or the *to*-alternation.

The Canonical Sequence is one of the Five-slot forms that cover the most common clause structures. A target verb that matches a clause template will obtain the label of that template and the matching collocates will obtain the collocate labels.

The first position in the Canonical Sequence belongs to the Agent. The second position occupies the target verb (finite and in the active voice). The third position belongs to the first noun phrase in the row or to a verb clause. This is also the right position for an adjective phrase that is not preceded by a noun phrase right of the target verb position. The fourth position hosts the second of two noun phrases, whenever they occur in the clause, or an adjective phrase preceded by a noun phrase right of the target verb, or a verb clause. The fifth position is meant for prepositional noun phrases, adverbs, verb particles (tagged as `RP`), and non-prepositional noun phrases identified as adverbials of time or quantity. We use a heuristic rule to identify these noun phrases. Our rule lists the most common lemmas of time/quantity information, such as names of weekdays, months and seasons, and quantity measures. Of course we do our best to avoid heuristic rules; this is an exception in our system.

As we are not able to differentiate between a prepositional object, obligatory modifier and a free adjunct, the position of the prepositional phrase is always optional in the query. Fig. 2 shows the visualizations of several clause templates.

4 Template sets

To find the clause templates in the corpus, we need the following information on the target verb:

- verb finiteness
- verb voice
- type of clause that it governs

We also need to find all words that can act as nouns and thus fill a position in the five-slot form, including their possible prepositions. Eventually, we want to identify adjectives and adverbs.

With these requirements we hit just between the part-of-speech tagging (Santorini 1990) and the syntactic labels provided by the parsers available to us. For instance a verb form marked as VBN (past participle) can represent a finite active verb form `(has/had read)`, a finite passive verb `form (is/was/is being/was being/has been/had been read)`, or an infinite passive verbform `to be read, to have been read`, etc., or the future tense `will be read` or `will have read`. The syntactic labels functions in their turn describe mostly the verb's syntactic relations to their governing syntactic elements. Therefore we have been creating our own labels. We have introduced a set of labels for the verbs, which we call Verb Form Templates. All verb forms are captured in approximately 40 templates. We keep a separate class for verbs combined with modal and a few auxiliary verbs, such as `be going to`, `used to` and `have (got) to`.

We have also sketched about 30 collocate templates *(Verb Argument Templates, VAT)*.

CLT_008.

1	2	3	4	?5+ (optional)
a	b	c	d	e
NP not WH_coref	TV act, not governed by NP	NP	ADJP	PP PP ING
Agent		Obj_1	Object Complement	
John	calls	Mary	dull	with pleasure

CLT_009.

1	2	3	4	?5+ (optional)
a	b	c		d
NP not WH_coref	TV act, not governed by NP	Quote, that-clause, subclause without subordinator, wh-clause	-	PP PP ING
Agent				
John	says	that it is raining	-	with pleasure
John	says	it is raining	-	
John	says:	"It is raining"	-	
John	says	what we want to hear		

Figure 2: Visualization of two clause templates

We distinguish the following VAT:

- noun phrase (including numbers, determiners and personal pronouns)
- possessive noun phrase (Saxon genitive and possessive forms of personal pronouns)
- relative expression in a wh-clause or a relative clause, antecedent identification added
- relative expression in a pseudocleft clause, antecedent identification added
- expletive `it`.

Fig. 3 shows the VFT of a lexical verb governed by a modal verb.

5 Overcoming parser errors with Five-slot forms

We have introduced the Five-Slot forms to overcome the weaknesses of the automatic parsing.

In traditional grammars, such as (Quirk et al. 2004), verbs are neatly grouped according to the number of objects. The problem is that the parsers available, unlike human experts, are not able to deal with structural ambiguities. Therefore they often give random results in syntactic labeling. For instance, a head noun following an active verb is mostly classified as an object, even when it is a subject complement or a temporal adverbial (e.g. `He arrived Sunday`).

Making use of the fixed word order in English, we use the structured parser output to provide relevant collocates with positional

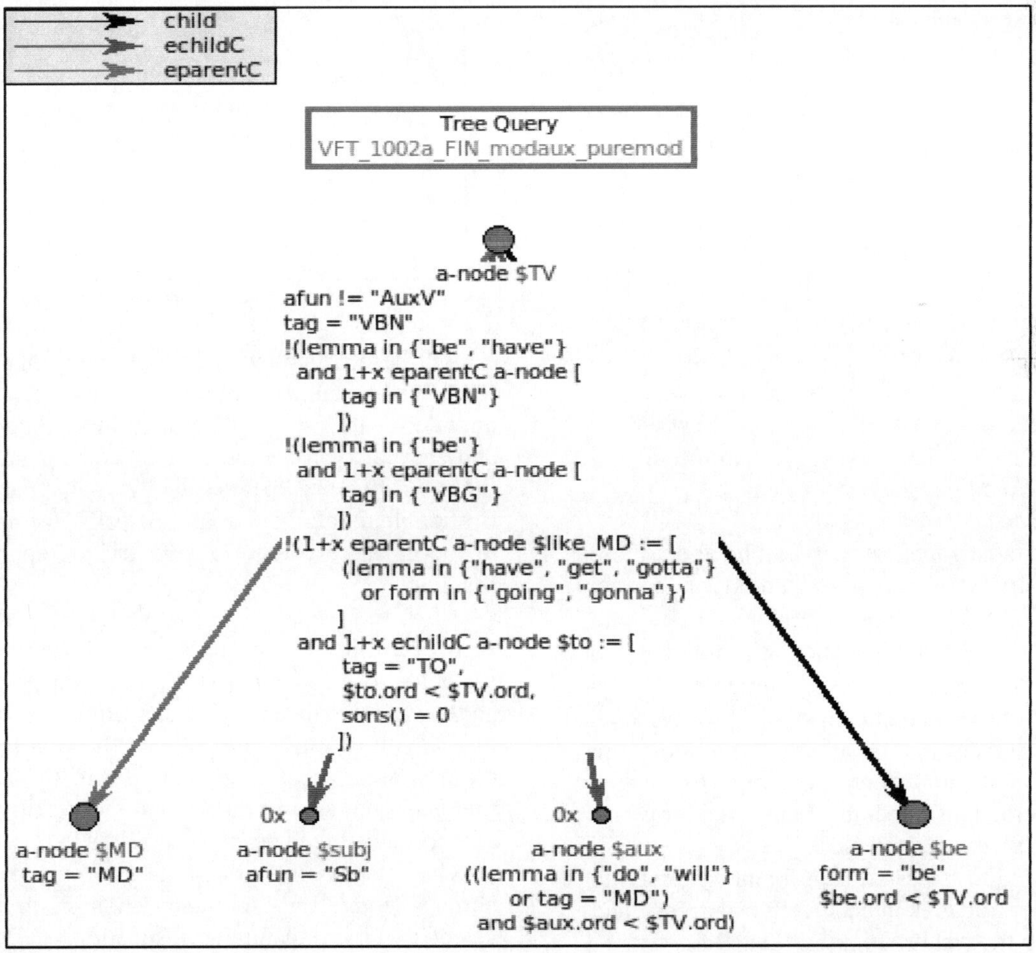

Figure 3: Verb form template of a lexical verb governed by a modal verb (regarded as a finite form of the lexical verb

labels. So we can bypass the errors in the syntactic analysis and are still able to compute occurrences of nouns.

We also have to deal with the fact that the parser is forced to overdo the semantic interpretation of a sentence to achieve a fully structured tree (and it often does it in a way a human never would). One interesting example of this sort is the to-infinitive following a noun phrase that follows the target verb.

There are three structure options for a number of structurally ambiguous cases. Cf.:

```
(7)   ... persuaded the
visitor to leave/... shut the
door to hide
(8)   ... hated the woman to
go
(9)   ... became the first
player to score
```

In the first case, `persuade` and `shut` have two complements each: `the visitor` and `leave (persuaded the visitor that the visitor should leave, shut the door in order to hide)`. Note that we ignore the labeling. In the first case, the infinitive clause with `leave` is a regular argument, while in the second clause `hide` is a free adjunct, that is, a purpose clause. In the second example, `hate` has only one argument – `go`, whereas `the woman` is the subject of `go (hated that the woman went)`. In the third case, the only argument of `become` is `player`, which is modified by the attributive infinitive `to score (became the first player who scored)`.

The statistical parser has learned about these three structures. It even produces correct results in verbs that occurred in the training data frequently enough, such as `expect` and `hate`. Nevertheless, the resulting structure is completely unpredictable in most verbs, and, even worse, the resulting structures are inconsistent in different occurrences of the same verb. This inevitably causes a strong bias in the collocation statistics.

We had to bypass this problem by querying all three structures in each verb occurrence and merging the results (Figures 4,5 and 6).

The parser provides labeling of syntax elements, but is often grossly wrong. For instance, prepositional phrases are typically labeled as adverbials: the prepositional objects of the verbs `rely` and `indulge` would be labeled as adverbials. On the other hand, non-prepositional adverbials, such as `last year` or `two miles` would be labeled as objects. Nor is the (i.e. any) parser particularly good at making a difference between the direct object of a bitransitive verb and the object complement expressed by a noun, and therefore we cannot retrieve them as two separate categories. Cf.:

```
John bought me a book.
John called me an idiot.
```

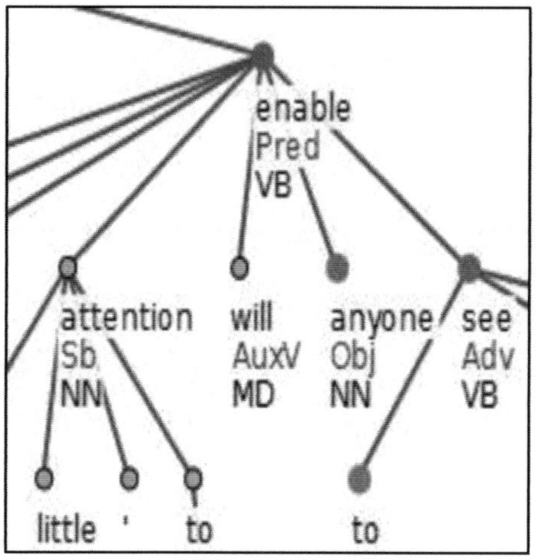

Figure 4: Control

All these structures are simple to recognize for a human, since the human uses their lexical knowledge to resolve the structural ambiguity, and they also make the human conceptualize the events in very different ways. As the parser is not able to tell them apart correctly, we have to merge these categories and try to separate them later.

Also, the parser very often picks the first verb form in the sentence to be the main predicate, even when it is a participial phrase and/or is introduced by a subordinator. The misindentification of the main predicate affects the argument recognition not just in the first predicate, but also in the second and further in an unpredictable way.

The issues mentioned above are both homogeneous and frequent enough to be detected by manual inspection. Their frequency slightly varies with respect to different verb lemmas, whose context we examine.

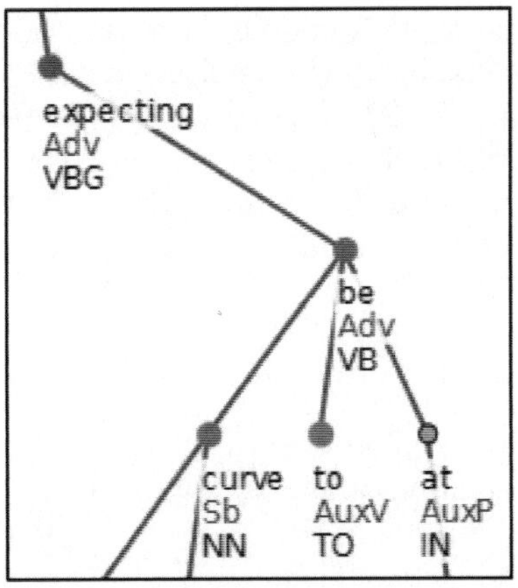

Figure 5: Raising

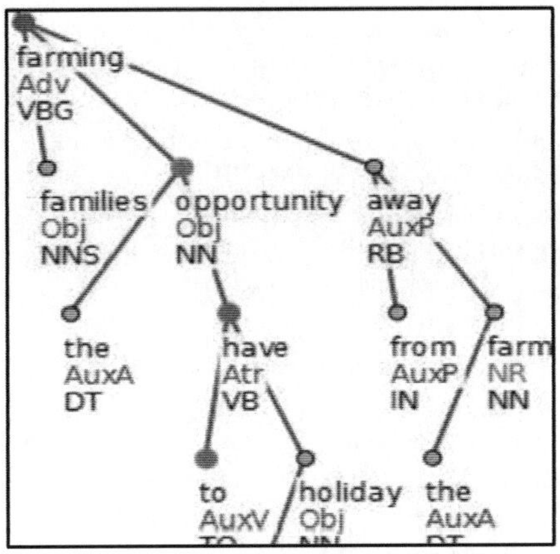

Figure 6: Attributive infinitive

6 The corpus

We perform the labeling on BNC50, a 50-million-token subset of BNC used in the Pattern Dictionary of English Verbs (Hanks and Pustejovsky 2005).

We have chosen to work with a syntactically parsed corpus, since our earlier (unpublished) preliminary study showed that collocation extraction has better recall on a parsed corpus than on a plain text corpus, with all tested parsers (McDonald, Lerman, and Pereira 2006); (de Marneffe, MacCartney, and Manning 2006) giving similar results. We use our in-house NLP infrastructure tool Treex (Žabokrtský 2011) to transform the outputs of different parsers into a uniform dependency representation in the annotation style of the Prague Dependency Treebank family (Hajič, 2004). The rules are tailored to the PDT-scheme and thus not specific to one of the original parsers, which means that they are applicable to any parser output processed by Treex. We have been using the MST parser.

At the beginning, we had to decide which annotation layer we should write our rules for, since Treex offers two different PDT-style linguistic representations. The PDT-like corpora have two different but interlinked syntax annotation layers: the analytical (i.e. surface syntax) and the tectogrammatical layer (i.e. underlying syntax with semantic labeling and coreference).

At first, the tectogrammatical layer was the apparent favorite, since it offers a straightforward extraction of verb arguments:

- It abstracts from regular syntactic alternations, such as passivization and reciprocity. Both active and passive clauses have the same tree representations and the same semantic labels (functors) of the arguments.
- Semantic labels (functors) distinguish arguments from adjuncts and give a semantic classification of the adjuncts.
- Missing verb arguments are substituted with labeled substitute nodes according to a valency lexicon. This feature compensates not only for textual ellipsis, but, more importantly, also for grammatical ellipsis; e.g. artificial subjects of controlled infinitives are inserted.
- Anaphora are resolved even in the grammatical coreference. For instance, the artificial subject node of a controlled infinitive contains a reference to a real node that would be the subject of the infinitive, if it were not controlled by another verb.

For all these enhancements, the tectogrammatical representation would have been our first choice, at least considering the manually annotated data (Hajič et al. 2012).

However, the automatic English tectogrammatical annotation is very unreliable, compared to the manual standard: the semantic labels are often wrong, and hardly any missing nodes are reconstructed. Besides, the tectogrammatical representation takes away word forms and auxiliary words. To retrieve the auxiliary words or word forms, one has to refer to the lower (analytical) layer, increasing the complexity of the corpus queries. Hence we preferred the analytical layer.

We had to reflect and compensate for systematic errors in the analytical parse. Most of them had propagated already from the constituency parser. By our manual estimation, all parsers known to us have similar problems, so we could not just switch the constituency parser at the beginning of the process pipeline to avoid these problems.

7 Future work

At the moment we are implementing the templates to be able to evaluate them. We have been testing the corpus queries continuously and revising the templates accordingly. However, we still have to do a quantitative evaluation. In the future we want to use the template labels as features in a model of selectional preferences of verbs.

8 Discussion

There are at least two well-working tools for collocation sorting for English: the Sketch Engine (Kilgarriff et al. 2004) and DeepDict (Bick 2009). However, the sorting we intend to do goes slightly beyond what they provide. To the best of our knowledge, neither the Sketch Engine nor DeepDict consider the collocates across different syntactic alternations. We believe that the quality of our syntactic labeling will rapidly increase with the growing data, so that collocate lists based e.g. on the English GigaWord (Graff and Cieri 2003) or CzEng (Bojar et al. 2012) will reflect the mapping of collocate positions between clause types well. A preliminary manual evaluation of the VFT and VAT annotation of several hundred sentences revealed minor inconsistencies, which are being fixed at the moment, but the labels proved generally appropriate. Inaproppriately labeled instances almost always occurred in trees with substantial parsing errors.

9 Conclusion

In this still initial investigation we have been labeling verb occurrences in a dependency treebank with clause types and their complements with numbers of positions they would occupy in the linear scheme of a finite statement clause with neutral word order. We have been pursuing this exercise because we believe that clause types and complement position labels will represent a useful set of features for statistical modeling of the selectional preferences of English nouns and verbs.

10 Acknowledgements

This work was supported by the Czech Science Foundation (grant No GAP103/12/G084).

References

Eckhard Bick. 2009. DeepDict - A Graphical Corpus-based Dictionary of Word Relations. In *Proceedings of NODALIDA* , 4:pp. 268–271. Tartu: Tartu University Library.

Ondřej Bojar , Zdeněk Žabokrtský, Ondřej Dušek, Petra Galuščáková, Martin Majliš, David Mareček, Jiří Maršík, Michal Novák, Martin Popel, and Aleš Tamchyna. 2012. The Joy of Parallelism with CzEng 1.0. In LREC Proceedings, 3921–3928. Istanbul, Turkey: European Language Resources Association.

Marie-Catherine De Marneffe, Bill MacCartney, and Christopher D. Manning. 2006. 'Generating Typed Dependency Parses from Phrase Structure Parses. In *Proceedings of the IEEE / ACL 2006 Workshop on Spoken Language Technology* Stanford University.

Charles J Fillmore. 2006. Frame Semantics. In *Encyclopedia of Language & Linguistics*, 613–620. Oxford: Elsevier.

John Rupert Firth. 1957. *Papers in Linguistics 1934–1951*. London: Oxford University Press.

David Graff, and Christopher Cieri. 2003. English Gigaword. *Linguistic Data Consortium, Philadelphia.*

Maurice Gross. 1994. The Lexicon Grammar of a Language Application to French. In *Encyclopedia of Language and Linguistics*, R. E. Ashe, 2195–2205.

Jan Hajič, Eva Hajičová, Jarmila Panevová, Petr Sgall, Ondřej Bojar, Silvie Cinková, Eva Fučíková, et al. 2012. Announcing Prague Czech-English Dependency Treebank 2.0. In LREC Proceedings, 3153–3160. Istanbul, Turkey: European Language Resources Association.

Patrick W. Hanks. 2013. *Lexical Analysis: Norms and Exploitations*. University Press Group Limited.

Patrick Hanks, and James Pustejovsky. 2005. A Pattern Dictionary for Natural Language Processing. *Revue Francaise de Linguistique Appliquée* 10 (2).

Michael Hoey. 2005. *Lexical Priming: A New Theory of Words and Language*. Routledge.

Richard Hudson. 2006. Word Grammar. In *Encyclopedia of Language & Linguistics*, 633–642. Oxford: Elsevier.

Adam Kilgarriff. 1997. "I Don't Believe in Word Senses". *Computers and the Humanities* 31 (2): 91–113.

Adam Kilgarriff, Pavel Rychly, Pavel Smrz, and David Tugwell. 2004. The Sketch Engine. In .

Beth Levin. 1993. *English Verb Classes and Alternations*. University of Chicago Press.

Ryan McDonald , Kevin Lerman, and Fernando Pereira. 2006. Multilingual Dependency Analysis with a Two-stage Discriminative Parser. In , 216–220. Association for Computational Linguistics.

OED Online. March 2013. Oxford University Press.

Petr Pajas, and Jan Štěpánek. 2009. System for Querying Syntactically Annotated Corpora. In , 33–36.

Martha Palmer, Dan Gildea, and Paul Kingsbury. 2005. The Proposition Bank: A Corpus Annotated with Semantic Roles. *Computational Linguistics Journal* 31 (1).

Randolph Quirk, Sidney Greenbaum, Geoffrey Leech, and Jan Svartvik. 2004. *A Comprehensive Grammar of the English Language*. Longman.

Beatrice Santorini. 1990. Part-of-Speech Tagging Guidelines for the Penn Treebank Project. *University of Pennsylvania 3rd Revision 2nd Printing* (MS-CIS-90-47): 33.

John Sinclair. 1991. *Corpus, Concordance, Collocation*. Oxford University Press.

Zdeněk Žabokrtský. 2011. Treex – an Open-source Framework for Natural Language Processing. In Information Technologies – Applications and Theory, 7–14.

A method to generate simplified Systemic Functional Parses from Dependency Parses

Eugeniu Costetchi
CRP Henri Tudor, Luxembourg, 29, J.F. Kennedy, 1855, Luxembourg
eugeniu.costetchi@tudor.lu

Abstract

Systemic Functional Linguistics provides a semiotic perspective on language. The text analysis described in Systemic Functional Linguistics (SFL) can be of critical value in real-world applications. But parsing with SFL grammars is computationally intensive task and parsers for this level of description to date have not been able to operate on unrestricted input. This paper describes a graph-based method to automatically generate simplified SFL mood and transitivity parses of English sentences from Stanford Dependency parses and a database providing transitivity categories for each verb.

1 Introduction

Broad coverage natural language components now exist for several levels of linguistic abstraction, ranging from tagging and stemming, through syntactic analyses, to semantic specifications. In general, the higher the degree of abstraction, the less accurate coverage becomes.

Transitivity descriptions[1] as developed within Systemic Functional Linguistics (SFL) offer a semantically-oriented decomposition of clauses that is still sufficiently closely tied to observable grammatical distinctions as to offer a powerful bridge for automatic analysis. Transitivity analyses, like those in Table 1, provide descriptions analogous to frame descriptions (Fillmore, 1985; Minsky, 1974) as found in FrameNet (Baker, Fillmore, & Lowe, 1998) or VerbNet (Kipper, Korhonen, Ryant, & Palmer, 2008) which are applied in Semantic Role Labelling tasks. CoNLL-2004/5(Carreras & Màrquez, 2005) shared tasks on SRL, revealed a major performance drop when when the test corpus differs from the training one. This can be due to the use of machine learning or due to annotation schemas. By contrast to VerbNet & FrameNet, the SFL transitivity descriptions enforce a further generalisation across the kinds of frame roles that can be used. This generalisation allows descriptions to be preserved when clauses are realised in different forms and also provides the basis for making a more robust connection to structural syntactic features of clauses.

Mood descriptions offer a functional syntactic decomposition of clauses that serves as a well-argued foundation for transitivity analysis (Halliday & Matthiessen, 2004).

SFL adopts a semiotic perspective on language and distinguishes different meaning-lines fused in the text. Therefore parsing in terms of mood and transitivity (e.g. Table 1) can be of tremendous value for Natural Language Understanding and Critical Discourse Analysis. Provided automatic mood and transitivity parsing can have applications well beyond those traditionally explored with automatic semantic and syntactic analysis.

example 1	**the duke**	**had**	**given**	**the teapot**	**to my aunt.**
mood	clause: [mood type: declarative; tense: past perfect simple; voice: active: polarity: positive]				
	subject	predicate: finite	predicate: predicator	complement	complement
transitivity	agent-carrier	possessive process		possessed	beneficiary
example 2	**the lion**	**caught**		**the tourist**	**yesterday.**
mood	clause: [mood type: declarative; tense: past perfect simple; voice: active: polarity: positive]				
	subject	predicator/finite		complement	adjunct
transitivity	agent-carrier	possessive process		affected-possessed	temporal location

Table 1 sample mood and transitivity analyses

Parsers for this level of description to date have not been able to operate on unrestricted input. To parse directly in terms of SFL is a computationally difficult task. However there have been successful attempts to produce SFL parses in two steps. This paper describes a method to automatically generate English sentences parses of mood and transitivity from Stanford Dependency parses (Marneffe, MacCartney, & Manning, 2006; Marneffe & Manning, 2008) and from the Process Type Database (Neale, 2002).

[1] Note that transitivity in SFL is a clause-level representation and not a verb property such as in traditional grammars.

Proceedings of the Second International Conference on Dependency Linguistics (DepLing 2013), pages 68–77, Prague, August 27–30, 2013.

Typed dependency grammars (like SD) and systemic functional grammars are different analysis approaches. The typed dependency analysis results in word pairs bound by a syntactic relation. The systemic functional analysis results in constituents and feature structures. The constituents are text chunks labelled with their functional grammatical role in the clause, while feature structures are sets of attribute-value pairs representing properties of constituents.

The main issues addressed here are: how to determine the boundaries of constituents and their (mood/transitivity) roles in a clause and how to further determine their features based on constituent position and lexico-grammatical resources. The Stanford Dependency Parser (SDP) offers a suitable backbone for bootstrapping mood analysis. The defined grammatical roles are syntactically compatible with functional grammar and contribute to the solving constituency problem (see Section 4.3). For the second problem we employ pattern graphs corresponding to choices in systemic networks together with lexical-semantic resources such as the PTDB to further enrich the constituents with semantic information.

The Process Type Database (PTDB) is a dictionary-like database of verb lexical items, each of which is bound to list of verb senses and corresponding semantic frames that dictate the process type and participant roles selection.

In the remainder of this paper we briefly introduce key SFL concepts with focus on mood and transitivity along with simplified MOOD[2] and TRANSITIVITY systems in terms of which we currently consider parsing (Section 2). Then, in Section 3, are presented the main contributions in SFL parsing followed, in Section 4, by description of our graph-based parsing approach detailed with parsing method, computational implementations and resources that support it. In Section 5 we conclude on presented approach.

2 SFL preliminaries

In Systemic Functional Linguistics there are three lines of meaning expressed in any clause: *textual, interpersonal* and *experiential*. Textually, a clause acts as a message (or an information unit) that contributes to the creation of the discourse as a whole. Interpersonally, a clause is a unit of exchange between speaker and listener, and so serves social relations and speech functions enacted in a clause. Within SFL, however, speech acts are expressed by means of typical grammatical variations and expressions, thus maintaining a tighter link between the speech act and the grammatical realization. *Mood analysis* provides the framework to grasp and use these grammatical variations. Experientially, a clause is the representation of some "*process in ongoing human experience*"(Halliday & Matthiessen, 2004, p. 170) and is described through *transitivity*.

Systemic Functional Grammar approach to syntactic structure is to focus on systematizing the *choice possibilities* a speaker has for construing her utterances. Each choice shapes the grammatical realization and is accompanied by a range of semantic implications. These choices are then structured in hierarchical system networks so that early choices restrict latter ones.

There are two large variants of Systemic Functional Grammars: the Sydney Grammar proposed by Halliday (Halliday & Matthiessen, 2004), who originated SFL, and the Cardiff Grammar proposed by Fawcett (Fawcett, 2008), who, based on Sydney Grammar, has constructed an alternative account focusing more directly on syntactic generalizations.

In the present paper, the Cardiff Grammar is used for transitivity analysis because the PTDB is build according to it and, a simplified version of Sydney Grammar is used for mood analysis as described in the next section.

2.1 Mood constituency and MOOD systemic network

Mood constituency analysis in SFL supports the interpersonal perspective on language and resembles the analysis of Quirk (1985) or that of Fawcett (2008) where the clause is syntactically split into constituting elements. We will refer to it as *mood constituency*, because, in SFL, all analyses have their own specific way of splitting the clause into constituents. An example of such analysis is exhibited in Table 1. The following is a brief description of clause constituents and their functional roles in exchange (argument) structure.

The *Finite* is a part of the verbal group expressing the tense or modality. It either precedes the Predicator (introduced below) or is conflated with it in present and past simple tenses. The role of the Finite is to make the clause finite by anchoring it into the here and now, so to speak, bringing the clause into the context of the speech event. This is done either by reference to the time

[2] Capitalized notation refers to a SFG system network whereas non-capitalized terms refer to concept s.

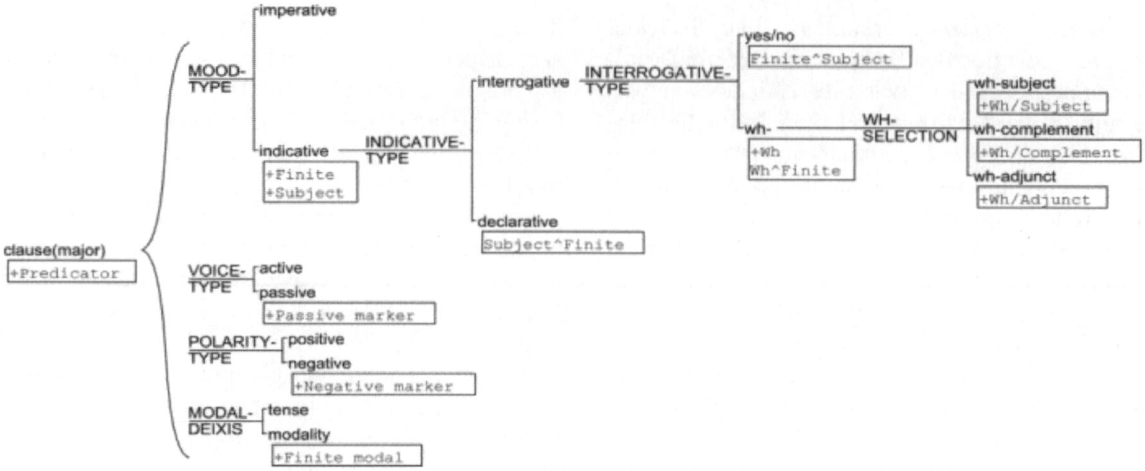

Figure 1 simplified MOOD system of Sydney Grammar

of speaking via tense or by reference to the judgment of the speaker via modality.

The *Subject* is the nominal group or a nominal clause that precedes the Predicator in a clause and it is something by reference to which the proposition can be affirmed or denied. It is considered to be "*modally responsible*" for the validity of what is being predicated (stated, commanded, questioned or offered) in the clause. Note that the predication is not interpreted as an experiential relation but as an interpersonal relation. Hence there is no interpretation in terms of truth values of a clause (because for e.g. offers, and commands cannot be attributed truth values).

The *Predicator* is the part of verbal group minus the finite constituent when they are not conflated. It specifies additional temporal and aspectual relations, voice and the process type (e.g. action, relation, mental process etc.) that is predicated about the Subject. It can contain one or more Main Verbs. The *Main Verb* is a non-auxiliary and non-modal verb at the end of the verbal group. If there is more than one Main Verb we say that it is a *complex clause*. To enforce the syntactic and functional analysis proposed in the Cardiff analysis methodology (Fawcett, 2008), the complex clauses need to be separated into individual clauses so that each comply with the "*one main verb per clause*" principle. Sentence division into clauses is explained in Section 2.5.

The *Complement* is a part of the clause that follows the Predicator and has the potential of becoming a Subject, i.e. it can become an axis of the argument. Usually it is a nominal group and rarely a prepositional phrase. For example in passive clauses the agent easily loses the preposition "*by*" to become Subject.

Complements correspond to "*objects*" in traditional grammars.

The *Adjuncts* are the last type of clause constituent. They do not have the potential of becoming a Subject; therefore arguments cannot be constructed around adjunct elements. They are realized by adverbial, nominal and prepositional groups.

The system of MOOD used in this paper (Figure 1) is a simplified version of Sydney

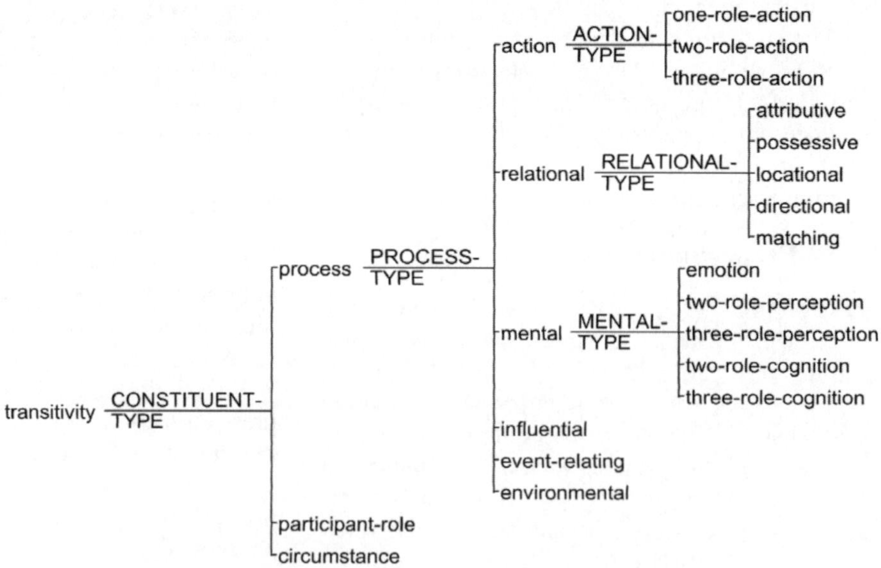

Figure 2 TRANSITIVITY system of Cardiff Grammar

Grammar mood. It focuses four features[3]: *mood type, voice type, clause polarity, and modal/temporal deixis*. These are clause-level features which are determined either by: (1) constituent presence, (2) constituent order, or (3) lexical items within a constituent. In section 4.3 is explained how to generate the mood structure and its features from the dependency graph.

2.2 Transitivity constituency and TRANSITIVITY systemic network

TRANSITIVITY (Figure 2) defines the *process types, participant roles* that correspond to each process type and *circumstances* that can occur in the language (English in this case). These are functional units of a configuration whose syntactic counterpart is the clause.

The *Process* is the central element of a configuration. Each *process type* (classification in Figure 2) provides its own model or schema for construing a particular domain of experience by defining a configuration of *participant roles* for that particular process type. The Process is filled by Finite and Predicator constituents but the Main Verb dictates systemic selection of the Process Type.

Participants are filled by Subject and Complement constituents and their roles are selected by the configuration schema. A configuration can have from one to three Participants just as a clause has a Subject up to two Complements. The vast majority of Processes require two Participants whereas only a small number of processes ask for one or three Participants.

The last unit type in a configuration is the *circumstance*. It introduces additional information about the configuration such as time, space, cause, manner, etc. Circumstances are filled by Adjunct constituents and are optional units in a configuration. The clause is syntactically valid if adjuncts are removed whereas if a Subject, Predicate or Complement is missing the clause changes its meaning or becomes syntactically invalid. The same holds for a configuration; if a participant or process is removed then it becomes another configuration or invalid.

One might argue that in "*John behaved well*", if we remove or substitute the adjunct "*well*", then the meaning of the entire clause is modified. The *Manner* is treated as circumstance in Sydney Grammar but in Cardiff grammar, it has been given a participant role. Since we are bond to the latter, syntactically manner is still an adjunct but semantically it becomes a participant role.

Due to space limitation, the detailed process type, participant role or circumstances classification are not covered further in the current paper. They are treated with great detail by Halliday and Matthiessen (2004), Neale (2002) and Fawcett (2009).

Seldom, a clause can be interpreted as corresponding to more than one configuration type which implies different participant role and process type selections. This principle, enounced by Halliday, is called *systemic indeterminacy* (Halliday & Matthiessen, 2004, p. 173) and applies to all systems but especially to TRANSITIVITY.

2.3 The Process Type Database

The Process Type Database (Neale, 2002) is the key resource in the automatisation of transitivity analysis because the selection of the process type during transitivity analysis is a semantically driven operation. PTDB provides information on what possible process types and participants can correspond to a particular verb.

The PTDB is a dictionary-like dataset of verb lexical items, each of them, bound to an exhaustive list of verb senses and the corresponding Process Configuration for each sense. It is the result of Neale's work (2002) on improving the TRANSITIVITY system of the Cardiff Grammar. She systematizes according to the Cardiff Grammar over 5400 senses (and process configurations) for over 2750 verbs. A small example is presented in *Table 2*. Each verb sense has its own Process Configuration and can coincide or differ from the Process Configurations of other verb senses.

verb form	*informal meaning*	*configuration*
calculate	work out by mathematics (commission will then calculate the number of casted votes)	cognition: Ag-Cog + Ph
	plan (newspaper articles were calculated to sway reader's opinions)	two role action: Ag + Cre
catch	run after and seize (a leopard unable to catch its normal prey)	possessive: Ag-Ca + Af-Pos
	(did you catch a cold?)	possessive: Af-Ca + Pos
catch (up with)	reach (Simon tried to catch up with others)	two role action: Ag + Ra

Table 2 sample PTDB entries (simplified)

[3] Feature values are further determined by their own sub-systems.

2.4 The interplay between mood and transitivity – the case of prepositional groups

There are cases in mood analysis when deciding the unit type is impossible by relying solely on syntactic analysis (including typed dependency analysis). Prominent cases are the *prepositional phrases*. These can fill both a Complement and an Adjunct role. For mood analysis this implies that the same syntactic unit can fill a Complement and an Adjunct, while for transitivity analysis, it implies that the same syntactic unit can fill a Participant or a Circumstance.

(1) *John goes home through London.*

(2) *John is building a house for Bob.*

(3) *her teardrop shines like a diamond.*

(4) *John is building a house for ten years now.*

(5) *John goes to London by fast train.*

In examples (1) and (2) the prepositional phrases "*through London*"[4] and "*for Bob*" are Complements and Participants (Path and Beneficiary roles) while in examples (3), (4) and (5), "*like a diamond*", "*for ten years now*" and "*by fast train*" are Adjuncts and Circumstances (of comparison, temporal duration and manner-means).

prep	*role*[5]	*Sydney grammar*	*Cardiff grammar*
by	Ag	material: actor; mental: phenomenon; relational: token	action: actor; mental (emotive): phenomenon; relational: token
to	Ben	material: recipient; verbal: receiver	action: client / receiver[6]
to	Dest	material: location / place	action: destination
for	Ben	material: client	action: receiver
as	Attr	relational: attribute	relational (attributive): attribute
on, in	Ra	material: scope; verbal: verbiage; material: locational / place	action: range / destination

Table 3 Prepositions introducing participants

To solve this problem of undetermined role allocation there are two complementary solutions. The first one is to mark the every prepositional phrase as Complement and as Adjunct. This just postpones the decision of selecting the right unit type, however.

The second solution is to decide based on the preposition and potential process type as specified in the PTDB. Most of prepositions introduce only circumstances and only a few prepositions can introduce participants as well. And when they do, it is for only specific process types. *Table 3* we present prepositions known to introduce participants for process types. This table is an extension of the one from (Halliday & Matthiessen, 2004, p. 278) and contains translations to Cardiff Grammar counterparts.

2.5 Sentence partition into clauses

Dependency Graphs (will be introduced in Section 4.2) are graphs of a whole sentence whereas transitivity analysis is at individual clause-level. This implies that DG need to be split into individual clauses before transitivity analysis. We propose to detect and delimit clauses during the mood analysis. For some commonly occurring situations we propose treatments aligned with Fawcett's (2008, 2009) methodology as follows.

When the clauses are connected by a conjunction and have their own subject/objects then the conjunction is the clause border marker.

(6) *The lion chased the tourist but she escaped alive.*

(6a) *The lion[Ag-Ca] chased[Pr] the tourist[Af-Pos]*

(6b) *she[Ag] escaped[Pr] alive[Ra]*

When the predicators are conjoined and share subject and/or objects then each predicator will form a new clause and borrow the subject/objects from the other clause.

(7) *The lion chased and caught the tourist.*

(7a) *the lion[Ag-Ca] chased[Pr] the tourist[Af-Pos]*

(7b) *the lion[Ag-Ca] caught[Pr] the tourist[Af-Pos]*

In the case of mental, influential and event relating processes (classification in Figure 2) the predicates are often complex. Verbs in these classes are known as control and raising verbs (Haegeman, 1991) where a superordinate controls subordinate non-finite verb and binds its participants (Subject/Complement).

In order to comply with "*one main verb per clause*" principle, each Main Verb of the complex clause becomes a governor of a distinct clause. The subordinate verb with all of its dependent nodes is assigned to a placeholder. The superordinate verb receives the placeholder as Complement with the role of Phenomena. If the subject is missing in the subordinate clause then it is copied from the superordinate one.

(8) *The lion wanted/began to chase the tourist.*

(8a) *the lion[Cog] wanted/began[Pr] X[Phen]*

---

[4] In Sydney Grammar it is a circumstance for a material process. However, in Cardiff Grammar for Directional and Locative Processes some circumstances are treated as participants therefore they are Complements (Fawcett, 2009).

[5] General functions defined in Sydney Grammar: Ag(Agent), Ben(Beneficiary), Dest(Destination), Attr(Attribute), Ra(Range), etc.

[6] Beneficiary and Client are not directly specified in Cardiff system. This role is identified as Destination in two and three role actions. The test distinguishing between beneficiary and destination is checking whether the participant is animate or non-animate.

(8b) *X= the lion[Ag-Ca] to chase[Pr] the tourist[Af-Pos]*

The meaning of complex clause decomposition can be expressed with an equivalent rephrasing by inserting "*something that is*" between the Main Verbs, as in example (9).

(9) *The lion wanted/began something that is to chase the tourist.*

3 Literature review

Most of the parsing attempts in SFL dealt with the Nigel grammar (Matthiessen, 1985), which is a large and complex natural language generation (NLG) grammar. One of the early attempts was done by Kasper (1988). He recompiles[7] the Nigel grammar as feature structures employing *Functional Unification Grammar* (FUG) (Martin Kay, 1985) which is a well-established and a formally understood representation. Kasper used phrase-structure trees which served as backbones to which were mapped systemic feature choices.

O'Donnell use a different approach to recompiling the Nigel grammar which allowed him to parse text directly without appeal to the phrase-structure backbone that Kasper had required (O'Donnell, 1993, 1994). However he could not parse with the entire Nigel grammar because of the sheer size of the grammar and its inherent complexity introduced by multiple parallel classifications (Bateman, 2008). O'Donnell (O'Donnell, 2005) subsequently, in UAM Parser, decided, for pragmatic reasons, to return to a syntactic backbone and restrict the grammar so that functionally only the Mood structure of clauses is accounted for.

In a very different style of approach, Honnibal and Curran (2005) constructed a parser to convert Penn Treebank into a corresponding SFGBank. This managed to provide a good conversion from parse trees into systemic functional representation covering sentence mood and thematic constituency (the third kind of analysis in SFL which has been mentioned in Section 2). Transitivity was not been covered because of its inherently semantic nature.

More recently, O'Donnell (2012) in UAM Corpus Tool, created a parser that uses Stanford Parser(Klein & Manning, 2003) output as a backbone, which then is transformed into mood parse and then further derives the Sydney Grammar transitivity parse. He uses a mood backbone and enriches this with semantic features that are derived based on lexical choices and structural patterns.

Our approach is aligned with Honnibal's and O'Donnell's work with respect to using mood constituency as a backbone and enriching it with syntactic and semantic features. When approaching transitivity, O'Donnell provides the possible process types that a verb can have by employing a large lexicon where each word has syntactic and semantic features. The approach described here differs both in terms of the lexical resource and parsing method used. We employ PTDB, which provides entire configurations (frames) for each verb sense and the parsing method is a graph-based pattern matching.

4 The parsing method

In this section implementations are proposed and their capacities described, as well as methods that perform mood and transitivity parsing. The Stanford Dependency Schema proposed in (Marneffe et al., 2006) and re-motivated in (Marneffe & Manning, 2008) constitutes the departing point of our current approach in building a Mood Constituency Graph (MCG). MCG is the structure reflecting mood analysis and serves as the backbone for performing transitivity analysis via Graph Matching operations. Our method involves three types of graph structures: (1) *Dependency Graphs*, (2) *Mood Constituency Graphs* and (3) *Pattern Graphs*. We now introduce the specifics of a generic graph structure and the operations that these graphs support and then we present the parsing algorithms.

4.1 The graphs and operations over them

Graphs are defined as usual as a data structure consisting of a finite set of directed *edges* connecting *node* entities. The nodes, however, are not atomic data but *Feature Structures* (Carpenter, 1992), whereas the edges are triples (x,y,f) where x and y are nodes being connected and f is the feature structure of the edge. A generic *feature structure* (FS) is a set of attribute-value pairs where the value can be of an atomic or a complex data-type such as list, dictionary or feature structure.

The literature on mood and transitivity analysis specifies a range of methods for detecting and selecting a particular feature (Fawcett, 2008, 2009; Halliday & Matthiessen, 2004). In order to support those methodological specifications the

[7] Recompilation is employed to adopt a resource for application needs. Nigel grammar was initially created for NL generation. That grammar structure is not applicable for the parsing task.

graphs need to allow a number of operations: (1) *querying* over nodes and edges, (2) *graph matching*, (3) *pattern matching* and (4) *pattern-based node extraction.*

Querying over the node or edge FS return nodes or edges that comply with the constraints of the query. For example one can ask for all nodes that contain an "*NP*" part of speech or all node pairs connected by "*det*" relation.

Graph matching enables answering questions of whether a graph is identical to a sub-graph of the second one. This is the *graph isomorphism problem,* and is known to be NP-complete. However, the available algorithm (Cordella, Foggia, Sansone, & Vento, 2004) nevertheless performs this task very quickly when the graphs addressed are of limited size. In our case the graphs are of (English) sentences composed in average of 15-20 words. This lies well within the limits of practical computability.

An extension of graph matching is the *pattern matching operation.* A *graph pattern* (GP) is a graph whose feature structures can either be under or over specified. In the case of underspecified FS, the attributes and/or their values can be omitted down to an empty feature structure. In the case of over specified FS, the values are a list of possible values for an attribute.

For example, Figure 3 depicts a GP for detecting present perfect continuous tense. The slash ("/") symbol stands for part of speech attribute, "at" ("@") stands for the lexeme attribute while square brackets ("*[,]*") indicate a list of values that are accepted for a match. Note that this pattern is underspecified for most attribute-value pairs and over specified for one edge indicating two acceptable edge types ("*[aux, auxpass]*") and for one node POS ("*[vbz, vbp]*").

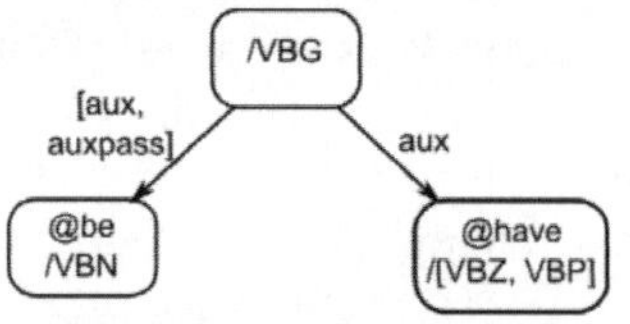

Figure 3 sample GP

The last operation is *pattern-based node extraction.* The purpose of the operation is returning nodes that have been marked in GP for extraction in the case of GP match. The matched nodes are returned together with the values of extraction markers in GP. An *extraction marker* is simply another attribute-value pair in the node's FS. This gives the possibility to assign new functional-semantic features to nodes, such as participant roles during transitivity parsing.

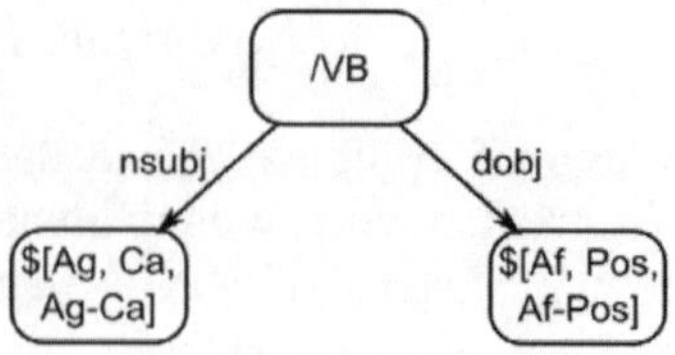

Figure 4 sample GP with marked nodes

For example, Figure 4 represents a GP used for transitivity analysis, where the dollar sign ("*$*") notation stands for an extraction marker. This means that whenever a verb is encountered that has a noun subject ("*nsubj*") and a direct object ("*dobj*"), then the subject node can receive agent, carrier or agent-carrier roles ("*[Ag,Ca,Ag-Ca]*"), while the object node can be attributed with affected, possessed or affected-possessed roles ("*[Af,Pos,Af-Pos]*").

4.2 The sentence dependency graph

Stanford Dependency Parser (Marneffe et al., 2006) generates, for each sentence, a set of typed dependencies between the words and the following information for each word token: *word, lemma, part of speech, named entity type* (if applicable) and *word index* in the sentence (for order preservation). This output can re-represented as a graph which we call *Dependency Graph* (DG). DG is instantiated from SDP output whose nodes and edge FSs are filled with corresponding information.

4.3 Generating mood parse

The *mood constituency graph* (MCG) is a directed graph which partitions the sentence into constituents at various hierarchical levels. A constituent has one corresponding MCG node. Therefore MCG node FS, among other attributes, contains the list of DG nodes which the constituent covers. The generation of MCG is executed in two phases: *creation* and *enrichment.*

A. *Creation* of MCG is based on breadth-first traversal of DG. The edge type, at every step decides what generative operation to execute on the MCG. The operation choices are: (1) *create a new constituent* (subject, predicator, finite, complement or adjunct as described in section 2.1), (2) *extend the current constituent* by a new token, (3) *create a subordinate clause constituent* and (4) *create a sibling constituent.*

Creation of a new constituent adds a new MCG node under the current one and fills it with the current DG node and all of its children. Extension of constituent means adding the current DG node to MCG node. This is a passive operation since the current DG node was added already when the new constituent was created. Creation of the clause constituent is similar to the creation of a simple constituent, but additionally, one more clause constituent is added under the former one and they both span over the same DG nodes. Sibling constituent creation adds a new constituent under the parent of the current one. The current DG node and all its children are moved from the current MCG node to a newly created sibling.

dependency relation	*operation on mcg*	*constituent type*
nsubj, nsubjpass, xsubj	new constituent	subject
csubj, csubjpass	new clause constituent	subject
attr, dobj, acomp	new constituent	complement
ccomp	new clause constituent	complement
agent	new constituent	complement agent
iobj	new constituent	complement dative
prep, prepc	new clause constituent	complement or adjunct
advcl	new clause constituent	adjunct
advmod, tmod	new constituent	adjunct
infmod, purpcl, rcmod, ref, rel, parataxis	new constituent	clause
expl, complm, mark	new sibling constituent	Marker
vb-dep-vb, vb-conj-vb,	new constituent	clause
amod, appos, aux, auxpass, cc, det, mwe, neg, nn, npadvmod, num, number, pobj, poss, possessive, preconj, predet, prt, punct, quantmod, xcomp	Extends current constituent	---

Table 4 rules for MCG creation

The decision of what operation to execute is based on the DG edge type, and in a few cases, on edge type plus the word's part of speech. Dependency types that require edge part of speech context are: "*dep*" and "*conj*". lists the rules binding (1) *Stanford Dependency relations*, (2) *generative operation in MCG* and (3) the *constituent type*. The following algorithm outlines how the MCG is created.

```
current_constit = create root node in mcg
bfs traverse DG:
 for each edge:
  oper_type,conit_type = get_rule(edge,nodes)
  new_constit = exec_oper(oper_type,
               contit_type, current_constit)
  current_constit = new_constit
```

B. In the *enrichment* phase Finite and Predicate components are added. Their creation requires more than one edge information available during the DG traversal and therefore, for the simplicity and clearness of the algorithm, these components have been left out of the creation phase. Moreover, in the cases of complex predicates the empty constituents need to be created according to subject/object control rules as described in Section 2.5 in order to constitute full clauses.

Finally, *voice, polarity, mood type and modal deixis features* are added to each clause. For each feature selection in the MOOD system (Section 2.1) a corresponding graph pattern is provided. The algorithm attempted to match these graph patterns in the MCG in order to determine which feature to add to the MCG clause constituent. The following algorithm outlines the enrichment phase of the MCG:

```
for each clause in MCG:
 create finite and predicate constituents
 create empty constituents
 match voice patterns & add features
 match polarity patterns & add features
 match mood type patterns & add features
 match modal deixis patterns & add features
```

4.4 Generating transitivity parse

MCG divides the sentence into clauses and their constituents and so it is an ideal structure to carry transitivity descriptions. Transitivity is a clause-level analysis that decorates the constituents with semantic roles, i.e. the Predicate with Process Type, the Subject and Complements with Participant Roles, the Adjuncts with Circumstances type (not covered here).

Transitivity parsing is very similar to enrichment phase of MCG generation. The following algorithm outlines how to enrich the MCG with transitivity descriptions:

```
for each clause in MCG:
  get process types (main verb)
  for each process type:
    get all configuration GPs
    for each configuration GP:
      if GP matches clause:
        add process type to clause
        extract marked nodes
        add roles to clause constituents
```

The graph patterns used in this task are called *Configuration Graph Patterns (CGP)*. They represent the graph form of the clause configurations as described by Fawcett (2009). Fawcett's configurations are given in a "*normalised*" form. It resembles Chomsky's *kernel sentences* which are of declarative mood type, active voice and unmarked positive polarity. This fixed functional feature set accompanying semantic descriptions of a configuration yields a particular realisation form. Any alternative feature set yields a predictable alternative realisation that can be grasped by the corresponding Graph Patterns for the same configuration. For example, a variation in voice of a two-role configuration would require two CGPs differing by participant positions. CGP with a passive voice would have switched participant roles between Subject and Complement constituents. So, every configuration may have several realization variations (as a result of conflation with other functions) and each configuration, therefore, has several corresponding CGPs covering those realisation variations.

In the Cardiff Grammar there are 16 distinct process types which cover 65 possible configurations. The process type dictates which configurations are allowed to occur and therefore the process type dictates which set of CGP shall be attempted for matching to clause DG. CGPs are grouped according to the process type and stored in a graph pattern repository.

Transitivity parsing process employs pattern-based node extraction. For each clause in MCG, process types are looked up in PTDB via Main Verb lexeme. Then, for each process type, all CGPs are matched against the clause MCG and in case of a successful match the marked nodes are extracted and enriched with semantic information carried in CGP. The final result is a MCG with a richer feature structure containing functional-semantic information specific for each clause constituent covered by the clause.

5 Conclusions

The present paper describes a graph-based approach to generate SFG mood and transitivity parses from the Stanford Dependency parse and Process Type Database. It is a computationally and linguistically viable text parsing approach for natural language understanding which encompasses framed semantic roles together with an adequate syntactic structure to support those semantic roles.

The presented method relies on correctness of dependency parse produced by SDP and on correctness of entries from PTDB. This constitutes a weak point because errors in SDP or PTDB can lead to decreased overall correctness. In case of missing verb items or verb senses for that verb items the parser will fail to produce transitivity analysis. Or if the verb sense has a faulty configuration specification then it will lead to incorrect semantic labelling. In case of incorrect dependencies or dependency types the mood parsing is likely to be erroneous as well. We cannot tell yet to what extend these limitations influence the correctness of our approach and it constitutes a future work.

A valuable investigation would be to check whether the Semantic Role Labelling with Cardiff Grammar suffers from the same limitation as the approaches describe in CoNLL-2005 which records a dramatic drop in parse correctness when the test corpus differs from the training corpus.

The semantic analysis provided by TRANSITIVITY covers process and participants. Currently no circumstance type has been taken into account as it would require additional lexicogrammatical resources.

No wide coverage parser employing the full Sydney Grammar has yet eventuated. However, the demand for systemic-oriented sentence analysis is on rise. Another increasing demand is for semantic text analysis to further support natural language understanding process. Concurrently there is a pragmatic need to work with unrestricted text and within reasonably small time for offline tasks like information extraction from large documents, and within significantly small time for online tasks like in the case of Dialogue Systems. The current method manages to satisfy demand for systemic sentence analysis via a trade-off between the richness of Sydney Grammar and pragmatic needs regarding coverage and execution time. Even so, a wide coverage systemic parser could have applications well beyond those traditionally explored with automatic semantic and syntactic analysis and become of critical value for solving real-life problems.

Bibliography

Baker, C. F., Fillmore, C. J., & Lowe, J. B. (1998). The Berkeley FrameNet Project. In C. Boitet & P. Whitelock (Eds.), *Proceedings of the 36th annual meeting on Association for Computational Linguistics* (Vol. 1, pp. 86–90). Association for Computational Linguistics.

Bateman, J. A. (2008). Systemic-Functional Linguistics and the Notion of Linguistic Structure: Unanswered Questions, New Possibilities. In Jonathan J. Webster (Ed.), *Meaning in Context: Implementing Intelligent Applications of Language Studies* (pp. 24–58). London, New York: Continuum.

Carpenter, B. (1992). *The logic of typed feature structures*. Cambridge: Cambridge University Press.

Carreras, X., & Màrquez, L. (2005). Introduction to the CoNLL-2005 Shared Task: Semantic Role Labeling. *Proceedings of the Ninth Conference on Computational Natural Language Learning CoNLL2005*, 152–164.

Cordella, L. P., Foggia, P., Sansone, C., & Vento, M. A (sub)graph isomorphism algorithm for matching large graphs. , 26 IEEE Transactions on Pattern Analysis and Machine Intelligence 1367–72 (2004). IEEE Computer Society.

Fawcett, R. P. (2008). *Invitation to Systemic Functional Linguistics through the Cardiff Grammar*. Equinox Publishing Ltd.

Fawcett, R. P. (2009). How to Analyze Process and Participant Roles. In *The Functional Semantics Handbook: Analyzing English at the level of meaning*. London: Continuum.

Fillmore, C. J. (1985). Frames and the semantics of understanding. *Quaderni di Semantica*, *6*, 222–254.

Haegeman, L. (1991). *Introduction to Government and Binding Theory. Blackwell Textbooks in Linguistics 1* (Vol. 2, p. 701). Blackwell.

Halliday, M. A. K., & Matthiessen, C. (2004). *An introduction to functional grammar*. London: Hodder Education.

Honnibal, M., & Curran, J. R. (2005). Creating a Systemic Functional Grammar Corpus from the Penn Treebank. In *Proceedings of the 5th Workshop on Important Unresolved Matters* (pp. 89–96). Association for Computational Linguistics.

Kipper, K., Korhonen, A., Ryant, N., & Palmer, M. (2008). A large-scale classification of English verbs. *Language Resources And Evaluation*, *42*, 21–40.

Klein, D., & Manning, C. (2003). Accurate unlexicalized parsing. (E. Hinrichs & D. Roth, Eds.)*Proceedings of the 41st Annual Meeting on Association for Computational Linguistics ACL 03*, *1*, 423–430.

Marneffe, M.-C., MacCartney, B., & Manning, C. D. (2006). Generating Typed Dependency Parses from Phrase Structure Parses. In *LREC 2006* (Vol. 6, pp. 449–454).

Marneffe, M.-C., & Manning, C. D. (2008). The Stanford typed dependencies representation. (P. Neittaanmäki, T. Rossi, K. Majava, & O. Pironneau, Eds.)*Coling 2008 Proceedings of the workshop on CrossFramework and CrossDomain Parser Evaluation CrossParser 08*, *1*, 1–8.

Martin Kay. (1985). Parsing In Functional Unification Grammar. In D.Dowty, L. Karttunen, & A. Zwicky (Eds.), *Natural Language Parsing*. Cambridge University Press.

Matthiessen, C. (1985). The systemic framework in text generation: Nigel. In James Benson and Willian Greaves (Ed.), *Systemic perspective on Discourse, Vol I* (pp. 96–118). Norwood, New Jersey: Ablex.

Michael O'Donnell. (2012). Transitivity Development in Spanish Learners of English. In *Proceedings of 39th International Systemic Functional Linguistics Conference*. Sydney, Australia.

Minsky, M. (1974). A framework for representing knowledge. In P. Winston (Ed.), *The Psychology of Computer Vision* (Vol. 20, pp. 211–277). McGraw-Hill.

Neale, A. C. (2002). *More Delicate TRANSITIVITY: Extending the PROCESS TYPE for English to include full semantic classifications*. Cardiff.

O'Donnell, M. (1993). Reducing Complexity in Systemic Parser. In *Proceeedings of the Third International Workshop on Parsing Technologies*. Tilburg.

O'Donnell, M. (1994). *Sentence Analysis and Generation: a systemic perspective*. Sydney.

O'Donnell, M. (2005). The UAM Systemic Parser. In *Proceedings of the 1st Computational Systemic Functional Grammar Conference*. Sydney: University of Sydney.

Quirk, R., Greenbaum, S., Leech, G., Svartvik, J., & Crystal, D. (1985). *A comprehensive grammar of the English language*. (R. Quirk, Ed.)*Computational Linguistics* (Vol. 1, p. 1779). New York, New York, USA: Longman.

Robert Kasper. (1988). An Experimental Parser for Systemic Grammars. In *Proceedings of the 12th Int. Conf. on Computational Linguistics*. Budapest.

Dependency distance and bilingual language use: evidence from German/English and Chinese/English data

Eva M. Duran Eppler
University of Roehampton, London
e.eppler@roehampton.ac.uk

Abstract

Closely related words tend to be close together in monolingual language use. This paper suggests that this is different in bilingual language use. The Distance Hypothesis (DH) proposes that long dependency distances between syntactically related units facilitate bilingual code-switching. We test the DH on a 9,023 word German/English and a 19,766 word Chinese/English corpus. Both corpora support the DH in that they present longer mixed dependencies than monolingual ones. Selected major dependency types (subject, object, adjunct) also have longer dependency distances when the head word and its dependent are from different languages. We discuss how processing motivations behind the DH make it a potentially viable motivator for bilingual language use.

1 Introduction

Corpus linguistic, computational linguistic and experimental language research has produced a considerable body of evidence over the past thirty years that there is a preference for linguistically related words to be close together in monolingual sentences (Gildea and Temperley 2010). Hudson (1995), Gibson (1998, 2000), Liu (2008) and others have worked on this from the comprehension side; Hawkins (1994, 2004), Temperley (2008) and collaborators have addressed the production side.

Most of this research captures the notion of linguistically 'closely related' and 'close together' with the concept of dependency distance/length. Dependencies are asymmetric syntactic relations between two words, a head/governor and a dependent. The head of each dependency is then the dependent of another word (unless it is the root of the sentence), forming a recursive structure which connects all the words of the sentence. Dependencies are (a) of a certain type, (b) directed, and (c) have a length.

(a) Dependencies can be semantic, morphological and/or syntactic. In this paper we are only looking at syntactic dependencies; the arrows representing dependencies are therefore labelled for grammatical functions, e.g. subject, adjunct etc.

(b) Dependency arrows point from the head to the dependent. Many languages have a dominant dependency direction: Arabic is predominantly head initial, Turkish head final; other languages like English, German and Chinese are more or less mixed.

(c) Every arrow spans a specific number of words (unless it indicates the root of the sentence). The linear distance between a head and its dependent, measured in terms of intervening words, is the dependency relation's distance[1] (Hudson 1995). The Mean Dependency Distance (MDD) of a sentence/text is the sum of its individual distances divided by the number of its dependencies.

Dependency distance (DD) is an important property of dependencies because of its implications for language production/processing. Constructing and interpreting sentences involves incrementally connecting words to arrive at meaning.

[1] Dependency distance can be quantified in different ways. Gibson (1998), for example, quantifies it in terms of new intervening discourse referents.

Proceedings of the Second International Conference on Dependency Linguistics (DepLing 2013), pages 78–87,
Prague, August 27–30, 2013.

This process consumes human/ computational resources; it is 'costly'. DD has been shown to correlate with the cognitive cost of processing syntactic relations in terms of the memory resources required to keep track of incomplete dependencies (Gibson 1998, 2000; Hudson 2010: 279); and in terms of the cost of connecting a new/incoming word to syntactically related ones. The computational cost of integrating a word into sentence structure has been shown to depend on the distance between a word and the most local head or dependent to which it attaches (Dependency Locality Theory DLT, Gibson 2000). The DLT predicts that structures with longer dependencies are more difficult to process. It can account for a number of processing complexity phenomena, e.g. the relative ease of subject- vs. object-extracted relative clauses; ambiguity resolution in e.g. prepositional phrase attachment decisions, heaviness effects, and processing overload effects of multiple center-embedded structures.

Considerations of parsing complexity have also been proposed to affect language production (Hawkins 1994, 2004, Temperley 2008). Synchronically and on the level of the individual speaker this seems to manifest itself mainly in phenomena of syntactic choice, e.g. default word order vs. extraction/extraposition (Temperley 2008); diachronically Liu (2009) and Gildea and Temperley (2010) suggest dependency length minimization may also play a role in the shaping of grammars, i.e. language evolution.

As DD has implications for the cost of language processing, factors influencing dependency length need to be considered. Liu (2008) suggests that projectivity, no crossing arches in the dependency graph of a sentence, influences DD. Liu compared the MDDs of natural languages with those of artificial random languages, projective and non-projective ones. He found that non-projective artificial grammars have the longest MDD, followed by projective artificial languages and natural ones. Liu interprets his results as showing "the usefulness of a no-crossing approach to dependency length reduction" (Liu 2008: 14) and the reduced DD of natural languages as a consequence of projectivity (see also Gildea and Temperley 2010: 307). Most well-formed strings in natural languages are projective (Marcus 2007: 159).

Another factor that has been proposed to influence DD is dependency direction. If each word in a sentence has exactly one dependent, uniformly head-first or head-last structures yield shorter dependency distances than ones with pre- and post-dependents (Frazier 1985, Hawkins 1994, Rijkhoff 1994). Predominantly head-first or head last-languages, such as Arabic and Japanese, should therefore have the shortest MDDs. Liu (2010) has shown that this is not the case. The reason is that words can and do have more than one dependent.

If a word has more than one dependent, and the grammar requires all dependents to point in the same direction, and there is syntactic choice in terms of constituent order (e.g. a verb that has two prepositional dependents), placing the shorter dependent (phrase) closer to the head results in shorter dependencies. Hawkins (1994, 2004) reports that the preference of placing the shorter dependent closer to the head is found in head-first and head-last languages.

If a head has several dependents, placing all of them on the same side of the head creates a kind of 'crowding' effect. German subordinate clauses, which are head final (rather than V2), illustrate that all dependents of the verbal head (*haben*) crowd to its left.

(1)

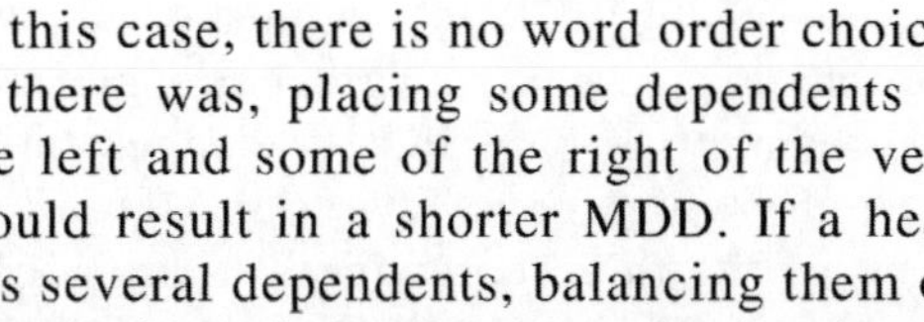

I forgot, dass wir eine neue partie angefangen haben.
that we all again a new game started have
Jen1.cha. line 2541

In this case, there is no word order choice; if there was, placing some dependents to the left and some of the right of the verb would result in a shorter MDD. If a head has several dependents, balancing them on either side of the head results in shorter dependency lengths (Temperley 2008).

Languages that have a prevailing dependency direction but allow some short dependent phrases to branch in the opposite direction have shorter MDDs than consistently same branching languages

(Dryer 1992, Liu 2010). English is generally regarded as a predominantly head-first language. In the Penn Treebank, however, only 48.8% of the English dependencies are head-first; German was found to be, on average, 54.5% head-first and Chinese 31.5% (Liu 2010: 1571). Of the three languages we are looking at in this study, English has the best balance between left and right dependents and should therefore have the shortest MDD (followed by German and then Chinese). Section 5 presents empirical support for this hypothesis.

So far we have established that DD is an appropriate and widely used measure for establishing the linear proximity of linguistically related words. DD can therefore be used to test whether closely related words tend to be close together in monolingual and bilingual language use. Other properties of dependencies, the type of relationship they encode and their direction, were discusses as factors influencing dependency distance. Most importantly, the effect DD seems to have on the computational resources required for language processing and production was reviewed. Keeping track of long incomplete dependencies is a burden on memory load, and the cost of linking a new word into sentence structure - by connecting it to a head and/or dependent - also seems to be influenced by DD (Gibson 1998, 2000).

In the next section we will look at DD in the three languages involved in our data.

2 DD in English, German and Chinese

MDDs differ cross-linguistically. Although there is considerable variation in the type of language data analyzed to date (spoken, written; formal, informal) and ways in which distance is measured and calculated[2], there is a surprising amount of agreement as to which languages have short, and which ones have long DDs.

Out of the three languages we are looking at, we anticipated English to have the shortest MDD, followed by German and Chinese. This is exactly what Liu (2008: 10) found: English (2.54) has a shorter MDD than German (3.35) and Chinese (3.66). Features of the three grammars that may account for this difference length will be looked at next.

The fact that English has fairly fixed word order and a prevailing dependency direction (head-first), but allows some short dependent phrases to branch in the opposite direction, seems to account for the short MDD of English (1.39, 1.49, 1.67 in Hiranuma's (1999), Eppler's (2010) and Wang and Liu's (2013) spoken data; 2.30 and 2.54 in the written data analysed by Gildea and Temperley (2010: 301) and Liu (2008: 12). In English, most words that are syntactically related are also adjacent; between 63% according to Collins (1996), 76% according to Pake (1998) and 78% according to Eppler (2010), but only slightly over 50% according to Liu (2008).

The mean distance between two syntactically related German words is longer than the mean distance between two related English words: 1.87 according to Eppler (2010), 3.07 according to Gildea and Temperley (2010), and 3.35 according to Liu (2008). The main reasons why German has a longer mean distance are the generally freer word order; the discontinuity between auxiliaries and their verbal complements (the Verbalklammer); and the different word orders in main (V2) and subordinate clauses (SOV). According to Liu (2008: 17) German has more adjacent dependencies than both Chinese and English.

Chinese has the longest MDD, not only of the three languages we are looking at in this paper, but also of the 20 languages Liu (2008) compared: 2.85 in spoken news data (Wang & Liu's 2013: 63), and 3.66 in written news data (Penn Chinese Treebank; Liu 2008: 12). The facts that Chinese has fewer mixed (head-first/head-last) dependencies than German and English and that Chinese is an isolating language, which marks e.g. tense, number and aspect with free (rather than inflectional) morphemes, has a significant influence on dependency length and the number of dependencies in a text.

[2] Eppler (2010) and Hiranuma (1999) measure dependency distance in terms of the number of intervening words; Liu (2008, 2009, 2010) in terms of the difference between the words' position numbers. Liu (2009) found the resulting difference in MDD to be small (1.81 vs. 1.89).

This brief cross-linguistic discussion of dependency length in English, German and Chinese has shown that rigidity of word order, consistency of dependency direction, and language type (isolating, inflecting) impact on a language's MDD. Collins (1996), Pake (1998), Eppler (2010) and Liu (2008) have looked into the relationship between dependency length and adjacency. These preliminary findings are difficult to interpret and more work needs to be done on this in the future.

The comparison of MDDs in different data sets furthermore supports the idea that DD is positively correlated with style (Liu et al. 2009: 171, Temperley 2008). Casual speech has shorter distances than more formal speech and writing, even when of the same genre (e.g. news, Liu 2009, Wang and Liu 2013). The average difference in dependency length between spoken and written data in English, German and Chinese is approximately one (1.02), with little variation between the three languages (Chinese 0.81, English 0.91 and German 1.34).

In the next sections we will look at bilingual data, speech which is constructed from lexical items and grammatical structures from typologically different languages (English and German, English and Chinese). We will test whether syntactically related words from different languages also prefer to be close together, or whether long dependency distances facilitate code-switching (DH); i.e. we will investigate the effects of DD on syntactic code-switching.

3 The data

The present paper is based on two bilingual corpora, a 9,023 word sample of a 93,235 word corpus of German/English (Eppler 2003), and a 19,766 word corpus of Chinese/English (Wang & Liu 2013). Both data sets were analyzed in the same dependency theoretic framework (Hudson 2007, 2010).

The German/English data was recorded in January 1993 among a close-knit network of members of the German-speaking Jewish refugee community who settled in London in the late 1930s. All speakers included in this sample are female and in their late sixties or early seventies. Their L1 is Austrian German. The age of onset of their L2, British English, was during adolescence (15-21 years of age) for all speakers. In informal settings like the ones recorded, the participants use a bilingual mode of interaction sometimes called 'Emigranto' (Eppler 2010). Linguistically this mixed code is characterized by frequent switching at speaker turn boundaries and heavy intra-sentential code-switching. The audio data were transcribed in the CHAT/LIDES (LIPPS Group 2000) format. The transcripts were manually annotated for word class, dependency type, dependency direction and dependency distance. See Table 1 for a summary of the data.

The Chinese/English data (Wang and Liu 2013) were audio-recorded from mainland China and Hong Kong TV or broadcasting programs from June to September 2011. Approximately 20% of the data are from interview programs; about 80% of the materials are news, social news, and entertainment news. Intra-sententially code-switched sentences were selected from the data, transcribed and syntactically annotated to build a Treebank containing the following information: linear position of the head and the dependent in the sentence, word class, language and a selected number of dependency types. The MDD of the corpus and of individual dependency types were calculated from the Treebank using formulae proposed by Liu (2009). See Table 1 for a summary of the data.

	German	English	Total	Chinese	English	Total
Word Tokens	5591	3432	9023	16267	3499	19766
Percentage	61.9	38.1	100	82.3	17.7	100

Table 1. Distribution of languages in the German/English and Chinese/English (Wang and Liu 2013) data

4 The Distance Hypothesis

In monolingual dependencies the head and the dependent are from the same language; in 'mixed' dependencies they are from different languages. The main point of interest for this paper is whether the MDDs of monolingual and mixed dependencies are similar or different. If they are significantly different, DD may have an effect on intra-sentential code-switching.

Theoretically the MDDs of mixed dependencies can be shorter, intermediate or longer than the MDDs of the monolingual dependencies. They would, for example, be shorter, if code-switching consumed additional processing resources which are counterbalanced by the reduced processing cost of short dependencies (Gibson 2000). Dussias (2001) found that complexity and switch frequency are inversely related. As the German/English data is heavily switched, its production is expected to have incurred not additional resources. Mixed MDDs might be between monolingual means, because syntactic dependency properties of both languages are involved. Or they might be longer, if the influence of a word's language on that of its dependent reduces with increased distance. In activation-based frameworks the activation level of a word and its properties (e.g. its sense or language) will decay with distance. Comprehension studies have shown that structural integration involves reactivating a word to a target threshold level so that aspects relevant for its integration can be retrieved from memory. This reactivation is not only costly (Gibson 1998), but may also be incomplete; information about a word's properties may degrade partially or completely. If we assume similar processes to drive production[3], we may hypothesise that long dependency distances (DD ≥ 2) increase the likelihood of an 'other' language dependent, i.e. a code-switch (DH).

A decay in activation levels of syntactically related words over distance is assumed to be the motivating factor behind code-switching. Both the head and the dependent need to be - or be made - active at the point in language production when the dependency between them is being established. Activation levels of words (and their properties) decay as intervening words are being produced. In long dependencies the processing load is therefore high (Gibson 1998, 2000) and the priming effect between the head and the dependent low. Mixed dependencies/code-switches may result from long DDs because the influence the head and the dependent have on each other decreases with increased distance. The DH is a syntactic processing hypothesis; evidence in its support would therefore shed light on grammatical and processing aspects of code-switching.

5 MDDs in the two corpora

The MDDs for monolingual and mixed dependencies in the German/English and Chinese/English copra are presented in Table 2.

	G	E	AVG	C	E	AVG
Mono	1.87	1.49	1.68	2.85	1.67	2.26
Mixed	1.85	2.26	2.06	3.54	2.81	3.18

Table 2: MDDs of monolingual and mixed dependencies with German, English and Chinese heads

The results for monolingual German and English support the hypothesis that monolingual German dependencies will be longer than monolingual English ones (made on the basis of the word order properties of the two languages in Section 2), and findings by Liu (2008) and Gildea and Temperley (2010).

The mean distances of mixed dependencies with a German head either indicate that heads do not have a more significant effect on dependency distance than dependents, or that German verbs, the word class that increases German MDD through bi-directional long-distance dependencies, are infrequently involved in mixed dependencies with a German head.

The mean distance of mixed dependencies with an English head suggests that English words enter into more remote syntactic relations with German dependents. We therefore expect a) English words to 'head' more dependency relations that are characterized by long distances (adjuncts, extractees and extraposees); and b) German dependents of English heads to be more frequently located at the clause periphery (Treffers-Daller 1994, Muysken 2000).

The highly significant difference between monolingual and mixed dependency distances ($p<0.001$) supports the idea that DD affects code-switching.

The recent analysis of a 19,766 word Chinese/English corpus (Wang and Liu 2013) supports the DH and has revealed interesting similarities and differences between the German/ English and Chinese/English data.

[3] Dussias' (2002: 98) study of the psycholinguistic complexity of code-switching revealed "a relatively clean convergence from [...] corpus analysis [which reflects production data] and on-line comprehension effects".

Chinese dependencies are longer than English ones ($p<0.005$). This was expected from the morphological and word-order properties of the two languages (Section 2) and supports findings by Liu (2008, 2009).

The MDD of mixed dependencies with a Chinese (L1) head and an English (L2) dependent is longer than that of monolingual Chinese dependencies ($p<0.001$; this is different to what we found in the German/English data), and also longer than the MDD of mixed dependencies with an English head and a Chinese dependent ($p<0.05$).

MDD increases more from monolingual English to mixed with an English head (+1.14) than from monolingual Chinese to mixed with a Chinese head (+ 0.69). This is similar to what we found in the German/English data, where the MDD between monolingual English and mixed dependencies with an English head increases by (+ 0.77); the MDD between monolingual German and mixed dependencies with a German head is virtually the same. Heads from the speakers' L1s (German and Chinese) therefore hold their dependents 'tighter' than L2 heads.

The mean distance of mixed dependencies with an English (L2) head and a Chinese (L1) dependent is also longer than that of monolingual English dependencies, but the difference is not quite as marked as in the German/English data ($p<0.05$ vs. $p<0.001$).

The average MDD of mixed dependencies (3.18) is longer than that of monolingual dependencies (2.26), and the average MDDs of mixed dependencies is longer than the MDDs of both English and Chinese monolingual dependencies ($p<0.05$).

In summary, the comparison of the MDDs from the German/English and Chinese/English data (Table 2) shows that

- MDDs are cross-linguistically different with English having the shortest MDD, followed by German and Chinese
- monolingual dependencies in mixed corpora are not significantly different to those found in comparable monolingual corpora
- the average MDDs of mixed dependencies are significantly longer than those of monolingual dependencies.

The patterns in the Chinese/English data (Wang and Liu 2013) largely correspond to those in the German/English data. Most importantly, greater DD also seems to increase chances of code-switching in Chinese/English bilingual speech. The findings from a typologically different language pair and data set therefore support the hypothesis that long DDs affect the language of dependents in that they render other language dependents more likely (DH).

6 MDDs of individual dependency types

In this section we will compare individual dependency types from the two data sets in terms of distance. The German/English data were analysed for the full range of syntactic relations used in Word Grammar (Hudson 2010). The Chinese/English data were analysed for four syntactic relations (subjects, objects, attributes and adverbials – both of the latter two are considered as adjuncts in the German/English data). To facilitate the comparison, we will focus on subjects, objects, and adjuncts. Section 6.1 briefly looks at monolingual dependencies, Section 6.2 compares monolingual L1 dependencies with mixed dependencies with an L1 head, and Section 6.3 compares monolingual L2 dependencies with mixed dependencies with an L2 head. The findings support the main idea outlined in the Section 5, the DH, and related findings from the code-switching literature (Treffers-Daller 1994, Mahootian and Santorini 1996, Muysken 2000).

6.1 Monolingual dependencies

Table 3 illustrates how individual dependency types contribute to the average DD of 1.87 for monolingual German and 1.49 for monolingual English dependencies in the German/English data.

	s <	> s	> o	o <	> a	a <	total
G-G	1.54 (142)	1.07 (45)	1.78 (54)	1.83 (36)	2.1 (100)	1.37 (86)	1.87 (754)
E-E	1.07 (130)	- (7)	1.5 (82)	- (0)	2.26 (72)	1.38 (44)	1.49 (596)

Table 3. MDDs and frequencies of selected monolingual German and English dependency types; s- subject; o- object; a - adjunct; left- (<) and right dependent (>)

The column entries of Table 3 demonstrate that different dependency types have different mean distances (Liu et al. 2009: 170); the rows show that MDDs differ cross-linguistically (Liu 2008, 2009) and that the German/English bilinguals' grammars seem to be intact in terms of topological fields: there are no English left-dependent objects (nor x-comps). The MDDs that differ most significantly between German and English are subjects (and x-comps). These differences are caused by the subjects of clause-final finite verbs (which are at almost opposite ends of subordinate clauses) and the Verbalklammer. Gildea and Temperley (2010: 301) also found that verb position contributes to the longer dependency distances in German, but stress that it is not specifically the distance from subject to verb that results in this effect. Given that subjects tend to be short and can frequently be placed on either side of the verb in German (s< or >s), this finding is in line with the interrelation between dependency direction and distance discussed in Section 1.

The biggest difference in mean distances between monolingual Chinese and English also lies in the subject relation (p<0.001).

	S	O	Atr	Adv	Average
C-C	2.55 (940)	2.74 (849)	1.59 (1505)	2.45 (3039)	2.33
E-E	1.41 (130)	1.65 (91)	1.17 (296)	1.92 (104)	1.54

Table 4. MDDs and frequencies of four monolingual Chinese and English dependency types

Chinese prepositional constructions, such as *bei, ba, jiang* or *ge* and the complement of *di,* which are used as adverbials, must follow the subject but precede the modified verb; this increases the DD between the subject and the root of Chinese sentences, as in Example (2) where the DD between the subject *wo* and the verb *dang* is 3 in Chinese; the DD between *I* and *treat*, on the other hand, is only 1.

(2) wo ba ta dang pengyou.
I PREP him treat friend
'I treat him as my friend.'

Wang and Liu (2013) found longer MDD of Chinese objects in comparison with English ones (p<0.001). Tense is realized by inflectional morphology in English; in Chinese tense is usually handled by function words which separate the object and the head. In Example (3) the DD between the object *book* and its head *bought* is 2. In Chinese, the DD between *mai* and *shu* is 4, because the complement of the classifiers *zhe* and *ben* and the perfect-tense auxiliary *le* intervene between the object and its verbal head.

(3) *wo mai le zhe-ben shu.*
I buy AUX this-CL book
'I bought the book.'

Examples like these raise the question what size unit DD should be measured in.

6.2 Monolingual L1 and mixed dependencies with an L1 head

Table 5 shows that in the German/English data the distances for most mixed syntactic relations (subjects, adjuncts and post-dependent objects) are longer than their monolingual German equivalents.

	s<	>s	>o	o<	>a	a<	total
G-G	1.54 (142)	1.07 (45)	1.78 (54)	1.83 (36)	2.1 (100)	1.37 (86)	1.87 (754)
G-E	1.7 (10)	1.5 (2)	2.38 (29)	1.5 (20)	3.9 (38)	1.52 (27)	1.85 (525)

Table 6. MDDs and frequencies of monolingual German and mixed dependencies with a G head

The slightly shorter mean distance of mixed dependencies with a German head is mainly due to the large number of borrowed English nouns complements of German determiners (> c: G-G MDD 1.65 (155) vs. G-E MDD 1.1 (309)).

That English post-dependent adjuncts are, on average, two words further away from their German head than monolingual German ones supports the notion that code-switching is favoured in adjoined peripheral positions (Treffers-Daller 1998, Mahootian and Santorini 1996, Muysken 2000), as in Example (3).

(3)
*MEL: *ich bin draussen # **as per usual**.*
%tra: I am out
Jen2.cha: line 185.

The MDD of mixed adverbials with a Chinese head is also much longer than that of monolingual Chinese adverbials (p<0.001), see Table7.

	S	O	Atr	Adv	Average
C-C	2.55 (940)	2.74 (849)	1.59 (1505)	2.45 (3039)	2.33
C-E	2.7 (161)	2.85 (310)	1.48 (43)	5.65 (54)	3.17

Table 7. MDDs and frequencies of monolingual Chinese and mixed dependencies with a Chinese head

The Chinese/English corpus furthermore contains data that support the notion that code-switching is favoured in clause peripheral positions. In Example (4) the English subject *fans* is dislocated from its default position (preceding *zhuanmen)* and moved to the left clause periphery. Because of extraposition and obligatory pre-posing of prepositional phrases before the verb, the distance between *fans* and its Chinese head *jisong* is 6; in the corresponding monolingual Chinese sentence, the distance between the Chinese subject *fensimen* and its head *jisong* is only 2.

(4) *Fans weile xiang ta zhijing zhuanmen jisong xianhua.*
Fans in order to to him pay their respects specially posted flowers
'In order to pay their respects to him, fans specially posted flowers.'

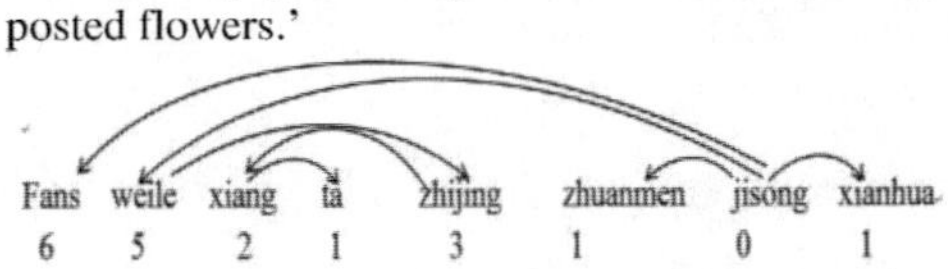

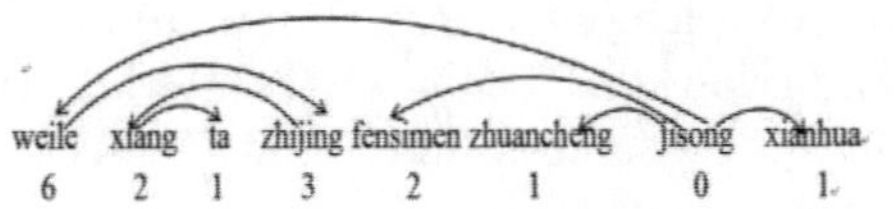

In Section 2 we suggested that the mean distance of mixed dependencies with a German head might be shorter than the mean distance of monolingual German dependencies because the word class that increases DD through a change in dependency direction, German verbal heads, is infrequently involved in mixed dependencies. An analysis of all German verbs in the German/English data revealed that, overall, German verbs are not significantly less frequently involved in mixed dependencies than monolingual ones (p=0.112). The same holds true for German main verbs (p=0.192). German auxiliaries and modals, however, are significantly more frequently involved in mixed dependencies than English ones (p<0.001). German auxiliaries are frequently in the V2 topological field in German, a position that frequently coincides with SVO. German AUX/MOD are therefore placed in congruence sites (Sebba 1998). Congruence sites have been identified as facilitators of code-switching (Muysken 2000).

6.3 Monolingual L2 and mixed dependencies with an L2 head

In Section 5 we suggested that mixed dependencies may be the result of distance. As a consequence of their long DDs, code-switches were expected to be more frequently located at the clause periphery in predominantly SVO and V2 languages.

More specifically, on the basis of the MMDs in the German/English data (Table 2) we proposed that English heads may enter into 'looser', literally more remote, syntactic relations with German dependents. We anticipated English words to 'head' more dependencies that are characterised by long distances, i.e. adjunct, extractee and extraposee relations, and predicted more German dependents of English heads to be located at the left or right clause periphery (Treffers-Daller 1994). This is what we find in the data.

	s <	> o	> a	a <	> x	x <	Total
E-E	1.07 (137)	1.5 (82)	2.26 (116)	1.38 (116)	1 (1)	2.3 (3)	1.64 (596)
E-G	1.9 (11)	1.18 (18)	2.33 (55)	1.78 (55)	1.45 (7)	4.5 (15)	2.06 (165)

Table 8. MDDs and frequencies of monolingual English and mixed dependencies with an E head; extraposee and extractee > x <

Table 8 demonstrates that all mixed dependencies with an English head (apart from objects) are longer than their monolingual English counterparts (this is unlike the MDDs of monolingual German and mixed dependencies with a German head; Table 6). Table 8 furthermore illustrates that all dependency relations that yield a significantly higher number of mixed tokens than monolingual ones (German adjuncts, extractees), are further away from their English heads than their English counterparts. This finding supports the DH.

Table 8 shows that the adjunct relation is very popular for switching between an English head and a German dependent.

(5)
*MEL: *als kind **I didn't like anything** aber **I love food** .*
%tra: as a child I didn't like anything but I love food
Jen2.cha, line 2058

The pre-adjunct in (5) is also moved out of its default word order position and extracted to the left clause periphery, which increases its DD by 4.

Example (6) illustrates a German long-distance clausal extraction.

(6) *was die Dorit wieder geschmissen hat, **I [/] I would have liked**.*

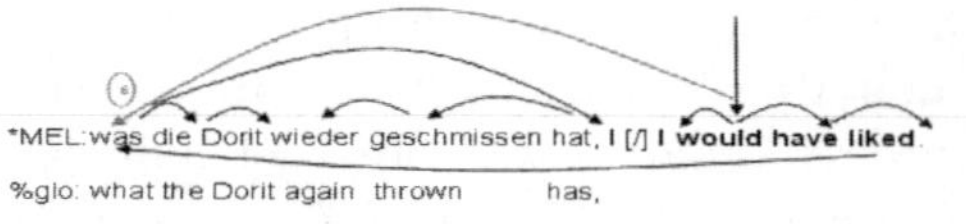

It appears that for reasons of syntactic choice (Temperley 2008), speaker MEL increases the distance of a mixed dependency relation from zero to six in Example (6).

The hypothesis that L2 heads predominantly enter 'looser' longer syntactic relations with L1 dependents is also supported by the Chinese/English data, both numerically and in terms of DD.

	S	O	Atr	Adv	Average
E-E	1.41 (130)	1.65 (91)	1.17 (296)	1.92 (104)	1.54
E-C	2.75 (87)	2.88 (32)	1.67 (446)	2.07 (311)	2.55

Table 9. MDDs of four monolingual English and mixed dependencies with an English head

The MDDs of all mixed dependencies with an English head is longer than that of monolingual English dependencies of the same type, and there are significantly ($p<0.001$) more switched Chinese adjuncts (Atr and Adv) than subjects and objects, like in the German/English data. Note, however, that the increase in MDD between monolingual and mixed dependencies is bigger in subjects and objects than in adverbials. This may indicate that, if close syntactic relations are switched, their distance may have to be even longer. The distance between the Chinese subject *tamen* and its head is 2 in Example (7), in its English translation the DD between *they* and *send* is only 1.

(7) *Tamen tiantian send E-mails.*
They everyday send
'They send E-mails everyday.'

In Example (8) the distance of *understand* and its object *yiqie* is 5; in its English translation the distance of *understand-everything* is 1.

(8) *I fully understand ni gaosu ta de yiqie*
you tell him AUX everything
'I fully understand everything that you tell him.'

The hypothesis that greater DD of syntactic relations increases the chances of code-switching appears to apply particularly to mixed dependencies with an L2 head. Mixed syntactic relations with an L2 head seem to pose a particular production difficulty for the German/English and Chinese/English bilinguals alike, and the activation of L2 heads appears to decay more rapidly than that of L1 heads. This seems to render the retrieval of features of the L2 head (e.g. its language) from memory more difficult and lead to the significantly larger number of mixed long distance syntactic relation with an L2 head in both corpora. The findings from the German/English data presented in Table 8 and those from the Chinese/English Treebank (Table 9) also support the notion that code-mixing is favoured in peripheral and adjoined positions (Treffers-Daller 1994, Mahootian and Santorini 1996, Mysken 2000).

7 Summary and Conclusion

We started from a well-established principle of monolingual language comprehension and production: closely related words tend to be close together in the sentence. We then suggested that this may be different in bilingual language use, i.e. that DD has an effect on whether both words in a dependency come from the same language or not. The Distance Hypothesis proposes that long dependency distances increase the likelihood of an 'other' language dependent, a code-switch. This syntactic processing claim is based on the rationale that both the head and the dependent need to be active at the point in the production process when the syntactic relation between them is being established. If the head and the dependent are far apart, the influence (priming effect) of a word's language on that of its dependent will decay with time/distance (the number of words intervening between them). The longer the dependency link, the less the priming influence, and the more likely a change in language.

The analysis of a 9,023 word corpus of German/English monolingual and bilingual speech revealed that mixed dependencies have a longer MDD than monolingual ones. In a 19,766 word corpus of a typologically very different language pair, Chinese/English, mixed dependencies also have longer MDDs than monolingual ones (Wang and Liu 2013). The MDDs of both corpora thus support the DH.

The analysis of individual syntactic relations in both corpora revealed that, with one exception in the Chinese/English corpus and three in the German/English data, all mixed dependency relations are, on average, longer than the corresponding monolingual ones. Both corpora contain considerable numbers of long-distance mixed adjuncts, and in the German/English data L2 heads predominantly enter into mixed long-distance syntactic relations that are not essential for building sentence structures (adjunction, extraction and extraposition). When L1 subjects and objects of L2 verbs are switched in the Chinese/English data, they have especially long dependency distances. In languages in which root verbs tend to occupy central sentence positions (SVO or V2), such as English, German and Chinese, long distance dependents will be located near the clause periphery. That code-switching is favoured in clause-peripheral positions has already been established in bilingualism research (Treffers-Daller 1994, Muysken 2000). The DH however, captures this notion on a more general syntactic processing level.

The results from the German/English and Chinese English data are promising. To establish DD between syntactically related units as a viable motivator for code-switching, the DH will have be tested on other bilingual corpora and with controlled psycholinguistic experiments to establish, e.g. that distance has similar effects in comprehension and production.

References

Michael J. Collins. 1996. A new statistical parser based on bigram lexical dependencies. *Proceedings of the 34th Annual Meeting on Association for Computational Linguistics. University of California, Santa Cruz 24-27 June 1996:* 184-191.

Matthew Dryer. 1992. The Greenbergian word order correlations. *Language*, 68: 81-138.

Paola E. Dussias. 2001. Psycholinguistics complexity in codeswitching. *International Journal of Bilingualism* 9(1): 87-101.

John A. Hawkins. 1994. *A Perfomance Theory of Order and Constituency.* Cambridge University Press, Cambridge.

John A. Hawkins. 2004. *Efficiency and Complexity in Grammar.* Oxford Univerisity Press, Oxford.

Eva M. Duran Eppler. 2010. *Emigranto. The syntax of German/English code-switching.* Braumüller, Vienna.

Eva M. Eppler. 2003. German/English data. http://talkbank.org/data/LIDES/Eppler.zip.

Edward Gibson. 1998. Linguistic complexity: Locality of syntactic dependencies. *Cognition* 68: 1-76.

Edward Gibson. 2000. The Dependency Locality Theory. In Y. Miyashita et al. (Eds.) *Image, Langauge, Brain.* MIT Press, Cambridge, MA, 92-126.

So Hiranuma. 1999. Syntactic difficulty in English and Japanese: A textual study. *UCL. Working Papers in Linguistics* 11: 309–322.

Richard A. Hudson. 1995. Measuring Syntactic Difficulty. Manuscript, University College London.

Richard A. Hudson. 2007. *Language Networks. The New Word Grammar.* Oxford University Press. Oxford.

Hitao Liu. 2008. Dependency distance as a metric of language comprehension difficulty. *Journal of Cognitive Science* 9(2): 161-174.

Hitao Liu, R. A. Hudson and Z. Feng, Z. 2009. Using a Chinese Treebank to measure dependency distance. *Corpus Linguistics and Linguistic Theory* 5(2). 161-174.

Sharzad Mahootian and B. Santorini. 1996. Code-Switching and the Complement/Adjunct Distinction. *Linguistic Inquiry* 27: 464-79.

Peter Muysken. 2000. *Bilingual Speech.* Cambridge University Press, Cambridge.

James Pake. 1998. The Marker Hypothesis. Edinburgh University [PhD thesis].

Mark Sebba. 1998. A congruence approach to the syntax of codeswitching". *International Journal of Bilingualism* 2(1): 1-19.

David Temperley. 2008. Dependency length minimization in natural and artificial languages. *Journal of Quarterly Linguistics* 15: 256-282.

Daniel Gildea and David Temperley. 2010. Do Grammars Minimize Dependency Length? *Cognitive Science* 34: 286-310.

Jeanine Treffers-Daller. 1994. *Mixing Two Languages: French-Dutch Contact in a Comparative Perspective.* de Gruyter, Berlin.

Lin Wang and Haitao Liu. 2013. Syntactic Variation in Chinese-English Code-switching. *Lingua* 123: 58-173.

Collaborative Dependency Annotation

Kim Gerdes
Sorbonne Nouvelle
ILPGA, LPP (CNRS)
Paris, France
kim@gerdes.fr

Abstract

This paper presents the Arborator, an online tool for collaborative dependency annotation together with a case study of crowdsourcing in a pedagogical university context. In greater detail, we explore what generally distinguishes dependency annotation tools from phrase structure annotation tools and we introduce existing tools for dependency annotation as well as the distinctive features and design choices of our tool. Finally we show how to setup a crowdsourced dependency annotation experiment as an exercise for university students. We explore constraints, results, and conclusions to draw.

1 Introduction

The importance of treebanks in today's data-driven linguistics cannot be overrated. All data-driven approaches to syntax require gold-standard annotations, and the need for (possibly machine-aided) hand annotation tools is more urgent than ever, as researchers want to go beyond the eternal Penn Treebank derivatives, because of interests in different languages, annotation levels, and theoretical backgrounds underlying the research.

In recent years, dependency treebanks have become the near-standard representation of annotation schemes in computational linguistics. However, the inherently non-local structure of dependencies make graphical annotation tools more difficult to develop and commonly less intuitive to use.

This paper presents an online annotation tool named Arborator, its features, and how it can be used in an educational surrounding at the same time for pedagogical purposes as well as with the goal to develop high-quality dependency treebanks.

2 Context

Even though a vast majority of dependency links are projective, even in so-called free word order languages, one of the major advantages of dependencies is not to presuppose the structure to have certain properties, like being projective. Phrase structure, on the contrary, is based on the underlying assumption of a coincidence between word order and government; contrary cases have to be taken care of by means of "traces" and "movements" (Gerdes 2005). Dependencies can thus represent more abstract relations, closer to semantics, which is arguably the main reason for today's success of dependency in NLP.

On the annotation level, however, dependency is a notably harder notion to handle than constituency. This holds for the file format because phrases can very easily be represented by simple bracketing or elaborated versions of bracketing like XML; dependency needs to separate tokens and links, the links referring back to the token objects. But this also holds for the manual annotation process as many tools exist for the exploration and editing of "tree"-like structures similar to "file/folder structures" – and dependency is somehow orthogonal to this kind of structure.

2.1 Existing tools

Still today, most dependency treebanks are derived from phrase structures by means of rule-based or statistical transformation of phrase structure. The manual quality control occurred on the phrase structure level with appropriate tools. For very small treebanks, some hand-woven approaches are still around (Chen et al. 2011), using for example a simple spreadsheet for annotation.

Only few dependency treebanks are directly constructed as such by use of well-adapted tools, in this section we will give a short overview over the existing graphical tools:

Proceedings of the Second International Conference on Dependency Linguistics (DepLing 2013), pages 88–97,
Prague, August 27–30, 2013.

The first tool that included dependency annotation was probably Annotate (Plaehn & Brants 2000), used for the development of the Tiger corpus. It applies Tiger's mixed syntactic structure: Labeled constituents with functionally labeled edges and crossing branches for non-projective structures.

At about the same time appeared the StrEd (Structure Editor, Boguslavsky et al. 2000), also an offline tool meant to facilitate the manual correction of already pre-annotated data. Its graphic representation has the particularity that each token is on a separate line, similar to the common CoNLL format, and the dependency tree is constructed on these tokens, thus turned by 90 degrees compared to more common representations with the root on top. To our knowledge, this is the first tool to use drag-and-drop creation of dependency links.

TrEd, the Tree Editor from Prague is an offline tool written in perl that helped to create and correct the Prague Dependency Treebank (Hajič et al. 2001, Hajič 2005) as well as other treebanks for other languages like English (Rambow et al. 2002) or more recently Persian (Seraji & Nivre 2012) . It includes an interface with a valency lexicon in order to keep the annotations coherent and scripting possibility for batch processing. Moreover, it was probably the first tool that includes visual comparisons between two annotators' trees, including the possibility to choose the correct structure.

NotaBene, developed by Mazziotta (2010) is an open-source (GPL) off-line tool written in Python that presents the above-mentioned file manager type interface. Elements are tokenized when entering data in the tool, but all other forms of automization are explicitely excluded. The tool includes sophisticasted feature handling, tree comparison and it follows RDF standards to capture multi-layer annotations. NotaBene is principally used in an ongoing annotation project of Ancient French.

DepAnn, written by Tuomo Kakkonen 2006 is another offline dependency annotation tool written in java. It can represent and modify the dependency representation of Tiger-XML. It includes a consistency checker and comparison of trees.

Other dependency treebank like the Danish Dependency Treebank, the Alpino Treebank (Van der Beek et al. 2002) or the Turin University Treebank have been elaborated with the help of bootstrapping approaches in a command line interfaces and special dependency tree viewers that allow for faster choices between different automatic parses of the same sentence.

More recently, MATE, a graph transduction workbench (Bohnet et al. 2000; Bohnet, 2006) has been used for the development of multistratal corpora in Meaning-Text style (Mel'cuk 1986) of Spanish and, with smaller scope, other European languages (Mille et al. 2009). MATE is written in java and includes a graphical editor for graph structures.

The most sophisticated tool and the closest in design to the Arborator is without any doubt the very recently presented tool "Brat" (Stenetorp, et al. 2012). Like the Arborator, Brat is a web-based application using SVG that allows for graphic drag-and-drop dependency-centric multiuser annotation of text corpora. It also has comparable user management, annotation comparison, Unicode support, and import and export capacities. Contrarily to the Arborator, it is not sentence-based, text appears continuously in multiline representation, and Brat thus allows for the annotation of intra-phrase relations like co-reference and discourse annotation. Also the segments are not fixed and any continuous chain of letters can be marked and then linked to other parts. Moreover it contains a constraint language that allows for on the fly checking of annotations. The Arborator's search and concordancer features seem to be slightly more developed as a search for specific feature is possible and Brat only includes plain text search. Also the Arborator's corpus distribution and user management seems to be more adapted to "uncooperative" surroundings like the classroom where it is important that the annotators and validators access only the texts that have been assigned to them. These features will be exposed in greater detail in the subsequent sections.

The only other web-based tool that we are aware of is EasyRef (De La Clergerie 2008). EasyRef has a constituent based representation even for dependencies: They are represented as (continuous) segments with a function label. This tool is designed for human evaluation of parser performance which makes it the only other tool including techniques for voting systems (see section 4).

3 Design of the Arborator

The Arborator has been developed over several years in a two-fold perspective: It was needed for the annotation of transcribed spoken language in the Rhapsodie treebank project (Gerdes et. al.

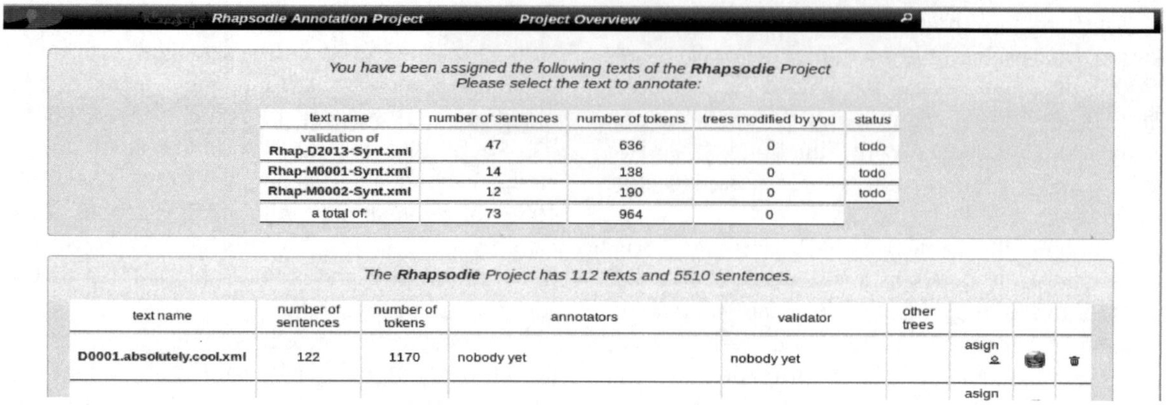

Rhapsodie Annotation Project Project Overview

You have been assigned the following texts of the **Rhapsodie** Project
Please select the text to annotate:

text name	number of sentences	number of tokens	trees modified by you	status
validation of **Rhap-D2013-Synt.xml**	47	636	0	todo
Rhap-M0001-Synt.xml	14	138	0	todo
Rhap-M0002-Synt.xml	12	190	0	todo
a total of:	73	964	0	

The **Rhapsodie** Project has 112 texts and 5510 sentences.

text name	number of sentences	number of tokens	annotators	validator	other trees			
D0001.absolutely.cool.xml	122	1170	nobody yet	nobody yet		asign		
						asign		

2012), and it is today used as a pedagogical and crowdsourcing tool in various universities. A description of such an experiment constitutes section 4 of the present paper.

This implies the following different design choices:

- Zero setup: The tool must run on any computer without any difficult adaptation or installation procedure.
- Central storage of texts and annotations.
- Multi-audience interface: For professional annotators, it needs to include numerous keyboard short cuts for all common annotation tasks, and for starters, the annotation process has to be graphical and self-explanatory.

These points exclude most existing tools and imply the development of a web-based application that does not use any plugins but runs directly in a standard-compliant browser. The graphical nature of the data including arrows forces us beyond simple HTML to an SVG representation of the corpus.

The Arborator can be used for the correction of automatically (or, less commonly, manually) pre-annotated corpora or for the creation of tree structures from scratch. Every token can depend on one (or more) governors and can have simple features attached to them. The choice of features to be shown (and to be modifiable) directly under the token is configurable, the most common ones being of course the syntactic category (POS) and the token's lemma.

Other technical design choices of the Arborator include:

- Development in Python with an underlying Sqlite database with client-side interactions in Javascript (Jquery).
- Runs on any Python-CGI capable Apache webserver.
- Optimized for the Firefox browser but runs reasonably well in other SVG capable browsers.
- Multi-level user hierarchy: site administrator, corpus administrator, validator, assigned annotator, visitor.
- The appearance of the dependency structures is highly configurable in simple configuration files.
- Of course, the Arborator is fully Unicode capable with non-ASCII characters being allowed in sentences, annotation schemes, and login names:

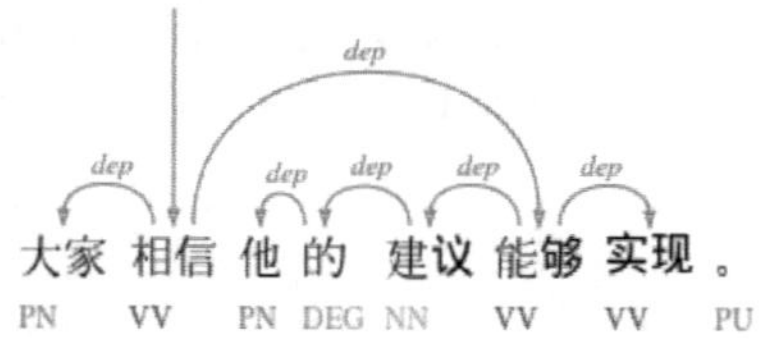

- The design choice of keeping the sentences "readable" with tokens being juxtaposed horizontally is debatable. The alternative, stemma-like structures like those used in the TrEd from Prague, makes the hierarchical structure of the trees more visible, whereas our choice emphasizes the linear sentence structure. We believe that this makes it easier for the annotator to understand the sentence and then to capture the sentence's syntactic structure. But of course, in this matter, beauty is in the eye of the beholder.

The Arborator is employed in different universities for annotation tasks, the main site being http://arborator.ilpga.fr – the main page also provides links to tutorial pages and the source code on Launchpad. The Arborator is distributed under the APGL license, the standard open-source license for server software.

3.1 The user experience

Before using the Arborator, the user has to create an account with email verification. The log-on brings him to the project page containing different option depending on the user level of the user. The normal annotator finds on top of the page the texts that have been assigned to him either as a validator or as an annotator[1]. Each text (and also each sentence) has a changeable status, which allows the annotator to indicate to the validator that the annotation process is terminated The center part of the project page contains a table with all the texts of the project. The administrator of the project can

- attribute any text to a user's annotation or

validation tasks,

- export the data in multiple formats and

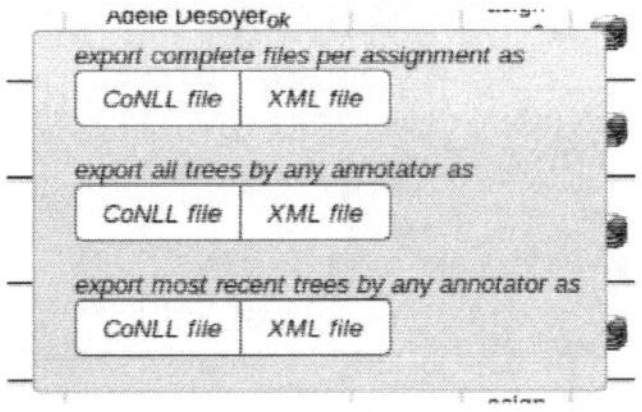

configurations

- add whole texts to the project, plain texts or pre-parsed data in CoNLL or Rhapsodie-XML format.
- Check the consistency of the annotation by obtaining tables of frequency distribution of features and 2-node connected sub-graphs of the dependency graph.
- Obtain an overview of each annotator's progress.

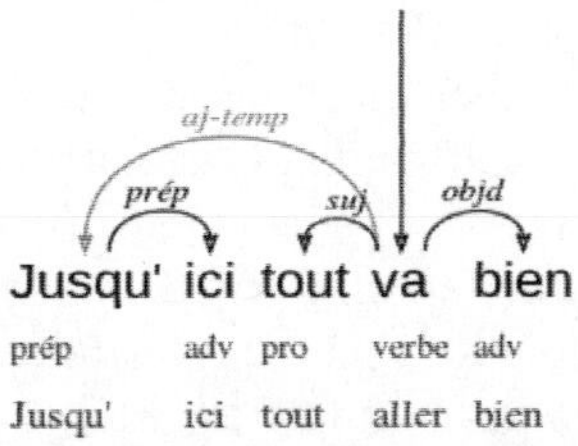

A click on the text name brings the user to the online editor. Depending on his role and the chosen setup of the annotation project, he will see only the words with his own annotation (if present), the standard annotation (for example the pre-parsed structures), or a list of all possible trees for each sentence.

Each token can be dragged and dropped on another token, thus creating a link in this direction. A context menu opens and the user has to choose the corresponding function name (the list of functions is set in the project configuration). When holding the *shift* key down when choosing the function name, the governor is added to the existing governor, allowing thus for the creation of cyclic graph structures.[2]

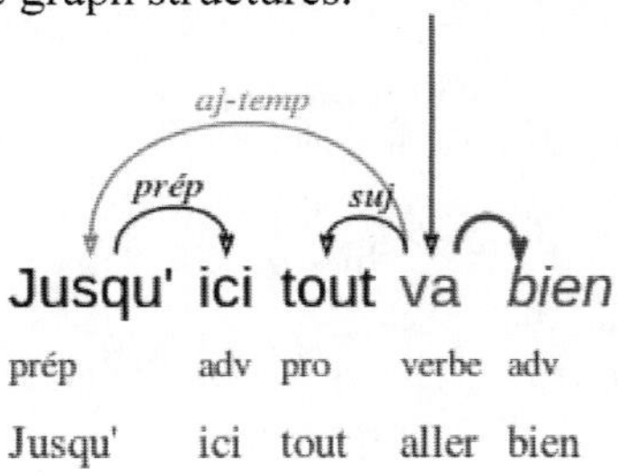

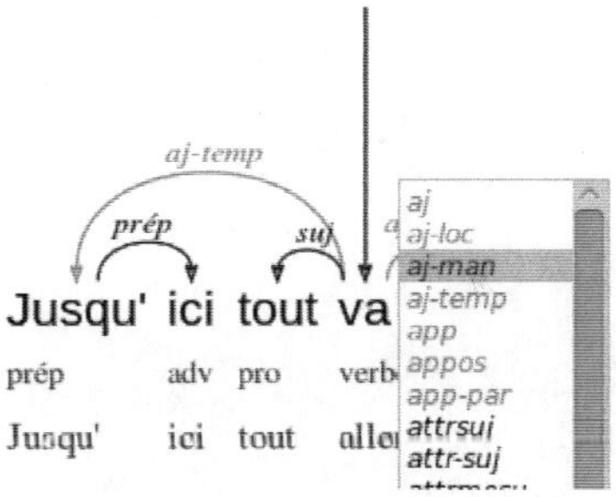

Equally, the shown features can be modified by means of a context menu that opens when the features are clicked upon. A double-click opens a table of other features, including, for administrators, the possibility to modify, add, or erase tokens.

[1] There are various setup options available to control the visibility of different annotations, but in the most basic configuration, the annotator only sees his own trees and the validator can see the trees of all annotators of the given text which allows her to compare between annotations and choose the correct tree.

[2] Some analyses of coordination or of relative phrases suppose double governors (for example because the relative pronoun is thought to play the role of the pronoun inside the relative clause and of the complementizer heading the relative phrase). Similarly, cycles have been proposed for the syntactic analysis of collocations and underspecified PP-attachment (Gerdes & Kahane 2011)

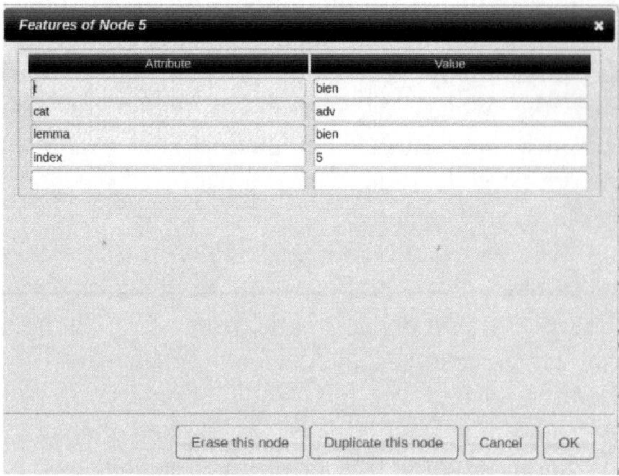

All modifications are undoable (during the annotation session – the Arborator does not yet provide automatic versioning) and the whole annotation (or correction) process can be done exclusively by means of keyboard shortcuts, without touching the mouse, which is often faster for experienced users.

If there is more than one tree visible to a user, he can graphically compare any set of annotations. The resulting graph shows in color the differences and grays out what is in common between the chosen analyses:

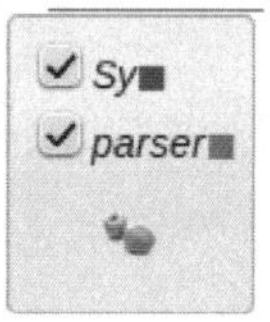

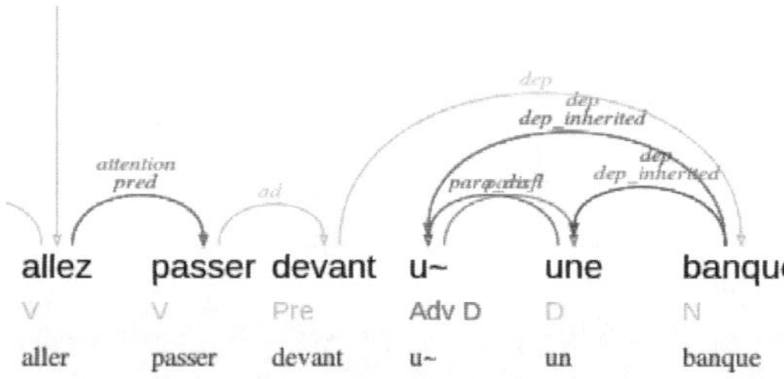

Each tree can individually be exported in the following formats. This allows for an easy integration of high-quality vectorial images for publications: SVG (Scalable Vector Graphics), PDF, PS, ODG, JPG, PNG, TIFF, CONLL (tab-separated text table), and XML (an idiosyncratic stand-up format that allows for the linking of the syntactic transcription to sound files)

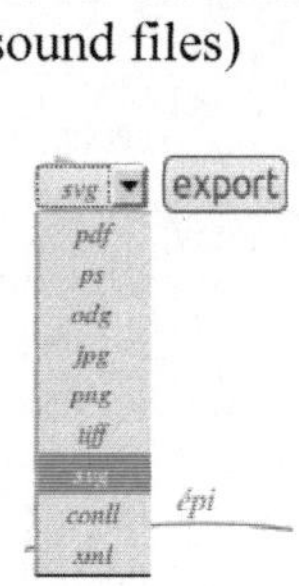

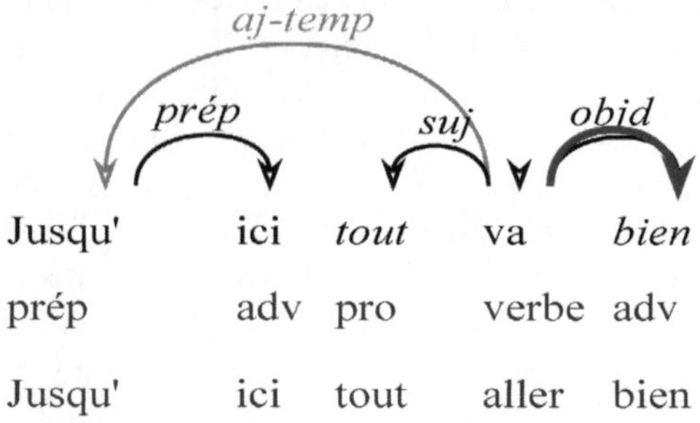

4 The experiment

The second part of this paper addresses the question of how good the dependency annotation of non-professional annotators can become, if we use a rover, i.e. a voting system (Fiscus 1997), to establish the best annotation among a series of annotations produced by semi-trained students.

This is interesting as many linguistic departments lack resources to train and pay professional annotators, but don't lack students with the desire to learn syntactic analysis.

4.1 Gaudium ex cathedra

Also from a pedagogical point of view, the use of a collaborative online annotation tool has many advantages:

First, the students are often taught in quite large classes and it is impossible for the teachers to systematically correct exercises composed of any larger amount of annotations. The Arborator allows for different types of exercises:

1. the gold-standard annotation is completely visible to the students – they can discover the structures.
2. an incomplete structure is left visible, but the gold-standard remains invisible. The teacher can thus oblige the student to complete parts of an analysis that was the subject of the current class.
3. The annotation is invisible to students, but scoring is public (so students can update their annotation until they hit 100%).
4. equal to mode 2 but the location of the errors are indicated on the sentence which guides the student more quickly to the right annotation.

The teacher, on the other hand can, with little effort, create interactive playful syntactic training sessions, and obtain, for free, a completely automatic list with student evaluations, thus forcing the students to work regularly. Of course, any e-learning environment allows for the creation of multiple choice tests, but it is difficult to make them as interesting and well-adapted to linguistic analysis.

Secondly, the task of annotation of raw data forces teacher and student to abandon easy handcrafted example sentences and allows them to face the cruel realities of language. When collaborative corpus annotation is taken as the main goal of a class, the questions and debates that come up in the classroom are of much more exiting and motivated nature than conventional teaching of syntax.

4.2 Context

The experiment was carried out with a class on corpus linguistics taught to about 60 3rd year linguistics majors in a French university, about 75% of which have French as their mother tongue. Only 3 main classes and 3 tutorial session in smaller groups were held on the subject of this project. Nearly all those students had have other classes on syntax, one of which was taught one year earlier by the same teacher specifically on dependency syntax, using very similar notational conventions as those used in the annotation guide for the experiment. The annotation guide was online and contained many concrete examples, also including the supposed analysis of language idiosyncrasies such as dates, numbers and punctuation, that are frequently encountered in Wikipedia and journalistic examples making up the essential parts of the texts to be analyzed.

4.3 Annotation task distribution

We have two sets of sentences:

- the mini gold-standard annotated by the researcher
- the non-annotated sentences, considered as unlimited

The goal is to distribute the sentence to the students in a just and reasonable manner. As online annotation does not provide the possibility to control the context in which the student annotate, it is important to make it difficult to blindly copy annotations from one student to the other (although theoretically cooperation of students during the annotation process could be useful to obtain better analyses of the syntactic structure). The system can distribute the sentences of the texts into task sets using the following parameters:

- t, total number of tokens per student to annotate (rounding up or down in order to distribute complete sentences)
- g, number of sentences from the pre-annotated mini gold-standard to mix into the student's task (to allow for evaluation)
- n, number of annotations per sentence (taken from the non-annotated sentences)
- p, percentage of sentences that can be equal from one task set to the other.[3]

The Arborator comes with a script that optimizes this distribution.

4.4 Setup

The students were presented with 48 sentences, mostly taken from two French Wikipedia articles and some constructed sentences that contain phenomena discussed in the class. The average length of 24.7 tokens per sentence reflects the "real world origin" of most sentences, very different from common example sentences from syntax classes or textbooks.

The tokenization is simply sign-based and was done automatically.[4] All sentences were also annotated by the teachers of the class. This is, of course, only necessary for this experimental

[3] If p=100%, n students receive equal tasks. When p decreases, for example to 50%, the first student will share 50% of her sentences with the second student, and another 50% with the third student, and so on.
Note that the total number of students is not part of these parameters, because in the natural setting of a class taught to a large number of students, many inscribed students will drop the class, and new students appear. Only when a student creates her account on the Arborator, her task is prepared. This minimizes the number of sentences that do not obtain n annotations in the end of the project.

[4] A more sophisticated tokenization would have been of use for a few special cases of French syntax. The most problematic case is the token *des* that can be the contraction of *de* 'of' and *les* 'the',or it can just be the plural article *des*. Other problematic cases include *parce que* 'because' and *c'est-à-dire* 'which means'. A production environment would in any case start of with the output of a parser that should do better on tokenization.

setup, and if the tool is to be used in an production environment, only a small number of sentences need to be annotated by the researchers, the rest will be done by the "crowd" of students.

This experiment is only concerned with simple dependency structures. The labels, i.e. the syntactic functions, are left aside for future research. One reason for this is that the results on functions appear, on a quick glance, much worse than the government structure. This is partly due to the fact that the students were told that the government structure is more central to the exercise than the choice of function; and the government structure was discussed in greater detail in the classes. Another reason is that the set of syntactic functions was unnecessarily (and uncommonly) large, including distinctions like locative, manner, temporal, and other adjuncts, etc.

We only kept annotations when 80% of the words were annotated (i.e. had a governor) and, in order to get reasonably good evaluations, we only kept the annotation of students who at least annotated 5 sentences. This left us with 42 student annotators. Using the evaluation based on all sentences, the quality of the dependency annotators ranges from 64% to 90% of correct government relations (F-score), the average being 79%. How many sentences do we have to take into account in the evaluation if we want to keep similarly precise evaluation scores of the student, needed for the rover? Interestingly, the student evaluation varies very little if we base it on the first half of the corpus only (less than 1% in average), the quality of the annotation is better (80%) on the first half, probably due to symptoms of fatigue of the annotators and discussions in class of problems the students encountered. If we decrease further the number of sentences that we base our evaluation on, the evaluation averages continue to grow, but the students' F-score decreases quickly.

Nr of sentences used for evaluation	48	24 (½)	12 (¼)	6 (1/8)	1 (1/48)
Min F-score	64%	67%	70%	73%	63%
Max F-score	90%	90%	90%	90%	100%
Average F-score	79%	80%	81%	83%	87%
Average difference from complete F-scores	0	1.2%	1.8%	3.5%	9.1%

Note that these F-scores are computed in the Arborator and can be exported and thus used directly for grading students. Let's now see how these scores are used in the voting system.

4.5 How many sentences for student evaluation?

When using one part of the trees for evaluation of the students, and constructing an optimal tree on the remaining sentences we obtain the following results. At the present state we always split into a first part for computing the students' scores and a second part which are the remaining sentences. Successive studies will try different jackknifing techniques.

The construction of an optimal tree is slightly complicated by the graph structure of the analysis, i.e. the possibility of double governors, as explained above. So the first step of the different voting systems is to decide on the number of governors, 1 most of the time, but sometimes 0 (errors in segmentation) or 2 (only relative pronouns with our annotation guidelines for French).

The *Scoring* voting system works as follows:

For every node, every proposal of a governor node gets the score the annotator obtained in the evaluation. Then the governor (or the two governors, if the first vote decided on two governors) with the highest score is chosen for the tree. Note that this does not include explicit coherence tests (like non-circularity etc.) but we have not discovered any circular tree with our data.

In this first version, only students can take part in the vote that have annotated ¼ of the trees that are used for evaluation.

Looking on these numbers, the first astonishing fact is the stability of the results independently of the number of sentences that are used for evaluation. Put differently: With only one tree to annotate, we already get a reasonable estimate of the student's capacities.

¼ have to be annotated				
Scoring algorithm part of sentences used:	Nr of students in	Precision	Recall	**F-score**
½ (24)	31	0.9465	0.9419	**0.9439**
¼ (12)	31	0.9472	0.9379	**0.9421**
1/8 (6)	39	0.9505	0.937	**0.9433**
1/48 (1)	42	0.9512	0.9405	**0.9454**

We also checked whether the threshold (of taking only evaluations into account that are based on a reasonable number of annotated sentences) has an impact on the results, but in fact the differences are very slight. This is astonishing when looking at the annotation quality seen in section 4.4, but can be explained by the stabilizing factor that *most* students try to do a good job.

½ have to be annotated				
Adding algorithm part of sentences used:	Nr of students in	Precision	Recall	**F-score**
½ (24)	19	0.945	0.9371	**0.9408**
¼ (12)	24	0.9495	0.94	**0.9444**
1/8 (6)	28	0.948	0.9357	**0.9414**
1/48(1)	42	0.9512	0.9405	**0.9454**

1/10 have to be annotated				
Adding algorithm part of sentences used:	Nr of students in	Precision	Recall	**F-score**
½ (24)	45	0.9464	0.9409	**0.9434**
¼ (12)	40	0.9476	0.9333	**0.9399**
1/8 (6)	50	0.9476	0.9333	**0.9399**
1/48(1)	42	0.9512	0.9405	**0.9455**

Unsurprisingly, not voting but just taking the best student for each tree gives quite unstable results, depending on the number of sentences annotated by the best students. The results are partly better, partly worse than the previous results.

1/10 have to be annotated				
Meritocracy algorithm part of sentences used:	Nr of students in	Precision	Recall	**F-score**
½ (24)	1 of 45	0.9702	0.9409	**0.9749**
¼ (12)	1 of 40	0.9704	0.9634	**0.9668**
1/8 (6)	1 of 50	0.8778	0.8538	**0.8647**
1/48(1)	1 of 42	0.8407	0.8403	**0.8396**

Of course it is unrealistic to have this many annotations per sentence. This leads us naturally to the exploration of how many annotations we actually need to keep up reasonable results.

4.6 Students to Quality

For a real-world annotation setting, we need to test systematically how many annotations we need for the required annotation quality.

We explored the range from 2 to 10 annotations per sentence by choosing arbitrarily for each sentence the annotators among the students that annotated the sentence (i.e. they attributed a governor to at least 80% of the words). We computed this score for 10 random attributions of each number of annotators. The results are reported in the diagram below.

On our data, the quality seems to quickly stabilize between 91 and 92% F-score. As we have seen, with higher numbers of annotators we don't get much beyond 94%. 4 or 5 annotations per sentence seems to be a reasonable number to obtain an F-score well-beyond 90%.

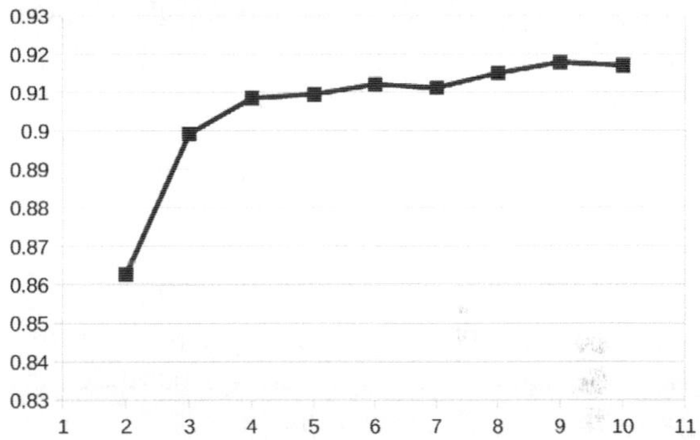

Average F-score
over 10 random attributions

5 Conclusion and outlook

In this paper we have presented the different features of the Arborator, a state-of-the-art online tool for collaborative dependency annotation. We have shown how most design choices were natural consequences of the annotation requirements.

We then showed that the application of the rover technique can give surprisingly good results, even though syntactic annotation is commonly considered as a task which is difficult to crowdsource (Munro et al. 2010). The reason is probably that the "crowd" is partly trained and the voting technique only has to pick out the "trained" good students. However, the data-set is too small and specific to draw more general conclusions.

We must also point out that an f-score of 0.94 and an average length of 25 tokens per sentence means that there are on average 1.5 errors per sentence, a result which is better than most automatic annotation on out of domain data but nothing we would want to call gold-standard. But then again, this is before any bootstrapping or pedagogical improvements taking into account the typical errors – it is a very good result for a first try.

While it seems practically impossible to use the Arborator in a "real" crowdsourcing task à la Mechanical Turk because the necessary training time is excessively high, it is possible to imagine crowd-sourcing of bootstrapping techniques in dependency syntax, too. It even seems easier than for phrase structure to find non-ambiguous paraphrases that Turks could vote on in order to decide between two equally probable analyses a parser provides.

The present experiment was carried out on raw text, i.e. students had to draw all dependency links, including trivial links for example from a noun to its determiner. The natural next step is to try out this "pedagogical crowd-sourcing" in a complete bootstrapping setup: The speed of the students and thus the output could probably be dramatically increased using statistical parsers that indicate uncertainty. This uncertainty can be rendered graphically in order to attract the students' attention to the problematic dependency link. And the corrections, after having been voted on, can then again be used to train the parser on bigger data. However, it is possible that the results would be different because detecting errors in a pre-annotated corpus is a different task than not making those errors when starting from scratch.

Another possible improvement of the result could stem from the application of more general machine learning techniques, that would, for example include lexical information in the predictions – or syntactic functions if they were included in the study. In other words, such an improvement should result in a system where a student that regularly gets the dependency links of coordinative conjunctions like "*and*" wrong, would have less voting rights when deciding on the best analysis around these words.

References

Bohnet, Bernd, Andreas Langjahr, and Leo Wanner. "A development environment for an MTT-based sentence generator." In Proceedings of the first international conference on Natural language generation-Volume 14, pp. 260-263. Association for Computational Linguistics, 2000.

Bohnet, Bernd, Textgenerierung durch Transduktion linguistischer Strukturen. DISKI 298. AKA, Berlin (2006)

Boguslavsky, Igor, Svetlana Grigorieva, Nikolai Grigoriev, Leonid Kreidlin, and Nadezhda Frid. "Dependency treebank for Russian: Concept, tools, types of information." In Proceedings of the 18th conference on Computational linguistics-Volume 2, pp. 987-991. Association for Computational Linguistics, 2000.

Brants, Thorsten, and Oliver Plaehn. "Interactive corpus annotation." In LREC'00. 2000.

Chen, Xinying, Xu Chunshan, Li Wenwen. "Extracting Valency Patterns of Word Classes from Syntactic Complex Networks." Proceedings of Depling 2011, Barcelona.

De La Clergerie, Éric Villemonte. "A collaborative infrastructure for handling syntactic annotations." In proc. of The First Workshop on Automated Syntactic Annotations for Interoperable Language Resources. 2008.

Van der Beek, Leonoor, Gosse Bouma, Rob Malouf, and Gertjan Van Noord. "The Alpino dependency treebank." Language and Computers 45, no. 1 (2002): 8-22.

Fiscus, Jonathan G. "A post-processing system to yield reduced word error rates: Recognizer output voting error reduction (ROVER)." In Automatic Speech Recognition and Understanding, 1997. Proceedings., 1997 IEEE Workshop on, pp. 347-354. IEEE, 1997.

Gerdes, Kim. "Sur la non-équivalence des représentations syntaxiques: Comment la représentation en X-barre nous amène au concept du mouvement." Cahiers de grammaire 30 (2006): 175-192.

Gerdes, Kim, and Sylvain Kahane. "Defining dependencies (and constituents)." In Proceedings of the International Conference on Dependency Linguistics, Depling 2011, pp. 17-27. 2011.

Gerdes, Kim, Sylvain Kahane, Anne Lacheret, Arthur Truong, and Paola Pietrandrea. "Intonosyntactic data structures: the Rhapsodie treebank of spoken French." In Proceedings of the Sixth Linguistic Annotation Workshop, pp. 85-94. Association for Computational Linguistics, 2012.

Hajič, Jan, Barbora Vidová-Hladká, and Petr Pajas. "The prague dependency treebank: Annotation structure and support." Proceedings of the IRCS Workshop on Linguistic Databases. 2001.

Hajič, Jan. 2005. "Complex corpus annotation: The Prague dependency treebank." Insight into the Slovak and Czech Corpus Linguistics (2005): 54.

Kakkonen, Tuomo. 2006. DepAnn - An Annotation Tool for Dependency Treebanks. Proceedings of the 11th ESSLLI Student Session at the 18th European Summer School in Logic, Language and Information (ESSLLI 2006), pp. 214-225. Malaga, Spain

Mel′čuk, Igor′ Aleksandrovič. Dependency syntax: theory and practice. State University of New York Press, 1988.

Mille, S., Burga, A., Vidal, V., & Wanner, L. (2009). Towards a rich dependency annotation of Spanish corpora. Proceedings of SEPLN'09, 325-333.

Munro, R., Bethard, S., Kuperman, V., Lai, V. T., Melnick, R., Potts, C., ... & Tily, H. (2010, June). Crowdsourcing and language studies: the new generation of linguistic data. Proceedings of the NAACL HLT 2010 Workshop on Creating Speech and Language Data with Amazon's Mechanical Turk (pp. 122-130). Association for Computational Linguistics.

Mazziotta, Nicolas. "Building the syntactic reference corpus of medieval French using notabene rdf annotation tool." In Proceedings of the Fourth Linguistic Annotation Workshop, pp. 142-146. Association for Computational Linguistics, 2010.

Stenetorp, Pontus, Sampo Pyysalo, Goran Topić, Tomoko Ohta, Sophia Ananiadou, and Jun'ichi Tsujii. "BRAT: a web-based tool for NLP-assisted text annotation." In Proceedings of the Demonstrations at the 13th Conference of the European Chapter of the Association for Computational Linguistics, pp. 102-107. Association for Computational Linguistics, 2012.

Rambow, Owen, et al. "A dependency treebank for English." Proceedings of LREC. Vol. 2. 2002.

Seraji, Mojgan, and Joakim Nivre. 2012. "Bootstrapping a Persian Dependency Treebank." Linguistic Issues in Language Technology 7.1.

Pragmatic Structures in Aymara

Petr Homola
Codesign, s.r.o.
Czech Republic
phomola@codesign.cz

Matt Coler
INCAS[3]
The Netherlands
MattColer@incas3.eu

Abstract

The paper describes overt marking of information structure in the indigenous Andean language Aymara. In this paper we show that although the word order is free, Aymara is not a discourse-configurational language (Kiss, 1994); instead, information structure is expressed only morphologically by pragmatic suffixes. The marking of 'topic' is more flexible that the marking of 'focus' (be it at the clause level or NP-internal). Since overt marking of information structure is partial, this paper also devotes considerable attention to the resolution of underspecification in Aymara.

1 Introduction

Chomsky's original approach to formal syntax assumes that sentences consist of constituents and that the type and order of these constituents define configurations that specify grammatical relations. As has been shown by Hale (1983), there are languages in which word order has no or limited relevance for grammatical relations and the respective constituent trees are flat. In most such languages, word order is said to specify information structure (hence the name discourse-configurational languages coined by Kiss (1994), as opposed to syntax-configurational languages). We show that Aymara is neither syntax-configurational nor discourse-configurational. In this language, information structure is expressed solely morphologically. This is very rare and therefore Aymara is very important for the research of information structure in general. As Bossong (2009) puts it (referring to Aymara and Quechua): "Cross-linguistically, grammemes explicitly expressing the function of theme are not very frequent; grammemes expressing the function of the rheme are a highly marked typological rarity [...]. Still more idiosyncratic is the combination of the thematic marker with a grammeme combining the two functions of *question* and *negation*."

We are not aware of any other language (except for, to some extent, Quechua) in which word order is irrelevant to information structure. Hardman (2000) says about Aymaran languages that "[t]he structural elements of a sentence may occur in any order and are at the disposal of the speaker for stylistic play." Hardman et al. (2001) say that word order in Aymara "affects only style, not the grammar nor basic semantics." Bossong (1989) says about Quechua (which is typologically very similar) that "word order is not only *free* but it is not primarily used as a means for expressing pragmatic functions as such." A detailed analysis of morphological information structure marking in Aymara can thus shed light on this module of grammar which is not expressed morphologically in most languages.

Section 2 presents basic facts about Aymara. Section 3 describes the overtly marked discourse categories in Aymara. Section 4 describes the means of morphosyntactic, semantic and pragmatic referent identification. Section 5 treats pragmatic marking in complex predicates. Finally, we conclude in Section 6.

2 Basic Facts about Aymara

Aymara is spoken by communities in a region encompassing Bolivia, Chile and Peru, extending north of Lake Titicaca to south of Lake Poopó, between the western limit of the Pacific coast valleys and eastward to the Yungas valleys. The language is spoken by roughly two million speakers, over half of whom are Bolivian. The rest reside in Peru and Chile. The Aymaran family (comprised of Aymara, Jaqaru, and Kawki) is a linguistic isolate with no close relative. Aymara is

Proceedings of the Second International Conference on Dependency Linguistics (DepLing 2013), pages 98–107,
Prague, August 27–30, 2013.

an affixal polysynthetic[1] language (according to Mattissen's (2006) classification) with a rich morphology. It is SOV with modifier-head word order. Aside from the morphologically unmarked subject, all syntactic relations are case-marked, typically on the NP head. Roots can be divided into nouns (including qualitative words), verbs, and particles. Suffixes, which may have a morphological or syntactic effect, can be classified as nominal, verbal, transpositional, independent, or pragmatic suffixes. The category of independent suffixes is comprised of three suffixes which are not classifiable as members of either nominal or verbal morphology which likewise cannot be said to be pragmatic suffixes. These suffixes generally occur prior to inflectional morphology and/or the pragmatic suffixes. Pragmatic suffixes, by comparison, typically suffix to the last word of the entire sentence and/or the NP or VP. As their name suggests, their function is overall pragmatic in nature. Nominal and verbal suffixes can be subdivided into inflectional and derivational categories, but given the ease with which category-changing transpositional suffixes attach to words of any category, often multiple times, it is common to find words with several nominal, verbal, transpositional, and independent suffixes.

Detailed information can be found in (Hardman et al., 2001; Briggs, 1976; Adelaar, 2007; Cerrón-Palomino and Carvajal, 2009; Yapita and Van der Noordaa, 2008).

3 Overt Marking of Information Structure

As mentioned in the introduction, word order in Aymara is not used to express information structure. As an example, consider the following sentences in English (syntax-configurational), Russian (discourse-configurational) and Aymara (subscript **N** marks contextually new, i.e. nonpredictable information):

(1)

(a) *Peter came*$_{N}$
It's Peter$_{N}$ *who came* (**Came Peter*)

(b) *Pëtr prišël*$_{N}$
Prišël Pëtr$_{N}$

(c) *Pedrox jutiwa*$_{N}$ or *Jutiw*$_{N}$ *Pedroxa*
Pedrow$_{N}$ *jutixa* or *Jutix Pedrowa*$_{N}$

[1]See (Baker, 1996).

Due to overt morphological marking of information structure, there are discontinuous phrases in which the "gap" is not motivated by pragmatics, such as (2)[2]. The corresponding tree is given in Figure 1.

(2) *Juma-n-x* *jiw-i-w*
you-GEN-REF die-SMPL$_{3\rightarrow3}$-NPRED
kimsa *ch'iyar* *phisi-ma-xa*
three black cat-POSS2-REF
"Your three black cats died."

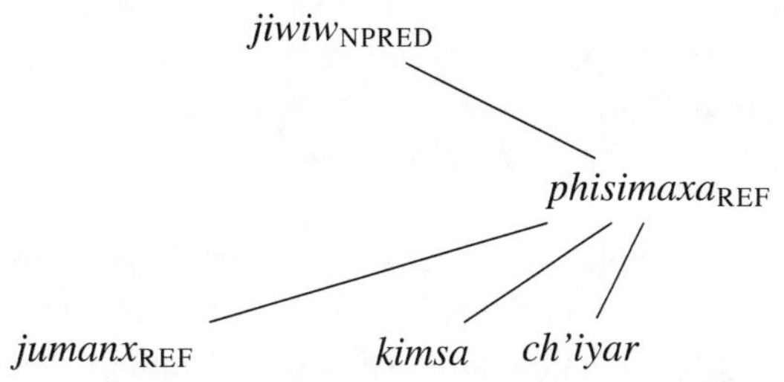

Figure 1: The surface syntax tree of (2) with a discontinuous noun phrase

Of course, the possessive pronoun *jumanx* could also form a continuous constituent with the rest of the NP. Or, it might be omitted since the possessiveness is already expressed with the suffix *-ma* (*phisi**ma**xa*).

Overt marking of information structure is obligatory in Aymara. A sentence without proper pragmatic suffixes (or with marking that would destroy intersentential cohesion) is considered ill-formed. It should also be noted that the marking of information structure is orthogonal to the morphosyntactic expression of evidentiality.[3]

3.1 Referentiality

Aymara has overt marking of referentiality. The notion of referentiality roughly corresponds to

[2]We use the following abbreviations in the glosses: ACC=accusative, AG=agentive, AGGR=aggregator, ALL=allative, BEN=benefactive, CAUS=causative, COM=comitative, CONJ=conjectural, DIR=directive, FUT=future tense, GEN=genitive, HON=honorific, HUM=human, IMPER=imperative, INCMPL=incompletive, INF=infinitive, LIM=limitative, LOC=locative, MIR=mirative, NEG=negative, NPRED=nonpredictable, PAST=past tense, PART=past participle, POSS=possessive, POSS1=1st person possessive, POSS2=2nd person possessive, POSS3=3rd person possessive, POT=potential, PROGR=progressive, QM=question marker, REF=referential, REFL=reflexive, SMPL=simple tense, TRGRDS=transgressive (different subject), TRGRSS=transgressive (same subject), VRBL=verbalizer

[3]Aymara has a three-way system of evidentiality: witnessed, knowledge through language, and inferred.

what Sgall et al. (1986) call ‘contextual boundedness’. We follow Sgall’s (2009) terminology here: “[Contextually bound] items are presented by the speaker as **referring** to entities assumed to be easily accessible by the hearer(s), in the prototypical case ‘given’. They refer to ‘established’ items, i.e. to those that were mentioned in the preceding co-text and thus still are sufficiently salient, or to the permanently established ones (indexicals, those given by the relevant culture or technical domain, etc.).”[4]

For the majority of bilingual speakers, referentiality is optionally marked with the suffix *-xa*,[5] however for monolinguals it is done so more consistently. There are also slight dialectal differences.

For example, in (3) the verb is marked as referential because the event is known from the context (the speaker supposes that the hearer knows that someone came, otherwise he would not ask).

(3) *Khiti-s* *jut-i-xa?*
who-QM come-SMPL$_{3\to3}$-REF
“Who did come?”

On the other hand, in (5) the verb is not marked as referential because it expresses an event which is apparently unknown to the hearer (since he has expressed surprise in (4)).

(4) *Aka-n-ka-sk-ta-sä*
this-LOC-VRBL-PROGR-SMPL$_{2\to3}$-MIR
“Oh, you are here!”

(5) *Jïsa,* *wasüru-w*
yes yesterday-NPRED
kutin-x-ta
return-COMPL-SMPL$_{1\to3}$
“Yes, I came back yesterday.”

The adverbial expression *wasüruw* “yesterday” is marked as nonpredictable[6] (even though it is inherently referential) because it is more salient than the verb[7] (B is surprised to see A because he thought that A had left or was about to leave). Nonetheless, the verb is nonpredictable, too, because B does not know what exactly happened (A may have come back earlier or may not have left at all).

Note that *-xa* marks referentiality, not known/given information, as illustrated in (6).

(6) *Qharüru-x* *sara-:-wa*
tomorrow-REF go-FUT$_{1\to3}$-NPRED
“I will go tomorrow.”

The adverbial expression *qharürux* “tomorrow” is marked as referential because it is inherently referential but there is no marking which would specify if it is predictable or not (the verb is already marked as nonpredictable and there can be at most one NPRED-marker per clause, as explained in the next subsection).[8]

It should be noted the the REF-marking is privative, i.e. the absence of *-xa* does not mean that the entity is not referential.

3.2 Nonpredictability

Entities are nonpredictable if they are ‘new’ to the hearer (cf. the usual dichotomy of information structure known/given vs. unknown/new).[9] Overt marking of nonpredictability in Aymara is much more consequent than that of referentiality. In affirmative sentences, the most salient nonpredictable entity is marked with the suffix *-wa*.[10] The placement of the NPRED-marker can be best explained by question/answer pairs, such as (7) and (8).

(7) *Khiti-taki-s* *ut-x*
who-BEN-QM house.ACC-REF
uta-ch-ta-xa
house-CAUS-SMPL$_{2\to3}$-REF
“For whom did you build the house?”

[4]We do not use the terminology ‘topic-focus’ or ‘theme-rheme’ because the paradigms of suffixes that express information structure do not correlate with it. For example, the two paradigms are not always mutually exclusive (two suffixes from different paradigms can mark the same word).

[5]In the literature this suffix is usually called “topic marker” or “attenuator”.

[6]This grammatical feature is described in the next subsection.

[7]“More salient” means that it is more important in the current context. Informally, we could also say “less predictable”. The scale of salience is important for intersentential referent identification.

[8]A reviewer suggested to compare pragmatic marking in Aymara with ‘topic’-markers in Japanese and/or Korean. First of all, whereas in the mentioned languages, topic marking interferes with case marking, in Aymara they are orthogonal. Also, in Aymara the use of pragmatic markers does not affect word order. Finally, there are no free topics as in the following sentence from (Iwasaki, 2013):

Zoo-wa$_{\mathrm{TOP}}$ *hana-ga*$_{\mathrm{NOM}}$ *nagai*
“The elephant; its nose is long.”

In Aymara, even if the word order of a NP is relaxed, all parts of the NP agree with each other.

[9]Again, we follow Sgall’s (2009) terminology: “[Contextually non-bound] items are presented as **not** directly **predictable** in the given context, as ‘new’ information (at least as chosen from a set of available alternatives).”

[10]In the literature this suffix is often called “affirmative”, “emphasizing”, or “declarative”.

(8) *Jilata-ja-taki-w*
brother-POSS1-BEN-NPRED
(uta-ch-t-xa)
house-CAUS-SMPL$_{1\to3}$-REF
"(I built it) for my brother."

In negative sentences, the NPRED-marker is usually attached to the negative particle *jani*, as in (9).

(9) *Jani-w* *kullaka-ma-r*
not-NPRED sister-POSS2-ALL
uñj-k-t-ti
see-INCMPL-SMPL$_{1\to3}$-NEG
"I did not see your sister."

However, if an argument of the verb is more salient than the verb (i.e., it is contrastive), it attracts the NPRED-marker, as in (10).

(10) *Kullaka-ma-ru-w* *jan*
sister-POSS2-ALL-NPRED not
uñj-k-t-ti
see-INCMPL-SMPL$_{1\to3}$-NEG
"It is your sister whom I did not see."

There are constructions in which NPRED-marks are disallowed, for example in imperative constructions or in those marked with the conjectural evidential suffix:

(11) *Chur-ita-ya*
give-IMPER$_{2\to1}$-HON
"Give it to me, please."

(12) *Jut-chi-ni*
come-CONJ-FUT$_{3\to3}$
"Maybe he will come."

NPRED-unmarked affirmative sentences in the future tense tend to have imperative meaning:

(13) *Sara-ñäni*
go-FUT$_{4\to3}$
"Let us go."

An affirmative sentence without NPRED-marking in the future tense does not alter the context of the present discourse and may have modal meaning (Hardman et al., 2001):

(14) *Nay* *sar-ä-xa*
I go-FUT$_{1\to3}$-REF
"I will go, right? / Should I go?"

Noun phrases introduced by *mä* "one" are indefinite and therefore always nonpredictable. Noun phrases with the determiners *aka* "this", *uka* "that", *khaya* (*khä*) "yonder" and *khuri* "away yonder" are definite and therefore usually predictable unless they are explicitly NPRED-marked (in which case they are contrastive). The following example illustrates that referentiality and nonpredictability do not exclude each other.

(15) *Aka* *warmi-mpi-w* *mä* *jisk'a*
this woman-COM-NPRED one small
marka-n *jiki-s-t-xa*
village-LOC meet-REFL-SMPL$_{1\to3}$-REF
"It is this woman whom I met in a small village."

In verbal complexes, the main (nonfinite) verb may be NPRED-marked, as in (16) and (17):

(16) *T'ant'* *ala-ñ-w*
bread.ACC buy-INF-NPRED
mun-ta
want-SMPL$_{1\to3}$
"I want to buy bread."

(17) *T'ant'* *al-iri-w*
bread.ACC buy-AG-NPRED
sara-sk-ta
go-PROGR-SMPL$_{1\to3}$
"I am going to buy bread."

3.3 Deeply Embedded Nonpredictable Elements

Nonpredictability is usually marked at clause level but it can occur inside a noun phrase[11] if it is required by the discourse context, as in (18) (from (Hardman et al., 2001)).[12]

(18) *Naya-n-x* *pusi-w*
I-GEN-REF four-NPRED
uta-ja-x *utj-itu*
house-POSS1-REF exist-SMPL$_{3\to1}$
"As for houses, I have four."

This example shows that REF and NPRED markers need not appear at the end of a (semantic) phrase. Similarly, a nominal modifier may follow

[11] Hajičová et al. (1998) call this kind of information-structural marking *proxy focus*.

[12] In this example, *pusiw* is not contrastive, it is simply an answer to the question *How many houses do you have?* Of course, one could say just *Pusiwa*.

its governor if its information structure status differs from that of its head in which case both words receive pragmatic marking, as in (19) (from (Hardman et al., 2001)).

(19) *Uka-x* *apilla-x*
that-REF oca-REF
luxu-cha-ta-wa
freeze-CAUS-PART-NPRED
"That is FROZEN oca."

Aymara is a radically nonconfigurational language.[13] However, even languages from this class may pose word order constraints on "deeply" embedded phrases. Indeed, in Aymara noun phrases have more rigid word order than clause constituents.[14] For example, while (20) is well-formed, (21) is ill-formed because the modifier *suma* "good" does not precede its head.

(20) *Suma* *chuq'i-w* *aka*
good potato-NPRED this
marka-n-x *ach-u*
village-LOC-REF grow-SMPL$_{3\to3}$
"In this village grow good potatoes."

(21) **Chuq'i-w* *suma* *aka*
potato-NPRED good this
marka-n-x *ach-u*
village-LOC-REF grow-SMPL$_{3\to3}$
Intended meaning: "In this village grow good potatoes."

Nevertheless the order of a nominal modifier and its head is not restricted if both have a pragmatic marker, as in (22)–(24).

(22) *Suma-w* *aka* *marka-n-x*
good-NPRED this village-LOC-REF
chuq'i-x *ach-u*
potato-REF grow-SMPL$_{3\to3}$
"GOOD potatoes grow in this village."

(23) *Uta-cha-ña-taki-x* *qala-x*
house-CAUS-INF-BEN-REF stone-REF
alluxa-w *apthapi-ña*
a-lot-NPRED gather-INF
"One must gather MANY stones to build a house."

[13] In terms of the generative grammar, languages with the rule $S \to C^+$ at clause level.

[14] Unlike, for example, in Latin, where the word order of NPs is less rigid although not completely free.

(24) *Qullq-x* *allux-w*
money.ACC-REF a-lot.ACC-NPRED
ap-kat-ta
put-DIR-SMPL$_{1\to3}$
"I collected A LOT of money."

Thus Aymara, like many nonconfigurational languages, allows discontinuous constituents. For example, in (22), the noun phrase *sumaw chuq'ix* "good potatoes" is discontinuous because *aka markanx* "in this village" is not part of its surface syntax subtree.

3.4 Focalizers

"Focalizers" (i.e. focusing operators, in English adverbs such as *only, even, also, always, at least,* etc., see (Hajičová et al., 1998)) are mostly expressed by suffixes in Aymara. In many cases, the word with a focalizing suffix attracts the NPRED-marking, as in (25)–(28).

(25) *Kimsa-ni-ki-w* *sar-i*
three-HUM-LIM-NPRED go-SMPL$_{3\to3}$
"Only three went."

(26) *Wawa-pa-x* *may-ni-ki-wa*
child-POSS3-REF one-HUM-LIM-NPRED
"He has only one child."

(27) *Iki-ña-k-w*
sleep-INF-LIM-NPRED
mun-t-xa
want-SMPL$_{1\to3}$-REF
"I only want to sleep."

(28) *Nay* *kuna-w* *sar-t-xa*
I what-NPRED go-SMPL$_{1\to3}$-REF
"Even I went."

Another pattern is attaching the independent aggregator *-sa* to the focalized word together with NPRED-marking of the verb, as in (29) and (30).

(29) *Naya-s* *sara-rak-t-wa*
I-AGGR go-'also'-SMPL$_{1\to3}$-NPRED
"I also went."

(30) *Juma-ki-s* *yati-sma-wa*
you-LIM-AGGR know-POT$_{2\to3}$-NPRED
"At least you should know it."

The focalizing negative particle *jani* "not" attracts the NPRED-marking in unmarked cases (but see (10)). Two focalizers can be combined, as in the case of *jani* and *puni* "always" which gives the form *janipuni* "never" or *jani* and *raki* "also" which gives the form *janiraki* "neither". Both forms attract the NPRED-marking.

3.5 Resolving Underspecification

As was demonstrated in the above description, overt marking of information structure in Aymara is partial, as it leaves some elements underspecified. Since Aymara is a radical pro-drop language[15] (any argument of the verb may be unexpressed, not only the subject), predictable arguments are often omitted. As a consequence, direct objects are usually omitted if they can be inferred from the context, as in (31).[16]

(31) *Tata-ja-taki-w*
father-POSS1-BEN-NPRED
ala-sk-t-xa
buy-PROGR-SMPL$_{1\rightarrow3}$-REF
"I am buying it for my father."

It follows that if a verb is NPRED-marked and has an overt object, the latter is nonpredictable, too, unless it is REF-marked, as in (32).

(32) *Naya-w* *um-x*
I-NPRED water.ACC-REF
wayu-ni-:-xa
carry-DIR-FUT$_{1\rightarrow3}$-REF
"It is me who will bring the water."

The same holds for other verbal arguments. The only ambiguity arises from inherently referential expressions which appear REF-marked or unmarked (e.g., *qharürux/qharüru* "tomorrow") and this marking does not correlate with their nonpredictability.[17]

3.6 Intersentential Cohesion

Overt marking of information structure, described in the previous section, has crucial importance for intersentential cohesion and can be helpful for coreference resolution. Consider, for example, the following two sentences:

(33) *Mä* *marka-n* *mä* *jisk'a* *imilla-w*
one village-LOC one small girl-NPRED
utj-i
exist-SMPL$_{3\rightarrow3}$
"There was a little girl in a village."

(34) *Jupa-x* *Mariya* *suti-ni-wa*
she-REF María name-POSS-NPRED
"Her name was María."

In (33), both noun phrases as well as the verb are nonpredictable. The noun *imilla* "girl" is NPRED-marked (i.e., marked as the most salient part of the utterance) because in (34), it is referred to by the pronoun *jupa* "he/she".

The analysis of utterances in texts such as stories and narratives reveals that Aymara speakers consequently take intersentential cohesion into account when they decide where to place pragmatic markers.

4 Referent Identification

Surface and deep syntax as well as semantics operate on isolated sentences. Now we will discuss the formalization of pragmatics, the level of discourse context.

For the purposes of this subsection we assume that we have a discourse that consists of sentences $s_1, \ldots, s_n$ and that we have the corresponding feature structures $f_1, \ldots, f_n$. An entity we call a feature structure that represents a person, an object or an event (an event may be dynamic if described by a verb or statal if described by a nominal predicate). Every entity has a special attribute, INDEX, to represent coreferences.

The discourse context is formally a list of indices (values of the INDEX attribute) $C = \langle i_1, \ldots, i_m \rangle$. The sentences are processed one by one. At the beginning, $C = \emptyset$. For every f_i, we do the following:

1. For every entity in f_i, we try to find its referent in C (we describe below how referents are identified). If a referent was found for an entity, its index in C is moved to the beginning of the list. Otherwise, a new index is assigned to the entity and prepended to the list.

2. The index of the NPRED-marked entity is moved (or prepended) to the beginning of C.

There are various strategies of identification of referents in the preceding discourse that can combine to resolve ambiguities.

[15] See (Cole, 1987).

[16] The sentence is an answer to the question *Who are you buying it for?*

[17] It is possible that the category of referentiality is undergoing a reanalysis as a result of language contact. A more detailed analysis of the speech of monolingual speakers is needed.

4.1 Morphosyntactic Referent Identification

Aymara has a rich system of switch-reference suffixes that help to identify referents in the discourse context. For example, the sentence

(35) *Tumasi-x*$_i$
Thomas-REF
klasi-n-ka-ska-:n-wa
class-LOC-VRBL-PROGR-PAST$_{3\to3}$-NPREF
"Thomas$_i$ was in the class room."

may be followed by the following sentence:

(36) *Yatichiri-x*$_j$ *manta-n-isin-x*
teacher-REF enter-DIR-TRGRSS-REF
nuw-i-wa
hit-SMPL$_{3\to3}$-NPRED
"When the teacher$_j$ entered, he$_j$ hit him$_i$."

The first sentence adds the index of the entity *Tumasix*$_i$ "Thomas" to C. The second sentence adds the index of the entity *Yatichirix*$_j$ "the teacher" to C. Furthermore, there are two unresolved (covert) pronouns that represent the actor and the patient of *nuwiwa* "to hit". In this case the switch-reference transgressive suffix *-sina* specifies that the actor of *nuwiwa* is the actor of *mantasinx* "entered", thus the actor of *nuwiwa* has the index i. The patient is coindexed with the next entity in C with which it agrees morphologically (e.g., in terms of animacy) or semantically. On the other hand, the sentence

(37) *Yatichiri-x*$_j$ *manta-n-ipan-x*
teacher-REF enter-DIR-TRGRDS-REF
nuw-i-wa
hit-SMPL$_{3\to3}$-NPRED
"When the teacher$_j$ entered, he$_i$ hit him$_j$."

changes the indexes of the pronouns in the matrix sentence because the switch-reference transgressive suffix *-ipana* specifies that the subject of *mantanipanx* is different from that of *nuwiwa*.

4.2 Semantic Referent Identification

If there is the sentence

(38) *Tumasi-mp*$_i$ *Marya-mp*$_j$
Thomas-COM Mary-COM
uñj-t-wa
see-SMPL$_{1\to3}$-NPRED
"I saw Thomas$_i$ and Mary$_j$."

followed by

(39) *Jani-w* *usuri-:-ta-p*
not-NPRED pregnant-VRBL-PART-POSS3
yat-k-t-ti
know-INCMPL-SMPL$_{1\to3}$-NEG
"I did not now that she$_j$ was pregnant."

the referent identification of the covert pronoun which is the actor of *usurïtap* "that she was pregnant" is not morphosyntactically restricted (Aymara has one pronoun, *jupa*, for both "he" and "she") but it is semantically restricted. It is obvious that the semantic information of this kind has to come from the lexicon. Likewise, there will be lexically encoded semantic gender for words such as *tayka* "mother", *jilata* "brother", *imilla* "girl", etc.

4.3 Pragmatic Referent Identification

As described in Subsection 3.6, explicitly NPRED-marked entities are more salient than other non-predictable entities in the same sentence. If there is the sentence

(40) *Tayka-ma-w*$_i$
mother-POSS2-NPRED
yatichiri-ma-mp$_j$ *jik-i-si*
teacher-POSS2-COM meet-SMPL$_{3\to3}$-REFL
"Your mother$_i$ met your teacher$_j$."

followed by

(41) *Usuta-:-ta-m-x*
sick-VRBL-PART-POSS2-REF
yat-x-i-wa
know-COMPL-SMPL$_{3\to3}$-NPRED
"She$_i$ already knew that you were sick."

the actor of *yatxiwa* "s/he already knew" is coindexed with *taykamaw* "your mother" because this entity is NPRED-marked in the first sentence and therefore more salient (it precedes other entities in C). If we move the NPRED-marker in the first sentence to the "teacher", the meaning of the second sentence will change:

(42) *Tayka-ma-x*$_i$
mother-POSS2-REF
yatichiri-ma-mpi-w$_j$
teacher-POSS2-COM-NPRED
jik-i-si
meet-SMPL$_{3\to3}$-REFL
"Your mother$_i$ met your teacher$_j$."

(43) *Usuta-:-ta-m-x*
sick-VRBL-PART-POSS2-REF
yat-x-i-wa
know-COMPL-SMPL$_{3\to3}$-NPRED
"He$_j$ already knew that you were sick."

5 Complex Predicates

A special case of pragmatic marking represent the so-called complex predicates, i.e. monoclausal predicates composed of (at least) two predicative elements. In such constructions, a (fully) semantic verb combines with a modal or auxiliary element to express complex predication such as causative, volitive, supine, etc. The concept of complex predicates, elaborated by Alsina (1996), has been applied to a number of phenomena and languages including, for example, Hindi light verbs (Mohanan, 1994) or Turkish causatives (Çetinoğlu et al., 2008). We will leave aside the rather complicated formal treatment of these constructions in unification-based grammars (Homola and Coler, 2013) and focus on the linguistic description of these form in Aymara from the pragmatic point of view here.

Sentences (16) and (17) are examples of complex predicates. The constructions contain only one NPRED-marker, i.e. they are monoclausal and should be represented by a single feature structure with a complex functor. For (16), we get:

(44) $$\begin{bmatrix} \text{FUNC} & \text{'muna-'} \\ \text{ARGS} & \left\langle \text{subj}_{act}, \begin{bmatrix} \text{FUNC} & \text{'ala-'} \\ \text{ARGS} & \langle \text{subj}_{act}, \text{dobj}_{pat} \rangle \end{bmatrix}_{pat} \right\rangle \end{bmatrix}$$

For (17), we get:

(45) $$\begin{bmatrix} \text{FUNC} & \text{'sara-'} \\ \text{ARGS} & \left\langle \text{subj}_{act}, \begin{bmatrix} \text{FUNC} & \text{'ala-'} \\ \text{ARGS} & \langle \text{subj}_{act}, \text{dobj}_{pat} \rangle \end{bmatrix}_{pat} \right\rangle \end{bmatrix}$$

In a more concise notation, (44) can be written as:

(46) $muna(\text{subj}_{act}, ala(\text{subj}_{act}, \text{dobj}_{pat})_{pat})$

Likewise, (45) can be written as:

(47) $sara(\text{subj}_{act}, ala(\text{subj}_{act}, \text{dobj}_{pat})_{pat})$

Unlike in languages with morphologically formed volitive verbal complexes, such as Guaraní, in Aymara such constructions are formed syntactically (i.e. the complex predicate value is not created in the lexicon). As for motion verbs, such as (45), there is a morphological alternative:

(48) *Jichha-x t'ant*
now-REF bread.ACC
ala-ni-rapi-:ma-wa
buy-DIR-BEN-FUT$_{1\to2}$-NPRED
"I will go to buy bread for you now."

Further evidence that such predicates are monoclausal is the fact that polypersonal agreement is expressed on the auxiliary or modal verb, not the full one, as in (49) and (50).

(49) *Ch'uq alja-ñ-w*
potato.ACC sell-INF-NPRED
mun-sma
want-SMPL$_{1\to2}$
"I want to sell potatoes to you."

(50) *Tump-iri-w jut-sma*
visit-AG-NPRED come-SMPL$_{1\to2}$
"I came to visit you."

It is noteworthy that a complex predicate with a motion verb can have two complements, namely a locative phrase and a verbal complement:

(51) *Al-iri-w Chukiaw*
buy-AG-NPRED La.Paz.ACC
sara :na
go-SMPL$_{3\to3}$
"He went to La Paz to buy it."

Even more evidence for monoclausality can be found in sentences like (52):

(52) *Chukiaw sara-ñ-w*
La.Paz.ACC go-INF-NPRED
mun-t-x irnaqa-ña-taki-xa
want-SMPL$_{1\to3}$-REF work-INF-BEN-REF
"I want to go to La Paz for work."

In (52), the nominalized verb *irnaqañatakixa* "to work" depends on *sarañw* "to go" creating a long-distance dependency. Without considering the verbal complex *sarañw muntx* a monoclausal predicate, it would be linguistically counterintuitive and computationally hard to parse the sentence.

It is obvious from the mentioned examples that the NPRED-marker tends to attach to the full verb. This fact supports the hypothesis that modal (deictic) syntactic elements should be considered synsemantic, i.e. at the level of deep syntax they should be represented as attributes of the nodes of their heads rather then autonomous nodes or feature structures. This approach, adopted by us, is consistent with (Sgall et al., 1986).

We omit from the discussion morphologically built complex predicates, such as causatives (e.g. (53)). In other languages where they are expressed syntactically, they would be treated in the same way as the constructions described above.

(53) *Jacha-y-t-wa*
cry-CAUS-SMPL$_{1\rightarrow3}$-NPRED
"I made him/her cry."

(54)
$$\begin{bmatrix} \text{FUNC} & \text{`caus'} \\ \text{ARGS} & \left\langle \text{subj}_{act}, \begin{bmatrix} \text{FUNC} & \text{`jacha-'} \\ \text{ARGS} & \langle \text{dobj}_{act} \rangle \end{bmatrix}^{pat} \right\rangle \end{bmatrix}$$

6 Conclusions

We have described the overt marking of information structure and its pivotal role both in intersentential cohesion in Aymara as well as coreference resolution. Through an analysis of morphological information structure marking with *pragmatic suffixes* in this language, we illustrate the irrelevance of word order for information structure. While overt marking of referentiality is not always consequent, nonpredictability is marked with strict regularity. Having demonstrated that nonpredictability can be marked both at clause level and inside a NP and that focalizing suffixes tend to attract NPRED morphology, we explained how underspecification is resolved, noting, for example, that the overt object of a NPRED-marked verb is also unpredictable unless it is REF-marked. We also treated the identification of morphosyntactic, semantic and pragmatic referents through a formalization of pragmatics. The specifics of pragmatic marking in complex predicates show how the NPRED-marker typically attaches to the full verb thus supporting the hypothesis that modal syntactic constructions should be considered monoclausal.

References

Willem Adelaar. 2007. *The Languages of the Andes*. Cambridge University Press.

Alex Alsina. 1996. *The Role of Argument Structure in Grammar: Evidence from Romance*. CSLI Publications.

Mark C. Baker. 1996. *The Polysynthesis Parameter*. Oxford University Press.

Georg Bossong. 1989. Morphemic marking of topic and focus. In Michel Kefer and Johan van der Auwera, editors, *Universals of Language*, pages 27–51.

Georg Bossong. 2009. Divergence, convergence, contact. In Kurt Braunmüller and Juliane House, editors, *Convergence and divergence in language contact situations*, pages 13–40.

Lucy Therina Briggs. 1976. *Dialectal Variation in the Aymara Language of Bolivia and Peru*. Ph.D. thesis, University of Florida.

R. Cerrón-Palomino and J. Carvajal Carvajal. 2009. Aimara. In M. Crevels and P. Muysken, editors, *Lenguas de Bolivia*. Plural Editores, La Paz, Bolivia.

Özlem Çetinoğlu, Miriam Butt, and Kemal Oflazer. 2008. Mono/bi-clausality of Turkish Causatives. In *Proceedings of the 14th International Conference on Turkish Linguistics*.

Peter Cole. 1987. Null Objects in Universal Grammar. *Linguistic Inquiry*, 18(4):597–612.

Eva Hajičová, Barbara H. Partee, and Petr Sgall. 1998. *Topic-focus articulation, tripartite structures, and semantic content*. Kluwer Academic Publishers, Dordrecht.

Kenneth L. Hale. 1983. Warlpiri and the grammar of non-configurational languages. *Natural Language & Linguistic Theory*, 1:5–47.

Martha Hardman, Juana Vásquez, and Juan de Dios Yapita. 2001. *Aymara. Compendio de estructura fonológica y gramatical*. Instituto de Lengua y Cultura Aymara.

Martha Hardman. 2000. *Jaqaru*. LINCOM EUROPA.

Petr Homola and Matt Coler. 2013. Causatives as Complex Predicates without the Restriction Operator. In Miriam Butt and Tracy Holloway King, editors, *Proceedings of the LFG Conference*.

Shoichi Iwasaki. 2013. *Japanese*. John Benjamins Publishing.

Katalin É. Kiss. 1994. *Discourse Configurational Languages*. Oxford University Press.

Joanna Mattissen. 2006. On the Ontology and Diachrony of Polysynthesis. In Dieter Wunderlich, editor, *Advances in the theory of the lexicon*, pages 287–354. Walter de Gruyter, Berlin.

Tara Mohanan. 1994. *Argument Structure in Hindi*. CSLI Publications.

Petr Sgall, Eva Hajičová, and Jarmila Panevová. 1986. *The Meaning of the Sentence in Its Semantic and Pragmatic Aspects*. D. Reider Publishing Company.

Petr Sgall. 2009. Where to look for the fundamentals of language. *Linguistica Pragensia*, 19(1):1–35.

Juan de Dios Yapita and J.T. Van der Noordaa. 2008. *La dinámica aymara. Conjugación de verbos*. Instituto de Lengua y Cultura Aymara.

Towards a psycholinguistically motivated dependency grammar for Hindi

Samar Husain
Department of Linguistics
Universität Potsdam
Germany
husain@uni-potsdam.de

Rajesh Bhatt
University of Massachusetts
Amherst, MA , USA
bhatt@linguist.umass.edu

Shravan Vasishth
Department of Linguistics
Universität Potsdam
Germany
vasishth@uni-potsdam.de

Abstract

The overall goal of our work is to build a dependency grammar-based human sentence processor for Hindi. As a first step towards this end, in this paper we present a dependency grammar that is motivated by psycholinguistic concerns. We describe the components of the grammar that have been automatically induced using a Hindi dependency treebank. We relate some aspects of the grammar to relevant ideas in the psycholinguistics literature. In the process, we also extract statistics and patterns for phenomena that are interesting from a processing perspective. We finally present an outline of a dependency grammar-based human sentence processor for Hindi.

1 Introduction

Human sentence processing proposals and modeling works are overwhelmingly based on phrase-structure parsing and constituent based representation. This is because most modern linguistic theories (Chomsky, 1965), (Chomsky, 1981), (Chomsky, 1995), (Bresnan and Kaplan, 1982), (Sag et al., 2003) use phrase structure representation to analyze a sentence. There is, however, an alternative approach to sentential syntactic representation, known as dependency representation, that is quite popular in Computational Linguistics (CL). Unlike phrase structures where the actual words of the sentence appear as leaves, and the internal nodes are phrases, in a dependency grammar (Mel'čuk, 1988), (Bharati et al., 1995), (Hudson, 2010) a syntactic tree comprises of sentential words as nodes. These words/nodes are connected to each other with edges/arcs. The edges can be labeled to show the type of relation between a pair of node. For example, in the sentence *John kissed Mary*, 'John' and 'Mary' are connected via arcs to 'kissed'; the former arc bears the label 'subject' and the latter arc the label 'object'. Taken together, these nodes with their connections form a tree. Figure 1 shows the dependency and the phrase structure trees for the above sentence.

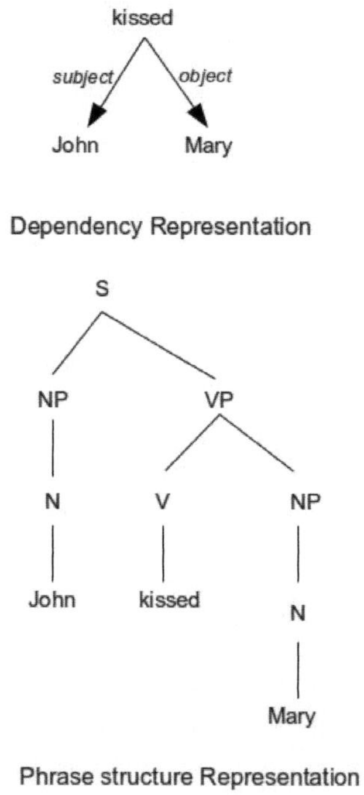

Figure 1: Dependency tree and Phrase structure tree

There have been some previous attempts to use lexicalized grammars such as LTAG, CCG, etc. in psycholinguistics. These lexicalized grammars have been independently shown to be related to dependency grammar (Kuhlmann, 2007). For example, Pickering and Barry (1991) used categorial grammar to handle processing of empty categories. Similarly, Pickering (1994) used dependency categorial grammar to process both local and non-local dependencies. More recenly, Ta-

Proceedings of the Second International Conference on Dependency Linguistics (DepLing 2013), pages 108–117,
Prague, August 27–30, 2013.

bor and Hutchins (2004) used a lexical grammar based parser and Kim et al. (1998) used lexicalized tree-adjoining grammar (LTAG) to model certain processing results. Demberg (2010) has recently proposed a psycholinguistically motivated LTAG (P-LTAG). Despite the success of dependency paradigm in CL, it has remained unexplored in psycholinguistics. To our knowledge, the work by Boston and colleagues (Boston et al., 2011), (Boston et al., 2008) is the only such attempt. There are some very interesting open questions with respect to using dependency representation and dependency parsers while building a human sentence processing system. Can a processing model based on dependency parsing paradigm account for classic psycholinguistic phenomena? Can one adapt a high performance dependency parser for psycholinguistic research? If yes, then how? How will the differences in different dependency parsing paradigms affect the predictive capacity of the models based on them?

This paper is arranged as follows, in Section 2 we mention some experimental works that have motivated the grammar design. Section 3 discusses the grammar induction process and lists out the main components of the grammar. In Section 4 we present statistics of Hindi word order variations as found in the treebank and point out some patterns that are interesting from a processing perspective. We also talk about prediction rules that are an important component in the grammar. Section 5 then presents a proposal for developing a human sentence processing system by adapting graph-based dependency parsing. Finally in Section 6 we discuss some issues and challenges in using dependency grammar paradigm for human sentence processing. We conclude in Section 7.

2 Motivation: Some relevant experimental work

Some crucial design decisions in our research have been inspired by psycholinguistic experimental work. In this section we will mention these works. But before that, we will briefly discuss Hindi, the language that we are working with.

Hindi is one of the official languages of India. Hindi is the fourth most widely spoken language in the world[1]. It is a free-word order language and is head final. It has relatively rich morphology with verb-subject[2], noun-adjective agreement. Examples (2) to (6) below show some of the possible word order variations possible with (1). These permutations are not exhaustive - in fact all 4! permutations are possible.

(1) malaya ne abhiisheka ko kitaaba dii
Malaya ERG Abhishek DAT book gave
'Malaya gave a book to Abhishek.' (S-IO-O-V)

(2) malaya ne kitaaba abhiisheka ko dii (S-O-IO-V)

(3) abhiisheka ko malaya ne kitaaba dii (IO-S-O-V)

(4) abhiisheka ko kitaaba malaya ne dii (IO-O-S-V)

(5) kitaaba abhiisheka ko malaya ne dii (O-IO-S-V)

(6) kitaaba malaya ne abhiisheka ko dii (O-S-IO-V)

A great deal of experimental research has shown that working-memory limitations play a major role in sentence comprehension difficulty (e.g., Lewis and Vasishth (2005)). We find numerous instances in natural language where a word needs to be temporarily retained in memory before it can be integrated as part of a larger structure. Because of limited working-memory, retaining a word for a longer period can make sentence processing difficult. Abstracting away from details, on this view, one way in which processing complexity can be formulated is by using metrics that can incorporate dependent-head distance (Gibson, 2000), (Grodner and Gibson, 2005). This idea manifests itself in various forms in the psycholinguistics literature. For example, Gibson (2000) proposes integration cost and storage cost to account for processing complexity. Lewis and Vasishth (2005) have proposed a working memory-based theory that uses the notion of decay as one determinant of memory retrieval difficulty. Elements that exists in memory without being retrieved for a long time will decay more, compared to elements that have been retrieved recently or elements that are recent. In addition to decay, the theory also incorporates the notion of interference. Memory retrievals are feature based, and feature overlap during retrieval, in addition to decay, will cause difficulty.

As opposed to locality-based accounts mentioned above, expectation-based theories appeal to the predictive nature of sentence processor. On this view, processing becomes difficult if the upcoming sentential material is less predictable. Surprisal (Hale, 2001), (Levy, 2008) is one such account. Informally, surprisal increases when a

[1](http://www.ethnologue.com/ethno_docs/distribution.asp?by=size).

[2]This is the default agreement pattern. The complete agreement system is much more complex.

parser is required to build some low-probability structure.

Expectation-based theories can successfully account for so called anti-locality effects. It has been noted that in some language phenomena, increasing the distance between the dependent and its head speeds up reading time at the head (see Konieczny (2000) for such effects in German, and Vasishth and Lewis (2006) for Hindi). This is, of course, contrary to the predictions made by locality-based accounts where such an increase should cause slowdown at the head. There is considerable empirical evidence supporting the idea of predictive parsing in language comprehension (e.g. Staub and Clifton (2006)). There is also some evidence that shows that the nature of predictive processing can be contingent on language specific characteristics. For example, Vasishth et al. (2010) argue that the verb-final nature of German subordinate clauses leads to the parser maintaining future predictions more effectively as compared to English. As Hindi is a verb-final language, these experimental results become pertinent for this paper. Locality-based results are generally formalized using the limited working memory model. Such a model enforces certain resource limitations within which human sentence processing system operates. On the other hand, expectation/prediction-based results have to be accounted by appealing to the nature of the processing system itself.

Hindi being a free word order language, experimental work that deal with the processing cost of word-order variation is also important to us. Experimental work points to the fact that human sentence processing is sensitive to word order variation (e.g. Bader and Meng (1999), Kaiser and Trueswell (2004)). However, it is still not clear as to why/how word order variation influences processing costs. Processing costs could be due to variety of reasons (such as, syntactic complexity, frequency, information structure, prosody, memory constraints, etc).

So, there are three streams of experimental research that are relevant for us: (a) locality effects, (b) anti-locality/expectation effects, (c) word-order variation effects. In section 3 and 4 we will discuss how insights from (b) and (c) inform some of our design decisions. Later in section 5 while discussing human sentence processing, we will touch upon the notion of locality in our parsing approach.

3 Inducing a grammar

To develop a dependency grammar we will make use of an already existing Hindi dependency treebank (Bhatt et al., 2009). The treebank data is a collection of news articles from a Hindi newspaper and has 400k words. The task of automatic induction of grammar from a treebank can be thought of as making explicit the implicit grammar present in the treebank. This approach can be beneficial for a variety of tasks, such as, complementing traditional hand-written grammars, comparing grammars of different languages, building parsers, etc. (Xia and Palmer, 2001), (Kolachina et al., 2010). Our task is much more focused, we want to bootstrap a grammar that can be used for a dependency-based human sentence processor for Hindi.

3.1 Lexicon

The lexicon comprises of syntactic properties of various heads (e.g. verbs). Based on *a priori* selection of certain argument relations (subject, object, indirect object, experiencer verb subject, goal, noun complements of subject for copula verbs) we formed around 13 verb clusters[3]. These clusters were then merged into 6 super-clusters based on the previously mentioned relations (this time acting as discriminators[4]). These clusters correspond to, (1) intransitive verbs (e.g. *so* 'sleep', *gira* 'fall'), (2) transitive verbs (e.g. *khaa* 'eat'), (3) ditransitives (e.g. *de* 'give'), (4) experiencer verbs (e.g. *dikha* 'to appear'), (5) copula (e.g. *hai* 'is'), (6) goal verbs (e.g. *jaa* 'go').

These 6 verb classes can be thought of as tree-templates and can be associated with various class specific constraints such as, number of mandatory arguments, part of speech, category of the arguments, canonical order of the arguments, relative position of the argument with respect to the verb, agreement constraints, etc. Figure 2 shows a simplified transitive template that can be associated with all the transitive verbs in the lexicon. Its

[3]Clustering originally gave us 31 classes that were manually checked to give us 13 correct classes. Although this filtering was done manually, most of the remaining 18 clusters could have also been identified automatically. The proportion of verbs associated with them is very low. These clusters are mainly due to annotation errors.

[4]Each of these clusters were then compared to each other in order to remove common verbs.

first argument (subject) is represented by a variable *i*, and its second argument (object) is represented by a variable *j*. The verb itself is shown as variable *x*. These variables (*i*, *j*, *x*) will be instantiated by those lexical items that are of a particular type. For example, *x* can only be instantiated by transitive verb class members[5]. Similarly, only those items that satisfy the dependent constraints can be instantiated as subject or object. These constraints can be of various kinds, such as the part of speech (POS) category, semantic type, etc. The tree-template in figure 2 also encodes the arity of the verbal head, as well as the canonical word order of its dependents (cf. figure 3). Lastly, the tree-template shows that adjuncts are not mandatory. Figure 3 shows a template for a transitive argument structure but with object fronting. In the figure, object is indexed with *j*, and its canonical position is shown by $\emptyset_j$. Note that the arc coming into the empty node ($\emptyset_j$) is not a dependency relation; the arc and the node are just a representational strategy to show word order variation in the tree-template.

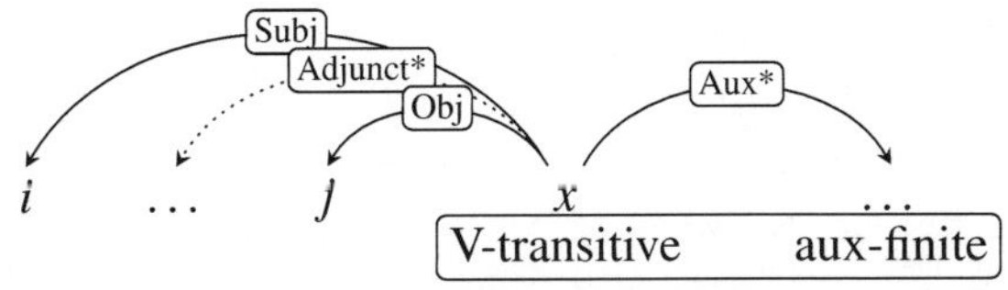

Figure 2: A simplified transitive tree-template. aux = Auxiliaries. * signifies 0 or more instances.

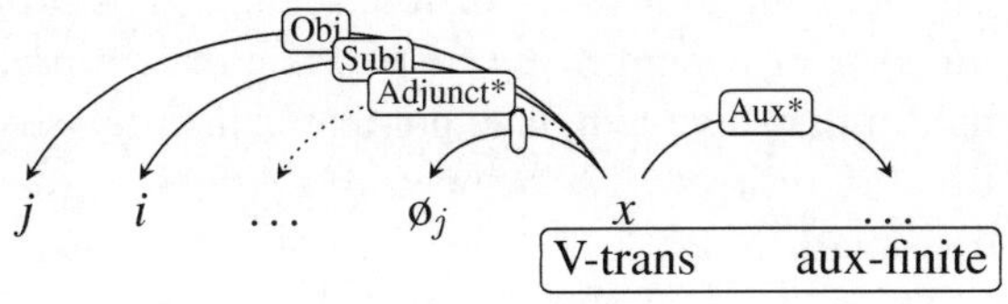

Figure 3: A simplified transitive tree template showing object fronting. trans = Transitive, aux = Auxiliaries, $\emptyset_j$ = canonical position of object *j*

3.2 Frame variations

The tree-templates we saw in section 3.1 have been induced automatically using the finite verb occurrences in the treebank. While inducing the clusters we neglected the differences in tense, aspect and modality (TAM) of the verbs (e.g. perfective, obligational) that sometime leads to different case-markings on the arguments. This is because we are focusing on the number of arguments, not the case-markings on the arguments. But, finite-templates cannot be used for non-finite verbs. This is because the surface requirements of non-finite verbs are different from that of finite verbs[6]. For example, when *khaa* 'eat' occurs as *khaakara* 'having eaten', its original requirement for a subject changes to mandatorily not taking any visible subject. In addition, it requires another finite or a non-finite verb as its head.

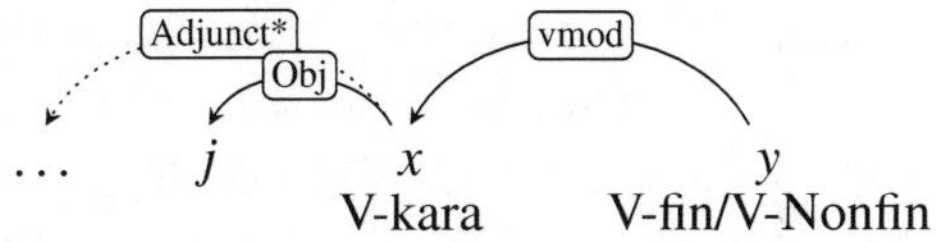

Figure 4: A -kara tree-template. fin = Finite.

One way to think about *-kara* template is that it is an outcome of transforming the transitive argument structure (Bharati et al., 1995). The transformation will perform a series of add/modify/delete operations on the transitive-template leading to the template shown in figure 4.

Another way to think about this would be basically a non-transformational account, where we assume that the non-finite templates are obtained independently of the transitive templates. This would amount to looking at only the non-finite verbs in the treebank and identifying some generalization about various non-finite instances, i.e. creating classes based on the inflections such *kara* (encodes causality/sequentiality), *e (hii)* (sequentiality), *taa huaa* (signifies co-occurring event), *naa* (gerundive form), etc.

From a grammar extraction perspective, the method that is used to get the non-finite templates is not that important. As long as one can extract the correct requirements of the non-finite verbs, it should suffice. On the other hand, such a distinction could, in fact, be very relevant from a lexical processing perspective. Do we build the *kara* template on the fly or do we just access its information from a stored entry? Such a design decision will have to await future investigation.

[5]Only finite verbs were considered to form the verb clusters. Syntactically, non-finite verbs in Hindi behave differently than their finite counterpart. This is not only reflected in the inflection, but also in the number of visible arguments. We discuss such cases in Section 3.2.

[6]This also holds true for passives.

3.3 Probability distribution of dependency types

Each verb class (*i*) is associated with a probability distribution of its dependents (j=1..n). The probability of a node (*x*) being a dependent of *i* with relation *r*, is computed as:

$$P_{x,r,i} = \frac{\lambda_{(x,r,i)}}{\sum_{j=1}^{n} \lambda_{(j,i)}} \quad (1)$$

where $\lambda_{(x,r,i)}$ is the count of i $\rightarrow$ x (with dependency relation *r*), and the denominator signifies the total count of all the dependents of *i*.

Such probabilities can be used to score a dependency tree at any given point during the parsing process. This is of course a simplification and as we will note in section 5, there are other ways to induce the probability model that can be used to score a dependency tree.

The dependency grammar that we have been building will be used to model a human sentence parser. The incrementality of the parser and the observation that many nouns can appear without any post-position makes it necessary to identify if the two nouns appearing together are collocations or independent arguments.

One way to compute the collocational strength between words x' and y' is by using pointwise mutual information (Manning and Schütze, 1999):

$$I(x', y') = log\frac{p(x', y')}{p(x')p(y')} \quad (2)$$

Again, as we will see in section 5, there might be other ways in order to incorporate this knowledge for parsing purposes.

3.4 Prediction rules

As each incoming word is incorporated into the existing structure, predictions are made about upcoming words based on current information. In order for the parser to proceed in such a fashion it must have ready access to such information. The grammar that we propose provides this information in the form of prediction rules. The kind of information that the (implemented) parser utilizes to make such predictions can be influenced by various theoretical assumptions (and/or experimental results). For illustrative purpose, while gathering statistics to formulate predictions shown in this section, we consider only verbal arguments. The presence of adjuncts has been neglected.

We begin with one simple cue, case of the arguments. Considering the occurrence of the first verbal argument in a sentence and its case, we tried to predict the verb class using the data in the Hindi dependency treebank. Here are some predictions based on frequent case-markings: *ne* (ERG) $\rightarrow$ transitive, *ko* (ACC) $\rightarrow$ transitive, *se* (INST) $\rightarrow$ ditransitive, *0* (NOM) $\rightarrow$ intransitive.

The verb classes that we get for *ne*, *se* and *0* reflect the default distribution of ERG, INST and NOM case-markers vis-à-vis the type of verbs they tend to occur with. Of course, predictions will become more precise as more words are processed. When the first two argument case-markers are considered we get:

0 0: copula
0 -: intransitive
0 se: transitive
0 ko: transitive
0 ne: transitive
ne 0: transitive
ne ko: transitive/ditransitive
ne se: ditransitive
ko 0: ditransitive
ko ko: ditransitive
ko se: ditransitive
ko ne: transitive
ko -: transitive
se 0: ditransitive
se ne: ditransitive

And as we get more information, we might have to revise our previous predictions and make necessary structural changes (or rerank multiple structures). For example, the first *ko* occurrence predicts a transitive-template, but that is later revised to a ditransitive if we happen to see a *0* or a *ko* case-marker.

The prediction rules shown above have been automatically extracted from the dependency treebank. Other than the case-marker, one can also use other features to make our predictions more realistic. For example, we could use features such as sentence position, animacy feature (using a resource such as WordNet), etc.

4 Processing concerns

Having discussed the main components of the grammar, in this section, we will raise some processing concerns based on the statistics gathered from the treebank.

4.1 Canonical and non-canonical structures

4.1.1 Argument structure variation

As mentioned previously, the tree-template for each verb class also encodes the canonical order in which its argument should appear. For example, in a transitive class, it is expected that the subject should precede the object, and that the object should immediately precede the verb. Such word order information can be extracted from the treebank.

Reflecting each verb class, following word orders were extracted from the treebank:

Transitive
- *Subj Obj*
- *Subj Obj-cm* (cm=case-marker; *ko* (ACC), *se* (INST))

Ditransitive
- *Subj Indirect-Obj Obj*
- *Subj Indirect-Obj Obj-cm*
- *Subj Indirect-Obj Obj-LOC*
- *Indirect-Obj Obj* (missing Subj)
- *Indirect-Obj Obj-LOC* (missing Subj)
- *Subj Indirect-Obj* (missing Obj)

Experiencer verbs
- *DAT NOM*

Copula
- *Subj Noun-complement*: Copula

Others
- *Subj Obj-LOC*: Verbs such as *jaa* 'go'
- *Object* verb collocation (whether the object appears immediately before the verb)
- *Object* verb order (the relative position of the object with respect to the verb; left or right)

Based on the above patterns, following are some main trends:

- Close to 11% of argument structures are non-canonical,
- Non-canonical order for "Subj Obj", "Subj Noun-complement" (for copula verbs) is rare; "Obj Subj" = 6.7% out of all "Subj Obj" instances, while "Noun-complement Subj" = 3.6% out of all "Subj Noun-complement" instances,
- When Obj is not case-marked it is more likely to appear next to the verb (82.2%), than when it is case-marked (47.2%)
- Total number of Obj appearing after the verb is extremely rare (.35% of all object verb instances)[7] (this is not considering clausal objects that occur with verbs such as *kaha* 'say').

The canonical order is encoded in the tree-template and non-canonical word order is therefore reflected in a separate tree. We can see this in the representations in figure 2 and figure 3. Figure 2 represents the canonical order and figure 3 the order with object fronting. To reflect that this is a non-canonical word order, a null node is also shown in object's canonical pre-verbal position and indexed to the fronted object.

As just noted, non-canonical word order due to changes in argument structure order is not so frequent. The occurrence of non-canonical word order has been attributed to information structure constraints. For example, (Butt and King, 1996) have argued for the following word position - discourse function mapping for Urdu/Hindi: Sentence initial → TOPIC, Pre-verbal (immediate) → FOCUS, Post-verb → BACKGROUND INFORMATION, Pre-verbal (others) → COMPLETIVE INFORMATION.

Other related work on Hindi word order (e.g. Kidwai (2000)[8], Gambhir (1981), Kachru (2006)) also have a discourse-centric explanation. There is some work that has investigated word order variation effects during sentence processing. Vasishth et al. (2012), Vasishth (2004) investigated the effect of discourse on word order variation, while Patil et al. (2008) looked at effects of word order and information structure on intonation.

4.1.2 Non-projective dependencies

A dependent and its head can sometimes be discontiguous; the constraint that the head-dependent pair is contiguous is called the projectivity constraint. More formally, an arc $i \rightarrow j$ is projective if, for node *i* with *j* as its child, any node *k*, such that $i < k < j$ (or $i > k > j$) is dominated by i ($i \rightarrow^* k$) (Nivre and Nilsson, 2005).

The dependency treebank being used has 3755 non-projective arcs. Amongst these, intra-clausal dependencies related to verbal heads account for 16.2% of non-projective arcs and 5% of such dependencies are due to intra-clausal dependencies with nominal head. While relative clauses (RCs)

[7] We note here that this pattern and the fact that non-canonical structures are rare, might be because our corpus is a written corpus. Spoken Hindi has more postverbal material and non-canonical structures than written Hindi.

[8] Kidwai (2000) has a syntactic explanation but her syntactic features have discourse motivations (topic, focus etc.).

account for close to 25% of all non-projective arcs. For a more detailed classification of non-projective dependencies in Hindi, see Mannem et al. (2009).

Embedded relative clauses and correlatives with canonical word order lead to projective structures, while right extraposed relative clauses such as the one shown in figure 5 are non-projective. A right extraposed relative clause can also be projective, this can happen in certain non-canonical configurations and is quite rare (see Table 1).

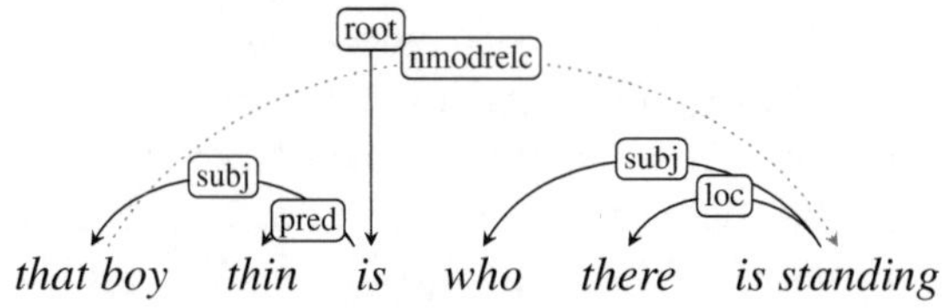

Figure 5: Right extraposed relative clause (non-projective).

Type	Projective	Non-projective	Total
Embedded	2.4	.2	2.6
Correlative	17.3	.5	17.8
Right extraposed	2.5	76.7	79.2

Table 1: Relative clause types (Occurrence in %). Total RC count = 1198.

Recently, Levy et al. (2012) have shown that extraposed RC structures in English are difficult to process. Such structures in English are non-projective and are quite rare[9]. As opposed to this, right-extraposed RCs in Hindi are the most frequently occurring structures amongst all relative clause types (cf. table 1). Like English, these structures are also non-projective in Hindi. The question then arises as to whether these non-projective structure are also difficult to process in Hindi, and if yes, why Hindi speakers prefer such configurations, as opposed to a projective structure of embedded relative clause or correlatives?[10]

At this point in time, we can pose the following questions:
- What is the difference between the processing of a canonical structure and its non-canonical counterpart in Hindi?
- How can we quantify this difference?

To answer these questions one needs to conduct targeted experiments. We need to investigate these questions because it will help us make more informed decisions to implement the grammar and the sentence processor. For instance, if it turns out that processing non-projective relative clause structures in Hindi is easy, then what does it say about the parser adaptability based on specific language patterns? And how will that knowledge affect the design of the parser?

4.2 Prediction rules

Given the observation that predictions made by the parser will go wrong and the parser will have to make revisions (or rerank), we need to ask:

- What is predicted?
- What are the different cues that are pooled to make a prediction?
- What is the processing cost when a prediction is incorrect?
- How can we quantify this cost?
- How does the prediction system interact with other aspects of the comprehension process?

Table 2 shows how our predictions based on case-markers (when the first two arguments have been seen) can vary in terms of correctness in word order and verb class. For example, after the 1st *ko* is seen, it predicts a canonical transtive-template, this prediction changes to non-canonical transitive template in case *ne* happens to be the next case-marker; on the other hand if a *0* case-marker was encountered instead, the parser revises its prediction to a canonical ditransitive-template. These predictions have been made before arriving at the verb, this means, sometimes these predictions could be incorrect. In such a case, the verb (or additional arguments) itself will eventually help make the final revision.

So, based on the above discussion, there are 2 factors that will influence the processing cost of a prediction:

- Correct/Incorrect verb-template prediction,
- Correct/Incorrect word-order prediction

[9]Table 1 in Levy et al. (2012), P(extraposedRC|context) is 0.00004, while P(RC|context) is 0.00561.

[10]Recently, Kothari (2010) in a judgement study found no effect of discourse in Hindi native speakers' preference for correlatives over right extraposed RCs. In another judgement study involving non-restrictive RCs, Kothari shows that Hindi native speakers prefer embeddings for short RCs while right extrapositions are preferred when the RC is long.

Prediction	CO	NCO
Correct prediction	Predicted → *0 0*: copula Correct → *0 0*: copula	Predicted → *ko ne*: transitive Correct → *ko ne*: transitive
Incorrect prediction (incorrect class)	Predicted → *0 0*: copula Correct → *0 0*: transitive	Predicted → *ko ne*: transitive Correct → *ko ne*: ditransitive
Incorrect prediction (incorrect word order)	Predicted → *ko ko*: ditransitive Correct → *ko ko*: ditransitive (NCO)	Predicted → ? Correct → ?
Incorrect prediction (incorrect class and word order)	Predicted → *ko 0*: ditransitive Correct → *ko 0*: transitive (NCO)	Predicted → ? Correct → ?

Table 2: Different prediction scenarios. Canonical order: CO, Non-canonical order: NCO

Based on the presented grammar design, the processing hypothesis about the cost of such a prediction is:

Correct prediction < *Incorrect prediction (argstr order or verb class)* < *Incorrect prediction (argstr and class)*

This hypothesis will of course need to be evaluated experimentally.

5 An outline of human sentence processing using dependency parsing

We will adapt the graph-based dependency parsing paradigm (Kübler et al., 2009) to model human sentence processing. The parser will be used to compute certain cognitive measures (such as surprisal, retrieval cost; cf. Boston et al. (2008), Demberg and Keller (2008)) that will in turn be used to predict processing difficulty.

Graph-based parsing data-driven models parameterizes directly on subtrees. Arc-factored models that only exploit single head-child node pair will be implemented. The parsing algorithm comprises of finding a maximal spanning tree (MST) out of a complete graph using the arc parameters. Note here that this formulation of the parsing algorithm (McDonald et al., 2005a), (McDonald et al., 2005b) needs to be modified in order to adapt it for the goals of this paper. In particular, the algorithm needs to be incremental. It is easy to see how this can be done. Instead of starting with the complete sentence, one needs to form complete graphs out of all the available words. If the length of the sentence is n, this will involve extracting an MST n-1 times, i.e., after hearing/reading each word. By doing so, the worst case complexity of the algorithm remains unchanged. Another modification that needs to be incorporated is the use of prediction rules within the parsing process; this will involve forming complete graphs using unlexicalized tree-template (that will be predicted by already seen tokens), and extracting MST out of it. The other important task after implementing the parser will be to use the parser to compute certain measures (such as surprisal, locality-based costs). These measures can then be used to predict processing difficulty. Within the graph-based parsing paradigm, a probability model can be induced using the method proposed by McDonald et al. (2005a), McDonald et al. (2005b)[11]. Once we have such a probability model, surprisal and locality-based costs can then be computed.

To the best of our knowledge the work by Boston and colleagues (Boston et al., 2008), (Boston et al., 2011) is the only other work that has employed dependency parsing to model human sentence processing difficulty. Unlike what has been proposed here, they used a transition-based dependency parsing model (Nivre, 2003). However, their parser will not be able to correctly analyse crossing/discontiguous dependencies. In addition, they have no notion of prediction explicitly built into their system.

The other work that bears similarity with our work is that of Demberg (2010). Demberg (2010), unlike us, used a variant of lexicalized tree-adjoining grammar (a psycholinguistically motivated LTAG called P-LTAG). And although, LTAG is related to dependency grammars (Kuhlmann, 2007), the choice of grammar has a considerable impact on the parsing system that one employs to model processing difficulty. Our predicted tree template looks similar to the prediction tree of Demberg (2010). But again, the operations and mechanisms that will be employed by us to construct the syntactic structure will be influenced by the constraints put in by the properties of dependency grammar and the graph-based parsing algorithm, and will be significantly different from the P-LTAG based operations such as substitution, adjunction (and verification).

6 Issues and Challenges

Our dependency grammar based human sentence processing system presents itself as an attractive alternative to phrase structure based models currently dominant in the psycholinguistic literature. This is because of its representational simplicity and availability of efficient dependency

[11] Such a probability model can be used as an alternative to the one mentioned in section 3.3

parsing paradigms. It seems to be well suited to model expectation-based psycholinguistic theories. However, there are certain issues that will need to be eventually addressed in order for the dependency model to have comprehensive coverage.

The first issue is related to the representational aspect of dependency structures. There is considerable evidence that while processing some dependencies, for example, filler-gap dependencies, anaphora resolution, etc., human sentence comprehension system uses certain grammatical constraints (Phillips et al., 2011). These constraints (e.g. c-command) have been traditionally formalized using phrase-structure representation. If it is true that the parser does employ configurational constraints such as c-command then it will be imperative to formulate a functionally equivalent definition of c-command within the dependency framework.

The second issue is related to parser adaptation. Adapting the graph-based dependency parser in order to effectively compute the cognitive measures will be the most challenging task of this work. In particular, the same parser has to be conceptualized to compute both locality-based as well as expectation-based measures (Boston et al., 2008). In addition, the prediction system needs to be seamlessly integrated within the parsing process.

7 Conclusion

In this paper we introduced our work towards building a psycholinguistically motivated dependency grammar for Hindi. We outlined the main components of such a dependency grammar that was automatically induced using a Hindi dependency treebank. We discussed certain language patterns that were interesting psycholinguistically. We sketched how a graph-based dependency parser can be used to model sentence processing difficulty. We finally mentioned some issues with using a dependency based human sentence processing model.

References

M. Bader and M. Meng. 1999. Subject-Object Ambiguities in German Embedded Clauses: An Across-the-Board Comparison. *Journal of Psycholinguistic Research.*, 28(2):121–143.

A. Bharati, V. Chaitanya, and R. Sangal. 1995. *Natural Language Processing: A Paninian Perspective*. Prentice-Hall of India, New Delhi.

R. Bhatt, B. Narasimhan, M. Palmer, O. Rambow, D. Sharma, and F. Xia. 2009. A Multi-Representational and Multi-Layered Treebank for Hindi/Urdu. In *Proceedings of the Third LAW*, ACL-IJCNLP '09, pages 186–189.

M. F. Boston, John T. Hale, U. Patil, R. Kliegl, and S. Vasishth. 2008. Parsing costs as predictors of reading difficulty: An evaluation using the Potsdam Sentence Corpus. *Journal of Eye Movement Research*, 2(1):1–12.

M. F. Boston, J. T. Hale, S. Vasishth, and R. Kliegl. 2011. Parallel processing and sentence comprehension difficulty. *Language and Cognitive Processes*, 26(3):301–349.

J. Bresnan and R. M. Kaplan. 1982. *The Mental Representation of Grammatical Relations.* The MIT Press, Cambridge, MA.

M. Butt and T. C. King. 1996. Structural topic and focus without movement. In *M. Butt and T. H. King, eds., The First LFG Conference. CSLI Publications.*

N. Chomsky. 1965. *Aspects of the theory of syntax.* MIT Press.

N. Chomsky. 1981. *Lectures on government and binding*. Dordrecht: Foris.

N. Chomsky. 1995. *The Minimalist Program.* The MIT Press.

V. Demberg and F. Keller. 2008. Eye-tracking corpora as evidence for theories of syntactic processing complexity. In *Cognition*, volume 109, pages 193–210.

V. Demberg. 2010. *A Broad-Coverage Model of Prediction in Human Sentence Processing*. Ph.D. thesis, The University of Edinburgh.

V. Gambhir. 1981. *Syntactic restrictions and discourse functions of word order in standard Hindi.* Ph.D. thesis, University of Pennsylvania, Philadelphia.

E. Gibson. 2000. Dependency locality theory: A distance-based theory of linguistic complexity. In *A. Marantz, Y. Miyashita W. O'Neil (Eds.), Image, language, brain: Papers from the first mind articulation project symposium. Cambridge, MA: MIT Press.*

D. Grodner and E. Gibson. 2005. Consequences of the serial nature of linguistic input for sentenial complexity. *Cognitive Science*, 29(2):261–290.

J. Hale. 2001. A probabilistic earley parser as a psycholinguistic model. In *Proceedings of the NAACL*, NAACL '01, pages 1–8.

R. Hudson. 2010. *An Introduction to Word Grammar.* Cambridge University Press.

Y. Kachru. 2006. *Hindi*. John Benjamins Publishing Company, Philadelphia.

E. Kaiser and J. C. Trueswell. 2004. The role of discourse context in the processing of a flexible word-order language. *Cognition*, 94:113–147.

A. Kidwai. 2000. *XP-Adjunction in universal grammar: Scrambling and binding in Hindi- Urdu*. Oxford University Press, New York.

A. Kim, B. Srinivas, and J. Trueswell. 1998. The convergence of lexicalist perspectives in psycholinguistics and computational linguistics. In *P. Merlo and S. Stevenson (eds.), Papers from the Special Section on the Lexicalist Basis of Syntactic Processing, CUNY Conference*.

P. Kolachina, S. Kolachina, A. K. Singh, V. Naidu, S. Husain, R. Sangal, and A. Bharati. 2010. Grammar Extraction from Treebanks for Hindi and Telugu. In *Proceedings of The 7th International Conference on Language Resources and Evaluation.*

L. Konieczny. 2000. Locality and parsing complexity. *Journal of Psycholinguistic Research*, 29(6):627–645.

A. Kothari. 2010. *Processing Constraints And Word Order Variation In Hindi Relative Clauses*. Ph.D. thesis, Stanford University.

S. Kübler, R. McDonald, and J. Nivre. 2009. *Dependency Parsing*. Synthesis Lectures on Human Language Technologies. Morgan & Claypool Publishers.

M. Kuhlmann. 2007. *Dependency Structures and Lexicalized Grammars*. Ph.D. thesis, Saarland University, Saarbrücken, Germany.

R. Levy, E. Fedorenko, M. Breen, and E. Gibson. 2012. The processing of extraposed structures in english. *Cognition*, 122(1):12–36.

R. Levy. 2008. Expectation-based syntactic comprehension. *Cognition*, 106(3):1126 – 1177.

R. L. Lewis and S. Vasishth. 2005. An activation-based model of sentence processing as skilled memory retrieval. *Cognitive Science*, 29:1–45.

P. Mannem, H. Chaudhry, and A. Bharati. 2009. Insights into non-projectivity in Hindi. In *ACL-IJCNLP Student Research Workshop*.

C. D. Manning and H. Schütze. 1999. *Foundations of Statistical Natural Language Processing*. MIT Press, june.

R. McDonald, K. Crammer, and F. Pereira. 2005a. Online large-margin training of dependency parsers. In *Proceedings of the 43rd ACL*, ACL '05.

R. McDonald, F. Pereira, K. Ribarov, and J. Hajič. 2005b. Non-projective dependency parsing using spanning tree algorithms. In *Proceedings of HLT/EMNLP*.

I. Mel'čuk. 1988. *Dependency Syntax: Theory and Practice*. State University of New York Press.

J. Nivre and J. Nilsson. 2005. Pseudo-projective dependency parsing. In *Proc. Of ACL 2005*.

J. Nivre. 2003. An efficient algorithm for projective dependency parsing. In *8th International Workshop on Parsing Technologies (IWPT)*, pages 149–160.

U. Patil, G. Kentner, A. Gollrad, F. Kuegler, C. Fery, and S. Vasishth. 2008. Focus, word order and intonation in Hindi. *Journal of South Asian Linguistics*, 1(1):55–72.

C. Phillips, M. W. Wagers, and E. F. Lau. 2011. Grammatical illusions and selective fallibility in real-time language comprehension. In *J. Runner (ed.), Experiments at the Interfaces, Syntax and Semantics*, volume 37, pages 153–186.

M. Pickering and G. Barry. 1991. Sentence Processing without Empty Categories. *Language and Cognitive Processes*, 6(3):229–259.

M. Pickering. 1994. Processing Local and Unbounded Dependencies: A Unified Account. *Journal of Psycholinguistic Research*, 23(4):323–352.

I. A. Sag, T. Wasow, and E. M. Bender. 2003. *Syntactic Theory: A Formal Introduction, 2nd edition*. CSLI.

A. Staub and C. Clifton. 2006. Syntactic prediction in language comprehension: Evidence from either ... or. *Journal of Experimental Psychology: Learning, Memory, and Cognition*, 32:425 436.

W. Tabor and S. Hutchins. 2004. Evidence for Self-Organized Sentence Processing: Digging-In Effects. *Journal of Experimental Psychology: Learning, Memory, and Cognition*, 30(2):431–450.

S. Vasishth and R. L. Lewis. 2006. Argument-head distance and processing complexity: Explaining both locality and antilocality effects. *Language*, 82(4):767–794.

S. Vasishth, K. Suckow, R. L. Lewis, and S. Kern. 2010. Short-term forgetting in sentence comprehension: Crosslinguistic evidence from head-final structures. *Language and Cognitive Processes*, 25(4):533–567.

S. Vasishth, R. Shaher, and N. Srinivasan. 2012. The role of clefting, word order and given-new ordering in sentence comprehension: Evidence from Hindi. In *Journal of South Asian Linguistics*, volume 5.

S. Vasishth. 2004. Discourse Context and Word Order Preferences in Hindi. In *R. Singh (ed.), The Yearbook of South Asian Languages and Linguistics*, pages 113–127.

F. Xia and M. Palmer. 2001. Converting dependency structures to phrase structures. In *Proceedings of the First International Conference on Human Language Technology Research*.

The syntax of Hungarian auxiliaries: a dependency grammar account

András Imrényi
Jagiellonian University, Cracow
Chair of Hungarian Philology
Poland
imrenyi.andras@gmail.com

Abstract

This paper addresses a hot topic of Hungarian syntactic research, viz. the treatment of "discontinuous" constructions involving auxiliaries. The case is made for a projective dependency grammar (DG) account built on the notions of *rising* and *catenae* (Groß and Osborne, 2009). Additionally, the semantic basis of the dependency created by rising is described with a view to analogy and constructional meaning.

1 Introduction

The topic of this paper is the word order pattern illustrated below.

(1) János el fog utazni Párizsba.
John away will.3SG travel Paris.to
'John will travel to Paris.'

(2) Részt akar venni a kiállításon.
part.ACC wants take the exhibition.on
'He/she wants to take part in the exhibition'

Both examples include a discontinuity, with the auxiliaries *fog* 'will.3SG' and *akar* 'wants' intervening between two parts of the complex verbs *elutazni* 'to travel away' and *részt venni* 'to take part', respectively. Under the standard assumption that the finite auxiliaries are the roots here, taking lexical verbs as their infinitival complements, the simplest DG analysis incurs a projectivity violation:

(3)

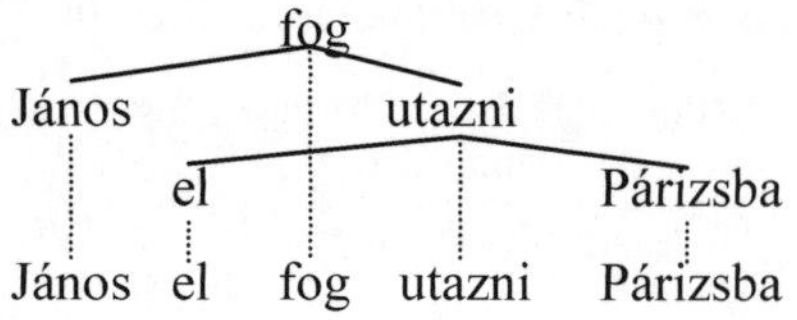

The goals of the paper are twofold.

Firstly, I will compare possible analyses of the construction, and argue for a projective DG account along the lines of Groß and Osborne (2009). In particular, it will be proposed that while *utazni* acts as the governor of *el* (licensing its appearance), the latter element takes the auxiliary as its head (a case of rising). Formal evidence in favour of the account will come from ellipsis, coordination, prosodic structure, and the placement of adverbs.

Secondly, with the above syntactic analysis in mind, I will turn to the issue whether the dependency created by rising has any associated meaning or function. It will be argued that it does, but in a way which crucially involves aspects of (clausal) constructional semantics.

The paper is concerned with a syntactic construction rather than the word class of auxiliaries. It has to be mentioned, though, that both traditional (Lengyel 2000) and generative approaches (Kenesei 2008) to Hungarian tend to narrow down the group to a few elements (including *fog* 'will' but excluding *akar* 'want', for example). I side with Kálmán C. et al. (1989), however, who identify Hungarian auxiliaries on the basis of syntactic and prosodic behaviour; roughly, appearance in the kind of construction illustrated in (1) and (2) above. I regard verbs which participate in this construction (in other words, which are collexemes of it in terms of Stefanowitsch and Gries, 2003) as auxiliaries, when and to the extent that they do so. However, this does not prevent them from being verbs, i.e. "auxiliary" is not viewed here as a distinct (let alone closed) word class of Hungarian.

In section **2**, I will present the relevant data, and make three observations against which the analyses will be matched. Section **3** compares four syntactic accounts, two each from the traditions of phrase structure grammar and dependency grammar. Section **4** addresses the relationship between rising and constructional meaning. Finally, summary and conclusions follow in section **5**.

Proceedings of the Second International Conference on Dependency Linguistics (DepLing 2013), pages 118–127,
Prague, August 27–30, 2013.

2 Data and observations

In this section, I make three observations about the construction, which will serve as a basis for evaluating analyses in section **3**. These observations are highlighted below for convenience.

1. There is a syntactic relationship between the verb modifier (VM, e.g. *el, részt*) appearing to the left of the root auxiliary and the infinitive (e.g. *utazni, venni*, with the *-ni* infinitive suffix) on its right.
2. There is also a syntactic relationship between the VM (e.g. *el, részt*) and the root auxiliary (e.g. *fog, akar*).
3. The three elements (i.e. the VM, the root auxiliary and the infinitive) form a grammatical unit, which, however, is subject to word order variation.

2.1 The link between VM and infinitive

The first, rather trivial observation is that in patterns like *el fog utazni* 'he/she will travel away' and *részt akar venni* 'he/she wants to take part', there is a syntactic relationship between the first and the third element. This relationship is one of licensing: the so-called verb modifiers (*el* 'away', *részt* 'part.ACC') could not occur in these structures were it not for the lexical verbs appearing in an infinitive form.

The two elements form a semantic unit with a higher or lower level of compositionality (cf. the oft-cited example *berúg* 'get drunk', where the VM *be* literally means 'in', and *rúg* literally means 'kick'). In addition, it is noteworthy that there is often a morphological dependency between the two elements: for example, the *-t* accusative suffix of *részt* 'part.ACC' is assigned by *venni* 'to take.' While morphological dependencies are considered separable in principle from syntactic ones (cf. Mel'čuk 1988), there is a clear tendency for such dependencies to hold between elements which are also syntactically related.

In Hungarian linguistics, the term "verb modifier"[1] (also known as "preverb") denotes a category of elements with the following properties: "(i) they occupy the position immediately preceding the verb,[2] and (ii) in the typical case they form semantically a complex verb with the base verb" (Kiefer 2003: 17). Thirdly, it can be added that the VM + verb sequence tends to behave as a single phonological word, with the word-initial stress of Hungarian falling on the first syllable of the unit.

VMs come in two subgroups, illustrated by the expressions in (4) and (5).

(4) a. moziba megy
cinema.to goes
'[he/she] goes to cinema'
b. újságot olvas
newspaper.ACC reads
'[he/she] reads newspaper' / '[he/she] is engaged in newspaper-reading'

(5) a. ki-megy
out-goes
'[he/she] goes out'
b. el-olvas
away-reads
'[he/she] reads [to the end]'

Whereas the VMs of the complex verbs listed in (4) satisfy an argument of the base verb, so-called verbal particles such as *el* 'away', *be* 'in' and *ki* 'out' fail to do so (cf. Kiefer ibid.). Nevertheless, there is considerable agreement in the literature that the two types of VMs are amenable to essentially the same syntactic analysis, cf. the analogous examples in (6).

(6) a. moziba fog menni
'[he/she] will go to cinema'
b. újságot akar olvasni
'[he/she] wants to read newspaper'
c. ki fog menni
'[he/she] will go out'
d. el akarja olvasni
away wants.DEF.OBJ read
'[he/she] wants to read it'

In conclusion, it would be hard to deny that there is a relationship between VMs and infinitives in the construction under study. The link is evident at several levels of analysis including the lexicon, morphology, syntax and semantics. From a syntactic perspective, the relationship can be defined as licensing, a point that will be taken up later in section **3**.

2.2 The link between VM and auxiliary

Less immediately apparent is the fact that there is also a syntactic relationship between the VM and the root auxiliary. Although the two ele-

[1] As a reviewer points out, the term may be misleading as VMs are not in fact modifiers (in the sense of being adjuncts). However, I still adopt it, following standard practice in Hungarian grammar (cf. É. Kiss, 2002: 67).

[2] At least in so-called neutral clauses, cf. section **2.3**.

ments are adjacent, adjacency alone is clearly insufficient to establish the link as syntactically significant. For instance, in *this obviously contrived example*, *this* and *obviously* have little to do with one another.

However, the following data strongly suggest that the VM and the root auxiliary are more intimately related.

(7) A: János el fog utazni Párizsba?
John away will.3SG travel Paris.to
'Will John travel to Paris?'

B: Igen, el fog.
yes away will.3SG
'Yes, he will.'

In speaker B's utterance, the VM and the root auxiliary together form a well-formed clause. This would hardly be possible in the absence of a direct syntactic relationship (more specifically, a dependency) between them.[3] In particular, the analysis in (3) is rendered unlikely, since it implies the possibility of eliding an intermediate element (*utazni* 'travel') while preserving the phonological content of elements both above and below it in the tree. We will see in section **3** that this goes against what seems to be a valid generalization about the relevant cases of ellipsis.

A second argument for a direct syntactic link between the VM and the root auxiliary comes from prosodic structure. As noted above, VMs immediately preceding their base verbs form a single phonological word with them; for example, *'elutazik* '[he/she] travels away' has a single stress assigned to the first syllable. Importantly, a similar situation holds when the VM is followed by an auxiliary. For example, in *'el fog 'utazni* '[he/she] will travel away', *el* and the first syllable of *utazni* are stressed, while *fog* is unstressed, presumably because *el* and *fog* belong to the same phonological word. Under the reasonable assumption that elements forming phonological words tend to be syntactically closely related, this suggests that there is a direct link between *el* and *fog* in the syntactic hierarchy.

Thirdly, the distribution of certain adverbs also supports the conclusion that the VM and the root auxiliary form a tightly integrated unit. For example, the epistemic adverb *talán* 'perhaps' cannot occur between the VM and the auxiliary (8a), only between the auxiliary and the infinitive (8b) or externally to the VM + auxiliary + infinitive pattern (8c, 8d).

(8) a. *János el talán fog utazni Párizsba.
b. János el fog talán utazni Párizsba.
c. János talán el fog utazni Párizsba.
d. János el fog utazni talán Párizsba.
'John will perhaps travel to Paris.'

Finally, the following coordination pattern also suggests the existence of a direct link between the VM and the auxiliary. Coordinating *el akar* and *el is fog* (where *is* means 'also') would hardly be possible if VM + auxiliary sequences were not grammatical units.

(9) J. el akar és el is fog utazni Párizsba.
J. away wants and away also will travel Paris.to
'John wants to, and also will, travel to Paris.'

All in all, ellipsis and coordination facts, prosody, and the distribution of adverbs such as *talán* 'perhaps' provide converging evidence that the adjacency between the VM and the root auxiliary is syntactically significant. Precisely how this can be incorporated in a DG analysis is an issue to be addressed in section **3**.

2.3 Evidence that the three elements form a grammatical unit

Finally, a third observation about the construction is that the VM, the auxiliary and the infinitive form some kind of grammatical unit. In this regard, note first that strings such as *el akar utazni* and *el fog utazni* can be substituted by one-word predicates with a similar discourse function (10, 11).

(10) a. János el akar utazni Párizsba.
'John wants to travel to Paris.'
b. János elutazna Párizsba.
John away.travel.COND.3G Paris.to
'John would [gladly] travel to Paris.'

(11) a. János el fog utazni Párizsba.
'John will travel to Paris.'
b. János elutazik Párizsba.
John away.travel.3SG Paris.to
'John is [soon] travelling to Paris.'

Secondly, the strings mentioned can be coordinated (12) or elided by gapping (13). In the latter example, *pedig* is a marker of topic shift.

[3] As a reviewer observes, disjointed elements may appear in answer fragments, cf. German [*Wem gefällt das?* 'Who likes that?] *Mir ~~gefällt das~~ nicht* 'Not me.' However, speaker B's utterance in (7) crucially includes the root auxiliary, whereas in the German example, the root verb is elided. It seems plausible to suppose that remnants which do include the root must be continuous.

(12) János el akar utazni és el is fog utazni P.-ba.
'J. wants to, and also will, travel to Paris.'

(13) J. el fog utazni Párizsba, Mari pedig Rómába.
'J. will travel to Paris, and Mary to Rome.'

Such facts are easiest to explain if the VM + auxiliary + infinitive pattern is treated as a grammatical unit. However, it is important to observe that the unit in question is highly flexible. In particular, the word order of its elements is subject to variation, as demonstrated by the examples below.

(14) János el fog Párizsba utazni.
'John will travel to Paris.'

(15) JÁNOS fog elutazni Párizsba.
'It is John who will travel to Paris.'

As (14) shows (compared with (1)), the relative position of the infinitive and its dependent is not fixed by the construction: *Párizsba* 'to Paris' may precede as well as follow its head *utazni* 'travel.' And as (15) illustrates, certain sentence types may also rearrange the order of the VM and the auxiliary. When an identificational focus (cf. É. Kiss 1998a) such as *JÁNOS* is present in the structure, it attracts the finite auxiliary to its right, and the VM is attached to the infinitive. More precisely, it is attached to the infinitive which licenses it, a qualification made necessary by examples such as (17).

(16) János el fog tudni utazni Párizsba.
John away will be.able travel Paris.to
'John will be able to travel to Paris.'

(17) JÁNOS fog tudni elutazni Párizsba.
'It is John who will be able to travel to P.'

In Hungarian linguistics, examples such as (14) and (16) are often called neutral clauses, whereas patterns like (15) and (17) are known as non-neutral ones. Roughly, whereas a neutral declarative clause answers the question *What happened?* or *What is the situation?*, a non-neutral one is felicitous under more special communicative circumstances. The generalization that VMs immediately precede the finite verb or auxiliary is construction-specific. Clauses with identificational foci, a negative particle, an interrogative pronoun, etc. display a different word order (see also section **4**).

To conclude this section, the facts are fairly complex but substitution, coordination and ellipsis tests do suggest that the VM + auxiliary + infinitive pattern forms some kind of grammatical unit. However, this unit is hardly a unitary block that always appears in exactly the same form. Rather, it is subject to significant variation regarding the word order of its elements. In section **3**, I will argue that this unit status combined with a high degree of flexibility can be best captured with the notion of catenae as proposed by Osborne et al. (2012).

3 Competing analyses

We are now in a position to assess competing syntactic analyses of the construction. The main criterion for evaluation will be the extent to which they comply with the observations made in the previous section. Of the four accounts to be considered, the first two come from the tradition of phrase structure grammar. These will be presented in **3.1**, followed by a comparison of two DG-based solutions in **3.2**.

3.1 Phrase structure grammar

In the last decades of the 20th century, phrase structure grammar enjoyed a virtual monopoly in analyses of Hungarian word order, so much so that even those not committed to Chomskyan generative grammar chose to adopt it for descriptive purposes. Thus in their classic paper on the system of Hungarian auxiliaries, Kálmán C. et al. (1989: 52) assigned the tree diagram in (19) to the sentence below.

(18) A MIGÉRT részt akart venni a kiállításon.
'MIGÉRT [name of Hungarian company] wanted to take part in the exhibition.'

(19)

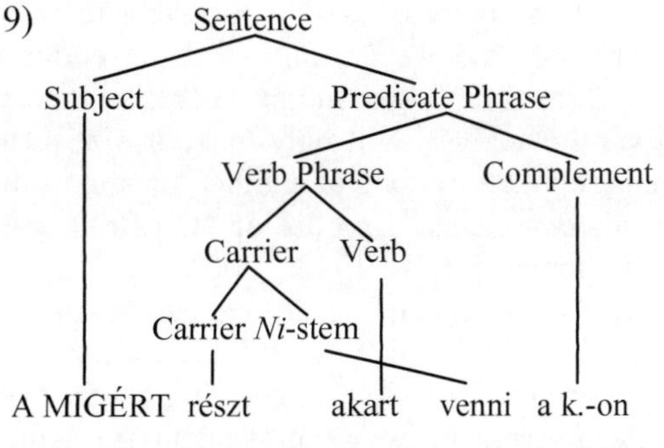

Dated as it undoubtedly is, the account is not without merits. Firstly, it captures the intuition that the three elements form a grammatical unit (**2.3**): specifically, *részt akart venni* 'wanted to take part' is analysed as a VP within the predicate phrase. Secondly, the relationship between the VM *részt* 'part.ACC' and the infinitive *venni* 'take' is signalled (cf. **2.1**), with the two forming a constituent called "carrier" in the VP.

On the other hand, the link betweeen the VM *részt* 'part.ACC' and the auxiliary verb *akart* 'wanted.3SG' is not directly indicated, despite evidence from prosodic structure (*'részt akart 'venni*), coordination (*részt akar és részt is fog venni* 'wants to, and will, take part') and the placement of adverbs.[4]

(20) a. *részt mindenképpen akart venni

b. részt akart mindenképpen venni

c. mindenképpen részt akart venni

d. részt akart venni mindenképpen
'wanted to take part by all means'

As shown in (20), the adverb *mindenképpen* 'by all means' has the same distribution vis-à-vis *részt akart venni* 'wanted to take part' as *talán* 'perhaps' did with respect to *el fog utazni* 'will travel away' in (8). This suggests that *részt* and *akart* form a tightly integrated unit.

The biggest problem with (19) though is that it violates the No Crossing Branches principle widely adopted in the tradition of phrase structure grammar. Kálmán C. et al.'s flexible approach to what passes as a well-formed tree is problematic because it grossly overgenerates the set of possible sentences. In the absence of clearly defined restrictions on the emergence of discontinuities, any word order is predicted to be possible, and the analysis is lacking explanatory power.

The second phrase structural analysis considered here is couched in transformational generative grammar. Rather than presenting a specific account found in the literature, I will attempt to come as close as possible to complying with the observations made in section **2** as well as the basic assumptions of the theory. Also, the analysis will only make use of ideas that are present in one or another version of the standard generative model of Hungarian (see in particular É. Kiss, 1998b, 2002).

Transformational generative grammar allows one to recognize the link between the VM and the infinitive at an underlying level of representation, and to let movement rules produce the surface word order. Thus, under the account in (21), the VM and the (non-finite) verb form a constituent at "deep structure" before the VM is moved out of the VP into a phrase called PredP, cf. É. Kiss (2008).

[4] The kind of ellipsis shown in (7) works perfectly with verbal particles (such as *el* 'away', *ki* 'out', etc.) but it is rather marginal with VMs like *részt*.

(21)
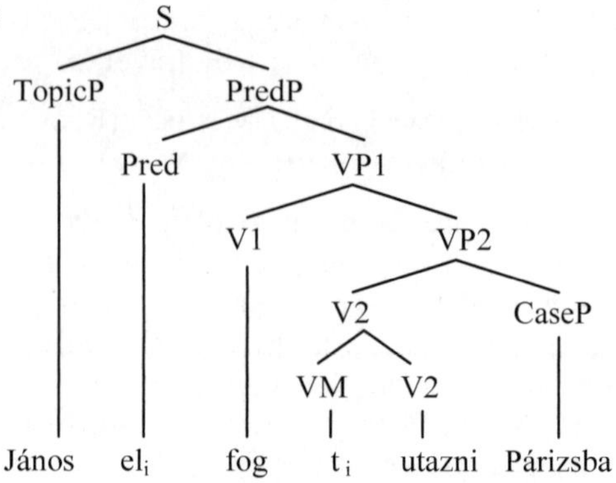

This analysis has the advantage of being more restrictive, and therefore theoretically more appealing, than the proposal of Kálmán C. et al. (1989).[5] The price paid for this is the introduction of underlying representations and transformations, which rival theories such as LFG and HPSG reject on account of their perceived lack of psycholinguistic plausibility and practical (computational linguistic) utility.

More importantly for the present discussion, while (21) is consistent with the observation that there is a syntactic link between the VM and the infinitive, and also goes some way toward recognizing the relationship between the VM and the auxiliary,[6] it fails to reflect the unit status of the VM + auxiliary + infinitive pattern. To the extent that the argumentation in section **2.3** was sound, this puts the account at a disadvantage.

3.2 Dependency grammar

As noted in the introduction, the simplest DG representation of the construction involves a projectivity violation.[7] The analysis is repeated in (22) below.

(22)
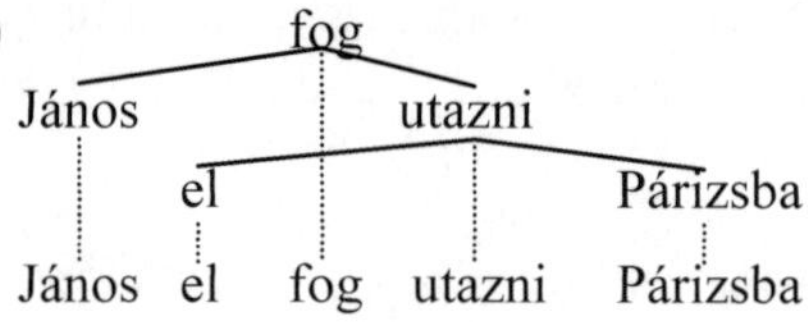

[5] The tree in (21) is simplified in ways that do not crucially affect the argumentation. Technically, the VM is in Spec,PredP, and Pred$_0$ may be the landing site of the finite verb (cf. É. Kiss 2008: 131). Thus, the VM and the finite verb may enter a Spec-Head configuration.

[6] This is so if the VM and the auxiliary are in a Spec-Head relationship, cf. footnote 5.

[7] In Nivre's formulation, "A dependency graph satisfies the constraint of projectivity with respect to a particular linear order of the nodes if, for every arc *h* [head]→ *d* [dependent] and node *w*, *w* occurs between *h* and *d* in the linear order only if *w* is dominated by *h*" (2005: 10).

The diagram signals the syntactic relationship between the VM and the infinitive, with *utazni* 'travel' identified as the head of *el* 'away.' Secondly, the root auxiliary, the infinitive and the VM form a dependency chain (cf. Hudson 1990: 99), hence a unit of DG. However, the tree in (22) implies that the adjacency of *el* and *fog* is merely a fact of word order; there is no direct dependency between them.

As is well known, versions of DG can be built either with or without the assumption of projectivity (cf. Nivre 2005: 10). Here, what needs to be established is whether there are any empirical reasons for rejecting (22). As suggested in **2.2**, the main counter-argument comes from the following type of ellipsis:

(23) A: János el fog utazni Párizsba?
John away will travel Paris.to
'Will John travel to Paris?'

B: Igen, el fog.
yes away will.3SG
'Yes, he will.'

Ellipsis is a hugely complex phenomenon, and a fully predictive account of when it is or is not possible may be an elusive research objective.[8] However, it seems fairly clear that given the structure in (22), one does not expect *utazni* to be elided while both its head *fog* 'will.3SG' and its dependent *el* 'away' are unaffected.

According to Rosta (2006: 176), "[e]llipsis involves the deletion of the phonological content of some syntactic structure, and it seems to operate rather as if (the phonology of) a branch of the syntactic tree were snipped off. Thus if the phonological content of one node is deleted, then so must be the phonological content of all nodes subordinate to it." Although this formulation is almost certainly too restrictive, as Rosta himself concedes (note especially gapping phenomena, cf. (13) and Osborne, 2005: 275–280), it does seem to be a valid generalization for the case at hand. When a sentence is reduced to a combination of elements including the root (let us call it its "core"), the core ought to be a "network within the network", with its internal structure describable by a continuous set of dependencies.

For this reason, and the further points made in **2.2**, I propose the following representation of the syntactic structure of (1), following Groß and Osborne (2009).[9]

(24)
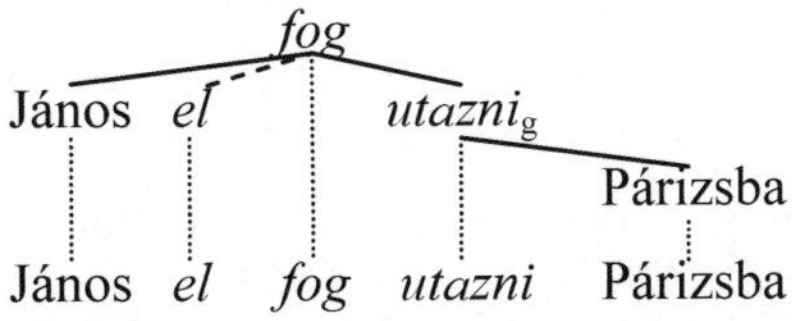

Groß and Osborne (2009: 53) crucially separate the notions of governor and head. A word's governor is the word licensing its appearance. By contrast, its head is the word that immediately dominates it. Although by default, the governor and the head are the same word, the two functions may also be associated with different nodes of the structure. In such cases, however, the head must be higher up in the tree than the governor; in other words, only "rising" can occur, not "lowering."[10]

The analysis in (24) expresses that the governor of *el* is *utazni*; this is marked by the *g* subscript of the latter. The dependency produced by rising is distinguished by a dashed dependency edge. Importantly, rising is understood only metaphorically here, since Groß and Osborne's approach is strictly non-derivational (cf. Groß and Osborne, 2009: 54). Hence, there is no such claim that the head of *el* should have been *utazni* at an underlying level of representation. For arguments supporting rising-based analyses of linguistic phenomena, see Groß and Osborne (2009: 56–64).

By separating governor and head, the analysis conforms to the observation that the VM is syntactically related to both the infinitive and the root auxiliary. Especially significant is the fact that the kind of ellipsis seen in (23) follows naturally from the proposal, which was not the case with (22). What is yet to be seen, though, is whether the grammatical unit status of the VM + auxiliary + infinitive pattern is accounted for under these assumptions.

---

[8] This is especially true for cross-linguistic predictions. As a reviewer remarks, similar word order configurations to the ones discussed in this paper exist in French, cf. *Jean l'a vu* 'John has seen it'/'John saw it', where the object clitic *l'* 'it' is licensed by the past participle *vu* 'seen' but it precedes and arguably depends on the auxiliary *a* 'has.' Still, the past participle cannot be elided (**Jean l'a ~~vu~~*). I assume that this is motivated by independent properties of French; parallel structures in different languages need not permit the same kinds of ellipsis.

[9] For a parsing-oriented approach along similar lines, see Barta et al., 2004.

[10] Groß and Osborne's concept of rising has many precedents in the literature including Duchier and Debusmann, 2001, Gerdes and Kahane, 2001, and Hudson, 2000 (cf. Groß and Osborne, 2009: 51). I adopt their approach because of its descriptive appeal; other frameworks may be seen as better developed from a model theoretic or computational linguistic perspective.

Broadly speaking, the issue is what kinds of units larger than the word a syntactic DG analysis can recognize. One traditional unit type is the DG equivalent of a phrase or constituent. In contrast with phrase structure grammar, DG treats constituents as units implied by a network of word-to-word relations (Hudson, 2007: 121) rather than as unique nodes of the tree. A theory-neutral definition of constituents, also applicable to DG, is as follows:

(25) Any node plus all the nodes that that node dominates. (Osborne, 2005: 254)

In (24), there are only two multi-word constituents: *utazni Párizsba*, and *János el fog utazni Párizsba*. By contrast, *el fog utazni* does not count as a constituent, since it does not include all the nodes that its root (*fog*) dominates.

Another established unit type recognized by DG is the dependency chain, i.e. a continuous non-branching line of $h \rightarrow d$ relations. According to Hudson (1990), "a word's phrase consists of the union of all its down-chains." In (24), the following complete down-chains of *fog* 'will.3SG' can be identified: *fog* → *János*; *fog* → *el*; and *fog* → *utazni* → *Párizsba*. Again, *el fog utazni* as analysed in (24) is not captured by the concept.

Recent years, however, have seen the recognition of a new, more inclusive unit type implied by the dependency network. Building on previous work (notably O'Grady, 1998, and Osborne, 2005), Osborne et al. (2012: 359) introduce a unit type called *catena* (Latin for 'chain'), defined over a D-tree as follows:

(26) A word, or a combination of words which is continuous with respect to dominance.

The catena concept is more inclusive than that of constituents/phrases because it does not require the unit to include all the nodes dominated by a given element. Also, it is more inclusive than traditional dependency chains since it also captures combinations of words consisting of a head and multiple dependents (schematically: $d_1 \leftarrow h \rightarrow d_2$). Finally, single words also count as catenae, which is again an extension on the previous concept of chains.

In this paper, it is not my goal to defend the catena concept (for this, see e.g. Osborne and Groß, 2012, and Osborne et al., 2012). Suffice it to say that there is considerable evidence (especially from ellipsis, analytic predicates, and idioms) suggesting that the concept is highly operational. For the present discussion, what is important is that *el fog utazni* is a catena (marked by italics in (24)). Hence, the analysis conforms not only to the observations made in **2.1** and **2.2** but also to the point that the three elements form a grammatical unit (**2.3**). Moreover, since the concept is defined in terms of dominance relations only, it is sufficiently flexible to accommodate word order variation. Thus, the examples in (14) and (15) can receive the following analyses, in which the three elements still form catenae.[11]

(27)

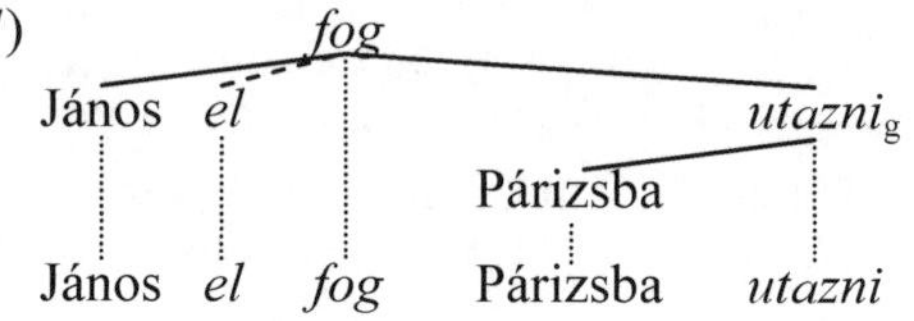

(28)

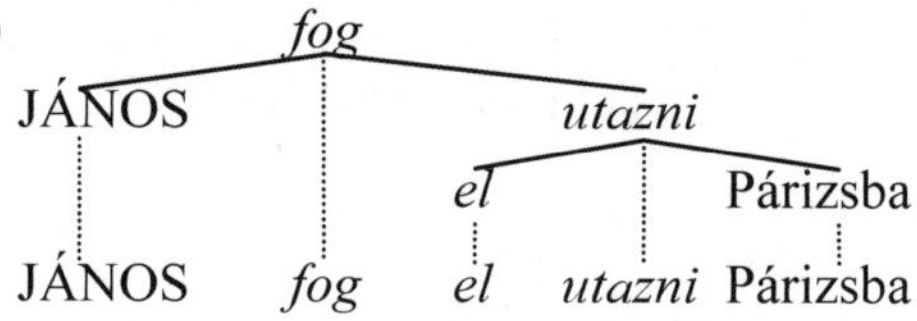

The proposal results from a happy marriage of empirical and theoretical considerations. On the one hand, there is strong empirical evidence for a direct link between the VM and the root auxiliary (cf. **2.2**), as signalled in (24) and (27). On the other, the independently motivated theory of rising and catenae provides a simple way of accounting for this as well as other relevant observations.

Also noteworthy is the fact that DG fares much better than phrase structure grammar in expressing the unit status of the VM + auxiliary + infinitive pattern. Constituency-based approaches either struggle to reflect this intuition but fail to produce a satisfactory account, cf. Kálmán C. et al. (1989), or ignore the issue altogether, cf. the analysis couched in transformational generative grammar. By contrast, the proposed DG account is flexible and restrictive enough to be faithful to the facts while also having strong theoretical appeal.

At the same time, a possible objection to the rising analysis still remains. In particular, under the assumption that dependencies ought to have an associated meaning or function, it is

[11] Two reviewers make the point that VMs may be analysable as clitics. If this is indeed the case, then the vertical projection lines of VMs have to be removed under the conventions of Groß (2011: 60). Since the dependency edges would still be the same, the basic validity of the analyses is not at stake. Whether a clitic analysis is necessary is an issue left for future research to resolve.

yet to be seen if the dependency created by rising also conforms to this requirement. In what follows, I argue that rising has a key role in coding aspects of constructional meaning.

4 Rising and constructional meaning

Since the inception of modern DG, the idea that dependencies have an associated meaning or function seems to be shared by most dependency grammarians. Tesnière already claimed that "there is never a structural connection without a semantic one" (1959: 44, my translation). And while Hudson rejects the view that dependencies are primarily a matter of meaning, he does contend that meaning is one of the properties that they "bring together", "along with word order, agreement, case choice, and so on" (2007: 130). Witness also the convergence between DG and construction grammar/CxG (Osborne and Groß, 2012, and references therein), which hinges on the notion that dependencies have a semantic side to them. After all, the basic tenet of CxG is that lexicon and syntax form a continuum, with syntactic constructions as well as morphemes, lexemes, etc. described as pairings of meaning and form.

Exceptions, however, have also been allowed by some theorists. Thus, Hudson argues that the "subject or object of a verb need not have any semantic relation to that verb at all" (2007: 130), _It seems_ *to be raining* being an example. Even more importantly for the present discussion, he posits an "extractee" dependency between *what* and *can* in the sentence below (2007: 131).

(29)
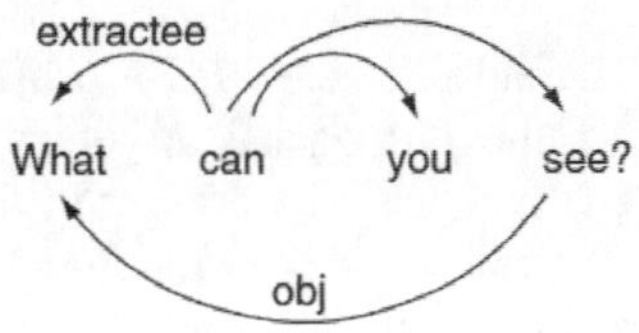

English non-subject wh-questions involve rising according to Osborne and Groß (2009: 52). In *What can you see?*, *can* is the head of *what* just as Hudson's surface analysis (above the string of words) has it. Therefore, it is significant that for Hudson, "such dependencies [as extractee] are concerned with very little but word order, and have little claim to semantic justification" (2007: 131). This suggests that the dependency created by rising perhaps does not, and need not, have an associated meaning.

Clearly, though, the word order of English wh-elements can at least receive semantic *motivation* (if not *justification*). Since they contribute a key aspect of constructional meaning (making a wh-question what it is), their prominent and distinctive linear position is natural. And while in non-projective versions of DG, the attested word order would not entail a dependency between the wh-word and the root auxiliary, there are independent reasons for subscribing to that account (e.g. the ellipsis in *What can you see and what can't you?*). In the final analysis, the dependency created by extraction or rising can be seen as "bringing together" both a semantic property (the special function of wh-questions as endowed to the construction by the wh-element) and formal ones (distinctive word order and prosody).

Generalizing from this, one may hypothesize that (certain) dependencies created by rising play a part in coding "global" aspects of constructional meaning, independently of any "local" (lexically motivated) semantic relationship between the two elements. More specifically, there may be a significant correlation between rising and sentence types (grounded in illocutionary force distinctions).[12]

As we return to Hungarian, it seems plausible to develop a similar account of the semantic background to the word order of VMs. To begin, note that whereas VMs immediately precede their base verbs in neutral positive declarative clauses lacking auxiliaries (30a), they follow them in sentence types which depart from this function in terms of illocutionary force or polarity:

(30) a. János el-utazott Párizsba.
John away-travelled.3SG Paris.to
'John travelled to Paris.'
b. Hova utazott el János?
where travelled.3SG away John?
'Where did John travel?'
c. PÁRIZSBA utazott el.
'It is to Paris that he/she travelled.'
d. Nem utazott el Párizsba.
not travelled.3SG away Paris.to
'He/she did not travel to Paris.'

[12] A similar reasoning may apply to other "meaningless" dependencies such as the subjects of English and German weather verbs (*it rains*, *es regnet*). As Jespersen remarks, "the need for this pronoun [English *it*, German *es*, etc.] was especially felt when it became the custom to express the difference between affirmation and question by means of word order *(er kommt, kommt er?*), for now it would be possible in the same way to mark the difference between *es regnet* and *regnet es?*" (Jespersen, 1924: 25).

The function of a neutral positive declarative clause such as (30a) is to profile the occurrence of an event relative to a mental space (in the sense of Fauconnier 1985). Here, the listener learns about the occurrence of a travelling event in the past (a mental space distinct from the present), involving John as the mover and Paris as the goal. At the core of the construct is the predicate *elutazott*, which has the function of a schematic clause. It may also stand by itself meaning 'He/she travelled away.' With respect to this clausal core, *János* 'John' and *Párizsba* 'to Paris' simply elaborate the mover and the goal, respectively.

By contrast, (30b,c,d) depart from the function of (30a) in one or another way. (30b) is used to inquire about John's destination; (30c) identifies Paris as the goal to the exclusion of other possibilities; and finally, (30d)'s speaker denies the occurrence of the travelling event. Although not all deviations from the neutral positive declarative clause type are signalled in this way, it is reasonable to suggest that the inversion of VM and finite verb plays a prominent role in coding clause type distinctions.[13]

From this perspective, the word order (and by implication, the rising) of the VM in the Hungarian auxiliary construction can be motivated by two interrelated facts. Firstly, the auxiliaries in question set up mental spaces in which an event unfolds. For example, *fog* 'will' sets up a space for talking about future events, *akar* 'want' a space for discussing somebody's intentions, etc. Since mental spaces are also implicit in the semantic structures of one-word predicates, it is natural to roll space-building verbs and verbs denoting events in those spaces into complex predicates. As noted in **2.3**, VM + auxiliary + infinitive patterns have a function analogous to that of VM + V sequences. The word order of the VM in the former can be seen as a reflex of complex predicate formation motivated by such analogies.

Secondly, the resulting word order has the advantage of allowing for a salient and regular way of expressing clause type distinctions. Consider the following parallels:

	positive	*negative*
past	elutazott 'he/she travelled away'	nem utazott el 'he/she did not travel away'
present	elutazik 'he/she is travelling away'	nem utazik el 'he/she is not travelling away'
future	el fog utazni 'he/she will travel away'	nem fog elutazni 'he/she will not travel away'

Table 1. Polarity and word order in Hungarian

In all three tenses, VM + finite verb/auxiliary order is associated with positive polarity, and a different linearization with its opposite. If the VM did not precede the root auxiliary in the future tense, *fog elutazni* and *nem fog elutazni* would stand in opposition, and the semantic contrast would be coded less saliently as well as less regularly across the paradigm.

To conclude, I have argued in this section that the word order (and assuming projectivity, the rising) of VMs codes important global aspects of constructional meaning. Firstly, it establishes a formal parallel between catenae with analogous functions (cf. the left-hand column in Table 1). Secondly, the VM + auxiliary pattern of neutral declarative clauses allows for a salient and regular way of coding sentence type distinctions (cf. the three rows in the table). It seems likely that other "meaningless" dependencies such as Hudson's "extractee" and the subject of English weather verbs (cf. footnote 12) may receive a similar motivation.

5 Conclusions

In this paper, I made the case for a projective DG analysis of the Hungarian auxiliary construction. In **2**, evidence was presented that in VM + auxiliary + infinitive patterns, there were syntactic links both between the VM and the infinitive and between the VM and the auxiliary. In addition, it was argued that the three elements formed a grammatical unit. In **3**, four analyses were compared, with the result that only the DG account based on rising and catenae conformed to all of the above observations. Finally, section **4** highlighted aspects of constructional meaning and analogy as motivating factors for the form of the construction.

Acknowledgments

The research reported here was supported by the Hungarian Scientific Research Fund

[13] Compare also Goldberg's (2006: 166–182) account of English subject-auxiliary inversion (SAI). According to Goldberg, SAI as a "sytematic difference in form" signals a "systematic difference in function" (178) vis-à-vis prototypical sentences (which are positive and declarative). However, "it is certainly not the only possible device" (181) in this capacity. For a more detailed account of English and Hungarian inversion, see Imrényi (2012).

(project no. K100717). I also thank Timothy Osborne and three anonymous reviewers for many insightful comments and suggestions. All remaining errors are my own.

References

Barta, Csongor, Ricarda Dormeyer and Ingrid Fischer .2004. Word order and discontinuities in a DG for Hungarian. *Proceedings of the 2nd Conference on Hungarian Computational Linguistics*. Juhász Nyomda, Szeged. 19–27.

Duchier, Denys and Ralph Debusmann. 2001. Topology dependency trees: A constraint based account of linear precedence. *Proceedings from the 39th annual meeting of the ACL*. 180–187.

É. Kiss, Katalin. 1998a. Identificational focus versus information focus. *Language* 74: 245–273.

É. Kiss, Katalin. 1998b. Mondattan. In: É. Kiss Katalin, Kiefer Ferenc and Siptár Péter, *Új magyar nyelvtan*. Budapest: Osiris. 1–184.

É. Kiss, Katalin. 2002. *The syntax of Hungarian*. CUP, Cambridge.

É. Kiss, Katalin. 2008. Tagadás vagy egyeztetés? *Magyar Nyelv* 104: 129–143.

Fauconnier, Gilles. 1985. *Mental spaces: Aspects of meaning construction in natural language*. MIT Press, Cambridge MA.

Gerdes, Kim and Sylvain Kahane. 2001. Word order in German: A formal dependency grammar using a topology model. *Proceedings from the 39th annual meeting of the ACL*. 220–227.

Goldberg, Adele. 2006. *Constructions at work: the nature of generalization in language*. OUP, Oxford.

Groß, Thomas. 2001. Clitics in Dependency Morphology. *Depling 2011 Proceedings*: 58–68.

Groß, Thomas and Timothy Osborne. 2009. Toward a practical dependency grammar theory of discontinuities. *SKY J. of Ling.* 22: 43–90.

Heine, Bernd. 1993. *Auxiliaries: cognitive forces and grammaticalization*. OUP, Oxford.

Hudson, Richard. 1990. *English Word Grammar*. Blackwell, Oxford.

Hudson, Richard. 2000. Discontinuities. In: Kahane, Sylvaine (ed.), *Les grammaires de dépendance. Traitement automatique des langues 41*. Hermes, Paris. 7–56.

Hudson, Richard. 2007. *Language networks. The new Word Grammar*. OUP, Oxford.

Imrényi, András. 2012. Inversion in English and Hungarian: comparison from a cognitive perspective. In: Hart, Christopher (ed.), *Selected Papers from UK-CLA Meetings, 1*. 209–228.

Jespersen, Otto. 1924. *The philosophy of grammar*. George Allen & Unwin Ltd, London.

Kálmán C., György, Kálmán László, Nádasdy Ádám and Prószéky Gábor. 1989. A magyar segédigék rendszere. *Általános Nyelvészeti Tanulmányok* XVII: 49–103.

Kenesei, István. 2008. A segédigék. In: Kiefer Ferenc ed. *Strukturális Magyar Nyelvtan 4. A szótár szerkezete*. Akadémiai Kiadó, Budapest. 615–620.

Kiefer, Ferenc. 2003. A kétféle igemódosítóról. *Nyelvtudományi Közlemények* 100: 177–186.

Lengyel, Klára. 2000. A segédigék és származékaik. In: Keszler, Borbála (ed.), *Magyar grammatika*. Nemzeti Tankönyvkiadó, Budapest. 252–258.

Mel'čuk, Igor. 1988. *Dependency Syntax: Theory and Practice*. The SUNY Press, Albany, N.Y.

Nivre, Joakim. 2005. *Dependency grammar and dependency parsing*. Vaxjo University.

O'Grady, William. 1998. The syntax of idioms. *Natural Language and Linguistic Theory* 16: 279–312.

Osborne, Timothy. 2005. Beyond the constituent: A dependency grammar analysis of chains. *Folia Linguistica* 39: 251–297.

Osborne, Timothy and Thomas Groß. 2012. Constructions are catenae. Construction Grammar meets Dependency Grammar. *Cognitive Linguistics* 23 (1): 163–214.

Osborne, Timothy, Michael Putnam and Thomas Groß. 2012. Catenae: Introducing a novel unit of syntactic analysis. *Syntax* 15 (4): 354–396.

Rosta, Andrew. 2006. Structural and distributional heads. In: Kensei Sugayama and Richard Hudson (eds.), *Word Grammar. New perspectives on a theory of language structure*. Continuum, London. 171–203.

Stefanowitsch, Anatol and Stefan Th. Gries. 2003. Collostructions: Investigating the inter-action between words and constructions. *International Journal of Corpus Linguistics* 8 (2): 209–43.

Tesnière, Lucien. 1959. *Éléments de syntaxe structurale*. Klincksieck, Paris.

Subordinators with Elaborative Meanings in Czech and English

Pavlína Jínová, Lucie Poláková, Jiří Mírovský
Charles University in Prague, Faculty of Mathematics and Physics
Institute of Formal and Applied Linguistics
Czech Republic
{jinova|polakova|mirovsky}@ufal.mff.cuni.cz

Abstract

This paper is focused on description of hypotactic constructions (constructions with subordinating conjunctions) with "elaborative" meanings. In dependency-based linguistic literature, they are referred to as *hypotactic coordinations* or also (a subset of) *false dependent clauses*. The analysis makes use of syntax- and discourse-annotated corpora of Czech and English and thus offers an empirically grounded contrastive study of the phenomena.

1 Motivation and Background

One of the basic means of expressing syntactic dependency are subordinating conjunctions (henceforth subordinators). They also signal the semantic type of the dependency relation, i.e. the semantic relation holding between the dependent and the governing clause. Some of them have several semantic interpretations. In this paper, we describe those uses of subordinators that operate between two syntactically dependent but semantically independent contents. In other words, the clause they introduce is formally dependent, but semantically it expresses an elaborative (coordinating, restating, etc.) meaning. For the purposes of this paper, we call them *hypotactic coordinations* (see Panevová 2012).[1]

The analysis is anchored in the theoretical framework of Prague School of structuralism and its extension – functional generative description (FGD, Sgall et al. 1986). It was carried out on 50 thousand Czech sentences from the Prague Discourse Treebank, and on a similar amount of English data from the Wall Street Journal – Penn Discourse Treebank.

In linguistic theories of dependency, there are several ways of understanding the relation between formal and semantic principles of a sentence composition. Czech linguistic tradition usually distinguishes hypotaxis and parataxis as two basic formal principles of combining clauses to create a compound sentence. In majority, the linguistic community agrees that **hypotaxis** corresponds mostly to the semantic relation of **determination** (one clause semantically complements or enriches the other, building together one content), and **parataxis** corresponds to the semantic principle of **coordination** (connecting two semantically autonomous contents – the second clause adds some new information to the first clause) (Hrbáček 2000). There are, however, discrepancies between these forms and their functions.

Such a phenomenon (correspondence between hypotaxis–determination, parataxis–coordination and also their discrepancies) was described earlier in structuralist works (Karcevskij 1929) and later in FGD for morphological and also syntactical level of linguistic analysis as asymmetric dualism of forms and functions (Panevová 1980, 2012). The phenomenon is depicted in Figure 1. The solid arrows symbolize the most common relations between the form and the meaning, the dashed arrows stand for other relations, i.e. coordination realized in the hypotactic form and determination realized in the paratactic form.

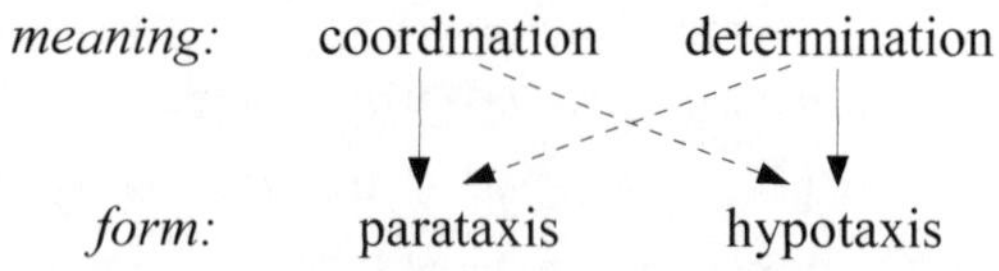

Figure 1: A schema of the asymmetric dualism between formal and semantic relations (Panevová 2012)

In the annotation of discourse structure, the account of semantic types[2] of relations between discourse units deliberately disregards the notion

[1] Primarily, the term *hypotactic coordination* was used on the level of a simple clause description, for constructions such as "mum with dad".

[2] e.g. temporality, causality, contrast

Proceedings of the Second International Conference on Dependency Linguistics (DepLing 2013), pages 128–136,
Prague, August 27–30, 2013.

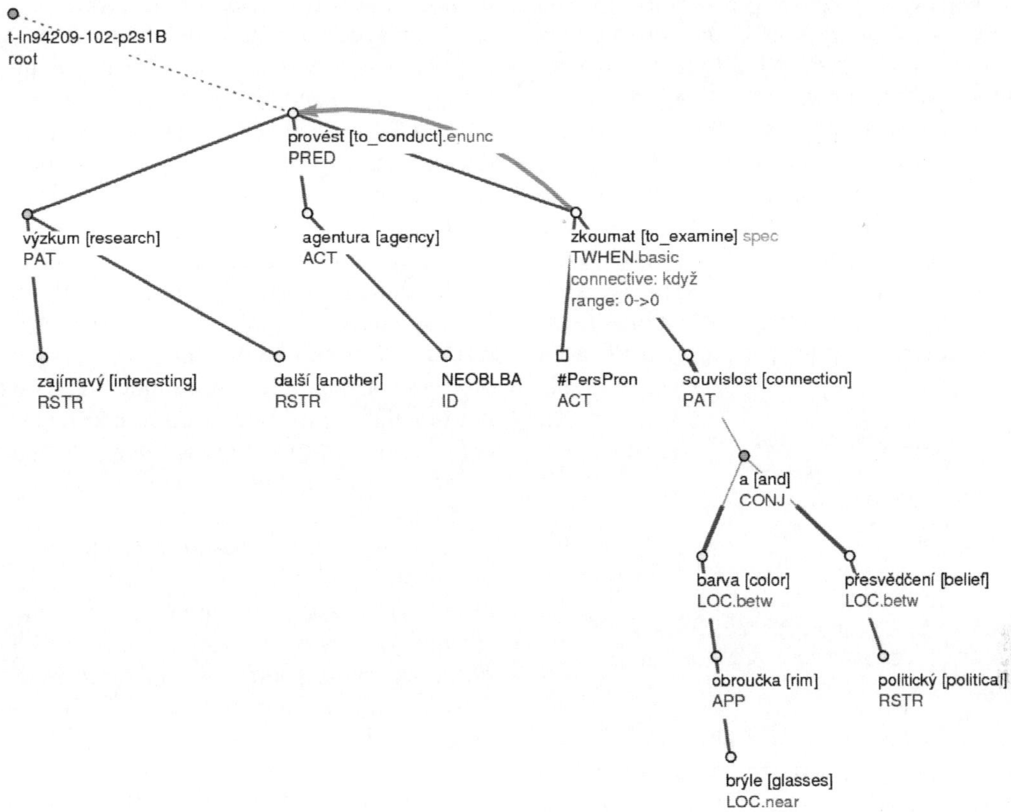

Figure 2: The dependency tree of the example sentence (1) with a thick arrow representing a discourse relation between two verbal nodes.

of syntactic parataxis/hypotaxis, in order to liberate the perception of discourse structure from the sentential syntax.

In this paper, we look back from the discourse structure to the sentential syntax. From this point of view, for one discourse-semantic (or cognitive) type (e.g. causality), there are several language means (forms) of expression (e.g. hypotactic and paratactic constructions on the inter-clausal level).

On the general level, we are interested in the question how discourse semantics is realized formally in the sentence, our specific question is to what degree the correspondence hypotaxis–determination and parataxis–coordination on the sentence level analysis holds also for the discourse level analysis. In other words, we want to see if e.g. causality, a basic semantic concept of connecting propositions in discourse, is a matter of hypotactic constructions or if it is rather a matter of parataxis. Jínová et al. (2011) offered an overview of intra- and inter-sentential distributions of discourse relations in the Prague Discourse Treebank. Here, we are interested in hypotactic/paratactic distributions of discourse relations[3] in order to either confirm or disprove that tendencies holding for the principles of sentence composition hold also for discourse composition.

In the study presented in this paper we focus on one part of the problem stated above – subordinators with elaborative meaning. The annotation of explicit[4] discourse connectives (with subordinators being a subset of them) and their discourse functions revealed some discrepancies in the perception of the sentence and discourse meanings. Subordinating connectives in constructions which we call *hypotactic coordinations* became one of the most visible differences between the sentence and discourse analysis in the Prague approach.

Only thanks to the more cognitive-based[5] discourse annotation against the background of the dependency-based syntactical tagging of the same data, we were first able to identify these constructions and study them empirically. As constructions with subordinating conjunctions,

[3] those realized within a compound sentence
[4] present on the surface
[5] or content-based, according to Panevová (2010)

they are tagged – accordingly to their form on the level of language meaning – as constructions with dependent clauses[6]. As discourse connectives, these subordinators are tagged in accordance with the elaborative meaning they express (the level of cognitive content), see Example (1) and Figure 2. The tree diagram shows the syntactic dependency of the clause introduced by *když* (*when*), and at the same time, the discourse tag "spec" for *specification*, which is a typical elaborative category (the prototypical temporal reading is considered inappropriate or marginal in this case).

(1) Další zajímavý výzkum provedla agentura NEOBLBA, **když** zkoumala souvislost mezi barvou obrouček u brýlí a politickým přesvědčením.

Another interesting research was conducted by the NEOBLBA agency **when** it examined a connection between the color of glasses rims and political beliefs.

Apart from the analysis of Czech subordinators, we were also interested in another theoretical issue, where the empirical data of the kind we had at our disposal could lead to other findings: Do other languages demonstrate the same or similar examples of the described asymmetric dualism? We were able to look into this issue on discourse- and syntax-annotated English data of the Penn Discourse Treebank.

The paper is structured as follows: in Section 2, the two corpora used for the analysis (Prague Discourse Treebank 1.0 and Penn Discourse Treebank 2.0) are briefly introduced. Section 3 presents the distribution of types of intra-sentential discourse relations (in total and in hypotactic constructions) in the Prague Discourse Treebank. Sections 4 and 5 are devoted to the analyses of Czech and English subordinators in *hypotactic coordinations*, respectively, and we summarize our findings in the concluding Section 6.

2 Resources used (PDiT and PDTB)

Prague Discourse Treebank 1.0[7] (PDiT, Poláková et al. 2012) is an annotation extension of the Prague Dependency Treebank 2.5[8] (PDT, Bejček et al. 2012). PDiT consists of approx. 50 thousand sentences of Czech newspaper texts manually annotated with discourse relations anchored by explicit (i.e. surface present) connectives. The annotation was carried out directly on the dependency trees (of the tectogrammatical (or syntactico-semantic) layer of PDT, see Sgall et al. 1986).

Penn Discourse Treebank 2.0[9] (PDTB, Prasad et al. 2008) is a manually annotated treebank of English texts from the Wall Street Journal, its size is comparable to the PDiT (again, approx. 50 thousand sentences). The annotation comprises both explicit and implicit discourse relations. In comparison with the Prague approach, the annotation was carried out on raw texts and only then mapped onto the syntactic trees.

Let us emphasize that all numbers and examples from PDiT that we present in this paper have been measured on and taken from the *training* and *development test* parts of the data (9/10 of the treebank, approx. 44 thousand sentences). The *evaluation test* part of the data thus remains unobserved.

3 Discourse relations and hypotactic structures in PDiT

In order to examine how discourse level analysis is related to the principles of sentence composition, all realizations of discourse relations within one (compound) sentence were measured over the data of PDiT. Then, as our interest here lies in subordinators, the percentage of subordinate structures among all intra-sentential realizations was measured.

Distribution of individual types of discourse relations[10] for subordinate structures is given in Table 1. It displays the total number of intra-sentential realizations for each semantic type of discourse relation and the percentage of subordinate structures for each type of relation. The remaining fraction consists of predominantly paratactic forms and a small number of parenthetical and other marginal structures. On the basis of these data, the following observations can be made.

First, all discourse intra-sentential relations whose syntactic parallels are treated by in Czech linguistic tradition as cases of **determination** (or content-dependency) – i.e. *purpose, condition – result of the condition, synchrony, conces-*

[6] For details on the annotation principles of the Prague Dependency Treebank, see Mikulová et al. (2005).

[7] http://ufal.mff.cuni.cz/discourse/

[8] http://ufal.mff.cuni.cz/pdt2.5/

[9] http://www.seas.upenn.edu/~pdtb/

[10] Because of their nature, we exclude pragmatic relations from the analysis. They represent other types of discourse meanings.

sion, precedence – succession and *reason – result* (Hrbáček 2000, Daneš et al. 1987) are realized in PDiT as subordinate structures in 50% of cases or more. The least distinctive is this result for the relation of *reason – result*, the most distinctive for the relation of *purpose* (*purpose* was only realized in the hypotactic structure).

type of discourse relation	number of occurrences within one sentence in PDiT[11]	hypotactic structures (in %)
purpose	372	100
condition – result of the condition	1,171	99
synchrony	140	84
concession	561	82
precedence – succession	495	68
confrontation	312	55
reason – result	1,428	51
explication	89	26
restrictive opposition	87	15
specification	453	13
exemplification	22	5
correction	300	4
opposition	1,235	4
conjunction	5,389	1
gradation	196	0.5
conjunctive alternative	62	0
disjunctive alternative	234	0
equivalence	38	0
generalization	8	0

Table 1: Intra-sentential discourse relations in PDiT

Second, with the exception of *confrontation* (see below in this section), all relations whose syntactic parallels are treated as cases of **coordination** (or content parallelism) are realized as hypotactic structures much less often than the first group. For four types of relations (*disjunctive* and *conjunctive alternative, equivalence* and *generalization*), no hypotactic realization was found in PDiT.

These findings corroborate the hypothesis about a symmetrical relation between hypotaxis and determination on one side, and parataxis and coordination on the other. Of course, with the exception of *purpose*, all discourse types whose syntactic parallel is treated as determination have also paratactic realizations documented in PDiT (for *reason – result*, they represent almost a half of the occurrences) and the majority of discourse types whose syntactic parallel is treated as content parallelism (coordination) was documented also as a hypotactic form. These hypotactic forms are, however, in sum much less frequent than paratactic forms of relations in the first group, and thus they represent a linguistically interesting phenomenon that has not been described yet on the basis of a larger corpus material. Therefore, in Section 4, we introduce a detailed analysis of types of these structures according to their formal characteristics. We call them *hypotactic coordinations* further on.

Before we proceed further, two types of the PDiT discourse relations, namely *confrontation* and *explication*, require a special comment. The syntactic parallel of *confrontation* is treated as a type of semantic coordination (Daneš et al. 1987, p. 462) – two pieces of content are put side by side and compared (see Example (8)). On the other hand, comprehensive description of Czech syntax distinguishes paratactic and hypotactic means of its realization (ibid.) and thus reflect its special status among coordinations. Our data confirms this status – the relation of *confrontation* is in 55 % of cases realized in hypotactic structures.

The second PDiT relation that deserves a special comment is *explication* – it is not a basic relation in grammatical descriptions of the Czech syntax, it was newly introduced for the discourse level analysis of PDiT. From the semantic point of view, it has a mixed nature between determination (an explanation of the content of one text unit is given in the second text unit) and content parallelism (these contents are somehow similar).[12] Because of this mixed nature, we ex-

[11] Please note again that all numbers related to PDiT refer to the training and development test parts of the data (9/10 of the treebank, 43,955 sentences).

[12] Cf. for example the context (A), where the dependent clause expresses an explanation of the fact of a late interest by saying what "late" means.

```
(A) O studium svého syna jste se
začal zajímat pozdě, protože ofi-
ciální termín přihlášek na střední
školy a učňovská zařízení vypršel
s koncem února.
```

clude *explication* from further analysis. Typical connectives for this relation in Czech are paratactic. Hypotactic realizations of this relation employ the same connectives as *reason – result* (26 % of intra-sentential realizations in PDiT).

4 Subordinators with elaborative meanings in PDiT

According to their formal structure, we can distinguish four main types of dependent clauses expressing elaborative meanings.

4.1 Clauses with a specific unambiguous structure

First, there are certain hypotactic formal means in Czech that only express one particular coordination relation and no others. We call them specific structures. These hypotactic structures are not very frequent in our data and they were only documented for *correction* (11 occurrences, connective *místo (toho,) aby* (*instead of*, lit. *instead of that, that*)) and *conjunction* (2 occurrences, connective *kromě toho, že* (*besides*, lit. *besides that, that*)). These structures are exemplified in (2) and (3).

(2) **Kromě toho, že** je kompatibilní s MS-DOS, podporuje řadu programů pro postižené osoby.

Besides being compatible with MS-DOS, it supports a variety of programs for disabled people.

(Lit: **Besides that, that** it is compatible with MS-DOS...)

(3) **Místo aby** clo od poslanců vymáhali, říkali jim "jen jeďte, jen jeďte".

Instead of exacting the customs from the members of parliament, they told them "just go, just go".

(Lit: **Instead that** the customs from the-members-of-parliament they-exacted, they-told them "just go, just go".)

These examples suggest that the specific status of these *hypotactic coordinations* is connected with the form of the subordinators – they are not regular conjunctions, they are composed of several elements: a preposition, (optionally of) a relative pronoun, and a conjunction.

4.2 Relative clauses

Second, some relative clauses are known to have other functions than only to determine the noun phrase. Rather, they provide additional information which can be expressed easily in a separate sentence (often they also express temporal succession of events). There is a possibility to consider these cases relevant for discourse analysis in our sense. In the Czech description of syntax, they are mostly called *false relative clauses* (Daneš et al. 1987, p. 533)[13], in English they are viewed as non-restrictive relative clauses (Quirk et al. 1992). As far as we know, however, there are no clear criteria for distinguishing semantically autonomous contents from determined contents in relative clauses, or, in our view, discourse-relevant cases from the other ones. Often it is impossible to say whether the relative clause only determines the noun phrase or continues the discourse. For the PDiT annotation, it was decided that only those cases are marked where there is (apart from the relative pronoun/adverb) an explicit connective present in the relative clause.

In PDiT data, we were able to document 45 cases of *opposition*, 24 cases of *conjunction*, 6 cases of *restrictive opposition*, 2 cases of *confrontation* and 1 case of *correction* expressed between a relative clause and its governing clause. Examples of such a realization of *opposition* and *conjunction* are given in (4) and (5).

(4) Chtěli jsme hrát nátlakový fotbal, **který však** ztroskotal na kvalitní obraně Benešova.

Lit: We wanted to play an aggressive football, **which however** failed on a high-quality defence of Benešov.

(5) Kuvajťan byl rychlou záchrannou službou převezen do pražské Thomayerovy nemocnice, **kde** byl **také** operován.

The Kuwaiti was transported by the ambulance to the Prague Thomayer hospital, **where** he **also** underwent a surgery.

You became interested in the studies of your son too late, **because** the official deadline for applications for high schools and secondary vocational schools has expired at the end of February.

[13] or *improper relative clauses*, in Czech *nepravé věty vedlejší*

4.3 Clauses formally equal to regular hypotactic structures

The third group of *hypotactic coordinations* is represented by structures formally indistinguishable from regular dependency structures. In Czech linguistic tradition, these types of dependent clauses are also often called “false” (or “improper”), as they formally signal dependency but semantically express an elaborative relation between two independent propositions. Table 2 lists all types and number of occurrences of these structures that we were able to document in the PDiT data.

Example (1) from the introductory section shows such a case of *specification,* which is formally expressed as a construction with a dependent temporal clause and the subordinator *když* (*when*), Example (6) below shows the same situation for *confrontation,* which is formally expressed as a construction with a dependent conditional clause and the subordinator *jestliže* (*if*).

(6) **Jestliže** v roce 1993 jich bylo 8650, což je vytížení kapacity lázní asi na 65 až 70 procent, **tak** v letošním roce by jich mělo být již 9745.

If there were 8,650 of them in 1993, which represents the capacity utilization of the spa to about 65 to 70 percent, **then** this year there should be already 9,745 of them.

relation	number of occurrences in PDiT	connectives
confrontation	9	2 *-li* (*if*), 2 *jestliže* (*if*), 3 *když* (*when*), 1 *i když* (*although*), 1 *přestože* (*although*)
conjunction	14	2 *aby* (*(as) to*), 11 *když* (*when*), 1 *jestliže* (*if*), 1 *zatímco* (*while*)
correction	1	1 *kdyby* (*if*)
exemplification	1	1 *například když* (*for example when*)
opposition	3	1 *zatímco* (*while*), 2 *i když* (*although*)
restrictive opposition	5	4 *i když* (*although*), 1 *když* (*when*)
specification	57	57 *když* (*when*)

Table 2: “False” dependent clauses in PDiT

The findings in Table 2 show that these structures are rather sparse. To illustrate how frequent the *hypotactic coordinations* are for each subordinator from Table 2, we measured types of relations which were expressed by each of them in PDiT. The results are summarized in Table 3.

connective	occurrences	dominant type of relation (in %)	hypotactic coordinations (in %)
aby	390	*purpose* (94)	0.5
-li	272	*condition* (97)	1
když	499	*condition* (42), *precedence – succession* (21), *synchrony* (16)	15
i když	166	*concession* (90)	4
jestliže	85	*condition* (92)	4
přestože	87	*concession* (98)	2
kdyby	155	*condition* (89), *concession* (10)	1
zatímco (regular use)	176	*confrontation* (90), *synchrony* (8)	92

Table 3: Subordinators in hypotactic coordinations in PDiT

Despite this rare use of subordinators in *hypotactic coordinations*, there is one subordinator in Czech, namely *zatímco* (*while*), which is used in *hypotactic coordinations* regularly and frequently. *Zatímco* in Czech either expresses temporal synchronicity (7) or confrontation (8) and both these uses are perceived as regular, in the sense not “false” or “improper”. The confrontational use, however, is treated as a semantic coordination, not determination, see Section 3. Therefore we claim that the connective *zatímco* in the confrontational use is the only regular form of expressing the asymmetric dualism in Czech on the syntax-discourse level of analysis. For comparison, it is added to Table 3 (the last row).

There are 160 occurrences of *confrontation* with the connective *zatímco* (*while*) documented in the PDiT data.

(7) [...] **zatímco** Sára ještě spí, zapřáhne osla.

[...] ***while*** *Sarah is still sleeping, he hithes up the donkey.*

(8) Prezident Václav Havel se těší důvěře 75 procent občanů, **zatímco** důvěra v premiéra Václava Klause klesla na 54 procent.

President Václav Havel enjoys the confidence of 75 percent of citizens, **while** the confidence in the Prime Minister Václav Klaus declined to 54 percent.

4.4 Connective *s tím, že* (*along with*)

One subordinator in Czech – *s tím, že* (roughly *along with* or *saying also that*, lit. *with that, that*) – is semantically vague and can serve as a connective for many relations (in PDiT data, there are eight different types of relation expressed by this connective). The type of the relation is inferable only from the context. From the point of view of *hypotactic coordination* in PDiT, it serves as a connective of *conjunction* in 14 cases and as a connective of *specification* in 3 cases. Examples of these contexts are given in (9) and (10), respectively.

(9) Doplněný návrh by měl obsahovat dvě varianty řešení **s tím, že** se k němu správní rada Českých drah znovu sejde 3. března.

The completed proposal should contain two variants of the solution **and** (lit. **with that that**) the Board of Czech Railways will reconvene to adress it again on the third of March.

(10) K oběma vraždám se přiznal **s tím, že** chtěl získat skromný majetek důchodců a drobné peněžní částky.

He confessed to both murders **saying that** he wanted to get the modest possessions of the retirees and small amounts of money.

5 Subordinators with elaborative meanings in PDTB

Thanks to Penn Discourse Treebank 2.0, we have at our disposal English subordinators annotated for their discourse semantics (Prasad et al. 2008). Having left their prevalent uses out of this analysis, we were able to draw (at least partial) parallels between their "non-standard" uses in Czech and in English.

We translated into English the Czech subordinators that took part in *hypotactic coordinations* (e.g. *když* = *when*; *jestliže* = *if*) and searched the PDTB for similar patterns. Even though such constructions may be language-specific, and, for English, they are scarcely documented in linguistic handbooks[14], some correspondence between Czech and English in our data is evident, compare Examples (11)–(13).

Subordinator: if, PDTB tag: Comparison:Contrast

(11) **If** Mr. Wilbur's translation is a finely ground lens through which we see the pettiness and corruption of 17th-century Paris, Mr. Falls's production is a mirror in which we see ourselves.

Subordinator: if, PDTB tag: Comparison:Contrast:Juxtaposition

(12) **If** the political establishment is reluctant to forgive sexual misadventures, the private sector sometimes will.

Subordinator: when, PDTB tag: Temporal:Synchrony/Expansion:Restatement:Specification

(13) In the same sentence he contradicts himself **when** he reports that the government still retains 40% of the total equity of the airline.

In these examples, the predominantly conditional *if* (11), (12) and the predominantly temporal *when* (13) express elaborative meanings – the same ones that we were able to document for Czech in Section 3.3, i.e. in Example (6) *confrontation*, in Example (1) *specification*.

A similar correspondence was documented for "false" relative clauses in English. Example (14) from PDTB shows a relative clause introduced by *which* that also contains a contrastive connective *nonetheless*. This co-occurrence in our view clearly signals the presence of a semantically autonomous content in the dependent clause (e.g. a coordination of the two contents rather than a determination) and so it corresponds to the Czech sentence in (4).

[14] with the exception of some non-restrictive relative clauses with a coordinative meaning (Quirk et al. 1992, p. 648), or "false" infinitives of purpose, such as: *I awoke to find the room flooded by sunshine.* (Dušková 1992, p. 562)

(14) Gemina, which owns 13.26% of Nuovo Banco, abstained in the final vote on Credit Agricole, **which** was **nonetheless** approved by a majority of shareholders.

Similarly as in Czech, the only subordinators that regularly signal a coordinative meaning are *while* and *whereas*: in terms of PDiT relations, they express *confrontation*. Of course, Czech *zatímco* and English *while* cannot be mapped 1:1 (e.g. the English *while* regularly expresses also causality) but for both languages they represent the most frequent subordinator with a coordinative meaning.

Having found evidence for parallels in use of subordinators in *hypotactic coordinations* in English and Czech, we are aware of the fact that the direction of analysis from Czech to English may have not revealed all such relevant structures in English. The existence of other types of *hypotactic coordinations* cannot be excluded and it is a possible topic for further linguistic research.

However, in spite of the assumed language-specificity in the repertoire of connective means and their use, our findings on a relatively small amount of data and a restricted language domain (financial journal) suggest that when subordinators deviate from their usual functions, they tend to do it in the similar way in Czech and English.

6 Conclusion

In this paper, we surveyed structures where subordinators convey coordinative meaning (*hypotactic coordinations*). These structures represent an irregular relation between formal and semantic principles of sentence composition, since coordinative meanings are prototypically realized in paratactic structures. On the basis of PDiT and PDTB, we described this phenomenon for Czech and we have drawn some comparisons of their use in English.

As the first step, the distribution of discourse relations as hypotactic versus paratactic structures in PDiT was measured to see to what extent the hypothesis of correspondence determination – hypotaxis, coordination – parataxis is also applicable for discourse semantics. We found that with the exception of *confrontation*, whose syntactic (and sentence-level semantic) counterpart is treated as coordination and which appears in our data quite regularly both as paratactic and hypotactic structures, relations whose syntactic counterpart is treated as coordination are realized as hypotactic structures rather rarely.

Further, we analyzed four types of *hypotactic coordinations* in Czech according to the characteristics of their respective subordinators. Some subordinators (e.g. *kromě toho, že* (lit. *besides that that*)) are specific only for coordination, a majority of them is used regularly for other relations than coordination (e.g. *jestliže* (*if*) is a regular subordinator for *condition*, some uses of it however express *confrontation*) etc.

Finally, subordinators whose "non-standard" meaning was documented for Czech (e.g. *jestliže* (*if*)) were translated and looked for also in the English data. Despite of the assumed language-specificity in connective functions, we were able to document English examples corresponding to the Czech structures.

Our findings are of course limited by the size and type of the language resources available for such a comparative study. Nevertheless, it should be highlighted that only the existence of such manually and specifically annotated corpora that gather linguistic information from different levels of language description makes it possible for the first time to carry out such a linguistic analysis.

Acknowledgments

We gratefully acknowledge support from the Grant Agency of the Czech Republic (grants P406/12/0658 and P406/2010/0875) and from the Ministry of Education, Youth and Sports in the Czech Republic (the LINDAT-Clarin project LM2010013). This research was also supported by SVV project number 267 314.

References

Eduard Bejček, Jarmila Panevová, Jan Popelka, Pavel Straňák, Magda Ševčíková, Jan Štěpánek, Zdeněk Žabokrtský. 2012. Prague Dependency Treebank 2.5 – a revisited version of PDT 2.0. In: *Proceedings of the 24th International Conference on Computational Linguistics (Coling 2012)*, Mumbai, India, pp. 231-246.

Libuše Dušková. 1992. *Mluvnice současné angličtiny na pozadí češtiny*. Praha: Academia.

Josef Hrbáček. 2000. Věta a výpověď. In: Čechová, M. et al. *Čeština – řeč a jazyk*.

Pavlína Jínová, Lucie Mladová, Jiří Mírovský. 2011. Sentence Structure and Discourse Structure: Possible Parallels. In: *Proceedings of the International Conference on Dependency Linguistics (Depling*

2011), Universitat Pompeu Fabra, Barcelona, Spain, ISBN 978-84-615-1834-0, pp. 233-240.

S. Karcevskij. 1929. Du dualisme asymétrique du signe linguistique. In: *Travaux du Cercle Linguistique de Prague, 1*, pp. 88–93. Czech translation by A. Bémová in: *Principy strukturní syntaxe 1* (1974). Praha: Státní pedagogické nakladatelství, pp. 26–30.

Marie Mikulová et al. 2005. *Anotace na tektogramatické rovině Pražského závislostního korpusu. Anotátorská příručka. Praha: ÚFAL MFF.* Available at: http://ufal.mff.cuni.cz/pdt2.0/doc/manuals/cz/t-layer/html/index.html.

Lucie Poláková, Pavlína Jínová, Šárka Zikánová, Eva Hajičová, Jiří Mírovský, Anna Nedoluzhko, Magdaléna Rysová, Veronika Pavlíková, Jana Zdeňková, Jiří Pergler, Radek Ocelák. 2012. *Prague Discourse Treebank 1.0.* Data/software, ÚFAL MFF UK, Prague, Czech Republic, http://ufal.mff.cuni.cz/discourse/, Nov 2012.

R. Prasad, N. Dinesh, A. Lee, E. Miltsakaki, L. Robaldo, A. Joshi and B. Webber. 2008. The Penn Discourse Treebank 2.0. In *Proceedings of the 6th International Conference on Language Resources and Evaluation (LREC 2008)*, Marrakech, Morocco, pp. 2961-2968.

Jarmila Panevová. 2010. Ke vztahu kognitivního obsahu a jazykového významu. In: *Korpus – gramatika – axiologie, Vol. 1, No. 1*, Gaudeamus, Hradec Králové, Czech Republic, ISSN 1804-137X, pp. 30-40.

Jarmila Panevová. 1980. *Formy a funkce ve stavbě české věty.* Praha: Academia.

Jarmila Panevová. 2012.*Koordinace vs. determinace (Forma nebo význam?).* Contributed talk, Zasedání Komise pro gramatickou stavbu slovanských jazyků při MKS, Univerzita Konštantína Filozofa Nitra, Nitra, Slovensko, Oct 2012.

František Daneš, Zdeněk Hlavsa, and Miroslav Grepl. 1987. *Mluvnice češtiny 3, Skladba.* Praha, Academia.

Lucie Poláková, Pavlína Jínová, Šárka Zikánová, Zuzana Bedřichová, Jiří Mírovský, Magdaléna Rysová, Jana Zdeňková, Veronika Pavlíková and Eva Hajičová. 2012. *Manual for Annotation of Discourse Relations in the Prague Dependency Treebank.* Technical report, UFAL MFF UK, Prague, Czech Republic. Available at: http://ufal.mff.cuni.cz/techrep/tr47.pdf.

Randolph Quirk, Sidney Greenbaum, Geoffrey Leech, Jan Svartvik. 1992. *A Grammar of Contemporary English.* England: Longman Group.

Petr Sgall, Eva Hajičová, Jarmila Panevová. 1986. *The Meaning of the Sentence in Its Semantic and Pragmatic Aspects.* Dordrecht: D. Reidel Publishing Company.

Predicative Adjunction in a Modular Dependency Grammar

Sylvain Kahane
Modyco, Université Paris Ouest Nanterre & CNRS, France
sylvain@kahane.fr

Abstract

This paper shows how to introduce predicative adjunction in a dependency grammar inspired from TAG, MTT and RG. The addition of predicative adjunction allows us to obtain a modular surface syntactic grammar, the derivation structures of which can be interpreted as semantic representations.

1 Introduction

The dependency grammar we propose is inspired by TAG (Joshi 1987), MTT (Mel'čuk 1988) and Relational Grammar (Perlmutter 1980). Like TAG, we combine elementary tree structures in order to generate the surface syntactic structures of sentences. Also like TAG, we want our derivation structures to be interpretable as semantic structures (Rambow & Joshi 1994, Candito & Kahane 1998). Like MTT, our syntactic structures are dependency trees and our semantic structures are graphs of predicate-argument relations between the lexical and grammatical meanings of the sentence. Like RG, the syntactic structures are constructed by strata and a syntactic function can be revaluated. Such a formalism has actually already been fully established (see Nasr 1995, Kahane 2001, Kahane & Lareau 2005, and Lareau 2008). Kahane 2006 exlores the underlying formalism, which we call Polarized Unification Grammar (PUG), and shows that rewriting systems (including CFG), TAG, HPSG or LFG can be strongly simulated by PUG.

In this paper, we propose to write a PUG with rules (i.e. elementary structures) that are simple (from a mathematical point of view), but that cover rather complex linguistic phenomena, like extraction and complex determiners. The grammar makes extensive use of predicative adjunction, an operation borrowed from TAG for combining structures. Predicative adjunction adjoins the syntactic governor to a node, which means that the syntactic governor is the semantic modifier of its dependent (Shieber & Schabes 1994). As far as we know, the formalism we propose is the first genuine dependency grammar using predicative adjunction. With the help of predicative adjunction, elegant rules are possible that directly interpret the derivation structure as a semantic representation.

2 The base formalism

Polarized Unification Grammar (PUG) generates a set of finite structures by combining elementary structures. A structure is based on *objects*, for instance, on nodes and dependencies in a dependency tree. Objects are linked to three kinds of elements: 1) other objects (like a dependency to its source and target nodes), 2) *atomic values* (labels or feature values), and 3) *polarities*. Polarities differ from atomic values in the way they combine.

When two (elementary) structures combine, at least one object of a structure must be identified with an object of the other structure (like with TAG substitution, whereby the root of one tree is identified with a leaf of the other tree). When two objects are identified, all the elements linked to them must be combined: objects and values are identified (this is traditionally called unification in unification-based formalisms), while polarities combine by a special operation called the *product on polarities*. We consider three polarities in this paper:

□ = white = unsaturated;
■ = black = saturated;
▪ = grey = invisible.

Only the white polarity can combine with other polarities and white is the identity element of the product:

·	□	■	▪
□	□	■	▪
■	■	⊥	⊥
▪	▪	⊥	⊥

Polarities can be interpreted as follows. White objects are unsaturated: they absolutely

Proceedings of the Second International Conference on Dependency Linguistics (DepLing 2013), pages 137–146,
Prague, August 27–30, 2013.

must combine with a non-white object. A final structure derived by the grammar must not contain any white object. Black objects are the elements of the structure constructed by the grammar. Grey objects are introduced during the derivation but are "invisible" in the end.[1]

Fig. 1 proposes five rules for our dependency grammar. These rules are based on Nasr 1995, with improvements proposed by Kahane & Lareau 2005. Lexemes are represented by nodes and labeled with small capitals (SLEEP, BOY…). Syntactic dependencies are represented by downward pointing arrows. A third kind of objects, represented by diamonds, correspond to *grammemes*, that is, to what are more or less inflectional morphemes (Mel'čuk 1988).

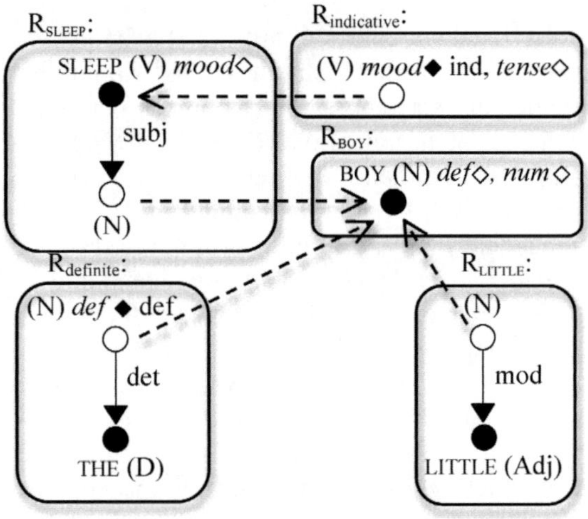

Figure 1. Sample rules and combination

The rule R_{SLEEP} indicates that the lexeme SLEEP needs a nominal subject and a mood (mood includes finiteness and its value can infinite as well as indicative). The subject dependency and the lexeme (polarized in black) are built by the rule, while the noun and the mood (polarized in white) are requests. The rule $R_{indicative}$ gives a verb the indicative mood and says that the indicative must combine with tense.[2] The rule R_{BOY} introduces the noun BOY and asks for definiteness and number for it. Note that the request for a grammeme of definiteness forces the noun to take a determiner. The rule $R_{definite}$ adjoins THE to a noun and gives it a clear value for definiteness. The rule R_{LITTLE} adjoins LITTLE to a noun. These five rules can combine together, as suggested in Fig. 1 (cf. dashed arrows), yielding the dependency tree in Fig. 2. The result of such a derivation is called a *derived structure*.

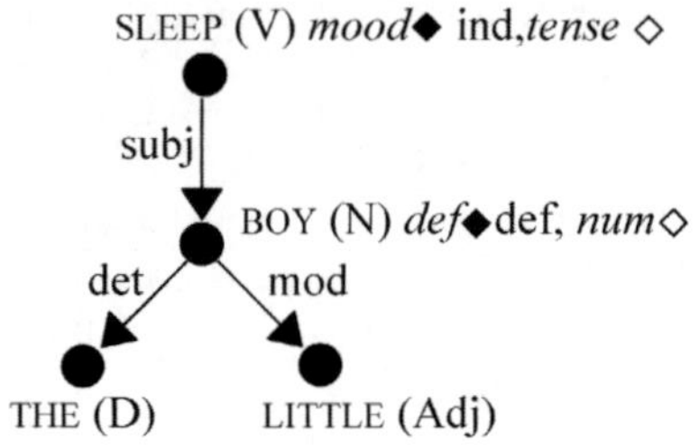

Figure 2. A (non-final) derived structure

Note that the tree in Fig. 2 is not saturated. It needs to combine with at least two more rules that introduce tense on SLEEP and number on BOY. We have also simplified the rule for the indicative mood: this mood not only asks for a tense, but for person and number agreement.

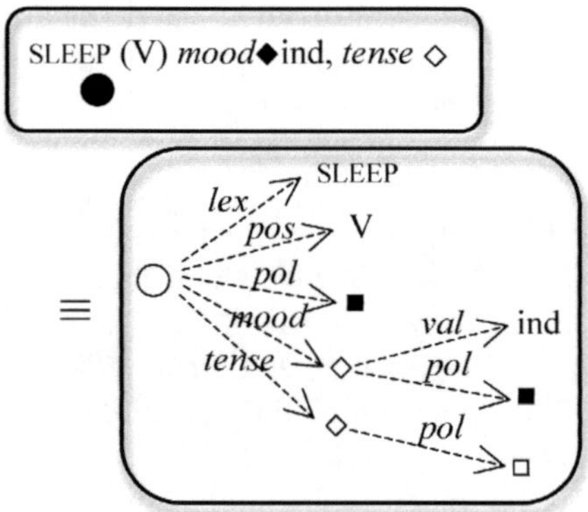

Figure 3. Our conventions[3]

Fig. 3 makes our formal conventions more precise. A black node has black polarity. The

[1] It is possible to write a powerful grammar using only black and white polarities. A grey object is in fact a saturated object that is invisible for the other modules of the grammar – for instance, the topological module ensuring the linearization of the syntactic tree. Each dependency thus bears a special polarity (called an *interface polarity*) indicating to the topological module whether it needs to be linearized or not (Kahane & Lareau 2005). From this point of view, a grey object in the present grammar is an object the interface polarity of which is saturated (Lareau 2008). Conversely a black object in the present grammar is visible, that is, it is an object the interface polarity of which is white and must be saturated by the topological module.

[2] In a PUG, it is easy, by using a dedicated polarity, to ensure that the structure is a tree and to specify which node is the root (Kahane 2006). This point will not be developed here however.

[3] Worth is noting that our formalism is not unlike other unification-based formalisms such as HPSG. The schema in Fig. 3 can be easily interpreted as a (recursive) feature structure and a dependency grammar of the kind presented here can be implemented in an HPSG-like formalism (Kahane 2009). Conversely, HPSG can be strongly simulated by PUG (Kahane 2006).

polarity is the value of a map we call *pol*. The lexeme name and the part of speech (pos) are atomic values. Grammemes are objects linked to the lexeme node by a map labeled by the name of the inflectional category (mood, tense…). These objects have their own polarities and values in turn. When the rules R_{SLEEP} and $R_{indicative}$ are combined, two nodes are identified and the values of the maps *pol, pos* and *mood* common to both of them are unified. The values of the map *mood* and *tense* are objects, so they must be identified and their own maps unified and so on.[4]

The structure showing the way of how the rules combine in a derivation is called a *derivation structure* (see Vijay-Shanker 1992 for TAG). We consider three ways of combining rules. The first way is by *substitution*: R_{BOY} substitutes in R_{SLEEP} because R_{BOY} saturates a leaf of R_{SLEEP}'s structure. The second way is by *adjunction*: R_{LITTLE} adjoins to R_{BOY} because R_{LITTLE} adds a dependency to a black node of R_{BOY}'s structure.[5] The third way is *grammatical completion*: $R_{definite}$ completes R_{BOY} by saturating a grammeme in R_{BOY}'s structure.

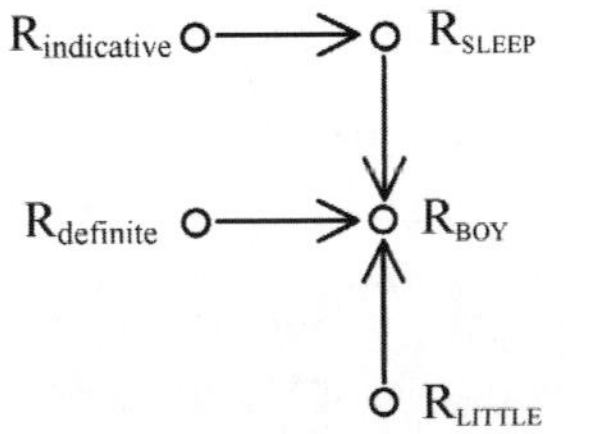

Figure 4. Derivation structure

Fig. 4 shows the derivation structure associated with the derivation suggested in Fig.1 giving the derived structure in Fig. 2. We adopt the following conventions: a substitution is represented by a downward arrow, an adjunction by an upward arrow, and an inflectional completion by a horizontal arrow. With these conventions, the derivation structure can be interpreted as a graph of predicate-argument relations (as shown in Candito & Kahane 1998 for TAG) and is the basis for a semantic representation (see Mel'čuk 2012). Indeed, each arrow in the derivation structure can be interpreted as a semantic dependency that points from a predicate to one of its arguments.

To conclude this section, it must be remarked that we focus on the syntax-semantics interface in this paper and we do not discuss word order. Gerdes & Kahane 2001 propose a formalism—*topological grammar*—for linearizing dependency trees, even for languages with non-projective constructions. It is possible to write a topological grammar in PUG and to combine it with the grammar presented here (see Kahane & Lareau 2005 for the combination of different modules in PUG).

3 Dependency rules

The first improvement to the base grammar that we propose is to separate the rules associated with the lexemes proper from the *dependency rules* ensuring the realization of a given dependency (see the nodal vs. sagittal rules of Kahane & Mel'čuk 1999). We modify our previous rules as a consequence and add separate rules for dependencies. See Fig. 5, which shows two rules the combination of which ($L_{SLEEP} \oplus D_{subject}$) results in R_{SLEEP}.[6]

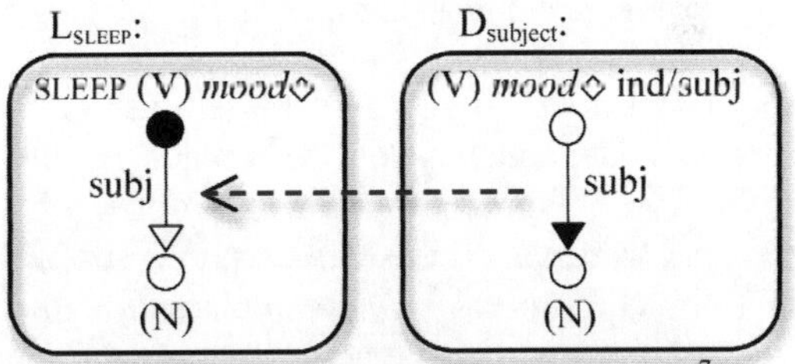

Figure 5. Lexical vs. dependency rules[7]

The dependency rule $D_{subject}$ constrains the subject dependency to be saturated only if the verb has the indicative or subjunctive mood. If

[4] We have slightly simplified Fig. 3. A map *host* from each grammeme to its lexeme is needed in order to ensure that the identification of two grammemes entails the identification of their host lexemes.

[5] This kind of adjunction is called *sister adjunction* by Rambow et al. 1995. Contrary to predicative adjunction, sister adjunction does not change the weak generative capacity of the formalism. One can note that the distinction between substitution and adjunction is small in PUG: in both cases, a black and a white node are identified. The only difference is the direction of the dependency, which is not really relevant in PUG (source and target are interchangeable from a graph-theoretical perspective).

[6] We will use the following conventions to name our rules: L for rules instantiating a lexeme, D for a dependency, G for a grammeme and S for structural rules that do not instantiate any object. R is an umbrella identifier used in Section 2, when lexical rules and dependency rules were not separated.

[7] In fact, a black dependency has to combine with a white one (if not, a second subject relation could be added to a verb). This can be easily solved by adding a second polarity: every black dependency will have a white additional polarity, while a white dependency will have a black one (see also positive and negative polarities in Kahane 2006).

the subject requirement is lexical (the subject is the first actant of the verb, cf. Tesnière 1959), the subject realization is controlled by the mood (mood includes finiteness) (cf. the position of the subject under IP in X-bar syntax). When the verb has another mood, like infinitive or participle, the subject requirement of L_{SLEEP} is not realized by a dependency on SLEEP. For instance, with a progressive form (*is sleeping*), the subject is lifted to the auxiliary BE. The subject requirement of SLEEP unifies with a grey polarity (and becomes invisible for other modules) and is replaced by a subject dependency on BE. Fig. 6 shows the rule ($G_{progressive}$) and the result of its combination with L_{SLEEP} ($L_{SLEEP} \oplus G_{progressive}$).[8]

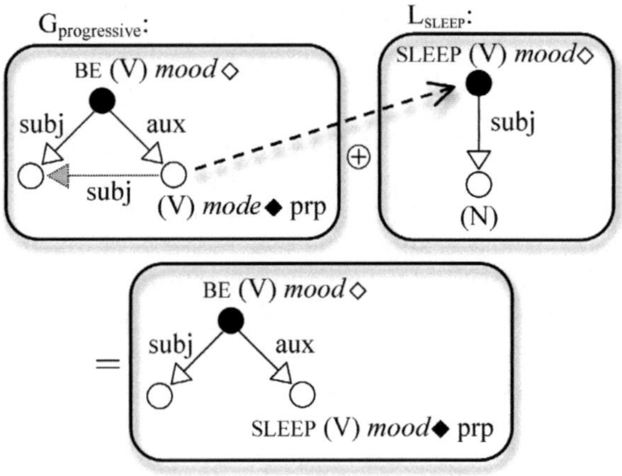

Figure 6. Invisible dependency.[9]

The fact that our formalism allows us to suppress a dependency and to replace it with another one is similar to what is proposed by RG. This leads us to consider deep and surface functions (Fillmore 1968). A *surface function* appears in a surface syntactic tree. A surface function must have been instantiated by a saturation rule, like $D_{subject}$ for the subject function (Fig. 5). A *deep function* is the initial function received by a lexeme, which can have been instantiated into an identical surface function or which may have been made invisible and replaced by another function.

Some deep functions will never be instantiated as surface functions. This is the case with the *to-obj* of TALK, which must be marked by the preposition TO. Fig. 7 shows the rule for the lexeme TALK and the *to-obj* dependency, as well as their combination ($L_{TALK} \oplus D_{to\text{-}obj}$). The last schema in Fig. 7 is a part of the derivation structure of the sentence *Aya talks to Bob*; it shows that L_{BOB} combines directly with L_{TALK}, while $D_{to\text{-}obj}$ is not interpreted as a lexical rule (TO is only a syntactic marker), but as a revaluation of the connection between two lexical rules. Such a rule is ignored when the derivation is interpreted at the semantic level.

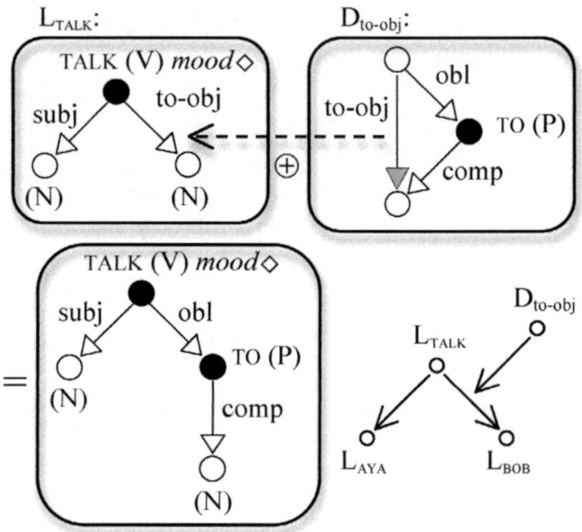

Figure 7. Governed preposition.

We choose not to introduce TO in the elementary structure of TALK contrary to what is done in TAG or in previous versions of our dependency grammar (Kahane 2001). We want our grammar to be as modular as possible, separating everything that can be separated. The government markers must be separated from the lexemes that call them for at least two reasons:

- they can be repeated in coordination: *Aya talks **to** Bob and **to** Dave.*
- they can have an alternative realization; for instance, in French, an indirect object is marked by the preposition À for a noun phrase, but by the dative case for a clitic pronoun (Fig. 8).[10] In English, a complementizer can be realized or not: *Aya knew* (*that*) *Bob came.*

[8] A similar rule has been proposed by Kahane (2001), where a grey dependency is called a quasi-dependency. The idea to consider a quasi-dependency as a dependency with a saturated interface polarity occured later (Kahane & Lareau 2005) and is explained in Lareau 2008.

[9] We do not represent grey objects in derived structures in order to simplify the figures and to emphasize the fact they are invisible for further treatments.

[10] The two constructions of PARLER 'talk' are:
(i) *Aya parle **à** Bob* 'Aya talks to Bob'
(ii) *Aya **lui** parle* 'Aya talks to him'

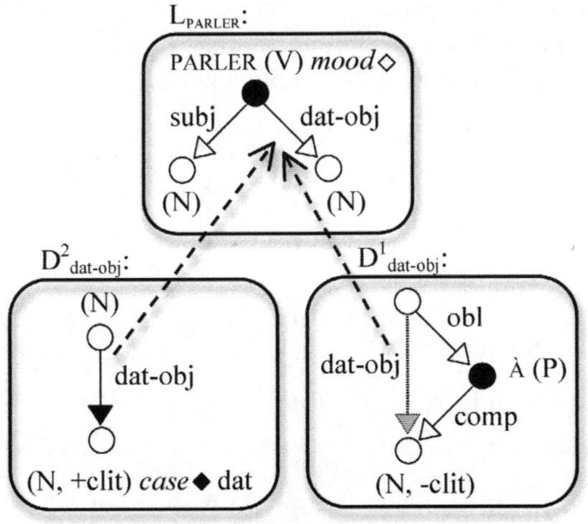

Figure 8. Indirect object in French

Therefore, we want the government markers to be realized by separate rules, but, for semantic reasons, we also want a predicative lexeme to combine directly with its arguments. We have solved these constraints thanks to the grey polarity and the invisible objects; as is shown in Fig. 7, the verb TALK has a direct connection with its semantic argument and it is only in the derived structure that the preposition appears between the verb and its argument.

The case of adjectives is interesting. Adjectives occur in two basic constructions. In the attributive construction they modify a noun (*the **red** book*) and in the predicative construction they form a verbal complex with the copula (*the book **is red***). In both cases, 'red' is a semantic predicate and 'book' is its semantic argument. But some adjectives take an event as argument and this argument can be realized by a verb (***reading this book** is tough*). Such adjectives cannot modify their verbal argument, but the direct object of this argument can be promoted (so-called *tough-movement*) and become the syntactic governor of the adjective (***a book** tough to read*). According to these facts, we cannot assume that the attributive construction is the base construction of every adjective, since this construction is impossible for adjectives taking a verbal argument. We thus propose that, in its base construction, the argument of the adjective has a special deep function we call subj' (Fig. 9). This deep function does not exist as a surface function, but at least three constructions can apply to it: the attributive construction ($D_{subj'}$), the predicative construction (S_{copula}) and the construction of tough-movement ($S_{tough\text{-}mvt}$). Note that the attributive construction can only apply if the argument is realized as a noun or after tough-movement, which promotes a noun as subj'.

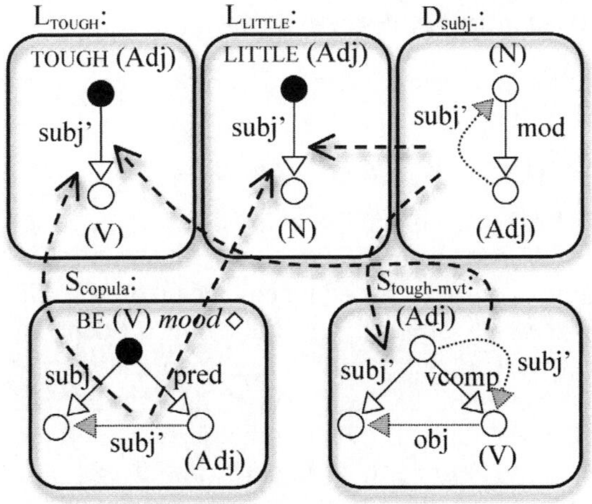

Figure 9. Adjectival constructions

The same deep function subj' is used for the passive past participle, which can enter into a predicative construction (*a book **has been stolen***) or an attributive construction (*the book **stolen by Bob***). The passive construction marked by the past participle inflection can be derived from a verbal base form by a rule using grey polarities again (Fig.10).

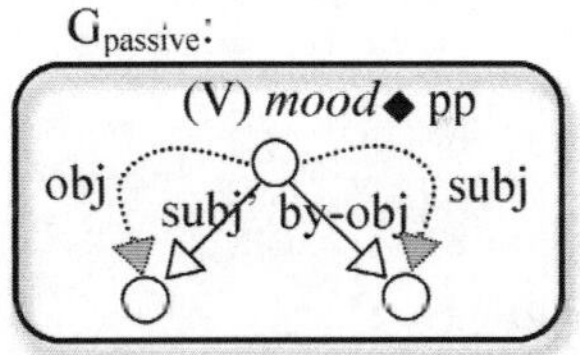

Figure 10. Passive voice

Intermediate conclusion: Thanks to the grey polarities, which allow us to make an object invisible (for other modules) and to replace it with another configuration, we are able to separate the rules describing the various constructions associated with a lexeme from the rule describing the lexeme itself. In a lexicalized grammar like TAG, an elementary structure describes a lexeme with one of its constructions and the set of elementary structures associated to a given lexeme must be generated by another module (like a metagrammar in Candito 1996). An advantage of the approach presented here is that the rules associated with the lexemes and their constructions are in the same formalism. They can be precompiled to obtain a lexicalized grammar or they can be triggered on-line during text analysis or synthesis.

We will now see how grey polarities can be used for modeling another way of combining lexemes: predicative adjunction.

4 Complex determiners

Numerous determiners are idiomatic constructions like *loads of* in (1):

(1) *Aya read* ***loads of*** *books.*

Such a construction causes a mismatch between the syntactic and the semantic structures: *loads* is the syntactic head of the NP *loads of books* and thus the syntactic dependent of *read*, but 'book' is its semantic head and the argument of 'read'. As a consequence, we want the derived tree and the derivation structure of (1) to be as in Fig. 11 (besides $S_{insertion}$, which is a technical rule introduced below).

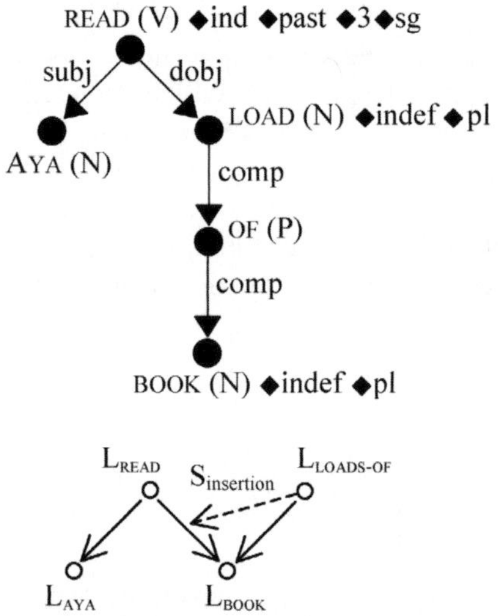

Figure 11. Derived tree and derivation structure for (1)[11]

This problem can be solved by *predicative adjunction*, as in the standard analysis of complex determiners in TAG (Shieber & Schabes 1994). A predicative adjunction is an adjunction where the adjunct is inserted in the syntactic governor position. This is making possible in our formalism by way of a special rule, $S_{insertion}$, allowing the insertion of a node and a dependency between two other nodes (Fig. 12). This rule can be compared to a rule like $D_{to\text{-}obj}$, which introduces a marker. But $S_{insertion}$ is a generic rule that can apply on any dependency ($r is a variable) and does not replace it but only inserts a dependency [*insert*:+] behind. The formalism forces us to replace the $r dependency by a new one, but in fact we just want to "move" it to a new dependent.

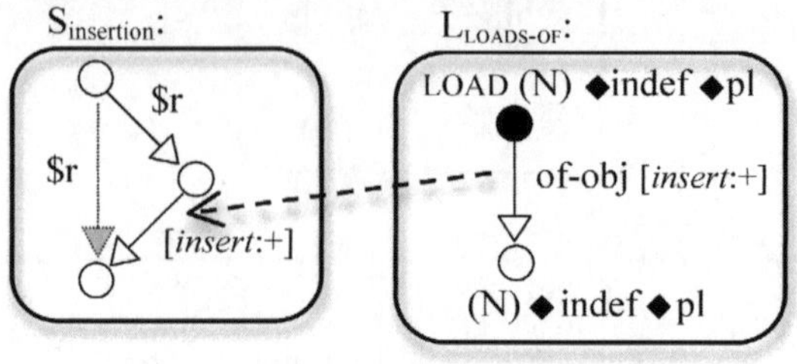

Figure 12. Predicative adjunction[12]

The predicative adjunction is indicated by a downward arrow in the derivation structure, like a substitution (Fig.11). A purely structural rule like $S_{insertion}$, which does not saturate any object, is represented by a dashed arrow. Note that L_{BOOK} substitutes in $L_{LOADS\text{-}OF}$ like in a normal substitution. Consequently, L_{BOOK} substitutes in two rules (L_{READ} and $L_{LOADS\text{-}OF}$), which is made possible by $S_{insertion}$. It is important to note that it is BOOK and not LOAD that fulfill the object position of READ. Therefore determiners that (predicatively) adjoin do not need to be nouns. In French there is a productive construction where the complex determiner is an adverb governing the noun (*trop de* N 'too_much of N', *moins de N* 'less of N' …). It is also possible to treat simple determiners, including articles, as syntactic governors of the noun they determine (Abney 1987, Hudson 2007). But even if in *read a book* the determiner A becomes the governor of BOOK, it is the noun of the unit *a book* that will combine with READ and it is not really legitimate to consider *a book* as a DP.

Note that the rule $S_{insertion}$ can be applied recursively, as in ***more than half of all*** *known species are insects*; indeed *half of* predicatively adjoins to *all known species* and *more than* predicatively adjoins to *half*.

5 Extraction

We will focus on relative clauses and start with *wh-relative clauses*, that is, with relative clauses marked by a wh-word, like in (2):

(2) (*the guy*) ***who*** *I invited.*

A relative clause depends on a noun (here *guy*), which is the antecedent of a wh-word (here *who*). Each wh-word will have its own

[11] We have simplified the derived tree by suppressing the attribute before the grammemes.

[12] Again the preposition (*of* in *loads of books*) is added by a separated rule.

rule: the rule S_{WHO} attaches the wh-word WHO to a noun bearing the feature +human (Fig. 13). The rule $D_{wh\text{-}rel}$ allows predicative adjunction on a wh-word.[13] The rule D_{rel} instantiates the dependency between the antecedent noun and the relative clause and forces the head of the relative clause to be a finite verb in the indicative or subjunctive mood (Fig. 14).

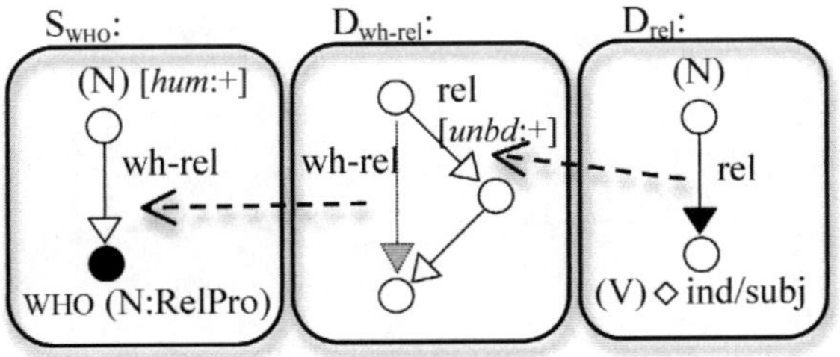

Figure 13. Rules for wh-relatives

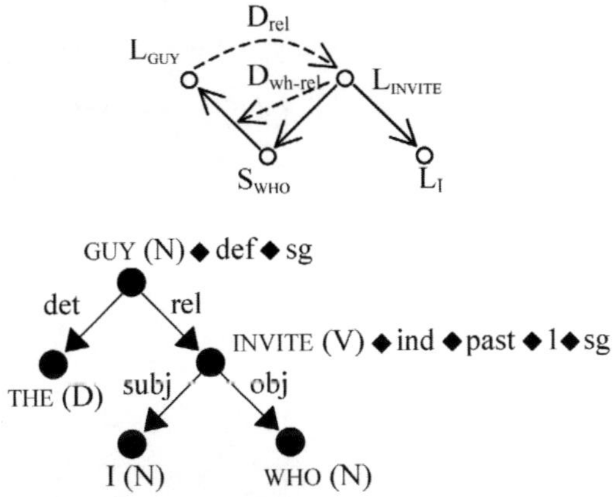

Figure 14. Derivation structure and derived tree for (2)

Tesnière 1959 argues that the wh-word occupies two positions in the dependency structure: it is both a complementizer (thus being the syntactic head of the relative clause) and a pronoun (filling the "extracted" position) (see additional arguments in Kahane 2002). Even though the wh-word occupies only the pronominal position in the derived tree in our account, the wh-word directly attaches to the antecedent noun (see S_{WHO} in Fig. 13 and in the derivation structures of Fig. 14 and 16) and thus carries out a complementizer role. It is even possible to not make invisible the wh-rel dependency between the antecedent noun and the wh-word and to obtain a dependency structure similar to Tesnière's stemma for extraction.

[13] We could have proposed a rule directly combining S_{WHO} and $D_{wh\text{-}rel}$, as it was done in previous works (Kahane 2001).

It has been well established since Ross 1967 that the string of dependencies between the antecedent noun and the "extracted" position (that is, the position filled by the wh-word) is potentially unbounded but nevertheless very constrained. In (3), the verb THINK has been added in the relative clause and has become the syntactic head of the clause.

(3) (*the guy*) *who* ***you think*** *I invited.*

Such a verb is called a *bridge verb*. We introduce a new rule, $S_{unbounded}$, allowing the predicative adjunction of a bridge verb (Fig. 15). Note that only syntactic dependencies labeled [*bridge*:+] can be inserted behind a dependency labeled [*unbd*:+]. This is comparable to the LFG's functional uncertainty (Kaplan & Zaenen 1989), where the constraints on extraction are also controlled at the syntactic function level.

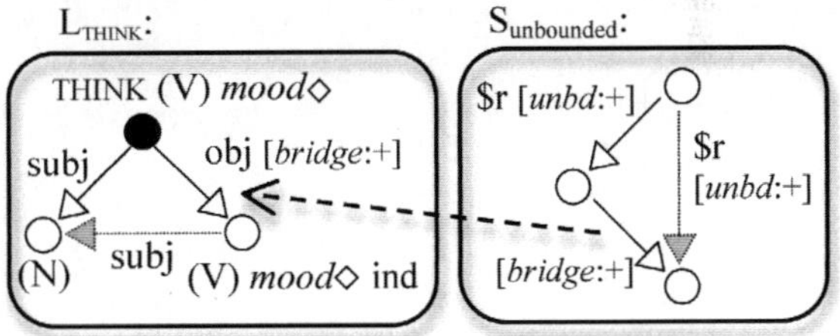

Figure 15. Rules for bridge verbs

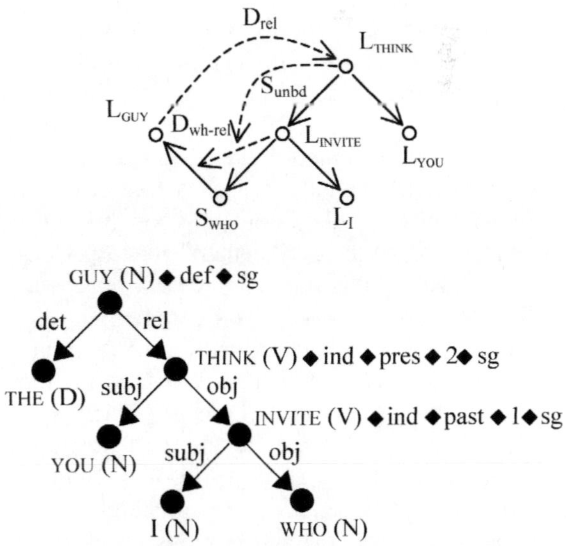

Figure 16. Derivation structure and derived tree for (3)

In the derivation of (3), who adjoins on GUY and substitutes into the object position of INVITE (Fig. 16). The latter is then inserted between WHO and GUY thanks to $S_{wh\text{-}rel}$, which introduces a rel(ative) dependency. In the same way, INVITE substitutes in the object position of THINK. As the object dependency bears a feature [*bridge*:+], the rule $S_{unbounded}$ can apply and insert THINK between GUY and INVITE, replacing the rel relation by a new one. This can be done recursively. At the end, the rel dependency is instantiated by D_{rel}.

Our analysis of wh-relative clauses is similar to the TAG analysis, where the bridge verbs predicatively adjoin (Kroch & Joshi 1986). It can also be compared to the analysis in other frameworks, in particular to LFG with the functional uncertainty, to the generative grammar with Move α, or to HPSG with the slash feature. Contrary to the Move α or slash analyses, it is not the wh-word that is moved, but the bridge verbs that are inserted, like in the functional uncertainty. Moreover, it is not the verb THINK that is a bridge, but only its object dependency, like in LFG again (Kaplan & Zaenen 1989). Nevertheless, $S_{unbounded}$ is a rule that moves the rel dependency from INVITE to THINK, which can be seen as movement of the complementizer role of the wh-word.

We will now contrast wh-relatives with *that-relative clauses*, like (4):

(4) (*the guy*) ***that*** *you think I invited.*

It has often been argued that that-relatives are syntactically different from wh-relatives, because 1) THAT also marks complement clauses (*you think **that** I invited this guy*), 2) it does not accept pied-piping (*the guy to whom I speak* vs. **the guy to that I speak*), 3) that-clauses alternate with unmarked clauses (*the guy you think I invited*), and 4), contrarily to wh-words, THAT does not have a "human" feature. Consequently, THAT is not analyzed as a pronoun like wh-words, but only as a complementizer, which marks the subordination of a finite clause. We thus necessitate different extraction rules for that-relatives, where the antecedent noun directly fills the "extracted" position: $D_{obj\text{-}extraction}$ and $D_{subj\text{-}extraction}$ (Fig. 17). Subject and object extraction are differentiated because 1) only the object extraction really accepts the predicative adjunction of bridge verbs (?**the guy that you think that invited me*), and 2) only the object extraction can be unmarked (*He is the guy *(that) invited me*). Consequently, only $D_{obj\text{-}extraction}$ can combine with $S_{unbounded}$ and $D_{unmarked\text{-}relative}$.

With this new set of rules we obtain a different syntactic structure (Fig. 18): THAT is the syntactic head of the relative clause and contrarily to WHO, THAT does not fill the "extracted" position and does not combine with INVITE in (4). THAT only intervenes to mark the subordination of the relative clause.

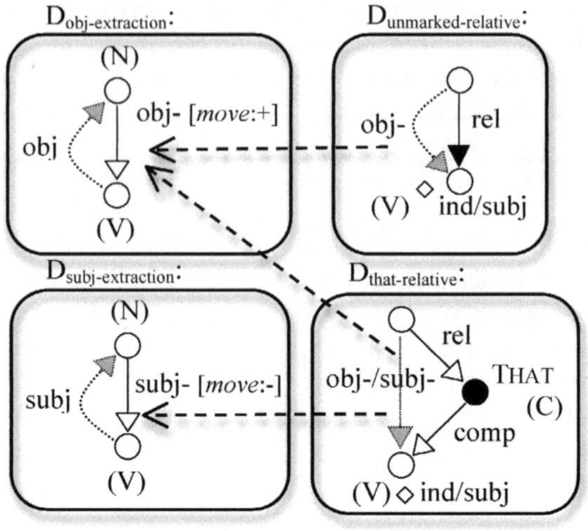

Figure 17. Rules for that-relatives

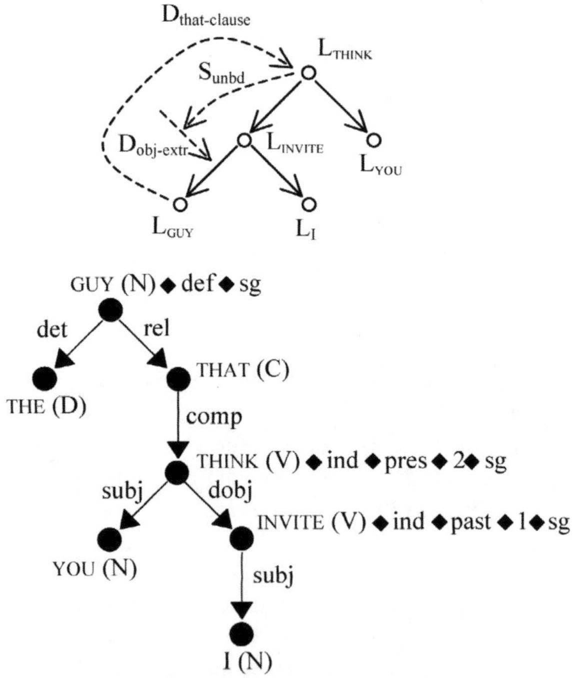

Figure 18. Derivation structure and derived tree for (4)

The case of French confirms the relevance of the distinction between wh-relatives and that-relatives. French has a +human wh-word QUI, comparable to WHO, but which can only be used after a preposition (*la fille à **qui** je parle* 'the girl to whom I talk'). In case of object extraction, the relative clause is marked by

QUE, which can be compared to THAT (*le livre* ***que*** *je lisais* 'the book that I read'); in particular, QUE is also the marker of complement clauses (*tu penses* ***que*** *j'ai invité ce gars* 'you think that I invited this guy') and no pied-piping is possible with QUE. Subject extraction is marked by a QUI form, different from the other QUI, because this one is not +human (*le livre* ***qui*** *est là* 'the book that is there'). Kayne 1975 argues that QUE is always a pure complementizer, even when it marks relative clauses. His main argument is the so-called *qui-que* alternation:

(5) (*la fille*) ***que*** *je pense* ***qui*** *m'a invité*
the girl that I think that invited me
'the girl that I think invited me'

In (5), the subject of the complement clause is extracted, but, contrarily to what might have been expected, the marker of the relative clause is QUE (*la fille que* ...) and moreover the marker of the complement clause is QUI (*je pense qui* ...). As a consequence, we can conclude that QUE and QUI are not exactly the subject and object relative markers and that they are not selected according to the "extracted" position they fill. We propose rather that these markers are selected according to the verb they complementize: QUI complementizes a verb without a realized subject, while QUE must complementize a verb with a subject. Such a solution can only be implemented in our formalism if QUI and QUE are treated as markers and connected to the verb they complementize in the syntactic tree (which is not the case for WHO in our analysis). Consequently, we propose subject and object extraction rules for French similar to the rules for English (of Fig. 17), but we add a ±subject feature on the subordinated verb indicating whether its subject has been extracted or not ($D_{subj\text{-}extraction}$ in Fig. 19). The QUI marker can only mark a relative clause if the main verb of the clause is [*subj*:-] ($D_{qui\text{-}relative}$ in Fig. 19).

The rule for relatives marked by QUE is similar ($D_{que\text{-}relative}$ in Fig. 20); the only difference is that the verb must have its subject and be marked [*subj*:+]. The rules for QUI and QUE could be merged assuming that *qui* and *que* are two forms of a same lexeme with an opposition of case (nominative for *qui* and oblique for *que*) (Kahane 2002). Moreover the two rules for QUE ($D_{que\text{-}relative}$ and $D_{que\text{-}complement}$ in Fig. 20) are almost identical: only the syntactic functions involved change. This corroborates Kayne's hypothesis that all these complementizers are one and the same.

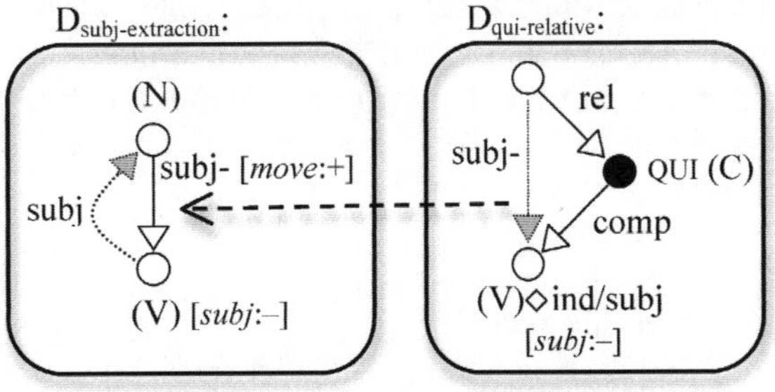

Figure 19. Rules for qui-relatives

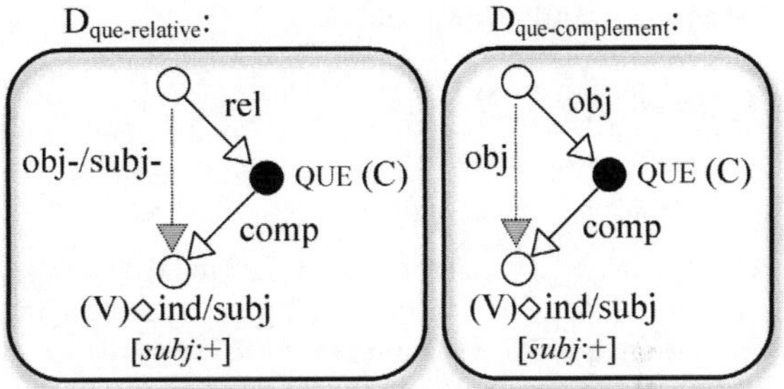

Figure 20. Rules for que-clauses

6 Conclusion

We have presented a dependency grammar that constructs syntactic dependency trees like any other dependency grammar. But this grammar accomplishes more than others. First, it takes into account the syntax-semantics interface: the derivation structure can be interpreted as a graph of predicate-argument relations, that is, as the skeleton of a semantic representation (in the sense of Mel'čuk 1988, 2012). Second, this grammar accomodates the syntax-text interface, that is, linearization and morphology. Even though the linearization rules are not presented here (see Kahane & Lareau 2005 or Gerdes 2004 for linearization rules in PUG), it could be shown that the derived structure contains all the surface syntactic dependencies necessary to calculate the linear order (Gerdes & Kahane 2001).

In other respects, the grammar presented here is very modular. Grammatical constructions have their own independent rules, separated from the lexical rules, which describe only the base construction of lexemes. From this point a view, this grammar enters in the paradigm of construction grammars (CxGs) and can even be seen as a formalization of the Relational Grammar (Perlmutter 1980).

Our formalism makes a big use of the invisible polarity and the predicative adjunction. Formally, the derived structure is a graph with a tree skeleton, which is the visible part of the derived structure (the objects polarized in black). The fact that we constantly maintain a tree skeleton during the derivation process is probably an important property from a computational point of view, but this has not been investigated further and the formalism has not been implemented.

Acknowledgments
I would like to thank Kim Gerdes, François Lareau and Tim Osborne for many valuable comments and corrections.

References

Abney S. 1987. *The English Noun Phrase in its Sentential Aspect*. PhD Dissertation, MIT.

Candito M.-H., Kahane S. 1998. Can the derivation tree represent a semantic graph? An answer in the light of Meaning-Text Theory, *Proc. TAG+4*, Philadelphia, 21-24.

Candito M.-H. 1996. A principle-based hierarchical representation of LTAGs. *Proc. COLING*, Copenhagen.

Fillmore Ch. J. 1968. The Case for Case. In Bach and Harms (eds.): *Universals in Linguistic Theory*. Holt, Rinehart, and Winston, New York, 1-88.

Gerdes K. 2004. Tree Unification Grammar Problems and Proposals for Topology, TAG, and German, *Electronic Notes in Theoretical Computer Science*, 53, 108-136.

Gerdes K., Kahane S. 2001. Word Order in German: A Formal Dependency Grammar Using a Topological Hierarchy. *Proc. ACL*, Toulouse.

Hudson R. 2007. *Language Networks: The New Word Grammar*, Oxford University Press.

Joshi A. 1987. Introduction to Tree Adjoining Grammar. In Manaster Ramer (ed.), *The Mathematics of Language*, Benjamins, Amsterdam, 87-114.

Kahane S. 2001. A fully lexicalized grammar for French based on Meaning-Text theory. *Proc. CICLing*, Mexico, Springer Verlag, 18-31.

Kahane S. 2002. A propos de la position syntaxique des mots qu-. In P. Le Goffic (ed.), *Interrogation, indéfinition, subordination*, Verbum, 24(4), 399-435.

Kahane S. 2006. Polarized Unification Grammars, *Proc. Coling-ACL,* Sydney.

Kahane S. 2009. On the Status of Phrases in Head-driven Phrase Structure Grammar: Illustration by a Fully Lexical Treatment of Extraction, in A. Polguère & I. Mel'čuk (eds.), *Dependency in Linguistic Description*, Benjamins,111-150.

Kahane S., Mel'čuk I. 1999. La synthèse sémantique ou la correspondance entre graphes sémantiques et arbres syntaxiques – Le cas des phrases à extraction en français contemporain, *T.A.L.*, 40(2), 25-85.

Kahane S., Lareau F. 2005. Meaning-Text Unification Grammar: Modularity and polarization. *MTT 2005*, Moscow.

Kaplan R., Zaenen A. 1989. Long-distance dependencies, constituent structure, and functional uncertainty. In M. Baltin and A. Kroch (eds.), *Alternative Conceptions of Phrase Structure.* Chicago University Press, 17-42.

Kayne R. 1975. *French Syntax: The Transformational Cycle*, Cambridge : MIT Press.

Kroch A., Joshi A. 1986. Analysing Extraposition in a TAG. In G. Huck & A. Ojeda (eds.), *Discontinuous Constituents*, Syntax and Semantics, vol. 20, Academic Press, 107-149.

Lareau F. 2008. Vers une grammaire d'unification Sens-Texte du français : le temps verbal dans l'interface sémantique-syntaxe, Ph.D. thesis, University of Montreal/University Paris 7.

Mel'čuk I. 1988. *Dependency Syntax: Theory and Practice*, SUNY, Albany.

Mel'čuk I. 2012, *Semantics: From Meaning to Text*, Benjamins, Amsterdam.

Nasr A. 1995. A Formalism and a Parser for Lexicalised Dependency Grammars, *Proc. IWPT*, Prague, 186-195.

Perlmutter D. 1980. Relational grammar. In E. Moravcsik & J. Wirth (eds.), *Syntax and semantics: Current approaches to syntax* (Vol. 13), Academic Press, New York, 195-229.

Pollard Carl, Sag Ivan, 1994, *Head-Driven Phrase Structure Grammar*, CSLI, Stanford.

Rambow O., Vijay-Shanker K., Weir D. 1995. D-tree grammars. *Proceedings of ACL,* Cambridge.

Tesnière L. 1959. *Éléments de syntaxe structurale.* Klincksieck, Paris.

Rambow O., Joshi A. 1994. A formal look at dependency grammars and phrase-structure grammars, with special consideration of word-order phenomena. In L. Wanner (ed.), *Current Issue in Meaning-Text Theory*, Pinter,London.

Ross J. 1967. *Constraints on Variables in Syntax.* PhD Thesis, MIT; 1985. *Infinite syntax !*, Reidel, Dordrecht.

Shieber S., Schabes Y. 1994. An alternative conception of tree-adjoining derivation. *Computational Linguistics,* 20(1), 91-124.

Vijay-Shanker K. 1987. *A Study of Tree Adjoining Grammars*. PhD thesis, University of Pennsylvania.

The Representation of Czech Light Verb Constructions in a Valency Lexicon

Václava Kettnerová and **Markéta Lopatková**
Charles University in Prague
Faculty of Mathematics and Physics
Institute of Formal and Applied Linguistics
Czech Republic
{kettnerova,lopatkova}@ufal.mff.cuni.cz

Abstract

Light verb constructions (LVCs) pose a serious challenge for both theoretical and applied linguistics as their syntactic structures are not solely determined by verbs alone but also by predicative nouns. In this contribution, we introduce an initial step to a new formal lexicographic representation of LVCs for the valency lexicon of Czech verbs, *VALLEX*.

The main idea underlying our representation is to decompose the information on an LVC between (i) the verbal valency frame and (ii) the nominal valency frame. Both deep and surface syntactic structures of LVCs can be easily derived from the information given in the verbal and nominal frames by application of formal rules as they are introduced in this contribution.

1 Introduction

Light verb constructions (LVCs) represent a type of complex predicate where two syntactic elements serve as a single predicate – for example, in Czech, light verbs combine with predicative nouns, ex. (1), adjectives, ex. (2), or adverbs, ex. (3) (LVCs are typed in bold). These combinations are characterized by ambivalent relations: from a syntactic point of view, a light verb is the governing component of the collocation; however, from a semantic point of view, it is the predicative noun that represents the governing component.

(1) *Petr* ***získal souhlas*** *od svého nadřízeného ke změně právního zástupce firmy.*
Eng. Peter **won approval** from his boss to change the legal representative of the company.

(2) *Jan* ***je podobný*** *svému otci.*
Eng. John **is like** his father.

(3) *Výpověď klíčového svědka by mohla* ***vnést*** *do případu* ***jasno****.*
Eng. Key witness testimony could **shed light** on the case.

Considering the wide range of issues, this study is limited to Czech LVCs based on the collocations of a light verb and a predicative noun, see ex. (1).

Despite being subject to many analyses, see esp. (Butt, 2010), a clear-cut definition of LVCs is still missing. In this paper, we follow both semantic and syntactic criteria for distinguishing LVCs. (i) The semantic operational criterion is based on the observation that a predicative noun (a predicative adjective or a predicative adverb) – as a semantic governing element – stands for the entire collocation of the predicative noun and a light verb; i.e, a predicative noun shows the same semantic distribution as the entire collocation. (ii) According to the syntactic criterion, some valency complementations of a light verb and a predicative noun have to be referentially identical, see esp. (Radimský, 2010) and (Kolářová, 2010).

Like other types of multiword expressions, LVCs pose a serious challenge for both theoretical and applied linguistics (Sag et al., 2002). As they require special treatment in NLP tasks, esp. in machine translation, their automatic recognition would bring a substantial benefit. Developing automatic recognition tools can be greatly assisted by lexical resources providing formal description of LVCs, see e.g. PropBank (Hwang et al., 2010), and WordNet (Vincze et al., 2012).

In this paper, we propose a formal representation of LVCs in the valency lexicon of Czech verbs, *VALLEX*.[1] The *VALLEX* lexicon is a collection of rich linguistically annotated data resulting from an attempt at a formal description of the valency behavior of Czech verbs. It provides the information on the valency structure of Czech

[1] http://ufal.mff.cuni.cz/vallex

Proceedings of the Second International Conference on Dependency Linguistics (DepLing 2013), pages 147–156,
Prague, August 27–30, 2013.

verbs in the form of valency frames, each valency frame corresponding to a single verbal lexical unit. For the description of valency, the valency theory formulated within the Functional Generative Description (FGD) – a dependency based framework – has been adopted (Sgall et al., 1986). Valency in FGD is related to the tectogrammatical layer – to a layer of linguistically structured meaning (roughly speaking, to a deep-syntactic layer). Five types of verbal actants – labeled by functors ACTor (ACT), PATient (PAT), ADDRessee (ADDR), ORIGin (ORIG), and EFFect (EFF) – have been determined. The first two – ACT and PAT – are distinguished on the syntactic basis. In assigning the remaining three actants – ADDR, ORIG and EFF – semantic criteria are taken into account as well, see esp. (Panevová, 1994).

The issue of LVCs (as well as other types of complex predicates) has remained underdeveloped in *VALLLEX* so far. The main motivation of this paper is to propose an adequate representation of this phenomenon in order to fill such serious gap in the description of valency behavior of Czech verbs. When designing an LVCs representation for *VALLEX*, we draw inspiration esp. from the Explanatory Combinatorial Dictionary of the Contemporary Russian Language elaborated within the Meaning-Text Theory, in which a strong emphasis is put on the systematic description of combinatorial potentials of lexical units, see (Mel'čuk and Žolkovskij, 1984). For the description of LVCs, several lexical functions – allowing to identify verbonominal collocations – are used, see (Mel'čuk, 1996).

We have carried out a detailed analysis of semantic and deep syntactic aspects (Section 2) as well as surface syntactic aspects (Section 3) of the given constructions. The analysis of the LVCs based on the combination of light verbs with predicative nouns can be conducted either (i) from the perspective of a light verb (Gross, 1981), or (ii) from the perspective of a predicative noun (Mel'čuk, 1996). Each of these analyses poses different challenging problems. Moreover, they can lead to more or less different interpretations of forming complex syntactic structure of LVCs.

The representation of LVC proposed in this article combines these two perspectives: (i) From the *semantic point of view*, it is a predicative noun that provides the LVC with its semantic participants; thus semantic aspects of LVCs are described from the perspective of a predicative noun here. (ii) On the other hand, *deep syntactic aspects* are described from the perspective of a (light) verb as it is a verb that provides its valency potential for semantic participants (evoked by the noun) and thus determines a core syntactic structure of a sentence.

The results of this analysis have been reflected in the representation of Czech LVCs in the *VALLEX* lexicon (Section 4). The proposed representation decomposes the information on LVCs between verbal and nominal lexicon entries, which are interlinked by a special attribute `-lvc`. Moreover, a special attribute `-map` attached to the verbal frame provides the information on the linking between verbal and nominal valency complementations referring to the same entities in LVCs. Based on this linking, deep and surface syntactic structure of LVCs can be derived by application of formal rules, which capture 'patterns' common to individual types of LVCs.

2 Semantic and (Deep) Syntactic Aspects

In this section, semantic and (deep) syntactic aspects of Czech LVCs are described in detail. When describing LVCs, it shows fruitful to distinguish:

(i) semantic participants involved in the situation expressed by a given LVC (related to semantic content),[2] roughly corresponding to semantic actants in MTT, see (Mel'čuk, 2004a; Mel'čuk, 2004b),

(ii) valency complementations (related to the deep syntactic layer), and

(iii) surface syntactic positions (related to the surface syntactic layer).

Here the relation between semantic participants (Subsection 2.1) and valency complementations in LVCs is discussed (Subsection 2.2).

2.1 Semantic Participants

Verbonominal collocations forming LVCs represent a type of complex predicates where two syntactic elements – a light verb and a predicative noun – serve as a single predicate. In contrast to a single predicating verb, in LVCs, semantic features are decomposed between a light verb and a predicative noun.

[2]Generally, whereas the inventory of units of syntactic layers have been well elaborated, the inventory of semantic participants has not been satisfactorily compiled so far in FGD. Here we have adopted semantic roles used in FrameNet for the description of semantic participants.

As to the distribution of semantic properties, a light verb appears to be a semantically incomplete element expressing only general semantic properties (esp. aspectual nuances). To be semantically complete, it enters into the combination with a predicative noun which contributes individual lexical-semantic properties into the resulting complex predicate (Macháčková, 1979).

The following examples make evident that it is the noun (not the light verb) that determines the number of semantic participants (indicated by their semantic labels) expressed in LVCs, ex. (4)–(5), and their semantic features, ex. (6)–(7).

(4) *Policista*$_{Speaker}$ ***podal hlášení*** *o akci*$_{Inform}$ *svému veliteli*$_{Recip}$.
'The officer$_{Speaker}$ – handed – a report – on the action$_{Info}$ – to his commander$_{Recip}$.'
Eng. The officer **reported** on the action to his commander.

(5) *Sportovec*$_{Agent}$ ***podal*** *v závodu velký* ***výkon***.
'The sportsman$_{Agent}$ – handed – in the race – a great performance.'
Eng. The sportsman **gave** a great **performance** in the race.

(6) *Tento počítač / člověk*$_{in/animate}$ ***dělá*** *hodně* ***práce***.
Eng. This computer/man$_{in/animate}$ **does** much **work**.

(7) *Tento *počítač / člověk*$_{in/animate}$ ***dělá*** *velkou* ***kariéru***.
Eng. This *computer / man$_{in/animate}$ **makes** a great **career**. (Radimský, 2010)

For instance, the light verb *obdržet* 'to receive' is depleted of individual semantic properties – including semantic participants, see ex. (9) – foregrounding only the abstract semantic facets (i.e., 'transferring') of its full verb counterpart; the latter expresses 'transferring a physical object from an agent to a recipient' characterized by three semantic participants, namely 'Recipient' (abbr. 'Recip'), 'Agent', and 'Theme', see ex. (8).

(8) *Výherce*$_{Recip}$ *od nás*$_{Agent}$ ***obdrží*** *drobný dárek*$_{Theme}$.
Eng. 'The winner$_{Recip}$ **will receive** a small gift$_{Theme}$ from us$_{Agent}$.'

(9) *Velitel*$_{Recip}$ ***obdržel hlášení*** *od policisty*$_{Speaker}$ *o akci*$_{Inform}$.
Eng. The commander$_{Recip}$ **received the report** on the action$_{Inform}$ from the officer$_{Speaker}$.

To be semantically complete, the light verb combines with the predicative noun *hlášení* 'report' that denotes the situation of 'conveying a piece of information to a recipient by a speaker'. This situation involves three participants – 'Speaker', 'Recip', and 'Information' (abbr. 'Inform'). As a result, the situation expressed by the collocation *obdržet hlášení* 'to receive report' is the situation of reporting, characterized by the semantic participants provided by the predicative noun, see ex. (9).

2.2 Valency Complementations

From a (deep) syntactic point of view, both a predicative noun and a light verb in an LVC preserve their own valency potentials (represented in a form of valency frames), i.e., they are characterized each by own sets of valency complementations. In case of predicative nouns, valency frames represent the usage of nouns in nominal structures. In case of light verbs, we observe that in Czech valency frames are prototypically identical with the frames of their full verb counterparts. Thus we assume that the valency frames of light verbs are inherited from the valency frames of the respective full verbs, see Subsection 2.3.2. As light verbs – entering into combination with predicative nouns – form multiword lexical units, their valency frames describe some kind of 'proto lexical units' (in contrast to valency frames of full verbs, where valency frames correspond to lexical units).

For instance, both the verb *obdržet* 'to receive' and the noun *hlášení* 'report' forming the LVC *obdržet hlášení* 'to receive report' are characterized by their own valency frames: (i) The valency frame of the verb is inherited from the valency frame of the full verb (10), see ex. (11). (ii) The valency frame of the noun (12) represents the usage of the noun in a nominal structure, see ex. (13).

(10) *obdržet* 'to receive' ... ACT PAT ORIG
The valency complementations of the full verb are mapped onto the semantic participants 'Recip', 'Theme', and 'Agent', respectively; see ex. (11).

(11) *Výherce*$_{ACT:Recip}$ *od nás*$_{ORIG:Agent}$ ***obdrží*** *drobný dárek*$_{PAT:Theme}$.
Eng. 'The winner$_{ACT:Recip}$ **will receive** a small gift$_{PAT:Theme}$ from us$_{ORIG:Agent}$.'

(12) *hlášení* 'report' ... ACT ADDR PAT
The nominal valency complementations are mapped onto the semantic participants 'Speaker', 'Recip', and 'Inform' respectively, see ex. (13).

(13) *Policistovo*$_{ACT:Speaker}$ ***hlášení*** *veliteli*$_{ADDR:Recip}$ *o akci*$_{PAT:Inform}$ *bylo stručné.*
Eng. The officer's$_{ACT:Speaker}$ **report** on the action$_{PAT:Inform}$ to his commander$_{ADDR:Recip}$ was brief.

The correspondence between valency complementations of a verb and those of a noun in LVCs is discussed in the following subsections.

2.3 Linking of Verbal and Nominal Valency Complementations

A predicative noun (as was shown above) contributes its semantic participants (linked with nominal valency complementations) to the LVC. On the other hand, the verbal complementations are not semantically saturated, see Subsection 2.1. To acquire semantic capacity, the verbal complementations are interlinked with nominal ones (saturated by nominal semantic participants).

The linking of verbal complementations with the nominal ones is reflected in the notions of fusion or merger posited in connection with LVCs by authors from different theoretical backgrounds, see esp. (Alsina, 1997) and (Mohanan, 1997). In FGD, this fact is tentatively referred to as sharing valency complementations between a verbal and a nominal valency frame which is indicated by a specific type of grammatical coreference – quasi-control, see esp. (Mikulová et al., 2006), (Kolářová, 2010), and (Cinková, 2009).

For instance, when the verb *obdržet* 'to receive' combines with the predicative noun *hlášení* 'report' into the LVC, the nominal valency complementations are still linked with nominal semantic participants (namely 'Speaker', 'Recip', and 'Inform', see (12) in Subsection 2.2). On the other hand, the verbal complementations do not correspond to any semantic participants. To acquire the semantic content, the verbal complementations are linked with the nominal complementations (and via them to the above given nominal semantic participants), see Fig. 1.

As to the mechanism of the linking: when the light verb *obdržet* 'to receive' combines with the

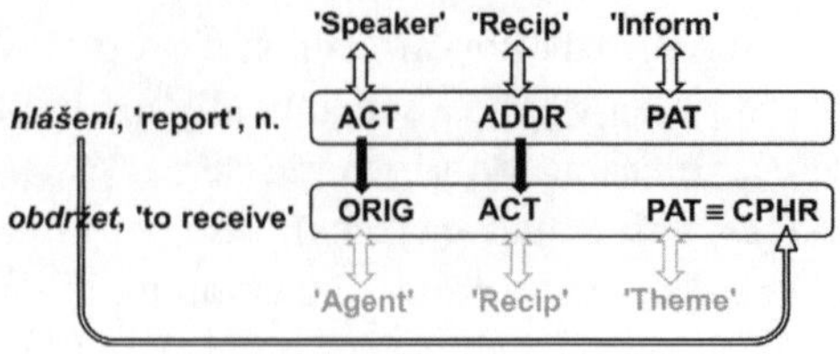

Figure 1: The linking of verbal valency complementations with nominal complementations (black arrows) and their saturation with the nominal semantic participants in the LVC *obdržet hlášení* 'to receive report'.

predicative noun *hlášení* 'report', the noun occupies the verbal valency 'PATient'. In accordance with FGD, we re-assign this valency complementation with the functor 'CPHR' ('CompoundPHRaseme') referring to a predicative component in complex predicates, see (Mikulová et al., 2006). The remaining valency complementations, 'ORIGin' and 'ACTor' in the verbal frame (10), are linked with the nominal complementations 'ACTor' and 'ADDRessee' in (12), respectively. As argued above, the linking allows the given verbal complementations to acquire semantic capacity from the nominal complementations.

2.3.1 Direction of Linking

With respect to the fact that a change of a light verb may trigger the changes in the linking of verbal and nominal valency complementations, we assume that it is the light verb that determines the linking of its complementation(s).

For instance, according to our suggestion, the arrangement of the links is evoked by the verb *obdržet* 'to receive' (not by the noun *hlášení* 'report') in the LVC *obdržet hlášení* 'to receive report', see Fig. 1. This hypothesis is supported by the following observation: when the noun *hlášení* 'report' enters into combination with another light verb, e.g., with the verb *podat* 'to hand' (resulting in the LVC *podat hlášení* 'to make report'), it leads to the rearrangement of the linking – in this case, the nominal 'ACTor' and 'ADDRessee' are linked with the 'ACTor' and 'ADDRessee' of the verb *podat* 'to hand', respectively, see ex. (14) and Fig. 2.

(14) *Policista*$_{ACT:Speaker}$ ***podal hlášení*** *o akci*$_{PAT:Info}$ *svému veliteli*$_{ADDR:Recip}$.
Eng. The officer$_{ACT:Speaker}$ **reported** on the action$_{PAT:Info}$ to his

commander$_{ADDR:Recip}$.

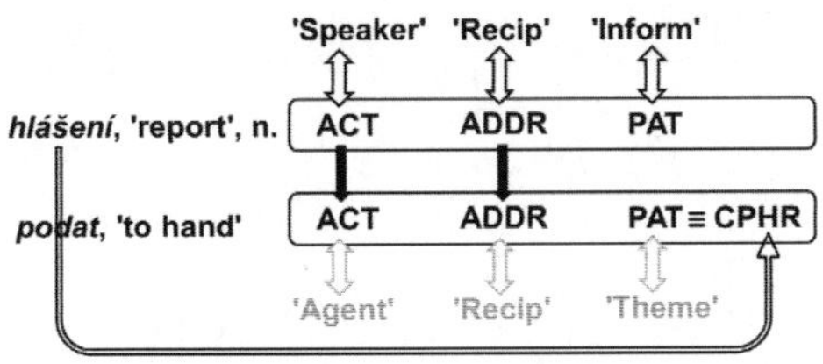

Figure 2: The linking of verbal valency complementations with nominal complementations (black arrows) and their saturation with the nominal semantic participants in the LVC *podat hlášení* 'to make report'.

2.3.2 Verbal Valency Frame of a Light Verb

Let us repeat that from our point of view, valency frames of light verbs are inherited from the valency frames of their full counterparts, i.e., the valency frames of light verbs are prototypically identical with the frames of the respective full verbs (with the only difference that the complementation referring to a predicative noun is marked with 'CPHR' functor), as was stated in Subsections 2.2 and 2.3.

There is only one additional exception. In comparison with the valency frames of full verbs, the number of valency complementations in the frames of light verbs can be reduced. According to our proposal, only those verbal valency complementations from the valency frame that acquire semantic content from nominal ones are retained in the valency frame. Thus in case of light verbs, only those valency complementations (in addition to 'CPHR') that acquire semantic capacity via the linking with nominal complementations are employed in the valency frame. Those verbal complementations that are depleted in any semantic content (i.e., those that remain unlinked with any nominal complementation) are removed from the valency frame.

These cases occur when the number of nominal complementations is lower than the number of verbal ones left in the verbal valency frame after a predicative noun occupies some verbal complementation. Let us exemplify this case on the verb *podat* 'to hand' when it enters into combination with the predicative noun *výkon* 'performance' (resulting in the LVC *podat výkon* 'to give performance'), see ex. (5). This predicative noun is characterized by a single valency complementation – 'ACTor' corresponding to the semantic participant 'Agent'. When this noun combines with the verb *podat* 'to hand', it fills the verbal 'PATient' (assigned with 'CPHR'). Then two verbal complementations – 'ACTor' and 'ADDRessee' – remain left in the verbal frame. The verbal 'ACTor' is linked with the nominal 'ACTor'; however, the verbal 'ADDRessee' remains unlinked. As a result, the 'ADDRessee' is deleted from the respective verbal valency frame, see Fig. 3.

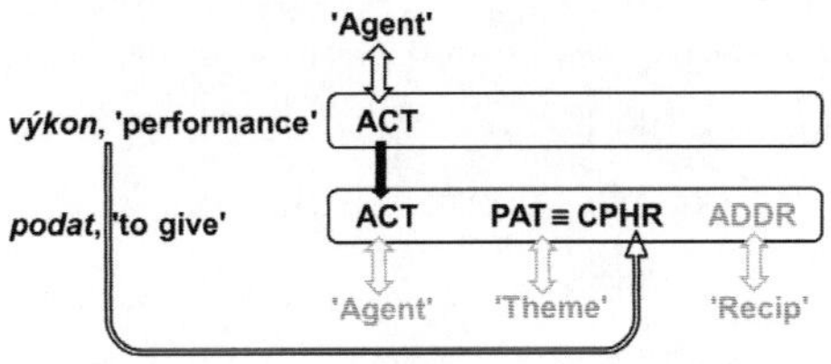

Figure 3: The linking of verbal valency complementations with nominal complementations (black arrows) and their saturation with the nominal semantic participants in the LVC *podat výkon* 'to give performance'; see esp. the unlinked (and thus deleted) verbal 'ADDRessee' (in gray).

3 Syntactic Expressions and Morphemic Forms of Valency Complementations

We have argued that both a light verb and a predicative noun retain their own valency potentials, i.e., they correspond to separate valency frames, see Subsection 2.2. These valency structures enter into interaction which results in a complex surface syntactic structure of a LVC.

In general, the number of valency complementations that can be expressed on the surface is determined by the number of semantic participants involved in the situation expressed by an LVC, plus one verbal complementation ('CPHR') that is reserved for a predicative noun.

Czech, as an inflectional language encoding surface syntactic relations via morphological cases, gives us an excellent opportunity to study the role of valency complementations of a light verb and a predicative noun in the complex surface structure formation. According to morphemic forms of valency complementations expressed on the surface in LVCs, we can infer that the surface syntactic structure of an LVC is typically partly formed by a verbal valency frame and partly by a nominal valency frame.

We formulate the following hypothesis: It is a verb that, in general, determines the syntactic structure of a sentence. Thus in case that a particular semantic participant is linked with both a nominal valency complementation (directly) and a verbal valency complementation (via the link to a nominal valency complementation), it is a verb (not a noun) that retains the complementation in the resulted surface structure (and thus prescribe the morphemic form of the complementation). As each semantic participant is prototypically expressed only once, we consider the respective nominal complementation as elliptic (i.e., as having zero morphemic realization).

Based on this hypothesis, the following rules can be formulated:

- From the verbal valency frame, those verbal valency complementations that are semantically saturated via linking with some nominal valency complementations can be expressed on the surface.
- From the nominal frame, those nominal complementations that remain unlinked with any verbal ones are expressed on the surface. On the contrary, the nominal complementation affected by linking with verbal complementation remains unexpressed on the surface.[3]

Let us exemplify the proposed rules on the example of the LVC *obdržet hlášení* 'to receive report', which expresses the situation of reporting characterized by three situational participants – 'Speaker', 'Recip', and 'Inform' (as discussed in Section 2). Thus three valency complementations can be surface syntactically structured in the LVC (in addition to the valency complementation occupied by the predicative noun), see ex. (19).

As to the valency behavior, the light verb *obdržet* 'to receive' is characterized by the valency frame (16) inherited from the frame of its full counterpart (15). The valency frame of the predicative noun *hlášení* 'report' (17) describes the usage of the noun in a nominal structure, as in ex. (18).

[3]In some cases, 'ACTor' can be expressed twice on the surface, i.e., as both a nominal and a verbal complementation, despite being interlinked, e.g., ***Nemocnice svůj** boj proti rušení akutních lůžek nevzdávají.* 'The **hospitals** do not give up **their** fight against eliminating acute beds.' However, the possibility of expressing the 'ACTor' twice in a surface structure is subject to strong stylistic constraints in Czech.

(15) *obdržet*: ACT_{nom} PAT_{acc} ORIG_{od+gen}

(16) *obdržet*: ACT_{nom} CPHR_{acc} ORIG_{od+gen}

(17) *hlášení*: $\mathrm{ACT}_{pos,gen}$ ADDR_{dat} PAT_{o+loc}

(18) *Policistovo*$_{ACT:pos}$ ***hlášení*** *veliteli*$_{ADDR:dat}$ *o akci*$_{PAT:o+loc}$ *bylo stručné.*
Eng. The officer's$_{ACT}$ **report** on the action to his commander$_{ADDR}$ was brief.

(19) *Velitel*$_{ACT:nom}$ ***obdržel hlášení***$_{CPHR:acc}$ *o akci*$_{PAT:o+loc}$ *od policisty*$_{ORIG:od+gen}$.
Eng. The commander$_{ACT}$ **received report**$_{CPHR}$ on the action$_{PAT}$ from the officer$_{ORIG}$.

1. When used in the LVC, one valency complementation of the verb *obdržet* 'to receive' – 'PATient' expressed in accusative case – is filled with the predicative noun *hlášení* 'report'; instead of 'PATient', this complementation is marked by the 'CPHR' functor distinguishing the light verb from the full verb, see above.

2. Five valency complementations – two from the verbal frame ('ACTor' and 'ORIGin') and three from the nominal one ('ACTor', 'ADDRessee', and 'PATient') – remain left in total for the expression of three semantic participants – 'Speaker', 'Recip', and 'Inform'. Two verbal valency complementations 'ACTor' and 'ORIGin' acquire semantic capacity from the nominal 'ADDRessee' and 'ACTor', respectively, see Subsection 2.2 and Fig. 1. Namely, the verbal 'ACTor' is linked with 'Recip' (via nominal 'ADDRessee') and the verbal 'ORIGin' is linked with 'Speaker' (via nominal 'ACTor'). According to our hypothesis, the verb retains these two complementations in the surface structure and it determines their morphemic forms, nominative and prepositional group *od*+genitive, respectively; see valency frame (15).

As a result, nominal 'ADDRessee' and 'ACTor', remain unexpressed on the surface, see Fig. 4 displaying the (simplified) dependency tree representing ex. (19) – the linked valency complementations are related by coreferential arrows going from the complementations unexpressed on the surface to the expressed ones.

3. The nominal 'PATient' – not being linked with any verbal complementation, see Fig. 1 – is expressed by the prepositional group *o*+locative modifying the noun as when the noun is used outside the LVC, see ex. (18) and (19).

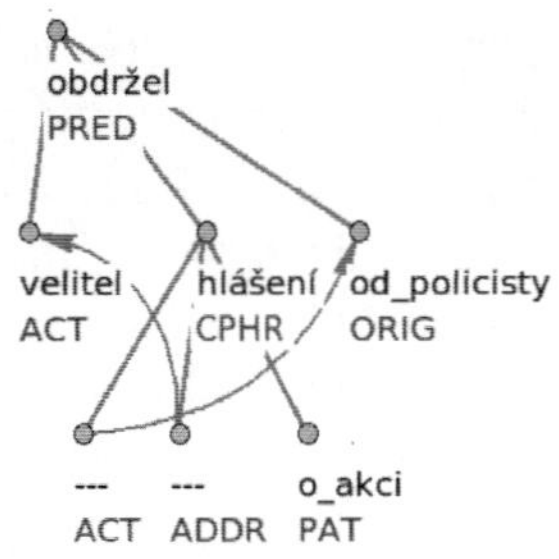

Figure 4: The (simplified) dependency tree for the LVC *obdržet hlášení* 'to receive report' in ex. (19).

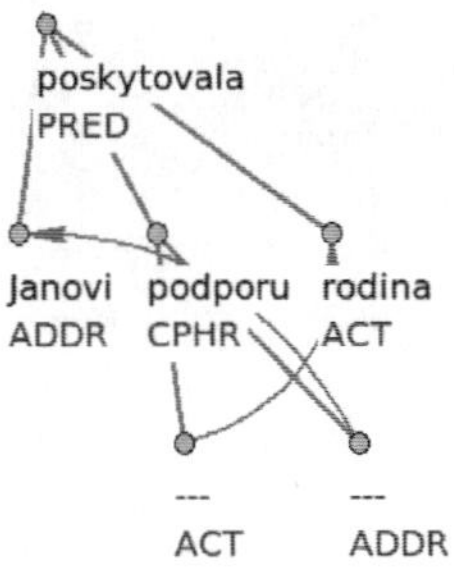

Figure 5: The (simplified) dependency tree for the LVC *poskytovat podporu* 'to provide support' in ex. (20).

The proposed hypotheses on the surface syntactic formation of LVCs deserve further examination on the corpus data.

3.1 Basic Typology of Syntactic Structures with Light Verb Constructions

We have identified three types of complex surface syntactic structures of LVCs in Czech (according to the linking criteria). They are briefly exemplified in the following paragraphs.

Type 1. All verbal complementations (excluding 'CPHR') are interlinked with the nominal ones and no nominal complementation remains unlinked. In this case, all the verbal complementations are expressed on the surface whereas all nominal complementations remain unexpressed. Compare with ex. (20) where the verbal 'ACTor' and 'ADDRessee' (linked with the nominal 'ACTor' and 'ADDResse', respectively) are realized in the resulting surface structure, whereas the respective nominal ones remain unexpressed (Fig. 5).

(20) *Janovi*$_{ADDR}$ ***poskytovala podporu***$_{CPHR}$ *rodina*$_{ACT}$.
Eng. John's family$_{ACT}$ **provided support**$_{CPHR}$ to him$_{ADDR}$.

Type 2. All verbal valency complementations (excluding 'CPHR') are linked with the nominal ones; however, some nominal complementations remain unlinked. In this case, the linked verbal complementations are expressed whereas the corresponding nominal complementations are unexpressed in the resulted surface structure (as in Type 1). Further, the unlinked nominal complementations remain expressed as nominal ones. Compare with ex. (21) where the verbal 'ACTor' (linked with the nominal 'ACTor') is expressed in the resulted surface structure, whereas the nominal 'ADDRessee' (being unlinked with any verbal complementation) is realized as a nominal complementation (expressed by the morphemic form determined by the given noun, Fig. 6).

(21) *Dceřin přítel*$_{ACT}$ *na nás*$_{ADDR}$ ***udělal dojem***$_{CPHR}$.
Eng. The daughter's boyfriend$_{ACT}$ **made an impression**$_{CPHR}$ on us$_{ADDR}$.

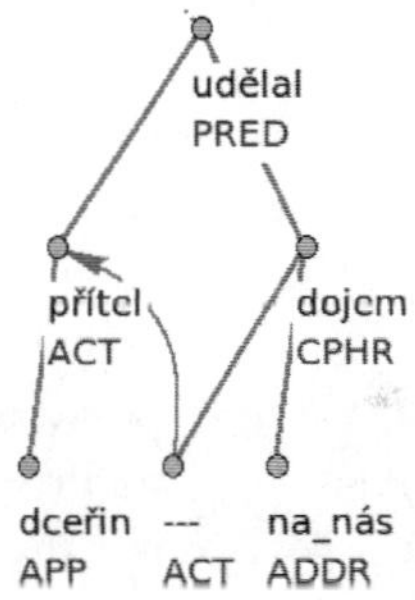

Figure 6: The (simplified) dependency tree for the LVC *udělat dojem* 'to make impression' in ex. (21).

Type 3. Not all verbal valency complementations (besides 'CPHR') are linked with the nominal ones, see Fig. 3. The linked ones are expressed on the surface whereas the unlinked ones are deleted from the verbal valency frame, see ex. (22) where the verbal 'ADDRessee' is not structured (Fig. 7), see also Subsection 2.3.2, Fig. 3.

(22) *Sportovec*$_{ACT}$ ***podal výkon***$_{CPHR}$.
Eng. The sportsman$_{ACT}$ **gave** a great **performance**$_{CPHR}$.

4 Light Verb Constructions in *VALLEX*

In this section, the lexicographic representation of LVCs is proposed for the valency lexicon of Czech

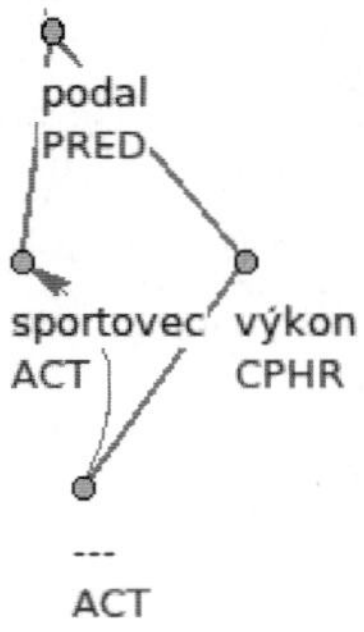

Figure 7: The (simplified) dependency tree for for the LVC *podat výkon* 'to give performance' in ex. (22).

verbs, *VALLEX*. As every light verb and predicative noun creating an LVC are characterized by their own valency potentials, we represent them by separate valency frames: (i) for light verbs (Subsection 4.1) and (ii) for predicative nouns (Subsection 4.2). These frames are interlinked by references so that the whole collocations can be easily obtained. A special attention is paid to the representation of the mapping between valency complementations of predicative nouns and light verbs.

In the current version *VALLEX 2.5*, there are roughly 2,730 verb lexeme entries containing together around 6,460 verb lexical units; under the term lexical unit, we understand a form-meaning complex with (relatively) stable and discrete semantic properties. A lexeme then represents an abstract two-fold unit associating lexical form(s) with lexical unit(s). The verbs were selected according to their frequency in (the part of) the Czech National Corpus[4] SYN2000 – the corpus coverage is approximately 98%. In building the lexicon, the main emphasis was laid on both human and machine readability – this is reflected in three formats of the lexicon: XML, HTML, and PDF formats.

The lexical entries of verbs in the *VALLEX* lexicon were exhaustively described in, e.g., (Žabokrtský and Lopatková, 2007). Let us shortly recapitulate here the basic information relevant for our explanation. Each lexical unit – represented by a lemma (or set of lemmas) – is characterized by obligatory attributes: gloss(es), a valency frame, and example(s). The valency frame, which provides the core information in the lexicon, is modeled as a sequence of valency slots. Each slot stands for one valency complementation; it is characterized by a functor (indicating the type of the semantic relation of a valency complementation to a verb), by obligatoriness (in superscript), and by a list of possible morphemic form(s) (in subscript). In addition, optional attributes may follow (providing the information on syntactico-semantic class, the information of applicable alternations, etc.).

[4] `http://ucnk.ff.cuni.cz`

4.1 Representation of Light Verbs

In this subsection, we describe the necessary modification of verb lexical entries for the purpose of the representation of light verbs. Let us stress that light verbs in the *VALLEX* lexicon will be represented by 'proto lexical units' (proto-LUs) (as light verbs form multiword lexical units only in combination with predicative nouns, see Subsection 2.2). These proto-LUs are characterized by valency frames inherited from the frames of their full verb counterparts. Proto-LUs have to provide the following types of information:

I. In the inherited frame, the verbal valency complementation that is filled with a predicative noun is specified – its functor is changed to 'CPHR'. In case that more verbal valency complementations can be filled by (different) predicative nouns, more inherited valency frames are determined, with different valency slots identified as 'CPHR'. This functor covers the similar information which is captured by lexical functions (namely $\texttt{Oper}_i$, $\texttt{Func}_i$, and $\texttt{Labor}_i, j, (k)$) in the Meaning-Text Theory, see esp. (Mel'čuk, 1996).

II. For each inherited valency frame, a list of possible linking(s) between the valency complementations of a light verb and those of a predicative noun is given in a special attribute `-map`, see Fig. 8.[5] The following information can be drawn from the linkings:

– which of the given valency complementation(s) is/are expressed in a surface structure as verbal modification(s) (those complementations that are linked (via nominal complementations) with semantic participants, see Section 3, Type 1, 2 and 3), and

– which verbal valency complementation(s) is/are deleted from the verbal frame (those that are not linked) and thus cannot be expressed on the surface (Section 3, Type 3).

[5] As it is a light verb that forms the syntactic structure of a sentence, this information is listed within verbal frames, see Subsection 2.3.

III. Moreover, each inherited valency frame of a light verb contains the references to possible predicative nouns that form LVCs with the given light verb. As the mapping may differ for different predicative nouns, these references are attached to individual types of linkings.

For instance, the verb *podávat*^{impf}, *podat*^{pf} 'to hand' as a full verb is characterized by the lexical unit displayed on the top of Fig. 8. The valency frame representing the full verb is inherited by the proto-LU of the light verb; this proto-LU is characterized by the valency frame displayed below. In this valency frame, the 'PATient' is filled by predicative nouns (and thus replaced by the 'CPHR' functor). Moreover, two possible types of linking between verbal and nominal complementations are specified. Both linkings are attributed with the list of predicative nouns forming respective collocations.

podávat ^{impf}**, podat** ^{pf} 'to give, to hand' **LU1**
-gloss: impf: dávat do ruky pf: dát do ruky 'to pass st to sb's hand'
-frame: **ACT** $^{obl}_{nom}$ **ADDR** $^{obl}_{dat}$ **PAT** $^{obl}_{acc}$
-example: impf: podávat cihly bratrovi 'to hand bricks to the brother'
pf: podat kolegovi šroubovák 'to hand a screwdriver to the colleague'
-class: exchange

podávat ^{impf}**, podat** ^{pf} 'to give, to hand' **proto-LU1**
-frame: **ACT** $^{obl}_{nom}$ **ADDR** $^{obl}_{dat}$ **CPHR** $^{obl}_{acc}$
-map$_1$: $ACT_V - ACT_N$; $ADDR_V - ADDR_N$
-lvc$_1$: hlášení, námitka, návrh, oznámení, pokyn, stížnost, vysvětlení, zpráva, ...
-map$_2$: $ACT_V - ACT_N$
-lvc$_2$: demise, výkon, výpověď, ...

Figure 8: The lexical unit of the full verb and the proto lexical unit of the light verb *podat, podávat* 'to hand' in *VALLEX*.

4.2 Representation of Predicative Nouns

The current version of the *VALLEX* lexicon covers only verbs, it does not comprise nouns. Thus for the purpose of the description of LVCs, it is necessary to enrich the lexicon with predicative nouns. The logical structure of *VALLEX* is designed in a way allowing for its further enriching with another part-of-speech.

As in case of verbs, each lexical unit of a noun is provided with a set of obligatory attributes providing the key information on the lexical unit – including a valency frame, gloss(es), and example(s). Again, the valency frame contains the core information on valency behavior of nouns. In case of predicative nouns, each noun is assigned the valency frame corresponding to the usage of the noun outside LVC(s), see, e.g., the valency frame of the noun *hlášení* 'report' given in (17), Section 3 describing the usage of the noun in ex. (18).

In addition, a list of optional attributes that are applicable only to relevant lexical units may follow. Each predicative noun entering into combination with a light verb is attached with the optional attribute `-lvc` containing references to possible light verbs forming LVCs with the given predicative noun;[6] see, e.g., the proposed *VALLEX* lexical unit for the noun *hlášení* 'report' in Fig. 9.

hlášení 'report'
-gloss: stručná zpráva, zvl. služební, úřední, vojenská apod.
'a short information, esp. official announcement/statement'
-frame: **ACT** $^{obl}_{pos,gen}$ **ADDR** $^{obl}_{dat}$ **PAT** $^{obl}_{o+loc}$
- example: policistovo hlášení veliteli o průběhu; hlášení policisty veliteli o průběhu akce 'the officer's report on the course of the action to his commander'
-lvc: verb: obdržet, podat, předat, přijmout, učinit, vypracovat, ...
-class: reporting

Figure 9: The proposed lexical unit in *VALLEX* describing the noun *podat* 'to hand'.

5 Conclusion

We have provided a detailed analysis of the semantic and deep syntactic aspects of light verb constructions – we have explained the role of semantic participants with nominal and verbal valency complementations and their interlinking. We have also addressed the issue of surface syntactic expressions of LVCs by giving an explanation of changes in morphemic forms of the valency complementations affected in these constructions.

Our hypotheses have been projected to the proposal of the representation of Czech LVCs in the *VALLEX* lexicon. We have proposed to decompose the information on LVCs between (i) verbal valency frames (corresponding to light verbs) and (ii) nominal valency frames (corresponding to predicative nouns). Both frames are interlinked by special attribute `-lvc`.

The proposed representation reflects the close interplay between two components of LVCs – a

[6]The list of relevant light verbs are obtained automatically from the verbal part of the *VALLEX* lexicon – we suppose that for human readers, it is highly relevant to provide this information (also) within the nominal frame; the automatic extraction of such lists reduces duplicity (and thus decreases possible inconsistencies in the lexicon).

light verb and a predicative noun. The information provided by the `-lvc` attribute assigned to proto-lexical units representing light verbs together with valency frames (inherited from full verbs) make it easy to derive both deep syntactic structure as well as surface syntactic structure and morphemic expressions of verbal and nominal valency complementations of LVCs.

As the future work, the proposed hypotheses on surface syntactic formation of LVCs will be further examined on the corpus data. Moreover, esp. three issues should be addressed in connection with LVCs: As for light verbs, a comprehensive inventory of their aspectual nuances should be compiled and included in their representation. As for predicative nouns, the restrictions imposed on the morphological category of number (e.g., *upadnout do rozpaků* 'to fall into embarrassment' where the Czech predicative noun can be used only in plural) deserve further theoretical research whose results should be covered in the lexicon as well. Further, the possibility of expressing some of valency complementations twice in the surface structure deserves further investigation.

Acknowledgments

This work has been using language resources stored and/or distributed by the LINDAT-Clarin project of MŠMT (project LM2010013). The research reported in this paper has been supported by GA ČR, grant No. GA P406/12/0557.

References

Alex Alsina. 1997. Causatives in bantu and romance. In Alex Alsina, Joan Bresnan, and Peter Sells, editors, *Complex Predicates*, pages 203–246. CSLI Publications, Stanford, California.

Miriam Butt. 2010. The Light Verb Jungle: Still Hacking Away. In Brett Baker Mengistu Amberber and Mark Harvey, editors, *Complex Predicates in Cross-Linguistic Perspective*, pages 48–78. Cambridge University Press, Cambridge.

Silvie Cinková. 2009. *Words that Matter: Towards a Swedish-Czech Colligational Dictionary of Basic Verbs*, volume 2 of *Studies in Computational and Theoretical Linguistics*. UFAL, Prague.

Maurice Gross. 1981. Les bases empiriques de la notion de prédicat sématique. *Languages*, 63:7–53.

Jena D. Hwang et al. 2010. Propbank annotation of multilingual light verb constructions. In *Proceedings of LAW 4*, pages 82–90, Uppsala, Sweden. ACL.

Veronika Kolářová. 2010. *Valence deverbativních substantiv v češtině (na materiálu substantiv s dativní valencí)*. Univerzita Karlova, Nakladateltsví Karolinum, Praha.

Eva Macháčková. 1979. *Analytická spojení typu sloveso + abstraktní substantivum (analytické vyjadřování predikátů)*. Ústav pro jazyk český ČSAV, Praha.

Igor A. Mel'čuk. 1996. Lexical Functions: A Tool for the description of lexical relations in a lexicon. In Leo Wanner, editor, *Lexical Functions in Lexicography and Natural Language Processing*, pages 37–105. John Benjamins, Amsterdam/Philadelphia.

Igor A. Mel'čuk. 2004a. Actants in semantics and syntax I: actants in semantics. *Linguistics*, 42(1):1–66.

Igor A. Mel'čuk. 2004b. Actants in semantics and syntax II: actants in syntax. *Linguistics*, 42(2):247–291.

Igor A. Mel'čuk and Alexander Žolkovskij. 1984. *Tolkovo-kombinatornyj slovar' sovremennovo russkovo jazyka*. Wiener Slawistischer Almanach, Sonderband 14, Wien.

Marie Mikulová et al. 2006. Annotation on the tectogrammatical level in the Prague Dependency Treebank. Annotation manual. Technical Report TR-2006-30, ÚFAL MFF UK, Prague.

Tara Mohanan. 1997. Multidimensionality of Representation: NV Complex Predicates in Hindi. In Alex Alsina et al., editor, *Complex Predicates*, pages 431–471, Stanford, California. CSLI Publications.

Jarmila Panevová. 1994. Valency Frames and the Meaning of the Sentence. In Philip A. Luelsdorff, editor, *The Prague School of Structural and Functional Linguistics*, pages 223–243. John Benjamins Publishing Company, Amsterdam, Philadelphia.

Jan Radimský. 2010. *Verbo-nominální predikát s kategoriálním slovesem*. Editio Universitatis Bohemiae Meridionalis, České Budějovice.

Ivan A. Sag et al. 2002. Multiword Expressions: A Pain in the Neck for NLP. In *Proceedings of CICLING 2002*, pages 1–15, Mexico City, Mexico.

Petr Sgall, Eva Hajičová, and Jarmila Panevová. 1986. *The Meaning of the Sentence in Its Semantic and Pragmatic Aspects*. Reidel, Dordrecht.

Veronika Vincze, Attila Almási, and János Csirik. 2012. Multiword verbs in wordnets. In Ch. Fellbaum and P. Vossen, editors, *Proceedings of the 6th International Global WordNet Conference*, pages 377–381, Brno. Tribun.

Zdeněk Žabokrtský and Markéta Lopatková. 2007. Valency information in VALLEX 2.0: Logical structure of the lexicon. *The Prague Bulletin of Mathematical Linguistics*, (87):41–60.

A Deterministic Dependency Parser with Dynamic Programming for Sanskrit

Amba Kulkarni
Department of Sanskrit Studies
University of Hyderabad
apksh@uohyd.ernet.in

Abstract

We describe a Deterministic Dependency Parser for Sanskrit. The parse is developed following a Depth First traversal of a graph whose nodes represent morphological analyses of the words in a sentence. During the traversal, relations at each node are checked for local compatibility, and finally for each full path, the relations on the path are checked for global compatibility. Stacking of intermediate results guarantees dynamic programming. We also describe an interface that displays multiple parses compactly and facilitates users to select the desired parse among various possible solutions with a maximum of $n-1$ choices for a sentence with n words.

1 Introduction

Past decade has witnessed a lot of dynamism and upsurge of activities in the field of Sanskrit Computational Linguistics. Several computational tools became available to the Sanskrit community as a web service through the internet[1]. With the availability of a wide coverage grammar for Sanskrit in the form of *Aṣṭādhyāyī*, there was a natural tendency to follow the grammar based approach towards the development of these tools (Huet, 2009; Kulkarni et al., 2010; Kulkarni and Ramakrishnamacharyulu, 2013; Goyal and Huet, 2013). Nevertheless, there were also notable efforts to use pure machine learning approaches for building these tools with a small manually tagged corpus as a boot-strap (Hellwig, 2009). At the same time, a combination of the grammar based approach supported by the statistical evidences to push the most likely solution to the top were also followed (Kumar et al., 2010; Kulkarni and Kumar, 2011).

Sanskrit being influenced by the oral tradition, Sanskrit texts are typically written as a continuous string of characters. Characters at the juncture of word boundaries undergo euphonic changes thereby merging the word boundaries. This makes it challenging to split a given string into grammatically acceptable words before taking up the task of parsing. The task of joining two words is deterministic but splitting a string of characters into well-formed words is non-deterministic. This non-determinism together with splits at more than one places in a given string leads to exponential possibilities. Huet (2002, 2009) proposed a novel way of augmenting the nodes of a Finite State Transducer with appropriate sandhi rules, and achieved the segmentation in linear transitions. He also developed a shallow parser using the sub-categorisation frames, and the agreement rules. This parser is useful to rule out the non-solutions before proceeding for the full fledged parsing. A purely statistical parser for Sanskrit also exists (Hellwig, 2009).

The first full fledged parser for Sanskrit based on Pāṇinian Grammar formalism is described in (Kulkarni et al., 2010). This parser is implemented as a constraint solver. In this model, a word in a sentence is represented as a node in a graph G, and the relations between the words as directed labelled edges. The task of parsing a sentence is modelled as finding a sub-graph T of G which is a directed labelled Tree. The problem of parsing is divided into three tasks:

1. The first task is to establish labelled edges between the nodes. The information of expectancy and agreement is used to establish these labelled edges.

2. Next a sub-graph T of G is identified, such that T is a directed Tree which satisfies the

[1] http://sanskrit.uohyd.ernet.in/scl
http://tdil-dc.in/scl
http://sanskrit.inria.fr
http://kjc-fs-cluster.kjc.uni-heidelberg.de/dcs/index.php

Proceedings of the Second International Conference on Dependency Linguistics (DepLing 2013), pages 157–166,
Prague, August 27–30, 2013.

following constraints.

- Every node can have at the most one incoming arrow.
- No two edges emerging from the same node have the same label.
- There are no loops.
- The resulting Tree is projective, i.e. if the nodes are arranged linearly according to the word order, then no two links cross each other.
- It is ensured that certain relations which always occur in pairs e.g. anuyogī-pratiyogī (relata-1 and relata-2), kartṛsamānādhikaraṇam-kartā (predicative adjective and subject[2]), etc. do have their counter-relatum present in the parse.

3. Finally in case there is more than one possible directed Tree, the solutions are prioritized.

The implementation of the parser is reported in Kulkarni et al. (2010). The graph G is represented as a 5D matrix C with a typical element $([i, j], R, [l, m])$, where R is the relation from the mth analysis of the lth word to the jth analysis of the ith word. In order to prioritize the solutions, every relation is assigned a weight. A simple Cost function is defined as Cost = $\sum w * |j - i|$, where w is the weight of the relation between the nodes i and j.

The main disadvantage of this approach is the complexity. The size of the 5D matrix is $N * M * K * N * M$, where N is the total number of words in a sentence, M is the maximum number of morph analyses for a word in a given sentence and K is the maximum number of distinct possible relations among the words in a given sentence. Sanskrit words being overloaded with morphological analysis, frequently occurring words tend to have several analyses possible[3]. Similarly though the average length of the sentences[4] is around 10, the sentences from literary texts tend to be longer with more than 20 words.

Sanskrit grammar texts discuss various relations, among words, necessary to interpret the meaning of a sentence. All these relations were compiled and classified by Ramakrishnamacharyulu (2009) and further they were investigated for their suitability for automatic parsing. Out of around 90 relations listed there, only those relations which one can predict based on the syntactico-semantic information available in a sentence are considered for automatic tagging (Kulkarni and Ramakrishnamacharyulu, 2013). There are around 35 of them. Thus R is one of these 35.

As the number of words in a sentence increases, or if a sentence has even a single word with considerable number of morph analyses, the size of the 5D matrix explodes, and the use of parser in real time applications becomes impractical.

Second disadvantage of the above method is that the constraints are applied globally to the matrix. However, we notice that some of the constraints are local to a node. Separating the local constraints from the global, and applying the local constraints at an early stage to rule out non-solutions should increase the efficiency of the system.

The importance and advantage of Dependency Parser over a constituency parser has been well recognised by the computational linguistic community and we see Dependency parsers for variety of languages such as English, Japanese, Swedish to name a few. More than half a dozen parsers exist for English alone that produce dependency parse. The existence of Pāṇinian grammar for Sanskrit is the strong motivation behind developing a Dependency based parser for Sanskrit. The current trend towards developing dependency parsers is more towards following the data driven approaches over the grammar based. However, we follow the grammar based approach. Some of the factors that motivated the design of the parser and choice of the approach are the following.

- Sanskrit does not have a tree bank of reasonable size so that we can use data driven approaches for Sanskrit.

- Sanskrit has a free word order, and hence the traditional POS taggers do not make any sense. Unlike modern Indian languages which are relatively free word order,

[2]We roughly translate kartā as a subject. This is not a faithful translation. Kartā and other kāraka relations represent the semantic information which can be extracted purely from the syntactic information available in the sentence.

[3]The word *te* has 16 possible analyses corresponding to its inflectional analysis. If we take into account the derivational information, the possibilities explode further.

[4]This figure is based on the SHMT corpus developed by the SHMT consortium project sponsored by DeitY, India (2008-12).

and which have a fixed word order for the adjective-substantive sequences, Sanskrit allows even the adjectives and genitives to float around in a sentence. This makes the usability of POS tagger for Sanskrit doubtful.

- The existence of almost exhaustive grammar for Sanskrit also demands from the users a justification for the analysis in terms of grammar rules.

We describe below a Deterministic Parsing algorithm which applies the local constraints locally, and also uses Dynamic Programming for efficient parsing. This parser differs from the Deterministic Dependency Parsers for English developed by Yamada and Matsumoto (Yamada and Matsumoto, 2003) and Nivre (Nivre and Scholz, 2004) in three major ways. These parsers for English use either a bottom-up or a combination of bottom-up and top-down algorithm. Our parser traverses the sentence from left to right guided by the possible paths among the nodes. Second major difference is that these parsers use shift-reduce parsing, while we check the relations for compatibility at each node. The third major difference is that we follow the grammar based approach while the above parsers for English are data driven.

2 Left-Right Deterministic Parsing with Dynamic Programming

Let $G_1 = (N_1, E_1)$ be a graph, where N_1 is the set of nodes corresponding to morphological analyses of the words in a given sentence. E_1 is the set of all directed weighted arcs (i, j, r) such that i^{th} node is related to j^{th} node through a relation r. With every relation r a weight w is associated, which reflects the preferences of relations over the other. The total number of nodes = $\sum m_i$, where m_i is the number of possible morphological analyses of the ith word.

Since a node in N_1 corresponds to a morphological analysis of a word, and not to the word, the constraint to choose only one analysis per word needs an information about how many analyses correspond to each word. This we specify through the adjacency information. For each word we provide indices of the morphological analyses of the word to the left as well as to the right. For the first word, the index of the left word is marked as 'S' (the starting node), and for the last word, the index of the right word is marked as 'F' (the final node).

From(j)	To(i)	relation(r)
2	4	karma (obj)
2	6	adhikaraṇa (loc)
2	7	adhikaraṇa (loc)
5	1	kartā (subj)
5	3	kartā (subj)
5	4	karma (obj)
6	4	karma (obj)
7	4	karma (obj)

Table 1: Possible Relations

This information of adjacency is represented as a graph $G_2 = (N_2, E_2)$, where $N_2 = N \cup \{S, F\}$ and E_2 is the set of directed edges (i, j) such that i and j correspond to the morphological analyses of adjacent words w_k and w_{k+1}. The direction of the edge is from i to j.

2.1 An example

We illustrate with an example the information content of the two graphs G_1 and G_2. Consider the following sentence.

San: *rāmaḥ vanaṁ gacchati.* (1)
gloss: Ram forest{acc.} goes.
Eng: Ram goes to the forest.

In this sentence, each of the two words *rāmaḥ* (Ram) and *vanaṁ* (forest) has two possible analyses, while the word *gacchati* (goes) has 3 possible analyses as shown below.

1. rāmaḥ = rāma {masc.} {sg.} {nom.}
2. rāmaḥ = rā {pr.} {1p} {pl.}
3. vanaṁ = vana {neu.} {sg.} {nom.}
4. vanaṁ = vana {neu.} {sg.} {acc.}
5. gacchati = gam {pr.} {3p.} {sg.}
6. gacchati = gam {pr. part.} {masc.} {sg.} {loc.}
7. gacchati = gam {pr. part.} {neu.} {sg.} {loc.}

Thus, G_1 has 7 nodes. Edges marking the relations are listed in Table 1. This is represented in the form of a graph as shown in Figure 1. The information of adjacency is shown in Table 2 and as a graph in Figure 2.

2.2 Local and Global constraints

A **path** P of a graph G_2 is a sequence of edges which connects the nodes from 'S' to 'F'. For example, S-1-3-5-F is a path in Figure 2.

Node no	node nos of left word	node nos of right word
1	S	3,4
2	S	3,4
3	1,2	5,6,7
4	1,2	5,6,7
5	3,4	F
6	3,4	F
7	3,4	F

Table 2: Adjacency

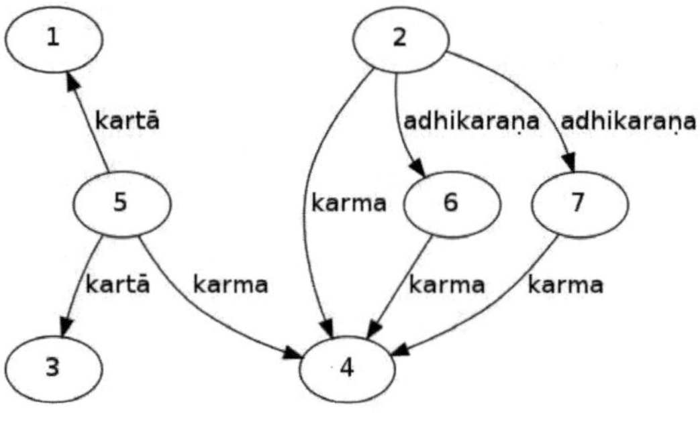

Figure 1: Possible Relations

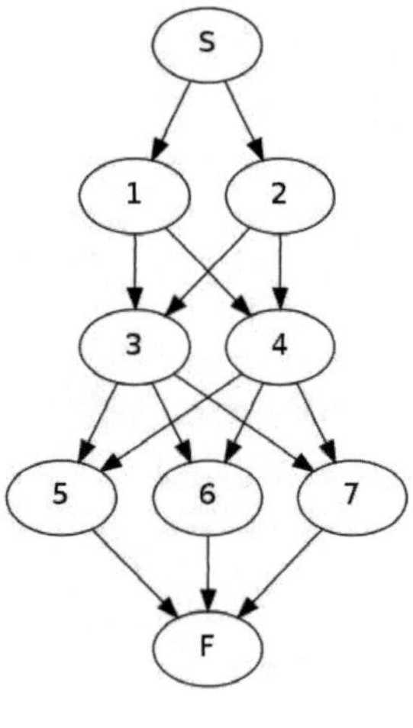

Figure 2: Adjacency and Possible paths

A relation (I, J, R) is **locally incompatible** with a set of relations R = $\{(i, j, r)|(i, j, r) \in E$ of $G_1\}$ under the following circumstances.
a. If for some $(i, j, r) \in E$ and $j = J$ and $r = R$, $i \neq I$. This ensures that no two words satisfy the same semantic role of a verb.
b. If for some $(i, j, r) \in E$ and $i = I$, either $j \neq J$ or $r \neq R$. This ensures that every word has at the most one semantic role[5].

A set of relations $R = \{(i, j, r)|(i, j, r) \in E$ of $G_1\}$ is said to be **locally compatible**, if no $(I, J, R) \in E$ is locally incompatible with the rest of the relations in R.

A set of labelled edges R = $\{(i, j, r)|(i, j, r) \in E$ of $G_1\}$ is **globally compatible** provided the following conditions are satisfied.
a. If the nodes of G_1 are arranged in an increasing order of their index, then the links do not cross.
b. For certain relations r such as *kartṛsamānādhikaraṇam* (predicative adjective) there is a matching relation *kartā* (subject).
c. The edges corresponding to the relations in R do not form a loop.

A sub-graph T of G_1 is a **parse** if
a. The nodes in T correspond to some path of G_2. This ensures that each node in T corresponds to a distinct word, and every word in the sentence is accounted for.
b. T is a Tree. This ensures that every word in a sentence is related directly to some other word.
c. The set of relations corresponding to the edge labels in T are both locally as well as globally compatible.

2.3 Parsing Algorithm

1. Starting from the node 'S' of the graph G_2 explore various paths of G_2 following the Depth-First-Traversal strategy. The stack keeps track of part of the paths visited so far.

2. At each node, refer to G_1 for various relations this node can have with other nodes. The stack, in our case, in addition to the information of paths visited so far, also keeps track of compatible relations at various nodes on this path.

[5]This condition is applied to only a few relations such as kartā (agent), karaṇa (instrument), etc.

3. For each of these relations
   - If the relation is locally compatible with the relations encountered on this path so far, add this relation to the stack and continue with the next node. The set of relations, at any point of time on the stack provides the current status of the partial solution / Tree explored.
   - If the relation is incompatible, declare this path to be incompatible, and proceed with other path, leaving this path further unexplored.
4. When you reach the node 'F', check the relations on this path for 'global compatibility'.
5. Each globally compatible set of relations, which is a sub-set of edges in G_1, forms a Tree and hence is a possible solution.
6. For each possible solution, compute the $Cost = \sum w * |j - i|$, where w is the weight associated with the relation between the nodes corresponding the jth and i^{th} word.

Traversing of the graph G_2 from 'S' to 'F' is equivalent to traversing the sentence from left to right for various combinations of morphological analyses. The parser is deterministic, and it is guaranteed to terminate after $\prod m_i$ paths are explored. At each node of G_2, the number of compatibility checks is equal to the number of incoming arrows at that node in graph G_1. Stacking of intermediate results ensures the dynamic programming. A Cost function is used to prioritize the solutions. Salient features of this algorithm are:

- We follow lattice programming to explore all possible paths.
- The parser deals with one word at a time starting from the first word. This is motivated by an approach [6] in the Indian theories of verbal cogniton and also confirms with Abney's (Abney, 1989) findings that the human operates this way.
- Since we do not want to miss any possible parse, we use dynamic programming which is upto 5 times faster than the conventional beam search (Huang and Sagae, 2010).
- Unlike the traditional based parsing which are typically breadth first, we follow a depth first strategy, stacking the intermediate results ensuring the effective dynamic programming.
- At each node we use constraints to check the compatibility of new relations with the stacked one.
- The weights for each relation are determined heuristically manually in the absence of any manually tagged reasonable sized data. The n-v relations expressing the kāraka (case) relations are given preferences over the non-kāraka relations.

[6] ādyaṃ padaṃ vākyaṃ

2.4 Evaluation

Sanskrit Tree bank corpus is developed under Government of India sponsored project 'Development of Sanskrit Computational Toolkit and Sanskrit Hindi Machine Translation system (2008-2012)'. The corpus consists of around 3000 sentences, a substantial part of it being modern short stories. A small part of the corpus contains sentences addressing various syntactic phenomena. The complete tagged corpus is still being cross checked for correctness. Hence the parser was tested only on 1316 sentences. We have a hierarchical tagset with 35 tags. Among these the sub-classification of 4 types of location (adhikaraṇa) and 3 types of objects (karma) is collapsed into one each resulting into a flat tagset of 30 tags.
Our parser produces all possible parses, ordered on cost. The one with minimum cost is shown as the first parse. For evaluation, we consider only the first parse. The correctness of parses is judged on several well established parameters.

- Relations with correct label and attachment (LAS)
  With 35 relations, the labelled attachments were correct in 63.1% cases, while with 30 relations, the score was 67.4%.
- Relations with correct attachment (UAS)
  If only attachments were considered, ignoring the labels, 80.26% attachments matched with the GOLD data.
- Sentences with matching dependency trees (MDT)
  This measure tells us in exactly how many cases the first tree matches the manually

tagged tree. Out of 1316 sentences, the first parse matched exactly in 569 (43.20%) sentences with a tagset of 35 tags, while with 30 tags, the first parse matched in 647 (49.1%) cases.

- Sentences with correct unlabelled dependency trees (UDT)
  Instead of complete tree match, now we check only for the attachments, and not the labels. Among 1316, the unlabelled dependency trees matched in 870 (66.05%) cases.

- Sentences with one wrong attachment (OWAS)
  It was found that out of 1316 sentences, 285 (21.6%) sentences had only one wrong labelled attachment. If this is rectified, the performance of the system for correct matches increases drastically.

3 Compact Display of Multiple Solutions

Sanskrit being a classical language demands certain special features with respect to its computational tools. Being an old classical language, most of the important texts in Sanskrit have been translated manually into several modern languages. So naturally, machine translation takes a back seat for Sanskrit. What a user needs is an access to the original text with the help of various online linguistic tools and resources so that he can himself interpret and understand the texts in original. From this aspect, displaying only the first parse does not serve the purpose. In fact, in more than 50% of the cases, the first parse is wrong. User might like to examine various possibilities and choose his own interpretation. It is also possible that the text is ambiguous with two or more readings, and user would like to go through each of them. Displaying all the parse trees would not serve any purpose, since the trees look almost similar with either a change in one or two branches, or with a change in the label.

In what follows we present a compact way of presenting all the solutions. This is an adaptation of the slim interface of Heritage segmenter (Huet and Goyal, 2013).

Let $T_i = (N_i, E_i)$, where $i = 1$ to n be n parses of a given sentence. Let $N = \cup N_i$, and $E = \cup E_i$. The display consists of 3 rows. The top row lists the words with their positions. The second row consists of morphological analyses corresponding to all the nodes in N. Analyses are written in n columns corresponding to each word. The third row consists of edges from E again displayed below the corresponding word/node.

The user can now choose either a node from the second row or an edge from the third row. Each choice calls the compatibility checker to remove the incompatible nodes and edges corresponding to the user's choice. Each choice results in the reduction of possible parses. At any point in time, a user can choose to display the graphs of current possible parses.

Here is an illustration of the interface. The input sentence is an anvaya of a śloka from Bhagvadgītā (8th śloka from the 4th chapter). The original śloka is
paritrāṇāya sādhūnām vināśāya ca duṣkṛtām dharma-samsthāpanārthāya sambhavāmi yuge yuge. (Bh.G.4.8)

The anvaya, an input to the parser, is:

sādhūnām paritrāṇāya duṣkṛtām vināśāya dharma-samsthāpanāya[7] *ca yuge yuge sambhavāmi.*

Fig 3 shows the summary of parses as a compact display[8]. The union of relations from all parses for each word are shown. User can choose either the correct morphological analysis or correct relation corresponding to the node. When he chooses the correct morphological analysis, all the relations in the relations row that are incompatible with this choice are removed from the display. Similarly, if a user chooses a relation in the relation row, all the relations that are incompatible with this relation, and all the morphological analyses that are incompatible with this choice of a relation are removed from the display. Thus, for example, the word *sādhūnām* has two morphological analyses in Fig 3. But, after selecting the appropriate analysis, in Fig 4, we notice that the relations under this word are also reduced. All those relations which has *sādhūnām* as one of the relata are removed from the display. Similarly, selecting the role of this word as *karma,2,2* (karma of the second analysis of the second word), not only removes all other relations below this word, but also removes the first

[7]The original word is dharma-samsthāpanārthāya, which we changed to dharma-samsthāpanāya, since the former is still not recognised by the morphological analyser.

[8]The display shows only first five columns.

Summary of Complete Parses

total filtered solutions = 556 of 26880

✓ Undo ✓ 556 filtered trees

sādhūnām(1)	paritrāṇāya(2)	duṣkṛtām(3)	vināśāya(4)	dharma-saṃsthāpanāya(5)
1. ✓ sādhu{pum}{6;bahu} 2. ✓ sādhu{napum}{6;bahu}	1. ✓ pari_trai1{kta;train;bhvādih;napum}{4;eka} 2. ✓ pari_trai1{lyut;train;bhvādih}{napum}{4;eka}	1. ✓ duskrt{pum}{6;bahu}	1. ✓ vināśa{pum}{4;eka}	1. ✓ dharma-samsthāpana{napum}{4;eka}
1. ✓ kartā,2,1 2. ✓ kartā,2,2 3. ✓ kartā,2,1 4. ✓ kartā,2,2 5. ✓ karma,2,1 6. ✓ karma,2,2 7. ✓ karma,2,1 8. ✓ karma,2,2 9. ✓ sasthīsambandhah,2,1 10. ✓ sasthīsambandhah,2,2 11. ✓ sasthīsambandhah,2,1 12. ✓ sasthīsambandhah,2,2 13. ✓ viśesanam,3,1	1. ✓ tādarthyam,3,1 2. ✓ tādarthyam,3,1 3. ✓ samuccitamprayojanam,6,1 4. ✓ samuccitamprayojanam,6,1 5. ✓ viśesanam,5,1 6. ✓ viśesanam,5,1 7. ✓ prayojanam,9,1 8. ✓ prayojanam,9,1	1. ✓ sasthīsambandhah,4,1	1. ✓ samuccitamprayojanam,6,1 2. ✓ tādarthyam,5,1 3. ✓ prayojanam,9,1 4. ✓ prayojanam,2,1 5. ✓ prayojanam,2,2	1. ✓ samuccitamprayojanam,6,1 2. ✓ prayojanam,9,1 3. ✓ prayojanam,2,1 4. ✓ prayojanam,2,2

Figure 3: compact display of solutions

Summary of Complete Parses

total filtered solutions = 556 of 26880

✓ Undo ✓ 292 filtered trees

sādhūnām(1)	paritrāṇāya(2)	duṣkṛtām(3)	vināśāya(4)	dharma-saṃsthāpanāya(5)
1. ✓ sādhu{pum}{6;bahu}	1. ✓ pari_trai1{kta;train;bhvādih;napum}{4;eka} 2. ✓ pari_trai1{lyut;train;bhvādih}{napum}{4;eka}	1. ✓ duskrt{pum}{6;bahu}	1. ✓ vināśa{pum}{4;eka}	1. ✓ dharma-samsthāpana{napum}{4;eka}
1. ✓ kartā,2,1 2. ✓ kartā,2,2 3. ✓ karma,2,1 4. ✓ karma,2,2 5. ✓ sasthīsambandhah,2,1 6. ✓ sasthīsambandhah,2,2 7. ✓ viśesanam,3,1	1. ✓ tādarthyam,3,1 2. ✓ tādarthyam,3,1 3. ✓ samuccitamprayojanam,6,1 4. ✓ samuccitamprayojanam,6,1 5. ✓ viśesanam,5,1 6. ✓ viśesanam,5,1 7. ✓ prayojanam,9,1 8. ✓ prayojanam,9,1	1. ✓ sasthīsambandhah,4,1	1. ✓ samuccitamprayojanam,6,1 2. ✓ tādarthyam,5,1 3. ✓ prayojanam,9,1 4. ✓ prayojanam,2,1 5. ✓ prayojanam,2,2	1. ✓ samuccitamprayojanam,6,1 2. ✓ prayojanam,9,1 3. ✓ prayojanam,2,1 4. ✓ prayojanam,2,2

Figure 4: Selection of a morphological analysis

Summary of Complete Parses

total filtered solutions = 556 of 26880

✓ Undo ✓ 44 filtered trees

sādhūnām(1)	paritrāṇāya(2)	duṣkṛtām(3)	vināśāya(4)	dharma-saṃsthāpanāya(5)
1. ✓ sādhu{pum}{6;bahu}	1. ✓ pari_trai1{lyut;train;bhvādih}{napum}{4;eka}	1. ✓ duskrt{pum}{6;bahu}	1. ✓ vināśa{pum}{4;eka}	1. ✓ dharma-samsthāpana{napum}{4;eka}
1. ✓ karma,2,2	1. ✓ tādarthyam,3,1 2. ✓ samuccitamprayojanam,6,1 3. ✓ viśeṣaṇam,5,1 4. ✓ prayojanam,9,1	1. ✓ ṣaṣṭhīsambandhaḥ,4,1	1. ✓ samuccitamprayojanam,6,1 2. ✓ tādarthyam,5,1 3. ✓ prayojanam,9,1 4. ✓ prayojanam,2,2	1. ✓ samuccitamprayojanam,6,1 2. ✓ prayojanam,9,1 3. ✓ prayojanam,2,2

Figure 5: selection of a relation

Summary of Complete Parses

total filtered solutions = 556 of 26880

✓ Undo ✓ Unique parse tree ✓ Save ✓ Translate into hindi

sādhūnām(1)	paritrāṇāya(2)	duṣkṛtām(3)	vināśāya(4)	dharma-saṃsthāpanāya(5)
1. ✓ sādhu{pum}{6;bahu}	1. ✓ pari_trai1{lyut;train;bhvādih}{napum}{4;eka}	1. ✓ duskrt{pum}{6;bahu}	1. ✓ vināśa{pum}{4;eka}	1. ✓ dharma-saṃsthāpana{napum}{4;eka}
1. ✓ karma,2,2	1. ✓ prayojanam,9,1	1. ✓ ṣaṣṭhīsambandhaḥ,4,1	1. ✓ prayojanam,9,1	1. ✓ prayojanam,9,1

Figure 6: Unique solution

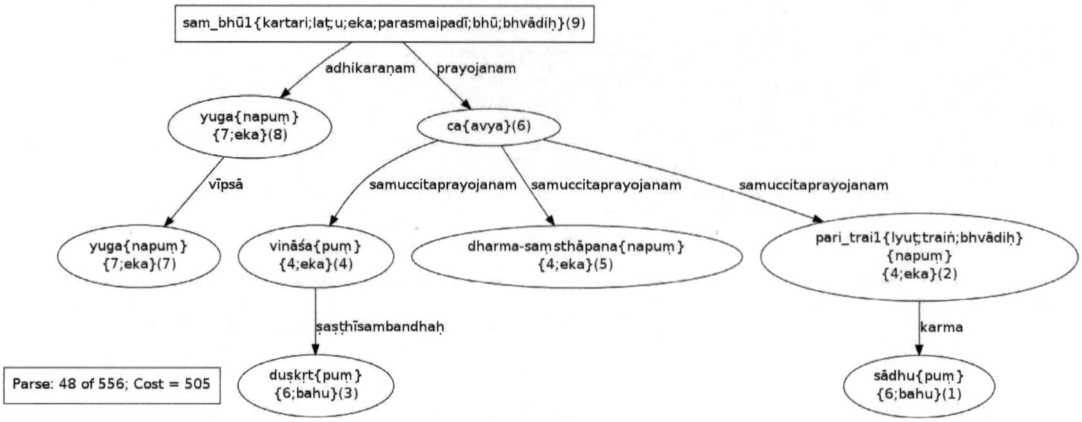

Figure 7: Dependency Graph

morph analysis of the second word, and all the relations having this analysis as one of the relata. The result of this is shown in Fig 5. Finally when we make all the choices, a unique parse is obtained (see Fig 6). Clicking on the check sign of unique parse, we get the rendering of the relations in the form of a dependency graph (see Fig 7).

The parse of a sentence with n words has $n - 1$ edges corresponding to the relations. Hence one can choose the correct parse from this compact display in maximum $n - 1$ choices. This interface thus can also be used for developing a tree bank for Sanskrit semi-automatically. Due to the limitations on space, we do not give the technical details of this interface here.

4 Using Shallow Parser for pruning

Normally the parsers for positional languages like English use a POS tagger to choose the morphological analysis in context before proceeding for the parsing. This reduces the search space of the parser substantially resulting in increase in the performance metric.

In case of Sanskrit which is morphologically rich and carries very little information in position, the POS taggers based on the positional information are of little value. On the other hand a shallow parser such as one developed by (Huet, 2007) makes sense. Because such a shallow parser, based on the agreement rules, subcategorisation of verbs into transitive and intransitive, co-ordination information, and certain restrictions on grammatical constructions rules out various possibilities and produces a sub-set of possible solutions. Thus it is desirable to use a shallow parser to filter out nonsensical combinations of the solutions before proceeding to a full fledged parsing. This shallow parser, in addition to resolving POS ambiguities, also does a little parsing to aid the full fledged parser.

As an example, consider the sentence (1) above. We have seen that there are 12 possible paths (Fig 2) for this sentence. The shallow parser produces two splits.

1. First split

    - 1. rāmaḥ = rāma {masc.} {sg.} {nom.}
    - 3. vanaṁ = vana {neu.} {sg.} {nom.}
    - 4. vanaṁ = vana {neu.} {sg.} {acc.}
    - 5. gacchati = gam {pr.} {3p.} {sg.}

    This corresponds to 2 paths: S-1-3-5-F and S-1-4-5-F (See Fig 8).

2. Second split

    - 2. rāmaḥ = rā {present tense} {1 per.} {pl.}
    - 3. vanaṁ = vana {neu.} {sg.} {nom.}
    - 4. vanaṁ = vana {neu.} {sg.} {acc.}
    - 6. gacchati = gam {pr. part.} {masc.} {sg.} {loc.}
    - 7. gacchati = gam {pr. part.} {neu.} {sg.} {loc.}

    This corresponds to 4 paths viz. S-2-3-6-F, S-2-3-7-F, S-2-4-6-F, and S-2-4-7-F (See Fig 8).

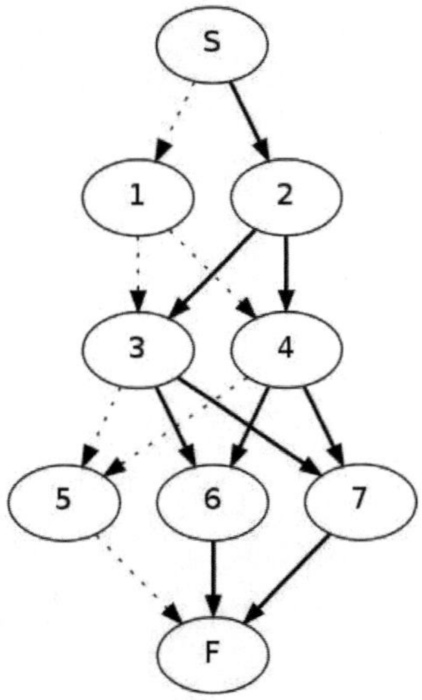

Figure 8: Partitioning of a graph

Thus the shallow parsing has reduced the number of paths from 12 to 6. Note that the POS ambiguities in the words *rāmaḥ* and *gacchati* are resolved. But the case ambiguity in the word *vanam* is not yet resolved.

5 Conclusion

The performance of the parser has confirmed our intuition that application of local constraints at an early stage improves the performance. The search space is further reduced by the use of shallow parser. Compact display is useful for a reader who wants to understand the text in original. This display can also be used for developing Sanskrit Tree bank semi-automatically. The algorithm described above is tested on Sanskrit. However it is general one and should work well for the modern Indian languages as well.

References

Steven P Abney. 1989. A computational model of human parsing. *Journal of Psycholinguistic Research*, 18:129–144.

Vāman Shivarām Apte. 1885. *The Student's Guide to Sanskrit Composition. A Treatise on Sanskrit Syntax for Use of Schools and Colleges*. Lokasamgraha Press, Poona, India.

Akshar Bharati, Vineet Chaitanya, and Rajeev Sangal. 1995. *Natural Language Processing. A Paninian Perspective*. Prentice-Hall of India, New Delhi.

Pawan Goyal and Gérard Huet. 2013. Completeness analysis of a Sanskrit reader. In *Proceedings, 5th International Symposium on Sanskrit Computational Linguistics*. D. K. Printworld(P) Ltd.

Pawan Goyal, Vipul Arora, and Laxmidhar Behera. 2009. Analysis of Sanskrit text: Parsing and semantic relations. In Gérard Huet, Amba Kulkarni, and Peter Scharf, editors, *Sanskrit Computational Linguistics 1 & 2*, pages 200–218. Springer-Verlag LNAI 5402.

Oliver Hellwig. 2009. Extracting dependency trees from Sanskrit texts. In Amba Kulkarni and Gérard Huet, editors, *Sanskrit Computational Linguistics 3*, pages 106–115. Springer-Verlag LNAI 5406.

L. Huang and K. Sagae. 2010. Dynamic programming for linear-time incremental parsing. In *In Proceedings of the 48th Annual Meeting of the Association for Computational Linguistics Uppsala, Sweden, July. Association for Computational Linguistics*, page 10771086.

Geŕard Huet and Pawan Goyal. 2013. Design of a lean interface for sanskrit corpus annotation. In *personal communication*.

Gérard Huet, Amba Kulkarni, and Peter Scharf, editors. 2009. *Sanskrit Computational Linguistics 1 & 2*. Springer-Verlag LNAI 5402.

Gérard Huet. 2007. Shallow syntax analysis in Sanskrit guided by semantic nets constraints. In *Proceedings of the 2006 International Workshop on Research Issues in Digital Libraries*, New York, NY, USA. ACM.

Gérard Huet. 2009. Formal structure of Sanskrit text: Requirements analysis for a mechanical Sanskrit processor. In Gérard Huet, Amba Kulkarni, and Peter Scharf, editors, *Sanskrit Computational Linguistics 1 & 2*. Springer-Verlag LNAI 5402.

S.D. Joshi, J.A.F. Roodbergen, and Bhandarkar Oriental Research Institute. 1990. *Patañjali's Vyākaraṇa-Mahābhāṣya Sthānivadbhāvāhnika: introduction, text, translation and notes*. Number v. 1 in Research Unit series. Bhandarkar Oriental Research Institute.

S.D. Joshi, J.A.F. Roodbergen, and Sāhitya Akādemī. 2004. *The Aṣṭādhyāyī of Pāṇini with Translation and Explanatory Notes*. Number v. 11 in The Aṣṭādhyāyī of Pāṇini. Sahitya Akademi.

Amba Kulkarni and Gérard Huet, editors. 2009. *Sanskrit Computational Linguistics 3*. Springer-Verlag LNAI 5406.

Amba Kulkarni and Anil Kumar. 2011. Statistical constituency parser for Sanskrit compounds. In *Proceedings of ICON 2011*. Macmillan Advanced Research Series, Macmillan Publishers India Ltd.

Amba Kulkarni and K. V. Ramakrishnamacharyulu. 2013. Parsing Sanskrit texts: Some relation specific issues. In Malhar Kulkarni, editor, *Proceedings of the 5th International Sanskrit Computational Linguistics Symposium*. D. K. Printworld(P) Ltd.

Amba Kulkarni and Devanand Shukl. 2009. Sanskrit morphological analyser: Some issues. *Indian Linguistics*, 70(1-4):169–177.

Amba Kulkarni, Sheetal Pokar, and Devanand Shukl. 2010. Designing a constraint based parser for Sanskrit. In G N Jha, editor, *Proceedings of the 4th International Sanskrit Computational Linguistics Symposium*. Springer-Verlag LNAI 6465.

Anil Kumar, Vipul Mittal, and Amba Kulkarni. 2010. Sanskrit compound processor. In G N Jha, editor, *Proceedings of the 4th International Sanskrit Computational Linguistics Symposium*. Springer-Verlag LNAI 6465.

J. Nivre and M. Scholz. 2004. Deterministic dependency parsing of english text. In *Proceedings of COLING 2004, Geneva, Switzerland, 64-70.*

H. Yamada and Y. Matsumoto. 2003. Statistical dependency analysis with support vector machines. In *Proceedings of IWPT, pages 195-206, Nancy, France.*

Reasoning with Dependency Structures and Lexicographic Definitions using Unit Graphs

Maxime Lefrançois and **Fabien Gandon**
Wimmics, Inria, I3S, CNRS, UNSA
2004 rte des Lucioles, BP. 93, 06902 Sophia Antipolis, France
{maxime.lefrancois,fabien.gandon}@inria.fr

Abstract

We are interested in a graph-based Knowledge Representation (KR) formalism that would allow for the representation, manipulation, query, and reasoning over dependency structures, and linguistic knowledge of the lexicon in the Meaning-Text Theory framework. Neither the semantic web formalisms nor the conceptual graphs appear to be suitable for this task, and this led to the introduction of the new Unit Graphs (UG) framework. In this paper we will overview the foundational concepts of this framework: the UGs are defined over a UG-support that contains: i) a hierarchy of unit types which is strongly driven by the actantial structure of unit types, ii) a hierarchy of circumstantial symbols, and iii) a set of unit identifiers. Based on these foundational concepts and on the definition of UGs, this paper justifies the use of a deep semantic representation level to represent meanings of lexical units. Rules over UGs are then introduced, and lexicographic definitions of lexical units are added to the hierarchy of unit types. Finally this paper provides UGs with semantics (in the logical sense), and pose the entailment problem, so as to enable the reasoning in the UGs framework.

1 Introduction

We are interested in a graph-based Knowledge Representation (KR) formalism that would allow for the representation, manipulation, query, and reasoning over dependency structures and linguistic knowledge of the Explanatory Combinatorial Dictionary (ECD), which is the lexicon at the core of the Meaning-Text Theory (MTT) (Mel'čuk, 2006).

Most past or current projects that aimed at implementing the ECD did so in a lexicographic perspective. One important example is the RELIEF project (Lux-Pogodalla and Polguère, 2011), which aims at representing a lexical system graph named RLF (Polguère, 2009), where lexical units are interlinked by paradigmatic and syntagmatic links of lexical functions (Mel'čuk, 1996). In the RELIEF project, the description of Lexical Functions is based on a formalization proposed by Kahane and Polguère (2001). Moreover, lexicographic definitions start to be partially formalized in the RELIEF project using the markup type that has been developed in the Definiens project (Barque and Polguère, 2008; Barque et al., 2010).

One exception is the proprietary linguistic processor ETAP-3 that implements a variety of ECD for Natural Language Processing (Apresian et al., 2003; Boguslavsky et al., 2004). Linguistic knowledge are asserted, and linguistic and grammatical rules are directly formalized in first order logic.

Adding to these formalization works, our goal is to propose a formalization from a knowledge engineering perspective, compatible with standard KR formalisms. The term *formalization* here means not only *make non-ambiguous*, but also *make operational*, i.e., *such that it supports logical operations* (e.g., knowledge manipulation, query, reasoning). We thus adopt a knowledge engineering approach applied to the domain of the MTT. The semantic web formalisms and the Conceptual Graphs formalism both seem to fit this task, but they actually present strong incompatibilities with the description of linguistic predicates (Lefrançois, 2013). These issues led to the introduction of the new graph-based Unit Graphs (UGs) KR formalism. In the UGs framework, the linguistic predicates are represented by unit types, and are described in a structure called the unit types hierarchy. Unit types specify through their

Proceedings of the Second International Conference on Dependency Linguistics (DepLing 2013), pages 167–176,
Prague, August 27–30, 2013.

actantial structure, i.e., actant slots, the ways in which their instances may be linked to other units in a UG.

The main research question of this paper is the following: *What semantics can be attributed to UGs, and how can we define the entailment problem for UGs ?*

The rest of this paper is organized as follows. We will first overview the issues of existing graph-based KR formalisms that led to the introduction of the new UGs framework (§2). The foundational concepts of this framework are then introduced (§3). From these foundational concepts we define the lexicographic definitions of Lexical Unit Types (LexUTs) (§4). Finally we provide UGs with semantics (in the logical sense), and pose the entailment problem (§5).

2 The Unit Graphs Formalism

At first sight, two existing KR formalisms seem interesting for representing dependency structures: semantic web formalisms (RDF[1], RDFS[2], OWL[3], SPARQL[4]), and Conceptual Graphs (CGs) (Sowa, 1984; Chein and Mugnier, 2008). Both formalisms are based on directed labelled graph structures, and some research has been done towards using them to represent dependency structures and knowledge of the lexicon (OWL in (Lefrançois and Gandon, 2011; Boguslavsky, 2011), CGs at the conceptual level in (Bohnet and Wanner, 2010)). Yet authors in (Lefrançois, 2013) showed that neither of these KR formalisms can represent linguistic predicates. Let us list the main drawbacks of these existing formalisms:

- The RDF is insufficient because its semantics is limited to that of oriented labelled graphs.
- In RDFS, OWL and the CGs, there is a strong distinction between concept types and relations. Yet, a linguistic predicate may be considered both as a concept type as it is instantiated in dependency structures, and as a relation as its instances may link other instances.
- RDFS and OWL only model binary relations, which is not the case of most linguistic predicates. One would need to use reification of n-ary relations, but then no semantics is attributed to such relations.
- CGs support n-ary relations, but the inheritance mechanism of relation types is such that two relations with different arities must be incomparable. Yet the Semantic Actant Slots (SemASlots) of a lexical unit are determined by linguistic criteria and may thus differ from those of the lexical unit from which its sense derives (Mel'čuk, 2004, p. 38). One thus cannot use the natural inheritance mechanism of CGs to model the meaning specialization of predicates.

As the CGs formalism is the closest to the semantic networks, the following choice has been made to overcome these issues: *Modify the CGs formalism basis, and define transformations to the RDF syntax for sharing knowledge and publishing over the web of data.* As we are to represents linguistic units of different nature (e.g., semantic units, lexical units, grammatical units, words), term *unit* has been chosen to be used in a generic manner, and the result of this adaptation is thus *the Unit Graphs (UGs) framework*.

3 Unit Graphs

For a specific Lexical Unit L, (Mel'čuk, 2004, p. 5) distinguishes considering L in language (i.e., in the lexicon), or in speech (i.e., in an utterance). KR formalisms and the Unit Graphs (UGs) formalism also make this distinction using types. In this paper and in the UGs formalism, there is thus a clear distinction between *units* (e.g., semantic unit, lexical unit), which will be represented in the UGs, and their *types* (e.g., semantic unit type, lexical unit type), which are roughly classes of units for which specific features are shared. It is those types that specify through actant slots how their instances (i.e., units) are to be linked to other units in a UG.

3.1 Support

Following the example of CGs, UGs are defined over a so-called *support*.

Definition 1. A UG *support* is denoted $\mathcal{S} \stackrel{\text{def}}{=} (\mathcal{T}, \mathcal{C}, \boldsymbol{M})$ and is composed of a hierarchy of unit types $\mathcal{T}$, a hierarchy of circumstantial symbols $\mathcal{C}$, and a set of unit identifiers $\boldsymbol{M}$.

Let us briefly introduce the components of $\mathcal{S}$.

[1] RDF - Resource Description Framework, c.f., http://w3.org/RDF/

[2] RDFS - RDF Schema, c.f., http://www.w3.org/TR/rdf-schema/

[3] OWL - Web Ontology Language, c.f., http://www.w3.org/TR/owl2-overview/

[4] SPARQL, c.f., http://www.w3.org/TR/sparql11-overview/

First, unit types and their actantial structure are described in a structure called *hierarchy* and denoted $\mathcal{T}$. Whether they are semantic, lexical or grammatical, unit types have *Actant Slots (ASlots)* with symbols. Moreover, ASlots may be optional, obligatory, or prohibited (Lefrançois and Gandon, 2013a). Let us briefly introduce two of the components of $\mathcal{T}$, and leave details for section 3.3.

- The core of $\mathcal{T}$ is the set of so-called *Primitive Unit Types (PUTs)*, denoted $\boldsymbol{T}$. Now a unit type may consist of several conjoint PUTs. In particular, it may be a lexical PUT and multiple grammatical PUTs, like $\{def, plur, \text{CAT}\}$. To represent this, we introduce the set $\boldsymbol{T}^{\cap}$ of possible *Conjunctive Unit Types (CUTs)* over $\boldsymbol{T}$ as the powerset[5] of $\boldsymbol{T}$.
- $\mathcal{T}$ contains a set of binary relation symbols of type predicate-argument called *Actant Symbols (ASymbols)*, and denoted $\boldsymbol{S}_{\mathcal{T}}$. $\boldsymbol{S}_{\mathcal{T}}$ contains numbers for the semantic unit types, and other "classical" symbols for the other levels under consideration (e.g, roman numerals I to VI for the MTT's Deep Syntactic level). Every unit type has an *actantial structure* that consists in a set of optional, obligatory and prohibited ASlots associated with some ASymbols. The actantial structure of a PUT specify how units of this type shall be linked to other units through so-called *actantial relations* in a dependency structure.

Second, there exists dependencies other than actantial: circumstantial relations (Mel'čuk, 2004). Circumstantial relations are considered of type instance-instance contrary to actantial relations. Example of such relations are the deep syntactic representation relations **ATTR, COORD, APPEND** of the MTT, but we may also use such relations to represent communicative dependencies for instance. Circumstantial relations are labelled by symbols chosen in a set of so-called *Circumstantial Symbols (CSymbols)*, denoted $\boldsymbol{S}_{\mathcal{C}}$, and their classes and usage are described in a hierarchy denoted $\mathcal{C}$. Section 3.4 details the hierarchy of CSymbols.

Finally, one actually needs symbols to identify units. We thus introduce a set of so-called *unit identifiers*, denoted $\boldsymbol{M}$. Every element of $\boldsymbol{M}$ identifies a specific unit, but multiple elements of $\boldsymbol{M}$ may identify the same unit.

[5]The powerset of X is the set of all subsets of X: 2^X

3.2 Definition of UGs

The UGs represent different types of dependency structures (e.g., semantic, syntactic). In a UG, unit nodes that are typed are interlinked by dependency relations that are either actantial or circumstantial.

Definition 2. A UG G defined over a support $\mathcal{S}$ is a tuple denoted $G \stackrel{\text{def}}{=} (U, \boldsymbol{l}, A, C, Eq)$ where U is the set of unit nodes, $\boldsymbol{l}$ is a labelling mapping over U, A and C are respectively actantial and circumstantial triples, and Eq is a set of asserted unit node equivalences.

Let us detail the components of G.

U is the set of *unit nodes*. Every unit node represents a specific unit, but multiple unit nodes may represent the same unit. Unit nodes are typed and marked so as to respectively specify what CUT they have and what unit they represent. The marker of a unit node is a set of unit identifiers, for mathematical reasons. The set of *unit node markers* is denoted $\boldsymbol{M}^{\cap}$ and is the powerset[5] of $\boldsymbol{M}$. If a unit node is marked by $\varnothing$, it is said to be *generic*, and the represented unit is unknown. On the other hand, if a unit node is marked $\{m_1, m_2\}$, then the unit identifiers m_1 and m_2 actually identify the same unit. $\boldsymbol{l}$ is thus a labelling mapping over U that assigns to each unit node $u \in U$ a couple $\boldsymbol{l}(u) = (t^{\cap}, m^{\cap}) \in \boldsymbol{T}^{\cap} \times \boldsymbol{M}^{\cap}$ of a CUT and a unit node marker. We denote $t^{\cap} = type(u)$ and $m^{\cap} = marker(u)$. Unit nodes are illustrated by rectangles with their label written inside.

A is the set of *actantial triples* $(u, s, v) \in U \times \boldsymbol{S}_{\mathcal{T}} \times U$. For all $a = (u, s, v) \in A$, the unit represented by v fills the ASlot s of the unit represented by u. We denote $u = governor(a)$, $s = symbol(a)$ and $v = actant(a)$. We also denote $arc(a) = (u, v)$. Actantial triples are illustrated by double arrows.

C is the set of *circumstantial triples* $(u, s, v) \in U \times \boldsymbol{S}_{\mathcal{C}} \times U$. For all $c = (u, s, v) \in C$, the unit represented by u governs the unit represented by v with respect to s. We denote $u = governor(c)$, $s = symbol(c)$ and $v = circumstantial(c)$. We also denote $arc(c) = (u, v)$. Circumstantial triples are illustrated by simple arrows.

$Eq \subseteq U^2$ is the set of so-called *asserted unit node equivalences*. For all couple (u_1, u_2) in Eq, u_1 and u_2 represent the same unit. The Eq relation is not an equivalence relation over unit nodes[6]. We thus distinguish explicit and implicit

[6]An equivalent relation is a reflexive, symmetric, and

knowledge. Asserted unit node equivalences are illustrated by dashed arrows.

For instance, figure 1a is a semantic representation of sentence *Peter tries to push the cat.* in which units are typed by singletons and ASymbols are numbers, in accordance with the MTT. Figure 1b is a simplified deep syntactic representation of *Peter is gently pushing the cat.* In this figure unit nodes u_2 and u_4 are typed by singletons, and only unit node u_2 is not generic and has a marker: $\{Peter\}$. P is composed of $(u_1, \mathbf{I}, u_2)$ and $(u_1, \mathbf{II}, u_3)$, where **I** and **II** are ASymbols. C is composed of $(u_1, \mathbf{ATTR}, u_4)$ where **ATTR** is a CSymbol. In the relation Eq there is (u_1, u_1), (u_2, u_2), and (u_3, u_3).

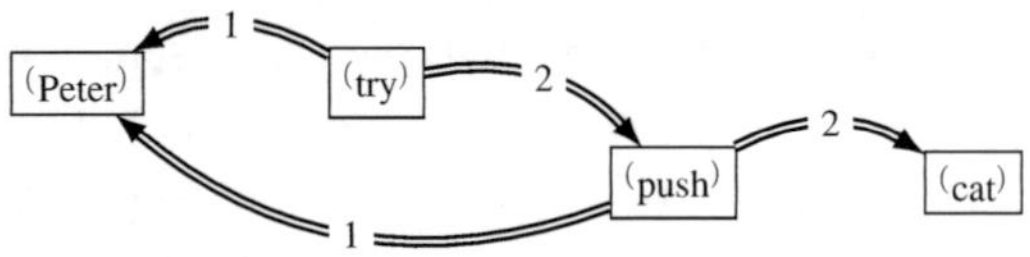

(a) Semantic representation of sentence *Peter tries to push the cat.*

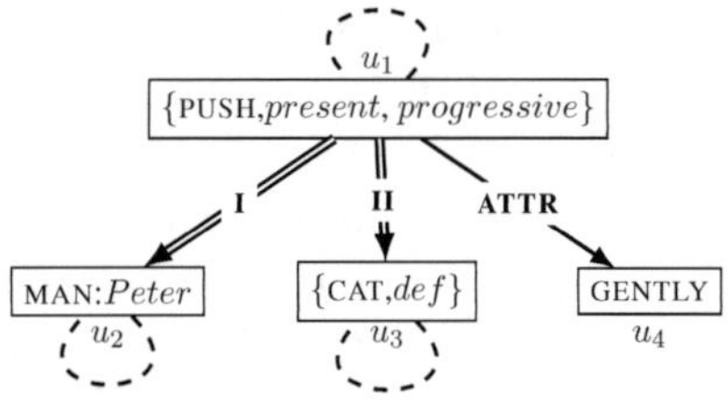

(b) Deep syntactic representation of sentence *Peter is gently pushing the cat.*

Figure 1: Examples of Unit Graphs.

UGs so defined are the core dependency structures of the UG mathematical framework. Before we present what they may be used for in more details, let us look more closely into components of the support on which UGs are defined: the unit types hierarchy and the CSymbols hierarchy.

3.3 Unit Types Hierarchy

As already stated in section 3.1, unit types and their actantial structure is described in the unit types hierarchy which is denoted $\mathcal{T}$.

Definition 3. A hierarchy of unit types, denoted $\mathcal{T}$, is a tuple $\mathcal{T} \overset{\text{def}}{=} (T_D, \boldsymbol{S}_{\mathcal{T}}, \boldsymbol{\gamma}, \boldsymbol{\gamma_1}, \boldsymbol{\gamma_0}, C_A, \perp^{\sqcap}_{A}, \{\varsigma_t\}_{t\in\boldsymbol{T}})$ that enables to construct a pre-ordered[7] set of Conjunctive Unit Types (CUTs) $\boldsymbol{T}^{\cap}$ with optional, obligatory, or prohibited ASlots.

This structure has been thoroughly described in (Lefrançois and Gandon, 2013a; Lefrançois, 2013). Let us overview its components.

T_D is a set of *declared Primitive Unit Types (PUTs).* This set is partitioned into linguistic PUTs of different nature (e.g., deep semantic, semantic, lexical). $\boldsymbol{S}_{\mathcal{T}}$ is a set of Actant Symbols (ASymbols). $\boldsymbol{\gamma}$ (resp1. $\boldsymbol{\gamma_1}$, resp2. $\boldsymbol{\gamma_0}$) assigns to every $s \in \boldsymbol{S}_{\mathcal{T}}$ its radix[8] (resp1. obligat[9], resp2. prohibet[10]) unit type $\boldsymbol{\gamma}(s)$ (resp1. $\boldsymbol{\gamma_1}(s)$, resp2. $\boldsymbol{\gamma_0}(s)$) that introduces (resp1. makes obligatory, resp2. makes prohibited) an Actant Slot (ASlot) of symbol s.

The set of *Primitive Unit Types (PUTs)* is denoted $\boldsymbol{T}$ and defined as the disjoint union of T_D, the range of $\boldsymbol{\gamma}$, $\boldsymbol{\gamma_1}$ and $\boldsymbol{\gamma_0}$, plus the *prime universal PUT* $\top$ and the *prime absurd PUT* $\perp$. $\boldsymbol{T}$ is then pre-ordered by a relation $\lesssim$ which is computed from the set of asserted PUTs comparisons $C_A \subseteq \boldsymbol{T}^2$. $t_1 \lesssim t_2$ models the fact that the PUT t_1 is more specific than the PUT t_2. A unit type may consist of several conjoint PUTs. We introduce the set $\boldsymbol{T}^{\cap}$ of possible *Conjunctive Unit Types (CUTs)* over $\boldsymbol{T}$ as the powerset[5] of $\boldsymbol{T}$. The set $\perp^{\sqcap}_{A}$ is the set of declared absurd CUTs that can not be instantiated.

The actantial structure of a unit type $t^{\cap}$ is a set of ASlots, whose symbols are chosen in the set $\boldsymbol{S}_{\mathcal{T}}$, and that may be optional, obligatory, or prohibited. Moreover, ASlots are signed. The signature of $t^{\cap}$ for one of its ASlots s is denoted $\boldsymbol{\varsigma}^{\cap}_{t^{\cap}}(s)$, and characterises the type of the unit that fills this slot. The set of signatures of $t^{\cap}$ is computed from the set of PUTs signatures $\{\varsigma_t\}_{t\in\boldsymbol{T}}$.

Finally the pre-order $\lesssim$ over $\boldsymbol{T}$ is extended to a pre-order $\overset{\cap}{\lesssim}$ over $\boldsymbol{T}^{\cap}$ as defined by Lefrançois and Gandon (2013a). Lefrançois and Gandon (2013b) proved that in the hierarchy of unit types, if $t^{\cap}_1 \overset{\cap}{\lesssim} t^{\cap}_2$ then the actantial structure of $t^{\cap}_1$ is more specific than that of $t^{\cap}_2$, except for some degenerated cases. Thus as one goes down the hierarchy of unit types, an ASlot with symbol s is introduced by the radix $\{\boldsymbol{\gamma}(s)\}$ and first defines an optional ASlot for any unit type $t^{\cap}$ more specific than $\{\boldsymbol{\gamma}(s)\}$, as long

transitive relation.

[7]A pre-order is a reflexive and transitive binary relation.

[8]radix is a latin word that means ⟨root⟩.

[9]obligat is the conjugated form of the latin verb obligo, 3p sing. pres., ⟨it makes mandatory⟩.

[10]prohibet is the conjugated form of the latin verb prohibeo, 3p sing. pres., ⟨it prohibits⟩.

as $t^{\cap}$ is not more specific than the obligat $\{\boldsymbol{\gamma_1}(s)\}$ (resp. the prohibet $\{\boldsymbol{\gamma_0}(s)\}$) of s. If that happens, the ASlot becomes obligatory (resp. prohibited). Moreover, the signature of an ASlot may only become more specific.

3.4 Circumstantial Symbols Hierarchy

As for any slot in a predicate, one ASlot of a unit may be filled by only one unit at a time. Now, one may also encounter dependencies of another type in some dependency structures: circumstantial dependencies (Mel'čuk, 2004). Circumstantial relations are considered of type instance-instance contrary to actantial relations. Example of such relations are the deep syntactic representation relations **ATTR**, **COORD**, **APPEND** of the MTT.

We thus introduce a finite set of so-called *Circumstantial Symbols (CSymbols)* $\boldsymbol{S_{\mathcal{C}}}$ which is a set of binary relation symbols. In order to classify $\boldsymbol{S_{\mathcal{C}}}$ in sets and subsets, we introduce a partial order $\overset{\mathcal{C}}{\lesssim}$ over $\boldsymbol{S_{\mathcal{C}}}$. $\overset{\mathcal{C}}{\lesssim}$ is the reflexo-transitive closure of a set of *asserted comparisons* $\boldsymbol{C_{S_{\mathcal{C}}}} \subseteq \boldsymbol{T}^2$. Finally, to each CSymbol is assigned a signature that specifies the type of units that are linked through a relation having this symbol. The set of signatures of CSymbol $\{\boldsymbol{\sigma}_s\}_{s \in \boldsymbol{S_{\mathcal{C}}}}$ is a set of couples of CUTs: $\{(domain(s), range(s))\}_{s \in \boldsymbol{S_{\mathcal{C}}}}$. As one goes down the hierarchy of PUTs, we impose that the signature of a CSymbol may only become more specific. We may hence introduce the hierarchy of CSymbols:

Definition 4. The hierarchy of Circumstantial Symbols, denoted $\mathcal{C} \overset{\text{def}}{=} (\boldsymbol{S_{\mathcal{C}}}, \boldsymbol{C_{S_{\mathcal{C}}}}, \mathcal{T}, \{\boldsymbol{\sigma}_s\}_{s \in \boldsymbol{S_{\mathcal{C}}}})$, is composed of a finite set of CSymbols $\boldsymbol{S_{\mathcal{C}}}$, a set of declared comparisons of CSymbols $\boldsymbol{C_{S_{\mathcal{C}}}}$, a hierarchy of unit types $\mathcal{T}$, and a set of signatures of the CSymbols $\{\boldsymbol{\sigma}_s\}_{s \in \boldsymbol{S_{\mathcal{C}}}}$.

3.5 UG Homomorphisms

Unit Graphs have an underlying oriented labelled graph. It is thus convenient for reasoning applications to introduce the notion of UGs homomorphism. Recall that for non-labelled graphs, an homomorphism from H to G, is an edge-preserving mapping from nodes of H to nodes of G. We will thus introduce the notion of homomorphism of UGs, based on homomorphism of their underlying oriented labelled graphs. Let us first introduce the notion of UGs mapping. Let $H = (U^h, \boldsymbol{l}^h, A^h, C^h, Eq^h)$ and $G = (U^g, \boldsymbol{l}^g, A^g, C^g, Eq^g)$ be two UGs defined over the same support.

Definition 5. A UGs mapping f from H to G, written $f : H \rightarrow G$, corresponds to a mapping of their underlying oriented labelled graphs, i.e., a mapping $f : U^h \rightarrow U^g$ from the unit nodes of H to the unit nodes of G.

Then there is a homomorphism of UGs if there is a homomorphism of their underlying oriented labelled graphs. To define such a homomorphism, one needs to choose pre-orders over labels for unit nodes and arcs. We use inclusion for unit node markers, $\overset{\cap}{\lesssim}$ for types, and $\overset{\mathcal{C}}{\lesssim}$ for circumstantial relations.

Definition 6. There is a *homomorphism* from H to G if and only if there exists a mapping $\pi : H \rightarrow G$ such that all of the following is true:

- $\forall u \in U^h, marker(u) \subseteq marker(\pi(u))$;
- $\forall u \in U^h, type(\pi(u)) \overset{\cap}{\lesssim} type(u)$;
- $(u, s, v) \in A^h \Rightarrow (\pi(u), s, \pi(v)) \in A^g$;
- $(u, s, v) \in C^h \Rightarrow \exists c \in C^g, arc(c) = (\pi(u), \pi(v))$ and $symbol(c) \overset{\mathcal{C}}{\lesssim} s$;
- $(u, v) \in Eq^h \Rightarrow (\pi(u), \pi(v)) \in Eq^g$.

4 Rules and Lexicographic Definitions

Now that we have defined the core structures of the UGs framework, and before we introduce semantics of UGs, we need to sketch some advance concepts of the UGs framework. Namely, the deep semantic representation level (§4.1), rules (§4.2), and unit types definitions (§4.3)

4.1 The deep-surface semantic interface

In the MTT, semantic ASymbols are numbers. For instance, the french lexical unit INSTRUMENT (en: instrument) has a SemASlot 1 that corresponds to the activity for which the instrument is designed. PEIGNE (en: comb) has a more specific meaning than INSTRUMENT, and also two SemASlots: 1 correspond to the person that uses the comb, and 2 is a split variable[11] that corresponds either to the hair or to the person that is to be combed.

As the specialization of PUTs implies the specialization of their actantial structure, the pre-order over semantic unit types can not correspond to a meaning specialization relation. Lefrançois and Gandon (2013a) hence defined a deeper level of representation for the MTT: the *deep semantic level*. At the deep semantic level, the pre-order

[11]See (Mel'čuk, 2004, p.43) for details about split SemASlots

over unit types may correspond to a meaning specialization relation. The *Deep Semantic Unit Type (DSemUT)* associated with a Lexical Unit Type (LexUT) L is denoted /L\, and the set of ASymbols that is used to symbolize ASlots is a set of semantic roles (e.g., $agent$, $experiencer$, $object$). For instance, the DSemUT /instrument\ associated with the LexUT INSTRUMENT may have an ASlot arbitrarily symbolized $activity$, which would be inherited by the DSemUT /peigne\. Then /peigne\ also introduces three new ASlots: one arbitrarily symbolized $possessor$ that corresponds to the ASlot 1 of ⁽peigne⁾, and two arbitrarily symbolized $combedhair$, and $combedperson$ that correspond to the ASlot 2 of ⁽peigne⁾.

4.2 Rules

One question one may ask at this point is: how to represent the correspondence between the actantial structure of a DSemUT, and the actantial structure of its associated Surface Semantic Unit Type (SSemUT)? First and parallel with CGs, we will define λ-UGs that enable to distinguish some generic unit nodes of a UG.

Definition 7. A *λ-UG* $L = \{u_1, \ldots, u_n\}G$ of size n defined over a support $\mathcal{S}$ is composed of a UG $G = (U, \boldsymbol{l}, A, C, Eq)$, and a set of n generic unit nodes of G, $\{u_1, \ldots, u_n\}$, denoted the free nodes of L.

λ-UG are actually generalized UGs, and a UG may be considered as a λ-UG of size 0. A rule may then be simply represented by two λ-UGs and a bijection between their free nodes.

Definition 8. A rule is a triple $R \overset{\text{def}}{=} (H, C, \kappa)$ where H and C are two λ-UGs of the same size defined over the same support, H is denoted the *hypothesis*, C the *conclusion*, and κ is a bijection from free nodes of H to free nodes of C.

A rule is said to be *applicable* to a UG G if and only if there exists a homomorphism from H to G. Let π be such a homomorphism from H to G. The application of R on G with respect to π is the UG obtained by merging C in G with respect to $\pi \circ \kappa^{-1}$, i.e.,

1. add C to G;
2. for all $(u^c, u^g) \in \pi \circ \kappa^{-1}$, merge u^c and u^g as follows: (i) add a new node u, with $type(u) = type(u^c) \cup type(u^g)$ and $marker(u) = marker(u^c) \cup marker(u^g)$; (ii) replace u^c and u^g by u in any dependency triple in $A \cup C$ and in any element of Eq.

Among other, rules enable to represent correspondences between representations of two adjacent levels, and they shall be automatically generated from the dictionary. Let us just note two issues with the definition of rules for the moment:

- in the correspondence between actantial structures of /peigne\ and ⁽peigne⁾, the ASlot 2 of ⁽peigne⁾ may correspond either to the ASlot $combedhair$ or to $combedperson$ of /peigne\. One thus need to define two different correspondence rules, one that assumes slot $combedhair$ is filled, and one that assumes slot $combedperson$ is filled.
- if a LexUT has an optional SemASlot, then one would need two different correspondence rules between its associated DSemUT and SSemUT: one that assumes the ASlot is filled and one that assumes the ASlot is not filled.

These remarks are valid not only at the deep-surface semantic interface, and the number of rules would grow in case of several optional ASlots, several split ASlots, or optional split SemASlots for instance. The semantic web SPARQL query language has OPTIONAL and UNION constructors that we could draw inspiration from to extend the definition of rules so as to factorize these cases. Now for the purpose of our presentation we will hold on the simple definition of rules given above, and rely on the fact that we do have means to compute all the possible correspondence rules.

4.3 Unit Types Hierarchy with Definitions

We formalize the notion of *definition* of a Primitive Unit Type (PUT) and include a set of PUTs definitions in the definition of the unit types hierarchy. Definitions are of special interest to represent lexicographic definitions of a LexUT L, which corresponds to the definition of its associated DSemUT /L\. Informally, a definition defines an equivalence between two λ-UG defined over the same support. One of them has a central free unit node typed with the defined PUT and some of its ASlots filled by free unit nodes. The other λ-UG is called the *expansion* of t. There is no circumstantial triple in these two λ-UG because they must not be part of the lexicographic definition of a LexUT.

Definition 9. A definition D_t of a PUT t is a triple $D_t \overset{\text{def}}{=} (D_t^-, D_t^+, \kappa)$ where:

- $D_t^- = \{u_t^-, v_1^-, \ldots, v_n^-\}(U^-, \boldsymbol{l}^-, A^-, \varnothing, \varnothing)$ contains only free unit nodes;
- u_t^- is called the the *central unit node* of D_t^-, and is typed $\{t\}$;
- the actantial triples of A^- are of the form (u_t^-, s_i, v_i^-) where the set of s_i is a subset of the ASlots of t;
- for all $(u_t^-, s_i, v_i^-) \in A^-$, the type of v_i^- corresponds to the signature of t for its ASlot s_i;
- $D_t^+ = \{u_t^+, v_1^+, \ldots, v_n^+\}(U^+, \boldsymbol{l}^+, A^+, \varnothing, \varnothing)$ is called the *expansion* of t;
- κ is a bijection from $\{u_t^-, v_1^-, \ldots, v_n^-\}$ to $\{u_t^+, v_1^+, \ldots, v_n^+\}$, such that $\kappa(u_t^-) = u_t^+$, and for all i, $\kappa(v_i^-) = v_i^+$;
- the type of u_t^+ is called the *genus* of t and is denoted $genus(t)$.

Figure 2 is an example of lexicographic definition of PEIGNE: an instrument that a person X uses to detangle the hair Y_1 of a person Y_2.

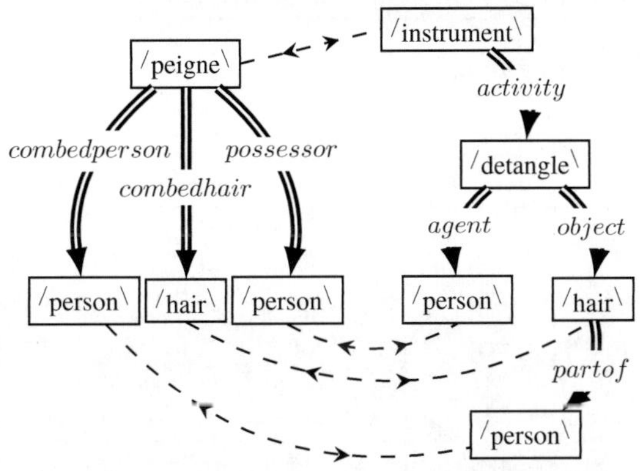

Figure 2: Lexicographic definition of PEIGNE.

Intuitively, a definition corresponds to two reciprocal rules: (D_t^-, D_t^+, κ) and $(D_t^+, D_t^-, \kappa^{-1})$. If there is the defined PUT in a UG then one may infer its definition, and vice versa. Again, there is currently an issue with the definitions with optional ASlots. In fact, one would need two different definitions, one with the ASlot filled, and one with the ASlot not filled. For the purpose of our presentation we will hold on the simple definition of definitions given above, and simply represent multiple definitions for a given PUT.

A set of PUTs definitions $\mathcal{D}$ may thus be added to the unit types hierarchy:

Definition 10. A hierarchy of unit types, denoted $\mathcal{T}$, is a tuple $\mathcal{T} \stackrel{\text{def}}{=} (T_D, \boldsymbol{S}_{\mathcal{T}}, \boldsymbol{\gamma}, \boldsymbol{\gamma_1}, \boldsymbol{\gamma_0}, C_A, \perp_A^{\sqcap}, \{\varsigma_t\}_{t \in \boldsymbol{T}}, \mathcal{D})$ that enables to construct a pre-ordered[7] set of unit types $\boldsymbol{T}^{\cap}$ with their actantial structure, and with $\mathcal{D}$ being definitions of some PUTs.

5 Semantics of UGs

5.1 Closure of a UG

The UGs framework makes the open-world assumption, which means that a UG along with the support on which it is defined represents explicit knowledge, and that additional knowledge may be inferred. Consider the UG $G = (U, \boldsymbol{l}, A, C, Eq)$ defined over the support $\mathcal{S}$ illustrated in figure 3a. Some knowledge in G is implicit:

1. two unit nodes u_1 and u_2 share a common unit marker $Mary$, so one may infer that they represent the same unit. (u_1, u_2) may be added to Eq.
2. every PUT is a subtype of $\top$, so one could add $\top$ to all the types of unit nodes in G.
3. there are two unit nodes v_1 and v_2 that fill the same ASlot $activity$ of the unit node typed /instrument\. So one may infer that v_1 and v_2 represent the same unit. Said otherwise, (v_1, v_2) may be added to Eq.
4. one may recognize the expansion of /peigne\ as defined in figure 2, so this type may be made explicit in the unit node typed /instrument\.

Each of the rules behind these cases explicit knowledge in G. More generally, table 1 lists a set of rules that one may use to explicit knowledge in any UG. Cases 1 to 4 respectively correspond to rules **mrk-eq**, **u-typ**, **a-fp**, and **def-**. The complete set of rules defines the axiomatization of the UGs semantics.

Definition 11 (Closing a UG)**.** The process of applying the set of rules of figure 1 on G until none of them has any effect is called *closing* G, and results in $cl(G)$.

Figure 3b illustrates the closure of G, where all of the inferable knowledge has been made explicit.

u-typ	For all $u \in U$, and $type(u) \overset{\sqcap}{\lesssim} t^{\cap}$	Add $t^{\cap}$	in $type(u)$
u-bot	For all $u \in U$, if $\bot \in type(u)$, ...	Error: inconsistency !	
eq-ref	For all $u \in U$	Add (u, u)	in Eq
eq-sym	For all $(u_1, u_2) \in Eq$	Add (u_2, u_1)	in Eq
eq-trans	For all (u_1, u_2) and $(u_2, u_3) \in Eq$	Add (u_1, u_3)	in Eq
eq-typ	For all $(u_1, u_2) \in Eq$	Add $type(u_1)$	in $type(u_2)$
eq-mrk	For all $(u_1, u_2) \in Eq$	Add $marker(u_1)$	in $marker(u_2)$
mrk-eq	For all $u_1, u_2 \in U$, if $marker(u_1) \cap marker(u_2) \neq \varnothing$,	Add (u_1, u_2)	in Eq
a-eq-g	For all $(u_1, s, v) \in A$ and $(u_1, u_2) \in Eq$	Add (u_2, s, v)	in A
a-eq-a	For all $(u, s, v_1) \in A$ and $(v_1, v_2) \in Eq$	Add (u, s, v_2)	in A
a-fp	For all (u, s, v_1) and $(u, s, v_2) \in A$	Add (v_1, v_2)	in Eq
a-radix	For all $(u, s, v) \in A$	Add $\boldsymbol{\gamma}(s)$	in $type(u)$
a-obl	For all $u \in U$ and $s \in \boldsymbol{S}_{\mathcal{T}}$, if $\boldsymbol{\gamma_1}(s) \in type(u)$	Ensure there exists (u, s, v) in A	
a-pro	For all $(u, s, v) \in A$, if $\boldsymbol{\gamma_0}(s) \in type(u)$,.............	Error: inconsistency !	
a-sig	For all $(u, s, v) \in A$	Add $\boldsymbol{\varsigma}^{\cap}_{type(u)}(s)$	in $type(v)$
c-eq-g	For all $(u_1, s, v) \in C$ and $(u_1, u_2) \in Eq$	Add (u_2, s, v)	in C
c-eq-c	For all $(u, s, v_1) \in C$ and $(v_1, v_2) \in Eq$	Add (u, s, v_2)	in C
c-dom	For all $(u, s, v) \in C$	Add $domain(s)$	in $type(u)$
c-rng	For all $(u, s, v) \in C$	Add $range(s)$	in $type(v)$
c-sop	For all $(u, s_1, v) \in C$ and $s_1 \overset{\mathcal{C}}{\lesssim} s_2$	Add (u, s_2, v)	in C
def+	For all $D_t \in \mathcal{D}$, if (D_t^-, D_t^+, κ) is applicable and $(D_t^+, D_t^-, \kappa^{-1})$ is not, apply (D_t^-, D_t^+, κ)		
def-	For all $D_t \in \mathcal{D}$, if $(D_t^+, D_t^-, \kappa^{-1})$ is applicable and (D_t^-, D_t^+, κ) is not, apply $(D_t^+, D_t^-, \kappa^{-1})$		

Table 1: Semantics of the Unit Graphs.

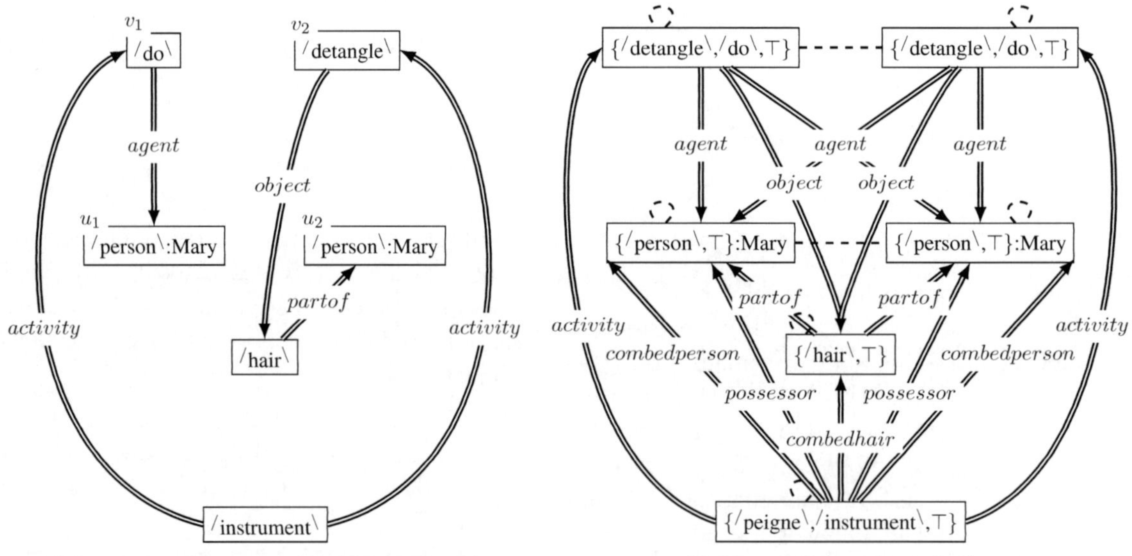

(a) Incomplete deep semantic representation G

(b) Closure of the unit graph G

Figure 3: Closure of a UG.

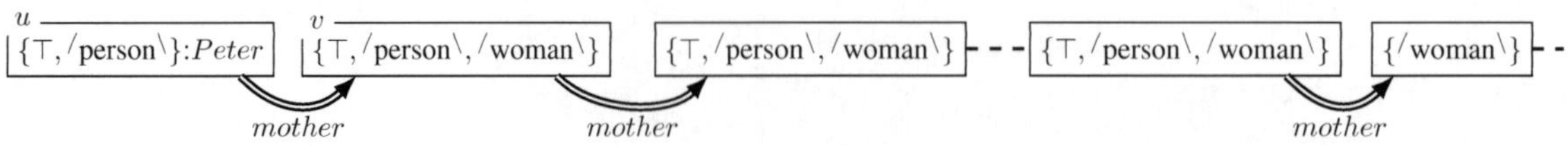

Figure 4: Illustration of an infinite closure of a simple Unit Graph

5.2 Reasoning with Homomorphisms

Now that we provided UGs with semantics and that we have means to explicit knowledge, we will define the prime decision problem of the UGs framework: *Considering two UGs G and H defined over the same support $\mathcal{S}$, does the knowledge of G entails the knowledge of H ?* The notion of *entailment* may intuitively be defined for UGs as follows: G entails H if and only if $cl(G)$ *includes* H.

There are two issues with this definition of entailment. The first is that one needs to define what is the precise meaning of *inclusion of a UG*. The second is that $cl(G)$ may be infinite, thus preventing decidability of entailment.

The answer to the first issue is straightforward as we already defined the UGs homomorphism. $cl(G)$ includes H if and only if there is a homomorphism from H to $cl(G)$.

Now, the second issue is more problematic. Indeed, the closure of a finite UG may be infinite, thus preventing decidability of the decision problem. This problem is illustrated on a simple example in figure 4, suppose one asserts that deep semantic PUTs /person\ has a obligatory ASlot $mother$ with $\varsigma_{/\text{person}\backslash}(mother) =$ /woman\, and of course, /woman\ $\lesssim$ /person\. Consider the UG $G = (\{u\}, \boldsymbol{l}, \varnothing, \varnothing, \{(u, u)\})$, such that $marker(u) = Peter$ and $type(u) = \{\top, /\text{person}\backslash\}$. One knows that the unit represented by u should have a unit of type /woman\ that fills its obligatory ASlot $mother$. So rule **add-a** is applicable and one could add a unit node v to represent that argument, with $(u, mother, v) \in A$. Rule **u-typ** will then make v be of type $\{\top, /\text{person}\backslash, /\text{woman}\backslash\}$, and rule **add-a** is again applicable on v. Thus $cl(G)$ is an infinite chain of unit nodes having type $\{\top, /\text{person}\backslash, /\text{woman}\backslash\}$ and that fill the ASlot $mother$ of one another.

In the set of inference rules of table 1, only three rules add unit nodes to the UG when triggered: **add-g**,**def-** and **def+**. An open problem is thus to find a sufficient condition on the unit types hierarchy and the set of definitions so that we are ensured that the closure of a finite UG is finite.

6 Conclusion

We studied how to formalize, in a knowledge engineering perspective, the dependency structures and the linguistic predicates, in order to represent, manipulate, query, and reason with linguistic knowledge.

We provided a rationale the introduction of the new graph-based Unit Graphs (UGs) KR formalism, and gave an overview of the foundational concepts of the UGs framework. The linguistic predicates are represented by unit types, and are described in a unit types hierarchy. Circumstantial relations are another kind of dependency relation that are described in a hierarchy, and along with a set of unit identifiers these two structures form a UGs support on which UGs may be defined. As UG have an underlying oriented labelled graph, one could introduce the notion of UG homomorphism which is useful to define the applicability of rules and the entailment problem.

The strong coherence in the unit types hierarchy justifies the introduction of a deep semantic representation level that is deeper than the semantic level, and in which one may represent the actual meaning of Lexical Unit Type (LexUT). It is at the deep semantic level that the lexicographic definitions of LexUTs shall be represented, and we gave a definition of the definition of the associated Deep Semantic Unit Type (DSemUT) of a LexUT.

Once we added a set of unit types definitions in the unit types hierarchy, we introduced the semantics of UGs and we posed the entailment problem for UGs. A UGs along with the support on which it is defined represents explicit knowledge, and additional knowledge may be inferred. We introduced a set of entailment rules that one may use to compute the closure $cl(G)$ of a UG G, i.e., make explicit all of the knowledge that is implicit. We then defined the entailment problem of H by G as a directed labelled graphs homomorphism problem between H, and the closure of G: $cl(G)$. In case $cl(G)$ is finite, the entailment problem is thus NP-complete.

In this paper we also sketched two directions for future research:

- Many rules may be needed to represent correspondences between the deep semantic and the semantic representation levels in case some Semantic ASlots are optional or split. More research is needed to adapt the SPARQL OPTIONAL and UNION constructors in these cases. The same can be said about definitions of DSemUTs that have optional ASlots.
- The closure may be infinite for finite UGs. If

that occurs it makes the closure undecidable, along with the entailment problem. We are currently working of the definition of restrictions of the unit types hierarchy and the set of definitions in order to ensure that any UG has a finite closure.

References

Juri Apresian, Igor Boguslavsky, Leonid Iomdin, Alexander Lazursky, Vladimir Sannikov, Victor Sizov, and Leonid Tsinman. 2003. ETAP-3 linguistic processor: A full-fledged NLP implementation of the MTT. In *First International Conference on Meaning–Text Theory (MTT'2003)*, pages 279–288.

Lucie Barque and Alain Polguère. 2008. Enrichissement formel des définitions du Trésor de la Langue Française informatisé (TLFi) dans une perspective lexicographique. *Lexique*, 22.

Lucie Barque, Alexis Nasr, and Alain Polguère. 2010. From the Definitions of the 'Trésor de la Langue Française' To a Semantic Database of the French Language. In Fryske Akademy, editor, *Proceedings of the XIV Euralex International Congress*, Fryske Akademy, pages 245–252, Leeuwarden, Pays-Bas. Anne Dykstra et Tanneke Schoonheim, dir.

Igor Boguslavsky, Leonid Iomdin, and Viktor Sizov. 2004. Multilinguality in ETAP-3: reuse of lexical resources. In Gilles Sérasset, editor, *Proc. COLING 2004 Multilingual Linguistic Ressources*, pages 1–8, Geneva, Switzerland. COLING.

Igor Boguslavsky. 2011. Semantic Analysis Based on Linguistic and Ontological Resources. In Igor Boguslavsky and Leo Wanner, editors, *Proceedings of the 5th International Conference on Meaning-Text Theory (MTT'2011)*, pages 25–36, Barcelona, Spain. INALCO.

Bernd Bohnet and Leo Wanner. 2010. Open source graph transducer interpreter and grammar development environment. In *Proceedings of the Seventh International Conference on Language Resources and Evaluation (LREC'10)*, pages 19–21, Valletta, Malta. European Language Resources Association (ELRA).

Michel Chein and Marie-Laure Mugnier. 2008. *Graph-based Knowledge Representation: Computational Foundations of Conceptual Graphs*. Springer-Verlag New York Incorporated.

Sylvain Kahane and Alain Polguère. 2001. Formal foundation of lexical functions. In *Proceedings of ACL/EACL 2001 Workshop on Collocation*, pages 8–15.

Maxime Lefrançois and Fabien Gandon. 2011. ILexicOn: Toward an ECD-Compliant Interlingual Lexical Ontology Described with Semantic Web Formalisms. In Igor Boguslavsky and Leo Wanner, editors, *Proceedings of the 5th International Conference on Meaning-Text Theory (MTT'2011)*, pages 155–164, Barcelona, Spain. INALCO.

Maxime Lefrançois and Fabien Gandon. 2013a. The Unit Graphs Framework: A graph-based Knowledge Representation Formalism designed for the Meaning-Text Theory. In *Proceedings of the 6th International Conference on Meaning-Text Theory (MTT'2013)*, Prague, Czech Republic.

Maxime Lefrançois and Fabien Gandon. 2013b. The Unit Graphs Mathematical Framework. Research Report RR-8212, Inria.

Maxime Lefrançois. 2013. Représentation des connaissances du DEC: Concepts fondamentaux du formalisme des Graphes d'Unités. In *Proceedings of the 15ème Rencontre des Étudiants Chercheurs en Informatique pour le Traitement Automatique des Langues (RECITAL'2013)*, Les Sables d'Olonne, France.

Veronika Lux-Pogodalla and Alain Polguère. 2011. Construction of a French Lexical Network: Methodological Issues. In *Proceedings of the International Workshop on Lexical Resources*, Ljubljana.

Igor Mel'čuk. 1996. Lexical Functions: A Tool for the Description of Lexical Relations in a Lexicon. In Leo Wanner, editor, *Lexical Functions in Lexicography and Natural Language Processing*, pages 37–102. Benjamins Academic Publishers, Amsterdam/Philadelphia.

Igor Mel'čuk. 2004. Actants in Semantics and Syntax I: Actants in Semantics. *Linguistics*, 42(1):247–291.

Igor Mel'čuk. 2006. Explanatory combinatorial dictionary. *Open Problems in Linguistics and Lexicography*, pages 225–355.

Alain Polguère. 2009. Lexical systems: graph models of natural language lexicons. *Language resources and evaluation*, 43(1):41–55.

John F Sowa. 1984. *Conceptual structures: information processing in mind and machine*. System programming series. Addison-Wesley Pub., Reading, MA.

Non-projectivity in the Ancient Greek Dependency Treebank

Francesco Mambrini
The Center for Hellenic Studies
Washington, DC
fmambrini@chs.harvard.edu

Marco Passarotti
Università Cattolica del Sacro Cuore
Milano, Italy
marco.passarotti@unicatt.it

Abstract

In this paper, we provide a quantitative analysis of non-projective constructions attested in the Ancient Greek Dependency Treebank (AGDT). We consider the different types of formal constraints and metrics that have become standardized in the literature on non-projectivity (planarity, well-nestedness, gap-degree, edge-degree). We also discuss some of the linguistic factors that cause non-projective edges in Ancient Greek. Our results confirm the remarkable extension of non-projectivity in the AGDT, both in terms of quantitative incidence of non-projective nodes and for their complexity, which is not paralleled by the corpora of modern languages considered in the literature. At the same time, the usefulness of other constraint (especially well-nestedness) is confirmed by our researches.

1 Introduction

The "free" word-order of Ancient Greek (AG) is a notorious problem for philologists and linguists. In spite of several studies devoted to the subject, the tendencies that govern the disposition of words and constituents in the sentence still lack a comprehensive explanation. Strictly connected to the word-order issue is the relevant amount of discontinuous constituents, which even casual readers of AG texts can experience[1].

The dependency-based treebanks of Classical languages (AG and Latin) that have been recently made available enable us to reconsider this long debate in the light of the abundant work on non-projective structures in dependency trees. Non-projectivity (see 2 for a formal definition) is a key issue in dependency grammar, both from the formal point of view and from a more descriptive linguistic perspective. From the standpoint of natural language processing, non-projectivity is also known to affect the efficiency of dependency parsers.

In a first attempt to improve parsing performances on AG, Mambrini and Passarotti (2012) reported that the amount of non-projective arcs occurring in the available treebanks of Classical languages is significantly higher than that attested in the corpora of modern languages used for CoNLL-X (Buchholz and Marsi, 2006, 155, tab. 1) and CoNLL 2007 shared tasks (Nivre et al., 2007, 920, tab. 1). Furthermore, the non-projective rate in the Ancient Greek Dependency Treebank is higher than in Classical and Medieval Latin (Passarotti and Ruffolo, 2010, 920, tab. 1).

In this paper, we want to discuss this claim in depth and substantiate it by applying to AG data the standard metrics for the different kinds of non projective constructions established in the literature.

The paper is organized as follows. Section 2 provides a definition of the formal constraints considered and of the metrics that will be used: non-projectivity, planarity, well-nestedness, on the one hand, and gap-degree and edge-degree on the other. Section 3 introduces the corpus that will be tested, the Ancient Greek Dependency Treebank (AGDT).

Section 4 presents the evidence provided by the data. In 4.1 we report the results for the different constraints and metrics defined in section 2. Results for the distribution of non-projectivity in the different genres of the corpus are given and commented in 4.2.

In section 5, we discuss some of the linguistic issues that cause non-projectivity. Finally, section 6 reports our conclusions and sketches possible directions for additional research.

[1] On AG word-order see more recently Dik (1995; 2007), with bibliography of previous studies. On discontinuous structures see Devine and Stephens (2000).

Proceedings of the Second International Conference on Dependency Linguistics (DepLing 2013), pages 177–186,
Prague, August 27–30, 2013.

2 Non-projectivity

A dependency tree is a rooted tree where the nodes represent the words of a sentence, the edges represent the syntactic dependencies and the linear order of the nodes stands for the sequence of words.

According to the so-called 'treeness constraint' (Debusmann and Kuhlmann, 2010), a dependency tree requires (a) that no word should depend on itself, not even transitively (i.e. the tree must be acyclic), (b) that each word should have at most one governor, and (c) that a dependency analysis should cover all the words in the sentence.

If a node j depends on a node i, j is called a 'child' of i, and, symmetrically, i is the 'parent' of j (we write $i \rightarrow j$). On the other hand, we write $i \leftrightarrow j$ whenever the edge is considered regardless of the direction of the relation (i can be either the parent or the child of j). If i precedes j in the word order, i lies to the left of j (we write $i < j$); conversely, j lies to the right of i ($j > i$). The set of all nodes that can be reached from a given node i by following a directed path of zero or more edges is called the set of 'descendants' of i. A subtree of a tree T at a node i is the restriction of T (nodes and edges) to the descendants of i.

The condition of **projectivity**, which was formally defined by Marcus (1965), requires each dependency subtree to cover a contiguous region of the sentence: a word and its transitive dependents must span a contiguous sequence in the linear order. We may define the constraint of projectivity with the following formula (Havelka, 2007, 609):

$$i \rightarrow j \,\&\, v \in (i, j) \Longrightarrow v \in Subtree_i$$

which must be read in this way: let i be the parent of j ($i \rightarrow j$); if a node v lies between i and j in the linear order of the sentence, then v belongs to the subtree of i. If this condition does not hold, then the edge is non-projective and v is said to be in a **gap** ($v \in Gap_{i \leftrightarrow j}$). Example 1 illustrates this construction with a simplified version of a sentence from the AGDT (the first sentence of the *Iliad*), which is also represented in fig. 1[2]. The edges *mēnin-Achilēos* and *mēnin-ouloménēn* are non-projective, since the nodes of *áeide* and *theá* are in a gap in both cases.

[2]The Greek words and lemmata in the AGDT are written in Greek characters, transcribed according to an ASCII-based convention known as "Beta Code" (TLG, 2010). All the trees reported in this paper are transliterated in Latin script by the authors for ease of reading.

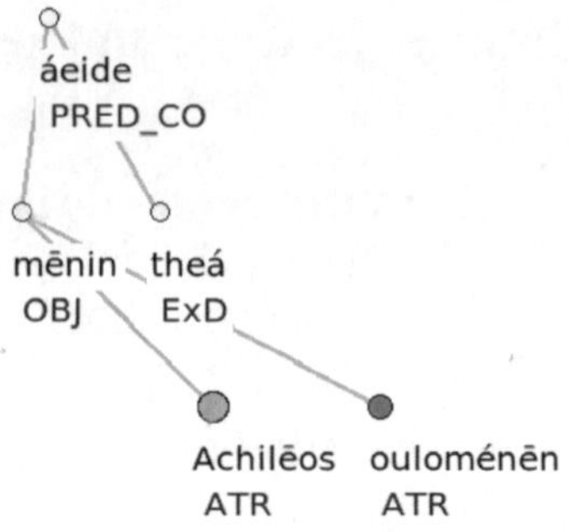

Figure 1: Non-projective edges: a simplified tree from the AGDT

(1) *mēnin* *áeide theá*
wrath.FEM.ACC sing Goddess.VOC
Achilēos *ouloménēn*
of-Achilles.GEN accursed.FEM.ACC
Sing, oh Goddess, the wrath of Achilles, the accursed wrath.
(simplified version of *Iliad* 1.1)

Non-projectivity, which was postulated by Marcus (1965) for the purposes of machine translation and language generation, is too strong a constraint for natural languages: a non-negligible number of constructions attested for many languages does not satisfy the condition. Several relaxations to the definition were subsequently introduced in order to better account for the linguistic data.

The condition of **planarity** involves two edges $i_1 \leftrightarrow j_1$ and $i_2 \leftrightarrow j_2$ and disallows any overlapping between them. Two edges are said to overlap if, for example, $i_1 > i_2 > j_1 > j_2$ or $i_1 < i_2 < j_1 < j_2$. Therefore, following Havelka (2007), a tree is non-planar if there are at least two edges $i_1 \leftrightarrow j_1$ and $i_2 \leftrightarrow j_2$ that meet the following condition:

$$i_1 \in (i_2, j_2) \,\&\, i_2 \in (i_1, j_1)$$

Example 2 (fig. 2) presents two non-planar edges from a tree of the AGDT.

(2) *mýri'* *Achaióis*
countless.NEUT.PL to-Achaeans.DAT
álge' *éthēke*
grieves.NEUT.PL (it)-caused.3rd.SG
(which) inflicted countless grieves to the Achaeans
(*Iliad* 1.2)

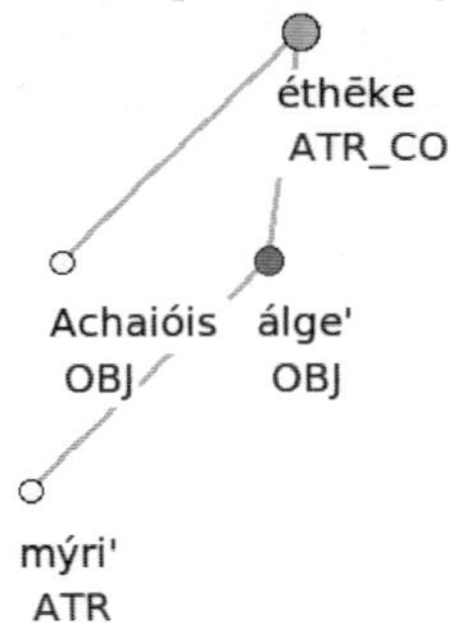

Figure 2: Non-planar (well-nested) edges

In the tree reported in fig. 2, the edges *éthēke* → *Achaióis* and *álge'* → *mýri'* are non-planar, because *éthēke* > *álge'* > *Achaióis* > *mýri'*.

Well-nestedness introduces a further relaxation to projectivity. A (sub)tree is said to be well-nested if, for each pair of overlapping disjoint edges, the source node of one of the edges is a descendant of the source node of the other; conversely (Havelka, 2007), the (sub)tree is ill-nested if, for two edges $i_1 \leftrightarrow j_1$ and $i_2 \leftrightarrow j_2$:

$$i_1 \in Gap_{i_2 \leftrightarrow j_2} \;\&\; i_2 \in Gap_{i_1 \leftrightarrow j_1}$$

One may note that the two edges in fig. 2 are well-nested, since *álge'* is the child of *éthēke*.

In addition to these constraints, two metrics have become standard measures for non-projectivity.

Given a non-projective edge, **edge-degree** represents the number of nodes that are in the gap. This metric was introduced by Nivre (2006), but was named *edge-degree* by Kuhlmann and Nivre (2006) and it corresponds to *component degree* in Havelka (2007). The edge-degree can be estimated either by counting the edges that match the definition in a treebank, or by using the tree as a basis, the edge-degree of a tree T being equal to the highest edge-degree among the edges of T.

On the contrary, **gap-degree** is not based on a single edge, but rather on the 'projection' (or on the 'blocks') of a node, which is defined as the longest non-empty sequence of nodes that goes down to a terminal node in a chain succession from father to child[3]. A gap (or interval) in the projection is a discontinuity such that, given a node j_k in the sequence, $j_k - j_{k+1} > 1$. The gap-degree corresponds to the number of gaps in the sequence (Kuhlmann and Nivre, 2006), while the gap-degree of a tree is equal to the highest gap-degree for each sequence in the tree[4].

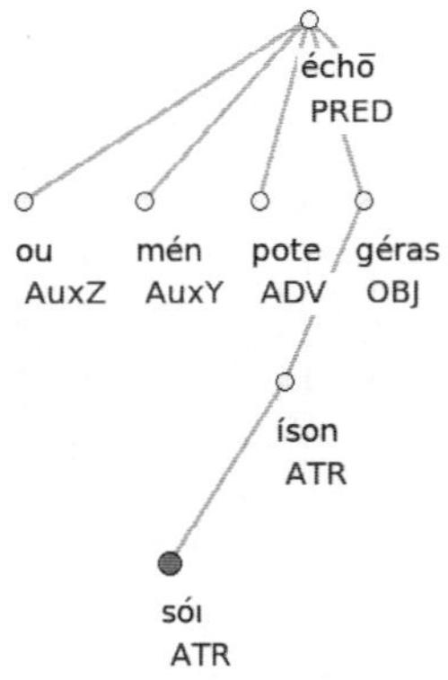

Figure 3: Gap-degree = 2

(3) *ou mén sói pote íson*
not PRTCL to-you.DAT ever equal.ACC
échō géras
(I)-have.1st.SG gift.ACC
Never do I get a gift that matches yours
(*Iliad* 1.163)

In fig. 3, which represents the tree of example 3, the segment *géras-íson-sói* is interrupted twice, namely by *échō* and *pote*. The words in the gaps do not form a single continuous interval in the linear order: the segment has therefore gap-degree = 2.

3 The corpus

The Ancient Greek Dependency Treebank (Bamman et al., 2009) is a dependency-based treebank of Greek literary texts of the Archaic and Classical age published by the Perseus Digital Library[5].

In its theoretical framework and guidelines, the AGDT is inspired by the analytical layer of the Prague Dependency Treebank of Czech (Böhmová et al., 2001). Currently, the last published version of the AGDT (1.7) includes 354,529 tokens. The collection is constituted by unabridged works that

[3]A projection of a node may consist of one or more 'blocks', i.e. maximal, non-empty intervals of descendants.

[4]**Interval-degree** is an edge-based version of the gap-degree (Havelka, 2007). Given a non-projective edge $i \rightarrow j$ with $v_{1,n}$ in the gap, the interval-degree corresponds to the number of intervals in the sequence $v_{1,n}$.

[5]Perseus Digital Library: http://www.perseus.tufts.edu/hopper/.

belong to three literary genres: epic poetry (the *Iliad*, the *Odyssey*, and the complete works of Hesiod), tragedy (the complete work of Aeschylus and five plays of Sophocles), philosophical prose (the *Euthyphro* of Plato). Chronologically, the texts range from the 8th to the 4th Century BCE. The composition of the AGDT 1.7 is resumed in table 1[6].

Author/Work	**Genre**	**Date**	**Tokens**
Iliad	Epic	8th(?)	128,102
Odyssey	Epic	8th(?)	104,467
Hesiod	Epic	7th(?)	18,881
Aeschylus	Drama	5th	48,261
Sophocles	Drama	5th	48,721
Plato	Prose	4th	6,097
Total			354,529

Table 1: AGDT 1.7

4 Results

4.1 Constraints and measures in the AGDT

Table 2 reports the number and percentage of the trees that do not respect the constraints of projectivity, planarity, and well-nestedness in the AGDT 1.7. The Ancient Greek data are compared with those of six other languages from the CoNLL-X shared task that display the highest rate of non-projective constructions (Havelka, 2007)[7]. The languages are sorted according to the percentage of non-projective trees in decreasing order.

As it may be seen, AG shows a remarkably high rate of non-projective trees in comparison with the other languages. Non-projective edges are found in almost three out of every four sentences of the AGDT, a distribution that nearly reverses that of German, Czech or Slovene. The abundance of non-projective constructions in the AGDT stands out even more clearly when one considers the rate of non-projective edges instead of non-projective trees. The numbers are reported in table 3; the comparative data are again taken from Havelka (2007).

Language	**Tot. edges**	**Non-proj. edges**	
		No.	%
A. Greek	301848	45731	15.15
Dutch	179063	10566	5.90
German	660394	15844	2.40
Czech	1105437	23570	2.13
Slovene	25777	550	2.13
Portuguese	197607	2702	1.37

Table 3: Non-projective edges in AG and other languages

Although AG is exceptional for the incidence of non-projective edges, if one considers the different conditions of relaxation of projectivity, AG data seem to reflect the same tendencies already observed in other languages (Kuhlmann and Nivre, 2006; Havelka, 2007). Non-planarity does not prove to mark a significant relaxation. On the contrary, well-nestedness is a very effective constraint in AG too. Although the absolute rate is higher than in the other languages, the number of ill-nested trees is considerably smaller.

AG deviates from the trend observed in other languages also for the complexity of non-projective structures, as measured by both gap- and edge-degree. The observations reported in table 4 highlight the main differences with the other languages studied[8].

The fact that in AG the percentages of gap-degree 0 and 1 appear to be almost inverted in comparison with those of the other languages is not surprising, given the general proportion of non-projective trees in the languages discussed. In all the languages but AG, a threshold set to gap-degree = 1 is a very strong constraint, which allows to account for more than 99% of the total of trees[9]. In AG, instead, the number of trees with gap-degree = 3 is still a non-negligible fraction (more than 6% of the total).

The rate of trees with edge-degree ≥ 1 is significantly higher in AG than in the other languages too. While in other treebanks an edge-degree = 2 is already sufficient to cover more than 99% of the

[6]The dates reported in the table refer to the century BCE. In some cases (like for the Homeric poems and the works of Hesiod), even this general chronology is very hypothetical.

[7]Note that in the CoNLL data format, each sentence is provided with a technical root node placed before the sentence (i.e. the root is the leftmost node in dependency trees for left-to-right languages). All the dependency analyses are attached directly, or indirectly to the root node. As edges from technical roots may introduce non-planarity, we disregard all such edges when counting trees conforming to the planarity constraint. Since the same is done by Havelka (2007, p. 21), this makes our data comparable with those reported there.

[8]The data for Danish and Czech are taken from Kuhlmann and Nivre (2006). Hindi and Urdu are two of the Indian languages studied by Bhat and Sharma (2012), whence the numbers were taken.

[9]Urdu with, 98.43%, is only a limited exception.

Language	Tot. trees	Non-proj.		Non-plan.		Ill-nested	
		trees	%	trees	%	trees	%
Ancient Greek	24825	18568	74.80	15334	61.77	656	2.64
Dutch	13349	4865	36.44	4115	30.83	15	0.11
German	39216	10883	27.75	10865	27.71	416	1.06
Czech	72703	16831	23.15	13783	18.96	79	0.11
Slovene	1534	340	22.16	283	18.45	3	0.20
Portuguese	9071	1718	18.94	1713	18.88	7	0.08

Table 2: Non-projective, non-planar, ill-nested trees in AG and other languages

Language	Trees	Gap-degree (%)					Edge-degree (%)				
		gd0	gd1	gd2	gd3	gd4	ed0	ed1	ed2	ed3	ed4
A. Greek	24825	25.20	68.33	6.17	0.28	0.02	25.20	43.73	14.15	7.07	3.88
Danish	4393	84.95	14.89	0.16	-	-	84.95	13.29	1.32	0.39	0.05
Czech	73088	76.85	22.72	0.42	0.01	<0.01	76.85	22.69	0.35	0.09	0.01
Hindi	20497	85.14	14.56	0.28	0.02	na	85.14	14.24	0.45	0.11	0.03
Urdu	3192	77.85	20.58	1.31	0.12	na	77.85	19.20	1.97	0.56	0.22

Table 4: Gap-degree and edge-degree

trees, it is only at edge-degree = 7 (0.84%) that the frequency of the AGDT trees drops under 1% of the corpus[10].

To sum up, we can conclude that, whereas well-nestedness appears to be an effective constraint in AG too, the thresholds of gap-degree 1 and edge-degree 2 in the AGDT do not have the same impact as that observed in other treebanks.

4.2 The role of genre

Genre difference is known to have a strong effect on the performances of dependency parsers for AG texts (Mambrini and Passarotti, 2012). It is important, therefore, to observe if the values reported above are at variance in the different genres included in the AGDT.

The frequencies of non-projective constructions in each of the three genres of the AGDT are reported in table 5. The most relevant fact is the difference between the poetic genres (epic and drama) on the one hand, and the philosophical dialogue in prose on the other. This difference can be appreciated especially when one looks at the rate on non-projective edges, which does not vary significantly between epic and drama (respectively, 15.30% and 15.09%), but it is quite different if prose is concerned (9.81%). Plato's *Euthyphro* (the sole prose work included in the corpus at the moment) is the only text where the number of non-projective trees is less than 50%, although the incidence of non-projectivity is still sensibly higher than in corpora of modern languages, as reported above.

These distributions may lead to the claim that the high number of discontinuous constituents is due to poetic style and, possibly, to the metrical constraints that operate in poetic language[11]. Unfortunately, no conclusions can be drawn on this matter. Limited as they are to one single author and text, the presently available data for prose language can hardly point to more than a working hypothesis for future research. It will be possible to test this hypothesis as soon as new texts of the same genre and/or author will be added to the corpus.

5 Discussion: linguistic causes of non-projective edges in the AGDT

In this section we discuss some of the linguistic causes of non-projective edges in the AGDT. We first analyze one specific kind of nodes in the gap (the clitics: 5.1); then we will focus on those non-projective edges in the AGDT that are governed by a verb or by a noun, also in the light of the typologies studied for Czech (Hajičová et al., 2004).

[10]The maximum edge-degree found in the AGDT is the abnormal value of 45, which however results from an annotation error.

[11]Sensible remarks (with minimal bibliography) about the question of linguistic and metrical constraints on word-order in AG tragedy can be read in Dik (2007, 3, 168-224).

Measures and constraints	Epic $T = 16359$ $E = 217539$	Drama $T = 8040$ $E = 79162$	Prose $T = 426$ $E = 5147$
non-proj trees (%)	82.25	60.95	49.77
non-proj edges (%)	15.30	15.09	9.81
non-planar (%)	66.67	52.70	44.84
ill-nested (%)	2.50	3.00	1.41
gap-deg = 0 (%)	17.75	39.05	50.23
gap-deg = 1 (%)	76.27	53.43	44.37
gap-deg = 2 (%)	5.78	7.00	5.40
edge-deg = 0 (%)	17.75	39.05	50.23
edge-deg = 1 (%)	50.21	31.64	23.00
edge-deg = 2 (%)	14.38	6.85	9.62
edge-deg = 3 (%)	7.51	3.09	4.69

Table 5: Measures and constraints in the AGDT, grouped by genre (T = tot. trees, E = tot. edges)

5.1 The role of clitics

As it is partly the case with the Czech conjunction *-li* (Hajičová et al., 2004), clitics are likely to have a strong role in non-projective structures of the AGDT. It is well known that in AG clitics tend to stick to a fixed position in the sentence or clause, in accordance to the so-called "Wackernagel's law", which is common to many Indo-European languages (Wackernagel, 1892; Ruijgh, 1990). The words that belong to the class of *postpositives* (i.e. the clitics and a few other words that cannot occupy the clause-initial position) tend to be placed in second position, even when this collocation breaks a syntactic constituent. In example 4, the coordinating particle *d'* (*dé*) is placed in second position and separates one of the two (non-coordinated) attributes (*pollás*) from the rest of the noun phrase (*iphthímous psychás*).

(4) *pollás* **d'** *iphthímous*
many.ACC.FEM **and** strong.ACC.FEM
psychás *Háidi* *proíapsen*
souls.ACC.FEM to-Hades (it)-sent

and (it) sent forth to Hades many valiant souls (*Iliad* 1.1)

This situation is normal also with the enclitic *te* (*and*, = Latin *-que*), which is regularly placed after the first word of coordinated clauses. Whenever the word that precedes *te* has one or more right descendants in the dependency tree, *te* comes to be in a gap.

Some facts hint that this tendency of clitics is a relevant issue for non-projectivity: we have resumed them in table 6. The first five most frequent words recurring in gaps belong all to the class of postpositives; in total, postpositives account for about 40% (39.16%) of the nodes attested in gaps[12]. As for the most frequent syntactic labels, coordinating conjunctions (COORD) and sentence adverbials (AuxY), which are the two typical functions of postpositives, are again the two groups ranking in the first and second place. Finally, second position (i.e. the one which is usually occupied by postpositives) is by far the most

		% nodes in gap
Lemmata	dé	25.85
	te	4.87
	mén	3.17
	gár	2.09
	án	0.69
Syntactic relations	COORD	22.78
	AuxY	15.35
	PRED	12.57
	ADV	9.47
	OBJ	6.91
Positions	2	18.63
	5	7.62
	4	7.00

Table 6: Most frequent lemmata, syntactic relations and positions in the sentences for words in a gap in the AGDT

[12]A list of postpositives can be found in Dik (1995, 32). Note that we left personal pronouns out of our analysis.

often attested for nodes in a gap[13].

5.2 Verb-headed and noun-headed non-projective edges in the AGDT

In this section we will focus on those non-projective edges that are governed by either a noun/pronoun or a verb, as they cover more than 76% of all the non-projective edges in the AGDT.

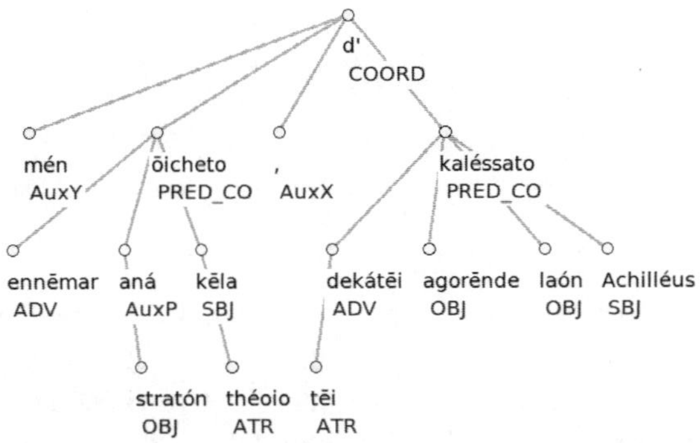

Figure 4: *Iliad* 1.53-4

Verb-headed edges: in the non-projective structures of the AGDT, verbal complementations precedes their verbal head in the 67.93% of the cases. Both arguments (subjects, predicatives and direct/indirect objects) and adjuncts (several kinds of adverbial modifications) are very frequently involved in such a movement of the complements to the left, which often results in non-projective constructions.

In Czech, this situation is produced notably by contrastive contextually bound elements moved towards the beginning of the clause. As the AGDT does not feature annotation of information structure yet, it is not easy for us to evaluate its quantitative impact in data, but a reading of the examples that can be extracted from the treebank suggests that the same tendency is at work also in AG[14].

In the two coordinated clauses of example 5 (fig. 4), for instance, the temporal complementations create a contrastive frame for the action (*ennēmar... tēi dekátēi*). In order to highlight their function, both complements are moved to the first position of their respective clauses. This movement causes non-projectivity, as the nodes for *mén* and *d'* result to be in a gap.

Another phenomenon that may generate non-projective constructions in AG is the raising of complementations of infinitive verbs that are moved to the left outside the subordinate clause. The importance of this pattern can be seen by measuring the distribution of verbal mood in the non-projective arcs. Indicative dominates in general (75% vs 14% of infintives), but if one considers the subset of cases with complement–head order and with a gap wider than one single clitic, then the rate of infinitives increases considerably (50% vs 42% of indicatives).

(5) *ennēmar mén*
for-nine-days on-the-one-hand
aná stratón ōicheto kēla
throughout camp went arrows
théoio, tēi dekátēi d'
of-the-god, (on-)the tenth while
agorēnde kaléssato laón Achilléus
to-assembly called army Achilles
For nine days the arrows of the god swept throughout the camp; on the tenth, Achilles called the army to the assembly (*Iliad* 1.53-4)

(6) *hoi mén epépleon hygrá*
they on-the-one-hand sailed-over watery
kéleutha, laoús d'
paths, men.ACC while
Atreídēs apolymáinesthai
son-of-Atreus.NOM to-purify.INF.REFL
ánōgen
commanded
So they sailed over the watery paths, while the son of Atreus commanded the men to purify themselves (*Iliad* 1.312-2, slightly simplified)

Example 6 (fig. 5) shows a combination of the two aforementioned phenomena: *laoús*, subject of the infinitive *apolymáinesthai*, is moved to the left of the main verb of the clause, outside the subordinate governed by the infinitive. At the same time, one may note the structure of the sentence, where two clauses are contrasted. In the first part, the departure of a small embassy of twenty selected

[13] The value of this observation is very limited. There are a number of cases (starting with those where a particle follows a coordinating conjunction and has the second coordinated clause in its scope) where the "second position" of clitics does not correspond to the second word of a sentence. However, it seems significant, also in light of the other observation reported above, that rank n. 2 scores so highly.

[14] It is also known that topic elements in AG tend to be placed at the beginning of the clause (Dik, 1995; Matić, 2003).

Greek soldiers (whose preparation is the subject of the preceding lines) is mentioned. In the second, the events at the Greek camp and the actions of the main army that remains at Troy are narrated. When the whole army is mentioned again, thus, the contrastive contextually bound word (*laoús*) is raised in prominent position and this movement causes non-projectivity, since the subject of the governing clause (*Atreídēs*) comes to be in a gap[15].

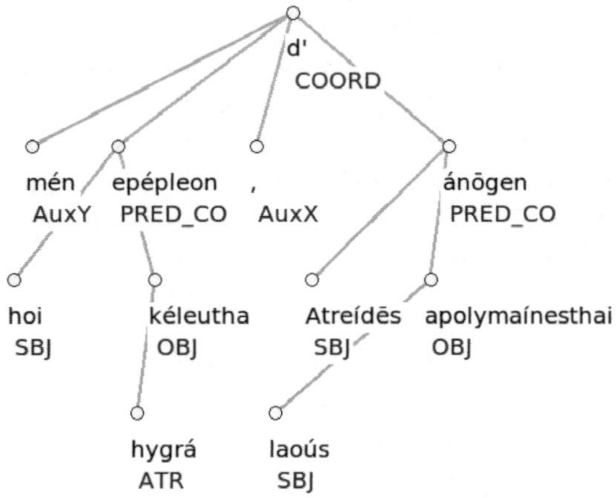

Figure 5: *Iliad* 1.312-3 (simplified)

Noun-headed edges: nouns can govern attributes (in the form of adjectives, nouns in genitives, or relative clauses), predicatives and valency complements (especially for deverbal nouns). In the case of nouns, the preference toward the complement–head order is less marked than with verbs (57% complement–head vs 43 head–complement%).

The head-noun of a non-projective edge can be the salient element moved toward the beginning of the sentence. This is the case in example 1 (fig. 1), where the noun *mēnis* ("wrath"), which introduces the main subject of the whole poem, is the focus of the sentence. This word is placed in first position, before the invocation to the Muse, and detached from the possessive genitive ("of Achilles"), of the epithet ("accursed") and of the long series of relative clauses that further specify the noun (not reported in the example above). The left-movement of the noun that isolates one of the key-themes in the poem occurs in the first sentence of each of the epic texts of the AGDT, with the only exception of the *Shield of Herakles*.

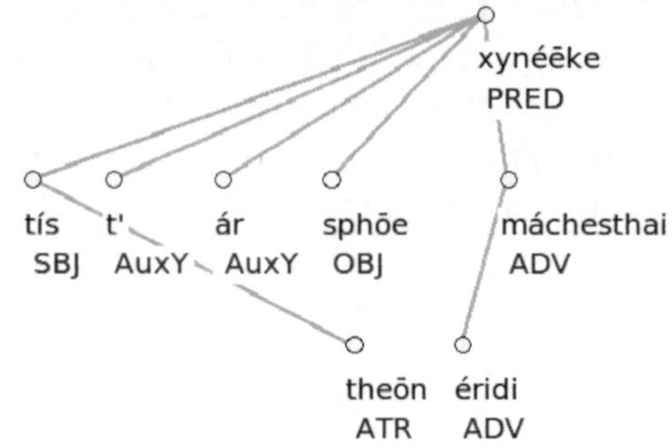

Figure 6: *Iliad* 1.8

Another case where we can observe the isolation of one focus element at the beginning of the sentence is with the interrogative pronoun *tís* ("who/which?"). Often, this left-movement separates the pronoun from the determiners that further specify it; in the case of example 7 (fig. 6) the pronoun is separated from the partitive genitive (*tís... theōn*) by two particles (*t'* and *ár*) and by the direct object of the verb (*sphōe*)[16].

(7) *tís t' ár sphōe*
who and then them-two.DU.ACC
theōn éridi xynéēke
of-the-gods with-strife pitted
máchesthai?
to-fight?
Who was it of the gods who pitted the two against each other so that they contended in strife? (*Iliad* 1.8)

Predicative adjectives, which specify the manner of the action expressed by the verb but agree with a nominal head, are very frequent in AG. They are syntactically dependent on the agreeing noun, but they modify semantically the verb as well. This sort of "double gravity" is a potential source of non-projective constructions. Often, as it is the case with *autómatos* ("of his initiative, unbidden") in example 8 (fig. 7), predicative adjectives convey the most salient information in the sentence and are therefore attracted toward a preeminent position.

[15]Note that even in the first clause the contrastive contextually bound subject (*hoi*) and the verb (*epépleon*) are noncontiguous, with the particle *mén* placed in the gap.

[16]The fact that the identity of the god is the focus of the question is evinced from the answers that is given (as nominal sentence) in the line that follows: "the son of Leto and Zeus. For he, angered against the king" etc.

(8) *autómatos dé hoi ēlthe boēn*
unbidden.NOM and to-him came cry
agathós Menélaos.
good Menelaos.NOM?

And Menelaos, good at the war-cry, came to him unbidden (*Iliad* 2.408)

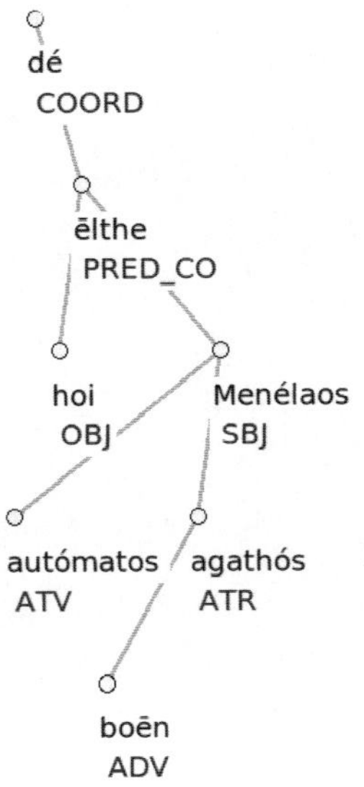

Figure 7: *Iliad* 2.408

6 Conclusions and future work

Our survey has confirmed the remarkable extension of non-projectivity in the Ancient Greek Dependency Treebank (1.7). The AGDT stands out for the relevant amount of both non-projective trees and edges, which are unmatched by the rate of discontinuous structures known from dependency treebanks of other languages and for the complexity of these constructions.

The edge-degree and gap-degree measures of non-projective trees from the AGDT are equally unmatched. In particular, the non-neglectable rates of trees with gap-degree ≥ 2 (which include more than 6% of the sentences in the AGDT) contradicts the assumptions that were inferable from other languages. On the other hand, in spite of these peculiarities, AG data confirm other conclusions that were drawn in previous literature, especially about the efficacy of the well-nestedness constraint.

The peculiar nature of these results may partially depend on the genres represented in the corpus, more than 98% of which is taken from poetic texts. The only prose work that is included in the collection shows a lesser degree of non-projective trees and edges, without conforming, however, to the rates known from other languages.

We have also isolated a number of specific constructions and we have tried to highlight some linguistic factors that can bring about syntactic discontinuity. Section 5 does not want to be an exhaustive classification of the linguistic aspects that stand behind non-projectivity: further work is required. Especially, on account of the well known influence of topic-focus articulation on AG word-order, this research would greatly benefit from the interaction of layers of syntax, pragmatics and information structure in annotated data.

References

David Bamman, Francesco Mambrini, and Gregory Crane. 2009. An ownership model of annotation: The Ancient Greek Dependency Treebank. In *Proceedings of the Eighth International Workshop on Treebanks and Linguistic Theories (TLT 8)*, pages 5–15, Milan. EDUCatt.

Riyaz Ahmad Bhat and Dipti Misra Sharma. 2012. Non-projective structures in Indian language treebanks. In *Proceedings of the 11th Workshop on Treebanks and Linguistic Theories (TLT11)*, pages 25–30, Lisbon. Colibri.

Alena Böhmová, Jan Hajič, Eva Hajičová, and Barbora Hladká. 2001. The Prague Dependency Treebank: A three-level annotation scenario. In Anne Abeillé, editor, *Treebanks: Building and Using Syntactically Annotated Corpora*, pages 103–127. Kluwer, Boston.

S. Buchholz and E. Marsi. 2006. CoNLL-X shared task on multilingual dependency parsing. In *Proceedings of the Tenth Conference on Computational Natural Language Learning (CoNLL-X '06)*, pages 149–164, Stroudsburg, PA, USA. ACL.

Ralph Debusmann and Marco Kuhlmann. 2010. Dependency grammar: Classification and exploration. In Matthew W. Crocker and Jörg Siekmann, editors, *Resource-Adaptive Cognitive Processes*, pages 365–388. Springer, Berlin and Heidelberg.

Andrew Devine and Laurence Stephens. 2000. *Discontinuous Syntax: Hyperbaton in Greek*. Oxford University Press, Oxford.

Helma Dik. 1995. *Word Order in Ancient Greek: A pragmatic account of word order variation in Herodotus*. J.C. Gieben, Amsterdam.

Helma Dik. 2007. *Word Order in Greek Tragic Dialogue*. Oxford University Press, Oxford.

Eva Hajičová, Petr Sgall, and Daniel Zeman. 2004. Issues of projectivity in the Prague Dependency Treebank. *Prague Bulletin of Mathematical Linguistics*, 81:5—22.

Jiří Havelka. 2007. Beyond projectivity: Multilingual evaluation of constraints and measures on non-projective structures. In *Proceedings of the 45th Annual Meeting of the Association of Computational Linguistics*, volume 45, pages 608–615, Prague. ACL.

Marco Kuhlmann and Joakim Nivre. 2006. Mildly non-projective dependency structures. In *Proceedings of the COLING/ACL 2006. Main Conference Poster Sessions*, pages 507–514, Sidney, Australia. ACL.

Francesco Mambrini and Marco Passarotti. 2012. Will a parser overtake Achilles? First experiments on parsing the Ancient Greek Dependency Treebank. In *Proceedings of the 11th Workshop on Treebanks and Linguistic Theories (TLT11)*, pages 133–144, Lisbon. Colibri.

Solomon Marcus. 1965. Sur la notion de projectivité. *Mathematical Logic Quarterly*, 11(2):181–192.

Dejan Matić. 2003. Topic, focus, and discourse structure: Ancient Greek word order. *Studies in Language*, 27(3):573–633.

J. Nivre, J. Hall, S. Kübler, R. McDonald, J. Nilsson, S. Riedel, and D. Yuret. 2007. The CoNLL 2007 shared task on dependency parsing. In *Proceedings of the CoNLL Shared Task Session of EMNLP-CoNLL 2007*, pages 915–932, Prague, Czech Republic. ACL.

Joakim Nivre. 2006. Constraints on non-projective dependency parsing. In *Proceedings of EACL-06. Trento, Italy*, pages 73–80, Trento. ACL.

Marco Passarotti and Paolo Ruffolo. 2010. Parsing the Index Thomisticus Treebank. Some preliminary results. In *Latin Linguistics Today. Akten des 15. Internationalem Kolloquiums zur Lateinischen Linguistik*, volume 137, pages 714–725. Institut fur Sprachwissenschaft der Universität Innsbruck.

Cornelis J. Ruijgh. 1990. La place des enclitiques dans l'ordre des mots chez Homère d'après la loi de Wackernagel. In Heiner Eichner and Helmut Rix, editors, *Sprachwissenschaft und Philologie. Jacob Wackernagel und die Indogermanistik heute*, pages 213–33. Reichert, Wiesbaden.

TLG. 2010. The TLG beta code manual 2010. http://stephanus.tlg.uci.edu/encoding/BCM2010.pdf.

Jacob Wackernagel. 1892. Über ein Gesetz der indogermanischen Wortstellung. *Indogermanische Forschungen*, 1:333–436.

More constructions, more genres: Extending Stanford Dependencies

Marie-Catherine de Marneffe*, **Miriam Connor, Natalia Silveira,**
Samuel R. Bowman, Timothy Dozat and Christopher D. Manning

*Linguistics Department
The Ohio State University
Columbus, OH 43210
mcdm@ling.osu.edu

Linguistics Department
Stanford University
Stanford, CA 94305
{mkconnor,natalias,sbowman,
tdozat,manning}@stanford.edu

Abstract

The Stanford dependency scheme aims to provide a simple and intuitive but linguistically sound way of annotating the dependencies between words in a sentence. In this paper, we address two limitations the scheme has suffered from: First, despite providing good coverage of core grammatical relations, the scheme has not offered explicit analyses of more difficult syntactic constructions; second, because the scheme was initially developed primarily on newswire data, it did not focus on constructions that are rare in newswire but very frequent in more informal texts, such as casual speech and current web texts. Here, we propose dependency analyses for several linguistically interesting constructions and extend the scheme to provide better coverage of modern web data.

1 Introduction

The Stanford dependency representation (de Marneffe et al. 2006, de Marneffe and Manning 2008b, henceforth SD) has seen wide usage within the Natural Language Processing (NLP) community as a standard for English grammatical relations, and its leading ideas are being adapted for other languages. This adaptation seems to be motivated by two principal advantages: (i) it provides a richer, more linguistically faithful typology of dependencies than the main alternatives and (ii) it adopts a simple, understandable, and uniform notation of dependency triples, close to traditional grammar. This combination makes it effective both for use by non-linguists working directly with linguistic information in the development of natural language understanding applications and also as a source of features for machine learning approaches. As a result, the representation has been variously used in relation extraction, text understanding, and machine translation applications.

While SD provides good coverage of core grammatical relations, such as subject, object, internal noun phrase relations, and adverbial and subordinate clauses, the standard remains underdeveloped and agnostic as to the treatment of many of the more difficult—albeit rarer—constructions that tend to dominate discussions of syntax in linguistics, such as *tough* adjectives, free relatives, comparative constructions, and small clauses. These constructions have been analyzed many times in various frameworks for constituency representation, and some have had some limited treatment in dependency grammar frameworks. Nevertheless, it is often not obvious how to analyze them in terms of dependencies, and currently the SD scheme does not offer explicit, principled analyses of these constructions.

Further, a current practical limitation is that the SD scheme was developed against newswire data, namely the Wall Street Journal portion of the Penn Treebank. It therefore gave relatively little consideration to constructions that are absent or rare in newswire, such as questions, imperatives, discourse particles, sentence fragments, ellipsis, and various kinds of list structures. Such constructions are, however, abundant in modern web texts. Emails, blogs, forum posts, and product reviews show a greater use of informal constructions, slang, and emoticons. It is important to handle these new genres by providing adequate dependency representations of the constructions which appear in such important modern genres.

Our goal in this paper is to address these two current limitations of Stanford dependencies. We extend the scheme to handle a wider array of linguistic constructions, both linguistically interesting constructions and those necessary to resolve practical problems in providing analyses for language use in modern web data.

Proceedings of the Second International Conference on Dependency Linguistics (DepLing 2013), pages 187–196,
Prague, August 27–30, 2013.

2 The Stanford dependencies

The set of grammatical relations used by SD is principally drawn from the grammatical-relation oriented traditions in American linguistics: Relational Grammar (Perlmutter 1983), Head-driven Phrase Structure Grammar (HPSG, Pollard and Sag 1994), and particularly Lexical-Functional Grammar (LFG, Bresnan 2001). However, the actual syntactic representation adopted follows the functional dependency grammar tradition (Tesnière 1959, Sgall et al. 1986, Mel'cuk 1988) and other dependency grammars such as Word Grammar (Hudson 2010) in representing a sentence as a set of grammatical relations between its words. The SD scheme deviates from its LFG roots in trying to achieve the correct balance between linguistic fidelity and human interpretability of the relations, particularly in the context of relation extraction tasks. This leads it to sometimes stay closer to the descriptions of traditional grammar (such as for *indirect object*) in order to avoid making unnecessary theoretical claims that detract from broad interpretability. The focus of the SD scheme is on semantically useful relations.

Automatic annotation of dependencies using the SD scheme can be obtained for English text with a tool distributed with the Stanford Parser.[1] The tool uses a rule-based strategy to extract grammatical relations as defined in the SD scheme via structural configurations in Penn Treebank-style phrase-structure trees. The tool performs well, but as with all automatic parsing, it is important to maintain a distinction between the annotations it produces and the theoretical standard of the SD scheme: there can be a difference between the relation that the scheme would assign to two words and the relation that gets assigned by the tool. In this paper, we address the ideal relation structures rather than discussing parser performance directly. The Stanford dependency representation makes available several variants, suited to different goals. One, the *basic* representation, is a simple dependency tree over all the words in the sentence, which is useful when a close parallelism to the source text words must be maintained, such as when used as a representation for direct dependency parsing (Kübler et al. 2009). The expanded representation adds additional relations that cannot be expressed by a tree structure but may be useful for capturing semantic relations between entities in the sentence. Here, we will draw such additional dependencies as dashed arcs.

[1] `http://nlp.stanford.edu/software/lexparser.shtml`

3 Data

We have started an annotation effort to construct a gold-standard corpus of web data annotated with this extended SD scheme.[2] To provide the community with a gold-standard corpus that better captures linguistic phenomena present in casual text genres, we are annotating the parsed section of the Google Web Treebank (Petrov and McDonald 2012). This corpus contains about 250,000 words of unedited web text and covers five domains: questions and answers, emails, newsgroups, local business reviews and blogs. For each domain, between 2,000 and 4,000 sentences have been annotated with phrase-structure trees in the style of OntoNotes 4.0 by professional annotators from the Linguistic Data Consortium.

4 Linguistic analyses adopted for different constructions

The SD scheme has been in use for seven years, but still lacks principled analyses of many of the difficult English constructions that have been a staple of the formal linguistic literature. However, we have found in our annotation work that some of these constructions now arise prominently in terms of cases for which the correct analysis is unclear. Here we try to resolve several of these interesting corner-cases of English grammar. Some of these cases, such as tough adjectives and free relatives, were also discussed in recent evaluations of dependency extraction systems (Rimell et al. 2009, Bender et al. 2011) where the goal was to recover long dependencies. The family of CoNLL dependency schemes for English (Buchholz and Marsi 2006, Johansson and Nugues 2007), another common dependency representation in NLP, largely does not provide satisfying analyses for any of the cases presented here. Small clauses are the one exception, and the CoNLL treatment of small clauses is similar to ours.

4.1 Tough adjectives

Tough adjectives, discussed in Bender et al. (2011), have posed challenges to nearly every syn-

[2] To date, except for the BioInfer corpus of biomedical texts (Pyysalo et al. 2007) and a small set of chosen long-distance dependency constructions (Rimell et al. 2009), there are no gold standard Stanford dependency annotations.

tactic formalism. For example, in (1a), the object of *find* can be "raised" to subject position in the main clause to form a tough adjective construction, as in (1b). One of the difficulties for generative grammar in modeling this construction is that the object being raised can be embedded arbitrarily deeply in the sentence, as in (1c).

(1) a. It was hard (for me) to find this address.

b. This address was hard (for me) to find.

c. This address was hard (for me) to work up the motivation to try to explain how to find.

In (1b), *this address* functions syntactically as the subject of *was hard*, but thematically as the object of *find*, and we want to represent both of these dependencies at some level. We simply give the surface subject (here *this address*) the expected *nsubj* label coming off the main predicate. We want to represent its relationship to the embedded verb as well though, since the surface subject is its thematic argument. Paralleling the existing *xsubj* dependency for the relationship between a verb and its controlling subject (which breaks the tree dependency structure), we introduce the *xobj* dependency to capture the relationship between a verb and its logical object when it breaks the tree dependency structure. So (1b) will have the dependency representation in (2), with an additional *xobj* dependency from *find* to *address*:

(2)
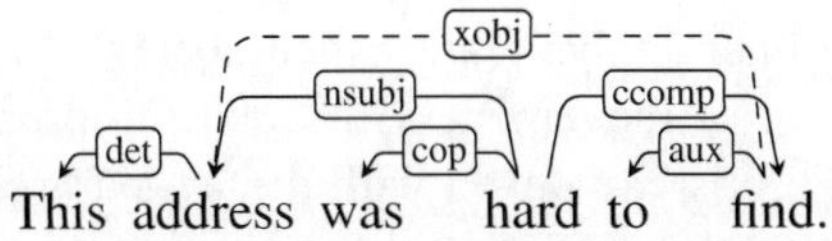

Further, there are two competing structural analyses for the optional *for NP* phrase. In one, the *for NP* is a PP complement of the main predicate, and in the other, *for* is a complementizer that takes a tense-less sentence. Chomsky (1973) argues on the basis of sentences like (3a–3b) that the experiencer *for NP* must be a true PP, not part of a complementizer.

(3) a. It is easy [$_{PP}$ for the rich] [$_{SBAR}$ for the poor to do all the work].

b. *All the work is easy [$_{PP}$ for the rich] [$_{SBAR}$ for the poor to do _]

When the *for* introduces an SBAR proposition (which is quite rare), the whole clause can "move" as a unit, as demonstrated in (4a), but when the *for* introduces a PP experiencer, the PP can "move" separately (4b), both supporting the hypothesis that the experiencer is not part of an SBAR.

(4) a. [$_{SBAR}$ For the poor to do all the work] is easy [$_{PP}$ for the rich].

b. X-server is difficult [$_{S}$ to set up] [$_{PP}$ for everyone].[3]

We conclude from data like this that the PP is usually a separate constituent, and should be annotated as such; (3a) and (4b) should therefore be assigned the dependencies shown in (5a–5b).

(5) a.
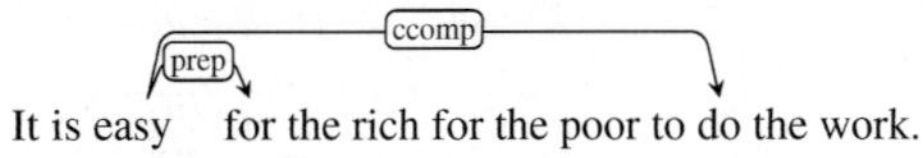

b.
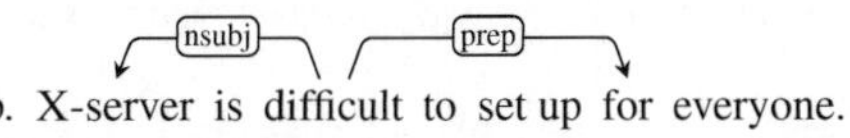

We opt to analyze *to find* in (1b) and *to set up* in (4b) as clausal complements (*ccomp*). Faithful to the original SD scheme, we reserve the use of the *xcomp* label for controlled complements in the LFG sense of functional control (Bresnan 1982) – where the subject of the complement is necessarily controlled by an argument of the governing verb. This is not the case here: the subject can be viewed as a covert PRO, which is coreferent with the *for PP* complement. We now have a complete analysis for *tough* adjectives. The dependency relations for the sentence in (1b) are given in (6) below.

(6)
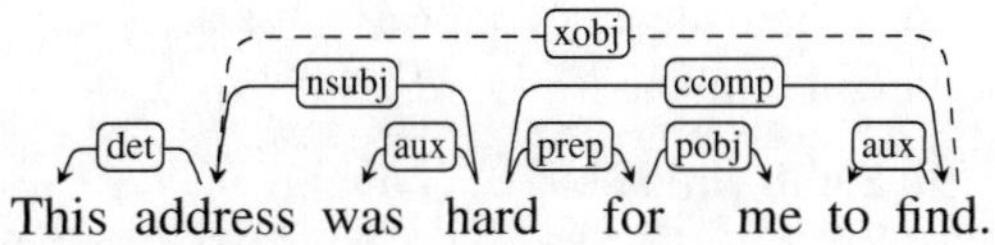

4.2 Free relatives

Free relatives, which are discussed in Rimell et al. (2009), are likewise challenging because while their surface resemblance to embedded interrogatives invites a transformational treatment parallel to *wh*-questions, certain of their syntactic properties point to an analysis in which the *wh*-phrase serves as the head rather than as a subordinate element. To illustrate these two conflicting analyses, we will explore the implications of each treatment using the free relative phrases (italicized) in (7) below as our chief examples.

[3] `https://mail.gnome.org/archives/gnome-accessibility-list/2003-May/msg00421.html`

(7) a. Put your bag down *wherever you see a spot*.

b. Sarah will talk to *whoever comes her way*.

c. I'll dress *however nicely you tell me to dress*.

An initially attractive approach to analyzing (7a–7c) is to treat the free relatives identically to embedded *wh*-interrogative complements. On this approach, *wherever* is an *advmod* of *see*, *whoever* is the *nsubj* of *comes*, and *however nicely* (with *nicely* being the head of the *wh*-phrase) is an *advmod* of *dress*, resulting in the following dependency structures:

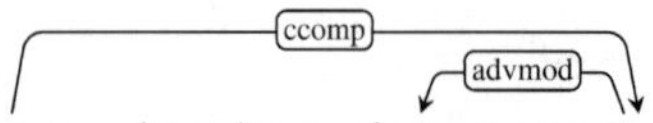

(8) a. Put your bag down wherever you see a spot

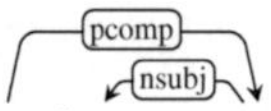

b. Sarah will talk to whoever comes her way

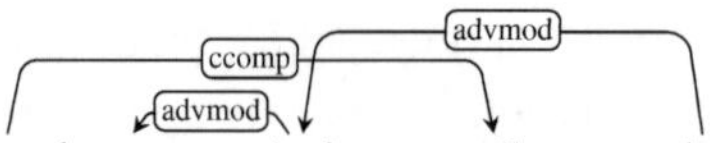

c. I'll dress however nicely you tell me to dress

The above treatment is analogous to a transformational analysis of free relatives in a phrase structure formalism. In such a treatment, the *wh*-phrase is generated inside the clause and moved to the clause-initial position through A′-movement. The Treebank II bracketing guidelines (Bies et al. 1995) take this approach, inserting a *T* node, indicating the trace of A′-movement, in the tree position where the *wh*-word was generated and coindexing it with the *wh*-word—see (9).

(9) Sarah will talk ...

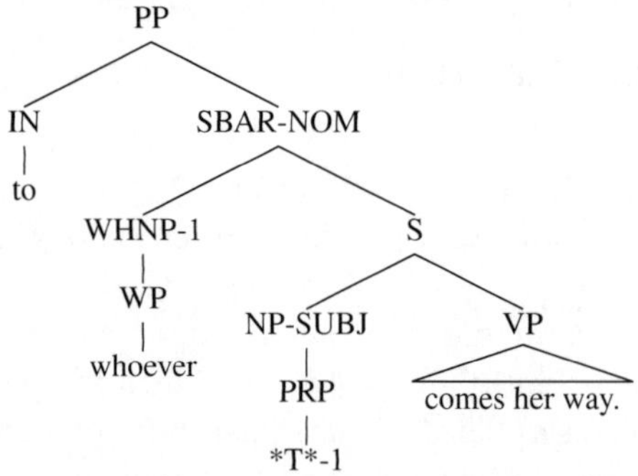

Under this analysis, we must treat *see* as a sentential complement of *put*, *comes* as a prepositional complement of *to*, and *tell* as a sentential complement of *dress*, as shown in (8a–8c) and (9).

However, as Bresnan and Grimshaw (1978) point out, this transformational analysis fails to capture certain key syntactic properties of free relatives. In particular, the free relative phrases in (7) do not really behave like sentential complements—in fact, substituting other sentential *wh*-complements for the free relative phrases in (7) leads to ungrammatical constructions:

(10) a. *Put your bag down *what table Al put his on*.

b. *Sarah will talk to *which person Fred talked to*.

c. *I'll dress *what dress I wore last time*.

We make better predictions if we analyze the free relatives like those in (7a), (7b), and (7c) as locative adverbial phrases, nominal phrases, and adverbial phrases, respectively. Substituting these phrase types for the free relatives in the original examples leads to perfectly natural constructions:

(11) a. Put your bag down *on the table*.

b. Sarah will talk to *that man over there*.

c. I'll dress *very nicely*.

In each example, the syntactic category assigned to the free relative phrase is identical to that of the *wh*-phrase within the free relative: *wherever* being locative, *whoever* being nominal, and *however nicely* being adverbial. Based on this observation (among others), Bresnan and Grimshaw (1978) argue for treating the *wh*-phrase as the head of the free relative. In their 1978 transformation grammar analysis, they then account for the appearance of movement with a deleted pronoun whose trace is coindexed with the *wh*-phrase and stipulate that the coindexed nodes must agree in certain grammatical features:

(12) a. Put your bag down [$_{\text{LocP}}$ wherever$_1$ [$_{\text{S}}$ you see a spot [*there*$\rightarrow \emptyset_1$]]].

b. Sarah will talk to [$_{\text{NP}}$ whoever$_1$ [$_{\text{S}}$ [*s/he*$\rightarrow \emptyset_1$] comes her way]].

c. I'll dress [$_{\text{AdvP}}$ [however nicely]$_1$ [$_{\text{S}}$ you tell me to dress [*so*$\rightarrow \emptyset_1$]]].

So rather than follow the Treebank II guidelines, we adopt the approach of Bresnan and Grimshaw (1978), analyzing the *wh*-phrase as the head of the free relative and treating the sentential portion of the free relative phrase as a relative clause modifier on the head. We also mark the relationships inside the relative clause, between the verb and the head of the *wh*-phrase, with additional dependencies, to preserve the semantic relationship between the two entities. The grammatical relations between the verb of the relative and the head of the *wh*-phrase correspond to the ones the traces would receive. Thus, we decompose the examples in (7a–7c) as follows:

(13) 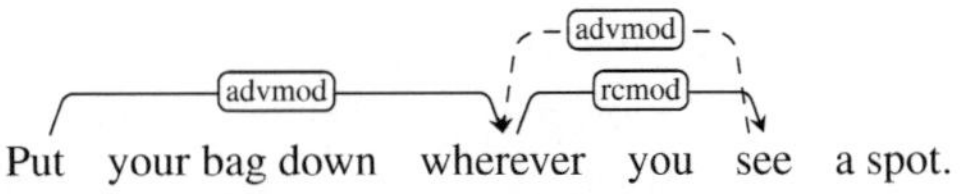

(14) 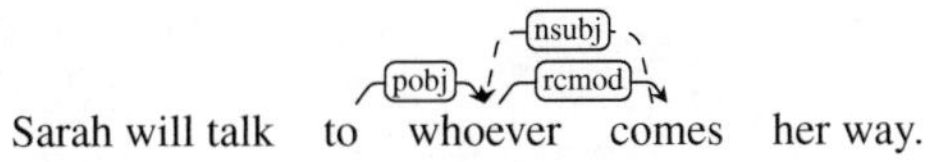

(15) 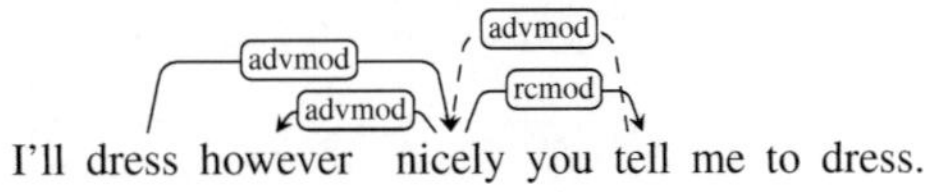

4.3 Comparative constructions

The syntax of comparative constructions in English poses various challenges for linguistic theory, many of which are discussed in Bresnan (1973). We devoted special attention to canonical (in)equality comparisons between two elements, of the form: as_1 *X* as_2 *Y* and *more X than Y*.

4.3.1 *as ... as* constructions

In constructions of the form as_1 *X* as_2 *Y*, *X* and *Y* can be of a range of syntactic types, leading to surface forms such as those exemplified below:

(16) a. Commitment is as important as a player's talent.

b. Get the cash to him as soon as possible.

c. I put in as much flour as the recipe called for.

Note that there are analogous constructions with inequality comparatives for all of these, briefly discussed below; the analysis argued for in this subsection will largely extend to those. *X* takes the form of an AdjP, an AdvP, and an NP in (16a), (16b) and (16c), respectively. We analyze the as_1 *X* as_2 *Y* expression as modification on the *X* phrase; notice that preserving only the head of the *X* phrase always yields a grammatical sentence, indicating that this head determines the syntactic type of the whole phrase:

(17) a. Commitment is important.

b. Get the cash to him soon.

c. I put in flour.

This suggests that the head of *X* is the head of the whole structure (and therefore depends on nothing inside it) and that the $as_1 \ldots as_2$ *Y* phrase modifies the inner *X* phrase. Our analysis expresses this by making as_1 dependent on a head inside *X*. However, clearly $as_1 \ldots as_2$ *Y* is a comparative modifier, and it modifies a gradable property. That property is not always denoted by the head of *X*; *flour*, for example, does not seem to be the target of the comparison in (16c). To reflect that, our next analytic decision is to make as_1 dependent on the adjective, adverb or quantifier that represents the gradable property targeted by the comparison. The relation is *advmod*, consistent with other types of degree modification, such as (18).

(18) a. Commitment is crucially important.

b. Get the cash to him very soon.

c. I put in too much flour.

With that, for (16a) we have:

(19) 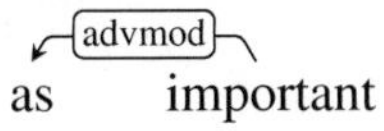

For (16c), we make as_1 dependent on *much*, not *flour*, as it is the quantity of flour that is the target of the comparison:

(20) 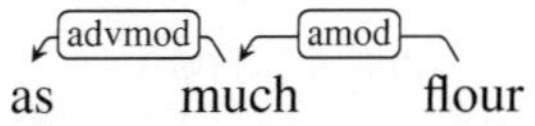

These decisions address the question of what the head of the entire phrase is, and how the comparative modifier interfaces with it. Next, we turn to questions about the internal structure of the comparative. It seems that as_1 has a privileged status over as_2, since it is possible to drop as_2 *Y* (21), but not as_1 (22):

(21) a. Commitment is (just) as important.

b. ?Get the cash to him (just) as soon.

c. I put in (just) as much flour.

(22) a. *Commitment is important as a player's talent.

b. *Get the cash to him soon as possible.

c. *I put in much flour as the recipe called for.

For this reason, and following other authors' syntactic analyses of the secondary term of a comparative as a complement (Huddleston and Pullum

2002), we make as_2 *Y* dependent on as_1. This still leaves the question of how to link *Y* with the rest of the phrase. It is clear that the material in as_2 *Y* can be clausal, as exemplified by (16c); it is also optional, as exemplified by (21). For that reason, we make it an *advcl*, dependent on as_1, with as_2 as a *mark*. This is consistent with the Penn Treebank annotations for these constructions. That gives us:

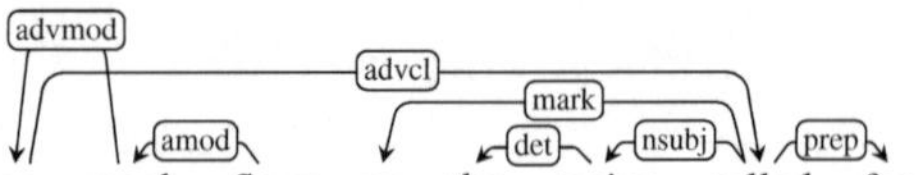

(23) as much flour as the recipe called for

In the case when *Y* is an NP, to remain consistent with the Penn Treebank annotations, we treat as_2 *Y* as a prepositional phrase. So we have:

(24) as important as a player 's talent

4.3.2 *more … than* constructions

The analysis we give to expressions like *more … than* or *less … than*, as in (25), is very similar to the analysis of *as … as* discussed above.

(25) I put in more flour than the recipe called for.

Again, we analyze the head of the *more X than Y* expression as the head of the *X* phrase, since keeping the head will yield a grammatical sentence, which in this case is exactly (17c). Also in parallel with the constructions above, we note that the relation between *more … than Y* and *X* has a parallel with other types of adverbial modifiers, as was shown in (18c). Therefore, we again label that relation *advmod*. As for *than Y*, again we take it to be an adverbial clause if *Y* is anything other than an NP. So we will have analyses such as:

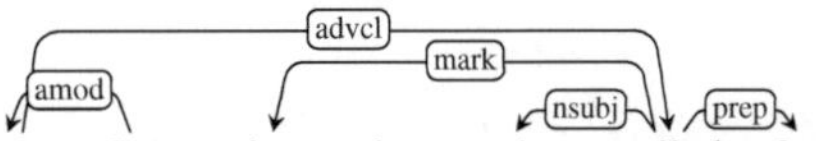

(26) more flour than the recipe called for

When *Y* is an NP, we essentially adopt the analysis of Bresnan (1973), in which an *-er* morpheme that expresses the comparative value combines with *much* to form *more*; this provides an explanation for why *much* appears in (16c), where it combines with *as*, but not in (25), where it combines with *-er*. This is relevant because the resulting *more* in (25) is, syntactically, an adjectival modifier, as is *much* in (16c). Also, in parallel with our analysis of as_1 *X* as_2 *Y* and consistently with the Penn Treebank analysis, we call *than Y* a prepositional phrase when *Y* is a noun phrase. We therefore arrive at the following analysis for the comparative expression below:

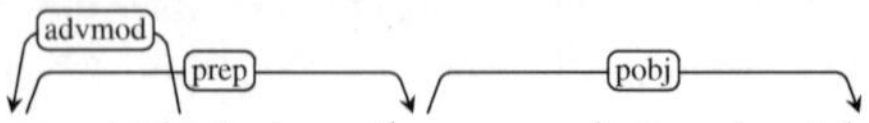

(27) more important than a player 's talent

4.4 Small clauses

In the world of phrase structure, *small clauses*, like the bracketed example in (28), have two competing analyses: in the analysis correlated with the lexicalist approach (28a), both the entity and the predicate depend on the main verb; and in the one correlated with the transformational approach (28b), the entity depends on the predicate.

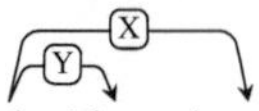

(28) a. We made [them leave].

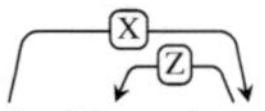

b. We made [them leave].

There is a substantial literature on small clauses and evidence for and against each structure (Borsley 1991, Culicover and Jackendoff 2005, Matthews 2007). The optimal analysis largely depends on the assumptions of the theory in question. The Penn Treebank adopts the analysis in (28b), putting both arguments of the main verb under an S node. Empirically, though, the small clause as a unit fails a considerable number of constituency tests, such as those in (29) (adapted from (Culicover and Jackendoff 2005)), which show that the small clause cannot move around in the sentence as a unit. So in the system we have been developing—which we aim to make as empirically motivated as possible—we choose to have both the entity and the predicate depend on the main verb (28a) as is also done in the CoNLL scheme, leading to the analysis in (30). This analysis also allows us to add an additional subject relation between the two components of the small clause when the small clause contains a verb (which CoNLL does not have). Adopting the other analysis, we would lose the link between the object and the higher verb.

(29) a. *What we made was them leave.

b. *We made without difficulty them leave.

c. *Them leave is what we made.

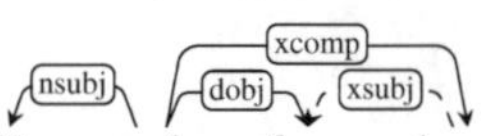

(30) We made them leave.

The Penn Treebank also recognizes small clause constructions where the predicate is a nominal or adjectival expression as in (31b) and (31c) respectively. We can extend the *xcomp* analysis to them by regarding the noun or adjective as also a predicate with a controlled subject. This is consistent with both the LFG analysis where the grammatical function XCOMP originated (Bresnan 1982) and the treatment of predicate nouns and adjectives in copula constructions in SD (de Marneffe and Manning 2008a).

(31) a. We made them leave.
  b. We made them martyrs.
  c. We made them noticeable.

For example (32a) has a parallel analysis to (32b):

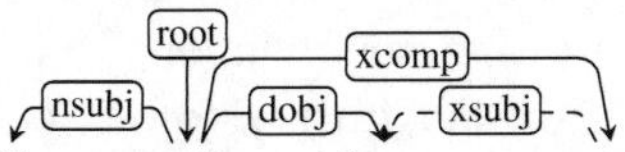

(32) a. We made them martyrs.

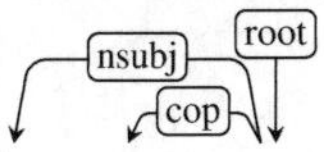

  b. They are martyrs.

Assigning the *xcomp* label offers a consistent analysis across all uses of the small clause construction and also emphasizes the fact that the second noun phrase is being used non-referentially, as a predicate instead of as an entity.

5 Extensions to the Stanford dependencies

In the process of annotating the Google Web Treebank, we also discovered a number of ways in which the SD standard needs to be modified to capture the syntax of a broader range of text genres. These changes, described in the following paragraphs, led to a new version of the extended SD scheme with 56 relations, listed in Figure 1.

5.1 New relations

discourse Colloquial writing contains interjections, emoticons, and other discourse markers which are not linked to their host sentences by any existing relation. We add a discourse element relation *discourse* which encompasses these constructions, including emoticons and all phrases headed by words that the Penn Treebank tags INTJ: interjections (*oh*, *uh-huh*, *Welcome*), fillers (*um*, *ah*), and discourse markers (*well*, *like*, *actually*).

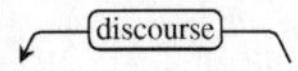

(33) Hello, my name is Vera.

- *root* - root
- *dep* - dependent
  - *aux* - auxiliary
    - *auxpass* - passive auxiliary
    - *cop* - copula
  - *arg* - argument
    - *agent* - agent
    - *comp* - complement
      - *acomp* - adjectival complement
      - *ccomp* - clausal complement with internal subject
      - *xcomp* - clausal complement with external subject
      - *obj* - object
        - *dobj* - direct object
        - *iobj* - indirect object
        - *pobj* - object of preposition
    - *subj* - subject
      - *csubj* - clausal subject
        - *csubjpass* - passive clausal subject
      - *nsubj* - nominal subject
        - *nsubjpass* - passive nominal subject
  - *cc* - coordination
  - *conj* - conjunct
  - *expl* - expletive (expletive "there")
  - *list* - list item
  - *mod* - modifier
    - *advmod* - adverbial modifier
      - *neg* - negation modifier
    - *amod* - adjectival modifier
    - *appos* - appositional modifier
    - *advcl* - adverbial clause modifier
    - *det* - determiner
    - *discourse* - discourse element
    - *goeswith* - goes with
    - *predet* - predeterminer
    - *preconj* - preconjunct
    - *mwe* - multi-word expression modifier
    - *mark* - marker (word introducing an *advcl* or *ccomp*)
    - *nn* - noun compound modifier
    - *npadvmod* - noun phrase adverbial modifier
      - *tmod* - temporal modifier
    - *num* - numeric modifier
    - *number* - element of compound number
    - *prep* - prepositional modifier
    - *poss* - possession modifier
    - *possessive* - possessive modifier (*'s*)
    - *prt* - phrasal verb particle
    - *quantmod* - quantifier modifier
    - *rcmod* - relative clause modifier
    - *vmod* - verbal modifier
    - *vocative* - vocative
  - *parataxis* - parataxis
  - *punct* - punctuation
  - *ref* - referent
  - *sdep* - semantic dependent (breaking tree structure)
    - *xsubj* - (controlled) subject
    - *xobj* - (controlled) object

Figure 1: Extended Stanford dependencies.

goeswith Unedited text often contains multiple tokens that correspond to a single standard English word, as a result of reanalysis of compounds ("hand some" for "handsome") or input error ("othe r" for "other"). The non-head portions of these broken words are tagged GW in the treebank. We cannot expect preprocessing steps (tokenization and normalization) to fix all of these errors, so we introduce the relation *goeswith* to reconnect these non-heads to their heads—usually the initial pieces of the words.

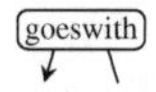

(34) They come here with out legal permission

list Web text often contains passages which are meant to be interpreted as lists of comparable items, but are parsed as single sentences. Email signatures in particular contain these structures, in the form of contact information. We label the contact information *list* as in (35). For the key-value pair relations that often occur in these contexts, we use the *appos* relation.

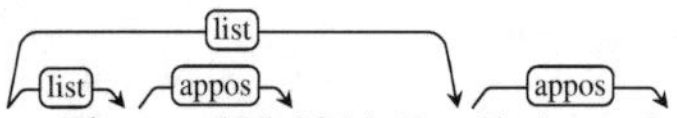

(35) Steve Jones Phone: 555-9814 Email: jones@abc.edf

vmod Since the distinction between *partmod* and *infmod* is straightforwardly reflected in the part-of-speech of the verb, we choose to cease duplicating information by merging these relations into a single one, *vmod*. We intend this to cover all cases of verb-headed phrases acting as modifiers, which are not full clauses.

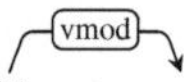

(36) I don't have anything to say.

vocative In writing that directly addresses a dialog participant (e.g., emails and newsgroup postings), it is common to begin sentences by naming that other participant. We introduce the *vocative* relation to link these names to their host sentences.

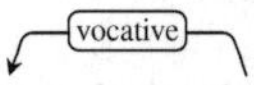

(37) Tracy, do we have concerns here?

xobj We introduce the relation *xobj* to capture the relationship between a verb and its displaced logical object. For further explanation, see the discussion of *tough* adjectives in section 4.1 above.

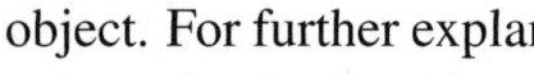

(38) Those were hard for him to find.

5.2 Modified and deleted relations

advcl Purpose clauses (*purpcl*) were singled out based on a semantic distinction, but distinctions were not made for other types of adverbial clause (temporal, causal, etc.). We make the scheme more uniform by collapsing purpose clauses with general adverbial clauses (*advcl*).

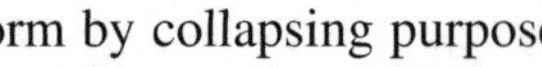

(39) She talked to him in order to secure the account.

amod Parenthetically marked ages have been treated as appositives (and marked *appos*), but we find that this violates the otherwise largely sound generalization that appositives fill the same semantic role as the NPs they modify, and essentially serve as alternative ways to identify the entities named by those NPs. Since, for example, it is not reasonable to infer (41) from (40), we choose to re-classify these cases as displaced adjectival modifiers, and label them *amod*.

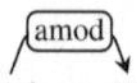

(40) John Smith (33) was from Kansas City, MO.

(41) 33 is from Kansas City, MO.

appos We abandon the *abbrev* relation and substitute *appos*: *abbrev* captured parenthetical expressions indicating abbreviations, but was used rarely, and provided little information not also captured by the more general *appos*.

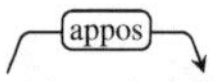

(42) The Australian Broadcasting Corporation (ABC)

attr In *wh*-questions such as (43), we treated the copular verb as the root, and the *wh*-word was an *attr*. We are abandoning the *attr* relation, leading to the following analysis which parallels that of affirmative copular sentences like (44) where the predicate is the root. Copular sentences are now treated more uniformly than before.

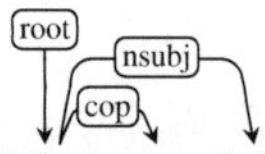

(43) What is that?

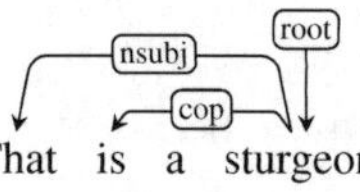

(44) That is a sturgeon.

mark The former *complm* relation captured overt complementizers like "that" in complement clauses (*ccomp*). We follow the intuition from HPSG that this relation captures approximately the same structural relation as *mark* in adverbial clauses (45), and provides no information that *mark* would not also provide. We thus abandon the *complm* relation, and substitute *mark* (46).

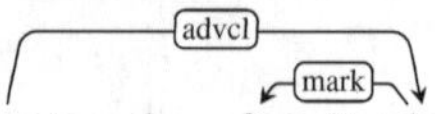

(45) I like to swim when it rains.

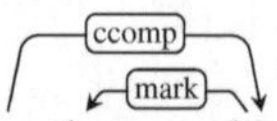

(46) He says that you like to swim.

mwe We have found several additional constructions that we believe meet the criteria to be considered multi-word expressions for the purposes of the *mwe* relation, which is intended for "multiword idioms that behave like a single function word." We add the following constructions:

> *at least, at most, how about, how come, in case, in order (to), of course, prior to, so as (to), so that, what if, whether or not*

This is in addition to already-recognized constructions such as:

> *rather than, as well as, instead of, such as, because of, instead of, in addition to, all but, such as, because of, instead of, due to*

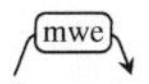

(47) Of course I'll go!

Ultimately, the choice of what to count as a *mwe* reflects a cut across the continuous cline of grammaticalization, and is necessarily arbitrary.

punct We do not follow Choi and Palmer (2012) in using the relations *hmod* and *hyph* for the non-head words of split-up hyphenated words and the hyphens respectively. We find the usage of hyphens is very inconsistent, and so we prefer to apply the most appropriate general relation that holds between the hyphenated components rather than adopt these labels. For the hyphen, when it is used to construct compound words (48), we treated it as punctuation and assign the *punct* relation, but when it is used in place of an en dash to indicate a range, as in (49), we treat it as a preposition and assign the *prep* relation.

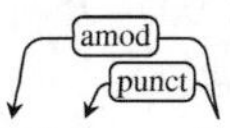

(48) short - term humanitarian crisis

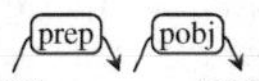

(49) French Indochina War (1946 - 1954)

rel *rel* has been used in a small number of constructions to mark the head words of *wh*-phrases introducing relative clauses. We are retiring the relation: we will mark the heads of *wh*-phrases in accordance with their role in the relative clause (usually *nsubj*, *dobj*, *pobj*, or *prep*), and any such head whose role cannot be identified will be marked with the generic relation *dep*.

xcomp The *xcomp* relation is specified in de Marneffe and Manning (2008a) to apply to any non-finite complement clause which has its subject controlled by the subject of the next higher verb. However, complement clauses with object control—wherein the object of the higher verb controls the subject of an embedded clause, as in (50)—structurally have more in common with subject control cases rather than with the canonical *ccomp* complement clause with which it would otherwise be classified. Further, these cases are grouped as XCOMP in LFG. In order to ensure that this crucial notion of external control is reliably captured, we expand the definition of *xcomp* to include cases of both subject and object control.

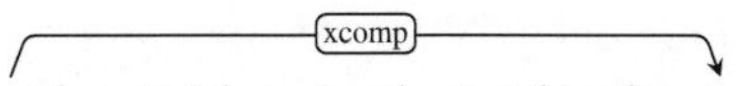

(50) It allowed material previously stored to decompose.

6 Conclusions

We extend the coverage of the SD scheme by presenting principled analyses of linguistically interesting constructions and by positing new relations to capture frequent constructions in modern web data. Our approach has been empirical: all the construction types discussed here appear in the Google English Web Treebank data that we are annotating. We are currently incorporating our extensions of the SD standard into the freely available converter tool associated with the scheme. So far, there has not been any quantitative evaluation of the tool: there has only been some qualitative analysis as well as a focus on some relations as reported in (Rimell et al. 2009, Bender et al. 2011), but ultimately the annotated gold standard corpus we are creating will enable a thorough evaluation of the converter tool.

Acknowledgment

Annotation of the English Web Treebank with gold Stanford dependencies has been supported by a gift from Google Inc. We thank the anonymous reviewers, John Bauer, and Joakim Nivre for helpful comments on the analyses we propose.

References

Bender, Emily M., Dan Flickinger, Stephan Oepen, and Yi Zhang. 2011. Parser evaluation over local and non-local deep dependencies in a large corpus. In *Proceedings of the Conference on Empirical Methods in Natural Language Processing*, pp. 397–408.

Bies, Ann, Mark Ferguson, Karen Katz, Robert MacIntyre, Victoria Tredinnick, Grace Kim, Mary Ann Marcinkiewicz, and Britta Schasberger, 1995. Bracketing guidelines for Treebank II style Penn Treebank project.

Borsley, Robert D. 1991. *Syntactic Theory: A Unified Approach*. Edward Arnold.

Bresnan, Joan. 1973. Syntax of the comparative clause construction in English. *Linguistic Inquiry* 4.

Bresnan, Joan. 1982. Control and complementation. In Joan Bresnan (ed.), *The Mental Representation of Grammatical Relations*, pp. 282–390. MIT Press.

Bresnan, Joan. 2001. *Lexical-functional syntax*. Blackwell.

Bresnan, Joan, and Jane Grimshaw. 1978. The syntax of free relatives in English. *Linguistic Inquiry* 9(3):331–391.

Buchholz, Sabine, and Erwin Marsi. 2006. CoNLL-X shared task on multilingual dependency parsing. In *Proceedings of the Tenth Conference on Computational Natural Language Learning*, pp. 149–164.

Choi, Jinho D., and Martha Palmer. 2012. Guidelines for the Clear style constituent to dependency conversion. Technical report, University of Colorado Boulder, Institute of Cognitive Science.

Chomsky, Noam. 1973. Conditions on transformations. In Stephen Anderson and Paul Kiparsky (eds.), *A Festschrift for Morris Halle*, pp. 232–286. New York: Holt, Rinehart & Winston.

Culicover, Peter W., and Ray Jackendoff. 2005. *Simpler syntax*. Oxford University Press.

de Marneffe, Marie-Catherine, Bill MacCartney, and Christopher D. Manning. 2006. Generating typed dependency parses from phrase structure parses. In *Proceedings of the 5th International Conference on Language Resources and Evaluation*, pp. 449–454.

de Marneffe, Marie-Catherine, and Christopher D. Manning. 2008a. Stanford typed dependencies manual. Technical report, Stanford University.

de Marneffe, Marie-Catherine, and Christopher D. Manning. 2008b. The Stanford typed dependencies representation. In *Proceedings of the COLING Workshop on Cross-framework and Cross-domain Parser Evaluation*, pp. 1–8.

Huddleston, Rodney, and Geoffrey K. Pullum. 2002. *The Cambridge Grammar of the English Language*. Cambridge University Press.

Hudson, Richard A. 2010. *An Introduction to Word Grammar*. Cambridge University Press.

Johansson, Richard, and Pierre Nugues. 2007. Extended constituent-to-dependency conversion for English. In *Proceedings of NODALIDA 2007*.

Kübler, Sandra, Ryan McDonald, and Joakim Nivre. 2009. *Dependency Parsing*, volume 2 of *Synthesis Lectures on Human Language Technologies*. Morgan & Claypool.

Matthews, Peter H. 2007. *Syntactic relations: A critical survey*. Cambridge University Press.

Mel'cuk, Igor A. 1988. *Dependency syntax: Theory and practice*. SUNY Press.

Perlmutter, David M. (ed.). 1983. *Studies in Relational Grammar*, volume 1. University of Chicago Press.

Petrov, Slav, and Ryan McDonald. 2012. Overview of the 2012 shared task on parsing the web. In *First Workshop on Syntactic Analysis of Non-Canonical Language*.

Pollard, Carl, and Ivan A. Sag. 1994. *Head-driven Phrase Structure Grammar*. University of Chicago Press.

Pyysalo, Sampo, Filip Ginter, Katri Haverinen, Juho Heimonen, Tapio Salakoski, and Veronika Laippala. 2007. On the unification of syntactic annotations under the Stanford dependency scheme: A case study on BioInfer and GENIA. In *Proceedings of BioNLP 2007: Biological, translational, and clinical language processing (ACL07)*, pp. 25–32.

Rimell, Laura, Stephen Clark, and Mark Steedman. 2009. Unbounded dependency recovery for parser evaluation. In *Proceedings of the 2009 Conference on Empirical Methods in Natural Language Processing*, pp. 813–821.

Sgall, Petr, Eva Hajičová, and Jarmila Panevová. 1986. *The meaning of the sentence in its semantic and pragmatic aspects*. D. Reidel Publishing Company.

Tesnière, Lucien. 1959. *Éléments de syntaxe structurale*. Librairie C. Klincksieck.

Why so many nodes?

Dan Maxwell
US Chess Center
Washington DC, USA
dan.n.maxwell@gmail.com

Abstract

This paper provides an analysis of the representation of various grammatical phenomena in both constituency structure and dependency structure (hereafter c-structure and d-structure), including agreement, case marking, and word order in transitive sentences, as well as three theoretical constructs, and the interface between the form of a sentence and its meaning. There is a crucial structural relationship for all of these phenomena in both constituency grammar and dependency grammar, but only the version used in dependency grammar is fully reliable. This insight evokes the following question: Why do linguists working with constituency grammars think that so many nodes are necessary? Upon examination, the extra nodes succeed only in confusing our understanding of syntactic phenomena.

1 Introduction

The obvious difference between constituency grammar and dependency grammar (for which the seminal work is Tesnière 1959) is that the former has more nodes due to the distinction it makes between lexical and phrasal categories. As first discussed in Hudson 1984:94-95, this distinction has an important consequence: nodes which are related to each other are directly connected to each other in dependency grammar, but only indirectly in constituency grammar. That is, they are **parent** and **child** in dependency grammar but at best **siblings** (the gender-neutral version of the more commonly used ‘sisters’) in a one-bar constituency grammar. A further problem is that the constituency grammars often use a system of two bars or more rather than a one-bar system. This contribution examines this fundamental difference and its consequences for the treatment of several kinds of linguistic phenomena and theoretical constructs to be treated in more detail below.

2 Agreement

In many languages, the form of one word varies according to the form of some other word in the same construction. These relationships include subject and verb, (more rarely) object and verb, noun and adjective, and noun and determiner. Highly inflected languages like Russian have all of these kinds of agreement. English has only two of them (and then only to a limited extent). So-called isolating languages like Vietnamese do not show agreement at all. The agreement can be in person, number, gender, and (for case-inflecting languages only) case.

English has agreement between the subject and the verb in the third person singular of the present tense, as shown by the contrast between (1a) on the one hand and (1b) and (1c) on the other:

(1) a. John *walks* slowly.
b. John and Sarah *walk* quickly.
c. I *walk* more quickly than they do.

The c-structures of these sentences assume that the subject NP (which is a parent of the noun which determines the form of the verb) is a sibling of the parent VP of the verb, so the structural relationship between this noun and this verb is something more complicated and indirect than that shown in dependency grammar and apparently varies according to the precise details of the construction or perhaps the system of X-bar theory (Jackendoff 1977) chosen by the grammarian, e.g.

(2)
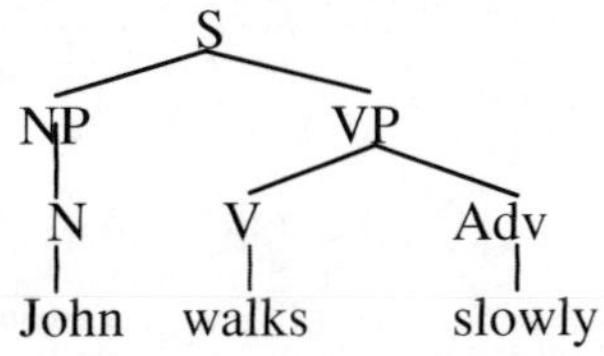

Neither the subject NP nor its child, the N *John* is a sibling of V, although this is the word with which the subject agrees.

In dependency grammar in contrast, there is of course neither an NP node nor a VP node. The verb is simply the parent of the noun, whatever kind it is. The nodes for these two words contain both the phonological information associated with them and, in the

Proceedings of the Second International Conference on Dependency Linguistics (DepLing 2013), pages 197–206,
Prague, August 27–30, 2013.

semantics, the associated words that make up the phrase of the same category.

(3)

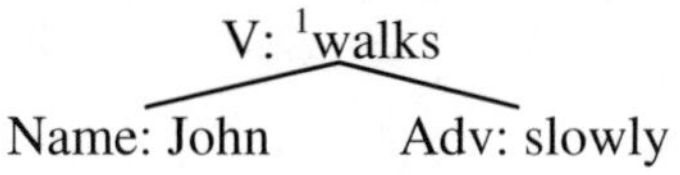

The V *walks* is the parent of the name *John.*

Agreement in number also occurs in English between common nouns and demonstrative determiners, as shown in the contrast between (4a) and (4b):

(4) a. this/that student

b. these/those students

In the most widely accepted analysis of the internal structure of the NP within constituency grammar frameworks, the determiner is a sibling of the N′, but not of the N that it agrees with. This is shown in (5):

(5)

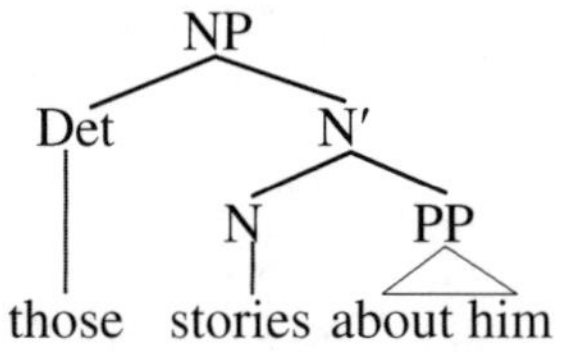

those agrees with *stories*, but the category Det of the former is a sibling of N′ rather than the category N of the latter.

In dependency grammar, either the N is the parent of the Det, or vice-versa, depending on which analysis is applied to the construction (NP vs. DP). The corresponding two competing treatments are also found in constituency grammar analyses. The more traditional N-as-head analysis is assumed here:

(6)

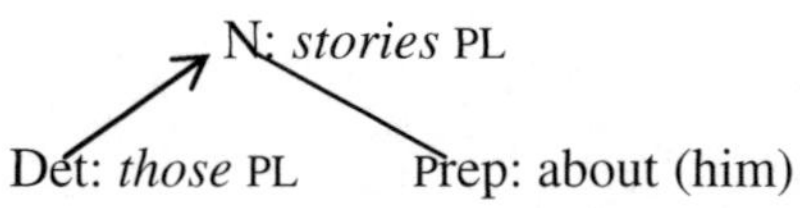

This shows that for the relationship between nouns and determiners, as between verbs and nouns, the source of the features and their target are directly connected to each other in DG as parent and child. In other words, they form a very restricted kind of *catena* (Osborne and Groβ 2012). A consequence of this is that the features can be expressed for both categories for whatever rule unites them.

In constituency grammar, on the other hand, the trees in (3) and (4) show that the N that is the source of the features is not always a sibling of the constituent that gets them from it. To allow such non-siblings to nevertheless get the features from the source noun, additional principles have been used. These include the ‘head feature convention’ in Generalized Phrase Structure Grammar (GPSG, Gazdar, Klein, Pullum, and Sag, 1984), the ‘head feature principle’ in Head-Driven Phrase Structure Grammar (HPSG, Pollard and Sag, 1994) or the ‘projection principle’ in Principles and Parameters (P&P, Chomsky and Lasnik, 1991). Lexical Functional Grammar (Bresnan, 2001) has a system of up-arrows and down-arrows to pass the features from the sibling node of the source of the features to the node that needs them. Such devices are not necessary in dependency grammar.

3 Case

Some languages that inflect for features like person, number, and gender, also inflect for case. If they inflect for case, they may also have agreement in case, as noted in the previous section. But how is case assigned in the first place? Unlike for features like person, number and gender, case cannot be inherent in nouns; it is, rather, clearly determined by the syntactic structure of the clause in which the nouns occur. More specifically, the case of a noun is determined by the verb or preposition (or occasionally a combination of both) which governs it. Just as with agreement, government is determined in dependency grammar by the parent-child relationship, but in constituency grammar, government is determined by a sibling relationship which requires some other grammatical device to pass the case feature between the word which ultimately gets case and the node which is the maximal extension of this word, e.g.

---

[1] Colons are used in this paper to separate a syntactic category and its associated phonology at a specific node in a dependency tree. On the other hand, the ‘AdvP’ in the same tree is used to label a parent node for a constituent consisting of more than one word and headed by an Adverb. This corresponds to the use of phrasal nodes to abbreviate a series of words in constituent grammars, when the internal details of these structures are not relevant to the point being made.

(7)

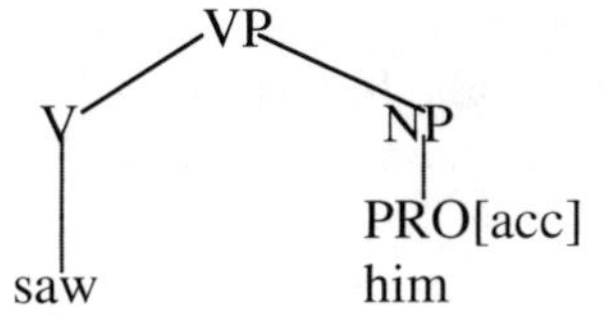

The accusative case of him is assigned by the verb saw. The sibling of the verb is the NP, not the PRO, so the feature must be passed to the PRO by some additional principle. Compare (7) with the direct connection between case assigner and case recipient in DG, as shown in (8):

(8)

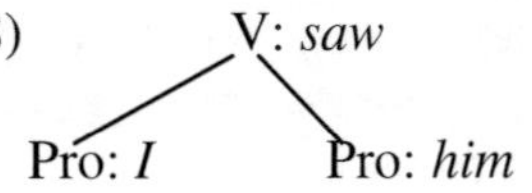

The nominative case of *I* and the case of *him* are both assigned by the parent verb *saw*.

4 Non-branching Phrasal Nodes[2]

Within a c-structure analysis, a PS rule may generate a phrasal node to allow for the possibility of a modifier or optional argument. But if this option is not taken, then the node appears to be superfluous. An example of such a situation is shown in (9).

(9)

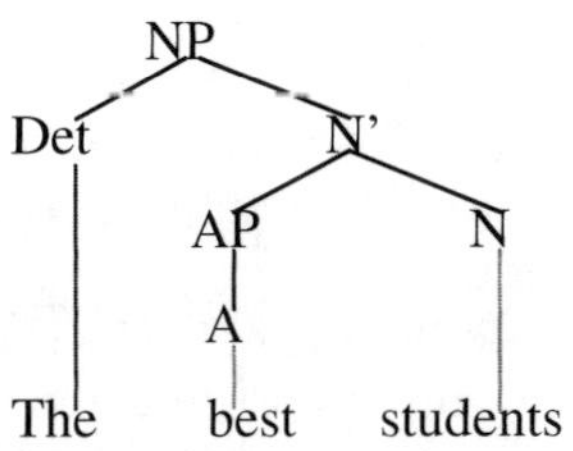

The AP(adjective phrase) does not branch. APs never branch unless they are modified, for example by a degree adverb such as *very* . If there were no adjective, then the N' node would likewise not branch.

Ross (1969) examines several other cases of non-branching nodes and suggests that such nodes should be removed by a rule of **pruning.** In its most general form, this rule results in all non-branching nodes being deleted. This is in fact Ross' initial proposal, but he goes on to find several problems with this due to the kind of transformational analysis which was in general use at the time of writing.

No such rule is necessary in d-structure grammars, since any node may or may not branch. Non-branching nodes are clearly not superfluous, since each one has phonological and/or semantic information (usually both) associated with a specific word. The d-structure which corresponds to (9) is shown in (10):

(10)

5 Word Oder: General

P&P is the most wide-spread c-structure framework and deals with variation of word order for a given sentence with transformations or some other derivational device. I will not go into this here, since such a solution appears to imply a distinction between 'deep structure' and 'surface structure'. P&P, the related Minimalist Program, Meaning-Text-Mapping (Mel'čuk 1988) and work within the Prague school tradition (Firbas 1992) still make this distinction, but both GPSG and HPSG, which are also c-structure frameworks, as well as Construction Grammar(Goldberg 2006), reject such a distinction. The first two of these, at least, have a different way of dealing with such word order variation. They distinguish between hierarchical structure and linear order and have separate sets of rules for each of these. In cases of discourse driven word order, as in the case of Russian (discussed in section 6) and similar languages, this distinction would allow them, when they deal with such phenomena[4], to create linearization rules which are sensitive to discourse information such as focus and topic.

But this is only a partial solution. Suppose we write linearization rules as follows: N1< N2, to mean N1 precedes N2, where N1 and N2 are any two nodes of the tree. As it stands, this needs to be interpreted. How do different rules of this sort interact with each other? What happens to the nodes dominated by N1 and N2?

[2] The essential point of this section is made in Hudson 2007:118

[3] The idea of using arrows as branches when the dependent is an adjunct is introduced in Osborne and Groβ 2009.

[4] Some work along these lines has been done in HPSG, notably Murphy (1995).

(11)

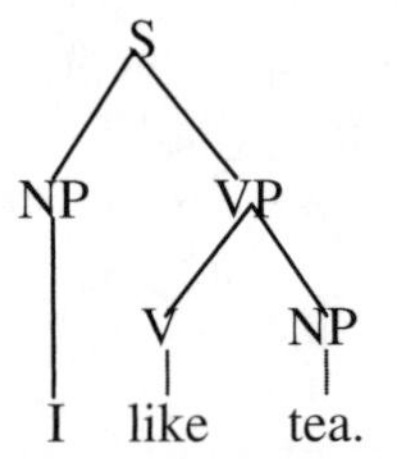

In this tree, the subject NP is the sibling of the VP, but not of the V, so no linearization rule can be written for the sequence of the Subject NP and V. Rather the subject NP must be linearized with respect to the VP. The object NP, on the other hand, is the sibling of the V, so writing a linearization rule is no problem for it: V < NP (V precedes the sibling NP).

To make the constituency grammar approach coherent, it is necessary to interpret these nodes as constituents and thereby include all the nodes they dominate in the linearization process. In the works cited above, their power is restricted to applying only to nodes in a sibling relationship, for example, between any preposition and the sibling NP that it governs, or between any verb and its direct object. One problem with this restriction is that it does not allow us to write a rule which determines the linear relationship between the verb and its subject, because they are not siblings in the tree. The subject NP is a sibling of the VP, not of the verb itself.

The so-called true tree principle (e.g. Schubert 1987:87-90) makes it impossible for different parts of a constituent C1 to be split apart by another constituent C2 which is not a part of C1. The constituent consisting of verb and object (the VP), for example, cannot be split apart by the subject, since the latter is not part of the VP. This has the consequence that in a sentence with VSO order, there can be no VP, at least not in surface structure, and accordingly not at all in any monostratal framework. It is therefore necessary to attach the verb and its arguments to the S node. This makes linearization easier.

The corresponding dependency grammar approach to the problem, shown in tree (12), would be to have linearization rules order the parent node with each of its child nodes.

(12)

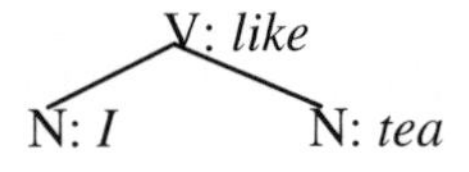

The verb is the parent of both the subject N and the object N, so the linearization rules can say that the verb follows one N and precedes the other: $N_{su} < V < N_{ob}$.

It turns out, however, that for languages like English, at least, linearization rules are not necessary at all, as has been shown by Groß and Osborne 2009 and numerous other publications. The linear relationship between the parent and its child in the D-structure tree can be determined by their linear relationship in the rule, assuming the rule corresponds closely to the resulting tree. The direction of the branch which unites parent and child provides this linear relationship. This is seen in the above tree.

Of course, it would be possible to eliminate the VP node of c-grammar and attach the verb and all its arguments directly to the S node at the top of the tree. This is the approach taken for all languages discussed in Starosta 1988, but has generally found little support within generative grammar. This approach solves the problem and makes the grammar more like a dependency grammar.

6 Free Word Order

All the data in this section is taken from Kallestinova 2007. From now on, this name followed by one or more numbers refers to a page or pages of this work.

Russian is one of quite a few languages which are often said to allow relatively "free" word order. According to a number of studies cited by Kallestinova, this freedom does not encode grammatical information, and accordingly does not affect truth conditions[5]. What this does mean is best illustrated with an example, which is taken from Kallestinova 1-2:

(13) a. Boris navestil Ivana. SVO
Boris-Nom. visited Ivan-Acc.[6]
'Boris visited Ivan.'

b. Boris Ivana navestil. SOV

c. Ivana navestil Boris. OVS

---

[5] In case of different word orders affecting the scope of adjuncts, truth conditions may be affected, as in the case of languages like English, but this is not the type of phenomenon under discussion here.

[6] I use the standard abbreviations for case-endings: acc. = accusative, instr. = instrumental, nom. =nominative

d. Ivana Boris navestil. OSV

e. Navestil Boris Ivana. VSO

f. Navestil Ivana Boris. VOS

These sentences show that the same idea can be expressed by more than one arrangement of a fixed set of words, in this case, there are three words in the set, and they can be arranged in any one of the logically possible six sequences of the Subject (S), Verb (V), and Object (O).

Furthermore, the different positions of the sentence are used to distinguish new information or **Foc(us)** from old information, or the **Top(ic)**. Old information goes at the beginning of the sentence, and new information at the end. For example, a subject-focus answer using a non-emotive strategy[7] requires an order with the subject at the end of the sentence, that is, either OVS or VOS. In a sentence using the non-emotive strategy, the only word order with a constituent other than the focused one in sentence final position to be found in significant numbers is SVO. The results of the perception experiment show, however, that one of the two orders found in the non-emotive strategy is distinctly preferred over the other. So in response to the question in (14a), (14b) is strongly preferred to (14c).

(14) a. Kto gryzjot kapustu?
Who bite cabbage-acc.
'Who is biting the cabbage?'

b. Kapustu gryzjot zajac.
cabbage-acc bite rabbit-nom
'The rabbit is biting the cabbage.'

c. ?Gryzjot kapustu zajac.

This shows that it is possible to place any of the major constituents of the verb at the end of the sentence, since any of these constituents can be the answer to such a question.

Representing some of the various possible word orders is no problem for a c-structure framework. As long as the verb and its dependents and modifiers are all siblings in the tree, linearization rules can determine their respective order. But in most c-structure frameworks, the subject is not considered to be a sibling of the verb. So if the subject intervenes between any of the constituents in the VP, this is a sequence which cannot be linearized using the assumptions mentioned so far. So of the six possible linear orders of the constituents (subject (S), verb (V), object (O)) of transitive sentences, two of them, namely VSO and OSV show these unlinearizable sequences. Do these orders really exist in Russian speech? The results of Kallestinova's perception experiment show that they are acceptable, although SVO is strongly preferred over VSO as a way of focusing on the O, and OVS is strongly preferred to VOS as a way of focusing on the S. Nevertheless, the two orders VSO and VOS occur often enough in Kallestinova's elicitation experiment that they cannot be attributed to chance.

There seems to be a further problem within constituency grammars of unifying the feature **Foc** with the final position of the sentence, in order to create responses that are appropriate in a given context. Once again, the problem is that transitive sentences in constituency grammars are created by a combination of two different phrase structure rules, one as an expansion of the S node and one as an expansion of the VP node. Either of these rules can be written to include this feature in its final constituent, and either of these rules can be linearized to place its two child constituents in either of the two logically possible orders. Then there needs to be a rule showing that whatever lexical constituent is in final position gets the feature **Foc,** and this rule needs to unify with the final position of the tree created by the above described phrase structure rules.

One problem with this is that few if any of the major c-structure frameworks mentioned earlier makes use of pragmatic features like [Foc].[8] This of course will change if and when they start incorporating more work on pragmatics into their grammars.

Another problem is the need to combine such a feature with a phonological feature such as '#'(clause final, corresponding to a break in the prosody). Because the phonology is generally taken for granted in work on syntax, there are not many examples of formal

---

[7] The emotive strategy, signaling the focus by prosodic means, allows speakers to use the basic SVO order. This is not treated here, however.

[8] Kallestinova (chapters 3 and 4) cites some analyses within the Minimalist Program which use phrasal nodes with the names FocP or TopP, thus apparently creating a pragmatic category rather than a syntactic one.

treatments involving interactions between it and syntax, semantics, or pragmatics. But cases of such interactions are discussed informally quite regularly, for example in discussions of sentences which are grammatical or have a specific meaning only in the presence of emphatic stress or a specific intonation. Goldberg 2006 postulates that representations of these different aspects of linguistic signs must always be paired together. There have been some attempts to incorporate such ideas into formal analyses, but no general agreement about how this should be done, even within one formal framework.

So far we have discussed word order when the subject, the object or the verb is focused. It is also possible to focus certain non-constituents: verb plus object or verb plus subject. In the following sentences (Kallestinova 60), (15b) shows an example of the former, which typically occurs in response to a question like (15a):

(15) a. Chto delaet devochka?
What does girl
'What is the girl doing?'

b. Devochka [podmetaet pol]-Foc.
Girl-Nom. sweeps-3sg. floor-Acc.
'The girl is sweeping the floor.'

The following data (Kallestinova 17) shows an example of verb-subject focus.

(16) a. What happened to the paintings?

b. Neskol'ko kartin [priobrel mestnyj muzej]-Foc.
a few paintings acquired local museum
'The local museum acquired a few of the paintings.'

c. Who acquired the paintings?

d. Neskol'ko kartin priobrel [mestnyj muzej]-Foc.
A few paintings acquired local museum
'The local museum acquired a few of the paintings.'

(16a) is the kind of question that requires an answer like the one in (16b), in which both the verb and subject are focused. (16c), on the other hand, requires an answer like the one in (16d), in which only the subject is in focus, since only the subject provides new information. The answers to the questions in (17a) and (17c) differ only in focus.

(17) a. Chto s oknom?
What with window-instr.
'What happened to the window?'

b. Okno [razbila Olja]
Window-Acc. broke Olja-Nom.
'Olja broke the window.'

c. ??Okno [Olja razbila].
Window-Acc. Olja-Nom. broke
'Olja broke the window.'

Sentence (17b) is the preferred answer to the question in (17a). Sentence (17c) is a less satisfactory answer, but is nevertheless possible. Both answers show the subject and verb in focus position at the end of the sentence. What is the structural relationship between a subject NP and its verb in a constituency grammar that has a VP? This varies according to the kind of X-bar system being used, but in the simplest kind, namely a one-bar system, the verb would be the niece/nephew of the subject NP. There is no one node which includes both of them and no other part of the sentence. This would appear to make any analysis linking [foc] in one node to the other quite awkward and ad hoc.

Recognizing such extended focus units as subject-verb and verb-object is also a problem for DG, but it is comforting that whatever solution is used for one of these can also be used for the other.

7 Heads

The head of a syntactic unit such as a phrase or sentence is the word which determines the category of the larger unit. Within a word, the head is the morph that determines the category of the word as a whole. The following examples show how this is represented in c-structure and d-structure. In the former, I will assume that superfluous nodes have been pruned away, as discussed in section 4.

(18) good idea

a.

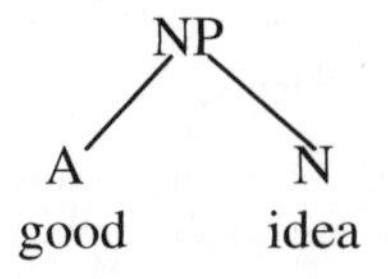

b.

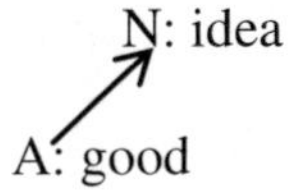

On the basis of these examples, there seems to be nothing new to say about the differences between c-structure and d-structure. In c-structure, the head is a sibling of its complement and has the same category as its parent. In d-structure the head is the parent of its complement.

However, a problem comes up for c-structure, if the complement has the same category as the head, as in (19):

(19) She wants to help.

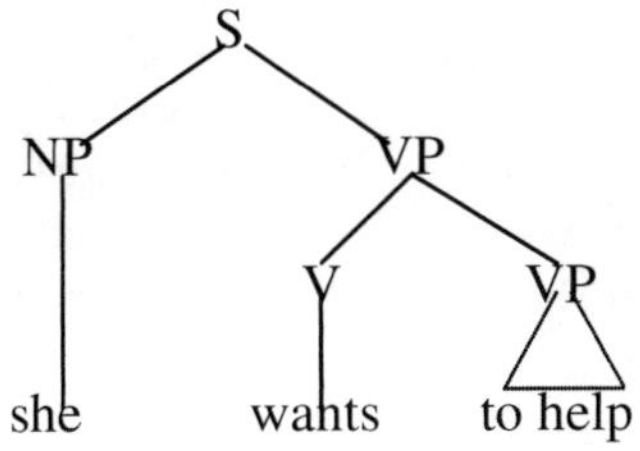

Both *wants* and *to help* have the category **verb.** They differ merely in bar level. How do we determine which one is the head of the higher VP? What formal criterion can be used to automate this selection? One way would be to say that in cases like this the lexical node is always the head. Another response to this question would be that taken in HPSG: the head is designated as H in the PS rule and inherits the category of the parent via the Head Feature Principle mentioned in section 3.

In any case, there is no such problem for d-structure. The head is always the parent of its complement rather than its sibling. So the category of the head is also the category of the entire phrase.

On the other hand, not every parent needs to be considered a head. I believe that the categories of words from small closed classes such as complementizers (*to, that)* do not determine the category of the entire phrase that they are part of and introduce and are therefore not heads. In any case, this question can and should be debated separately from the questions dealt with in this paper.

8 Catenae: a necessary part of Ellipsis and Idioms

Osborne and Groß 2012 provide evidence that ellipsis and idioms always meet a specific structural condition which is easily formulated in dependency grammars, but not in constituency grammars. This is that the missing words of any construction involving ellipsis as well as the idiomatic part of a sentence always form a **catena** (plural: **catenae).** They define this as part of a dependency tree which is "continuous with respect to dominance." In other words, the nodes of a catena are all connected to each other. Osborne and Groß claim that the idiomatic part of any sentence must form a catena.[9]

Tree (20) shows a c-structure representation of the WXDY construction (Kay and Fillmore 1999), which as far as I can determine from their discussion would be the one provided by the authors, if they had been using tree diagrams of this sort[10].

(20)

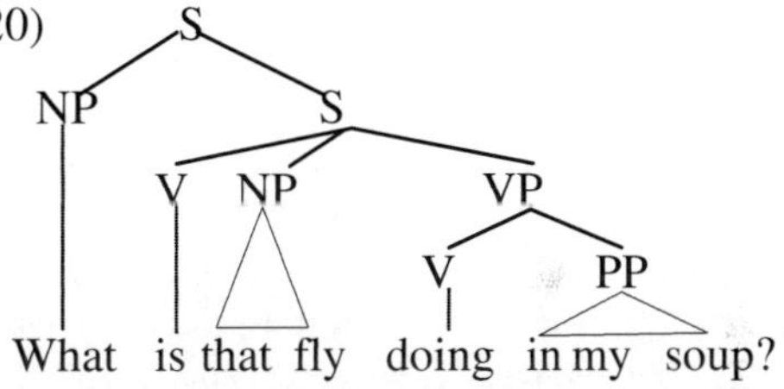

Tree (21) shows the same sentence in a d-structure tree (I have omitted the lexical categories).

(21)

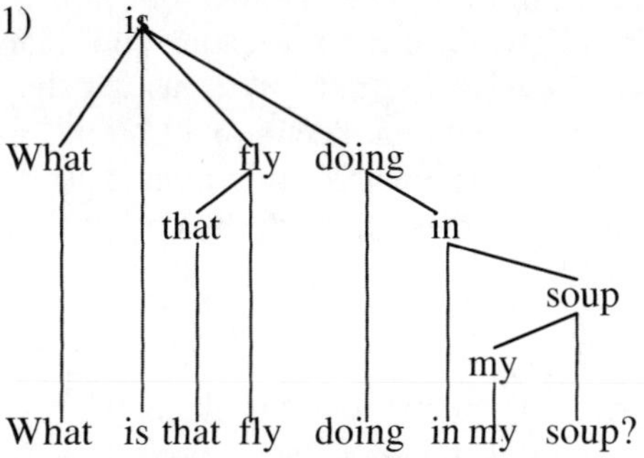

[9] They note that there are a few idioms, such as *spill the beans*, which in their passive form (*the beans were spilled*) do not form a catena due to the intervening auxiliary verb. To get around this, one might suggest that the passive and active forms of the idiom are generated by the same lexical entry, which necessarily is an idiom.

[10] They in fact use matrices, specifically attribute-value matrices.

Kay and Fillmore consider the following words to be the idiomatic part of this sentence: *What, is, doing*. In other versions of this idiom, *is* can be replaced by any finite form of the verb *be*, depending on what is required for agreement with the subject. *This fly* and *in my soup* are the non-idiomatic parts of the construction. The idiomatic words are all connected to each other as a catena in the d-structure. It is clear from a glance at (20) that no two of the three nodes corresponding to *what, is*, and *doing* in the c-structure are in a sibling relationship. This apparently removes the justification for connecting these nodes directly. The alternative is to connect them by going through the three phrasal nodes. It is necessary to go through both S nodes and the VP in order to connect *What* to the other two words of the idiom. But once we allow catenae to go through any number of phrasal nodes as well as the required lexical nodes, it appears that any combination of words can be considered a catena. This would make the concept meaningless. This is not the case in d-structure trees. For example, the combination of *what* in (21) with any word in the sentence except *is* does not form a catena.

Note that the extended focus units (verb-subject and verb-object) discussed in the previous section do form catenae, thus perhaps providing the basis for a solution to the problem discussed there. This is not the place to go into details of this, however.

The significance of catenae for ellipsis is that the elided material, no matter how many words it consists of, always forms a catena. This is dealt with in detail in Osborne and Groβ 2012. I summarize this point with the following examples, taken from Osborne and Groβ 2012:

(22)

a. Fred will attempt to help you, and
b. Tom [will attempt to help] me
c. Tom [will attempt] to help me

(23)

a. she may take a picture of me, and
b. he [may take a picture] of me
c. he [may take] a picture of me

(24)

a. Mom intends to require me to mow the front lawn this week, and
b. Dad [intends to require me to mow the front lawn] next week
c. Dad [intends to require me to mow] the back lawn next week

The a clauses show the first clause of a coordinate structure. The b and c clauses show various forms of the second clause. The bracketed material can be omitted in each case. And in these cases, the words of the omitted material form a catena.

9 Interface with Semantics

Words in a sentence combine with each other to create meanings of larger units such as propositions. Within a constituency grammar, this is thought to happen (Partee 1975) by combining meanings of the lexical nodes at the bottom of the tree to form the meanings of the constituent(s) represented by the immediately dominating phrasal node(s). The meanings at such nodes then combine with each other to create the meanings of the phrasal nodes that dominate them, and so on, until the meaning at the top of the tree is created. Given this situation, it appears that the way nodes combine depends on the nature of these nodes. So for every different phrase structure rule, there would be a specific rule combining the meanings of each constituent. The view that meanings combine this way is known as the rule-to-rule hypothesis.

The rule-to-rule hypothesis works differently in dependency grammar, since the parent node has its own contribution to the meaning of the sentence and this meaning needs to combine with the meanings of the child or children. If the child nodes are complements of their head, they combine with the parent as its arguments. So the parent node in DG would generally serve a double function as both the head child of the construction and place where the meanings of this head and the children are shown.

These two scenarios are shown in the following two figures:

(25)

a.

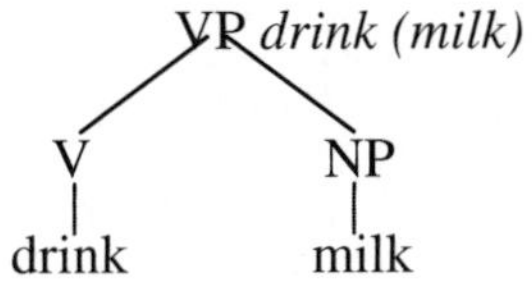

In c-structure, the italicized words show how the SEM (semantics) of the verb combines with the SEM of the NP to create a predicate-argument structure.

b.

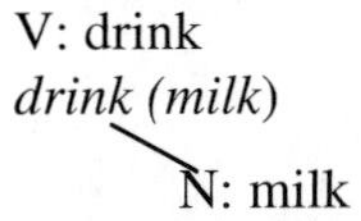

In d-structure, the same node is used both to store the predicate *drink* and the combination of the SEM of this word with that of its complement noun. The d-structure in (b) shows one general pattern found in many specific d-structures: the head node is the predicate, and the complements its arguments. The other general pattern is the one used for adjuncts or adjunct phrases: they take their head (and its complements, if it has any) as their argument. The c-structure version of this is shown in (26a) without a VP and (26b) with a VP.

(26)

a.

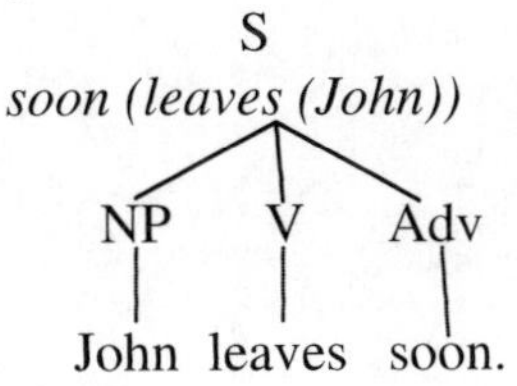

b.

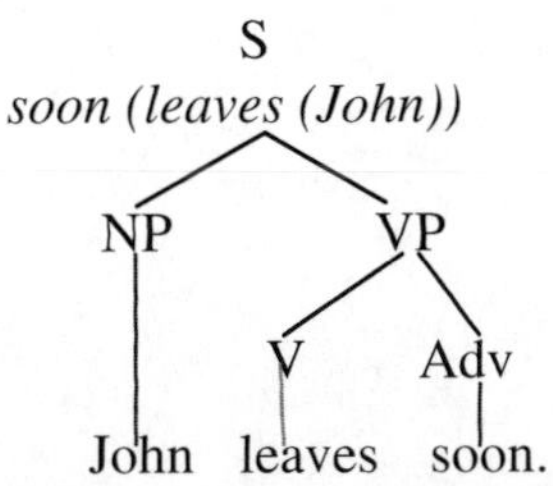

In the predicate-argument structures which must result from both of the above trees, the adjunct *soon* takes the meaning of the rest of the sentence as its argument.

The problem for c-structure is shown in (26b). What meaning is stored at the VP? It should be just the combination of the two SEMs which are in its child nodes, that is *soon (leaves)*; *leaves* still has not combined with its argument *John,* which becomes available only in the next step up the tree. But *John* is also a complement of *leaves*. So it seems to be necessary to leave a placeholder slot in the argument position of the V to signal that just the subject does not immediately fill the V's argument slots, allowing it to remain empty until the next step up the tree is made. This empty slot is then filled by the subject in that next step. This can be done, but it seems to be an unnecessary complication. In the d-structure, or in the c-structure without the VP, all of the argument slots are immediately available.

10 Conclusion

I have argued that c-structure faces problems that d-structure does not face in the areas of agreement, case marking, word order (especially free word order), eliminating or otherwise dealing with superfluous nodes, defining catena, and combining meaningful parts to create predicate-argument structures. It is true that these problems could be reduced by eliminating an intermediate level of the phrasal projection (the VP node and the N' node), but the fact these intermediate levels have become firmly entrenched in frameworks based on c-structure militates against this happening. In fact, in the Minimalist Program the trend has been in the opposite direction – to more nodes and more structure, making their representations of sentence structure still less like those provided by dependency grammars. These additional nodes guarantee further complications in creating meaning representations in ways which have been shown in this paper.

Acknowledgements

I wish to thank Tim Osborne for comments on the first draft of this paper and three anonymous referees for comments on the submitted version. This final version has been influenced by all of these comments.

References

Joan Bresnan. 2001. *Lexical Functional Syntax*. Oxford: Blackwell.

Noam Chomsky and Howard Lasnik. 1993. "The theory of Principles and Parameters". In Jacobs, J.; von Stechow, A.; Sternefeld, W. et al. *Syntax: An international handbook of contemporary research*. Berlin: de Gruyter.

Jan Firbas. 1992. *Functional Sentence Perspective in written and spoken communication.* Cambridge University Press. republished in 2006, edited by John Alges and Bas Aarts.

Gerald Gazdar, Evan Klein et al. 1985. *Generalized Phrase Structure Grammar*. Oxford: Basil Blackwell.

Adele Goldberg. 2006. *Constructions at Work: The Nature of Generalization in Language.* Oxford University Press.

Thomas Groß and Timothy Osborne. 2009. Toward a practical dependency grammar of theory discontinuities. *SKY Journal of Linguistics* 22, 43-90.

Richard Hudson. 1984. *Word Grammar.* Oxford University Press.

Richard Hudson. 2007. *Language Networks: the New Word Grammar*. Oxford University Press.

Ray Jackendoff. 1977. *X-bar Theory*. MIT Press.

Elena Kallestinova. 2007. *Aspects of Russian Word Order.* University of Iowa Dissertation. http://ir.uiowa.edu/etd/165.

Paul Kay and Charles Fillmore. 1999. Grammatical Constructions and Linguistic Generalizations. *Language*: 75:1-34.

Igor Mel'čuk. 1988. *Dependency Syntax: Theory and Practice.* Albany: State University of New York Press.

Patrick Murphy. 1995. Word Order, Themes and Discourse in Head-Driven Phrase Structure Grammar. www.unc/~murphy/research

Timothy Osborne and Thomas Groß. 2012. Construction Grammar meets Dependency Grammar of syntactic analysis. *Cognitive Linguistics* 23.1: 364-396.

Barbara Partee. 1975. Montague grammar and transformational Grammar. *Linguistic Inquiry* 6 (*1975*): 203-300.

Carl Pollard and Ivan Sag. 1994. *Head-driven Phrase Structure Grammar.* Chicago University Press.

John Robert Ross. 1969. A Proposed Rule of tree Pruning. 288-299. In Modern Studies in English. *Readings in Transformational Grammar.* Edited by David A. Reibel and Sanford Schane. Prentice-Hall:Englewood cliffs, New Jersey.

Klaus Schubert. 1987. *Metataxis: Contrastive dependency syntax for machine translation.* Dordrecht: Foris Publications.

Stanley Starosta. 1988. *The case for lexicase: an outline of lexicase grammatical theory*. Open Linguistics Series, ed. by Robin Fawcett. London: Pinter Publishers Limited; Cassell.

Lucien Tesnière. 1959. *Éléments de syntaxe structural.* Paris: Klincksieck, Paris 1959.

Grammatical markers and grammatical relations in the simple clause in Old French

Nicolas Mazziotta
Universität Stuttgart
Institut für Linguistik/Romanistik
Germany
nicolas.mazziotta@ulg.ac.be

Abstract

The focus of this paper is the description of the surface syntax relations in the simple clause in Old French and the way they can be described in a dependency grammar. The declension system of Old French is not reliable enough to cope with the identification of the dependents of the main verb, but it remains true that related grammatical markers are still observable and obey rules that forbid them to appear in specific syntactic positions.

This study relies on three previous accounts; Igor Mel'čuk's "criteria B", the criteria that are used to determine which is the syntactic governor in a syntactic dependency relation, Thomas Groß's intraword analysis, which grants morphs node status in the tree, and the concept of *specification* as used by Alain Lemaréchal, who understands grammatical markers as a set of formal constraints that stack over a relation.

I demonstrate that the structure of the nominal dependents of the verb is highly unstable, ranging from explicit marking of the relation to constructions that do not make use of any segmental marker: some structures use bound morphemes, some others use free morphemes and some use only semantic features to express the relations. Moreover, markers are mainly optional and can stack up in a hierarchical way, which results in variable structural organization of the nominal phrase.

1 Introduction

This paper investigates the grammatical markers at work in the structure of the simple clause in Old French (henceforth "OF") and the way they can be described in a dependency framework (henceforth "DF"). As an introduction, I will first give a quick overview of OF (1.1), and define the focus of this study (1.2).

1.1 Old French: an overview

The term *Old French* roughly corresponds to a continuum of romance varieties that were spoken in the northern half of France, in Wallonia and in England during the Middle Ages (9th-13th C.). To carry on a description of OF, one has to systematize the common ground that all these idioms share as well as the major differences that distinguish the varieties. The paper will focus on that common ground, which can be seen as the direct ancestor of modern French.

From a grammatical point of view, OF is much more analytic than Latin is: many relations are introduced by prepositions. The traditional description of the nominal inflection tells us that Latin declension had shrunk in OF to a simple two-fold opposition between the nominative (Fr. *cas sujet*) and a universal oblique case (Fr. *cas régime*). Periphrastic verbal tenses had developed and the whole aspectual system had changed; the system had become clearly dominated by the opposition between bare forms and compound verbs (expressing aspectual/temporal anteriority).

The distribution of the major constituents of the clause tends to express information-structural properties rather than grammatical ones. Therefore, word order was a lot freer than it is in modern French.

1.2 Question

Others have demonstrated that the declension system of OF is not reliable enough to cope with the identification of dependents[1] of the verb. Several

[1] In the remainder of this paper, when no additional precision is given, the terms *dependency*, *governor*, *dependent*, *actant*, *tree*, etc. as well as the → symbol between a governor

Proceedings of the Second International Conference on Dependency Linguistics (DepLing 2013), pages 207–216,
Prague, August 27–30, 2013.

studies have shown: 1/ that the valence of the verb as well as the semantic properties of the actants are more important than the declension patterns (Schøsler, 1984); 2/ that the declension pattern is so heterogeneous that it cannot be described as a systematic tool (Chambon, 2003; Chambon and Davidsdottir, 2007); 3/ that case markers are an additional mean to express dependencies that would exist without them.[2]

General grammatical descriptions acknowledge these conclusions, but still deliver long lists of tables describing the different "paradigms" (Buridant, 2000).

As unreliable as declension is, it is nevertheless a fact that related grammatical markers are still observable and appear to obey at least some rules. These rules ensure that declension is well integrated with the rest of the grammar, which is invoked as a whole during the communication process (Schøsler, 2013, 173-175). Apparently, the rules block the markers from appearing in certain specific syntactic positions. The purpose of this paper is to describe the syntactic structure of the constructions where they appear. I will make use of DF to model grammatical relations between words (and morphemes, see 2.2), focusing mainly on verbal dependents of the intransitive and transitive minimal clause. As it will appear in the following sections, identifying the dependencies is not a trivial matter, because one has to cope with an unreliable declension system. Even the simplest examples involve complex phenomena inside the noun phrase, that have not yet been described under the scope of DF.[3]

To achieve a proper description, three major theoretical choices (2) will be used to carry out the analyses (3).

2 Theoretical grounds

My study relies on three primary sources:

- Igor Mel'čuk's "criteria B", which, given a pair of forms united by a syntactic dependency relation, are used to distinguish between the governor and the dependent (2.1);
- Thomas Groß's intra-word analysis, which treats morphs (surface expression of morphemes) in the syntactic tree (2.2);
- the concept of *specification* as employed by Alain Lemaréchal, who understands grammatical markers as a set of formal constraints over a relation (2.3).

2.1 Mel'čuk's criteria for finding dependencies

Given two forms f_1 and f_2, united by a dependency, which form is the governor? This crucial issue has been debated by so many scholars in many different frameworks that it would not be possible to name them all. From the DF perspective, it seems fair to assume that Arnold Zwicky (1985) has played a major role in clarifying things. Many criteria have been investigated since his work, but it seems that Igor Mel'čuk (2009) has given the most rigorous hierarchized list so far. There are three criteria: namely, in order of importance, B1, B2 and B3.[4] It is important to note that these criteria are initially meant to be used when f_1 and f_2 are *words* (see sec. 2.2 about morphs).

B1. Igor Mel'čuk claims that the orientation of a dependency between f_1 and f_2 mainly depends on the syntactic criterion based of what he calls *passive valence*:

> Passive syntactic valence of a lexeme/of a phrase: a set of syntactic roles which the lexeme/the phrase can take in larger constructions (maybe with some inflectional modifications). In other words, the passive syntactic valence of a lexeme/a phrase is its syntactic distribution. (Mel'čuk, 2009, 4)

The main idea is that the governor controls the passive valence; i.e., f_1 S-governs f_2 if the distribution of the phrase $f_1 + f_2$ is more the one of f_1 than the one of f_2. In ex. 1, the word *horse* governs the word *white*, because the distribution of *white horse* is more the distribution of *horse* than of *white* (which can be deleted). Note that Igor Mel'čuk speaks about *syntactic* distribution only, without any reference to word order.

and a dependent, will fall under the scope of surface syntax (Mel'čuk, 2009, 6-7)

[2] Given the high level of instability of the system, some authors even claim their main purpose is sociolinguistic and indicates that "the speaker is well-integrated in the speech community" (Detges, 2009, esp. 117).

[3] As explained by Peter Stein and Claudia Benneckenstein (2006) (who mainly focus on the verb), as far as OF is concerned, hardly any question has been described under the scope of DF so far. Nevertheless, the works of Lene Schøsler, starting with her thesis (1984), makes use of Lucien Tesnière's approach (1966).

[4] C criteria (used to discriminate different dependencies) will not be discussed here (Mel'čuk, 2009, 34-40). A criteria (used to find dependencies between words) are discussed in sec. 2.2.

(1) *the white horse*

One should not confuse this criterion with the omissibility property. Most of the time, governors are not omissible, but it is not always the case; e.g.: in English, the subordination marker *that* constrains the distribution of the clause when it is present, but can be omitted in some cases (Mel'čuk, 2009, 42).

This criterion is a genuinely syntactic one. As such, it must be used first: B2 and B3 must be invoked only if B1 fails. B1 will be extensively used in sec. 3.

B2. Sometimes, B1 simply does not work, because both forms are required in a given context and it is not possible to tell which of the two forms is the one that most constrains the syntactic distribution. In such cases, Igor Mel'čuk invokes the morphological properties of the forms involved: the governor is either the form that controls agreement or morphological government outside of the phrase, or the form that is morphologically governed from outside the phrase.

E.g., the French finite clause must have a subject and the relation between the main verb and the subject is compulsory. Therefore, the distribution of the clause is constrained by both the subject and the verb and B1 does not apply. However, if the clause is subordinate, it is the verb in the subordinate clause that is morphologically dependent of the governing verb. Here, the syntactic governor is the *morphological contact point* of the phrase.

(2) *Je veux qu' il vienne*
I want that he comes-SUBJUNCTIVE
"I want him to come"

In ex. 2, the subjunctive mood of *vienne* morphologically depends on the word *veux*. Therefore, at the syntactic level, *vienne* governs *il* and *qu'* governs *vienne*.

B3. If both B1 and B2 fail, one may then have a look at semantics. The governor is the form that expresses the referential class of the phrase most accurately.

(3) *I eat this jam sandwich*

Take *jam sandwich* in ex. 3; both terms have the same distribution (B1) and neither of the two words is the morphological contact point to some agreement outside the phrase (B2), but *jam sandwich* "refers to a kind of sandwich, rather than a kind of jam (Mel'čuk, 2009, 31), quoting (Hudson, 1990). Hence, *sandwich* → *jam*.

2.2 Thomas Groß's intra-word analysis

Expanding the Meaning-Text Theory (henceforth "MTT") model (Mel'čuk, 2009) to handle intra-word syntactic dependencies can help produce a more explicit analysis of the relations between segmental units. Thomas Groß's (2011) suggestion will lead to reconsider some of the basic definitions provided by Igor Mel'čuk.

Grammatical markers in MTT. According to Igor Mel'čuk (2009, 23-24), there are only four linguistic means to express meaning:

- lexemes (free words);
- order of lexemes;
- prosody;
- inflection.

For Igor Mel'čuk, there are no other means; excepting inflection, they are all used in all languages in every sentence, and they can express semantic meaning as well as syntactic relations. Igor Mel'čuk also posits out that only lexical units ("full" words or "empty" ones, e.g. prepositions and conjunctions) must be represented in the tree. The order of the lexemes, the prosody and the inflection are not part of the tree: they merely permit one to build it. Let us have a look at a simple German example (ex. 4) from (Groß, 2011, 48).

(4) *mit Kind -er -n*
with child PLURAL DATIVE
"with children"

Fig. 1 displays the classic MTT tree of this phrase, where the bound morphemes expressing the plural and the dative are merged with the lexeme into a single word-form.

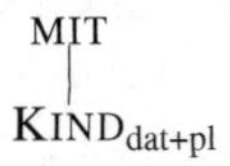

Figure 1: MTT analysis of Germ. *mit Kindern*

Extending DF trees to morphology. Thomas Groß (Groß, 2011) suggested that bound morphs too should be represented as well in trees (we will focus only on inflectional morphology, leaving aside constructional morphology). In other words, morphs can be granted node status in surface syntactic representations. The distinction between *morpheme* (abstract unit) and *morph* (surface realization of this abstract unit) is very important here: only morphs, are considered. The idea is not new, since that Leonard Bloomfield (1933, ch. 10) already considered immediate constituents can be bound or free morphemes and that analysis acknowledging inflection as a *functional head* is widely spread in the Government and Binding paradigm (Haegemann, 1994, esp. ch. 11).

The main argument backing the idea of an intra-word syntax is that bound morphs, which are segmental units, behave similar to grammatical words such as prepositions and conjunctions. Most of these morphs constrain the distribution of the word they are attached to (B1). Consequently, trees should represent intra-word dependencies, i.e. the relation between the lexeme and the bound morphs. This conception is very close to Gilbert Lazard's idea of *tripartition of syntax* (Lazard, 1984). Gilbert Lazard distinguishes three levels: clause level, phrase level and intra-word level. The intra-word level is traditionally called *morphology*, but these classical terms fails to express the rules of distribution and the combination contraints that morphs undergo with regard to the organization at higher level (syntax). Thomas Groß suggests the tree in fig. 2 to represent the dependencies at work in ex. 4.[5] The German preposition *mit* governs a dative complement, because the dative marker is compulsory with this preposition. The distribution of the dependent of *mit* is the one of any dative noun, but *only* dative nouns: an accusative form would not be grammatically correct. Therefore, *-n* governs the whole nominal phrase (B1). The plural marker *-er* also governs the lexeme, because *-n* must dominate a plural word.

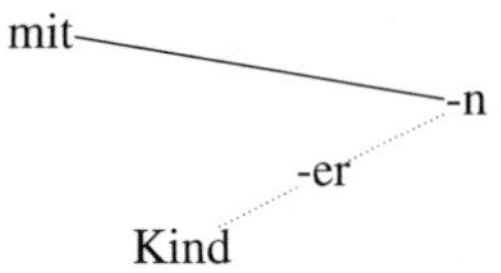

Figure 2: Groß's analysis of Germ. *mit Kindern*

Syntactic vs. morphological dependencies. One must pay attention to the distinction between morphological and syntactic dependencies[6]. Following Igor Mel'čuk (Mel'čuk, 2009, 12), one can define *morphological dependency* as follows:

> The wordform *w2* is said to morphologically depend on the wordform *w1* in the given utterance if and only if at least one grammeme of *w2* is selected depending on w1.

On the other hand the existence of a syntactic dependency between two forms (f_1 and f_2) can be checked by the means of two criteria (A1 and A2) that must be met (2009, 25-27):

1. A1: the linear arrangement of f_1 and f_2 must be linearly constrained in a neutral utterance.
2. A2: the combination of f_1 and f_2, or the combination of f_1 and the subtree governed by f_2 must form a potential prosodic unit (which is equivalent to a *phrase* in the MTT framework).

Of course, a morphological dependency can affect the same forms as a syntactic dependency; e.g.: in *It is blue*, the agreement between the verb and the subject is a morphological dependency, but there also exists a syntactic relation between *it* and *is*.

From the moment one chooses to split words in the syntactic dependency tree, the definition of morphological dependency cannot work any longer and must be revised. With bound morphs, there are fewer problems with A1 than with free lexemes. As far as A2 is concerned, it helps clarify things. In a phrase like *mit Kindern*, it is quite clear that *mit* and *-n* do not form a phrase, but the fact that *-n* governs the rest of the word is enough to ensure that A2 is met. There is no problem either with other intra-word dependencies. The main issue is about inter-word agreement. E.g., in ex. 5 (Groß, 2011, 59), the genitive marker *-es* licenses the occurrence of the word *Dankes*, but it also implies that the article has the form *des* (which could even be split in $d \rightarrow es$). However, the tree (fig. 3) does not display this dependency, but rather $Word \rightarrow des$.

(5) *mit Wort -er -n des*
with word PLURAL DATIVE the-GEN
Dank -es
thank GEN
"with words of gratitude"

[5] The dotted lines represent intra-word dependencies and the hyphen represents lack of phonological autonomy. Also note that the tree somewhat represents word order. Although this aspect is not crucial for this paper, using this convention enhances readability.

[6] The third major type of dependency, namely, semantic dependency, does not deal with morphs and does not need to be scrutinized here.

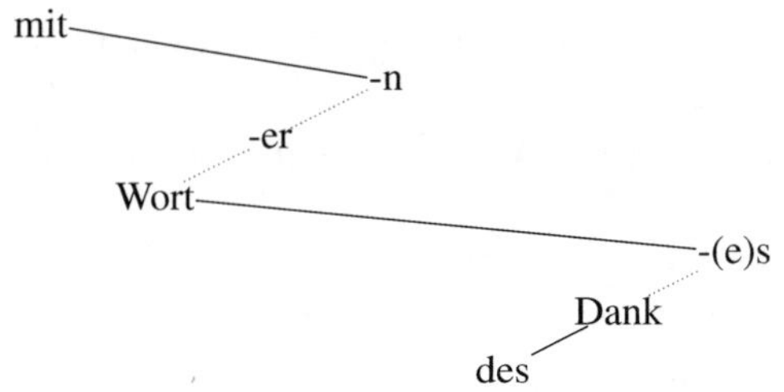

Figure 3: Groß's analysis if Germ. *mit Wortern des Dankes*

This appears to be quite right because of criterion A2: the reason why *-es* $\rightarrow$ *des* is not a syntactic dependency is that it does not form a potential prosodic unit (phrase). Therefore, agreement is not a syntactic dependency. Agreement is not sufficient to bring together enough blocks of syntactic units to form a proper phrase. This lets us clearly define the distinction between morphological and syntactic dependencies in the case of form determination: in the case of a syntactic dependency, the form determination constrains the distribution at a higher level and must apply to the head of a phrase; in the case of a morphological dependency, form determination does not necessarily apply to the head of a phrase. This distinction is very different from the one proposed by Igor Mel'čuk.

The only problem that remains is that the presence of one case marker is sometimes compulsory in languages (e.g.: for most Latin nouns, case marking is compulsory). Nouns cannot form a phrase without inflection. Hence, if there is some adjective depending on the noun, such as *carum* in Latin *carum amicum* – see ex. 6 (indices distinguish between forms in the demonstration) and fig. 4 –, the dependency *amic* $\rightarrow$ *-um$_2$* seems not to satisfy the A2 criterion (it does not form a phrase).

(6) *Amic -um$_1$ car -um$_2$ video*
friend ACC dear Acc I see
"I see (my) dear friend"

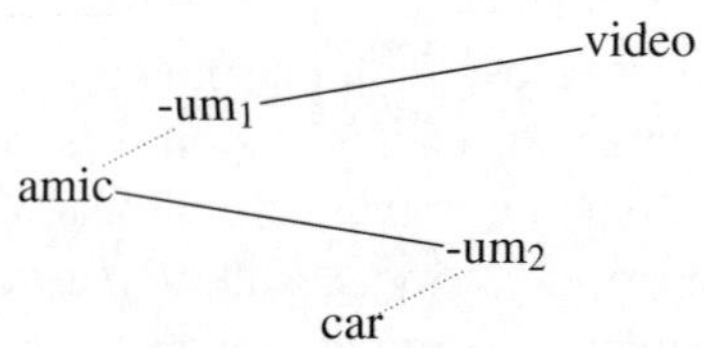

Figure 4: Analysis of Lat. *Amicum carum video*

To solve this kind of problem without loosing the benefit of the A2 criterion, we have to posit:

> Let $f_1 \rightarrow f_2$ be a compulsory intra-word syntactic dependency. For all inter-word dependencies f_2 — f_3, A2 holds if either $f_1 f_2 f_3$ or $f_1 f_2$ and the subtree governed by f_3 forms a potential prosodic unit (= phrase).

Since *-um$_1$* $\rightarrow$ *amic* is a compulsory intra-word dependency and *um$_2$* is the governor of *car*, there exist a relation between *amic* and *um$_2$* because *carum amicum* is a potential prosodic unit. However, there is no syntactic relation beween *um$_1$* and *um$_2$* because *-um carum* is not a phrase – and *-um carum video* is not a phrase either.

2.3 Alain Lemaréchal's *specification*

Hierarchy of markers. My third theoretical milestone is the concept of *specification* as used by Alain Lemaréchal in his works (1997). The main assumption is that grammatical markers are hierarchized and that the parts of speech also play a role in the way the markers interconnect. Hence, the grammatical markers are the following, in decreasing order of importance:

1. integrative markers (prosody);
2. lexeme order;
3. part of speech compatibilities;
4. segmental units (free relational morphemes and inflection).

This hierarchy is based on the fact that the only compulsory markers are prosodic ones and that words can be connected simply because of their respective part of speech; e.g.: *John slept* (simple past) works because *John* is a noun and *slept* is a verb. In this conception, segmental markers are added at the very last level and are the least important for the relation to exist.

Markers and government. Alain Lemaréchal's view basically contradicts the idea that prepositions, conjunctions and bound morphemes should often be seen as the governor of the relation. His point is that these markers are added to an existing relation and that they form a *stack* of grammatical constraints that *specify* the relation, both syntactically and semantically. Specifications are not compulsory to establish relations. In this framework, a morpheme such as a preposition behaves similar to what Lucien Tesnière calls a *translatif* (Tesnière, 1966): it changes the part of speech of the words it combines with – e.g.: a preposition can change a noun to an adverb and allow this noun to be an adjunct.

Even if it belongs to a dependency framework, this analysis does not follow the same theoretical guidelines as the ones introduced in sec. 2.1 and sec. 2.2. However, Alain Lemaréchal (1997, 117) also adds a very important detail in his presentation: markers may not be compulsory, but if they appear, *they have to be the right ones*. He compares ex. 7 and 8. In ex. 7, the verbal form carries no segmental marker expressing the person and the sentence remains understandable (although not very satisfactory). In ex. 8, the bound morph *-ons* conflicts with the 3rd pers. sg. of the proper name. Hence, the sentence is not understandable at all.

(7) **Alfred chanter*
Alfred to sing

(8) **Alfred chantons*
Alfred we sing

If this point is transferred to the B1 criterion, it means that when such a specific marker is present, it firmly constrains the syntactic distribution of the construction.

Stacking markers. One other important point in Alain Lemaréchal's model is the concept of *marker stacking* (Fr. *cumul des marques*). His idea is that homonyms do not exist among grammatical markers (Lemaréchal, 1983). Markers can be ambiguous, because they are not specific enough on their own. E.g., traditionally, in French, *que* has been described as a pronoun (*L'homme que tu vois* "The man you see") or as a conjunction (*Je veux que tu viennes* "I want you to come"). If one takes into account that the clause beginning with *que* works with a noun (*homme*) or with a verb (*veux*), this ambiguity disappears. In other words, there is a stacking of markers that gradually specify the relation between words: instead of two different *que* one should see an undespecified *que* that stacks with part of speech compatibilities to specify several different relations.

3 Major relations in the clause in OF

This section investigates the grammatical means of expressing dependencies in the OF clause. The theoretical aspects described above will prove useful in order to achieve a description that encompasses the main characteristics of the phenomena under study. The description reveals the striking instability of the system: DF trees will help demonstrate this lack of systematicity in a rigorous way.

I will give the classical idealized approach of the declension system in OF and underline the main problems (3.1). Then, we will see that the definite article plays an important role in the syntactic organization of the clause (3.2) and that some nouns have a syntactically specialized theme (3.3). Some structures that completely lack overt markers will also be introduced (3.4). I will conclude with a synthesis and point out historical concerns (3.5).

3.1 Classical approach to declension in OF

Ideal system. The traditional analysis of the declension system in OF relies on the fact that a few nouns are marked with a bound morpheme that indicates whether they assume the role of the subject or not. Following this point of view, OF distinguishes between two cases: the nominative case *cas sujet* and the universal oblique case *cas régime* (which is used for all functions but the subject).

Therefore, the minimal sentence in ex. 13 clearly shows that the noun *Charle* has an *-s* morph at the end.

(9) *Charle -s respunt*
Charles NOM answers
– Roland (Moignet, 1972, v. 156)

The resulting analysis would thus be the one shown in fig. 5.

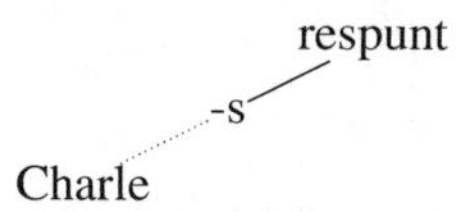

Figure 5: Analysis of OF *Charles respunt*

Problems. However, even with little knowledge of OF, one feels that the traditional analysis oversimplifies things.

The first issue is that the ideal system as described only affects a comparatively small subset of nouns: most feminine nouns do not follow any syntax-driven declension rule and nominal lexemes ending with *-s*/*-z* are invariable. Traditional description adopt a paradigmatic approach to this problem, in effect, multiplying nominal paradigms, with regard to the way they behave in the declension "system".

The second issue is that the presence of *-s* is not compulsory even for the nouns that generally have a marked nominative form. Nevertheless, "inverse mistakes", where *-s* appears in the oblique case are very seldom (Schøsler, 1984, 237-8), which means that Alain Lemaréchal's prediction holds, that is, the markers must be correct when they do appear (sec. 2.3).

But there is a third problem: *-s* is highly syncretic in the grammar of OF, because it is also used to mark the plural form of the oblique case of the nouns that do follow the declension rules (for other nouns, *-s* merely marks the plural). In a nutshell, the classical paradigm is the one shown in tab. 1 (Moignet, 1988, 19). This paradigm contrasts with the one of most feminine nouns ending in *-e* (tab. 2).

	sg.	pl.
NOM	-s	–
OBL	–	-s

Table 1: Ideal case marker paradigm in OF

	sg.	pl.
NOM/OBL	–	-s

Table 2: Case marker paradigm for OF feminine nouns in *-e*

If one accepts that there is only one *-s* (last paragraph in sec. 2.3) that, as it will appear, may stack with other markers, one can say that the distribution of the nominal phrase is constrained by *-s*, *modulo* the syntactic distribution is not homogeneous, because the marker is underspecified.

3.2 Definite article

A more reliable marker. The definite article is a marker that can optionally specify the noun phrase in OF.[7] It is more reliable than nominal inflection in determining the case, but, unlike its modern counterpart, it is by no means compulsory – all nouns can be used as a complete phrase without a determiner: when the latter is absent, the meaning is general (Moignet, 1988, 105-11).[8]

Some of the forms of this article are specific: for masculine nouns, *li* reliably corresponds to the nominative (singular and plural), *le* corresponds to the oblique singular and *les* corresponds to the oblique plural. Therefore, let us assume that relations are most likely to be oriented this way: *li/le/les* → noun.

Marker stacking. Since the *-s* does not reliably fixate the distribution, it has to be demoted at least one level below the article when both markers are present. Still, one must bear in mind that "inverse mistakes" are rare, and that this *-s* does not have a random distribution. In ex. 12, *-s* does not mark the case, but when the article is present, *-s* may only appear if the article is compatible.

(10) *Li* *nain* *-s* *[...] vient*
The-NOM dwarf "stacking" *-s* comes
"The dwarf comes" – Erec (Roques, 1952, v. 161)

It becomes clear that *-s* is a mere optional agreement with its morphological governor *li*. The resulting tree is shown in fig. 6. Note that the form

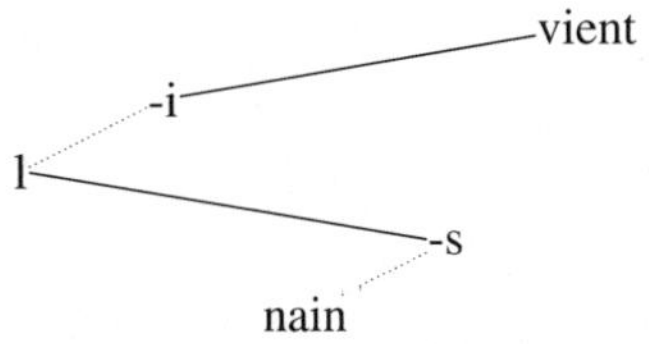

Figure 6: Analysis of OF *Li nains vient*

determination relation between *-i* and *-s* is purely morphological, according to the revision of the A2 criterion (sec. 2.2).

Intra-paradigm discrepancies. Nevertheless, feminine forms are not case-specific at all. Therefore, while *li* and *le* clearly constrain the

	MASC.		FEM.	
	sg.	pl.	sg.	pl.
NOM	li	li	la	les
OBL	le	les		

Table 3: Definite article paradigm in OF

syntactic distribution of the noun phrase, *la* and *les* do not (tab. 3); they are left completely underspecified with regard to the distribution of the nominal phrase. The result is that the articles are set in different positions in the tree. Thus, the analysis of ex. 11 is given in fig. 7.

[7] Although this paper only discusses the definite article, OF has a wide range of determiners that can accompany the noun.

[8] The fact that a morph can be omitted does not mean it does not qualifies as a governor (see sec. 2.1).

(11) *La reïne [...] voit*
The-FEM queen sees
le chevalier
the-MASC-DIROBJ knight
– Erec (Roques, 1952, v. 149)

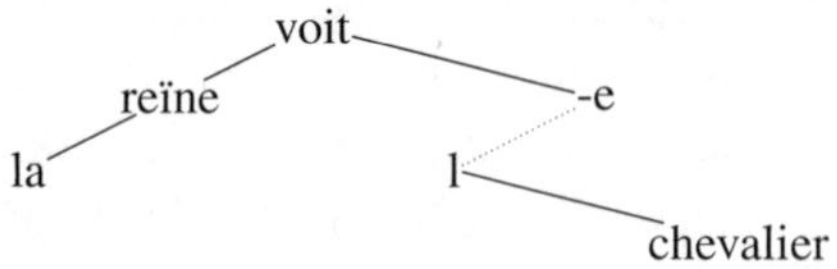

Figure 7: Analysis of OF *La reïne voit le chevalier*

While it is true that *le* → *chevalier*, because of the existence of the phrase *li* → *chevalier(s)*, that has another distribution (subject), one must posit *reïne* → *la*, because B1 does not apply well and *reïne* serves as a morphological contact point for the feminine category (B2).

3.3 Theme variation

Another important feature of OF is the existence of variable nominal themes. A subset of nouns have two themes: one specifically corresponds to the nominative singular (the form is specialized in this function), the other is not specialized. Considering examples where the specialized form stacks with a specialized definite article, such as in ex. 12. In this example, *ber* is specifically a singular nominative (plural forms and accusative forms are built on another theme: *baron*).

(12) *Cunquerrantment si finereit li*
As a hero so would end the-NOM
ber -s
noble man-NOM SG -s
"The noble man would end like a hero"
– Roland (Moignet, 1972, v. 2867)

In this example, both *ber* and *li* are specialized. Both of them correspond to the syntactic distribution of the phrase and B1 does not work well. Again, B2 works better, since it is the noun that would morphologically govern optional predicative adjectives in constructions using a copula – the copula would syntactically govern the adjective. Therefore, the hierarchy would be the one shown in fig. 8. The position of *-s* can be justified by at least two arguments: fistly, *ber* is the most specific form and should dominate the whole nominal phrase (sec. 2.1); secondly, *li* ... *-s* would not form a phrase and the relation between *-i* and *-s* is purely morphological (see sec. 2.2, 2.2).

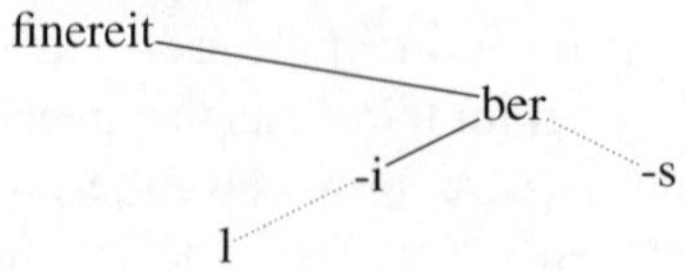

Figure 8: Analysis of OF *finereit li bers*

3.4 No overt marker at all

As a result of phenomena exposed in sec. 3.1 and sec. 3.2, segmental markers can be completely absent. A sentence where the subject and the object are both feminine nouns in *-e* displays no overt contrast between the dependents of the main verb – ex. 13 and ex. 14 (Schøsler, 1984, 34 and 41).

(13) *La nouvele oït l'abesse*
The news heard the abbess
"The abbess heard the news"

(14) *La dame esme la comtesse*
The lady thinks highly of the countess
"The lady thinks highly of the countess" or
"The countess thinks highly of the lady"

Lene Schøsler claims that the semantic properties of the dependents is the only available clue within the scope of ex. 13 (*abesse* is animate, whereas *nouvele* is not), but to understand the structure of ex. 14, only contextual clues can help. This possibility also provides strong support to the claim that markers must be seen as an additional mean to express argument structure of sentences that are mostly understandable without them (Detges, 2009).

3.5 Synthesis and diachronics

As demonstrated in the previous sections, the structure of the nominal dependents in OF is highly unstable, ranging from a completely specified construction (ex. 12) to a completely underspecified one (ex. 14). Moreover, the level of specificity of the markers is also variable. This variable specificity entails that the presence of a more specific marker automatically demotes less specific ones through a stacking mechanism (sec. 3.2 and sec. 3.3).

Through this synchronic variation, change has chosen to favor the less specified construction over the others: modern French does not use nominal inflection to mark the dependents of the verb. Therefore, a regular utterance such as ex. 15 looks exactly like ex. 14.

(15) *Le chat voit la souris*
The cat sees the mouse

Much as in English, the dependency type is expressed by the relative position of the phrases around the main verb and morphological agreement: the subject, with which the verb agrees, to the left, the object to the right[9]. The DF analysis of ex. 15 is sketched in fig. 9. The typological

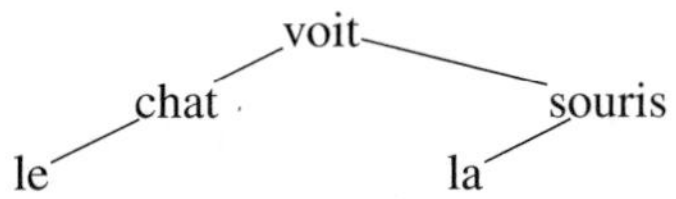

Figure 9: Analysis of Fr. *Le chat voit la souris*

contrast between Old French and modern French is strikingly clear. In the noun phrase, all morphemes (bound or free) intended to mark the relation between the verb and its arguments have disappeared. The immediate consequence of this language change is that the structure of the French noun phrase is now completely homogeneous.

4 Conclusion

DF is a great tool to emphasize the differences between the analyses of the various simple noun phrases that are described above. There is a temptation to simplify everything to give it a more coherent look and feel. From the point the perspective of this paper, this would clearly be a mistake because that would reduce syntax to a mere paradigmatic system. Why would one treat members of the same morphological paradigm exactly the same way if they behave differently at the syntactic level? On the contrary, I find it more interesting to redefine paradigms taking into account syntactic behavior.

By not smoothing trees too much, one also benefits from a powerful tool that helps discover underspecified markers. These markers are used in different trees and are demoted to lower levels when they stack with more specific ones. Therefore, DF is able to model the syntactic behavior of units that have always been problematic for traditional descriptions simply by using its core mechanics: *hierarchy*.

[9] Assuming that one accepts Willy Van Langendonck's demonstration (1994), the definite article has to be defined as a dependent of the noun. Note that transferring the idea that the determiner is the governor – "DP hypothesis", see the introduction in (Haegemann, 1994, 607-611) – from the Government and Binding framework to syntactic dependency does not change much to the conclusions of this paper: the form of the determiner does not distinguish between verbal dependents.

Acknowledgements

I would like to thank, for their suggestions and corrections (in no particular order): Thomas Groß, Sylvain Kahane, Timothy Osborne and Lene Schøsler, as well as the anonymous reviewers of the Depling conference.

References

Leonard Bloomfield. 1933. *Language*. George Allen & Undwin Ltd., London.

Claude Buridant. 2000. *Grammaire nouvelle de l'ancien français*. Sedes, Paris.

Jean-Pierre Chambon and Rosa Davidsdottir. 2007. Approche de la déclinaison des substantifs en ancien français: de moignet à skøarup (lecture critique et suggestions). *Bulletin de la Société de Linguistique de Paris*, 102(1):173–192.

Jean-Pierre Chambon. 2003. La déclinaison en ancien occitan, ou: comment s'en débarrasser? une réanalyse non orthodoxe de la flexion substantivale. *Revue de linguistique romane*, 67:342–363.

Ulrich Detges. 2009. How useful is case morphology? the loss of the old french two-case system within a theory of preferred argument structure. In Jóhanna Barđdal and Chelliah Shobhana, editors, *The Role of Semantic, Pragmatic, and Discourse Factors in the Development of Case*, number 108 in Studies in Language Companion Series, pages 93–120. Benjamins, Amsterdam.

Thomas Groß. 2011. Catenae in morphology. In Kim Gerdes, Elena Hajičová, and Leo Wanner, editors, *Proceedings of Depling 2011, International Conference on Dependency Linguistics, Barcelona*, pages 47–57. Barcelona.

Lilinane Haegemann. 1994. *Introduction to Government and Binding Theory*. Blackwell, Oxford and Malden, 2nd edition.

Richard Hudson. 1990. *English word grammar*. Blackwell, Oxford.

Gilbert Lazard. 1984. La distinction entre nom et verbe en syntaxe et en morphologie. *Modèles linguistiques*, 6(1):29–39.

Alain Lemaréchal. 1983. Sur la prétendue homonymie des marques de fonction: la superposition des marques. *Bulletin de la Société de Linguistique de Paris*, 78(1):53–76.

Alain Lemaréchal. 1997. *Zéro(s)*. Linguistique nouvelle. Presses universitaires de France, Paris.

Igor Mel'čuk. 2009. Dependency in natural language. In Alain Polguère and Igor Mel'čuk, editors, *Dependency in linguistic description*, pages 1–110. John Benjamins, Amsterdam and Philadelphia.

Gérard Moignet, editor. 1972. *La chanson de Roland*. Bordas, Paris, 3rd edition.

Gérard Moignet. 1988. *Grammaire de l'ancien français. Morphologie – Syntaxe*. Number 2 in Initiation à la linguistique. Série B. Problèmes et méthodes. Klincksieck, Paris, 2nd edition.

Mario Roques, editor. 1952. *Chrétien de Troyes, Erec et Enide*. Number 80 in Classiques français du moyen âge. Champion, Paris.

Lene Schøsler. 1984. *La déclinaison bicasuelle de l'ancien français: son rôle dans la syntaxe de la phrase, les causes de sa disparation*. Number 19 in Etudes romanes de l'Université d'Odense. Odense University Press, Odense.

Lene Schøsler. 2013. The development of the declension system. In Deborah L. Arteaga, editor, *Research on Old French: the state of the art*, pages 167–186. Springer, London.

Peter Stein and Claudia Benneckenstein. 2006. Historische fallstudie: Altfranzösisch. In Vilmos Àgel, Ludwig M. Eichiner, Hans-Werner Eroms, Peter Hellwig, Hans Jürgen Heringer, and Henning Lobin, editors, *Dependenz und Valenz. Ein internationales Handbuch der zeitgenössischen Forschung. 2. Halbband*, Handbücher zur Sprach- und Kommunikationswissenschaft, pages 1508–1515. Walter de Gruyter, Berlin and New York.

Lucien Tesnière. 1966. *Éléments de syntaxe structurale*. Klincksieck, Paris, 2nd edition.

Willy Van Langendonck. 1994. Determiners as heads? *Cognitive Linguistics*, 5(3):243–259.

Arnold M. Zwicky. 1985. Heads. *Journal of linguistics*, 21:1–29.

AnCora-UPF: A Multi-Level Annotation of Spanish

Simon Mille[1] **Alicia Burga**[1] **Leo Wanner**[1,2]
[1] Natural Language Processing Group, Pompeu Fabra University, Barcelona, Spain
[2] Institució Catalana de Recerca i Estudis Avançats (ICREA)
firstname.lastname@upf.edu

Abstract

There is an increasing need for the annotation of multiple types of linguistic information that are rather different in their nature, e.g., word order, morphological features, syntactic and semantic relations, etc. Quite frequently, their annotation is combined in a single structure, which not only results in inadequate annotations of treebanks and consequent low-quality applications trained on them, but also is deficient from a theoretical (linguistic) perspective. We present a new corpus of Spanish annotated on four independent levels, morphology, surface-syntax, deep-syntax and semantics, as well as the methodology that allows for obtaining it with fewer cost while maintaining a high inter-annotator agreement.

1 Introduction

There is an increasing need in stochastic dependency-oriented NLP applications (among them, semantic role labeling or semantic analysis, sentence generation, abstractive summarization, etc.) to deal not only with syntactic, but also with semantic information. This need implies that dependency treebanks must be annotated with both syntactic and semantic information, as, e.g., the Prague Dependency Treebank (PDT) 2.0 for Czech (Hajič, 2004; J.Hajič et al., 2006) and the Italian Syntactic-Semantic Treebank (S.Montemagni et al., 2003). However, most of the widely-known treebanks contain only one layer of annotation, namely the syntactic one; see, e.g., the dependency version of the Penn TreeBank (Johansson and Nugues, 2007) for English, Talbanken05 for Swedish (Nilsson et al., 2005), and SynTagRus for Russian (Apresjan et al., 2006). To also offer semantic annotation, some corpora have been enriched a posteriori by semantic information; cf., e.g., Penn Treebank/PropBank (Palmer et al., 2005)/NomBank (Meyers et al., 2004) or Ancora (Taulé et al., 2008). The disadvantage of such amendments is that they risk to intermingle syntactic and semantic information in the same annotation scheme, which then negatively affects the applications trained on them. This is true in particular for Natural Language Generation: see for instance (Bohnet et al., 2010) and the first Surface-Realization Shared Task (Belz et al., 2011), who both needed to separate semantic and syntactic annotations for their experiments.

In this paper, we propose a genuinely multilevel corpus annotation scheme for Spanish and discuss a sample annotation of the corpus (Ancora-UPF), the current version of which contains 3,513 sentences (100,892 tokens).[1]

2 The layers in our annotation

Our annotation intends to ensure that (i) a level of representation does not percolate into another one, and (ii) the annotation is complete in order to allow for easy automatic processing at each layer. Following the levels of the linguistic model in the Meaning-Text Theory (Mel'čuk, 1988), we annotate four different layers on top of the sentence level: morphological, surface-syntactic, deep-syntactic, and semantic.

2.1 Morphological layer

The morphological layer is a simple chain of surface lexical units bearing morpho-syntactic information. Surface lexical units are all the items of the vocabulary, that is, words as they appear in any monolingual dictionary, and their inflected variants. In Table 1, all possible values of all morpho-syntactic features used in our annotation are detailed. In addition to features such as gender and number, we use three different tagsets for Part-of-Speech: a coarse-grained one, *dpos*, and two fine-grained ones: *pos* and *spos*. The difference between *pos*, which is a subset of the PoS tagset from the Penn TreeBank set (Marcus et al., 1993), and *spos* is minor, although, for instance, in parsing

[1]It includes the 3,510 sentences that AnCora comprised at the time we launched this project back in early 2008, and three additional sentences we used for early tests. For downloads, see http://www.taln.upf.edu/content/resources/495.

Proceedings of the Second International Conference on Dependency Linguistics (DepLing 2013), pages 217–226,
Prague, August 27–30, 2013.

Features	Possible values	#
dpos	A, Adv, N, V	88,873
spos	adjective, adverb, auxiliary, conjunction, copula, determiner, foreign_word, formula, interjection, interrogative_pronoun, noun, number, percentage, preposition, pronoun, proper_noun, punctuation, relative_pronoun, roman_numeral, verb	100,892
pos	CC, CD, DT, IN, JJ, N, NN, NP, PP, RB, SYM, UH, VB, VH, VV, WP, formula	100,892
id	1 to ∞	100,892
surface form	any	100,892
lemma	any	100,892
gender	C, FEM, MASC	41,735
number	PL, SG	53,608
mood	IMP, IND, SUBJ	8,116
person	1, 2, 3	8,132
tense	FUT, PAST, PRES	8,070
finiteness	FIN, GER, INF, PART	11,176

Table 1: Morpho-syntactic features

experiments reported upon in (Ballesteros et al., 2013), *spos* performed better than *pos* for labeled relation attachment. Table 2 shows the repartition of the morpho-syntactic features that not all nodes carry, while Table 3 allows for visualizing the difference between the two fine-grained part-of-speech tags.[2]

FEAT	V	N	Adj	Det	Pro	Other
finiteness	99.91	0.01	0.06	0	0	0.02
gender	2.02	46.72	14.31	32.33	4.37	0.25
mood	99.95	0.01	0	0	0	0.04
number	16.74	36.57	15.15	27.1	4.25	0.19
person	99.98	0.01	0	0	0	0.01
tense	99.98	0	0	0	0	0.02

Table 2: Distribution of features (%)

pos	spos
CC	**conjunction**
CD	cardinal number
DT	determiner
IN	**conjunction** preposition
JJ	adjective
NN	common noun
NP	proper noun
PP	personal pronoun
RB	adverb
SYM	punctuation percentage
UH	interjection
VB	**auxiliary** copula
VH	**auxiliary**
VV	verb
WP	interrogative pronoun relative pronoun
Formula	formula
-	foreign word

Table 3: Correspondences between *pos* and *spos*

[2]There are only 88,873 *dpos* features because punctuations do not receive any.

2.2 Surface-syntactic (SSynt) layer

This layer is annotated with unordered dependency trees in which labelled dependencies link pairs of surface lexical units. Thus, the nodes have a one-to-one correspondence with the nodes of the morphological level. The 47 language-specific surface-syntactic relations used for the annotation of this layer are given and briefly explained in Table 4.[3] In the corpus, 14 of these relations occur more than a thousand times; these are, from the most frequent to the less frequent: *prepos*, *det*, *punc*, *adv*, *modif*, *subj*, *obl_obj*, *dobj*, *conj*, *coord*, *aux_phras*, *attr*, *copul*, and *relat*. Depending on the application, one can need more or less tags in the annotation. In order to allow for tuning the granularity of the tagset, we organized the relations in a hierarchy (see (Mille et al., 2012) for illustration).

2.3 Deep-syntactic (DSynt) layer

The structures at this layer are dependency trees in which labelled dependencies link pairs of *deep* lexical units. To the lexical units, deep-syntactic grammemes are assigned. The deep-syntactic dependency relations (cf. Table 5) are language-independent and thus also more abstract than the surface-syntactic ones. In our corpus, the deep-syntactic layer contains only 66,980 nodes since all punctuation signs and functional nodes have been removed. In the following, the four particular cases of node-removal are listed.[4]

(a) Governed elements

The presence of a governed preposition is imposed by the subcategorization ("valency") characteristics of its head, as, e.g., the appearance of TO in *give it TO your friend*), in the sense that the preposition TO is required by 'give'. TO in itself is here void of own meaning and should thus not appear in the deep-syntactic structure. This is different in, for instance, *to go INTO/IN FRONT OF/NEXT TO/... your house*, where the preposition is meaningful (even though it is governed) and thus should appear in the deep-syntactic structure. The depen-

[3]So far, we do not have special relations for ellipses; we add a syntactic empty node in order to deal with "impossible" dependencies only in case of what is commonly known as "gapping" and "right-node-raising".

[4]Some nodes are also added in the deep-syntactic structure. Thus, when there is an empty subject, we introduce a node with the person and number information as first argument of the verb (since the verb takes that information for being inflected), and when necessary link that new node to another one with a coreference relation.

DepRel	Distinctive properties
abbrev	abbreviated apposition
abs_pred	non-removable dependent of an N making the latter act as an adverb
adv	mobile adverbial
agent	promotable dependent of a participle
analyt_fut	Prep *a* governed by future Aux
analyt_pass	non-finite V governed by passive Aux
analyt_perf	non-finite V governed by perfect Aux
analyt_progr	non-finite V governed by progressive Aux
appos	apposed element
attr	right-side modifier of an N
aux_phras	multi-word marker
aux_refl	reflexive Pro depending on a V
bin_junct	for binary constructions
compar	complement of a comparative Adj/Adv
compl1	non-removable adjectival object agreeing with subject
compl2	non-removable adjectival object agreeing with direct object
compl_adnom	prepositional dependent of a stranded Det
conj	complement of a non-coordinating Conj
coord	between a conjunct and the element acting as coordination conjunction
coord_conj	complement of a coordinating Conj
copul	cliticizable dependent of a copula
copul_clitic	cliticized dependent of a copula
det	non-repeatable left-side modifier of an N
dobj	verbal dependent that can be promoted or cliticized with an accusative Pro
dobj_clitic	accusative clitic Pro depending on a V
elect	non-argumental right-side dependent of a comparative Adj/Adv or a number
iobj	dependent replaceable by a dative Pro
iobj_clitic	dative clitic Pro depending on a V
juxtapos	for linking two unrelated groups
modal	non-removable, non-cliticizable infinitive verbal dependent
modif	for Adj agreeing with their governing N
num_junct	numerical dependent of another number
obj_copred	adverbial dependent of a V, which agrees with the direct object
obl_compl	right-side dependent of a non-V element introduced by a governed Prep
obl_obj	prepositional object that cannot be demoted, promoted or cliticized
prepos	complement of a preposition
prolep	for clause-initial accumulation of elements with no connectors
punc	for non-sentence-initial punctuations
punc_init	for sentence-initial punctuation
quant	numerical dependent which controls the number of its governing N
quasi_coord	for coordinated elements withthe no connector
quasi_subj	a subject next to a grammatical subject
relat	finite V that modifies an N
relat_expl	adverbial finite clause
sequent	right-side coordinated adjacent element
subj	dependent that controls agreement on its governing V
subj_copred	adverbial dependent of a V agreeing with the subject

Table 4: 47 dependency relations used at the surface-syntactic layer

dents involved in the following SSynt-relations are concerned: *agent*, *compar*, *dobj*, *iobj*, *obl_compl*, and *obl_obj*. We also remove all subordinating conjunctions *que* 'that' when they introduce an argument of a predicate.

(b) Auxiliaries

An auxiliary is a functional element and therefore should not appear as such in a "deep" structure. However, it expresses semantic grammatical significations, namely tense (past: *haber* 'have' + past participle; future: *ir* 'go' + preposition *a* 'to' + infinitive), aspect (progressive: *estar* 'be' + present participle) or voice (passive: *ser* 'be' + past participle). These significations must be reflected in the deep-syntactic structure. For this purpose, corresponding attributes have been introduced to capture tense, aspect and voice: 'tense' for tense (with as possible values *present*, *future* and *past*); 'tem_constituency' for aspect (with as possible values *simple*, *progressive*, *perfect*, *perfect progressive*); and the attribute 'voice', with the values *active* or *passive*. However, since there are two ways to realize passive voice in Spanish (one with an auxiliary and one with a reflexive pronoun), the mapping between a deep-syntactic verb with "voice=passive" and its superficial counterpart is not straightforward.

(c) Determiners

Definite *el* 'the' and indefinite *un* 'a' determiners (at least) should be removed from the deep-syntactic annotation: they indicate degrees of givenness, and in this respect account for a part of the information and coreference structures. The determiners can be replaced by attribute/value pairs assigned to the governing noun (*given* VS *new*). However, we are conscious that there is no reliable way to identify automatically the givenness of nouns, since there is no systematic correlation between the presence or the absence of a determiner for a noun and its givenness. A manual annotation of givenness would be needed for some tasks; for instance, for a generator to learn correctly how to deal with the introduction of determiners in a superficial structure. For now, we only annotate definiteness on nouns so as to encode the presence of a definite or indefinite determiner at the surface. All other determiners (demonstrative, possessives, etc.) are kept in the deep annotation because they can encode more than mere givenness: possessives can receive any edge in deep-syntax since they can stand for a modifier (*su silla* 'his/her chair') or an argument (first argument: *su traducción* 'his/her translation (of something)'; second argument: *su elección* 'his/her election (by someone)', etc.) of the governing noun. The determiners that are maintained in DSynt receive the dependency relation *ATTR*.

(d) Relative Pronouns

Relative pronouns with antecedent should be substituted by their antecedent in the deep-syntactic structure, and a coreference link added between them. Given how we annotate relative clauses (see Figure 1), we can always find the antecedent of the pronoun as the governor of the *relat* relation.

DepRel	Short description
I	first argument
II	second argument
III	third argument
IV	fourth argument
V	fifth argument
VI	sixth argument
APPEND	backgrounded modifier
ATTR	regular modifier
COORD	coordinate
coref	special coreference relation

Table 5: 9 dependency relations used at the deep-syntactic layer

The deep-syntactic grammemes comprise the features of the more superficial layers (see Table 1), and some additional features specific to this level (see Table 6). We see that the feature(s) *id_ssynt* store the correspondence between the DSynt node and one or more SSynt nodes.

DSynt Feature	Possible values
coref_id	1 to ∞
definiteness	DEFINITE | INDEFINITE | N/A
id_ssynt1	1 to ∞
id_ssynt2	1 to ∞
id_ssyntn	1 to ∞
tem_constituency	SIMPLE | PROGRESSIVE | PERFECT | PERFECT PROGRESSIVE
voice	ACTIVE | PASSIVE

Table 6: Additional (compared to SSynt) grammemes used in the DSynt annotation

2.4 Semantic (Sem) layer

A semantic structure is an acyclic predicate-argument graph. The nodes at the semantic level in our corpus are the same as the nodes at the deep-syntactic level. In other words, in the first version of the corpus, we do not generalize the word labels: different words which have identical meanings keep a different label in semantics. However, we add six different types of meta-nodes in order to encode information stored as feature/values in the previous layers or to connect non-predicative units to the rest of the structure:[5]

ROOT: it has only one argument, and simply indicates which node of the semantic structure is the most important; it directly relates with the main node of the sentence, that is, usually, the main verb of the main clause.

TENSE: the first argument is by convention the event, and the second argument indicates whether it was in the past, is in the present, or will be in the future.

NUMBER: following the same model as *TENSE*, the first argument is the semantic number, and the second argument is the value *SINGULAR* or *PLURAL*. Note that this should concern semantic number only, and not lexical number. For instance, the number of the word *paro* 'unemployment' in Figure 1d is *lexical*; it cannot vary. As a result, it should not be an argument of a node *NUMBER*. However, in this version of the corpus, all nouns receive a number.

TEM_CONSTITUENCY: again, the first argument is by convention the event, and the second argument indicates whether it is progressive, perfect, both or none.

ELABORATION: this meta-node is used to connect to the semantic graph those non-predicative deep-syntactic nodes that receive the relations ATTR or APPEND. The node ELABORATION takes the dependent as its second argument, and the governor as its first one. It is mainly used in the case of apposition. In Figure 1c, there are two predicative attributes, *este* 'this' and the head of the relative clause, *engrosar* 'make swell'; in both cases, their syntactic governor is their first argument and, therefore, no ELABORATION node is needed to connect them to the semantic structure. However, in some appositive constructions, for instance, the apposed element cannot take its DSynt governor as argument: in *Pipo, mi perro* 'Pipo, my dog', we have Pipo-*ATTR*→perro, and *perro* is not a predicate. An extra node is therefore needed to connect it to the structure. The attributive relation in this case stands for the fact that the governor is the name given to the dependent; subsequently,

[5]Meta-nodes are shown in upper case in Figure 1d, while regular nodes are in lower case.

we should have at the semantic level 'Pipo'←2-NAME-1→'perro'. However, since we did not undertake a manual revision of the semantic layer as yet, we use for now the generic label *ELABORATION* in all cases, considering that the second argument somehow elaborates on the first one.

POSSESS: as already mentioned in Section 2.3, when the possessive determiner is not an argument, it usually stands for a possession relation between the governor, which will be the second semantic argument, and the dependent, which will be the first one.[6]

These predicates are called "meta" because they encode information that is necessary at the semantic level of representation, but that should not be considered the same as other nodes, since they should not be realized as words in the final sentence. If we would not differentiate one type of node from the other, Figure 1d could result in a sentence like "The document, the number of which is singular, suggests in a present time that ...".[7] Finally, the semantic features are (i) a unique individual ID, (ii) an ID that indicates the correspondence with DSynt nodes, and (iii) an attribute that encodes the definiteness of some nouns.

The nomenclature of predicate-argument relations is given in Table 7;[8] an example of each annotation level is shown in Figure 1.

DepRel	Short description
1	first argument
2	second argument
3	third argument
n	nth argument

Table 7: Predicate-argument relations used at the semantic layer

2.5 Format

In order to facilitate the processing of the superficial layers of the annotation, the sentence, morphological and surface-syntactic layers are pre-

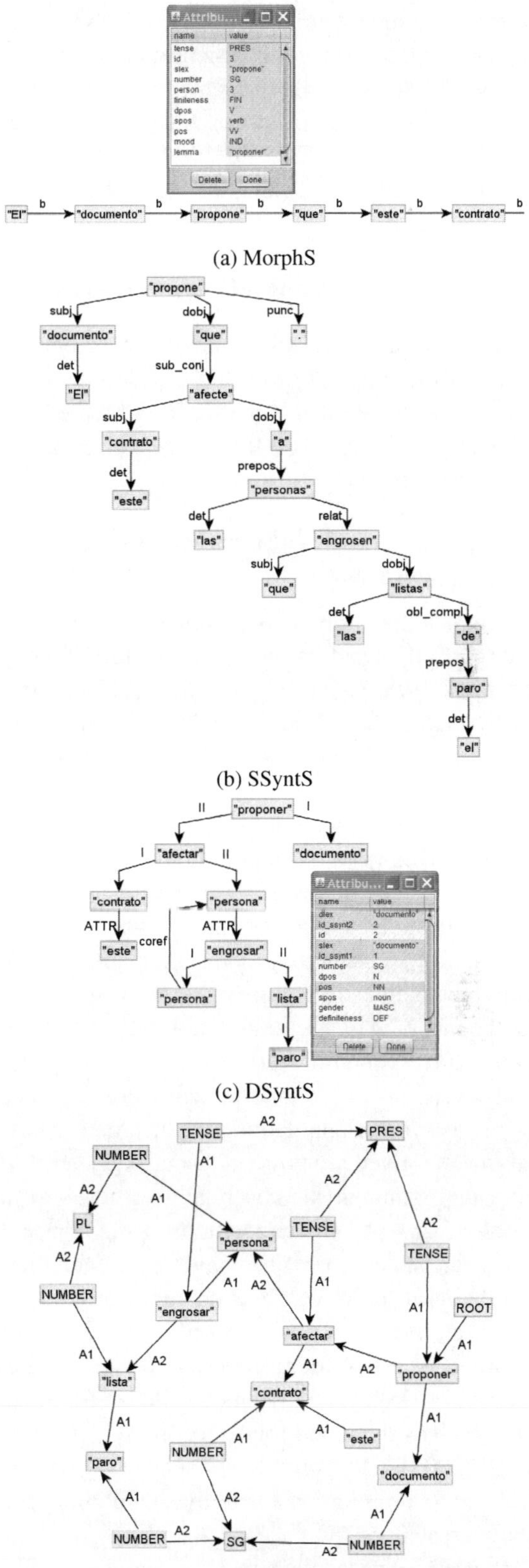

(a) MorphS

(b) SSyntS

(c) DSyntS

(d) SemS

Figure 1: The four levels of annotation for the sentence *El documento propone que este contrato afecte a las personas que engrosen las listas del paro* 'The document suggests that this contract affect the persons who make the unemployment lists swell'

[6]These three last meta-nodes are not shown in Figure 1d in order to make the figure more readable.

[7]Technically, the information encoded until now in the semantic structure is still not sufficient to regenerate the sentence as it was on the surface: the information structure also constrains the realization of the semantic graph. However, as we consider the superimposing of an information structure on a semantic network as a different task, this is out of the scope of this paper.

[8]Note that unlike the semantic annotation of PTB/PB, the semantic structure in MTT has transparent semantic frames, in the sense that no difference is made between external or internal arguments.

sented in a single standard 14-column CoNLL file. The deep-syntactic layer is also provided in a separate CoNLL file, while the semantic layer is presented in the HFG format used in the Surface-Realization Shared Task in 2011 (Belz et al., 2011). The different layers are connected thanks to the IDs of the nodes.

3 Multilayered annotation in practice

Annotating such a corpus manually can seem too costly at the first sight. In this section, we show that a solid theoretical framework and the use of adequate tools can allow for significant reduction of the manual workload.

3.1 The advantages of our theoretical framework

As already mentioned, our annotation model is strongly influenced by the Meaning-Text Theory (Mel'čuk, 1988). Its rich stratification facilitates a clear separation of different types of linguistic phenomena and thus a straightforward handling for various NLP-applications. Equivalent annotations for other theoretical frameworks can be easily derived from our representations—which is why we believe that MTT in general has considerable advantages. But on top of that, the MTT model is a transductive model (Kahane, 2003). This means that it also provides the instruments for the mapping of a representation at a given level to the corresponding representations at the adjacent levels. This has an interesting consequence as far as corpus annotation is concerned: starting from a given stratum and a manually created mapping grammar (the coverage does not need to be broad at first), the annotations at the adjacent strata can be easily obtained, and they can on their turn be used to derive the annotations at the next strata, and so on. In other words, with a corpus of SSyntSs, it is straightforward to derive parallel corpora of DSyntSs and SemSs using an adequate tool, such as the graph transducer MATE (Bohnet et al., 2000). The process of annotation can be reduced to a minimal manual revision of automatically created structures.

For the surface-syntactic annotation, we use our detailed annotation schema that allows for relatively easy dependency relation identification, based on easy-to-use criteria. The annotation schema has been defined taking into account that (a) the schema should cover only criteria that are related to the *syntactic* behaviour of the nodes; (b) the granularity of the schema should be balanced in the sense that it should be fine-grained enough to capture language-specific syntactic idiosyncrasies, but be still manageable by the annotator team.[9] The latter led us target a set of around 50 SSyntRels. For details on when we establish a dependency between two nodes as well as its direction, and to see which criteria we used for labelling dependencies, see (Burga et al., 2011).

3.2 Annotation of the morphological and surface-syntactic layers

The dependency treebank from which we started is AnCora-DEP-ES in its 2008 version (Taulé et al., 2008). The surface-syntactic annotation procedure comprised two stages: (1) an automatic projection of the annotations of the sentences from AnCora onto rudimentary surface-syntactic structures (see (Mille et al., 2009) for more details); (2) multiple manual revisions of the structures obtained in Stage 1. For the revision work carried out by a small team of trained annotators, the graph editor of the graph transducer MATE was used (Bohnet et al., 2000).

To facilitate the annotation of the deeper levels, we split 14 of the relations shown in Table 4 into more fine-grained relations which also encode predicate-argument information. Those labels are used to derive automatically rather complete deep-syntactic structures (see Section 3.3), but are not retained in the surface-syntactic annotation, which only includes the 47 original labels. That is, in order to label the dependencies, the annotator has to follow the syntactic guidelines, and when annotating some of the relations in the DepRel column of Table 4, add or not a suffix to the label, based on three criteria:

(1) What is the configuration of the underlying predicate-argument structure? (5 DepRel→ 25)

For the DepRel *iobj*, *iobj_clitic*, *obl_compl*, *obl_obj*, the goal is to associate to the dependent a slot in the valency frame of its governor: by convention, we number the argument slots from 0 to 5, although they correspond to the first to the sixth arguments. For this, we asked the annotators to (i) consider the definition of the predicate, which can only be complete if all its arguments are mentioned, and (ii) evaluate the importance of each ar-

[9] We refer here, first of all, to decision making and inter-agreement rate.

gument with respect to this predicate, which allows for assigning them a slot in its valency. At the first glance, the task may appear subjective and thus difficult. However, the very large majority of predicates have between one and three arguments. This makes the task easier, especially for verbs, for which the subject (in active voice) is always considered the first argument,[10] and the direct object the second. In case of oblique or indirect objects or oblique complements (see Table 4 for more details), the decision can be harder to make. But the high inter-annotator agreement rate obtained for the task (see Section 3.5) indicates that the intuition of the annotators coincides to a large extent. Consider, for example, the predicate *proponer* 'suggest': its definition would be something like "an entity E1 giving an idea I to another entity E2 for E2 to consider I". In other words, *proponer* has three arguments, E1, I, E2; E1 and I are almost never omitted, which makes them higher in the argument hierarchy than E2, and the entity "who does" is considered more important than what is done. As a result, we have E1=Arg1 (subject), I=Arg2 (direct object), and E2=Arg3 (oblique object 2).

In addition to object and complement DepRel, the reflexive auxiliary *aux_refl* tag is subdivided into four groups: direct (the pronoun is the second argument of the verb and has a coreference link with its subject), indirect (same as direct but the pronoun is third argument), passive (the pronoun is not an argument but triggers an inversion of first and second arguments in the DSyntS), and lexical (the pronoun is just a part of the verb's lemma).

(2) Is the dependent parenthetical?(6 DepRel→ 12)
This criterion is used in order to distinguish between two levels of modification for basic modifiers, one being closer to the governor than the other. For instance, the *adv* DepRel below a verb indicates the presence of a circumstancial element related to the verb itself, while the *adjunct* DepRel indicates that the circumstancial operates at the sentence level: (normalmente←*adjunct*-corre-*adv*→[cada dia] 'usually he runs every day'). For nominal governors (*appos*, *attr*, *modif*, *quant*, *relat*), the descriptive extension is usually granted to groups separated by a comma from their head.

(3) Is the dependent quoted? (3 DepRel→ 6)
In simple terms, it is the group formed by the dependent and all its dependents surrounded by quotation marks, which indicate an actual quotation. Consider, for illustration, the difference between *dijo "me voy"* 'he said "I'm going"' (quote), and *¡Mira, el "presidente" llega!* 'Look, the "president" is arriving!', in which the quotation marks are a stylistic way of making fun of someone. Three DepRel are concerned: *subj*, *dobj* and *prepos*.

As a result, instead of 14 DepRel, the annotator has to consider 43, that is, 29 more. So far, this gives us 76 different tags (47 + 29). In addition, we further split for testing reasons (which we do not have space to detail in this paper) the label *conj* into *sub_conj* and *compar_conj*, and added a third label *restr* when splitting the DepRel *adv*. Thus, the total tagset which represents the base of our annotation process comprises **79 different tags**. We refer to this tagset as the "Annotation SSynt DepRel" tagset (SSynt DepRel$_A$).

As for the annotation at the morphological layer, it was mostly derived automatically from the AnCora annotation.

3.3 Annotation of the deep-syntactic layer

As mentioned in Section 2, the deep-syntactic layer has the form of an unordered dependency tree. The edges encode explicit valency relations, and also coordination and modifications, while only meaning-bearing units are accepted as nodes. Multi-word expressions are fused into single nodes. Sentence-internal coreferential links are superimposed on the annotation. All surface-syntactic relations (except *det*, see Section 2.3) have a direct correlation with deep-syntactic configurations.

Taking this into account, together with the syntactic properties of each DepRel (e.g., *obl_obj* points to a governed preposition, i.e., to a functional node which does not carry any meaning on its own), the mapping between SSynt and DSynt can be largely automatic (for instance, the DSyntS shown in Figure 1c has required no manual modification, although this is not always the case). The workload of the annotator is reduced to (i) addition of coreferences between nodes of the same sentence, (ii) definition of the argument slot of possessive pronouns when necessary, and (iii) repair of possible erroneous rule applications. There are currently 129 rules in the SSynt-DSynt mapping grammar, and its coverage is not yet complete,

[10]This is why there is no extension 0 for verbal relations (iobj, iobj_clitic, obl_obj), and also why by default we start numbering the arguments from the second.

as some very specific configurations are still not taken into account. However, we intend to expand the coverage as much as possible in the future. An average-length sentence (around 30 nodes) takes an annotator around one and a half minutes to process (while without the automatic annotation derivation it takes her/him about 10 minutes).

SSynt	DSynt	SSynt	DSynt
abbrev	ATTR	iobj_clitic1	II
abs_pred	ATTR	iobj_clitic2	III
adjunct	APPEND	iobj_clitic3	IV
adv	ATTR	iobj_clitic4	V
adv_mod	ATTR	iobj_clitic5	VI
agent	I	juxtapos	APPEND
analyt_fut	-	modal	II
analyt_pass	-	modif	ATTR
analyt_perf	-	modif_descr	APPEND
analyt_progr	-	num_junct	COORD
appos	ATTR	obj_copred	ATTR
appos_descr	APPEND	obl_compl0	I
attr	ATTR	obl_compl1	II
attr_descr	APPEND	obl_compl2	III
aux_phras	-	obl_compl3	IV
aux_refl_dir	II	obl_compl4	V
aux_refl_indir	III	obl_compl5	VI
aux_refl_lex	-	obl_obj1	II
aux_refl_pass	-	obl_obj2	III
bin_junct	ATTR	obl_obj3	IV
compar	II	obl_obj4	V
compar_conj	II	obl_obj5	VI
compl1	II	prepos	II
compl2	III	prepos_quot	II
compl_adnom	ATTR	prolep	APPEND
coord	COORD	punc	-
coord_conj	II	punc_init	-
copul	II	quant	ATTR
copul_clitic	II	quant_descr	APPEND
copul_quot	II	quasi_coord	COORD
det	any	quasi_subj	I
dobj	II	relat	ATTR
dobj_clitic	II	relat_descr	APPEND
dobj_quot	II	relat_expl	APPEND
elect	ATTR	restr	ATTR
iobj1	II	sequent	ATTR
iobj2	III	sub_conj	II
iobj3	IV	subj	I
iobj4	V	subj_copred	ATTR
iobj5	VI		

Table 8: Mapping of the 79 SSynt DepRel$_A$ onto DSynt DepRel

Table 8 indicates that some SSynt DepRel$_A$ are not mapped to any DSynt DepRel. This is due to the fact that some nodes (namely the functional ones) are removed from the deep-syntactic structure. The idea is that from the perspective of Natural Language Generation (NLG) from abstract structures, the system will only have access to non-linguistic data; see, e.g., (Bouayad-Agha et al., 2012). This implies that a system that generates statistically from those abstract representations MUST be able to learn when to introduce functional words (i.e., words that carry a grammatical content, but no own lexical meaning). Therefore, a corpus claimed to be suitable for training statistical NLG modules should always take this

SSynt DepRel$_A$	Changes in DSynt
analyt_fut	remove Gov and Dep add tense=FUT
analyt_pass	remove Gov invert I and II add voice=PASS
analyt_perf	remove Gov add tense=PAST
analyt_progr	remove Gov add tem_constituency=PROGR
aux_refl_dir	replace node label with antecedent's add coreference between I and II
aux_refl_indir	replace node label with antecedent's add coreference between I and III
aux_refl_lex	remove Dep add *se* at the end of Gov's lemma
aux_refl_pass	remove Dep invert I and II add voice=PASS
det	**IF Dep=ellun** remove Dep add definiteness=DEF/INDEF
	IF Dep=possessive replace node label with antecedent's edit DSynt DepRel add coreference link with antecedent
	IF Dep=other map *det* to *ATTR*
dobj/iobj1-5/obl_compl0-5 obl_obj1-5	remove Dep if governed preposition
relat/relat_descr	replace node label with antecedent's add coreference link with antecedent
..._conj	remove Dep if governed preposition

Table 9: More complex SSynt to DSynt mappings

into account. In addition, the removal of functional nodes allows the generators to deal with different surface realizations when several realizations are possible (e.g., *give something to Mary* VS *give Mary something*). Having in parallel two layers, one with all the words, and one without the functional words, is one way to provide the basis for statistical models.

Since, as we have seen in Section 3.3, not all surface-syntactic nodes are mapped to the deep-syntactic level, some configurations imply non-typical equivalences. Table 9 completes Table 8 by summarizing all mappings of SSynt DepRel$_A$ to something else than a single DSynt DepRel.

3.4 Annotation of the semantic layer

Since in the deep-syntactic layer all grammatical units are removed from the structure, the mapping to a connected acyclic graph entirely composed of predicate-argument relations that connect any meaning-bearing unit used in the sentence (which includes DSynt nodes and some additional meta-nodes) is much easier. A different mapping grammar from the one detailed in Section 3.3 can transform the deep-syntactic structure in Figure 1c into a semantic structure shown in Figure 1d.

During this second mapping, all nodes from the deep-syntactic structure are transferred, except nodes which have a coreference relation with another node. Only one node that stands for all coreferring nodes appears in the semantic structure; all edges that point to a node which is removed are transferred to that one node.[11]

Most relations can be derived in a straightforward way: Roman numerals map to Arabic numerals, and *ATTR*, *APPEND* and *COORD* edges are inverted and relabelled with *1* when the DSynt dependent is a predicate. Otherwise, we introduce meta-predicates like, for instance, *ELABORATION* or *POSSESS* in order to connect the equivalent of the DSynt dependent to the graph (see Section 3.4).

In the procedure of obtaining the annotation at the semantic layer, the mapping grammar does all the work, and there is no need for manual revision at all.

3.5 Inter-annotator agreement

Due to the still preliminary nature of our deep-syntactic and semantic annotations, we evaluated the inter-annotator agreement so far only for the surface-syntactic annotation. However, we used the 79-relation tagset, which facilitated the automatic derivation of the deeper annotations; see Section 3. This tagset thus allows us to indirectly obtain the deep layer inter-annotator agreement (while the 47-relation tagset gives us the SSynt-layer inter-annotator agreement)—with the exception of possessive determiners, which are mapped to a variety of different deep-syntactic relations (ATTR, I, II, etc.). Therefore and given that possessive determiners represent only 1% of the total number of dependencies in the corpus, we decided not to take them into account in the deep evaluation.

To obtain the material for the inter-annotator agreement evaluation, we parsed with Bohnet's parser (Bohnet, 2009), trained on the surface-syntactic annotation the *lingüística* 'linguistics' wikipedia page,[12] 72 sentences in total (2,443 tokens). Two annotators then post-edited in separate sessions every sentence using the 79-tag tagset as described in Section 3.2. Drawing upon the surface-syntactic tag hierarchy described in (Mille et al., 2012), the resulting two annotations were further generalized to 47, 31 and 15 tags, such that we obtained parallel annotations for four different annotations.

Taking one annotation of each pair as gold standard and the other as "predicted", we ran the CoNLL'08 evaluation and calculated the LAS. The results are displayed in Table 10.

	79	47	31	15
UAS (%)	96.15	96.15	96.15	96.15
LAS (%)	89.40	92.26	92.51	92.80

Table 10: Inter-annotator agreement.

Since the successive mappings from 79 to 15 DepRel only concern the edge labels, it is normal that the Unlabeled Attachment Score remains the same for all tagsets. As expected, the agreement rate correlates with the number of tags in the tagset. Thus, we reached 89.4%, including predicate-argument identification 92.26%, with the 47 DepRel given in Table 4 in Section 2.2, and up to 92.8% with the reduced tagset of 15 DepRels. All inter-annotator agreement figures oscillate around the 90% threshold recommended in the OntoNotes project (Hovy et al., 2006).

4 Conclusions and future work

In this paper, we report on the results of the annotation of a Spanish corpus, in which the different levels of annotation are clearly separated. We show that thanks to a sound theoretical framework and appropriate tools, it is possible to reduce the manual workload and, at the same time, achieve a high inter-annotator agreement rate on all evaluated levels (more than 92% for syntax and more than 89% for syntax and semantics). These figures are largely due to the fact that the criteria that define each dependency relation have been carefully selected and are exclusively linguistically motivated. However, the 3-point difference between semantic and syntactic tagsets confirms that predicate-argument structures are less easily identifiable than syntactic dependencies since the criteria that define them are not as straightforward as syntactic criteria. In the future, we aim to augment the size of our tree bank, work on improving the predicate-argument identification, and add the dimension of the information structure. Both the treebank and all resources developed during the annotation (guidelines, software, etc.) will be made available to the community.

[11]Our mapping grammar actually has a parameter that allows for keeping the coreferring nodes separated in the SemS. This can be useful for experiments on information structure.

[12]Prior to parse it, the page has been cleaned.

Acknowledgements

We would like to thank warmly Bernd Bohnet, Roberto Carlini, Gabriela Ferraro, Kim Gerdes, Antónia Martí, and Igor Mel'čuk. It is because of them that this work became possible.

References

J. Apresjan, I. Boguslavsky, B. Iomdin, L. Iomdin, A. Sannikov, and V. Sizov. 2006. A syntactically and semantically tagged corpus of Russian: State of the art and prospects. In *Proceedings of LREC*, pages 1378–1381.

M. Ballesteros, S. Mille, and A. Burga. 2013. Exploring morphosyntactic annotation over a spanish corpus for dependency parsing. In *Proceedings of DepLing*.

A. Belz, M. White, D. Espinosa, E. Kow, D. Hogan, and A. Stent. 2011. The first surface realisation shared task: Overview and evaluation results. In *Proceedings of the Generation Challenges Session at ENLG*, pages 217–226.

B. Bohnet, A. Langjahr, and L. Wanner. 2000. A development environment for an MTT-based sentence generator. In *Proceedings of INLG*, pages 260–263.

B. Bohnet, L. Wanner, S. Mille, and A. Burga. 2010. Broad coverage multilingual deep sentence generation with a stochastic multi-level realizer. In *Proceedings of COLING*, pages "98–106".

B. Bohnet. 2009. Efficient Parsing of Syntactic and Semantic Dependency Structures. In *Proceedings of CoNLL-2009*.

N. Bouayad-Agha, G. Casamayor, S. Mille, M. Rospocher, H. Saggion, L., and L. Wanner. 2012. From Ontology to NL: Generation of Multilingual User-Oriented Environmental Reports. In *Proceedings of NLDB*, Groningen, The Netherlands.

A. Burga, S. Mille, and L. Wanner. 2011. Looking Behind the Scenes of Syntactic Dependency Corpus Annotation: Towards a Motivated Annotation Schema of Surface-Syntax in Spanish. In *Proceedings of DepLing*, pages 104–114.

J. Hajič. 2004. Complex corpus annotation: The prague dependency treebank. Bratislava, Slovakia. Jazykovedný ústav L'. Štúra, SAV.

E. Hovy, M. Marcus, M. Palmer, L. Ramshaw, and R. Weischedel. 2006. Ontonotes: The 90% solution. In *Proceedings of HLT/NAACL*, pages 879–884, USA, June.

J.Hajič, J. Panevová, E. Hajičová, P. Sgall, P. Pajas, J. Štěpánek, J. Havelka, M. Mikulová, and Z. Žabokrtský. 2006. Prague Dependency Treebank 2.0. Linguistic Data Consortium, Philadelphia.

R. Johansson and P. Nugues. 2007. Extended constituent-to-dependency conversion for English. In *Proceedings of NODALIDA*, pages 105–112, Tartu, Estonia, May 25-26.

S. Kahane. 2003. The Meaning-Text Theory. In *Dependency and Valency. Handbooks of Linguistics and Communication Sciences*, volume 1-2. De Gruyter.

M.P. Marcus, B. Santorini, and M.A. Marcinkiewicz. 1993. Building a large annotated corpus of English: The Penn Treebank. *Computational Linguistics*, 19(2):313–330.

I. Mel'čuk. 1988. *Dependency Syntax: Theory and Practice*. State University of New York Press, Albany.

A. Meyers, R. Reeves, C. Macleod, R. Szekely, V. Zielinska, B. Young, and R. Grishman. 2004. The NomBank Project: An interim report. In *Proceedings of the NAACL/HLT Workshop on Frontiers in Corpus Annotation*.

S. Mille, L. Wanner, V. Vidal, and A. Burga. 2009. Towards a rich dependency annotation of Spanish corpora. In *Proceedings of SEPLN*, San Sebastian, Spain.

S. Mille, A. Burga, G. Ferraro, and L. Wanner. 2012. How does the granularity of an annotation scheme influence dependency parsing performance? In *Proceedings of COLING*, Mumbai, India.

J. Nilsson, J. Hall, and J. Nivre. 2005. MAMBA meets TIGER: Reconstructing a Swedish treebank from antiquity. In *Proceedings of NODALIDA*, pages 119–132.

M. Palmer, P. Kingsbury, and D. Gildea. 2005. The Proposition Bank: An annotated corpus of semantic roles. *Computational Linguistics*, 31.

S.Montemagni, F. Barsotti, and M. Battista et al. 2003. Building the Italian syntactic-semantic treebank. In Anne Abeillé, editor, *Building and Using Syntactically Annotated Corpora*, pages 189–210.

M. Taulé, M. A. Martí, and M. Recasens. 2008. Ancora: Multilevel annotated corpora for Catalan and Spanish. In *Proceedings of LREC*, Marrakech, Morocco.

Towards Building Parallel Dependency Treebanks: Intra-Chunk Expansion and Alignment for English Dependency Treebank

Debanka Nandi, Maaz Nomani
Jamia Hamdard, New Delhi, India
debanka.nandi0@gmail.com, maaz_nomani@hotmail.com

Himanshu Sharma, Himani Chaudhary, Sambhav Jain, Dipti Misra Sharma
IIIT-H, Hyderabad, India
{himanshu.sharma,himani,sambhav.jain}@research.iiit.ac.in
dipti@iiit.ac.in

Abstract

The paper presents our work on the annotation of intra-chunk dependencies on an English treebank that was previously annotated with Inter-chunk dependencies, and for which there exists a fully expanded parallel Hindi dependency treebank. This provides fully parsed dependency trees for the English treebank. We also report an analysis of the inter-annotator agreement for this chunk expansion task. Further, these fully expanded parallel Hindi and English treebanks were word aligned and an analysis for the task has been given. Issues related to intra-chunk expansion and alignment for the language pair Hindi-English are discussed and guidelines for these tasks have been prepared and released.

1 Introduction

Recent years have seen an increasing interest in research based on parallel corpora. Statistical machine translation systems use parallel text corpora to learn pattern-based rules. These rules can be simple or sophisticated, based on the level of information present in the corresponding parallel corpus. Earlier research in statistical MT utilized just sentence and lexical alignment (Brown et al., 1990) which requires merely a sentence and word aligned parallel text. Later, to acquire these rules the alignment of a parsed structure in one language with a raw string in the other language emerged (Yamada and Knight, 2001; Shen et al., 2008). Of late, the focus has been on exploring these rules from the alignment of source/target language parse trees (Zhang et al., 2008; Cowan, 2008). Also, mapping from a source language tree to a target language tree offers a mechanism to preserve the meaning of the input and producing a target language tree helps to ensure the grammaticality of the output (Cowan, 2008). Thus there is a need for aligned parallel treebanks with alignment information on top of their parsing information.

And, with the availability of a number of treebanks of various languages now, parallel treebanks are being put to use for analysis and further experiments. A parallel treebank comprises syntactically annotated aligned sentences in two or more languages. In addition to this, the trees are aligned on a sub-sentential level. (Tinsley et al., 2009). Further, such resources could be useful for many applications, e.g. as training or evaluation corpora for word/phrase alignment, as also for data driven MT systems and for the automatic induction of transfer rules. (Hearne et al., 2007)

Our work using two parallel dependency treebanks is another such effort in this direction. It includes:

1. Intra-chunk expansion of the English treebank previously annotated with Inter-chunk dependencies, for which there exists a fully expanded parallel Hindi dependency treebank.

2. An analysis of the inter-annotator agreement for the chunk expansion task mentioned in (1) above.

3. Alignment of the two treebanks at sentence and also at word level.

A chunk, by definition, represents a set of adjacent words in a sentence, which are in dependency relation with each other, and where one of these words is their head. (Mannem et al., 2009). The task of dependency annotation is thus divided into: inter-chunk dependency annotation (relations between these chunks) and intra-chunk

Proceedings of the Second International Conference on Dependency Linguistics (DepLing 2013), pages 227–235,
Prague, August 27–30, 2013.

dependency annotation (relations between words inside the chunk).

Some notable efforts in this direction include the automatic intra-chunk dependency annotation of an inter-chunk annotated Hindi dependency treebank, wherein they present both, a rule-based and a statistical approach to automatically mark intra-chunk dependencies on an existing Hindi treebank (Kosaraju et al., 2012). Zhou (2008) worked on the expansion of the chunks in the Chinese treebank TCT (Qiang, 2004) through automatic rule acquisition.

The remainder of the paper is organized as follows: In Section 2, we give an overview of the two dependency treebanks used for our work, and their development. Section 3 describes the guidelines for intra-chunk dependency annotation. In Section 4, we talk about issues with the expansion and our resolutions for them. Further, it presents the results of the inter-annotator agreement. Section 5 comprises our work on alignment of parallel Hindi-English corpora and the issues related to that. We conclude and propose some future works towards the end of the paper.

2 Treebanks

We make use of the English dependency treebank (reported in Chaudhry and Sharma (2011)), developed on the Computational Paninian Grammar (CPG) model (Bharati et al., 1995), for this work. This treebank is parallel to a section of the Hindi Dependency treebank (reported in Bhatt et al. (2009)) being developed under the Hindi-Urdu Treebank (HUTB) Project and was created by translating the sentences from HUTB. The English treebank is much smaller in size, with around 1000 sentence (nearly 20K words) as compared to its Hindi counterpart which has about 22800 sentences (nearly 450K words). There is a difference in size of nearly 1000 words between the English treebank and its parallel Hindi treebank from which it was translated. This is because the translations involve both literal and stylistic variations.

The annotation labels used to mark the relations in the treebank conform to the dependency annotation scheme reported in Chaudhry and Sharma (2011), which is an adaptation of the annotation scheme given by Begum et al. (2008), for Hindi. Further, as per these annotation schemes, dependency relations in the treebank are marked at chunk level (between chunk heads), instead of being marked between words.

The Hindi treebank also had intra-chunk dependency relations marked on it, along with the inter-chunk dependencies. And since the English dependency treebank used here, is relatively much newer, there was scope for further work on it. We thus expanded this treebank at intra-chunk level, annotating each node within the chunk with its dependency label/information. Annotating the English treebank with this information brings it at par with the parallel Hindi treebank, making them better suited for experimentation on parallel treebanks.

Further, the earlier version of the treebank was annotated only with the inter-chunk dependencies. Consequently, this enforced a restriction to interpret the chunk merely as a group of words with the head of the group as its representative. The relations among other nodes inside the chunk remained unaccounted for. Now, with the intra-chunk dependencies also marked, the treebank has complete sentence level parsing information, giving access to the syntactic information associated with each node in the tree.

Additionally, the dependency annotation is done using Sanchay annotation interface, and the data is stored in Shakti Standard Format (SSF).[1] (Bharati et al., 2006).

3 Intra-chunk Expansion

As mentioned earlier, the English dependency treebank used here, is relatively much smaller than its parallel Hindi treebank. Given this, we manually expanded this treebank at intra-chunk level, and performed an inter-annotator analysis for this task. Preparation of a set of guidelines for the expansion is another aspect of this effort.

This section of the paper reports our annotation of intra-chunk dependencies (dependency relations among the words within chunks) on the English dependency treebank (described in Section-2) in which inter chunk dependencies are already marked using the CPG model. Adding the intra-chunk annotation provides a fully parsed dependency treebank for English.

The intra-chunk dependencies for this task, were annotated manually (by two annotators). Inter-annotator agreement values for this intra-chunk annotation were then calculated. Both of these tasks are reported in this section, as also, a

[1] http://ltrc.iiit.ac.in/mtpil2012/Data/ssf-guide.pdf

discussion of the types of issues encountered in the annotation.

For the purpose of intra-chunk annotation, the chunk expansion guidelines for the Hindi Treebank expansion were taken as a point of reference and adapted to suit the requirements of the English treebank. The guidelines thus prepared, were used to annotate the intra-chunk dependencies in the English treebank. After the initial annotation and a subsequent analysis of the encountered ambiguous cases, they have been updated accordingly.

The guidelines thus prepared, serve to ensure consistency across multiple annotations. There are a total of 18 intra-chunk tags in the guidelines. The tags are of three types: (a) normal dependencies, eg. nmod__adj, jjmod__intf, etc., (b) local word group dependencies (lwg), eg. lwg__prep, lwg__vaux, etc., and (c) linking part-of dependencies, eg. pof__cn. (Table 1)

Local Word Groups (lwg) are word groups formed on the basis of 'local information' (i.e. information based on adjacent words) (Bharati et al., 1995). 'lwg' dependencies occur due to adjacency of words in a local word group. These are of two types: simple-lwg dependencies and linking-lwg dependencies (termed as 'linking part-of dependencies' above). Linking-lwg dependencies are marked for words that are parts of an LWG, and don't modify each other (usually used in compound nouns, named-entities etc.). Normal dependencies are marked for individual words and don't represent a relation with the complete local word group. For Ex. nmod_adj relation is for a **Noun modifier** of the type **Adjective**. Here the association of the adjective is not with the complete 'lwg', but with a particular noun which may or may not restrict the meaning of the 'lwg'.

Label Type	Label Description
nmod__adj	Noun modifier of the type adjective
nmod__n	Noun modifier of the type noun
jjmod__intf	Adjective modifier of the type intensifier
lwg__det	A determiner associated with an LWG
lwg__inf	An infinitive marker associated with LWG
lwg__prep	A preposition associated with LWG
lwg__neg	A negation particle associated with LWG
lwg__vaux	An auxiliary verb associated with LWG
lwg__rp	A particle associated with LWG
lwg__uh	An interjection particle associated with LWG
lwg__poss	A possession marker associated with LWG
lwg__adv	An adverb associated with LWG
lwg__ccof	Arguments of a conjunct associated with LWG
lwg__emph	An emphatic marker associated with LWG
lwg__v	Verbal nouns (participials, gerunds etc.) associated with LWG
pof__cn	Part-of relation expressing continuation
pof__redup	Part-of relation expressing reduplication
rsym	Symbols

Table 1: Label Types and Descriptions

4 Inter-Annotator Agreement: Evaluation and Analysis

4.1 Evaluation Criteria

The guidelines for Intra-chunk Expansion were created by studying different possible cases of chunk expansion. The guidelines, in total, list 18 different intra-chunk tags. These intra-chunk labels along with 34 inter-chunk labels make a total of 52 dependency tags. Inter-Annotator Agreement was then calculated on these fully expanded dependency trees for the 2 annotators.

Fleiss's Kappa (Fleiss, 1971) is used to calculate the agreement, which is a commonly used measure for calculating agreement over multiple annotators. Table 3 shows the agreement strength relative to the kappa statistic. The Fleiss's kappa is calculated as :

$$\kappa = \frac{Pr(a) - Pr(e)}{1 - Pr(e)}$$

The factor 1 - Pr(e) gives the degree of agreement that is attainable above chance, and, Pr(a) - Pr(e) gives the degree of agreement actually achieved above chance.

$$Pr(a) = \frac{1}{Nn(n-1)} \sum_{i \in N} \sum_{j \in k} (n_{ij}^2 - Nn)$$

$$Pr(e) = \sum_{j \in k} p_j^2 \qquad \text{where,}$$

$$p_j = \frac{1}{Nn} \sum_{i \in N} n_{ij}$$

Along with the Fleiss Kappa, we also calculate the Unlabelled Attachment and Labelled Attachment accuracies for the fully expanded trees in Table 4. The inter-chunk labels were not excluded for calculating the above mentioned statistics. This is because identifying the head in a chunk is also an important step in creating a fully connected tree. It has been further analysed in Section 4.2 and shown that identifying a different head might lead to different fully expanded trees, and therefore, must be included in the calculation of final statistics.

Edge Pairs	Unlabelled Attachment (UA)	Label Accuracy	Labelled Attachment
1718	1605 (93.42%)	1611 (93.77%)	1554 (90.45%)

Table 4: Attachment and Label Accuracy

Edge Pairs	Agreement	Pr(a)	Pr(e)	Kappa
1605	1554	0.955	0.061	0.952

Table 2: Kappa statistics for Inter-Annotator Experiment

Kappa Statistic	Strength of agreement
<0.00	Poor
0.0-0.20	Slight
0.21-0.40	Fair
0.41-0.60	Moderate
0.61-0.80	Substantial
0.81-1.00	Almost perfect

Table 3: Coefficients for the agreement-rate based on (Landis and Koch, 1977).

4.2 Analysis

Besides calculating the inter-annotator agreement, cases with disagreement were analysed for possible errors and cases of ambiguities in the guidelines. The observed cases which led to percentage error in inter-annotator agreement were then resolved and the guidelines were updated, so as to reduce potential errors arising due to these in future. A few of the observed cases have been discussed below:

1. **Named Entity Handling**

   Since the treebank doesn't have Named Entity (NE) annotation, the handling of NEs induced an element of disagreement between the two annotations. Ex. In the case below, **The Indian Council of Medical Research** is an NE, but it has been handled differently by the two annotators.

   Whether it should be treated as a frozen unit (A compound noun with no further analysis in the structure of the name), or it should be treated as a phrase that is analysed for the association of constituents is the issue here.

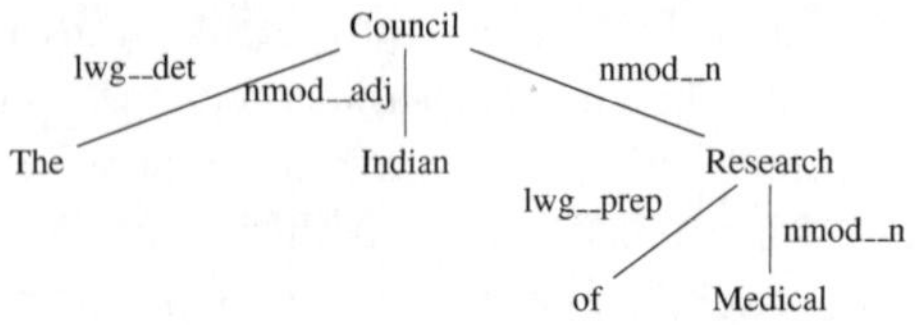

S1 : The Indian Council of Medical Research (Chunk Analysis)*

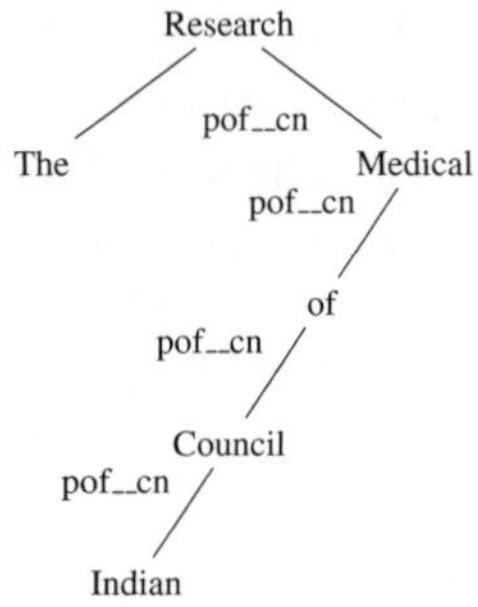

S2 : The Indian Council of Medical Research (Frozen)

We chose to consider structure-2 as the appropriate one. This decision is motivated by the observation that Named Entities are frozen expressions and may or may not always be analysable in parts. This will thus help maintain consistency in annotation of NEs across the treebank.

2. **Appositives**

   Appositives are grammatical constructions where two noun-phrases are placed adjacent to each other and one modifies or restricts the other. In the PP phrase below, **to Talib's mother Khushnuda**, there are two noun phrases **Talib's mother** and **Khushnuda** (name) and any of them can be considered as the head of the chunk. Further, the preposition **to** can attach to any of the two noun phrases.

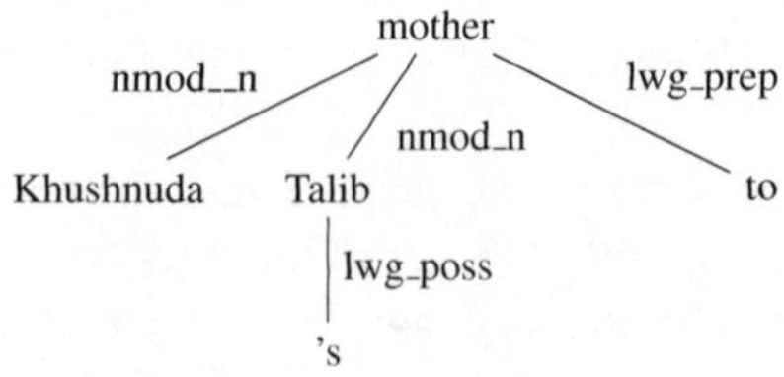

S1 : to Talib's mother Khushnuda*

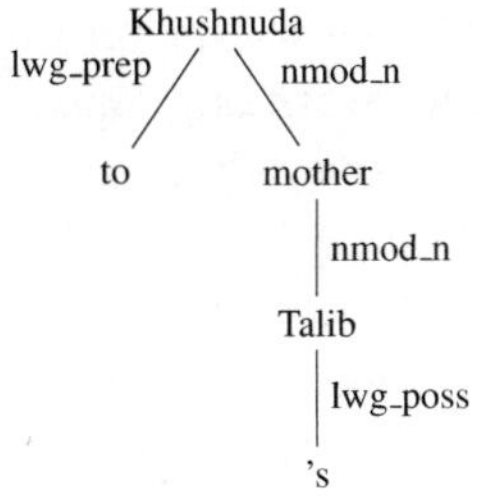

S2 : to Talib's mother Khushnuda

For these cases, the noun phrase that most specifically describes the object of discussion is taken to be the primary noun phrase and the secondary ones as its modifiers. For the above example, **Khushnuda** is the NP that specifies the head of the phrase more clearly and is thus considered to be the head, and the preposition **to** is attached to **Khushnuda**, rendering *S2* as the correct analysis.

In cases of abbreviations, where both noun phrases are different representations of the same name, we consider the expanded name to be the head and the abbreviation is attached as a modifier of the head noun. In the example below, since **The Indian Council of Medical Research** is being considered a Named Entity, **Research** is the head of the phrase and the abbreviation **ICMR** is attached to it as a modifier.

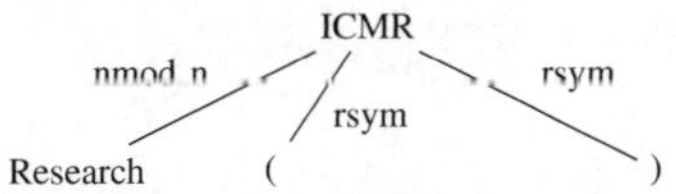

S1 : The Indian Council of Medical Research(ICMR)*

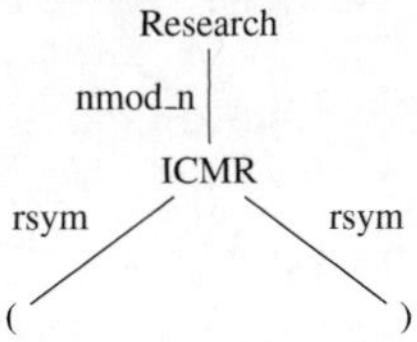

S2 : The Indian Council of Medical Research(ICMR)

3. **Head-Identification**

While annotating relations between tokens, identifying the head of a constituent is a crucial step and decides the structure of the fully expanded tree. Ex. in the PP phrase **in the next one or two days**, the most probable head is **days**. In our scheme, the coordinator is considered to be the head of the coordinated phrase, hence **or** is regarded as the head of **one** and **two** (*S1*). Another possibility is to add a NULL element in the first argument of conjunction and make the phrase **in the next one NULL or two days**, where the **NULL** is a copy of the features of **days** (*S2*).

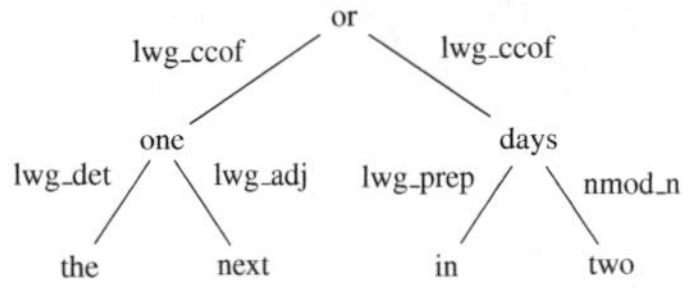

S1 : in the next one or two days*

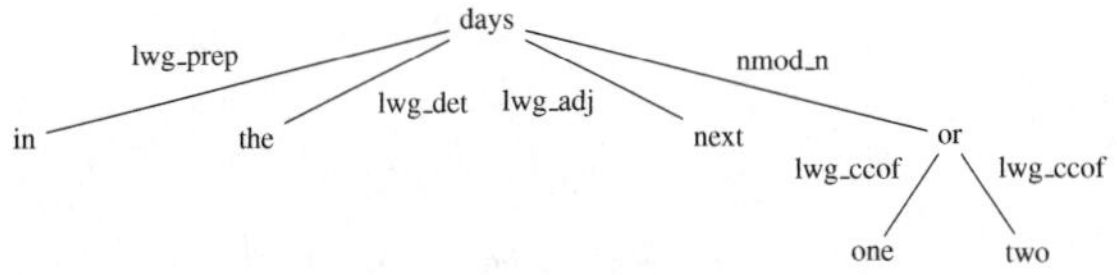

S2 : in the next one or two days

However, in the inter-chunk dependency annotation scheme NULLs are inserted only if they are crucial for representing the dependency structure. Following this, *S2* was preferred over *S1* for such cases. Also, in *S2* the association of cardinals **one** and **two** with **days** is easily visible and can be interpreted if required.

4. **Phrasal Verbs**

Phrasal verbs are verbs that include particles or prepositions. Their meaning is non-compositional, as it cannot be retrieved by individually handling the lexical items. Ex. **look after** : verb+preposition , **brought up** : verb+particle , **put up with** : verb+particle+preposition . For these cases, the verb is considered to be the head of the chunk. A clear distinction between prepositions and particles in a verb phrase has been made in our guidelines by way of different annotation labels. The associated labels are: *lwg_prep* (local-word-group preposition) and *lwg_rp* (local-word-group particle). A few examples of this are:

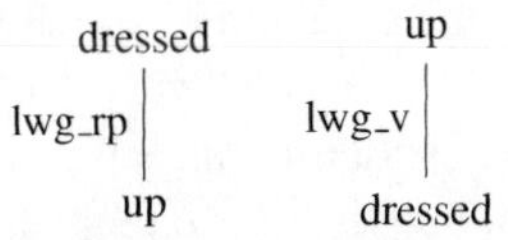

dressed up *dressed up**

5. **Genitives**

We observed disagreement between the two annotations where there were instances of multiple consecutive genitives in a single chunk. However, this cannot be resolved at the level of guidelines since the decisions in such cases would depend on the world knowledge of annotators and would have to be resolved contextually and individually. The example below illustrates this further.

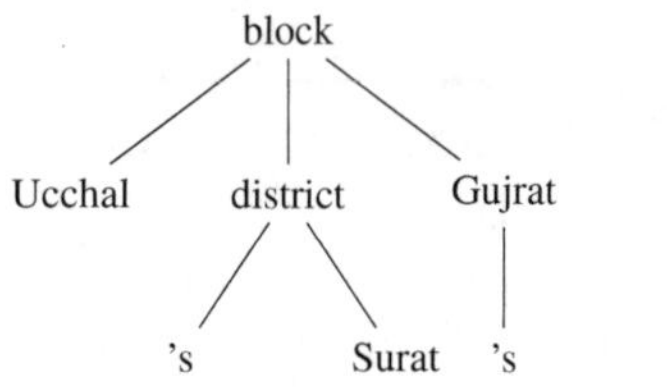

S1 : Gujrat's Surat district's Ucchal block*

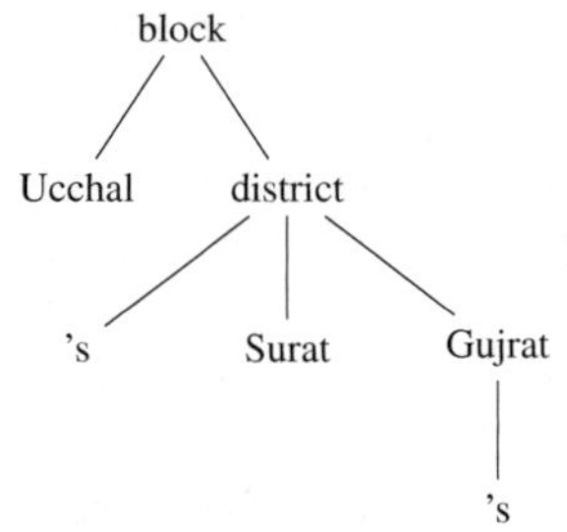

S2 : Gujrat's Surat district's Ucchal block

Here the knowledge whether **Surat** is a **district** in **Gujrat** or not is important in deciding if **Gujrat** should modify **District** (in *S2*) or **block** (in *S1*). Here, since **Surat** is a district in **Gujrat**, **Gujrat**, *S2* would be the correct analysis rejected.

5 Alignment

In this task, the fully expanded English dependency trees, obtained after the intra-chunk expansion, were aligned with their respective counterparts in the Hindi Dependency Treebank(Fully expanded Hindi dependency trees).

Due to limitations of the available annotation tools, one cannot align trees from one language to the other directly in a structural manner. Thus, we chose to align the data at the textual level and then incorporated them in the already existing treebank. *Sanchay*[2] was chosen as the alignment tool after experimenting with some openly available tools such as GATE, Cairo etc.

The alignment was done in two stages :

1. *Sentence Alignment* : First, parallel text files (Hindi and English) were aligned on the sentence level.

[2]Sanchay : http://www.sanchay.co.in

2. *Word Alignment* : A set of guidelines were created for word alignment, by doing a pilot study on a small dataset. As we encountered issues during the alignment, these guidelines were updated accordingly.

After the two alignment tasks, the word aligned data was merged with the respective treebanks.

5.1 Issues in Alignment

5.1.1 Sentence Alignment Issues

For sentence alignment, a basic postulate was that all the events must be captured in a sentence aligned pair [(source sentences)-(target sentences)]. As is commonly observed in studies of parallel corpora, the target language sometimes removes argument information, or adds extra arguments to provide a sound translation. These cases are not considered as a divergence at the level of sentence alignment, since the selection criteria is strictly limited to event information. In our task, we encountered 4 types of sentence alignment structures. These are :

1. *One-to-One Mapping* : When all the events in a source sentence are mapped to events in the target sentence, we say that there is a One-to-One mapping. For instance, in Figure-1, all the source sentences are mapped to exactly one target sentence, although crossed.

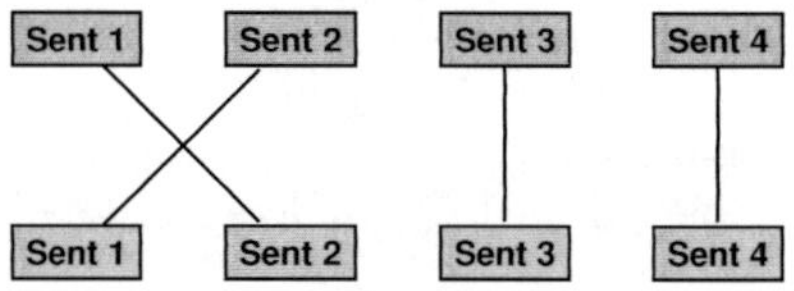

Figure 1: One-to-One Alignment

2. *Many-to-One Mapping* : Cases where multiple source sentences map to a single sentence in the target language, i.e. events in multiple source sentences are incorporated into a single target sentence. In Figure-2, Sent-2, Sent-3 and Sent-4 of the source language go to Sent-3 of the target Language.

3. *One to Many Mapping* : Single source language sentence is divided into multiple target language sentences. In Figure-2, Sent-1 of source language is aligned to both Sent-1 and Sent-2 of the target language.

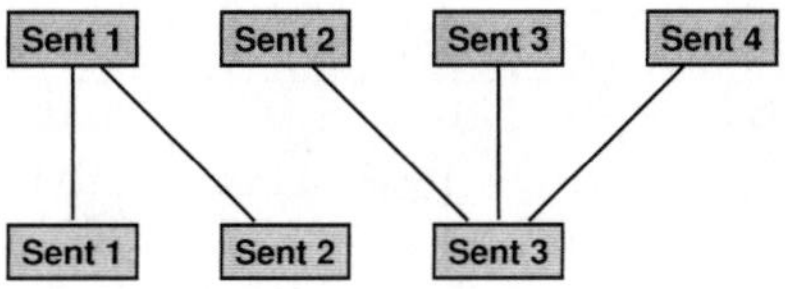

Figure 2: One-to-Many, Many-to-One Alignment

4. *Many to Many Mapping* : Events are distributed unevenly in source and target sentences. In example x, for a pair of source and target sentences, the mapping resembles a 'Z' structure. Such sentences were altered to convert them into one of the above three types. Figure-3 shows the Z-structure observed in those cases. This particular case can be resolved by changing the sentence alignments as per Figure-4.

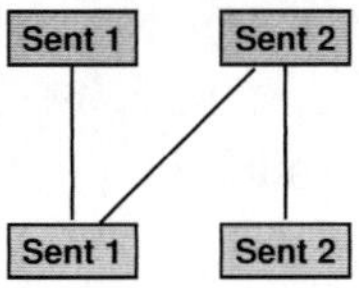

Figure 3: Many-to-Many Alignment

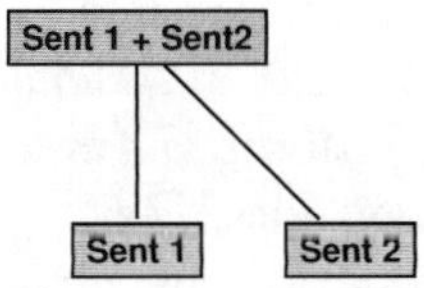

Figure 4: Many-to-Many Alignment(Altered)

5.1.2 Word Alignment Issues

During word alignment, the main focus was on the maintaining the syntactic and semantic functions of the words across the language pair. For many cases, it was not possible to syntactically align the words, as is observed in stylistic translations, idiomatic usages, multi-word expressions etc. The similarity in the semantic function of the words was the deciding factor for these cases.

During the course of annotation and while developing the guidelines, few issues related to word alignment were encountered. Given below is a summary of the types of divergences that were found, with a few examples.

1. **Multi Word Expressions(MWE)** :
   Multi word expressions in source languages are translated to another MWE in the target language or vice-versa. These are divided into two types :

   - *Many-to-One* OR *One-to-Many* alignments are the those where MWE in one language maps to a single word in another language. In such cases, all the constituting words of the MWE are mapped to that single word in the target language. Ex. Hindi : ***'aguvAI karne vAle'*** goes to English ***'heading'*** in Example-1.

     (1) .. *xala* *kI* ***aguvAI*** ***karne***
     .. group of head do
     vale *KAna* ..
     ATTR Khan ..
     ".. Khan **heading** the group .."

   - In cases of *Many-to-Many* alignment, where the MWE is literally translated with/without retaining the sense, we map each individual token of the MWE to their respective mappings in the other language. Thus, essentially reducing the problem to either *One to One*, *One to Many* or *Many to One*. For cases, where MWEs are not literally translated, we map all the tokens in the source language MWE to the head of the MWE chunk in the target language.

2. **Mismatched syntactic categories** :
   Many syntactic categories like determiners, infinitives are realized differently (syntactically/structurally) in Hindi. Ex. English determiner ***'A'*** goes to Hindi ordinal ***'eka'*** sometimes, and doesn't have a mapping for other cases . These functional categories are mapped to either the token aligned with the head of their chunk (category) or to the element which is functionally similar. In Example-2, English determiner ***'every'*** is mapped to Hindi noun ***'kaxama'***. In this particular case, Hindi employs the use of reduplication to get the same meaning as the determiner ***'every'***.

   (2) .. ***kaxama*** ***kaxama*** *para*
   .. step step at
   BraStACAra *hE* ..
   corruption is ..
   ".. corruption is at **every step** .."

Tag	RP	CC	NEG	J	N	QF+	QC	DEM	RB	V	PSP	PRP
FW	0	3	0	0	4	0	0	0	0	0	0	0
V	10	3	11	133	287	4	2	2	7	1323	114	8
PRP+	4	2	0	6	21	0	0	8	0	8	10	237
DT	6	4	8	73	445	24	40	93	5	9	24	55
RP	0	0	0	2	7	0	0	0	2	17	5	0
NNC	0	0	0	0	5	0	0	0	0	0	2	0
TO	2	3	0	6	8	0	0	0	2	37	123	2
RB+	68	24	52	20	48	10	5	3	29	14	36	50
CC	2	163	0	0	2	0	0	2	2	0	7	2
J	4	2	5	229	104	24	11	5	9	28	34	8
N	3	0	7	80	2457	13	16	16	7	44	161	20
IN	14	132	5	10	115	8	5	6	10	49	661	27
CD	2	0	0	3	18	0	82	0	0	2	0	0
MD	4	0	4	8	3	0	0	0	2	85	3	0

Table 5: POS Mappings

3. **Syntactic difference** :
   In cases where a certain word/phrase is present in the source language, while its equivalent is absent in the target. These differences arise due to many reasons including stylistic variation, syntactic differences (word-order), Many to One MWE mappings etc. For Ex. Post-positions in Hindi have a certain mapping to prepositions in English. Though, the prepositions don't always realize. For Ex. *Hindi chunk: rAma ne* is aligned to *English chunk: Ram*. Here, there is no preposition to align with the post-position *ne*. In such cases, the dependents are attached to the word in the target language aligned to it's head element. Thus, the post-position *ne*, here, is aligned to *Ram*.

   It may be noted that, this issue is different from (2) (Mismatched Syntactic Categories) where the meaning of the phrase was being realized in the sentence via some other word that belongs to a category different from the category of the source-word. Here, it is not possible to align individual words due to position, word-order, nature of MWE (literal/metaphorical) and other issues which arise due to syntactic differences between the two languages.

5.1.3 POS Tag

For the purpose of analysis and manual alignment quality evaluation, the POS tag mappings were recorded in a table (Table-5). The POS tagsets are different for English and Hindi treebanks. The English Treebank uses Penn POS Tagset (Marcus et al., 1993), while Hindi treebank is annotated as per Bharati et al. (2006). Keeping the large number of POS categories and differences in tagsets in view, some POS category columns have been merged in the table. For Ex. We merged the categories for JJ,JJR,JJS into J (Adjective) for English POS tagset and JJC,JJ into J for Hindi POS tagset for comparison and error analysis over broad syntactic categories. Major categories such as verbs, adjectives, adverbs, nouns etc. have a considerable mapping ratio in the word aligned data. All the odd POS alignment pairs, such as PostPosition-Determiner, Verb-Preposition, Question Words-Prepositions and many more, were studied and wherever deemed possible, errors in POS tags of these cases were corrected. Cases related to the above-mentioned issues were documented and will be available with the parallel treebank.

Conclusion and Future Work

In this paper we reported our work on Intra-Chunk Annotation and Expansion of the English Treebank, inter-annotator studies over the same, and furthermore, alignment over the expanded parallel data. The reported inter-annotator reliability measure value for intra-chunk expansion was $\kappa = 0.95$. A further analysis of the ambiguous cases was done and the guidelines were further improved so as to resolve the cases of confusion. We extended this work with alignment over parallel Hindi-English fully expanded dependency treebanks in the CPG formalism. A set of guidelines are also prepared for manual alignment of data in Hindi-English language pair. The POS Matrix analysis could provide some insights in the divergences between the two languages. This work could prove helpful in bi-text projections, language divergence studies and statistical machine translation and we hope to take these as our future work.

Acknowledgments

We gratefully acknowledge the provision of the useful resource by way of the Hindi Treebank developed under HUTB, of which the Hindi treebank used for our research purpose is a part, and the work for which is supported by the NSF grant (Award Number: CNS 0751202; CFDA Number: 47.070). Also, any opinions, findings, and conclusions or recommendations expressed in this material are those of the author(s) and do not necessarily reflect the views of the National Science Foundation.

References

R. Begum, S. Husain, A. Dhwaj, D.M. Sharma, L. Bai, and R. Sangal. 2008. Dependency annotation scheme for indian languages. In *Proceedings of IJCNLP*.

Akshar Bharati, Rajeev Sangal, and Vineet Chaitanya. 1995. *Natural Language Processing: A Paninian Perspective*. Prentice-Hall of India.

Akshar Bharati, D.M. Sharma, Lakshmi Bai, and Rajeev Sangal. 2006. Anncorra: Guidelines for pos and chunk annotation for indian languages. Technical report, IIIT-H.

R. Bhatt, B. Narasimhan, M. Palmer, O. Rambow, D.M. Sharma, and F. Xia. 2009. A multi-representational and multi-layered treebank for hindi/urdu. In *Proceedings of the Third Linguistic Annotation Workshop*, pages 186–189. Association for Computational Linguistics.

P.F. Brown, J. Cocke, S.A.D. Pietra, V.J.D. Pietra, F. Jelinek, J.D. Lafferty, R.L. Mercer, and P.S. Roossin. 1990. A statistical approach to machine translation. *Computational linguistics*, 16(2):79–85.

H. Chaudhry and D.M. Sharma. 2011. Annotation and issues in building an english dependency treebank.

B.A. Cowan. 2008. *A tree-to-tree model for statistical machine translation*. Ph.D. thesis, Massachusetts Institute of Technology.

J.L. Fleiss. 1971. Measuring nominal scale agreement among many raters. *Psychological bulletin*, 76(5):378.

M. Hearne, J. Tinsley, V. Zhechev, and A. Way. 2007. Capturing translational divergences with a statistical tree-to-tree aligner.

P. Kosaraju, B.R. Ambati, S. Husain, Sharma, D.M., and R. Sangal. 2012. Intra-chunk dependency annotation: Expanding hindi inter-chunk annotated treebank.

J.R. Landis and G.G. Koch. 1977. The measurement of observer agreement for categorical data. *Biometrics*, pages 159–174.

P. Mannem, H. Chaudhry, and A. Bharati. 2009. Insights into non-projectivity in hindi. In *Proceedings of the ACL-IJCNLP 2009 Student Research Workshop*, pages 10–17. Association for Computational Linguistics.

Mitchell P. Marcus, Mary Ann Marcinkiewicz, and Beatrice Santorini. 1993. Building a large annotated corpus of english: the penn treebank. *Comput. Linguist.*, 19(2):313–330.

Z. Qiang. 2004. Annotation scheme for chinese treebank. *Journal of Chinese Information Processing*, 18(4):1–8.

L. Shen, J. Xu, and R. Weischedel. 2008. A new string-to-dependency machine translation algorithm with a target dependency language model. *Proceedings of ACL-08: HLT*, pages 577–585.

J. Tinsley, M. Hearne, and A. Way. 2009. Exploiting parallel treebanks to improve phrase-based statistical machine translation. *Computational Linguistics and Intelligent Text Processing*, pages 318–331.

K. Yamada and K. Knight. 2001. A syntax-based statistical translation model. In *Proceedings of the 39th Annual Meeting on Association for Computational Linguistics*, pages 523–530. Association for Computational Linguistics.

M. Zhang, H. Jiang, A. Aw, H. Li, C.L. Tan, and S. Li. 2008. A tree sequence alignment-based tree-to-tree translation model. *Proceedings of ACL-08: HLT*, pages 559–567.

Q. Zhou. 2008. Automatic rule acquisition for chinese intra-chunk relations. In *Proceedings of International Joint Conference of Natural Language Processing (IJCNLP)*.

Annotators' Certainty and Disagreements in Coreference and Bridging Annotation in Prague Dependency Treebank

Anna Nedoluzhko
Charles University in Prague
Faculty of Mathematics and Physics
Institute of Formal and Applied Linguistics
Czech Republic
nedoluzko@ufal.mff.cuni.cz

Jiří Mírovský
Charles University in Prague
Faculty of Mathematics and Physics
Institute of Formal and Applied Linguistics
Czech Republic
mirovsky@ufal.mff.cuni.cz

Abstract

In this paper, we present the results of the parallel Czech coreference and bridging annotation in the Prague Dependency Treebank 2.0. The annotation is carried out on dependency trees (on the tectogrammatical layer). We describe the inter-annotator agreement measurement, classify and analyse the most common types of annotators' disagreement. On two selected long texts, we asked the annotators to mark the degree of certainty they have in some most problematic points; we compare the results to the inter-annotator agreement measurement.

1 Introduction

The coreference and bridging annotation in the Prague Dependency Treebank (PDT) is one of the largest existing manually annotated corpora for pronominal, zero and nominal coreference and bridging relations. Contrary to the majority of similarly aimed corpus projects (Poesio 2004, Poesio – Artstein 2008, Poesio et al. 2004, Recasens 2009, Krasavina – Chiarchos 2007, etc.), coreference and bridging relations have been annotated directly on the syntactic trees and technically they are a part of the tectogrammatical (complex semantic) layer of PDT. This approach allows us to include relevant syntactic phenomena annotated earlier (such as e.g. appositions, coreference relations between subject and predicate nominals, etc.) into the coreference representation, and to take advantage of the syntactic structure itself (resolution of elliptical structures, coordinations, parentheses, foreign expressions and identification structures, direct speech, etc.)[1]. Also, from the perspective of querying and visualizing the treebank, all the different types of linguistic information are interlinked, available and visible at once. One of the important advantages is that PDT includes information on topic-focus articulation (Hajič et al. 2006) and discourse annotation (Mladová 2011).

Comparing the results of inter-annotator agreement in manual annotations of language phenomena at different language levels makes evident that the degree of agreement goes down when proceeding from phonological to "higher" language levels. On the one hand, relations that cross the sentence boundary are not so systematically described both in classical linguistics and in annotation guidelines, causing disagreements due to different understanding of terms. On the other hand, such relations are much more vague and in many cases ambiguous. Both these problems influence the measurement of the inter-annotator agreement. In this paper, we present results of the inter-annotator agreement measurement for nominal coreference and bridging relations for Czech and compare them to the degree of certainty the annotators had while marking these relations.

2 The Annotation Scheme

Within the bounds of coreference-like phenomena, three types of relations are marked in PDT:

a) grammatical coreference (coreference of relative and reflexive pronouns, verbs of

[1] The benefits of the tectogrammatical structure for coreference annotation are described in detail in Nedoluzhko – Mírovský (2013).

Proceedings of the Second International Conference on Dependency Linguistics (DepLing 2013), pages 236–243,
Prague, August 27–30, 2013.

control arguments, arguments in constructions with reciprocity and verbal complements),

b) pronominal and nominal textual coreference (including zero anaphora), which is further specified into coreference of specific (type SPEC) and generic (type GEN) noun phrases, and

c) bridging relations, which mark some semantic relations between non-coreferential entities.

The following types of bridging relations are distinguished: PART-OF (e.g. *room - ceiling*), SUBSET (*students - some students*) and FUNCT (*state - president*) traditional relations (see e.g. Clark 1977), CONTRAST for coherence relevant discourse opposites (*this year - last year*), ANAF for explicitly anaphoric relations without coreference, e.g. for metalinguistic references (*rainbow - that word*) and the further underspecified group REST[2].

Grammatical coreference typically occurs within a single sentence, the antecedent being able to be derived on the basis of grammar rules of a given language. For this reason, grammatical coreference is the least ambiguous among the coreference types, its annotation is the most reliable, being close to other grammatical phenomena annotated in PDT.

3 Solving Coreference Ambiguity in Similar Projects

Problems of low inter-annotator agreement and ambiguity in annotation of coreference and bridging relations have been topics of active discussions during the last few years. Shortcomings of straightforward definitions of coreference were pointed out in Poesio and Artstein (2005). They were later analyzed in detail using linguistic and computational methods in Versley (2008), and Recasens et al. (2010, 2011). The group of so called "near-identity" relations, where the discourse entities to which the noun phrases refer cannot be called coreferential in all senses but still are rather coreferential than not, was separated from the cases of full-coreference. Coreference was thus redefined as a scalar relation between linguistic expressions that refer to discourse entities considered to be at the same granularity level relevant to the linguistic and pragmatic context (Recasens et al. 2011). The "near-identity" relation holds e.g. between *several hundred disabled people* and *the congregated* in Versley's (2008) example (1). The groups of people addressed by these noun phrases are not the same but the difference is neutralized by the context:

(1) *For a "barrier-free Bremen," several hundred disabled people went onto the streets yesterday—and demonstrated for "Equality, not Barriers." . . . "Why always us" the congregated asked on the posters.*

However, the attempt to annotate "near-identity" explicitly has proved to be unreliable, because it is difficult for annotators to recognize such relations (Recasens et al. 2012). Also ambiguity seems to be much better identified not by asking annotators to code ambiguous expressions but by comparing the annotations produced by different annotators (Poesio and Artstein 2005). Explicitly marked ambiguity is annotated in the PoCoS corpus for German (Krasavina – Chiarchos 2007) but was not analysed in detail yet.

4 Evaluation of Parallel Annotations

F-1 on textual pronominal coreference (including zeros)	0.86[3]
F-1 on textual coreference for specific NPs	0.705
F-1 on textual coreference for generic NPs	0.492
F-1 on bridging relations	0.455
new textual kappa of agreement on type	0.759
bridging kappa of agreement on type	0.889

Table 1: Evaluation of parallel annotations

In order to evaluate the inter-annotator agreement on selected texts annotated by two or more annotators, we used F_1-measure for the agreement on arrows and Cohen's κ (Cohen 1960) for the agreement on types of arrows. During the annotation period, 11 measurements between two coders have been

[2] For a detailed classification of identity coreference and bridging anaphora used in PDT, see e.g. Nedoluzhko - Mírovský (2011).

[3] As reported in a technical report from the annotation of PDT (Kučová et al. 2003).

provided for (in total) 1,606 sentences in 39 documents.

Table 1 shows average results of the inter-annotator agreement measurements for all types of textual coreference and bridging relations.

5 Cases of Typical Disagreement

Proceeding to further phases of the annotation process didn't give us any dramatic enhancement of the inter-annotator agreement. Some later measurements have shown even lower agreement than the earlier ones, although the quality of annotating was very high. That indicated that the results primarily depend neither on the annotators' experience in the field nor on their ability to follow the guidelines.

Technically, as for the annotators, four general issues appeared to be difficult to decide: whether the relation is to be annotated for coreference/bridging at all, what is the correct antecedent of a given noun phrase, to distinguish between the bridging anaphora and the textual coreference and to select the type of the bridging anaphora or the textual coreference. These issues are closely analysed in the sections 5.1 to 5.4, with real-data examples.

5.1 Annotating / not annotating a relation

There is a relatively high degree of disagreement in the very recognition of a coreference or bridging relation in some typical cases.

The most frequent example is a general reference of noun phrases, which may and may not be annotated as coreferential.

(2) *A když už byla knížka hotova, tak se zjistilo, že je praktická i pro rodiče. V této knize je poučení, jak snášejí děti_rozvod a jak na něj reagují, a návod, jak se mají rodiče chovat, aby se utrpení dětí snížilo. (=After the book had been already written, it was clear, that it is quite useful for parents too. The book contains explanations, how children go through divorce, how they react to it, and the instructions how parents should behave to minimize the suffering of their children..)*

The disagreement is even more likely if the generic antecedent is relatively far from the noun phrase in question (example 3):

(3) *Preferuji širší předvedení s mnoha vnitřními souvislostmi, protože nám chybějí kritéria pro hodnocení současné české výtvarné kultury.* {11 sentences inbetween} *Měli bychom se znovu pokusit ... získávat současné umění, abychom jednou měli autentický soubor naší doby (= I prefer wider demonstration with many internal connections because we lack criteria for evaluation of contemporary Czech art. We should try ... to acquire the contemporary art again, in order to get an authentic set of our time.)*

5.2 Different selecting the antecedent / anaphoric element

Compare (4) - (6) for identity coreference. In (4), the anaphoric noun phrase *the new structure* corefers with *the type F railing* in one coder's annotation and with *the G Street Bridge* in the other's.

(4) *In Richmond, Ind., the type F railing is being used to replace arched openings on the G Street Bridge. Garret Boone, who teaches art at Earlham College, calls the new structure ``just an ugly bridge" and one that blocks the view of a new park below.*

The measure in (5) corefers with *the House bill on airline leveraged buy-outs* in one coder's annotation and with the extended noun phrase *legislation similar to the House bill on airline leveraged buy-outs* in the other annotation:

(5) *While the Senate Commerce Committee has approved legislation similar to the House bill on airline leveraged buy-outs, the measure hasn't yet come to the full floor.*

The following example (6) demonstrates disagreement in constructions with measure and time-period words. *The year earlier* may corefer with *prior-year* or *the prior-year period*:

(6) *That compares with operating earnings of $132.9 million, or 49 cents a share, the year earlier. The prior-year period includes...*

In (7), *Tajikistan* is linked by the bridging SUBSET relation by both coders but they chose different antecedents: one coder linked it to *these countries* (thus coreferring it to the whole coordinating construction *post-*

communist countries of Eastern Europe and the republics of the former USSR.), while the other coder made a more precise decision and linked *Tajikistan* to *the republics of the former USSR*, i.e. just to one element of the coordination. Both annotations are empirically correct, the decision depends on the coder's world knowledge.

(7) *Tiskárny bankovek mají i nové zákazníky, především v postkomunistických zemích východní Evropy a republikách bývalého SSSR. Bankovky v těchto zemích jsou náchylné na padělání a mají zastaralý design. Kanadská firma CBNC bude tisknout nové bankovky pro Tádžikistán* (= *They have new clients, first of all in the post-soviet countries of East Europe and in the republics of the former USSR. Banknotes in these countries can be easily falsified. The CBNC Company will print banknotes for Tajikistan.*)

5.3 Distinguishing between the bridging relations and the textual coreference

Disagreement in choosing between bridging relations and identity coreference relations are often the case when noun phrases have a generic or unspecific reference. In (8), the relation between *banknotes* and *undamaged banknotes* is understood as coreference by one coder and as bridging SUBSET by the other one.

(8) *I přes klesající inflaci ve světě ... je tisk bankovek a výroba bankovkového papíru jedním z nejlukrativnějších odvětví.* [...] ... *Rozšíření bankovních automatů vyžaduje neustálý přísun nepoškozených bankovek.* (= *Although inflation in the world rather decreases, ... printing banknotes and production of banknote paper is still one of the most profitable areas. Mass expansion of ATMs calls for permanent increase of undamaged banknotes.*)

5.4 Selecting the type of the bridging anaphora or the textual coreference

As for bridging relations, some relations can be disagreed on in different contexts, e.g. the relation between *Slovakia* and *Bratislava* in (9) may be understood from two different points of view. One coder marked it geographically (Bratislava is a part of Slovakia – relation PART-OF), the other understood the relation from the point of view of its function (Bratislava is the capital of Slovakia – relation FUNCT).

(9) *Slovensko po několika měsících diskusí devalvovalo svou měnu o deset procent. [...] Spíše je otázkou, zda Bratislava nepřistoupila k akci poněkud pozdě. (=After several months of discussions, Slovakia devalued its currency by ten percent. [...] The question is whether Bratislava was not somewhat late with this decision.)*

For identity coreference, types SPEC and GEN were distinguished (see section 2) according to which noun phrases the coreference relation was applied to. However, in real corpus examples, the distinction is not always clear and coders may mark it differently.

6 Reasons for Disagreement

The evaluations of parallel annotations of selected texts brought up some interesting observations. The nature of disagreements corresponds to the general problem of a formal description on such a high level of language, namely – the texts sometimes allow for different, equally relevant interpretations. Moreover, the guidelines restrict us by the number of arrows leading from one node, and only a few formalized types of coreference and bridging relations are annotated in PDT, thus it does not fully reflect the real situation of text cohesion. See e.g. (4), where the semantically correct decision would be to annotate both relations as (near-)coreference, but not disposing such rich annotation guidelines, coders have to choose one variant and disagreement is to be expected.

Reflecting the results, we were able to distinguish two main textual factors for disagreement: the text size and the degree of its abstractedness. Especially long texts with a large number of generic nouns, abstracts and deverbatives have the lowest inter-annotator agreement.

A detailed manual comparison of parallel annotations revealed that almost three quarters of the coders' disagreements come from the text ambiguity (the relations may be empirically ambiguous as in (5), where coreferring with different antecedents may change the meaning, or rather near-identical in the sence of Recasens (2010), when different interpretations are possible that do not actually change the meaning of the text as a whole).

Constructions with nouns of measure and time periods appear to be hard to agree on (see e.g. 6) – in spite of quite detailed descriptions in the guidelines, coders tend to mark them differently in different types of context according to their intuition in every particular case. Generic noun phrases, abstract nouns and deverbatives cause really rich ambiguity in almost all coreference annotation projects. However, for Czech, it results in even more disagreements (examples (2), (3) and (8)), because Czech does not have grammatical means to mark definiteness, thus forcing not to make any distinction in marking coreference between definite and indefinite noun phrases.

Marking coreference between indefinite noun phrases results in a further reason of disagreement, and that is a different level of thoroughness of the coders' interpretation. For example, in (3), the antecedent for *the contemporary art* was used 11 sentences before, the noun phrase in question is positioned as new (it has focus value in the TFA-annotation) and a coder doesn't need to see any serious reason to connect it by a coreference relation with such a distant antecedent. The similar situation is in (10) where, although not distant, the identity of *the safety and health deficiencies* and *the hazards* is up to the coder's intuition.

(10) *Gerard Scannell, the head of OSHA, said USX managers have known about many of the safety and health deficiencies at the plants for years, ``yet have failed to take necessary action to counteract the hazards."*

The rest of the coders' disagreements are caused be either a coder's mistake (cca 15% of occurences) or guidelines inconsistency (cca 10% of occurences).

7 Certainty of the Manual Annotations

To find out which part of problematic cases the coders are aware of, we organized one special inter-annotator agreement measurement. We asked the annotators to annotate the data as usual and also mark the certainty they had in several parts of the task.[4]

They were asked to mark the certainty for their annotation decisions on the scale of 1 to 3 (1 means quite certain, 2 means moderately certain, 3 means not really certain). The certainty was marked for four types of decision (tasks), according to cases of frequent disagreement described in sections 5.1-5.4, i.e. certainty in the presence of a relation, certainty in selecting the antecedent, certainty in distinguishing between the bridging relation and the textual coreference and certainty in selecting the type of the bridging anaphora or the textual coreference.

The certainty and the inter-annotator agreement were then measured separately for these tasks and (where applicable) also separately for various levels of certainty.

7.1 Certainty in the presence of a relation

Table 2 shows the average certainty the annotators expressed in various situations in the task of detecting the presence of a relation.

measurement	average certainty
one annotator marked a relation (bridging), the other has not marked any	1.88
one annotator marked a relation (coref-text), the other has not marked any	1.44
one annotator marked a relation (any relation), the other has not marked any	1.68
both annotators marked a relation (bridging)	1.35
both annotators marked a relation (coref-text)	1.17
both annotators marked a relation (any relation)	1.25

Table 2: Average certainty in the task of detecting the presence of a relation

The numbers show that the lower the agreement is, the less sure the annotators are. However, if we look at the absolute numbers of (non-)annotating textual coreference, we see that the number of cases where the annotators didn't mark uncertainty but still disagreed exceeds all other cases. In the analysed documents, uncertainty was marked in 26 cases of disagreement. In another 30 cases where only one coder annotated a coreference relation, the uncertainty was not marked.

7.2 Certainty in selecting the antecedent

Table 3 shows the inter-annotator agreement in the task of choosing the antecedent of the

[4] This measurement was performed on 190 sentences in 2 documents.

relations, depending on the relation and the certainty declared by the annotators. It is measured on the cases where both the annotators marked a relation at the given position in the data.

measurement	certainty declared by the annotators	agreement
bridging relations	both 1	48%
coref-text relations	both 1	67%
any relation	both 1	62%
bridging relations	at least one of them 2 or 3	33%
coref-text relations	at least one of them 2 or 3	36%
any relation	at least one of them 2 or 3	41%

Table 3: The inter-annotator agreement in the task of choosing the antecedent

Again, the numbers show a lower agreement in cases where the annotators were not sure about the antecedent. However, from 27 disagreements in choosing the antecedent, only 16 were marked as uncertain by at least one annotator.

7.3 Certainty in distinguishing between the bridging anaphora and the textual coreference

Table 4 shows the inter-annotator agreement in the decision whether the relation is a bridging anaphora or a textual coreference, depending on the certainty declared by the annotators. It is measured on the cases where both the annotators marked a relation at the given position in the data.

measurement	certainty declared by the annotators	agreement
any relation	both 1	97%
any relation	at least one of them 2 or 3	84%

Table 4: The inter-annotator agreement in the decision whether the relation is the bridging anaphora or the textual coreference

The difference in agreement between "certain" and "uncertain" relations in this case is not so relevant. As seen from the table, the agreement is very high. In most cases (21 out of 32), the annotators marked ambiguity but still made the same decision.

7.4 Certainty in selecting the type of the bridging anaphora or the textual coreference

The following table shows the inter-annotator agreement in the task of choosing the type of the bridging anaphora or the textual coreference, depending on the relation and the certainty declared by the annotators. It is measured on the cases where both the annotators marked a relation at the given position in the data.

measurement	certainty declared by the annotators	agreement
bridging relations	both 1	97%
coref-text relations	both 1	96%
any relation	both 1	92%
bridging relations	at least one of them 2 or 3	75%
coref-text relations	at least one of them 2 or 3	73%
any relation	at least one of them 2 or 3	63%

Table 5: The inter-annotator agreement in the task of choosing the type of the bridging anaphora or the textual coreference

8 Discussion

Analyzing the inter-annotator agreement together with the results of annotators' certainty about the relations reveals the following challenging issues:

Firstly, it points out the complexity of real corpus data which can never be reflected by any annotation guidelines in full detail. See e.g. examples (2), (4) and (6) that are not empirically ambiguous but cannot be captured by single yes/no identity rules. The same is true for bridging anaphora: a small set of relations which can yet be reasonable in large-scale corpora annotation cannot capture all cases of text cohesion. Unlike syntax, annotation of "higher" levels (coreference, bridging relations, discourse, etc.) does not reflect a language phenomenon as a whole. It rather excerpts a part of it, which is relevant for a certain task, and formalizes it to a reasonable degree. Contra-intuitivity, such formalized decisions result in a lower inter-annotator agreement. Also the annotators' certainty is lower in cases where intuition goes against the guidelines. Entities might seem to be very coherent, but there may be no good formal relation to be identified.

Secondly, empirical ambiguity seems to be more frequent on text level than on syntax level and lower. However, a detailed analysis of our data confirms the Recasens' at al. (2010) and Poesio-Artstein's (2005) statements: ambiguity is much better seen when comparing parallel annotations than when asking annotators to mark it by themselves.

Thirdly, weak points of the annotation guidelines are revealed. Not having precise and exhaustive rules, annotators naturally doubt more. In our case, this concerns first of all classifying generic noun phrases, abstract nouns and deverbatives. Also noun phrases with measures of different kind, time periods and some language specific constructions appear to be problematic. Annotators are much less certain about relations between generic and abstract nouns. Also the inter-annotator agreement for these cases is always lower than that for specific nouns with concrete meaning. Generally, we can say that in Czech, the most frequent reason for inter-annotator disagreement is not so much metonymy and different cases of near-identity relations in the sense of Recasens, but rather the relations between noun phrases with a generic and an abstract meaning. An improvement of such a problematic area would be to have the semantic information assigned to nouns themselves, as a part of tectogrammatical information. However, this task is very time-consuming.

Comparing the parallel annotations also shows that annotators are more sure about relations between noun phrases in topic and contrastive topic than about those in focus. More than other nouns, this fact concerns generic and abstract nouns and deverbatives. Coreference of these types of nouns in focus is not always obvious. Presented as new, coreference relation with a preceding noun phrase referring to the same type loses its relevance. However, this statement is rather a hypothesis, it needs further investigation.

9 Conclusion

We presented an evaluation and analysis of disagreements in the annotation of coreference and bridging relations in the Prague Dependency Treebank. As demonstrated by the results of parallel annotations, the agreement decreases in the direction from pronominal and zero coreference towards bridging relations. We extracted four most frequent types of problematic cases, exemplified them and described the possible reasons of inter-annotator disagreements. Then we asked annotators to mark the certainty they had in these cases and compared the results to the results of inter-annotator agreement. Although the percentage numbers were quite predictable (the less sure the annotators were, the lower was the agreement), the absolute numbers indicate that there remain many disagreements where uncertainty was not marked by any annotator.

Acknowledgments

We gratefully acknowledge support from the Grant Agency of the Czech Republic (grants P406/12/0658 and P406/2010/0875).

References

Herbert Clark. 1977. Bridging. In Johnson-Laird and Wason, editors, *Thinking: Readings in Cognitive Science*. Cambridge, pp. 411–420.

Jacob Cohen. 1960. A coefficient of agreement for nominal scales. *Educational and Psychological Measurement*, 20(1), pp. 37–46.

Jan Hajič et al. 2006. *Prague Dependency Treebank 2.0*. Philadelphia: Linguistic Data Consortium.

Olga Krasavina and Christian Chiarcos. 2007. PoCoS – Potsdam Coreference Scheme. *Proc. of ACL 2007*, Prague, Czech Republic.

Lucie Kučová, Veronika Kolářová, Zdeněk Žabokrtský, Petr Pajas, Oliver Čulo. 2003. *Anotování koreference v Pražském závislostním korpusu*. ÚFAL Technical Report TR-2003-19.

Lucie Mladová. 2011. *Annotating Discourse in Prague Dependency Treebank*. A presentation at the workshop Annotation of Discourse Relations in Large Corpora at the conference Corpus Linguistics 2011 (CL 2011), Birmingham, Great Britain, July 2011.

Anna Nedoluzhko and Jiří Mírovský. 2013. How dependency trees and tectogrammatics help annotating coreference and bridging relations in Prague Dependency Treebank. *Proceedings of the International Conference on Dependency Linguistics (Depling 2013)*, Prague, Czech Republic (in press).

Anna Nedoluzhko and Jiří Mírovský. 2011. *Annotating Extended Textual Coreference and Bridging Relations in the Prague Dependency Treebank.* Annotation manual. Technical report No. 44, ÚFAL, Charles University in Prague.

Massimo Poesio and Ron Artstein. 2005. The reliability of anaphoric annotation, reconsidered: Taking ambiguity into account. *Proceedings of the ACL Workshop on Frontiers in Corpus Annotation II*. Ann Arbor, pp. 76–83.

Massimo Poesio, Rodolfo Delmonte, Antonella Bristot, Luminita Chiran, Sara Tonelli. 2004. *The Venex corpus of anaphora and deixis in spoken and written Italian*. Manuscript.

Massimo Poesio. 2004. The MATE/GNOME Proposals for Anaphoric Annotation, Revisited. *Proceedings of The 5th SIGdial Workshop on Discourse and Dialogue,* Boston.

Massimo Poesio, Ron Artstein. 2008. Anaphoric annotation in the ARRAU corpus. *Proceedings of LREC 2008*, Marrakech.

Marta Recasens, M. Antònia Martí. 2009. AnCora-CO: Coreferentially annotated corpora for Spanish and Catalan. *Language Resources and Evaluation.*

Marta Recasens, Eduard Hovy, M. Antònia Martí. 2010. *A typology of near-identity relations for coreference (NIDENT)*. In Proceedings of LREC 2010, Valletta.

Marta Recasens, Eduard Hovy, and M. Antònia Martí. 2011. Identity, Non-Identity, and Near-Identity: *Addressing the complexity of coreference*. Lingua, 121(6), pp. 1138–1152 2011.

Marta Recasens, M. Antònia Martí, Constantin Orasan. 2012. Annotating Near-Identity from Coreference Disagreements. *Proceedings of the Eight International Conference on Language Resources and Evaluation (LREC'12)*, Istanbul.

Yanick Versley. 2008. Vagueness and referential ambiguity in a large-scale annotated corpus. *Research on Language and Computation 6*, pp. 333–353.

How Dependency Trees and Tectogrammatics Help Annotating Coreference and Bridging Relations in Prague Dependency Treebank

Anna Nedoluzhko
Charles University in Prague
Faculty of Mathematics and Physics
Institute of Formal and Applied Linguistics
Czech Republic
nedoluzko@ufal.mff.cuni.cz

Jiří Mírovský
Charles University in Prague
Faculty of Mathematics and Physics
Institute of Formal and Applied Linguistics
Czech Republic
mirovsky@ufal.mff.cuni.cz

Abstract

In this paper, we explore the benefits of dependency trees and tectogrammatical structure used in the Prague Dependency Treebank for annotating language phenomena that cross the sentence boundary, namely coreference and bridging relations. We present the benefits of dependency trees such as the detailed processing of ellipses, syntactic decisions for coordination and apposition structures that make possible coding coreference relations in cases that are not so easy when annotating on the raw texts. We introduce the coreference decision for non-referring constructions and present some tectogrammatical features that are useful for annotation of coreference.

1 Introduction

The dependency syntax is one of the most influential linguistic theories. However, its benefits are mainly explored for research of linguistic phenomena that do not cross the sentence boundary and may be illustrated within a single dependency tree. In this paper, we will explore how dependency trees and tectogrammatical structure can help in the annotation of coreference and bridging relations in the Prague Dependency Treebank.

The Prague Dependency Treebank (henceforth PDT, Hajič et al. 2006) is a large collection of linguistically annotated data and documentation. In PDT 2.0, Czech newspaper texts are annotated on three layers: morphological, syntactic and complex semantic (tectogrammatical). In addition to syntax, the tectogrammatical layer includes the annotation of topic-focus articulation, discourse relations[1], coreference links and bridging relations. Benefits of tectogrammatics in the annotation of discourse structure were examined in Mírovský et al. (2012), we will focus on coreference and bridging relations.

When we say that we take certain advantages from the tectogrammatical layer, we should realize that the advantages of two kinds are possible: we can take advantage from the dependency structure itself, independently of the PDT conception, and we can use the information included in the tectogrammatical layer as a specific contribution of the Prague Dependency Treebank. In this paper, when we describe benefits that can be obtained for coreference and bridging annotation using the dependency structure, our examples are syntactically analyzed using the PDT tectogrammatical annotation strategy and are seriously influenced by this approach. However, we suppose that in principle any dependency analyzer would be able to solve these problems in a similar way.

2 The Coreference and Bridging Relations in PDT

There are three types of relations annotated in PDT: (a) grammatical coreference (coreference of relative and reflexive pronouns, arguments of verbs of control, arguments in constructions with reciprocity and verbal complements), (b) pronominal and nominal textual coreference (including zero anaphora), which is further specified into coreference of specific (type SPEC) and generic (type GEN) noun phrases, and (c) bridging relations, which mark some associative semantic relations between non-coreferential entities. The following types of bridging relations are distinguished: PART-OF (e.g. room - ceiling), SUBSET (students - some students) and FUNCT (state - president)

[1] The annotation of discourse and bridging relations is a later addition to the data of PDT, see http://ufal.mff.cuni.cz/discourse/

Proceedings of the Second International Conference on Dependency Linguistics (DepLing 2013), pages 244–251,
Prague, August 27–30, 2013.

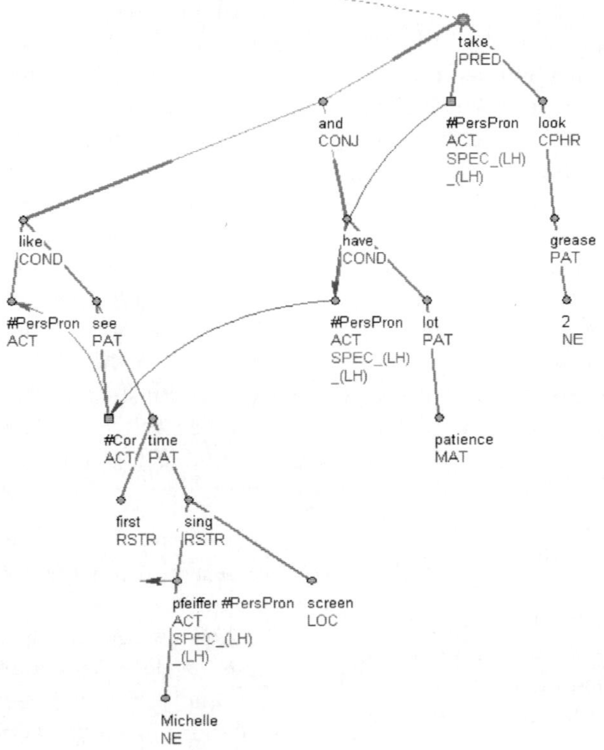

Figure 1: *If you'd like* {#Cor.ACT} *to see the first time Michelle Pfeiffer sang on screen, and you have a lot of patience,* #PersPron *take a look at Grease 2.*

traditional relations, CONTRAST for coherence relevant discourse opposites (this year - last year), ANAF for explicitly anaphoric relations without coreference (rainbow - that word) and the further underspecified group REST[2].

Coreference relations are marked between the whole subtrees of the antecedent/anaphoric expressions that are the subject to annotation.

3 The Annotation Tool

The primary format of PDT 2.0 is called PML. It is an abstract XML-based format designed for annotation of treebanks. For editing and processing data in PML format, a fully customizable tree editor TrEd has been implemented (Pajas and Štěpánek 2008). For the coreference and bridging annotation, a special extension was used, included into the system as a module.

Technically, the coreference extension module of TrEd allows annotation both on raw texts and on dependency trees. However, annotation on dependency trees is more comfortable as it gives more visual information about the function of the annotated noun phrases in the sentence structure, about being in the governing or dependent position in the coreferring expression, about being a part of an appositional or a coordinative construction and so on.

4 Benefits of Dependency Trees and Tectogrammatics

One of the technical advantages of gold dependency trees is the automatic extraction of elements to be annotated for coreference, including so called minimal markables (MIN-IDs) that are always the governing expression of full span markable expressions. Of course, it does not solve the problem for coreference resolution systems, but it makes the manual annotation easier, reducing it to a single step of coding coreferential links between already identified markables.

4.1 Syntactic zeros

In so-called 'pro-drop' languages such as most Romance languages, Japanese, Greek, most Slavonic languages, etc., a phonetic realization is not required for anaphoric references in contexts where they are syntactically or pragmatically inferable. The problem of syntactic zeros is the

[2] For a detailed classification of coreference and bridging relations used in PDT, see e.g. Nedoluzhko et al. (2011).

subject of research in many different linguistic theories (see e.g. the elaboration of different aspects in generative grammar (Roberts 1997), Prague dependency grammar (Panevová 1986, Růžička 1999), Moscow structuralismus (Meľčuk 1974), etc.). There is not much theoretical disagreement concerning such elements (at least in case of zero anaphoric pronouns and control constructions), but they raise a lot of problems with annotation of their relations to coreferential expressions and automatic resolution of these relations. Thus, only a few coreference annotation projects reconstruct the ellided expressions and annotate them for coreference (see e.g. Xue et al. 2005, Pradhan et al. 2007). However, for example, with tools such as MMAX (Müller and Strube 2001), the only option is to have 'verbal markables' as done e.g., in VENEX (Poesio et al. 2004) and LiveMemories (Rodriguez 2010) annotation (i.e., annotate a relation between the immediately following verbal element and the antecedent). In AnCora (Recasens and Martí 2010), zero subjects were added as extra 'empty' tokens, and these were used for annotating coreference.

Consequent annotation of such arguments is better possible with annotation tools that use as a base layer a full syntactic annotation or an argument structure. As TrEd is one of such tools, its benefits are used for reconstructing ellided

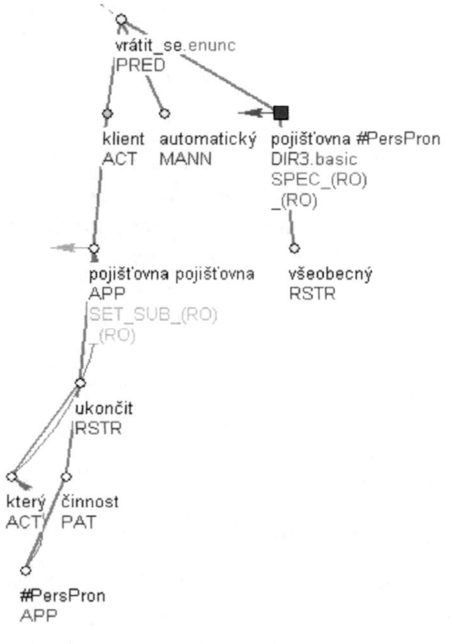

Figure 2: *Klienti pojišťoven, které ukončí svou činnost, se automaticky vrátí k* *__Všeobecné__*. (=lit. *Clients of insurance companies which shut down will automatically return to* *__the General {one}__*.)

expressions, their coreference relations being further consistently annotated. Zero arguments are reconstructed using the PDT Valency Lexicon VALLEX (Hajič et al. 2003), which for each autosemantic, valency-capable word provides its valency information.

According to the detailed classification of ellipses introduced in Mikulová (2011), PDT uses a rich variety of newly established nodes occupying positions of all kinds of modifications. The classification of these nodes corresponds to the ability of different types of newly established nodes to take part in coreference relations. Newly established nodes that are subjects to coreference annotation are the following:

- **#PersPron**. This lemma is assigned to nodes representing personal or possessive pronouns. It applies both to newly established nodes and to those present at the surface level. In most cases, nodes with #PersPron lemma, especially those representing personal pronouns in the third person, are connected with their antecedents by coreference relations (the rare exceptions are mostly generic uses of pronouns used once in the text without further reference). Cf. Fig. 1.
- **#Cor**. This lemma is assigned to newly established nodes representing the (usually inexpressible) controllee in control constructions. These nodes are always connected by a grammatical coreference link with its controller, cf. coreference of unexpressed actor of the verb in Fig. 1.
- **#QCor**. This lemma is assigned to newly established nodes representing a (usually inexpressible) valency modification in constructions with so-called quasi-control. This case can be found with multi-word predicates the dependent part of which is a noun with valency requirements, cf. *He offered Jan* {#QCor} *protection.* The valency of the verb *offer* as well as the modification of the noun *protection* has the same referent *Jan.* This shared modification can only be present once at the surface level (it is impossible to say: **He offered Jan protection of Jan*). These nodes are always connected by a grammatical coreference link with its controller.
- **#Rcp**. This lemma is assigned to newly established nodes representing participants that are left out as a result of reciprocation. There is always a grammatical coreference

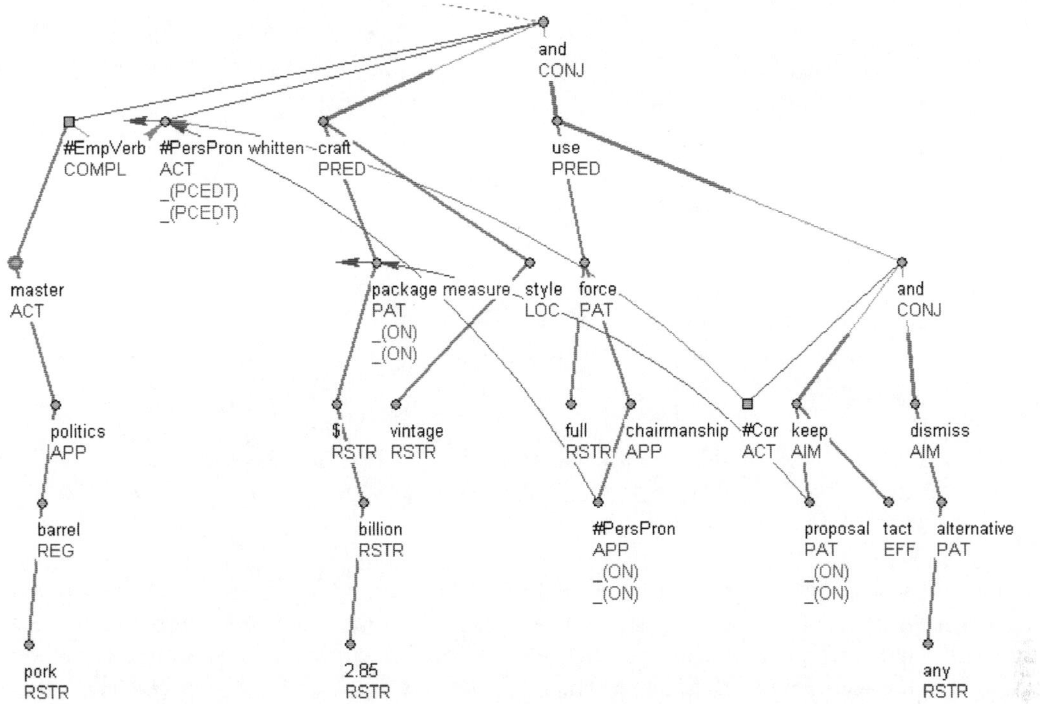

Figure 3: <u>*A master of pork-barrel politics*</u>, <u>*he*</u> *had crafted the $2.85 billion package in vintage style and used the full force of his chairmanship to keep the proposal intact and dismiss any alternative*.

relationship indicated in the tectogrammatical tree, going from the node with the #Rcp t-lemma to the node with which it is in the reciprocal relation: *The lovers kissed* {#Rcp.PAT}.

- If it is clear (and possible to find in the text) which noun has been omitted in the surface structure of the sentence (the case of textual ellipsis), a copy of the node representing the same lexical unit as the omitted element is inserted into the appropriate position. Cf. Fig. 2.

Other newly established nodes are not supposed to be linked by coreference. These are e.g. **#Gen** for a general participant (*Houses are built* {#Gen.ACT} *from bricks.*), **#Unsp** for valency modifications with vague (non-specific) semantic content (*U Nováků* {#Unsp.ACT} *dobře vaří. (=They cook well at Nováks'.*)), **#EmpNoun** for non-expressed nouns governing syntactic adjectives, which are not the case of textual ellipsis (*Přišli jen* {#EmpNoun.ACT} *mladší. (=lit. Came only {#EmpNoun} younger.*)), **#Oblfm** for obligatory adjuncts that are absent at the surface level (*Ta vypadá.* {#Oblfm.MANN} *(=lit. That.fem looks; meaning: She looks awful/so strange...*)) and some other newly established nodes used in comparative constructions.

Such a detailed linguistically elaborated method provides very consistent information of the analyzed language and thus a reliable base for a theoretical linguistic research, but corpora annotated in this way are problematic for many automatic resolving systems, as the state of the art at extracting full syntactic structure / argument structure from text is still not good enough. However, the results for #PersPron resolution in PDT are not so bad. A rule-based system employed in Nguy and Žabokrtský (2007) to resolution of pronominal textual coreference got the success rate of 74 % (F1-measure). Applying machine learning methods, particularly perceptron ranking in Nguy et al. (2009) on the same task outperformed the rule-based method with F1-measure over 79 %.

4.2 Processing non-referring expressions

Non-referring expressions such as appositions, verbal complements and noun phrases in predicative positions are a special problematic issue in coreference annotation projects that mark coreference on raw texts. Coding coreference on dependency trees may solve the problem. In PDT, appositions, verbal complements and noun phrases in predicative

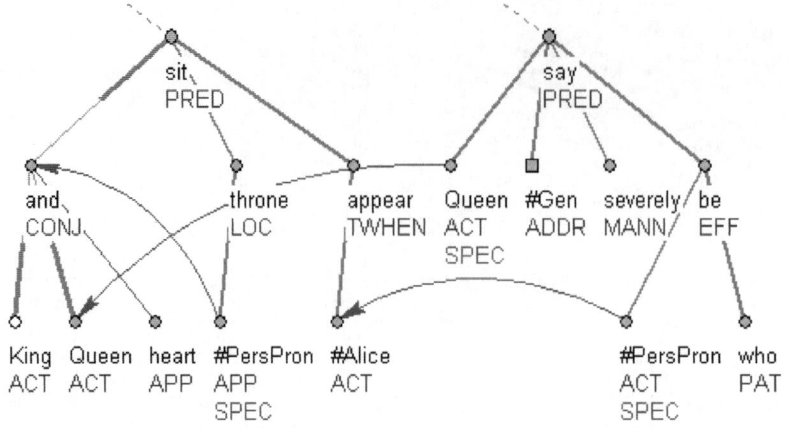

Figure 4: *The King and Queen of Hearts were sitting on their throne when Alice appeared. The Queen said severely "Who is she?"*

positions are resolved on the syntactic level and they do not need to be additionally annotated for coreference. This information can be easily extracted from the tectogrammatical layer. Thus, for appositions, the whole construction serves as a markable for coreference annotation, its parts beeing connected with a node with a special tectogrammatical functor APPS. The predicative relation is obvious. For verbal complements, the functor COMPL is used, the dependency on a noun being additionally represented by means of a special attribute compl.rf, in TrEd visualized by a (non-coreference) arrow (see Fig. 3).

4.3 Coordinative constructions

Coordination structures and their connection with plural reference are another difficult issue for processing coreference relations. E.g. the semantics of plural reference to a coordination like *John and Mary met. They had not seen each other for a long time* is fairly uncontroversial from a semantic point of view and can be solved satisfactorily by any annotation system (the coordination construction as a whole and its parts separately may be lined by coreference relations). On the contrary, the problem of multiple antecedents for *they* in *John visited Ellen, and they went to the seaside* will present a problem for all, no matter if dependency-based or raw-text annotations. Still, there are coordinative constructions that are complicated for annotation on texts (a special split-antecedent mechanism is needed) and have an elegant solution on dependency trees.

Annotating coreference link for *the Queen* in Fig. 4[3] on the raw text is problematic because of its modifier *of Hearts* is common for both NPs, *The King* and *the Queen*. In PDT tectogrammatics, this is resolved by a dependency structure, as shown in Fig. 4.

The reconstruction of a complex syntactic construction makes it possible to refer to a coordination *Latitude or Longitude* in Fig. 5.

4.4 Contribution of tectogrammatics

There are some additional helpful features that do not necessarily depend on the dependency structure of the text representation but are present in the tectogrammatical level of the Prague Dependency Treebank and are very useful for the consistent annotation of coreference and bridging relations and its further analysis. According to its semantic part of speech, each node contains grammatical information about gender, number, resp. person, tense, mood, etc. Direct speech and parenthesis are marked in a special attribute. Discourse annotation supplies the information about which expressions are parts of titles or subtitles. Very important for the analysis of text cohesion is the topic-focus articulation that is annotated manually for the whole PDT.

Furthermore, PDT uses a special approach to the syntactic annotation of quantifiers, measure NPs and constructions with similar semantic meaning. In PDT annotation guidelines, they are called nouns with a 'container' meaning. Their

[3] For examples Fig. 4 and Fig. 5, the sentences from the discussion on the workshop RAIS are used (http://wiki.ims.uni-stuttgart.de/RAIS/Stuttgart-Workshop).

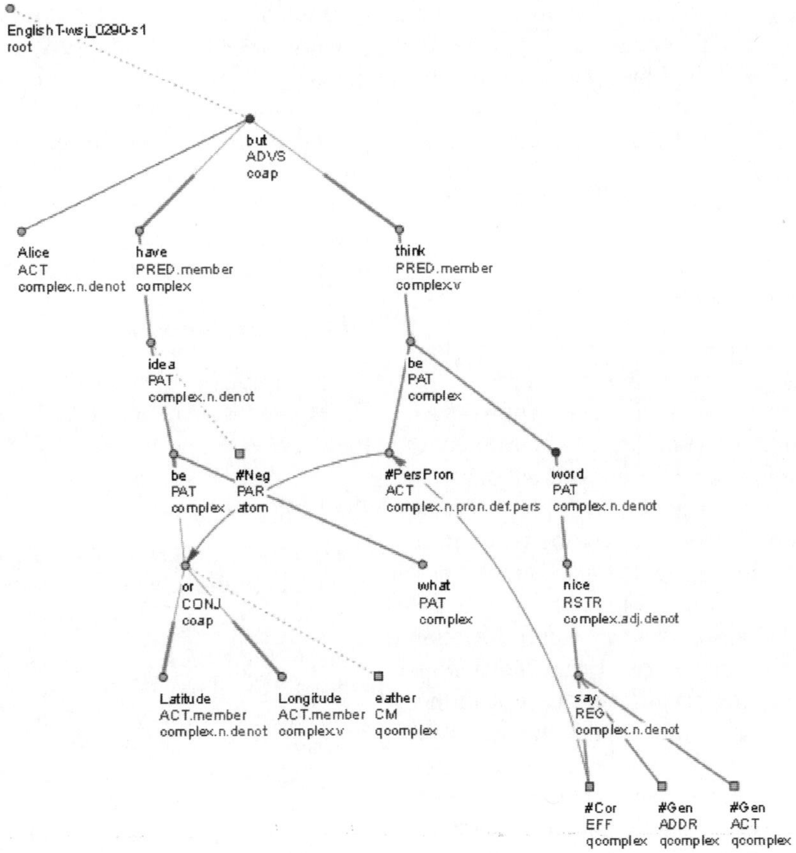

Figure 5. *Alice had no idea what Latitude was, or Longitude either, but thought they were nice grand words to say.*

arguments have typical semantic label MAT and can be easily recognized in the dependency tree. This fact was widely exploited for coreference annotation. The 'container' words were basically considered to be markables for coreference relations, their dependent elements were annotated for coreference only in some special (rare) cases where annotation to 'containers' was not possible for technical or semantical reasons (Nedoluzhko 2011).

Also information about the tectogrammatical functors of potentially coreferring nodes is widely explored for annotation of coreference and bridging relations. In PDT, functors mainly represent the semantic values of syntactic dependency relations, they express the functions of individual modifications in the sentence. As mentioned above, functors for appositive, predicative and coordinative constructions, as well as the special functor for verbal complements, are of great use for consequent coreference annotation. Moreover, when annotating coreference and bridging relations, there should be considered such functors as ID, ACMP, AUTH etc.

4.4.1 The ID functor

The functor ID (identity) is used as a functor for an identifying expression, which is represented as an identification structure. The ID functor is assigned to adnominal adjuncts representing meta-language expressions, proper nouns and names of animals, objects and events, e.g. *v případu Kott - Kutílek* (= *in the case of Kott - Kutílek*); *agentura Reuters* (=*Reuters agency*); *pojem čas* (=*notion of time*). In such cases, noun phrases do not refer to objects but to themselves. For this reason, all constructions containing expressions with the ID functor are annotated for coreference as one unit. The coreference arrow links the governing node to the node with the ID functor (i.e. *agency* in case of *Reuters agency*, *notion* in case of *notion of time* and so on).

4.4.2 The ACMP functor

The ACMP functor (accompaniment) is a functor for such an adjunct which expresses manner by specifying a circumstance (an object, person, event) that accompanies (or fails to accompany) the event or entity modified by the adjunct. The meaning of the ACMP functor may appear in conflict with some bridging relations (mainly SUBSET). In this case, the bridging relations are not annotated. Cf. *válečná plavidla včetně bojových letadel*.ACMP *a bitevních vrtulníků*.ACMP (=*warships including air force* ...).

5 Problematic Issues

Of course, dependency trees and tectogrammatics do not solve all coreference annotation problems. One of the problematic issues that remains daunting for coreference annotation is the identity of prepositional phrases and included noun phrases. In PDT, prepositions are hidden in sub-functors and can be taken into account if annotating on tectogrammatical trees only by looking at these subfunctors. Although the semantic distinction between prepositional phrases with the same head and different preposition is very important, we ignore it in the annotation. So, if two noun phrases are coreferential, we mark coreferential relation between them also in case when they are parts of prepositional phrases which are not coreferential. Although contraintuitive, the following expressions will be marked as coreferential: *Prague – near Prague, before the war – during the war – after the war*. The distinction between PPs and NPs beeing in Prague tectogrammatics complicated (though technically possible), the question about the ability of PPs to corefer still remains open, so our decision to mark coreference for NPs ignoring PPs still remains quite consequent.

6 Conclusion

In this paper, we demonstrated how manual annotation of coreference relations may benefit from the use of dependency trees and the tectogrammatical structure of the Prague Dependency Treebank. We considered separately the contribution of dependency trees and the tectogrammatics. Although dependency syntactic annotation is quite costly and time-consuming, it gives good structural solutions for processing coreference in predicative, appositive and coordinative structures, constructions with ellipses of different kinds and so on. The connection to the syntactico-semantic analysis of the tectogrammatical layer in the Prague Dependency Treebank appears as a rather convenient tool. In addition to issues already mentioned, it makes it possible to work with already established and coherent solutions of typical syntactic constructions and tectogrammatic functors. Along with other similar tasks being performed on the same PDT level (topic-focus articulation, discourse annotation), it creates a reliable basis for a deeper linguistic research in the field of language phenomena that cross the sentence boundary.

Acknowledgements

We gratefully acknowledge support from the Grant Agency of the Czech Republic (grants P406/12/0658 and P406/2010/0875).

Bibliography

J. Hajič et al. 2006. Prague Dependency Treebank 2.0.CD-ROM, Linguistic Data Consortium, LDC Catalog No.: LDC2006T01, Philadelphia.

J. Hajič, J. Panevová, Z. Urešová, A. Bémová and V. Kolářová. 2003. PDT-Vallex: Creating a Large-coverage Valency Lexicon for Treebank Annotation. In Proceedings of The Second Workshop on Treebanks and Linguistic Theories, 57-68. Vaxjo University Press.

I. Meľčuk. 1974. O sintaksicheskom nule. In Cholodovich A.A. (ed.) *Tipologija passivnych konstrukcij. Diatezy i zalogi*. Leningrad.

M. Mikulová. 2011. *Významová reprezentace elipsy.* ÚFAL, Prague, 230 pp.

M. Mikulová, A. Bémová, J. Hajič, E. Hajičová, J. Havelka, V. Kolářová, M. Lopatková, P. Pajas, J. Panevová, M. Razímová, P. Sgall, J. Štěpánek, Z. Urešová, K. Veselá, Z. Žabokrtský, L. Kučová. 2005. *Anotace na tektogramatické rovině Pražského závislostního korpusu. Anotátorská příručka (t-layer annotation guidelines)*. Technical Report TR-2005-28, ÚFAL MFF UK, Prague.

J. Mírovský, P. Jínová, L. Poláková. 2012. Does Tectogrammatics help the Annotation of Discourse? In *Procedings of the 24th International Conference on Computational Linguistics* (COLING 2012), Mumbai, India.

L. Mladová, Š. Zikánová, E. Hajičová. 2008. From Sentence to Discourse: Building an Annotation Scheme for Discourse Based on Prague Dependency Treebank. In *Proceedings of the 6th International Conference on Language Resources and Evaluation (LREC 2008)*, Marakéš, Maroko.

Ch. Müller, M. Strube. 2001. Annotating anaphoric and bridging relations with MMAX. In *Proceedings of the 2nd SIGdial Workshop on Discourse and Dialogue*. Aalborg, Denmark, pp. 90–95.

A. Nedoluzhko. 2011. *Rozšířená textová koreference a asociační anafora. Koncepce anotace českých dat v Pražském závislostním korpusu.* ÚFAL, Prague.

G. L. Nguy, Z. Žabokrtský. 2007. Rule-based Approach to Pronominal Anaphora Resolution Applied on the Prague Dependency Treebank 2.0 Data. In *Proceedings of the 6th Discourse Anaphroa and Anaphor Resolution Colloquium*, Lagos, 2007.

G. L. Nguy, V. Novák, Z. Žabokrtský. 2009. Comparison of Classification and Ranking Approaches to Pronominal Anaphora Resolution in Czech. In *Proceedings of the SIGDIAL 2009 Conference*, London.

P. Pajas, J. Štěpánek. 2008. Recent advances in a feature-rich framework for treebank annotation. In *The 22nd Interntional Conference on Computational Linguistics – Proceedings of the Conference*. Manchester, pp. 673-680.

J. Panevová. 1986. The Czech infinitive in the function of objective and the rules of reference. In Mey J. (ed) *Language and discourse: Text and protest*. Amsterdam; Philadelphia: John Benjamins.

M. Poesio, R. Delmonte, A. Bristot, L. Chiran, S.Tonelli. 2004. *The VENEX corpus of anaphoric information in spoken and written Italian*. Manuscript.

M. Poesio. 2004. The MATE/GNOME Scheme for Anaphoric Annotation, Revisited. In *Proc.of SIGDIAL*, Boston.

M. Poesio, R. Artstein. 2008. Anaphoric annotation in the ARRAU corpus In *Proceedings of the Sixth International Conference on Language Resources and Evaluation (LREC)*. Marrakech, Morocco.

S. Pradhan, L. A. Ramshaw, R. M. Weischedel, J. MacBride, L. Micciulla. 2007. Unrestricted Coreference: Identifying Entities and Events in OntoNotes. In *Proceedings of the International Conference on Semantic Computing (ICSC '07)*. 446-453.

M. Recasens, A. Martí. 2010. *AnCora-CO: Coreferentially annotated corpora for Spanish and Catalan*. In Language Resources and Evaluation.

I. Roberts. 1997. *Comparative syntax*. London: Arnold.

K. J. Rodriguez, F. Delogu, Y. Versley, E. Stemle and M. Poesio. 2010. Anaphoric Annotation of Wikipedia and Blogs in the Live Memories Corpus. In *Proceedings of the Seventh International Conference on Language Resources and Evaluation (LREC)*, Valletta, Malta, May 2010.

R. Růžička. 1999. *Control in grammar and pragmatics: a cross-linguistic study*. John Benjamins Publishing.

Nianwen Xue, Fei Xia, Fu-Dong Chiou, and M. Palmer. 2005. The Penn Chinese TreeBank: Phrase structure annotation of a large corpus. *Natural Language Engineering*, 11(2):207–238.

Predicting conjunct propagation and other extended Stanford Dependencies

Jenna Nyblom[1], **Samuel Kohonen**[1], **Katri Haverinen**[1,2],
Tapio Salakoski[1,2] and **Filip Ginter**[1]
[1]Department of Information Technology, University of Turku, Finland
[2]Turku Centre for Computer Science, Turku, Finland
`first.last@utu.fi`

Abstract

In this work, we present a data-driven method to enhance syntax trees with additional dependencies as defined in the well-known Stanford Dependencies scheme, so as to give more information about the structure of the sentence. This hybrid method utilizes both machine learning and a rule-based approach, and achieves a performance of 93.1% in F_1-score, as evaluated using an existing treebank of Finnish. The resulting tool will be integrated into an existing Finnish parser and made publicly available at the address `http://bionlp.utu.fi/`.

1 Introduction

Dependency-based analysis of syntax has recently become popular within natural language processing. It has been argued to be preferable over constituency analysis in both parser evaluation and further applications (Lin, 1998; Clegg and Shepherd, 2007), and indeed both dependency treebanks and parsers have emerged in recent years.

Dependency formalisms usually require that all valid analyses must be *trees*, meaning that each token in a sentence must only have one governor, and the whole sentence must have one head word. Tree structures, however, do not necessarily allow the explicit representation of a number of relevant phenomena. This is demonstrated by the well-known Stanford Dependencies (SD) scheme (de Marneffe and Manning, 2008), which is defined in multiple *variants*. The *basic* variant requires sentence structures to be trees, and the other variants can then be used to add further dependencies on top of the tree structure, making the resulting structures graphs rather than trees. Phenomena that are further analyzed in the non-basic variants of SD include relative clauses, open clausal complements, coordinations and prepositional phrases.

The dependencies present in non-basic variants of SD can be useful for applications that build on top of the syntactic analysis. For instance, the clinical domain pilot study of Haverinen et al. (2010) has shown that these dependencies can be used in annotating argument structures of verbs using the popular PropBank scheme (Palmer et al., 2005). Also, Yuret et al. (2012) have used the propagated and collapsed variant of the SD scheme to retrieve as semantically meaningful dependencies as possible in the context of textual entailments. The non-basic variants of SD are also extensively applied in information extraction, as seen for example in the BioNLP shared tasks on event extraction, where a number of top-ranking systems relied on SD analyses (Kim et al., 2011).

In this work, we are concerned with three phenomena represented in the non-basic variants of SD. Most importantly, we consider the dependencies that are the result of *conjunct propagation*. They resolve, at least partially, ambiguities known as *coordination scope ambiguities*. These are ambiguities where there are multiple ways to understand the scope of a coordination; for instance, in the phrase *old men and women* either both the men and the women are old, or alternatively, only the men. Additionally, we consider dependencies that reveal the *syntactic functions of relativizers* and *external subjects* of open clausal complements.

We present a method that, given the basic syntactic tree of a sentence, predicts these additional dependencies as defined in the SD scheme using machine learning. As training data, we use morphological and syntactic information gathered from an existing treebank of Finnish, which has human annotated conjunct propagation and additional dependencies present. We begin with a discussion of related work and the treebank used as training material. We then move on to the details of the method itself and present a thorough evaluation of the pipeline. We make comparisons with

Proceedings of the Second International Conference on Dependency Linguistics (DepLing 2013), pages 252–261,
Prague, August 27–30, 2013.

several baseline methods, and conclude that the proposed method achieves a performance clearly superior to each of these baselines. In particular, the method demonstrates performance clearly superior to that achieved by the commonly used Stanford tools.

2 Related work

The general problem of *coordination scope ambiguity* is a widely studied, difficult problem. It is frequently tackled by utilizing lexical parallelism and selectional preferences, as for instance in the works of Kawahara and Kurohashi (2011) and Resnik (1999). In the domain of requirements engineering, Chantree et al. (2005) disambiguate coordinations using heuristics based on the distributions of the words appearing in them. Goldberg (1999) has presented an unsupervised model for a limited range of coordination phenomena, and Agarwal and Boggess (1992) introduce a simplified algorithm for recognizing the correct conjuncts for coordinations. Kawahara and Kurohashi (2007) and van Noord (2007) have incorporated disambiguation methods into parsers of Japanese and Dutch, respectively.

In dependency representations, there are multiple ways to treat coordination structures, and the chosen treatment also affects coordination scope ambiguities. The Stanford Dependencies scheme (de Marneffe and Manning, 2008) used in this work considers the first coordinated element the head of the coordination, and uses an additional layer of dependencies to represent the propagation of conjunct dependencies (see Figures 1 and 2). As a point of comparison, for instance the Link Grammar scheme (Sleator and Temperley, 1993) makes the coordinating conjunction the head word of the coordination, thus partially resolving the scope ambiguities using tree structures only as will be shown in greater detail in Section 5.2.

The Stanford tools[1] are able to produce output with the additional dependencies of the SD scheme present, but according to de Marneffe and Manning (2008), this part of the tools performs imperfectly. While the English resource PARC 700 (King et al., 2003), annotated in the LFG-formalism (Bresnan, 2001), contains dependencies similar to those considered in this work,

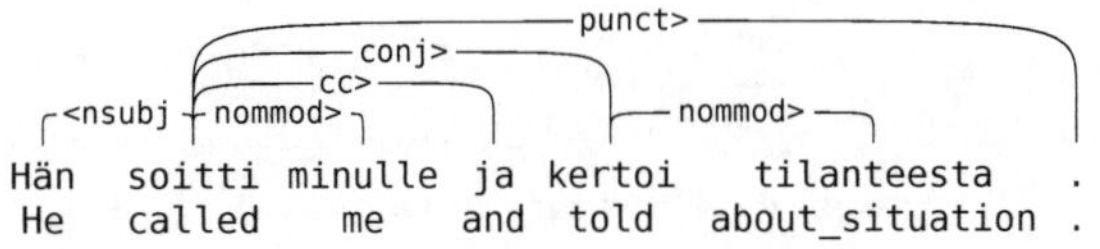

Figure 1: The basic variant of the Stanford Dependencies scheme on a Finnish sentence. The example can be translated as *He called me and told me about the situation.*

to our knowledge the Turku Dependency Treebank (Haverinen et al., 2011) is the only existing manually annotated resource that contains conjunct propagation as described in the SD scheme.

In addition to the post-processing approach implemented in the Stanford tools, also methods to directly parse dependency graphs involving tokens with multiple governors have been studied. McDonald and Pereira (2006) introduce a modification of the Maximum Spanning Tree algorithm to infer secondary dependencies in the Danish Dependency Treebank, and Sagae and Tsujii (2008) present a modification of the Shift-Reduce algorithm, which can parse directed acyclic graphs.

3 Data

3.1 Turku Dependency Treebank

As both the training and testing data of this study, we use the Turku Dependency Treebank (TDT) (Haverinen et al., 2011), which is a publicly available treebank for Finnish. TDT contains 15,126 sentences (204,399 tokens) from ten different genres or text sources, including for instance Wikipedia, EU-text and amateur fiction.

TDT has been annotated using the SD scheme, which was originally developed to be used with the English language. Thus it has been slightly modified in order to be able to capture the specific features of Finnish. The Finnish-specific SD scheme contains 53 different dependency types, and has been thoroughly described in the annotation manual of Haverinen (2012).

3.2 Conjunct propagation and additional dependencies

TDT contains two annotation layers. The first layer is based on the *basic* variant of the SD scheme and represents the structure of a sentence as a tree. Figure 1 illustrates the first annotation layer. The second layer gives extra information about specific phenomena: *conjunct propagation*,

[1] `http://nlp.stanford.edu/software/lex-parser.shtml`

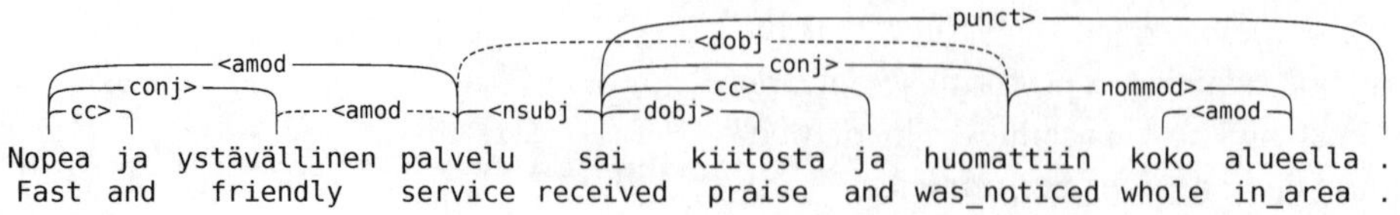

Figure 2: Conjunct propagation in the SD scheme. The base-layer dependencies are marked with solid lines, and the propagated dependencies are dashed. The example sentence can be translated as *The fast and friendly service received praise and was noticed in the whole area.* Note that the noun *palvelu* (*service*) serves as the subject of the first clause and the object of the second, which causes the type of the propagated dependency to change.

external subjects and *syntactic functions of relativizers*. Approximately 9% (18,926/208,417) of all dependencies in the treebank are part of the second layer. The second annotation layer adds dependencies on top of the existing first layer, thus making the resulting analyses directed graphs, rather than trees.

Conjunct propagation is related to coordination structures. In the SD scheme, the first coordinated element is considered to be the head of the whole coordination, and all other coordinated elements depend on it. Therefore, if a sentence element depends on the first element of a coordination, it can alternatively modify only the first element, some coordinated elements, or all of them. If a sentence element modifies multiple conjuncts, it should be propagated to them, as illustrated in Figure 2. Similarly, some or all conjuncts can modify another sentence element. If a modifier serves a different role for different conjuncts, or if coordinated elements are of different parts-of-speech, the type of the propagating dependency may change during the propagation. This is also illustrated in Figure 2.

External subjects occur with so called *open clausal complements*, where two verbs share a subject (also known as *subject control*). Due to the treeness restriction, in the basic layer of annotation it is not possible to convey the information that the subject of the first verb is also the subject of the second verb. Therefore, these subjects are marked in the second annotation layer, using the dependency types *xsubj*, for external subjects, and *xsubj-cop*, for external copula-subjects.

Syntactic functions of relativizers give additional information about relative clauses. The phrase containing the relative pronoun is marked simply as a *relativizer* (*rel*) in the first layer of annotation. However, the relativizer also always has a secondary syntactic function; for instance, it can

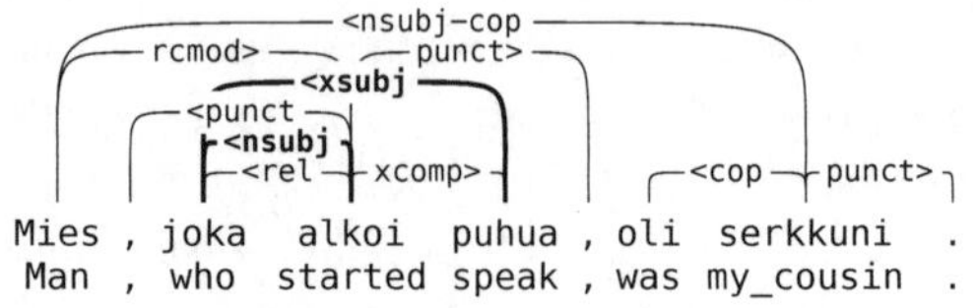

Figure 3: Syntactic functions of relativizers and external subjects. The relative pronoun *joka* (*who*) also acts as the subject to the main verb of the relative clause, as well as the subject of its open clausal complement. The example sentence can be translated as *The man who started to speak was my cousin.*

be the subject of the relative clause. This is marked in the second annotation layer with an additional dependency, which takes one of the dependency types defined in the first annotation layer. Due to the fact that the governor of the relativizer dependency is always the main predicate of the relative clause, the second layer dependency does not necessarily have the same governor. Both external subjects and relativizers are illustrated in Figure 3.

External subjects and syntactic functions of relativizers also interact with conjunct propagation. External subjects can propagate, and propagated subjects can produce new external subjects. Relativizers can also propagate, but note that if the relativizer dependency and the corresponding second layer dependency are between the same tokens, they always propagate together. Finally, if a relativizer acts as the subject of a predicate, it can also act as the external subject of another predicate.

4 Methods

We now proceed to describe the method that automatically infers the propagated and other additional dependencies based on the first layer of syntax annotation in the treebank. We have divided the task into three different subproblems: conjunct propagation, syntactic functions of relativizers, and external subjects. The first two are solved using machine learning, whereas the third problem is easily approached with a rule-based method.

4.1 Conjunct propagation

In conjunct propagation, as is the case of the other two tasks as well, it is possible to exhaustively enumerate all candidate governor–dependent pairs between which may exist a dependency resulting from conjunct propagation. This is the case also for recursive coordination structures, in which the dependencies propagate along chains of two or more conjunct dependencies. We can therefore cast the problem as a multi-class classification task, whereby each of the candidate governor-dependent pairs is assigned the type of the propagated dependency, or alternatively classified as a negative example in case the dependency does not propagate. A simple binary classification into dependencies that do or do not propagate does not suffice, as this would not account for the 2.3% of cases in which the type of the propagated dependency differs from the original base-layer dependency, as discussed earlier in Section 3.2. In preliminary experiments, we have also tested a combined approach of binary classification (propagate or not) followed by a multiclass classification (assign type to propagated dependencies), but found that such a combined approach gives no additional advantage.

The set of possible classes consists of 49 dependency types from the SD scheme (for four SD types, *punct*, *conj*, *cc* and *ellipsis*, propagation is not allowed), plus the negative class and a number of compound types for relativizers. As mentioned in Section 3.2, the relativizer and its corresponding second layer dependency propagate together. Due to this, we have performed the propagation in two steps. First, the two dependency types are merged into one compound type, such as *rel-nsubj*, and after the propagation, they are separated again into two distinct dependencies. This merging increases the number of classes by ten, as only functions of relativizers that actually occur in the training data are allowed. Discounting dependency types that in fact never propagate in the training data and are thus never predicted to do so, the total number of possible classes is 51.

A number of features, extracted from both the tokens and the underlying dependency structure, are used in the classification. *Token features* include the lemma of the token, its main POS, and a separate feature for each its morphological tags that belong to one of several relevant morphological categories. These are *Subcategory*, *Case*, *Number*, *Person*, *Voice* and *Infinitive*, as selected based on preliminary experiments. Token features are extracted separately for the candidate governor and dependent, as well as the head of the coordination. The lemma of the coordinating conjunction itself, if such a conjunction is present, is also used as a feature. *Tree features* include the type of the dependency which is being propagated, whether the dependency governs or modifies the head of the conjunction, whether the target of the propagation already has a dependent with the same type (only relevant in cases where a dependent is propagated, not the governor), the set of outgoing dependency types for the candidate governor and dependent, the dependency type governing the head of the dependency being propagated, whether the linear direction of the candidate propagated dependency is the same as the linear direction of the dependency being propagated (possible values being both-left, both-right, and differing-directions), and finally the number of coordinated items in the coordination expressed as a binary feature (i.e. one binary feature for every discrete value).

Prior to classification, all possible feature pairs are explicitly generated, simulating the use of a second-degree polynomial kernel. For instance, a feature vector (f_1, f_2, f_3) is turned into $(f_1f_1, f_1f_2, f_1f_3, f_2f_2, f_2f_3, f_3f_3)$ prior to classification. As will be shown in the feature ablation study in Section 5.1, this technique improves the classification accuracy. Finally, prior to the classification the feature vectors are normalized to unit length.

4.2 Syntactic functions of relativizers

As discussed in Section 3.2, every relativizer is assigned a syntactic function in the second annotation layer of the treebank. This is expressed as an additional dependency that governs the relativizer (see Figure 3) and in the majority of cases (95.4%) has the same governor as the relativizer dependency in the first annotation layer. As with conjunct propagation, we approach the task as a machine learning problem. For each relativizer dependency, we predict an additional dependency type which represents the syntactic function of the relativizer. A new dependency with this type is then created governing the relativizer word.

To account for certain cases of object control and raising, we identify cases where the governor of the relativizer has an infinite clausal complement (i.e. governs an *iccomp* dependency) and the head of the complement does not already have a dependent of the predicted type. If so, we post-process the new dependency to be governed by the head of the complement. This is a heuristic to treat the most common situation where the governor of the *relativizer* dependency differs from the governor of the corresponding second layer dependency. In all other cases, the second layer dependency is predicted between the governor and dependent of the base syntax relativizer dependency.

The feature representation in this task is comparatively simple. Separately for the governor and dependent, we generate their token features (the same features as in conjunct propagation) and the set of types of dependencies they govern. As with conjunct propagation, explicit feature pair generation as well as normalization of feature vectors to unit length are employed.

4.3 External subject assignment

Unlike in the two previous tasks, we find that assignment of external subjects is best approached by a simple rule-based method, since only clausal complements governed by an *xcomp* dependency have an external subject. As noted by Campbell (2004), in some highly restricted linguistic problems rule-based approaches are sufficient. The rule assigning external subjects only needs to account for whether the external subject dependency type is the regular subject type *xsubj* or the copular subject type *xsubj-cop*. Further, chains of clausal complements with external subjects must be correctly addressed, so that each open clausal complement correctly receives an external subject.

4.4 Combining predictions

As mentioned earlier in Section 3.2, the three tasks are not independent of each other: First, if the predicted syntactic function of the relativizer is a subject, the newly inserted subject dependency can produce an external subject dependency as well. Second, both external subjects and the dependencies encoding relativizer functions may propagate in coordinations. Third, propagated subject dependencies may again produce new external subject dependencies.

	P	R	F
Conj. propagation	93.1	92.9	93.0
Relativizer prediction	94.5	92.4	93.5
External subjects	90.0	97.3	93.5
All tasks combined	93.0	93.2	93.1

Table 1: Performance of the combined second layer prediction, as well as the individual tasks measured in terms of precision, recall, and F_1-score on the gold-standard base syntax trees.

The combined prediction of the entire second annotation layer is thus carried out in four separate steps. First, we predict the syntactic functions of relativizers, then the external subjects. After this, the conjuncts are propagated, and finally, the external subjects are predicted again, in order to cover external subjects produced by propagated subject dependencies.

4.5 Machine learning method and parameter selection

The underlying classifier for both the conjunct propagation and the relativizer syntactic function prediction is the multi-class support vector machine implemented in the *SVM-multiclass* package of Joachims (1999). The fast training algorithm implemented for linear kernels in SVM-multiclass is also the reason why we explicitly generate feature pairs, instead of directly utilizing the quadratic kernel. The available data is divided into training (80%), parameter optimization (10%), and test (10%) sets, this division being constant in all reported results. Further, the division is done on document level, i.e., all sentences from a single document in the treebank are assigned to the same set. This is to avoid any possibility of sharing information about the behavior of rare lexical items between the training and test sets. All reported results are obtained by optimizing the SVM regularization parameter C on the parameter optimization set, and using the resulting model on the test set. This optimization is done separately for each task.

5 Evaluation

We evaluate the performance of the predictions in terms of precision (P), recall (R), and F_1-score (F) of the predicted second layer dependencies. Precision is defined as the proportion of dependen-

	P	R	F
Full method	93.3	93.0	93.1
- feature pairs	92.5	92.1	92.3
- lemma	92.5	92.2	92.3
- lemma & morph	90.7	93.4	92.1
- lemma & morph & POS	87.9	91.9	89.9

Table 2: Feature ablation study. *Feature pairs* refer to the second-degree polynomial expansion described in Section 4.1, and *morph* refers to features extracted from morphological tags other than the main POS.

Method	P	R	F
Always	48.5	97.4	64.8
Type	61.8	51.6	56.2
Type and direction	83.5	64.1	72.6
Stanford parser alg.	83.7	57.7	68.3
Proposed method	93.3	93.0	93.1

Table 3: Performance of the proposed machine learning method in terms of precision, recall and F_1-score of propagated dependencies. The performance is compared to the four baselines defined in Section 5.1.

cies in the evaluated output also present in the gold standard, and recall as the proportion of dependencies in the gold standard also present in the evaluated output. Using these, F_1-score is defined as $F = \frac{2PR}{P+R}$. In addition to evaluating the performance using the gold-standard base layer annotation in the treebank, we also perform an evaluation with the base syntax layer produced by a dependency parser, discussed further in Section 5.2.

5.1 Performance and baselines

The evaluation results of the combined second layer prediction are shown in Table 1. The performance on the gold standard base syntax is high, with an overall F_1-score of 93.1%.

For conjunct propagation, which is the largest (71.4% of all second layer dependencies in the treebank are propagated) and arguably most important subtask, we perform several further analyses. Using the gold-standard syntactic information, also including gold-standard relativizer functions and external subjects, we estimate the contribution of the various feature types to the classification performance of the conjunct propagation subtask in a feature ablation study. The results of this study are shown in Table 2. Interestingly, an F_1-score of 89.9%, only 3.2pp lower than the full method, can be achieved only based on the features extracted from the syntactic tree, with no token-derived information whatsoever. Further, we see that using explicit feature pair generation improves the results by 0.8pp.

Next, we compare the performance of the machine learning conjunct propagation method to several baselines. The trivial baseline is to *always propagate*. We also implement a *propagate type* baseline, in which a dependency is propagated only if its type is more likely to propagate than not in the training data, regardless of whether the propagated dependency governs the head of the coordination, or depends on it. Taking into account the fact that dependencies governing the head of the coordination are considerably more likely to propagate (96.5% propagate) compared to those modifying it (32.9% propagate), in the *propagate type and direction* baseline a dependency is propagated only if dependencies with the same type and direction (i.e. govern or depend on the head of the coordination) are more likely to propagate in the training data.

As the primary baseline, we implement a close approximation of the conjunct propagation method in the Stanford Parser,[2] the "reference standard" for the SD scheme. The Stanford Parser conjunct propagation algorithm is relatively conservative, aiming at high precision at the cost of recall. All dependencies governing the head of the coordination are propagated, unless involved in a complex coordination of two relative clauses. Only subject dependencies governed by the head of the coordination are propagated, unless the propagation target already has a subject of its own. The type of a propagated subject dependency may change to/from the passive subject, depending whether the target of the propagation is active or passive. Our implementation differs in the handling of propagation in passive structures, since Finnish does not have passive subjects but rather direct objects.

The performance of the proposed method as well as the four abovementioned baselines is summarized in Table 3. In terms of F_1-score, the proposed method outperforms all baselines by a wide margin. Of particular interest is the gain over the algorithm used in the Stanford parser, the current

[2] `http://nlp.stanford.edu/software/lex-parser.shtml`, version 2.0.4

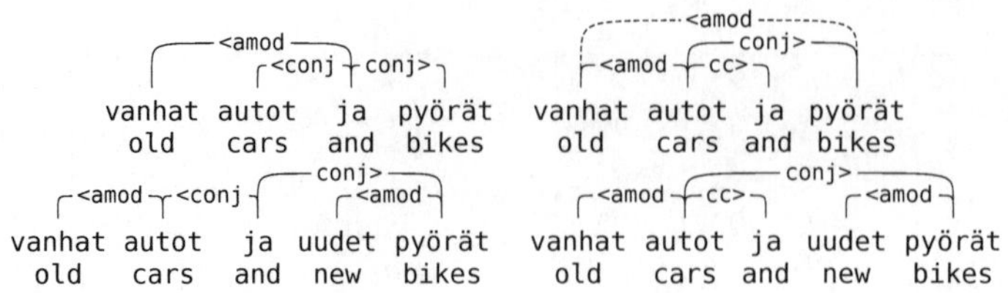

Figure 4: Left: the conjunction-as-head analysis, akin to the Link Grammar scheme. Modifiers of all coordinated elements are attached to the conjunction, while modifiers of a single coordinated element are attached to the element itself. In the top analysis, the adjective *vanhat* (*old*) modifies the whole coordination, and in the bottom analysis, only the first conjunct. Right: the corresponding analyses in the SD scheme. The example can be translated as *the old cars and (the new) bikes.*

widely-used reference implementation of conjunction propagation in the SD scheme.

5.2 Performance on parser output

Next, we discuss the performance of the proposed method on input produced by a dependency parser, as opposed to gold standard syntactic trees. This will also allow us to test one additional baseline, the conjunction-as-head analysis, discussed later in this section.

The parser used in the evaluation is a combination of the HunPOS tagger (Halácsy et al., 2007) with the Mate-Tools statistical dependency parser of Bohnet (2010), a second-order graph-based parser that achieves a state-of-the-art performance on a number of different languages; an earlier version of this parser ranked first on English and German in the CoNLL shared task in 2009 (Hajič and others, 2009). With a labeled attachment score of 81%, this combination represents the best dependency parser currently available for Finnish as tested on the Turku Dependency Treebank, outperforming for instance the popular MaltParser (Nivre et al., 2007) by several percentage points.[3]

When parser output is considered, a drop in performance is to be expected, seeing that coordination is one of the hardest phenomena to parse, and the parser often fails to produce the dependencies needed in order to generate the propagated dependencies. The evaluation on top of the parser output is presented in Table 4. The overall F_1-score is 61.8% (compared to 93.1% on gold standard syntax), and on the coordination propagation task only, the F_1 score is 58.4% (compared to 93.0% on gold standard syntax). This performance drop can be attributed to the accuracy of the underlying parse trees, since the correct base syntax structure is present only for 66.1% of the propagated dependencies in the gold standard, thus imposing a severe restriction on the recall of the conjunct propagation method. This reflects the intrinsic difficulty of syntactically parsing coordination structures. In contrast, 89.1% of relativizer dependencies are correctly recovered by the base parser, allowing a much higher recall on this task. Out of all errors in all three subtasks, approximately 79.2% can be attributed to the parser output not containing the required base structure, meaning that in fact, the performance of the machine learning method itself does not degrade notably when applied to parser output.

	P	R	F
Conj. propagation	58.1	58.6	58.4
Relativizer prediction	85.5	83.3	84.4
External subjects	67.5	73.0	70.1
All tasks combined	61.3	62.2	61.8

Table 4: Performance of the combined second layer prediction, as well as the individual tasks measured in terms of precision, recall, and F_1-score on top of statistical parser output.

We also repeat the baseline experiments discussed above using parser output rather than gold standard dependencies. Since reliable external subject and relativizer function dependencies are not available for the parser output, we disregard these. The results are given in Table 5, demonstrating that the performance of the proposed method is clearly superior to all of the baselines also on parser output.

As a final point of comparison, we test a joint approach to parsing and conjunct propaga-

[3]A detailed description of the parser pipeline is out-of-scope for this paper. The parser is described in a manuscript currently under review.

Method	P	R	F
Always	30.5	62.3	40.9
Type	37.9	29.8	33.4
Type and direction	50.9	38.2	43.6
Stanford parser alg.	54.1	38.5	44.9
Proposed method	57.3	58.0	57.7

Table 5: Performance of the method as compared to the baselines of Section 5.1 on top of parser output.

tion, by adopting an analysis where the conjunction is the head of the coordination structure, as has been done for instance in the Link Grammar parser (Sleator and Temperley, 1993). In this scheme, a dependent modifying a single coordinated element is governed by this element whereas a dependent modifying all of the coordinated elements is governed by the coordinating conjunction. This approach is illustrated in Figure 4. The most important property of this representation is that in both cases, the resulting analysis is a tree, which in turn can be used to train a dependency parser, thus combining base syntax parsing with conjunct propagation as a single joint task.

We have developed a forward and backward conversion to the conjunction-as-head style. Note that this conversion is not lossless, as there are several structures which this analysis cannot express: dependents modifying multiple but not all coordinated elements, and cases where the governor to the head of the coordination does not propagate. Further, dependencies whose type changes as a result of the propagation cannot be represented either. A difficulty is also presented by cases where no explicit conjunction is stated in the text, nor is there a punctuation symbol (such as a comma) which would serve its role. These cases, however, only occur in 0.5% of all sentences, which we subsequently discard. Applying the forward and backward conversion to the gold-standard data results in a precision of 92.6% and a recall of 92.3% in propagated dependencies, demonstrating that the majority of cases are within scope for the conjunction-as-head analysis. Finally, note that this style cannot directly represent the other second layer dependencies like external subjects.

Using again the Mate-Tools parser of Bohnet (2010), trained on the treebank transformed in the conjunction-as-head style, the performance on propagated base layer dependencies is shown in Table 6 and compared to the proposed machine learning method, re-trained to match the input data (i.e. no external subjects or relativizer syntactic functions present). Here we see that the joint parsing and propagation perform notably worse in comparison with the proposed method. This agrees with the results of Schwartz et al. (2012), who show in their studies about learnability of different syntactic schemes that making the first conjunct of coordination as a head improves parsing results significantly. It is also important to remember that the conjunction-as-head analysis incurs a notable penalty for not being able to represent approximately 7% of the conjunct propagation cases in the data, as demonstrated by the recall of the forward and backward conversion.

	P	R	F
Conj. as head	43.7	42.6	43.1
Proposed method	58.2	58.8	58.5

Table 6: Comparisons of results obtained by reverse converting to SD the output of a statistical parser trained to produce the conjunction-as-head style of analysis, with the proposed method.

5.3 Discussion

When examining the results presented in this paper, two issues should be noted. First, although the conjunct propagation of the SD scheme is indeed closely related to the resolution of coordination scope ambiguity, it is not the entirety of this difficult disambiguation problem. Consider, for instance, the English phrase *corn and peanut butter*. This phrase contains a coordination ambiguity: either it describes butter made of corn and peanuts, or one of the items described is corn and the other peanut butter. However, this ambiguity lies deeper than the conjunct propagation layer of the SD scheme, as illustrated in Figure 5. As a result, when the method presented in this paper is applied, this particular ambiguity has already been resolved by the parser that has produced the base-syntactic trees.

Second, a similar note applies to the specific nature of the Finnish language, or the Finnish compound nouns in particular. Unlike for instance in English, in Finnish it is customary to write compounds as one word. As a consequence, this particular ambiguity is not very problem-

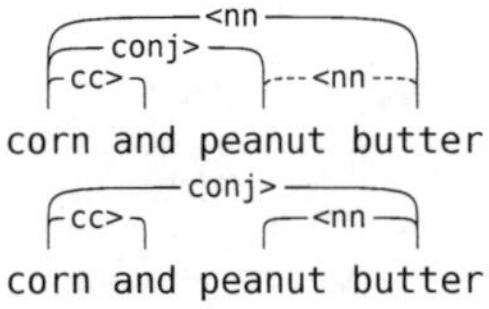

Figure 5: The ambiguity of the phrase *corn and peanut butter* is to be resolved in the *basic* variant of the SD scheme, not in the conjunct propagation layer. Top: the reading where the butter is made of corn and peanuts. Bottom: the reading where corn is combined with peanut butter. Note that while there is a propagated dependency present in the top reading, the decision whether this dependency should be generated or not does not represent the ambiguity of the phrase, and in fact, there is no valid reading where the propagated dependency would be absent, that is, a reading where the butter would be made of corn but not peanuts.

Figure 6: The difference between a simple noun coordinated with a compound and a two-part compound is surface-marked in Finnish using a dash. The top phrase can be translated as *a pine and fir forest* and the bottom phrase as *a pine and a fir forest*.

atic in Finnish, since the difference is surface-marked using a dash. For instance, the coordination *mänty- ja kuusimetsä* (*a pine and fir forest*) describes a forest growing both pines and firs, whereas *mänty ja kuusimetsä* (*a pine and a fir forest*) is the coordination of a single pine combined with a fir forest. Also, as breaking compound words into their components during the syntax annotation is not allowed, the analyses of the two Finnish phrases in TDT would in fact be identical, as illustrated in Figure 6, and would not involve propagation of dependencies.

6 Conclusion

In this paper, we have introduced a method for inferring additional sentence structure information from a dependency parse tree in the Stanford Dependencies scheme, most importantly *propagation of conjunct dependencies*, which is related to resolving *coordination scope ambiguities*. This machine learning based method uses the syntactic trees and morphological information to predict the additional dependencies, which can be highly useful in for instance the construction of a PropBank, as previously demonstrated by Haverinen et al. (2010).

On gold standard syntactic trees, the method achieves 93.1% F_1-score. When evaluated on top of actual parser output rather than gold standard trees, the performance predictably suffers a penalty, but an analysis of the errors reveals that 79.2% of all errors, when evaluated on parser output, are due to the parser not producing the correct base structure and thus disallowing the method from retrieving the correct dependencies.

In addition, we have also separately evaluated the largest and most important subtask, the conjunct propagation by comparing it against several baseline methods, including the method used in the original Stanford tools. We find that the proposed method clearly outperforms all baselines, and in particular, it achieves improved results over the method used in the original Stanford tools, which are widely used for producing the additional dependencies in applications, and can thus serve as its more accurate replacement in all applications that rely on syntactic analysis in the SD scheme. Interestingly, we also find that when using no token-based information, an F_1-score of 89.9% can be achieved for this subtask, only 3.2pp lower than the full, lexicalized set of features. This demonstrates that much of the necessary information for the task is contained in the syntactic trees themselves.

The software used in this work will be integrated with the existing Finnish parser and made publicly available at the address `http://bionlp.utu.fi/`, under an open licence. The training data will be available for the public in the final version of the Turku Dependency Treebank.

Acknowledgments

This work was supported by the Academy of Finland and the Emil Aaltonen Foundation. Computational resources were provided by CSC – IT Center for Science.

References

Rajeev Agarwal and Lois Boggess. 1992. A simple but useful approach to conjunct identification. In *Proceedings of ACL'92*, pages 15–21.

Bernd Bohnet. 2010. Top accuracy and fast dependency parsing is not a contradiction. In *Proceedings of COLING'10*, pages 89–97.

Joan Bresnan. 2001. *Lexical-functional syntax*, volume 16 of *Blackwell Textbooks in Linguistics*. Blackwell.

Richard Campbell. 2004. Using linguistic principles to recover empty categories. In *Proceedings of ACL*, pages 646–653.

Francis Chantree, Adam Kilgarriff, Anne de Roeck, and Alistair Willis. 2005. Disambiguating coordinations using word distribution information. In *Proceedings of RANLP'05*.

Andrew B. Clegg and Adrian Shepherd. 2007. Benchmarking natural-language parsers for biological applications using dependency graphs. *BMC Bioinformatics*, 8(1):24.

Miriam Goldberg. 1999. An unsupervised model for statistically determining coordinate phrase attachment. In *Proceedings of ACL'99*, pages 610–614.

Jan Hajič et al. 2009. The conll-2009 shared task: syntactic and semantic dependencies in multiple languages. In *Proceedings of CoNLL'09*, pages 1–18.

Péter Halácsy, András Kornai, and Csaba Oravecz. 2007. HunPos – an open source trigram tagger. In *Proceedings of ACL'07, Companion Volume*, pages 209–212.

Katri Haverinen, Filip Ginter, Veronika Laippala, Timo Viljanen, and Tapio Salakoski. 2010. Dependency-based propbanking of clinical Finnish. In *Proceedings of LAW IV*, pages 137–141.

Katri Haverinen, Filip Ginter, Veronika Laippala, Samuel Kohonen, Timo Viljanen, Jenna Nyblom, and Tapio Salakoski. 2011. A dependency-based analysis of treebank annotation errors. In *Proceedings of Depling'11*, pages 115–124.

Katri Haverinen. 2012. Syntax annotation guidelines for the Turku Dependency Treebank. Technical Report 1034, Turku Centre for Computer Science, January.

Thorsten Joachims. 1999. Making large-scale SVM learning practical. In *Advances in Kernel Methods - Support Vector Learning*, pages 169–184. MIT Press.

Daisuke Kawahara and Sadao Kurohashi. 2007. Probabilistic coordination disambiguation in a fully-lexicalized Japanese parser. In *Proceedings of EMNLP-CoNLL'07*, pages 306–314.

Daisuke Kawahara and Sadao Kurohashi. 2011. Generative modeling of coordination by factoring parallelism and selectional preferences. In *Proceedings of IJCNLP'11*, pages 456–464.

Jin-Dong Kim, Sampo Pyysalo, Tomoko Ohta, Robert Bossy, Ngan Nguyen, and Jun'ichi Tsujii. 2011. Overview of bionlp shared task 2011. In *Proceedings of BioNLP Shared Task 2011 Workshop*, pages 1–6. Association for Computational Linguistics.

Tracy Holloway King, Crouch Richard, Stefan Riezler, Mary Dalrymple, and Ronald M. Kaplan. 2003. The PARC 700 dependency bank. In *Proceedings of LINC'03*, pages 1–8.

Dekang Lin. 1998. A dependency-based method for evaluating broad-coverage parsers. *Natural Language Engineering*, 4(2):97–114.

Marie-Catherine de Marneffe and Christopher Manning. 2008. Stanford typed dependencies manual. Technical report, Stanford University, September.

Ryan McDonald and Fernando Pereira. 2006. Online learning of approximate dependency parsing algorithms. In *Proceedings of the 11th Conference of the European Chapter of the Association for Computational Linguistics (EACL)*, pages 81–88.

Joakim Nivre, Johan Hall, Jens Nilsson, Atanas Chanev, Gülşen Eryiğit, Sandra Kübler, Svetoslav Marinov, and Erwin Marsi. 2007. MaltParser: A language-independent system for data-driven dependency parsing. *Natural Language Engineering*, 13(2):95–135.

Martha Palmer, Daniel Gildea, and Paul Kingsbury. 2005. The Proposition Bank: An annotated corpus of semantic roles. *Computational Linguistics*, 31(1):71–106.

Philip Resnik. 1999. Semantic similarity in a taxonomy: An information-based measure and its application to problems of ambiguity in natural language. *Journal of Artificial Intelligence Research*, 11:95–130.

Kenji Sagae and Jun'ichi Tsujii. 2008. Shift-reduce dependency dag parsing. In *Proceedings of the 22nd International Conference on Computational Linguistics (Coling 2008) - Volume 1*, pages 753–760.

Roy Schwartz, Omri Abend, and Ari Rappoport. 2012. Learnability-based syntactic annotation design. In *Proceedings of the 24th International Conference on Computational Linguistics (Coling 2012)*, pages 2405–2422.

Daniel Sleator and Davy Temperley. 1993. Parsing English with a Link Grammar. In *Proceedings of IWPT'93*, pages 277–291.

Gertjan van Noord. 2007. Using-self-trained bilexical preferences to improve disambiguation accuracy. In *Proceedings of IWPT'07*, pages 1–10.

Deniz Yuret, Laura Rimmell, and Aydin Han. 2012. Parser evaluation using textual entailments. *Language Resources and Evaluation*, pages 1–21.

A Look at Tesnière's *Éléments* through the Lens of Modern Syntactic Theory

Timothy Osborne
615 6th Street Apt. 110
Kirkland, WA 98033
USA

tjo3ya@yahoo.com

Abstract

A recent project to produce a much belated English translation of Lucien Tesnière's *Éléments de syntaxe structurale* has provided the opportunity for an in depth look at Tesnière's theory of syntax. This contribution examines a few aspects of Tesnière's work through the lens of modern syntactic theory. Tesnière's understandings of constituents and phrases, auxiliary verbs, prepositions, gapping, right node raising, propositional infinitives, and exocentric structures are all briefly considered. Concerning some of these areas, we see that Tesnière was visionary with his analysis, whereas in other areas, modern syntactic theory now rejects his account. Of particular interest is the fact that Tesnière's theory was not entirely dependency-based. His account of *transfer* (Fr. *translation*) acknowledged exocentric structures, which means his system was also employing constituency. In this regard, one can, surprisingly, classify Tesnière's theory as a hybrid dependency-constituency grammar.

1 Introduction

Lucien Tesnière (1893-1954) is widely considered to be the father of modern dependency grammars (DGs). While the dependency concept certainly existed in varying forms in the works of numerous grammarians that preceded him, Tesnière (1959) was the first to fully utilize the concept of direct word-word dependencies in a comprehensive manner and to illustrate these dependencies using tree representations (stemmas) that left no doubt about the analysis of syntactic structure being proposed. In particular, Tesnière appears to have been the first prominent theoretician to have rejected the binary division of the clause into a subject and predicate and to have replaced this division with verb centrality. The placement of the verb as the root of all syntactic structure was the all-important novelty (and the main act of genius) in his theory. Given verb centrality, the theory of syntax that Tesnière was proposing could not help but be construed as a DG.

Despite the fact that Tesnière is widely acknowledged as the father of an entire stream of syntactic theory, most syntacticians and grammarians lack exposure to his work. Few grammarians have actually read Tesnière's *Éléments de syntaxe structurale*, largely because an English translation of the *Éléments* is absent from the world of linguistics. Spanish, Italian, and German translations of the *Éléments* exist, but surprisingly, no English translation is yet available. With this lacuna in mind, a recent project to translate the *Éléments* into English has been initiated and is continuing at present. This project is providing an in depth look at Tesnière's theory and has motivated the current contribution.

Tesnière's *Éléments* is large in size, 670 pages with hundreds of tables and tree diagrams (stemmas). Tesnière addresses many aspects and phenomena of syntax, whereby he employs examples from approximately two dozen languages, many of which he actually spoke – Tesnière was a true polyglot. In this respect, the intent of the current contribution is to briefly consider only a few important areas of the *Éléments*, these areas being the ones that stuck out during the translation work. Certain aspects of Tesnière's understanding of constituents and

Proceedings of the Second International Conference on Dependency Linguistics (DepLing 2013), pages 262–271,
Prague, August 27–30, 2013.

phrases, auxiliary verbs, prepositions, gapping, right node raising, propositional infinitives, and exocentric structures are considered below.

Two highlights can be mentioned here up front. First, Tesnière rejected much of the terminology of syntax that preceded him, declaring that morphologists had imposed their nomenclature on the study of syntax and thus confused our understanding of syntax (ch. 15). In this regard, Tesnière had a penchant for introducing new terms, many of which have not become established. One can therefore speculate about the reduced impact of his work due to his unfortunate use of terminology. Second, Tesnière never actually employed the term *dependency grammar* (Fr. *grammaire de la dépandence*). In fact it seems likely that he was not aware of the difference between dependency and constituency, since that distinction would be established later during the reception of his work.[1] In this respect, he did not shy away from employing constituency in his theory of *transfer* (Fr. *translation*), a fact that may have been overlooked until now.

To conclude this introduction, a note concerning the citation practice employed below for Tesnière's book is necessary. The *Éléments* is split into 278 chapters, whereby each paragraph in a chapter is numbered. When citing specific passages, the chapter (ch.) and paragraph (§) are given (e.g. ch. 3, §3) instead of the page number. This practice avoids confusion that might arise if page numbers were cited due to the various editions of the *Éléments* in various languages (French, German, Spanish, Italian, and soon English as well).

2 Constituents and phrases

The constituent is the basic unit of syntactic analysis assumed by most constituency grammars. A constituent is typically defined as *a node plus all the nodes that that node dominates* (for similar definitions, see Napoli 1993:167; Jacobson 1996:55; Haegeman and Guéron 1999:51; Carnie 2008:37). Given such a definition, the number of constituents in a given tree structure matches the number of nodes. In the past, many DGs seem to have overlooked the fact that the definition is applicable to dependency structures as well and that it identifies subtrees as constituents. A subtree that consists of a single node is simply a *word*, whereas a subtree consisting of more than one word is a *phrase*. In other words, DGs can and do acknowledge constituents and phrases just like constituency grammars do, the only difference being that DGs acknowledge many fewer of both.

Tesnière certainly saw the need to acknowledge the status of subtrees as particular units of syntax, but his use of terminology in the area was not consistent and this inconsistency has probably contributed to the confusion about whether dependency grammars acknowledge constituents and phrases.

Tesnière defined the node (Fr. *nœud*) as follows:

> "We will define the *node* as a group consisting of a governor and all the subordinates that are to some degree either directly or indirectly dependent on that governor. The governor joins these nodes into a single cluster." (ch. 3, §3)

It should be apparent from this definition that Tesnière saw any subtree of a tree as a node, which in turn means that he was acknowledging constituents and phrases, although the terminology he was using to denote these units (*nœud*) was different from modern usage (*constituent*, *phrase*).

In fact Tesnière's use of terminology was, as stated, inconsistent in this area.[2] While his original definition suggested that his node was to be understood as a subtree, his later (and preferred) use of the term points to the meaning 'vertex'. In other words, Tesnière usually meant just 'vertex' when he wrote *nœud* despite the fact that he had defined the node to be a subtree, i.e. a constituent. The contradiction in his use of terminology is seen most vividly in the passage where he is comparing the node to the *nucleus*:

> "The *node* is nothing more than a geometric point, whereas the *nucleus* is a collection of multiple points,..." (ch. 22, §12)

[1] According to Jurafsky and Martin (2000:489), David Hays (1964) may have been the first to employ the term *dependency grammar*.

[2] This statement may be unfair. The *Éléments* was published posthumously. The inconsistency in the use of the term *nœud* may have arisen as the manuscript was being prepared for publication by others.

Comparing this passage with the previous one where Tesnière initially defines the node, the contradiction should be apparent.

The pertinent question now concerns the extent to which Tesnière's inconsistent use of terminology has contributed to the fallacious perception that DGs do not acknowledge constituents and phrases. They of course can and do acknowledge such units, although they have not been clear about their use of the associated terminology.

3 Auxiliary verbs

Most modern DGs assume that auxiliary verbs dominate main verbs, and in this respect, they are consistent with most constituency grammars. In the Government and Binding framework (Chomsky 1981), for instance, a finite verb resides in I, which projects up to IP, the root node of the clause, and in the Head-Driven Phrase Structure Grammar framework (Pollard and Sag 1994), a finite auxiliary verb is the head daughter in the clause, which means it passes its features up to the root node of the clause, the clause being a greater VP in a sense.

Tesnière, in contrast, did not explicitly state that given a two-word string such as *has gone*, the auxiliary verb *has* governs the main verb *gone*. He instead positioned the two in one and the same *split nucleus* (*nucleus dissocié*, ch. 23). The auxiliary verb *has* guarantees the syntactic contribution of the split nucleus and the full verb *gone* guarantees its semantic contribution. Tesnière drew a bubble around the two words in order to indicate that the two belong to one and the same nucleus. He illustrated this state of affairs with the diagram of the sentence *Alfred a oublié son chapeau hier* 'Alfred forgot his hat yesterday' (ch. 31, stemma 39):

(1)

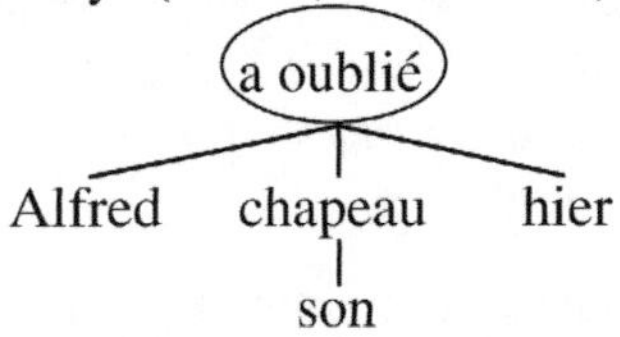

Given this analysis, Tesnière, if he were alive today, might object to the widespread assumption that sees the auxiliary verb governing the main verb.

On the other hand, he might actually approve of the modern practice, since he drew another distinction that can be interpreted as accommodating the modern analysis. He distinguished between *constitutive* and *subsidiary* words inside nuclei (ch. 29). A constitutive word guarantees the syntactic integrity of the nucleus, whereas the subsidiary word is a satellite of the constitutive word. He also states (ch. 38, §13) that in a split nucleus consisting of an auxiliary verb and a full verb, the auxiliary verb is constitutive. Further, he explains that from an etymological point of view, the constitutive word once governed the subsidiary word (ch. 29, §18) and that this fact can be shown inside a nucleus by positioning the constitutive word above the subsidiary word. This practice would result in tree representations like the following one (my rendition, not Tesnière's):

(2)

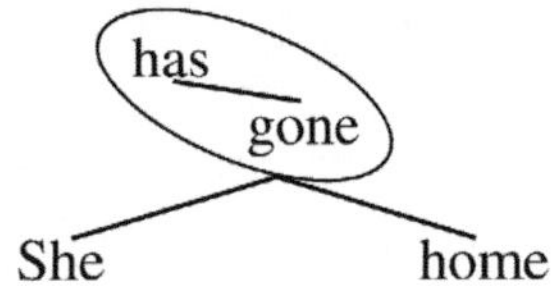

The step from this tree to the modern analysis is not so great. By positioning the subject as a direct dependent of the finite verb and the adverb as a direct dependent of the participle, one accommodates directly in the tree both subject-verb agreement and the lack of object-verb agreement:

(3)

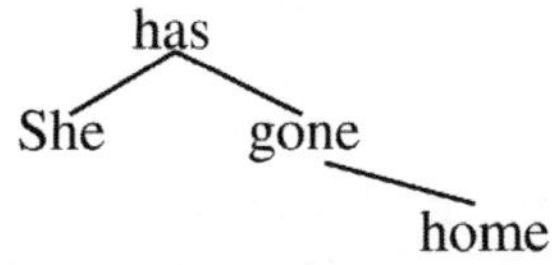

These considerations suggest that the modern practice in both constituency and dependency grammars of positioning the auxiliary verb as head over the full verb is not necessarily contrary to Tesnière's theory. In fact Tesnière's analysis can be construed as presaging the modern analysis of auxiliary verbs, which did not take full hold until the 1980s – in Transformational Grammar, the auxiliary verb was originally construed as a daughter of S (but not as the head daughter).

4 Prepositions

While Tesnière's account of auxiliary verbs presaged the modern analysis, his account of prepositions was entirely contrary to modern assumptions. He classified many prepositions as semantically empty (Fr. *mot vide*) (ch. 28, §18) and syntactically subsidiary (Fr. *mot subsidiaire*) (ch. 29, §4). For Tesnière, prepositions were *translatives* (ch. 40, §4), which meant they served to transfer a word of one class into a word of another class, e.g. a noun to an adjective. The fact that these words were subsidiary means that for Tesnière, they could be analyzed as etymologically dependent on a constitutive word within a nucleus (ch. 29, §18). What this means is that from an etymological point of view, Tesnière took the preposition to be a dependent of the noun inside a split nucleus, e.g.

(4)

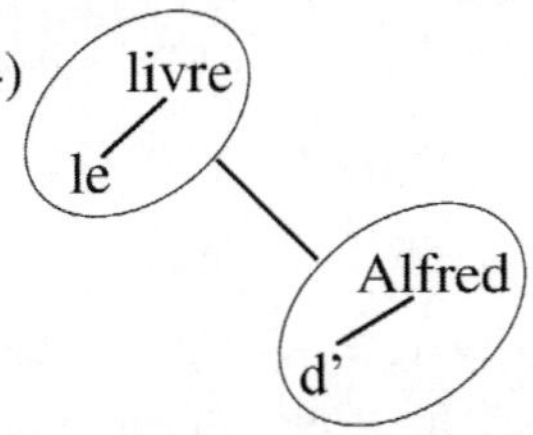

le livre d' Alfred
'Alfred's book'

This tree has been adapted from stemma 32 (ch.29) to show the etymological dependencies inside the nuclei. The important point is that the status of the preposition *d'* in Tesnière's system as a subsidiary word requires one to view it in an etymological sense as a dependent of the prepositional object. This analysis is, however, quite contrary to modern accounts, which almost unanimously take the preposition to be head over its object.

To be fair, Tesnière's analysis of prepositions was not entirely unlike the syntactic analysis of prepositions of his day. For instance, Bloomfield's original analysis of prepositional phrases (1933) took them to be exocentric constructions, meaning that neither the preposition nor its object noun could be construed as the head of the phrase. Section 8 below has more to say about the distinction between endo- and exocentric constituents.

5 Gapping and right node raising

The part of Tesnière's theory that was perhaps most ahead of its time regards coordination (*Jonction*, Part II of the *Éléments*). In particular, Tesnière identified and produced an analysis of two aspects of coordinate structures, *gapping* and *right node raising*, that would not be acknowledged and explored until much later in the works of Ross (1970), Jackendoff (1971), and Postal (1974). Tesnière recognized key traits of gapping and right node raising and his analysis of these phenomena remains largely consistent with more modern DG accounts (e.g. Hudson 1988, 1989, Osborne 2008), although there are certainly differences in the details.

Tesnière called gapping *double bifurcation* (*bifidité double*, ch. 146). He interpreted it to be a combination of both *catadidymic* and *anadidymic* coordination (Fr. *jonction catadidymes et anadidymes*, ch. 145, §13). Catadidymic coordination obtains when one or more shared dependents appear to the immediate right of the coordinate structure, whereas anadidymic coordination obtains when one or more shared dependents appears to the immediate left of the coordinate structure, e.g.

Catadidymic

(5) [R. picks] and [B. cracks] the chestnuts.

Anadidymic

(6) A. [loves cake] and [detests punishment].

The expressions *catadidymic* and *anadidymic* are obscure terms that Tesnière borrowed from biology. He describes their meaning with a metaphor as follows:

> "..., catadidymic sentences are comparable to the dragon with multiple heads in the fable (cf. La Fontaine, *Fables*, I, 12), and anadidymic sentences to the dragon with multiple tails." (ch. 145, §14)

While Tesnière's analysis of these examples was insightful, his choice of obscure terminology has probably hindered the spread of his theory of coordination (and otherwise) more than anything. The modern English designation for instances of coordination like the one in (5) is *right node raising*, a term that is due to Postal (1974). While this modern term is also not ideal (because Postal's original analysis of the phenomenon is no longer defended), it at least contains "right", this adjective pointing to the fact that the shared material appears to the right of the coordinate structure.

Tesnière took instances of gapping to be a combination of both catadidymic and anadidymic coordination. He therefore coined the term *anacatadidymic* to denote the phenomenon, e.g.

Anacatadidymic
(7) The one carries his armor, the other his shield.

He characterized anacatadidymic coordination with the following metaphor:

> "This sentence behaves like a dragon that has both multiple heads and multiple tails, but just one trunk. Or even like Siamese twins who are conjoined together back to back." (ch. 146, §4)

We again sense that Tesnière's choice of terminology was poor, since the term *anacatadidymic* does not evoke any associations. The modern term for such instances of coordination, i.e. *gapping*, is much more appropriate, since one clearly senses the presence of a "gap"; the verb is gapped from the non-initial conjuncts.

Tesnière's primary insight in cases of gapping was that the verb is shared in a sense, a point that nobody would dispute. He rendered such cases of gapping with the French version of the following stemma:

(8)
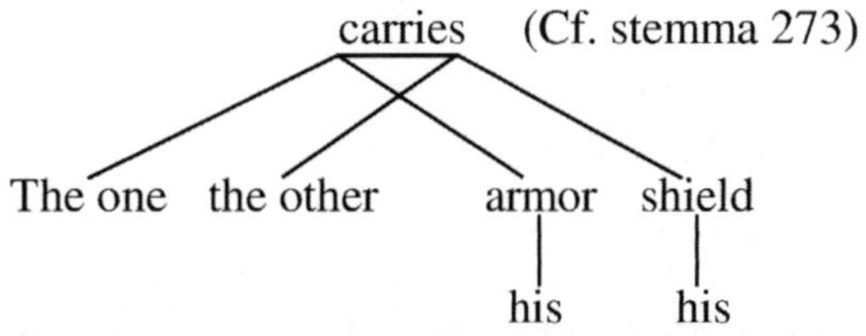

This stemma indicates important aspects of interpretation and meaning; it shows that the first subject and object share the verb in the same manner as the second subject and object. Furthermore, it shows that the verb has two subject actants and two object actants. Tesnière also correctly observed (ch. 146, §12) that the remnants in the gapped conjunct can be adjuncts (*circonstants*) as well as arguments (*actants*).

While Tesnière's analysis of gapping was brief (ch. 146 only), it correctly identified key aspects of the gapping mechanism. The reason Tesnière is not credited with his insightful analysis may in part be his unfortunate choice of terminology. His penchant for obscure grammatical terms certainly did not promote the accessibility of his account.

6 More on right node raising

As mentioned in the previous section, Tesnière also identified the mechanism of *right node raising*. His analysis was, again, characterized in terms of bifurcation, whereby the particular type of bifurcation he assumed in cases of right node raising was catadidymic, i.e. the shared dependents appeared to the right of the coordinate structure (a dragon with two heads but just one tail).

Tesnière produced the following dependency analysis of the sentence *Raton picks and Bertrand cracks the chestnuts*:

(9)
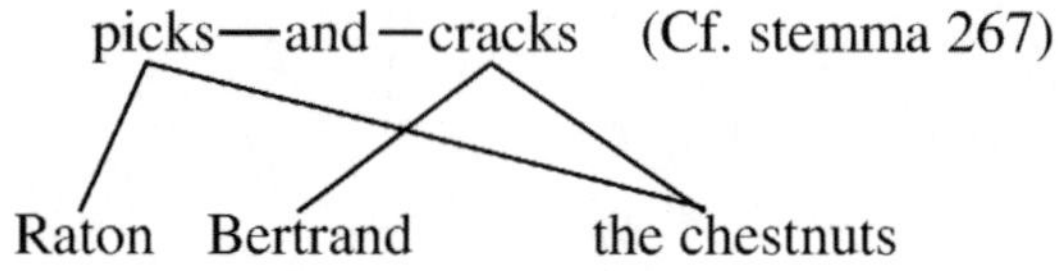

This stemma correctly reflects some of the key traits of right node raising. It shows the manner in which the object *the chestnuts* is shared by the verbs at the same time that the verbs do not share a subject. It also correctly indicates that coordination occurs at the highest level, i.e. with the verbs.

Another important aspect of the analysis in (9) is that it does not rely on some notion of deletion or ellipsis, and in this respect, it is congruent with certain data where we can see that an ellipsis or deletion analysis contradicts observation, e.g.

(10) a. [I sang] and [you hummed] the same tune.

b. *[I sang ~~the same tune~~] and [you hummed the same tune].

The deletion analysis indicated in (10b) cannot be correct, since the non-elided version of the sentence would mean something different from (10a). In other words, *I sang the same tune and you hummed the same tune* does not correctly reflect the intended meaning of (10a), since it necessitates that the tune referenced appear in the preceding context, whereas sentence (10a) is not referencing a tune in the previous context.

While Tesnière's analysis of right node raising and other phenomena of coordination did not posit deletion or ellipsis, he did make clear that at a semantic level, coordination involves the 'addition' of numerous underlying sentences.

His comment in this regard was that coordination is a very powerful device that allows for great economy of expression, a statement that no one who has studied coordination would dispute.

7 Propositional infinitives

In modern syntactic theory, the analysis of certain *to*-infinitives is a matter of controversy.

(11) a. I believe her to be a genius.

b. You assumed me to know the answer.

There are essentially two competing analyses of the underlined strings: either the object nominal and the *to*-infinitive phrase form a constituent or they do not. If they do not, both are construed as dependents of the matrix verb. The two competing analyses are illustrated as follows:

(12)

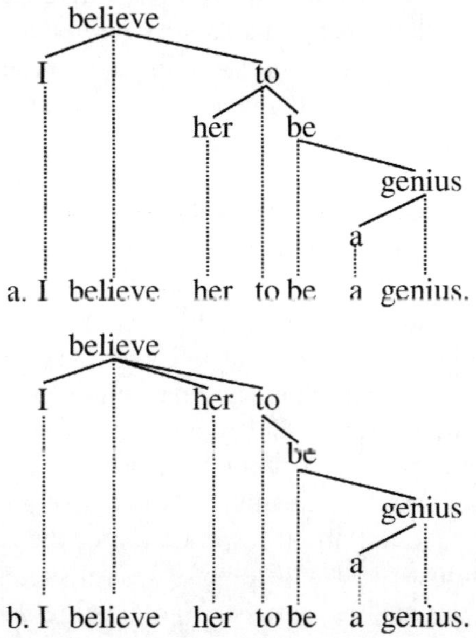

The main distinction here is whether the object nominal (here *her*) is construed as a dependent of the matrix verb or of the embedded verb (here of the particle *to*). Modern transformational/derivational accounts of such data are assocated with *small clauses*, and they prefer an analysis like the one in (12a) (e.g. Chomsky 1986:20, Ouhalla 1994:109ff., Haegeman and Guéron 1999:108ff.), whereas representational grammars, which tend to be accepting of flatter structures, prefer the analysis in (12b) (e.g. Culicover and Jackendoff 2005:131ff.).

Surprisingly, Tesnière's account of such data is more supportive of the analysis shown in (12a) than of the one in (12b). This is surprising because the very nature of dependency-based analyses of syntactic structure is that they must in many cases assume relatively flat structures. Tesnière called the small-clause-like constructions illustrated with (11-12) *propositional infinitives* (ch. 182). Based primarily on data from Latin and Greek, he construed the propositional infinitive as the root of a clause-like substructure.

The particular analysis he assumed is illustrated with the Latin sentence *Credo Deum esse sanctum* 'I believe God to be holy'.

(13) (stemma 307)

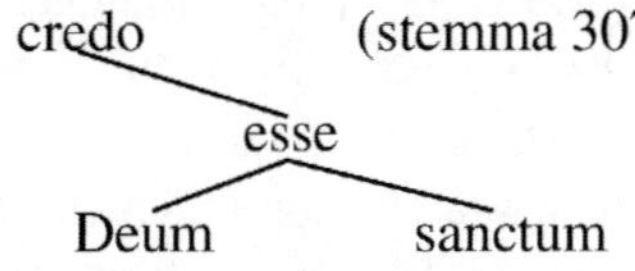

The thing to note about this example is the fact that Tesnière construed *Deum* 'God' as a dependent of *esse* 'be'. His analysis was therefore similar to the analysis in (12a), both trees showing the (*to*-)infinitive as the root of an infinitival clause. The main piece of evidence that he produces in favor of the analysis in (13) is that the entire propositional infinitive phrase can function as subject, whereby the logical subject of the infinitive, *Deum* in (13), remains in the accusative case. Tesnière illustrated this fact with a different Latin sentence:

(14)

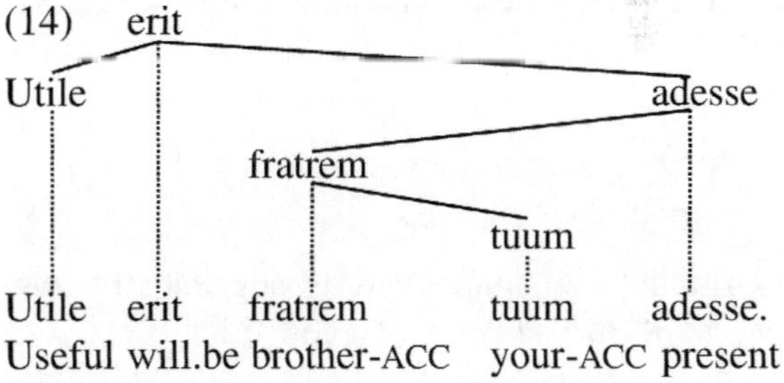

Useful will.be brother-ACC your-ACC present
'Your brother's presence will be useful.'

The fact that *fratrem tuum* remains in the accusative case suggests strongly that *fratrem tuum* is indeed a dependent of *adesse* as shown in (14), for if *fratrem tuum* were a dependent of *erit*, we would expect to find the nominative case, *frater tuus*. In other words, the nominative *frater tuus* instead of the accusative *fratrem tuum* would be necessary if *fratrem tuum* were a dependent of the finite verb *erit*. It would be functioning syntactically like a normal subject and would therefore have to appear in the nominative.

Tesnière also notes that propositional infinitives occur in English (and French). The English example he produces is *I suppose my friend to be very rich* (ch. 182, §14). While he did not produce a tree to illustrate his structural analysis of this sentence, we can assume that he would have extended his analysis of the Latin examples to English, whereby the noun phrase *my friend* would be construed as a dependent of the split nucleus *to be*.

While Tesnière's analysis of propositional infinitives seems correct for the Latin and Greek data that he discussed, it is debatable whether the analysis shown in (13) can be extended to English examples. In fact there is strong evidence suggesting that his analysis of the Latin and Greek examples does not extend to English. In other words, Tesnière's analysis of small clause-like constructions was probably incorrect for English. A number of facts demonstrate this to be the case. For instance, the propositional infinitive cannot function as the subject in English, e.g.

(15) a. *My friend to be very rich is supposed.

But the object nominal can become the subject in the passive-like counterpart:

(15) b. My friend is supposed to be very rich.

Furthermore, the object nominal can be a reflexive pronoun that is co-referential with the subject:

(15) c. My friend supposes himself to be very rich.

And finally, constituency tests suggest that *my friend to be very rich* is not a constituent, e.g.

(16) a. *My friend to be very rich I suppose. - Topicalization

d. *It is my friend to be very rich that I suppose. - Clefting.

e. ??What I suppose is my friend to be very rich. - Pseudoclefting

f. What do I suppose? ??– My friend to be very rich. - Answer fragment

If the object nominal were a dependent of the propositional infinitive, we would expect these constituency tests to identify the infinitival clause as a constituent. These data therefore point to the validity of the analysis in (12b), where the pronoun *her* and the infinitival phrase *to be a genius* do not form a constituent.

The conclusion to be drawn from this dicussion is that Tesnière's analysis of propositional infinitives was perhaps correct for Latin and Greek, but it cannot be extended to English (and not to French). His analysis was therefore not nuanced enough. A syntactic construction that was productive in Latin and ancient Greek has become largely lexicalized in modern English, meaning that only a relatively small number of predicates in English (e.g. *assume*, *believe*, *suppose*, *take*) subcategorize for such a propositional infinitive.

8 Exocentric structures

As stated in the introduction, Tesnière never employed the term *dependency grammar* (Fr. *grammaire de dépandence*). In fact Tesnière rarely used the term *dependent* in the sense that it is understood today in modern DGs; he preferred the term *subordinate* instead. What this means is that at the point in time when Tesnière was developing his theory, the distinction between dependency- and constituency-based grammars did not yet exist. Or, to be more exact, the world of linguistics was not yet aware of the distinction. In this respect, one cannot assume that Tesnière was explicitly against the modern understanding of constituency as it is employed in phrase structure grammars today. While he was very explicit about his rejection of the binary division of the clause into a subject and a predicate (ch. 49) – this division being at the core of most constituency grammars – this fact did not prevent him for employing constituency elsewhere in his theory.

The modern understanding of dependency and constituency sees all dependency-based structures as endocentric (Osborne et al. 2011:325). In this regard, the adoption of X-bar Theory in the 1970s can be interpreted as a step in the direction of DG, since X-bar Theory does not allow for exocentric structures. The distinction between endo- and exocentric structures is illustrated with the following representations:

(17) a. b. - Endocentric

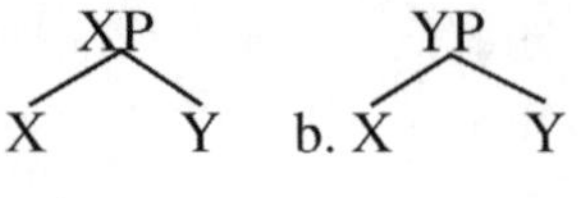

c. 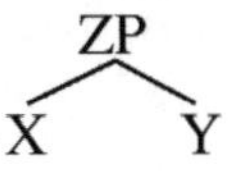

- Exocentric

An exocentric structure bears a category label that is unlike either of its constituent parts. Thus the structure in (17c) is exocentric because ZP is not XP or YP. Dependency by its very nature cannot acknowledge exocentric structures like the one in (17c); only endocentric structures are possible:

(18) 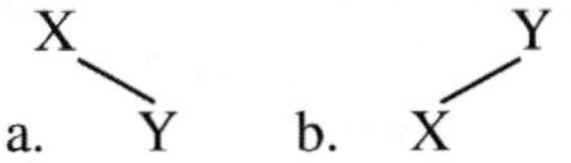

- Endocentric

Dependency's rejection of the phonologically null nodes of constituency structures prevents dependency-based structures from acknowledging exocentric constituents. In other words, a given constituent in DG always bears the category label of its root node.

The fact that Tesnière was (probably at least somewhat) unaware of these distinctions (dependency vs. constituency, endocentric vs. exocentric) means that nothing prevented him from positing the existence of exocentric structures, for he was not attempting to produce a purely dependency-based theory of syntax. In fact, his theory of transfer (Fr. *translation*), which occupies the second half of his book (300 pages), frequently employs constituency in order to indicate transfer which, upon close examination, is revealed as an exocentric construction. This fact, i.e. that Tesnière utilized constituency to accommodate the exocentric structures that he was positing, seems to have been overlooked in the reception of Tesnière's work. In the more than 50 years since the *Éléments* was first published, the fact that Tesnière was actually proposing a hybrid dependency-constituency model of syntax is not acknowledged.

The theory of transfer starts with Tesnière's claim that in European languages, there are only four basic categories of content words (ch. 33): nouns (O), adjectives (A), verbs (I), and adverbs (E). The abbreviations O, A, I, and E are a mnemonic device; they correspond to last letter of the Esperanto equivalents (ch. 33, §3). Tesnière took other word categories that most modern theories of grammar acknowledge (adpositions, determiners, conjunctions, pronouns, etc.) to be *indices*, *junctors* (j), or *translatives* (t) (ch. 38). Indices serve simply to indicate reference; they are typically clitic pronouns; junctors indicate the presence of coordination (Fr. *jonction*); and translatives serve to transfer the category of a given word to another category.

According to Tesnière, translatives are empty words and as such, they appear intra-nuclear, i.e. inside a split nucleus with a full word (ch. 40). They transfer the syntactic category of the full word in their nucleus to another category. For instance, the French preposition *de* 'of' often transfers the syntactic category of its object, which is a noun, to an adjective. The French subordinate conjunction *que* 'that' often transfers the syntactic category of its complement, which is a verb, to a noun.

Tesnière employed special devices in his stemmas to indicate the presence of transfer. He positioned the base word and its translative equi-level as sisters. He drew a vertical line separating the two, whereby the line was slanted at its base toward the translative. He drew a horizontal line above the two and placed the category resulting from the transfer medially on top of the line (ch. 155). For example:

(19) 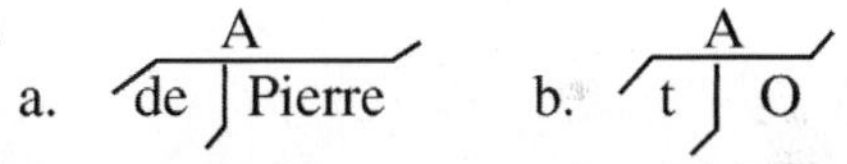

Example (19a) is a concrete stemma, whereas (19b) is "virtual" (ch. 33), since it shows just the categories involved in the instance of transfer. Tesnière employs these graphic devices frequently. For instance, he fills 16 pages at the end of his book with large tree diagrams (stemmas 354-366), most of which contain multiple instances of transfer.

The diagrams (19a) and (19b) show that *Pierre* is a noun (O), *de* is a translative (t), and that the two together function as an adjective (A). It should be apparent that these graphic representations are manifestations of constituency, not of dependency. Constituency is evident insofar as *de* (t) and *Pierre* (O) are positioned as equi-level sisters that are dominated by the category that they become together. Constituency is also evident in the fact that there are three category labels (A, t, O) but only two words (*de* and *Pierre*). Furthermore, the entire unit is an adjective, a category distinct from either of the parts, which means that an exocentric constituent obtains.

If one renders example (19a) using modern conventions for constructing trees, this is what one gets:

(20)

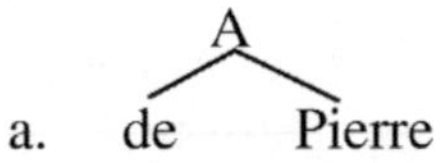

This tree is entirely constituency-based, a fact that is evident in that there are three nodes but only two words and in that the whole is an adjective, a category distinct from either of its parts (t and O). The only clear difference that distinguishes this tree from modern constituency-based trees is the lack of "P", which would indicate that the whole has the status of a phrase.

Since Tesnière made massive use of transfer in his stemmas – a fact that is illustrated with the reproduction of stemma 357 below – means that one cannot argue that he sparingly augmented his dependency-based stemmas with constituency in order to accommodate some rare phenomena. Instead, one is forced to acknowledge that his theory of sentence structure is a true hybrid that frequently combines dependency and constituency.

(21) (stemma 257)

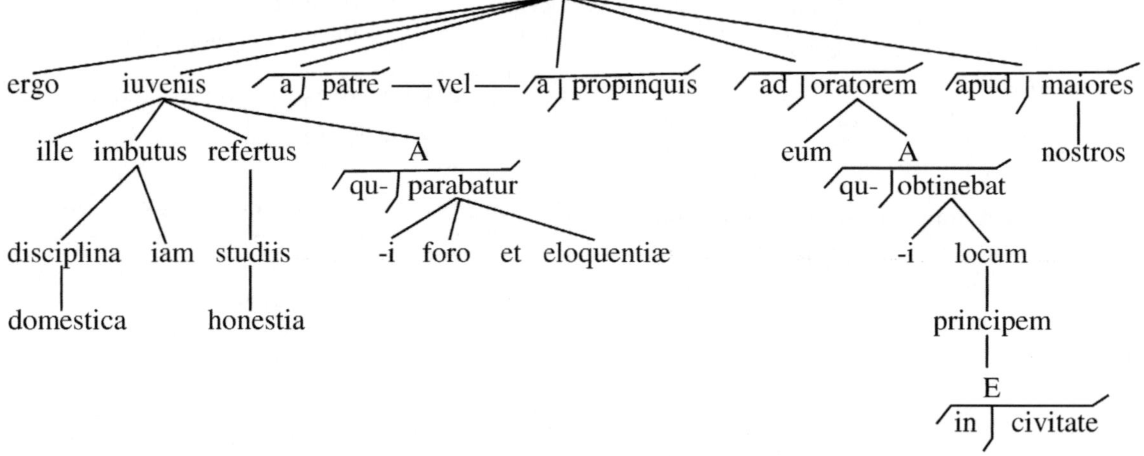

Ergo apud majores nostros iuvenis ille, qui foro et eloquentiae parabatur, imbutus iam domestica disciplina, refertus honestis studiis deducebatur a patre vel a propinquis ad eum oratorem, qui principem in civitate locum obtinebat. (Tacitus, *Dialogue of Orators*, 34)

9 Conclusion

This contribution has considered a few interesting and noteworthy aspects of Tesnière's theory of syntax. The motivation for the exploration has been a recent translation project, whereby Tesnière's central work, *Éléments de syntaxe structurale*, is finally being translated into English. This project has provided the current author with the opportunity to take a detailed look at Tesnière's ideas. As a result, the strengths and weaknesses of Tesnière's theory are now becoming more apparent.

Arguably, Tesnière's most brilliant insight was two-fold: he rejected the binary division of the clause into a subject and predicate, and in place of this division, he chose to position the verb as the root of all clause structure. This move allowed Tesnière to produce a truly novel theory of syntax. To the best of my knowledge, no one before Tesnière had thought to do this as clearly and as consistently as he did. The brilliance of Tesnière's theory is also evident in the fact that his analysis of certain phenomena was visionary. His hierarchical analysis of auxiliary verbs, for instance, is basically accepted by most work in modern syntax. He also correctly identified the gapping and right node raising mechanisms, an accomplishment for which he rarely receives credit.

On the other hand, certain weaknesses in Tesnière's system have also come to light. Tesnière employed the term node (*nœud*) inconsistently, which may have contributed to the misconception that dependency-based structures do not acknowledge constituents and phrases, and he had an unfortunate penchant for introducing obscure terminology. This practice may also have had a negative impact on the reception and spread of his ideas. Furthermore, Tesnière's analysis of certain structures has not survived into modern theories of syntax, for instance he failed to see that prepositions are the heads of prepositional phrases and that a flat analysis of small-clause-like constructions in languages like English is more defensible than the more layered analysis he proposed.

Finally, the most noteworthy insight gained so far during the translation project occurred in the second half of the *Éléments*, where Tesnière presents his theory of transfer in great detail. He employed a graphic representation that is constituency-based. In other words, he employed constituency to accommodate his exocentric analysis of certain phrase types. What this means is that Tesnière was actually not proposing a purely dependency-based model of syntax, but rather he was proposing a hybrid dependency-constituency system.

References

Bloomfield, Leonard. 1933. *Language*. Henry Holt, New York.

Andrew Carnie. 2008. *Constituent Structure*. Oxford University Press, Oxford.

Chomsky, Noam 1981. *Lectures on Government and Binding: The Pisa Lectures*. Mouton de Gruyter.

Noam Chomsky. 1986. *Barriers*. MIT Press, Cambridge, MA.

Peter Culicover and Ray Jackendoff. 2005. *Simpler Syntax*. Oxford University Press, Oxford, UK.

Daniel Jurafsky and James Martin. 2000. *Speech and Language Processing: An introduction to Natural Language Processing, Computational Linguistics, and Speech Recognition*. Pearson Education, New Delhi, India.

David Hays. 1964. Dependency theory: A formalism and some observations. *Language* 40, 511-525.

Liliane Haegeman, L., Guéron, J., 1999. *English Grammar: A Generative Perspective*. Basil Blackwell, Oxford.

Ray Jackendoff. 1971. Gapping and Related Rules. *Linguistic Inquiry* 2, 21-35

Pauline Jacobson. 1996. Constituent Structure. In: *A Concise Encyclopedia of Syntactic Theory*. Pergamon, Cambridge.

Donna Napoli. 1993. *Syntax: Theory and Problems*. Oxford University Press, New York.

Richard Hudson 1988. Coordination and grammatical relations. *Journal of Linguistics* 24, 303-342.

Richard Hudson 1989. Gapping and grammatical relations. *Journal of Linguistics* 25, 57-94.

Igor Mel'čuk. 1988. *Dependency Syntax: Theory and Practice*. The SUNY Press, Albany, N.Y.

Timothy Osborne. 2008. Major constituents: And two Dependency Grammar constraints on sharing in coordination. *Linguistics* 46, 6, 1109-1165.

Timothy Osborne, Michael Putnam and Thomas Groß. 2011. Bare phrase structure, label-less structures, and specifier-less syntax: Is Minimalism becoming a dependency grammar? *The Linguistic Review* 28, 315-364.

Jamal Ouhalla. 1994. *Transformational Grammar: From Rules to Principles and Parameters*. Edward Arnold, London.

Carl Pollard and Ivan Sag. 1994. *Head-Driven Phrase Structure Grammar*. University of Chicago Press, Chicago.

Paul Postal. 1974. *On Raising*. MIT Press, Cambridge, MA.

John Ross. 1970. Gapping and the order of constituents. In M. Bierwisch and K. Heidolph (eds.), *Progress in Linguistics: A Collection of Papers*, pp. 249–259. Mouton, The Hague.

Lucien Tesnière. 1959. *Éléments de syntaxe structurale*. Klincksieck, Paris.

Lucien Tesnière. 1959. *Elements of structural syntax*. [Translated by Timothy Osborne and Sylvain Kahane, Benjamins, to appear].

The Distribution of Floating Quantifiers
A Dependency Grammar Analysis

Timothy Osborne
615 6th Street Apt. 110
Kirkland, WA 98033
USA

tjo3ya@yahoo.com

Abstract

This contribution provides a dependency grammar analysis of the distribution of floating quantifiers in English and German. Floating quantifiers are deemed to be "base generated", meaning that they are not moved into their surface position by a transformation. Their distribution is similar to that of modal adverbs. The nominal (noun or pronoun) over which they quantify is an argument of the predicate to which they attach. Variation in their placement across English and German is due to independent word order principles associated with each language.

1 Introduction

The quantifiers *all* (in English) and *alle* (in German) in the following sentences are "floating":

(1) a. They have *all* understood.
b. Sie haben *alle* verstanden.

The noteworthy trait of these quantifiers is that they are positioned at a distance from the definite nominal (noun or pronoun) over which they quantify. In the examples here, *all* and *alle* are separated from the pronouns *they* and *sie* by the finite verbs *have* and *haben*. This situation is contrary to expectation, since the modifiers of nominals generally appear adjacent to them. Data such as (1a-b) are, however, a frequent occurrence, and the term *floating quantifier* has long been established in order to denote the phenomenon. Typical quantifiers that float in English are *all*, *both* and *each*, and in German *alle* 'all' and *beide* 'both'.[1]

For the most part, there are two possible and competing theoretical analyses of floating quantifiers. The one is associated with transformational syntax, the assumption being that the quantifier and nominal form a constituent at some underlying level of representation or stage of a derivation (e.g. Sportiche 1988, Carillo 2009). The quantifier ends up "floating" because its host nominal is moved out of its base position up the structure, whereby the quantifier remains behind. This approach is called the *movement approach* here. The other approach assumes that there is no movement (e.g. Dowty and Brodie 1984, Bobaljik 2003, Hoeksema 2012), but rather floating quantifiers are a type of adverbial, and their distribution is similar to that of, for instance, modal adverbs (*e.g. certainly*, *probably*, *mainly*). This approach is called the *adverb approach* here.

Of these two approaches, this contribution rejects the first in favor of the second. It rejects the movement approach for two reasons, the first being that movement is not consistent with the tradition of dependency grammar (DG), a majority of DGs rejecting the movements and derivational processes associated with transformational syntax, favoring representations instead. The second reason for rejecting the movement approach is empirical. There are a number of problems with the movement approach (see Bobaljik 2003 and Hoeksema 2012), not the least of which is the fact that floating quantifiers at times quantify

[1] Partitive quantifiers can also float, e.g. *They were all of them deceived.* The distribution of partitive quantifiers is not examined in this contribution, although they behave similarly to their non-partitive counterparts.

Proceedings of the Second International Conference on Dependency Linguistics (DepLing 2013), pages 272–281,
Prague, August 27–30, 2013.

over material with which they cannot be construed as forming a constituent at some underlying level or point in a derivation, e.g.

(2) a. Bob, Bill, and Tom have *all* called.
b. **All* Bob, Bill, and Tom have called.

Based on the unacceptability of (2b), it is difficult to see how the quantifier *all* in (2a) could be construed as forming a constituent with the subject *Bob, Bill, and Tom* at some underlying level or point in a derivation.

The adverb approach is more congruent with the DG tradition, since it sees the quantifier as "base generated" in its surface position. More importantly, it is supported by a number of empirical considerations, not the least of which is the simple observation that floating quantifiers have a distribution that is similar to that of modal adverbs:

(3) a. ?The kids *likely* will have been seen.
b. The kids will *likely* have been seen.
c. The kids will have *likely* been seen.
d. ??The kids will have been *likely* seen.

(4) a. ?The kids *all* will have been seen.
b. The kids will *all* have been seen.
c. The kids will have *all* been seen.
d. ??The kids will have been *all* seen.

The adverb approach is supported by the similar acceptability judgments across these two groups of sentences. The movement approach, in contrast, comes up short when confronted with these data, since it has no reason to put floating quantifiers on par with modal adverbs.[2]

This contribution presents a DG analysis of the distribution of floating quantifiers in English and German, whereby the adverb approach is pursued. It will be demonstrated that the principle of distribution is consistent across the two languages. The differences that do exist across English and German are due to independent principles of word order that have little to do with floating quantifiers.

[2] Note that by claiming that floating quantifiers distribute like modal adverbs, I am not claiming that floating quantifiers *are* modal adverbs. A similar distribution does not necessitate that the two types of words belong to the same syntactic class.

2 Floating?

An analysis of floating quantifiers must first be in a position to distinguish between quantifiers that are and are not floating. In a DG, this task can be accomplished if one sees the quantifier as floating when its position in relation to the nominal it quantifies over would constitute a projectivity violation:

Floating quantifier (initial version)
A quantifier is floating if interpreting it as a dependent of a nominal that it quantifies over would mean the presence of a projectivity violation in the dependency tree.

Given this guideline, any time a quantifier is separated from the noun it quantifies over by one or more words that dominate the noun, that quantifier must necessarily be "floating", e.g.

(5)
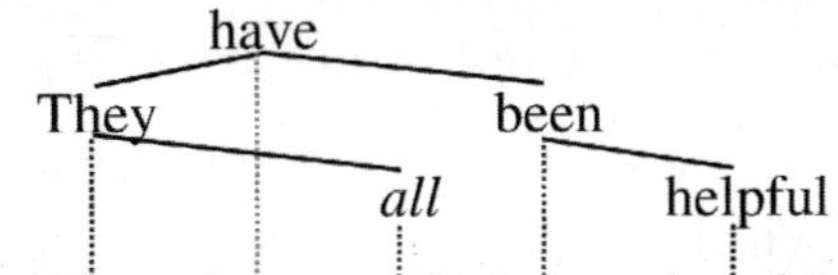

a. They have *all* been helpful.

The crossing lines in this tree identify a projectivity violation, which means the quantifier is floating.

The status of *all* as a floating quantifier in examples like (5) is beyond contention. There are other cases, however, where one might overlook the fact that the quantifier is floating, e.g.

(6) The boys all left.

Since the quantifier *all* is adjacent to the noun *boys* and it quantifies over *boys*, the guideline above does not necessitate that it be viewed as floating. Further considerations, however, demonstrate that *all* is not a dependent of *boys* in (6), which means it must be floating. When a quantifier attaches to the noun over which it quantifies, it attaches as a predependent, never as a postdependent, and when it appears as a dependent of a pronoun, it is always a postdependent, never a predependent. These facts are visible in the following sentences:

(7) a. Fred liked all the candies.
b. *Fred liked the candies all.

c. *Fred liked all them.

d. Fred liked them all.

These sentences show that when a quantifier attaches to the noun it quantifies, it must be a predependent, but when it attaches to a pronoun, it must be a postdependent. These traits of nouns, pronouns, and quantifiers are probably motivated by prosodic factors, the quantifier preferring to attach as a postdependent to prosodically weak elements.

The V2 principle of German delivers support for the conclusion. The V2 principle requires one and only one constituent to appear as the predependent of the finite verb in standard declarative matrix clauses and w-constituent questions, e.g.

(8) a. *Die Leute alle kennen es.
The people all know it

b. Wir alle kennen es.
we all know es

(9) a. *Welche Leute alle hast du gehört?
Which people all have you heard?

b. Wen alles hast du gehört?
who all have you heard

When the left-most constituent before the finite verb is an NP, the quantifier cannot immediately follow it, but if that element is a pronoun, the quantifier CAN immediately follow it. The V2 principle predicts that the b-sentences would be bad like the a-sentences if the quantifier were floating in the b-sentences, for two constituents, not just one, would be preceding the finite verb.

The same sort of acceptability contrast shows up in English:

(10) a. *Which people all did you see?

b. Who all did you see?

This contrast is explained in part if we assume that in English as well, only one constituent can precede the finite verb in such *wh*-questions.

The following contrast further supports the general insight:

(11) a. ?The boys all had done their work.

b. The boys had all done their work.

(12) a. They all had done their work.

b. They had all done their work.

Sentence (11a) is marginally acceptable, the word order in (11b) clearly being preferred. This contrast in acceptability disappears in (12), where both word orders are fine. The difference is explained in part if one assumes that the quantifier *all* is floating in (11a), but it is a postdependent of the pronoun *they* in (12a).

This peculiar asymmetry between nouns and pronouns with respect to quantifiers is, again, probably explained by prosodic considerations; the quantifier prefers to immediately follow a prosodically weak element (such as a pronoun or an auxiliary verb). This asymmetry must be kept in mind when exploring the distribution of floating quantifiers. What it means is that the guideline above is not completely accurate. The relevant criterion for identifying floating quantifiers is not whether its position necessitates a projectivity violation, but whether the quantifier can be construed as a dependent of the nominal that it quantifies over. If it cannot, then it is floating. Thus in the case of (6), which is repeated here as (13a) with the dependency structure added, the quantifier *all* is floating because it is a dependent of the verb, not of the noun:

(13)

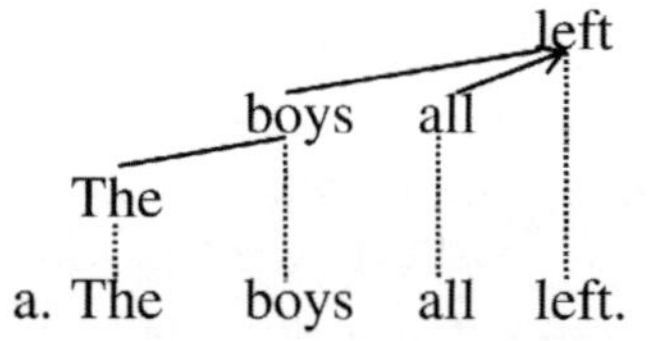

(The arrow dependency edge marks a constituent that is not selected or subcategorized for by its head – in other words, it marks an adjunct.) But if the subject is a pronoun, the quantifier is a postdependent of the pronoun:

(13)

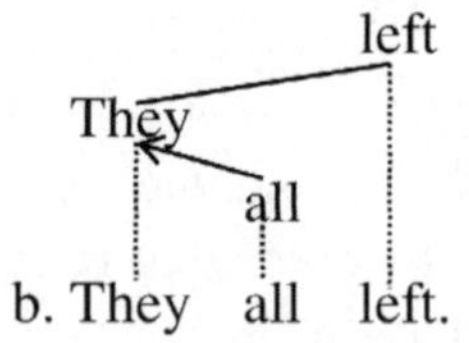

Note that the analysis shown in (13b) does not prohibit the quantifier from floating if need be, e.g.

(13)

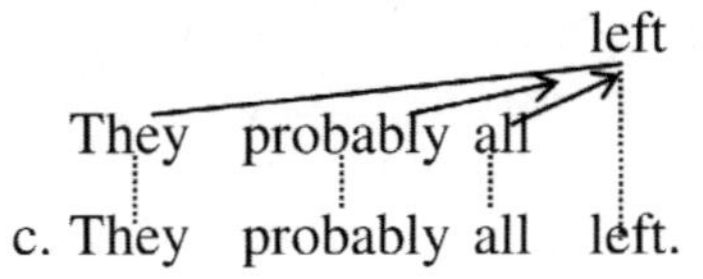

These points motivate a reformulation of the guideline for identifying floating quantifiers:

Floating quantifier (final version)
A quantifier is floating if, for whatever reason, it cannot be construed as a dependent of the nominal that it quantifies.

3 Rising?

A widespread means of addressing projectivity violations like the one shown in (5) is to assume that the displaced constituent climbs up the structure and attaches to a word that dominates its governor (e.g. Duchier and Debusmann 2001, Gerdes and Kahane 2001, Bröker 2003:294). Groß and Osborne (2009) call this mechanism *rising*, and they indicate its presence in dependency trees using a dashed dependency edge to mark the "risen" constituent and a g subscript to mark the governor of the risen constituent.[3] On a rising analysis, the tree for sentence (5) might be as follows:

(14)

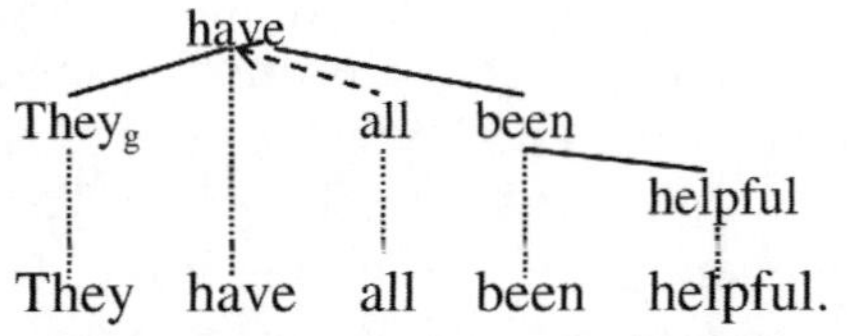

This sort of analysis has been shown to be valid for the major types of discontinuities acknowledged in the literature (extraposition, scrambling, topicalization, wh-fronting) – see Groß and Osborne (2009) and Osborne et al. (2012). The analysis cannot, however, be valid for floating quantifiers. We know it cannot be valid for floating quantifiers because floating quantifiers can appear much lower down in the syntactic hierarchy, a fact that a rising analysis really cannot accommodate, since it would necessitate more than one instance of rising, e.g.

(15)

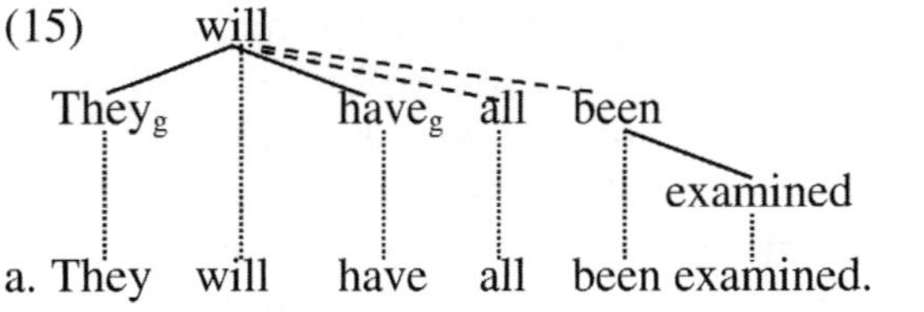

The rising analysis shown in this tree is implausible because it sees both the quantifier *all* and the nonfinite VP *been examined* rising. There is no independent evidence that nonfinite VPs headed by an auxiliary verb can rise in this manner.

A more plausible approach is to assume that the quantifier attaches as a postdependent to the infinitive auxiliary *have*:

(15)

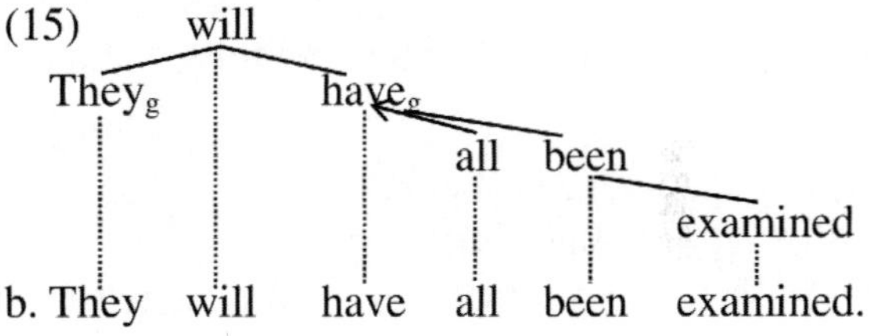

An alternative analysis here that attaches the quantifier *all* as a predependent to the participle *been* is implausible for reasons that will be made clear further below.

The greater point to these examples is that many floating quantifiers appear too low in the syntactic hierarchy to allow an analysis in terms of rising. This insight leads immediately to the following question: then what is a float ing quantifier? As stated in the introduction, the current contribution follows an established tradition in assuming that floating quantifiers are essentially a type of adverb that has a distribution similar to that of modal adverbs.

4 Why float?

Floating quantifiers have similar quantificational powers to the corresponding nonfloating quantifiers. They are quantifying over a nominal, restricting or expanding the set of entities that can be denoted by the nominal. Thus the following two sentences translate to the same formula of predicate logic:

(16) a. All the guests were hungry.
b. The guests were all hungry.
$\forall x\ ((\text{guest}\ (x)) \rightarrow (\text{hungry}\ (x)))$

[3] Groß and Osborne (2009) emphasize that the term *rising* should not be understood as indicating a transformational approach. They use the term as a convenient metaphor to denote a constellation in which the head of a given constituent is not its governor.

Given this complete overlap in meaning, one can ask why floating quantifiers exist: what do they accomplish? The answer to this question is that they can disambiguate utterances.

Dowty and Brody (1984) demonstrate that the use of a floating quantifier can disambiguate an utterance. Floating quantifiers do not, namely, allow the scope ambiguities associated with their non-floating counterparts. The following sentence is ambiguous depending on whether the quantifier scopes over the negation, or vice versa:

(17) a. *All* the women didn't protest.
$\forall x\ ((\text{woman}\ (x)) \rightarrow \neg\ (\text{protest}\ (x)))$
$\neg\ \forall x\ ((\text{woman}\ (x)) \rightarrow (\text{protest}\ (x)))$

When the quantifier floats, in contrast, the ambiguity disappears:

(17) b. The women *all* didn't protest.
$\forall x\ ((\text{woman}\ (x)) \rightarrow \neg\ (\text{protest}\ (x)))$
$*\ \neg\ \forall x\ ((\text{woman}\ (x)) \rightarrow (\text{protest}\ (x)))$

c. The women didn't *all* protest.
$*\ \forall x\ ((\text{woman}\ (x)) \rightarrow \neg\ (\text{protest}\ (x)))$
$\neg\ \forall x\ ((\text{woman}\ (x)) \rightarrow (\text{protest}\ (x)))$

When a quantifier floats, scope is determined strictly by linear order; the logical operator that appears first in the left-to-right sequence takes scope over an operator that follows.

The ability of floating quantifiers to disambiguate utterances justifies their existence.

5 C-command?

The fact, however, that a floating quantifier is often not adjacent to the nominal that it quantifies over should motivate one to question how it picks out its argument. Why, for instance, is the quantifier incapable of quantifying over the italicized constituent in the following sentence?

(18) **His parents'* idea has both upset him.

This sentence fails obviously because the quantifier *both* cannot pick out *his parents'* as its argument, but why not?

Some constituency grammars might seek to answer this question by appealing to c-command, the assumption being that the argument of a floating quantifier must c-command its antecedent (e.g. Radford 2004:239, Cirillo 2009:2). Given a DP analysis of noun phrases, however, it is not obvious that an explanation in terms of c-command will work, since such an analysis might take *his parents'* to be a determiner that heads the phrase and thus c-commands out of it.

An approach to the distribution of floating quantifiers in terms of c-command will clearly not work for languages such as Dutch and German, as pointed out by Hoeksema (2012:3), because these languages allow the floating quantifier to precede its nominal, as the following examples from German, taken from Hoeksema, demonstrate:

(19) a. *Alle* haben sie gelogen.
all have they lied
'They have all lied.'

b. *Beide* waren sie dabei.
Both were they present
'They were both present.'

The pre-verb position is widely believed to be the most prominent syntactic position, the one position that c-commands everything to its right. Thus there is no way that the subject pronouns *sie* and *sie* in these sentences can be construed as c-commanding the quantifiers.[4]

The relevant insight concerning sentence (18) is that *his parents'* is not an argument of the matrix predicate, but rather it is embedded in an argument of the matrix predicate. In order to be an argument of the matrix predicate, it would have to be directly dependent on it. The rule of quantifier binding is therefore that a floating quantifier can quantify only over an argument of the predicate to which it attaches:

Principle of floating quantification
A floating quantifier can quantify only over an argument of the predicate to which the quantifier attaches.

It is important to note that predicates in dependency structures are often multi-word *catenae* (Osborne et al. 2012), that is, they consist of a word or a combination of words that are chained together by dependencies. Thus what

[4] Unlike German, English never allows a floating quantifier to precede its nominal. The difference across the two languages probably has to do with differences in how topicalization occurs.

this principle says is that a floating quantifier can quantify over a given nominal only as long as it attaches to any part of the predicate for which that nominal is an argument.

The catena concept as it bears on predicates is illustrated using the following structure:

(20)
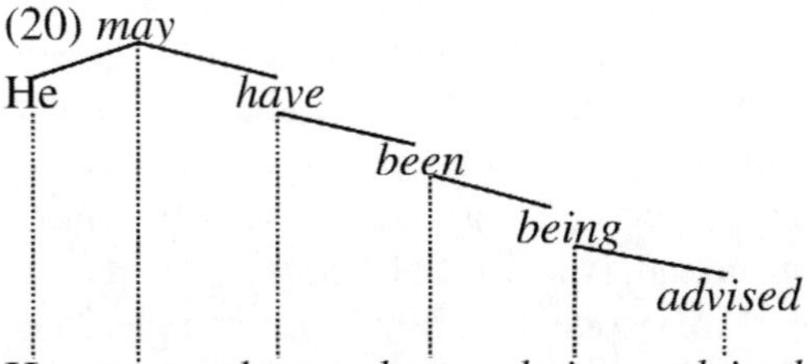

He *may* *have* *been* *being* *advised.*

The matrix predicate is in italics. Each of the auxiliary verbs, starting with the modal auxiliary, is part of the matrix predicate. We know that these verbs are part of the matrix predicate because they do not select any arguments and they thus do not each constitute a separate predicate. They certainly subcategorize for specific syntactic categories, but they do not semantically select any arguments; they contribute only functional meaning to the core of the predicate represented by *advised*. Hence what the principle of floating quantification says is that by attaching to any one of the words of such a predicate catena, a floating quantifier is quantifying over one of the arguments of that multi-word predicate catena.

The principle allows a floating quantifier to attach to a predicate that is embedded under a dominant control predicate, e.g.

(21)
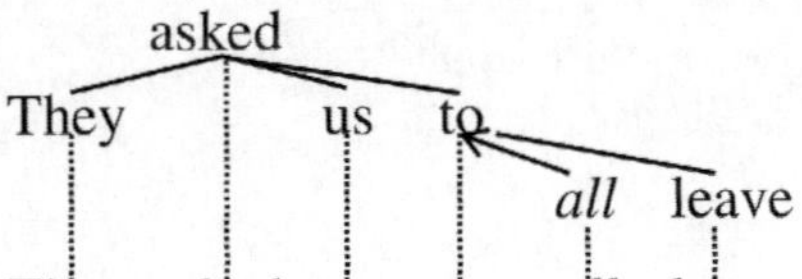

a. They asked us to *all* leave.

b. *They asked him to all leave.

Since the position of the quantifier between *to* and *leave* prevents it from attaching to the matrix predicate *asked*, the quantifier is restricted to quantifying over the argument of the embedded predicate *to...leave*, that argument being *us/him*.[5] This explains the fact that *all* cannot quantify over *they*, for *they* is an argument of *asked*, not of *to...leave*. Note that a basic trait of control predicates liked *asked* in (21) is that they assign one of their arguments to also be the subject argument of the infinitive predicate that they embed. What this means is that a floating quantifier can attach to an embedded predicate yet still quantify over a dependent of the matrix predicate, as shown in (21).

The principle is also valid for German, e.g.

(22)
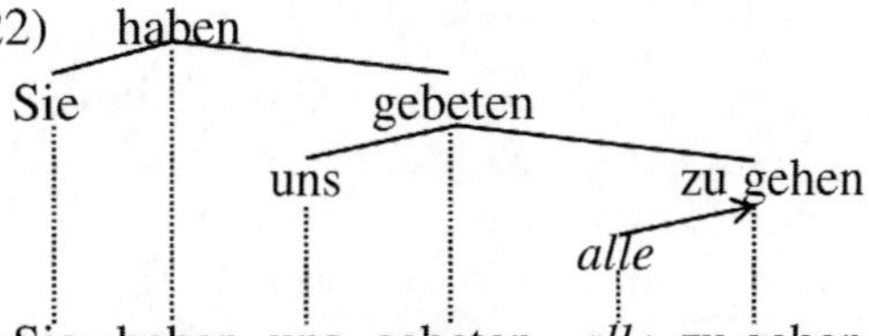

a. Sie haben uns gebeten, *alle* zu gehen.
they have us asked all to leave

b. *Sie haben ihn gebeten *alle* zu gehen.
they have him asked all to leave

We again see that when the quantifier attaches to the embedded predicate, it is capable of quantifying over only the one argument of the embedded predicate, *uns/ihn* in this case. Note the status of *all* in (21) as a postdependent of *to* in contrast to *alle* in (22), which is a predependent of *zu gehen*. *Zu*-infinitives in German behave as single words in every respect, hence they are granted just a single node here.

6 Pre- or postdependents?

An aspect of floating quantifiers that has not been addressed so far in this contribution concerns their status as either pre- or postdependents. Do they prefer to be pre- or postdependents of their heads? The answer to this question is not obvious. In fact, an examination of the data suggests that floating quantifiers obey language specific constraints; they are at times predependents of their heads, and at other times postdependents, depending in part on the extent to which the language at hand prefers centrifugal (right branching) or centripetal (left branching) structures.

The fact that quantifiers cannot attach to nouns as postdependents, as illustrated with

[5] The quantifier in (21) is shown as a postdependent of the particle *to*. This analysis is plausible for a couple of reasons, the one being that English prefers right-branching structures, and the other is that there is no evidence that floating quantifiers can attach as predependents to infinitives embedded under a finite verb. The issue is touched on below.

examples (7a-b), impacts the analysis of floating quantifiers in relation to auxiliary and full verbs. In particular, it helps motivate the insight that floating quantifiers only reluctantly attach as a predependent to finite auxiliary verbs in English, but they readily attach as predependents to finite full verbs:

(23) a. ?The workmen all will show up.

b. The workmen will all show up.

(24) The workmen all showed up.

Sentence (23a) is marginal, the order in (23b) clearly being preferred, whereas sentence (24), where the floating quantifier also immediately precedes the finite verb, is perfectly fine. The reason for this contrast between auxiliary verbs and full verbs is not entirely clear, although as stated above, it probably has to do with prosodic differences between auxiliary verbs, which tend to be unstressed, and full verbs, which tend to be prosodically more prominent. Floating quantifiers prefer to attach as postdependents to prosodically weak words in English. If such a word is not available, only then do they readily attach as a predependent to a prosodically more prominent word.

Despite the fact that sentence (23a) is not very good, examples like (24) demonstrate that floating quantifiers can easily attach to verbs as predependents. But this insight does not clarify whether a floating quantifier that appears between two verbs of a predicate catena is a pre- or postdependent. For instance, which of the following two analyses is correct?

(25)

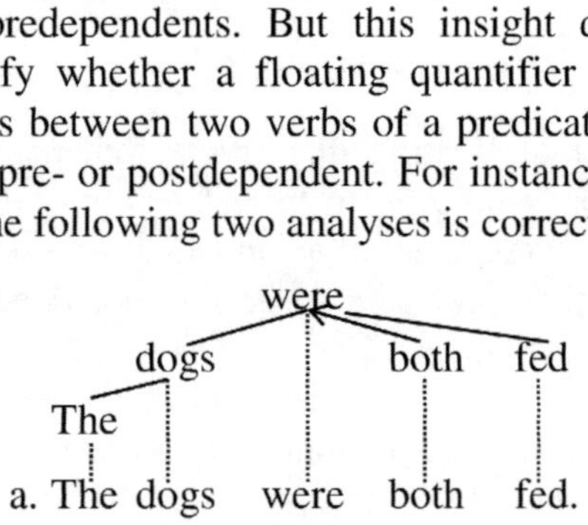

Three considerations support the analysis shown in (25a) over the one in (25b). The first is that English VPs are by and large right branching. In this regard, the analysis in (25b) would necessitate viewing *both fed* as a left-branching VP, which does not seem right for English.

The second consideration supporting (25a) over (25b) has to do with the category status of the floating quantifier. One can make a case that floating quantifiers can be nominals, since quantifiers can appear as argument dependents of verbs, e.g. *All is good*, *We saw both (of them)*, etc. Nominals do not generally attach to nonfinite verbs as predependents in English. The analysis in (25a) accommodates this fact, whereas the analysis in (25b) contradicts it.

The third consideration supporting (25a) over (25b) is evident when a measure adverb appears in addition to the floating quantifier, e.g.

(26) a. The dogs are all completely fed.

b. *The dogs are completely all fed.

Measure adverbs attach directly to the predicate word that they modify. They can be displaced with their head, e.g. *Completely fed, the dogs definitely were*. If *all* were a predependent of *fed* in (26), we would expect both sentences to be acceptable. Since only (26a) works, we can assume that *all* is not attaching to *fed* as a predependent, but rather it must be a postdependent of *are*.

The analysis can be extended to similar cases such as (15) above, which is repeated here as (27):

(27)

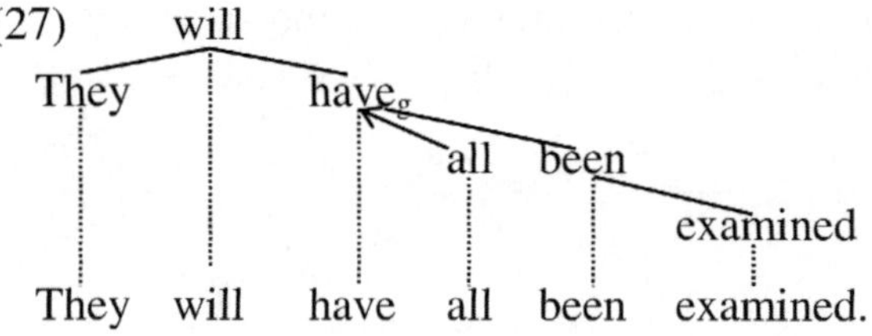

The floating quantifier is taken as a postdependent of *have* as opposed to as a predependent of *been*. The three considerations enumerated for examples (25) and (26) extend to this case, where the quantifier appears lower in the structure.

Applying the reasoning to further cases, the account here sees floating quantifiers as pre- and postdependents of finite verbs, but generally only as postdependents of nonfinite verbs in English (overlooking an exception discussed below). This analysis does not extend to German, however, since there is clear evidence that floating quantifiers can be predependents of nonfinite verbs in German. Example (22) from above is repeated here as (28):

(28)

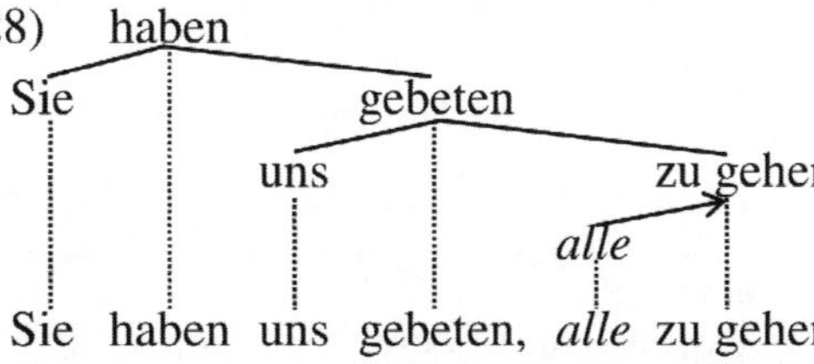

a. Sie haben uns gebeten, *alle* zu gehen.
they have us asked all to leave

The analysis shown here, where *alle* is a predependent of *zu gehen*, is the only plausible analysis for two reasons: because *zu*-infinitive phrases tend to behave as single constituents in German and because the only alternative would be to position the quantifier as a postdependent of *gebeten*, which cannot be correct, since the nonverbal dependents of nonfinite verbs in German are by and large predependents, not postdependents.

The long and the short of these considerations is that nonfinite verbs in English take floating quantifiers as postdependents in line with the tendency for nonfinite VPs in English to be right branching. In German in contrast, floating quantifiers attach to nonfinite verbs as predependents in line with the tendency for nonfinite VPs in German to be left branching.

7 Predicate catenae

The observations and reasoning employed above do not make the correct prediction for floating quantifiers in nonfinite clauses. When the floating quantifier appears in a clausal constituent the head of which is a participle, for instance, the quantifier has the option to precede or follow the participle, e.g.

(29) a. The beers all tasting the same, …
b. The beers tasting all the same,…

(30) a. The boys both having been examined,..
b. The boys having both been examined,...

The same optional position occurs in nonfinite clauses even when the predicate is not a verb form, e.g.

(31) a. With the two girls both in love with it,..
b. With the two girls in love with it both,..

These data suggest that the generalization arrived at in the foregoing section cannot be correct. Nonfinite verb forms can in fact take floating quantifiers as predependents in English, as the a-sentences in (29-31) demonstrate.

To accommodate these additional data, the role of predicate catenae can be acknowledged. The relevant criterion for determining when a floating quantifier can be a predependent concerns the root word of the predicate catena involved. A floating quantifier can precede or follow the root word of a predicate catena, regardless of whether this root word is a finite verb or not. Below this root word, however, a floating quantifier can attach to a nonfinite verb only as a postdependent:

> **Distribution of floating quantifiers in English**
> Floating quantifiers in English can attach as a pre- or postdependent to the root word of a clause predicate, or as a postdependent to a nonfinite verb below the root.

The principle is similar for German, the only difference being that the quantifiers attach as predependents to the nonfinite verbs below the root, not as postdependents:

> **Distribution of floating quantifiers in German**
> Floating quantifiers in German can attach as a pre- or postdependent to the root word of a clause predicate, or as a predependent to a nonfinite verb below the root.

Of course this rule cannot flout the V2 principle, meaning that floating quantifiers in German cannot precede the finite verb of a matrix V2 (or V1) clause – see example (8a) above. They can easily precede a finite verb in VF clauses, though, e.g.

(32)

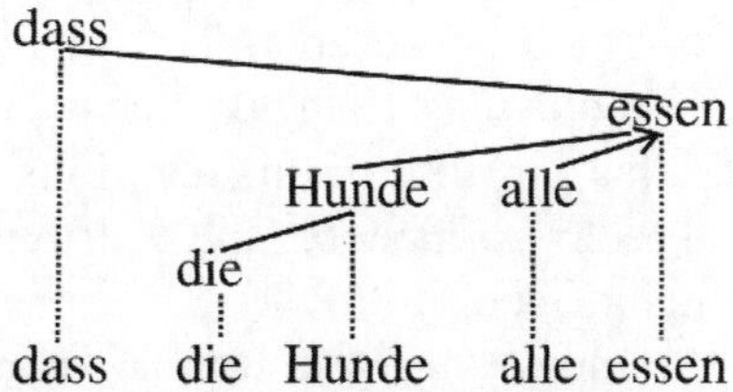

dass die Hunde alle essen
that the dogs all eat
'that the dogs are all eating'

In sum, the distribution of floating quantifiers in English and German is similar, the same basic principle of distribution determining where they can appear. The differences that do exist across the two languages are explained by overarching principles of word order, i.e. SV vs. V2 word order and left vs. right branching VPs.

8 Enigmatic behavior

The two principles just produced are necessary conditions on the distribution of floating quantifiers, but they are not sufficient ones. There are a couple of outstanding issues that can now be addressed, however briefly. The first concerns the special behavior of *all*. As noted a couple of times above, the distribution of *all* seems to be determined in part by prosodic factors; it prefers to attach as a postdependent, rather than a predependent, to a prosodically unstressed element. Other quantifiers are more flexible, e.g.

(33) a. They will all solve the problem.
b. *They will solve the problem all.
c. They will solve the problem all before noon.

(34)a. They will both solve the problem.
b. ?They will solve the problem both.
c. They will solve the problem both before noon.

The contrast in acceptability across the b-sentences must be due to prosodic factors, the weak quantifier *all*, which lacks an onset, seems to be prosodically reliant on some other word in context; it cannot appear in the prosodically prominent spot at the end of sentence. The quantifier *both*, in contrast, which has an onset, can appear in sentence final position, although its appearance there is also not so good. When something follows the quantifier as in the c-sentences, acceptability improves markedly in both cases. Thus these data demonstrate that prosodic considerations are an additional factor influencing the distribution of floating quantifiers.

Perhaps the most enigmatic trait of floating quantifiers in English is their reluctance to appear as a postdependent of a nonfinite form of the auxiliary *BE*, e.g.

(35) a. The guests will each be fed.
b. ??The guests will be each fed.

(36) a. They will all be trying hard.
b. ??They will be all trying hard.

(37) a. The two will have both been sneaky.
b. ??The two will have been both sneaky.

There is a significant decrease in acceptability moving from the a- to the b-sentences. The source of this decrease is unclear, though, since the quantifier can easily attach as a postdependent to a form of *HAVE*, which is also an auxiliary like *BE*, as example (37a) demonstrates.[6]

While it is unclear at this point why a nonfinite form of the auxiliary *BE* does not readily accept a floating quantifier as a postdependent, one should note that the problem is not restricted to quantifiers. Modal adverbs are also reluctant to appear immediately after a nonfinite form of *BE*, e.g.

(37) a. They will probably be helpful.
b. ??They will be probably helpful.

(38) a. She has certainly been doing the work.
b. ?She has been certainly doing the work.

What these examples show is that the unwillingness of floating quantifiers to attach to nonfinite forms of *BE* is not restricted to them, but rather it is an aspect of the distribution of certain adverbial elements in general. These elements dislike the position between nonfinite *BE* and a full verb or other part of the predicate.

9 Conclusion

To conclude, the four highlights of the DG account of floating quantifiers presented above are repeated here:

[6] One possible explanation might have to with the fact that nonfinite *have* cliticizes to other words, whereas nonfinite *be*, *been*, and *being* never do, e.g.

(i) We would've done it.
(ii) *We would'e happy.
(iii) *We would have'n happy.

This observation suggests that nonfinite forms *HAVE* may in fact be prosodically weaker than nonfinite forms of *BE*.

Floating quantifier
A quantifier is floating if, for whatever reason, it cannot be construed as a dependent of the nominal it quantifies over.

Principle of floating quantification
A floating quantifier can quantify only over an argument of the predicate to which it attaches.

Distribution of floating quantifiers in English
Floating quantifiers in English can attach as a pre- or postdependent to the root word of a clause predicate, or as a postdependent to a nonfinite verb below the root.

Distribution of floating quantifiers in German
Floating quantifiers in German can attach as a pre- or postdependent to the root word of a clause predicate, or as a predependent to a nonfinite verb below the root.

And to restate these highlights in other words, a quantifier is floating if it cannot be construed as a dependent of the nominal over which it quantifies. Floating quantifiers attach to predicates and quantify over an argument of these predicates. Their category status is that of a nominal, which means they distribute like nominals. In English, they tend to appear as postdependents of nonfinite verbs just like other nominals, and in German, they tend to appear as predependents of nonfinite verbs just like other nominals. When they attach to the root of a predicate catena, they can be a predependent or a postdependent, whereby prosodic factors can influence which is preferred.

A final comment considers the DG approach to floating quantifiers presented above in comparison to previous accounts, all of which are, to the best of my knowledge, constituency-based. While notions such as *catena*, *head*, *dependent*, *predicate, predependent*, and *postdependent* can be defined over constituency-based structures, doing so is more laborious, since the phrasal nodes complicate matters. In this respect, the DG approach presented here can claim superiority by virtue of its minimalism.

References

Robert Cirillo. 2009. *The syntax of floating quantifiers: Stranding revisited.* Doctoral dissertation, University of Amsterdam. Utrecht: LOT.

David Dowty and Belinda Brodie. 1984. A semantic analysis of floated quantifiers in transformational grammar. *Proceedings of the West Coast Conference on formal linguistics 3.* Stanford: Stanford Linguistics Association, Stanford University.

Denys Duchier and Ralph Debusmann. 2001. Topology dependency trees: A constraint based account of linear precedence. *Proceedings from the 39th annual meeting of the Association Computational Linguistics (ACL) 2001*, Toulouse, France, 180-187.

Gerdes, K. and S. Kahane. 2001. Word order in German: A formal dependency grammar using a topology model. *Proceedings from the 39th annual meeting of the Association Computational Linguistics (ACL) 2001*, Toulouse, France, 220-227.

Thomas Groß and Timothy Osborne. 2009. Toward a practical dependency grammar theory of discontinuities. *SKY Journal of Linguistics* 22: 43-90.

Jack Hoeksema. 2012. Floating quantifiers, partitives and distributivity. Freely downloadable from ebooks (March 2013).

Timothy Osborne, Michael Putnam, and Thomas Groß. 2012. Catenae: Introducing a novel unit of syntactic analysis. *Syntax* 15(4): 354-396.

Andrew Radford. 2004. *English Syntax: An Introduction.* Cambridge, UK: Cambridge University Press.

Dominique Sportiche. 1988. A theory of floating quantifiers in transformational grammar. *Linguistic Inquiry* 19: 425-449.

Jonathan Bobaljik. 2003. Floating quantifiers: Handle with care. In Lisa Cheng and Rint Sybesma (eds.),*The Second GLOT International State-of-the-Art Book.* Mouton de Gruyter. Freely downloadal from ebooks (March 2013)

Dependency and constituency in translation shift analysis

Manuela Sanguinetti and **Cristina Bosco** and **Leonardo Lesmo**
Universitá di Torino
Dipartimento di Informatica
Italy
{manuela.sanguinetti;cristina.bosco;leonardo.lesmo}@unito.it

Abstract

Exploiting data from a parallel treebank recently developed for Italian, English and French, the paper discusses issues related to the development of a dependency-based alignment system. We focus on the alignment of linguistic expressions and constructions which are structurally different in the languages that have to be aligned, and on how to deal with them using dependency rather than constituency. In order to analyze in particular the shifts related to syntactic structure, we present a selection of cases where a dependency-based and a constituency-based representation has been applied and compared.

1 Introduction

In the last few years several resources have been developed for improving Machine Translation tools, applying corpus-based approaches. Among them, there are parallel multilingual treebanks, which are also valuable for the extraction of linguistic knowledge and for translation studies. Their usefulness can be strongly improved by data alignment in particular on the syntactic level, but this task is very time-consuming if manually performed and especially challenging for automatic systems.

The main challenge for such kind of systems is the alignment of linguistic constructions which are expressed by different structures in different languages. Based on past work on translational divergences, or *shifts* – according to Catford's terminology (Catford, 1965) – we thus present in this paper a corpus-based analysis and a comparison, with respect to translation shifts and their possible alignment, of parse tree pairs represented both in a dependency and constituency-based format. The aim of our research is to create a syntax-driven alignment system for parallel parse trees. Our intuition is that, as it has been shown for other tasks, the use of syntactic information on dependency relations and on the predicative structure provided by annotated corpora can be useful while tackling the alignment task, and, as a result, for translation purposes. We therefore developed an alignment system based on dependency information. While our alignment system is now at a prototyping stage, what we intend to define in this paper is a feasibility study on the information that could be exploited by such system. Moreover, in order to examine whether and to what extent the dependencies are able to capture parallelisms, we compared them to a constituency representation. The observations emerged from this study, as well as being the main focus of this paper, constitute the theoretical framework upon which our alignment system can be based. For the preliminary nature of our research, the approach is strongly rule-based, and this allows us to have more control over what information is actually relevant, and which is not.

The paper is organized as follows: after a presentation of the main contributions presented in the last decade concerning parse tree alignment, we describe the linguistic resource we used for our study, focusing on both size and annotation formats applied to the treebank. In the last sections we provide some detailed analyses of the data, and we present a selection of shifts where dependency and constituency-based representations have been compared, with final remarks on the observations emerged from the comparison.

2 Parse tree alignment and related work

When it comes to parse tree alignment, the structures involved are mostly represented in the form of syntactic constituents. Alignment of constituency trees typically includes a sub-sentential level: first, a lexical mapping is performed to terminal nodes (i.e. words), then the non-terminal nodes (i.e. phrases) are aligned so that ances-

Proceedings of the Second International Conference on Dependency Linguistics (DepLing 2013), pages 282–291,
Prague, August 27–30, 2013.

tor/descendant in the source tree are only aligned to an ancestor/descendant of its counterpart in the target tree (Tiedemann, 2011; Tinsley et al., 2007; Wu, 1997). Constituency paradigm is still the most common and widespread in the field of parsing and treebank development, and phrase alignments are considered useful for Syntax-based Machine Translation (which is, in fact, the main use of aligned parallel resources) (Chiang, 2007; Tiedemann and Kotzé, 2009), or for annotating correspondences of idiomatic expressions (Volk et al., 2011). Furthermore, they were also used to make explicit the syntactic divergences between sentence pairs, as in Hearne et al. (2007). In this work in particular the major benefit from aligning phrase structures is claimed to be the opportunity to infer translational correspondences between two substrings in the source and target side by allowing links at higher levels in the tree pair.

Our hypothesis is based on the fact that certain equivalence relations, despite divergences in translations, can be detected using dependency trees. This hypothesis is supported in literature by some previous work on the alignment of deep syntactic structures. For example Ding et al. (2003) developed an algorithm that uses parallel dependency structures to iteratively add constraints to possible alignments; an extension of such work is that of Ding and Palmer (2004), who used a statistical approach to learn dependency structure mappings from parallel corpora, assuming at first a free word mapping, then gradually adding constraints to word level alignments by breaking down the parallel dependency structures into smaller pieces. Mareček et al. (2008) proposed an alignment system of the tectogrammatical layer of texts from the Prague Czech-English Dependency Treebank[1] with a greedy feature-based algorithm that exploits some measurable properties of Czech and English nodes in the corresponding tectogrammatical layers. Among these works, three in particular presented a common approach consisting in the creation of an initial set of word alignment which is then propagated to the other nodes in the source and target dependency trees using syntactic knowledge, formalized in a set of alignment rules (Menezes and Richardson, 2001; Ozdowska, 2005) or extracted by means of unsupervised machine learning techniques (Ma et al., 2008).

Our approach to the alignment task has been largely inspired by such works. What we seek to verify is how such an approach can be a valid alternative to classical phrase-based ones, especially when encountering translational shifts and linguistic differences of various nature.

3 Annotations and data

In this section we describe the data exploited in our study, focusing on the dependency and constituency formats applied to the parallel treebank, together with a brief overview of its size and content.

3.1 Annotation formats

The resource exploited in this study, i.e. ParTUT[2], is a parallel dependency treebank annotated according to the principles and using the same tags for Part of Speech (PoS) and syntactic labels of the Italian monolingual treebank TUT (Turin University Treebank[3]), whose format has been the reference for parsing evaluation campaigns[4], on which is currently defined the state-of-the-art for Italian. TUT trees can be partially compared to surface-syntactic structures (*SSyntS*) as proposed in the Meaning-Text Theory (Melčuk, 1988) and to the analytical layer in the Prague Dependency Treebank style (Böhmová et al., 2003).
As far as the native TUT dependency format is concerned, it uses projective structures whose nodes are labeled with words, and whose arcs are labeled with the names of syntactic relations. Figure 1 shows an example of a typical TUT tree. The arc labels include two components: the second one specifies if the dependent is an argument (ARG) or a modifier (in this case there are only *restrictive* modifiers: RMOD). The first component is the category of the governing item, in case the relation is ARG, or of the dependent, in case of RMOD. In some cases, the subcategory (type) is also included (after the plus sign). So PREP-RMOD should be read as *prepositional restrictive modifier* and DET+DEF-ARG as *argument of a definite determiner*. Note that, in TUT, the root of noun groups is the Determiner (if any), while the root of a prepositional group is the Preposition, as prescribed in the *Word Grammar* (Hudson, 1984) theoretical framework. In the actual TUT

[1] http://ufal.mff.cuni.cz/pcedt2.0/

[2] http://www.di.unito.it/~tutreeb/partut.html

[3] http://www.di.unito.it/~tutreeb

[4] http://www.evalita.it/

there is a third component (omitted here) concerning the semantic role of the dependent with respect to its governor. An important feature is that the format is oriented to an explicit representation of the predicate-argument structure, which is applied to Verb, but also to Nouns and Adjectives; to this end, a distinction is drawn between modifiers and subcategorized arguments and between surface and deep realization of any admitted argument. TUT format is also enhanced by a trace filler mechanism to deal with discontinuous structures, pro-drops and elliptical constructions. Furthermore, compound nouns and contracted forms are split into their components, with an associated node in the parse tree for each of them. The same happens for multi-word espressions, where each of their components is associated with a different node, although in this case they share the same lexical (i.e lemma) and morpho-syntactic information. This means, for example, that the Italian preposition in the example Figure "*dei*", resulting from the contraction between the preposition "*di*" (*of*) and the masculine plural article "*i*" (*the*), is split in two distinct nodes for each of their components.

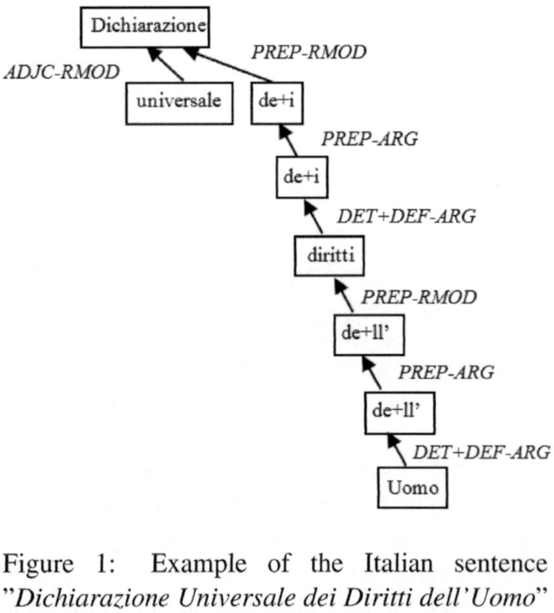

Figure 1: Example of the Italian sentence "*Dichiarazione Universale dei Diritti dell'Uomo*" (*Universal Declaration of Human Rights*) annotated in the TUT format.

The resource has been made available by conversion also in other formats, among them TUT-Penn, a format compliant (except for a few aspects described below) with the English Penn Treebank (PTB) standard. TUT-Penn has a richer morpho-syntactic tag set than Penn format, but it implements almost the same syntactic structure. With respect to the syntactic annotation, it differs from PTB only for some particular constructions and phenomena. It features, for example, a special representation for post-verbal subjects: though a quite common phenomenon in Italian, this is typically challenging for phrase structures (since the subject is considered as external argument of the VP). The standard PTB inventory of null elements is also adopted in TUT–Penn, but while for English null elements are mainly traces denoting constituent movements, in TUT–Penn they can play different roles: zero Pronouns, reduction of relative clauses, elliptical Verbs and also, as said before, the duplication of Subjects which are positioned after Verbs.

These two types of representation, i.e. TUT and TUT-Penn, are those used in our study (in Figure 2 the two formats are shown in parallel)[5]; the observations emerged during their comparison with respect to the alignment issue are described in Section 5.1.

3.2 Data set size and content

ParTUT includes 3,184 sentences corresponding to 85,821 tokens: 28,772 for Italian, 30,118 for French and 26,931 for English, organized in different sub-corpora and text genres, as outlined in Table 1. The content of each corpus varies from legal texts, namely legislative texts of European Community (JRCAquis)[6], to texts extracted from the proceedings of the European Parliament (Europarl)[7] and the Creative Commons license (CC)[8], from the Universal Declaration of Human Rights (UDHR)[9] to instructions on how to create a new Facebook account (FB) and multilingual transcriptions of TED talks[10] (WIT3)[11].

Although the limited size of the treebank, which is still far from being a representative resource of the languages involved, the variety of genres included in the collection also allows to detect some

[5] While for the implementation of the alignment tool we use data annotated with TUT labels but formatted in CoNNL tabs.

[6] `http://langtech.jrc.it/JRC-Acquis.html`

[7] `http://www.statmt.org/europarl/`

[8] `http://creativecommons.org/licenses/by-nc-sa/2.0`

[9] `http://www.ohchr.org/EN/UDHR/Pages/SearchByLang.aspx`

[10] `http://www.ted.com/talks`

[11] `https://wit3.fbk.eu/`

relevant linguistic phenomena and their regularity.

Corpus	sentences	tokens
JRCAcquis_It	181	5,984
JRCAcquis_En	179	4,705
JRCAcquis_Fr	179	6,580
UDHR_It	76	2,072
UDHR_En	77	2,293
UDHR_Fr	77	2,329
CC_It	96	3,252
CC_En	88	2,507
CC_Fr	102	3,097
FB_It	115	1,893
FB_En	114	1,723
FB_Fr	112	1,964
Europarl_It	505	14,051
Europarl_En	515	14,204
Europarl_Fr	480	14,480
WIT3_It	97	1,520
WIT3_En	92	1,499
WIT3_Fr	99	1,668
total	3,184	85,821

Table 1: Corpora and size of ParTUT

4 Data analysis

We applied several different analyses to the data using a set of tools which take, as input, data in the native TUT format. The assumptions of our analysis are based on preliminary studies (Sanguinetti and Bosco, 2012) on the presence, and their classification, of translation shifts in the dataset. The results of those studies had shown that, as expected, the highest number of shifts occurred essentially on the morpho-syntactic and, especially, structural level (see Section 5 for their description). In order to both support and integrate those preliminary studies, in the current analysis we focused our attention basically on the degree of structural complexity of the texts in the different languages, described in terms of word order and dependency distance (Hudson, 1995). We also selected these two metrics as they are good indicators of potential cross-linguistic differences and translational divergences, as well as discrepancies in the structural representation using different formalisms.
As a side effect of the application of these tools, we also obtained a validation and an improved quality of the data set.

4.1 Word order

As for the word order (whose statistics are summarized in Table 2), although the high number of contributions in literature on the matter, it is difficult to find quantitative and cross-language results about the behavior of languages with respect to the movement of major constituents within the sentence structure. A reliable and wide study about word order should be based on a carefully balanced very large dataset, and this goal is beyond the scope of this work. The limits of our analysis are those imposed by the limited size and content of the dataset currently available, the results obtained, however are in line with common knowledge on typical behaviours of English, Italian and French with respect to this issue.
In our analysis, we focused mainly on four elements, i.e. Verb, Subject, Object and Complement[12] and on their relative positions within the sentence. We excluded in advance from the analysis data such as marked structures, interrogative and relative clauses, or infinitival structures, in order to concentrate our attention on unmarked declarative clauses only. For the same motivations we did not consider expletive, progressive and passive structures. The remaining verbal structures consist of 782 clauses for English, 886 for French and 597 for Italian distributed within the three monolingual treebanks. The far smaller amount of verbal structures taken into account for Italian is motivated by the exclusion of structures affected by pro-drop, i.e. the absence of subject in finite clauses, which occurs 32.6% of unmarked declarative verbal structures.
The most frequent word order for all the three languages is the classical SVO, as assumed in literature (Dryer, 1998); however, if we focus our attention on the relative position of Subject and Verb, a typical issue that can be problematic for constituency-based formats, we can see that this phenomenon is quite rare in French (4.7%) and English (7.3%), but far more frequent in Italian (17.1%) verbal structures. Such figures, as far as Italian language is concerned, are in line with the results obtained in previous studies on the influence of the constituent order on data-driven parsing (Alicante et al., 2012), where the Subj/Verb order is attested at 79.10% and its inverted order

[12]We encompassed on the label Compl the Indirect Object, the Agent complement, predicatives and other indirect complements that act as arguments of the verb encountered.

at 20.90%.

Language	order	frequency
Italian (597)	Subj/Verb(/Obj)	74.5%
	Subject after Verb	17.1%
	Compl between	9.9%
French (886)	Subj/Verb(/Obj)	82.4%
	Subject after Verb	4.7%
	Compl between	9.4%
English (782)	Subj/Verb(/Obj)	88.5%
	Subject after Verb	7.3%
	Compl between	1.02%

Table 2: Word order in the ParTUT languages.

The well-known assumption that English is featured by a fixed word order, with respect to French or Italian, is clearly attested by our results also observing that in the former it is very rare that a Complement or an Object is positioned between Subject and Verb. In Italian and French various kinds of Complements can be positioned between Subject and Verb[13], thus making the structure more complex.

4.2 Dependency distance

Concerning the results obtained in the analysis of dependency distance, which is measured here as the distance between words and their parents in terms of intervening words (Hudson, 1995), we considered also its correlated measure, that of dependency direction, i.e the contrast between governor-initial (which means that the position number of the governor is lower than that of the dependent) and governor-final dependencies (see Table 3). In view of a comparison with a constituency representation, this measure is a good indicator of how the relationship between a dependent and its head, within a dependency framework, is still preserved despite their distance, and the direction of this distance. This seems even more important when we have to find correspondences between parallel parse trees in different languages.

The distance is reported in terms of percentage of dependencies, while the direction is expressed by the labels POS (POSITIVE, i.e. governor-initial cases) and NEG (NEGATIVE, i.e. governor-final cases). With respect to this matter, we observed that English has a higher number of dependency relations with governor-final cases (25.19%), although their distance is lower if compared to Italian and French. This could be easily explained by the higher frequency of English premodifiers, with respect to Italian and French.

Despite the small amount of data available for our experiments, from a comparison of the data for the Italian in ParTUT and those extracted from the TUT monolingual treebank[14] (a more extended dataset, with a different text composition from the multilingual treebank) there is a substantial similarity with respect to dependency distance and its direction (see the rightmost column in Table 3). In light of this, we expect similar results for English and French as well, once we can rely on a larger dataset.

Distance	En.	Fr.	It.	TUT
POS	74.81	81.91	81.01	76.65
POS <=10	98.12	97.89	97.72	97.88
10 > POS < 20	1.43	1.64	1.72	1.62
POS >= 20	0.45	0.47	0.56	0.49
NEG	25.19	18.09	18.99	18.59
NEG <=10	95.70	92.81	93.62	92.24
10 > NEG < 20	2.99	4.91	4.54	5.17
NEG >= 20	1.31	2.28	1.84	2.58

Table 3: The table shows statistics on dependency distance and direction distributed per language, with a comparison of Italian data of ParTUT with the overall figures extracted from the monolingual treebank TUT.

5 Translation shifts and their alignment

The search for matches between pairs of non-isomorphic trees requires an extended knowledge (whether formalized by a set of rules or learned automatically) on the divergences, or shifts, that may occur during the translation process. While designing our alignment system, we attempted in a first step to determine what types of shifts may be encountered in ParTUT. The classification was made on a sample of the treebank sentences extracted from each of the sub-corpora that compose the collection.

This comparison led to a first basic classification[15] which includes essentially three levels:

[13]Such complements are mainly in the form of clitics expressing a direct or indirect object ("***me l'ont demandé***" – *I was asked to*), or predicative complements ("*non **lo** sono mai*" – *they are never like that*)

[14]The treebank currently consists of 3,542 sentences and 102,150 tokens.

[15]It was difficult to establish a clear-cut disticntion for each

morpho-syntactic (*Category Shifts*) and syntactic level (*Strucutral Shifts*) on one hand, and that of meaning (*Semantic Shifts*) on the other[16].

Category Shifts may involve a change in the Part of Speech;

Structral Shifts are the most complex and include a number of different situations that can be determined both by linguistic constraints imposed by the respective languages, or, more simply, by individual translator's choice. Structural shifts may thus comprise cases of:

- different word order and discontinuous correspondences;
- passivization/depassivization;
- function word introduction/elimination;
- conflation (i.e. tre translation of two words using a single word equivalent in meaning);
- paraphrases; – idioms.

Semantic Shifts mainly concern the level of meaning; they include cases of:

- addition/deletion (i.e. the introduction or elimination of pieces of information);
- mutation (whenever the correspondence is characterised by a high degree of fuzziness, or the content substantially differs).

In order to handle properly with such divergences, we therefore designed an alignment system that starting from a lexical mapping of the nodes in the tree pair, it moves outwards to the unaligned nodes using the information available on syntactic structure, with a focus in particular on the argument structure (which, in ParTUT is applied to Nouns and Adjectives as well).

The algorithm, which is currently in a prototype implementation stage, includes two distinct steps, respectively referring to the lexical level and to syntactic dependencies.

Step 1: lexical correspondences are identified and stored in lexical pairs; the mapping of source and target nodes is carried out by means of a probabilistic dictionary created using the IMB Model 1 implementation in the Bilingual Sentence Aligner (Moore, 2002).

Step 2: starting from the lexical pairs obtained in the first step, correspondences between neighbouring nodes are verified comparing in parallel the respective relational structure, such that:

$$d_s > d_t \text{ if:}$$
$$(w_s;w_t)$$
$$rel\ (w_s;d_s) = rel(w_t;d_t)$$

where d_s and d_t are a source and a target node of a tree pair whose governors are the word w_s and its counterpart w_t; d_s and d_t can be aligned ($d_s > d_t$) whenever their governors are selected as anchor pair ($w_s;w_t$) during the lexical mapping step, and the syntactic relation $rel\ (w_s;d_s)$ between the source anchor word w_s and its dependent d_s is the same as $rel(w_t;d_t)$, i.e. that between the target anchor word w_t and its dependent d_t. This means that, for example, in the expressions "*no one*" – "*nessun individuo*", given the anchor pair (*no; nessun*), and the syntactic relations ARG(*no; one*) and ARG(*nessun; individuo*), then the alignment can be expanded to the dependents (*one;individuo*).

Our hypothesis is that tree alignment of dependency structures could work because, besides lexicon, it is based on predicative structure, which (provided that this is shared by the two parse trees) will remain stable in different languages despite variations in the realization of the constituents; as a result, whenever the algorithm attempts to search for correspondences between a source and a target dependency tree, it may be able to find, within a reasonable distance from the head of a predicative structure, the relations that make up that structure. This reasonable distance can be approximated by taking into account the elements we reported in the analysis on word order and dependency distance.

5.1 Constituency and dependency: cross-linguistic comparison

In the previous section, we described the overall framework of our alignment system; in this section, we attempt to describe its strengths and weaknesses while comparing trees in ParTUT as represented in the dependency-based TUT format and in the constituency-based converted format TUT-Penn. The comparison mainly deals with the types of shift introduced in Section 5. What emerged from this investigation is that the choice to compare sentence pairs considering their deep structure and relations, rather than grouping them together into constituents, can help

kind of shifts, especially when multiple divergences cooccurred. Their classification was made based on the predominant aspects that characterize each shift.

[16]This classification is similar in spirit to the work by Cyrus (2006), Dorr (1994) and Melčuk and Wanner (2006), and partially adopts their terminology and definitions. In particular, like in Cyrus (2006), we opted for maintaining the notion of *shift* as, in our view, particularly conveying the idea of the transfer that takes place during the process of transposition of meaning from one language to another.

to overcome some of the limitations imposed by such non-isomorphism. This proved true in the case of category shift. With respect to the classic case of nominalization, for example, while a hierarchical costituency representation gives rise to two different phrases, dependents identification of corresponding heads is facilitated by the fact that, as mentioned in Section 3.1, even Nouns are assigned a predicative structure. Dependents are therefore labeled as arguments of a same predicative structure, as in the example below[17]:

(1a) TUT:

1-improving[TOP] *2-the*[1;OBJ] *3-efficiency*[2;ARG]

1-l'[TOP] *1-amélioration*[1;ARG] *3-de*[2;OBJ] *4-l'*[3;ARG] *5-efficacité*[4;ARG]

(*The improvement of the efficiency*)[18]

(1b) TUT-Penn:

(VP (V *Improving*) (NP (ART *the*) (N *efficiency*)))

(NP (ART *L'*) (NP (N *amélioration*) (PP (PREP *de*) (NP (ART *l'*) (N *efficacité*)))))

As they include linguistic aspects of various nature, structural shifts require broader and more articulated considerations. On the one hand the dependency structure, and in particular the predicative structure as encoded in TUT, once again may be useful in overcoming translational divergences and reducing them to a common structure. This is the case, for example, for long-distance dependencies - which are difficult to represent as such in a phrase structure - but also for word order. Below we report an English-Italian bisentence that may exemplify this issue:

(2a) TUT:

1-the*[18;SUBJ]** *2-exchange*[1;ARG] *3-of*[2;RMOD] *4-information*[3;ARG] *5-on*[4;RMOD] *6-environmental*[9;RMOD] *7-life*[8;RMOD] *8-cycle*[9;RMOD] *9-performance*[5;ARG] *10-and*[5;COORD] *11-on*[10;COORD2ND] *12-the*[11;ARG] *13-achievements*[12;ARG] *14-of*[13;RMOD] *15-design*[16;RMOD] *16-solutions*[14;ARG] *17-is*[18;AUX] ***18-facilitated[TOP]

1-è[2;AUX] ***2-agevolato*[TOP] *3-uno*[2;SUBJ]** *4-scambio*[3;ARG] *5-di*[4;RMOD] *6-informazioni*[5;ARG] *7-su*[6;RMOD] *8-l'*[7;ARG] *9-analisi*[8;ARG] *10-di*[8;RMOD] *11-la*[10;ARG] *12-prestazione*[11;ARG] *13-ambientale*[12;RMOD] *14-di*[12;RMOD] *15-il*[14;ARG] *16-ciclo*[15;ARG] *17-di*[16;RMOD] *18-vita*[17;RMOD] *19-e*[7;COORD] *20-su*[19;COORD2ND] *21-le*[20;ARG] *22-realizzazioni*[21;ARG] *23-di*[22;RMOD] *24-soluzioni*[23;ARG] *25-di*[24;RMOD] *26-progettazione*[25;ARG]

(*is facilitated an exchange of information on the analysis of the environmental life cycle perfomance and on the achievements of design solutions.*)

(2b) TUT-Penn:

((S (NP (NP (ART *The*) (N *exchange*)) (PP (PREP *of*)(NP (NP (N *information*))(PP (PP (PREP *on*)(NP (NP (NP (N life)) (N *cycle*)) (NP (ADJ *environmental*) (N *performance*))))(CONJ *and*)(PP (PREP *on*)(NP (NP (ART *the*) (N *achievements*))(PP (PREP *of*)(NP (NP (N *design*)) (N *solutions*)))))))))(VP (V *is*)(VP (V *facilitated*)))))

((S (VP (V *é*) (VP (V *agevolato*)(NP (ART *uno*)(N *scambio*))(PP (PREP *di*)(NP (NP (N *informazioni*))(PP (PREP *su*)(NP (NP (ART *l'*)(N *analisi*))(PP (PREP *di*)(NP (ART *la*)(NP (N *prestazione*))(ADJP (ADJ *ambientale*)(PP (PREP *di*) (NP (NP (ART *il*) (N *ciclo*)) (PP (PREP *di*)(NP (NP (N *vita*))(CONJ *e*)(PP (PREP *su*)(NP (NP (ART *le*) (N *realizzazioni*))(PP (PREP *di*)(NP(NP (N *soluzioni*))(PP (PREP *di*)(NP (N *progettazione*))))))))))))))))))))))

The English sentence presents a standard Subj-Verb order, although their dependency distance (as measured with the tools used for analysis described in Section 4) equals to 17; on the contrary, its Italian counterpart shows a Verb-Subj order with a positive dependency distance of 1. While such figures affected the phrase structure representation, mainly because of the post-positioned Subject in the Italian version, this was not the case in dependency analysis, where the respective arguments of the corresponding verbs were appro-

[17]The examples are here represented in a compact form where only the major annotated information is shown: for each dependency node we provide information on *position-word[governorposition;relation]*, while for constituency only some phrase label is abbreviated. Each example reports a sentence pair where the source language is always English and the target language is Italian or French. Bold characters are used to highlight the dependency distance between a head and its dependent in the linear order of the sentence (see example 2a and 2b).

[18]The glosses for non-English examples are intended as literal and do not necessarily correspond to the correct English expression.

priately assigned, despite the high distance of the Subject from the main verb in English, thus preserving the parallelism between the two structures, and as a result, their alignment.

The same can be said for passivization, which can be easily detected and aligned by means of the explicit representation of deep relations. Considering the bisentence below, for example, a common predicative structure can be observed for the main verbs in the respective languages, although in the passive form surface syntactic roles are also expressed, so as to specify that the verb has undertaken a transformation: the surface Subject is thus linked to its predicate with the relation [OBJ/SUBJ], meaning that it corresponds to a deep Object. While in the phrase structure the arguments of the predicate are moved during transformation, resulting in a different realization.

(3a) TUT:

1-we$_{[2;SUBJ]}$ *2-allow*$_{[TOP]}$ *3-accounts*$_{[2;OBJ]}$

1-gli$_{[4;OBJ/SUBJ]}$ *2-account*$_{[1;ARG]}$ *3-sono*$_{[4;AUX]}$ *4-consentiti*$_{[TOP]}$

(*accounts are allowed*)

(3b) TUT-Penn:

((S (NP (PRO *we*)) (VP (V *allow*) (NP (N *accounts*)))))

((S (NP (ART *gli*) (N *account*)) (V *sono*) (VP (V *consentiti*))))

A more tricky cases are those of paraphrases, idioms and the conflation of two lexical items into a single item semantically equivalent. In Figure 2 we represented in a graphic form an example of paraphrase, where a Verb in English is expressed with a Verb followed by the nominalized form of the English Verb in Italian, and of an idiom in English and its translation in French. In the sub-class of idioms we also included multiword expressions: although their overall presence in the treebank is not so relevant (1,15% in Italian, 0,86% in French and 0,05% in English), it is a phenomenon that we should take into account, as they share with idioms the features of non-compositionality and an idiosyncatic use, which make them a very complex linguguistic phenomenon for several NLP tasks, not only in the alignment issue. It should also be pointed out that, despite the problematic identification of a multi-word unit, in the TUT format a number of these linguistic items are already recognized as such. This means that the aligner also can take advantage of this information, as it is provided in the annotation.

All the aspects mentioned here share some peculiarities that require particular consideration: the difficult identification of these cases, by virtue of both the absence of a direct lexical mapping and a different syntactic realization, may see the need to introduce a more extensive hierarchical notion, such as that of dependency substructure, or *treelet*, introduced in Ding and Palmer (2004)[19]. This could be useful in order to capture possible translational matches at a higher level, abstracting away from pure relations between individual nodes (supporting, though from a dependency perspective, what suggested in Hearne et al. (2007), also reported in Section 2).
Contrarily, for example, to Mel'čuk and Wanner (2006), where the level considered (i.e. the deep-syntactic structure, *DSyntS*) is abstract enough to avoid all types of lexical and syntactic divergences, the dependency format considered in this study, despite the explicit annotation of argumental roles, is more oriented to the representation of the surface dependency structure. The observations posed above, and the examples in Figure 2 suggested us the hypothesis that to overcome these limitations while attempting to map divergent (though translationally equivalent) structures, it is necessary to integrate the current alignment system with an additional layer of abstraction, such that:

$$d_{(s1,\dots,sn)} > d_{(t1,\dots,tn)} \text{ if:}$$
$$(w_s;w_t)$$
$$rel\,(w_s;d_{(s1,\dots,sn)}) = rel(w_t;d_t)$$

where n is the number of nodes comprised in the substructure, and $(w_s;\ w_t)$ is the lexical pair used as the closest anchor point from which the alignment can be expanded. This means that more than one node that goes down from w_s could be aligned to the subtree that goes down from d_s; i.e., for example, that in the expression given in Figure 2 "*to bring that home*" – "*pour vous faire comprendre*", given the anchor pair (*to; pour*) and the syntactic relations ARG(*to; bring*) and ARG(*pour; faire*) the descending nodes could then be aligned.

[19]As pointed out by the authors, the choice of the term *treelet* was made in order to avoid confusion with *subtree*, as treelets do not necessarily go down to every leaf.

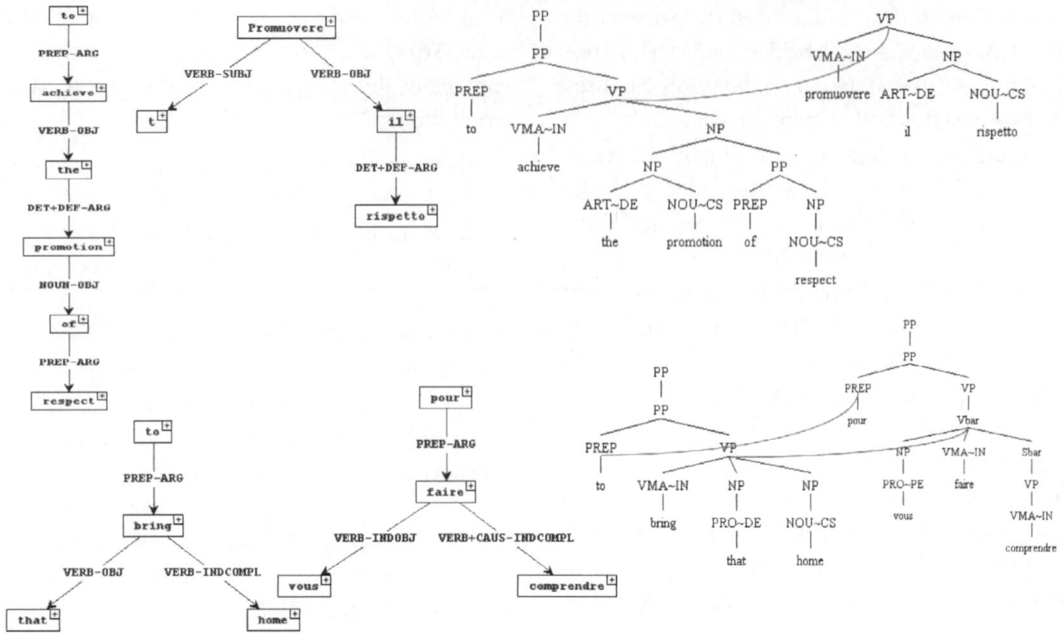

Figure 2: Graphic representations in TUT (on the left side) and TUT-Penn (on the right) of two tree pairs. The first reports a paraphrase in English, "*to achieve the promotion*", of a single Italian verb, "*promuovere*" ("*to promote*"); the second one represents an English idiom,"*to bring that home*", and its French translation, "*pour vous faire comprendre*" ("*to let you understand*"). While an alignment link can be drawn between the correspondent phrases in the constituency format, we are not able to do the same for the nodes in the dependency structures.

5.2 Discussion

Comparing the TUT dependency format to a converted version in the standard Penn Treebank, we came to the conclusion that a number of shifts could be handled with a simple approach that directly uses dependency relations expressed in the format at issue. Structural shifts when the same argumental roles are shared by the parallel trees, or wirh differences in the linear word order or distance are easily linked. However, other cases required a different treatment. Some classes of shifts, in particular those where divergences are due to differences in the idiosyncratic use between the languages or to the low compositionality of the expressions, may require the integration of a more abstract notion of substrucutre, or treelet (which can be partially assimilated to that of constituency subtree) in order to link the entire substructure to its equivalent node, that is to capture translational equivalence between these complex expressions and their counterpart in the other language. This seems to us a viable solution that could balance the limits imposed by the format with the useful linguistic information it provides.

6 Conclusion and future work

In this paper we presented a comparative study between dependency and costituency representation of parallel structures with the aim of verifiyng how and to what extent dependencies are a valuable support in the alignment task. The aim of our research, in fact, is laying the ground for the development of a more linguistically motivated treebank alignment system which could properly exploit linguistic information on dependency structures in order to handle properly translational divergences, or shifts, that may occur on different levels (morpho-syntactic, syntactic or semantic). The linguistic resource we used is a parallel multilingual treebank, ParTUT, where dependency representation is more oriented to the surface order of nodes in the input sentence, rather than a deep semantic representation. Besides the extension of the treebank, in order to make it a more balanced and reliable linguistic resource, the next steps in our research will consist in improving the implementation of the alignment system so that it could consider the notion of treelet, and, in a further stage, in testing more extensively this method also to other shifts, such as semantic shifts, which constitute an even greater challenge.

References

Anita Alicante, Cristina Bosco, Anna Corazza and Alberto Lavelli. 2012. A treebank-based study on the influence of Italian word order on parsing performance. In *Proceedings of the Eight International Conference on Language Resources and Evaluation (LREC'12)*, pp. 1985–1982.

Alena Böhmová, Jan Hajič, Eva Hajičová and Barbora Hladká. 2003. The Prague Dependency Treebank. In *Treebanks*, pp. 103-127, Springer Netherlands.

John C. Catford. 1965. *A linguistic theory of translation: An essay on applied linguistics*, University Press, Oxford.

David Chiang. 2007. Hierarchical phrase-based translation. In *Computational Linguistics*, volume 33, number 2, pp. 201–228, MIT Press, Cambridge, MA, USA.

Lea Cyrus. 2006. Building a resource for studying translation shifts. In *Proceedings of Language Resources and Evaluation Conference (LREC '06)*, Genoa, Italy.

Yuan Ding, Daniel Gildea and Martha Palmer. 2003. An algorithm for word-level alignment of parallel dependency trees. In *The 9th Machine Translation Summit of the International Association for Machine Translation*, pp. 95–101.

Yuan Ding and Martha Palmer. 2004. Automatic learning of parallel dependency treelet pairs. In *Proceedings of The First International Joint Conference on Natural Language Processing (IJCNLP-04)*, Hainan Island, China, pp. 233–243.

Bonnie J. Dorr. 1994. Machine translation divergences: a formal description and proposed solution. In *Computational Linguistics*, volume 20, number 4, pp. 597–633.

Matthew S. Dryer. 1998. Aspects of Word Order in the Languages of Europe. In *Constituent Order in the Languages of Europe*, pp. 283 - 319.

Mary Hearne, John Tinsley, Ventsislav Zhechev and Andy Way. 2007. Capturing translational divergences with a statistical tree-to-tree aligner. In *Proceedings of the 11th Conference on Theoretical and Methodological Issues in Machine Translation (TMI-07)*.

Richard Hudson. 1984. *Word Grammar*. Basil Blackwell, Oxford and New York.

Richard Hudson. 1995. Measuring syntactic difficulty. Unpublished paper. http://www.phon.ucl.ac.uk/home/dick/difficulty.htm

Yanjun Ma, Sylwia Ozdowska, Yanli Sun, Andy Way. 2008. Improving word alignment using syntactic dependencies. In *Proceeding of the Second ACL Workshop on Syntax and Structure in Statistical Translation (SSST-2)*, pp. 69–77.

David Mareček, Zdeněk Žabortský and Václav Novák. 2008. Automatic alignment of Czech and English deep syntactic dependency tree. In *Proceeding of the 12th EAMT Conference*, Hamburg, Germany.

Igor Mel'čuk. 1988 *Dependency Syntax: Theory and Practice.*. The SUNY Press, Albany, N.Y.

Igor Melčuk and Leo Wanner. 2006. Syntactic mismatches in machine translation. In *Machine Translation*, volume 20, number 2, pp. 81–138 .

Arul Menezes and Stephen D. Richardson. 2001. A best-first alignment algorithm for automatic extraction of transfer mappings from bilingual corpora. In *Proceedings of the Workshop on Data-driven Methods in Machine Translation at ACL-2001*, pp. 39–46.

Robert C. Moore. 2002. Fast and accurate sentence alignment of bilingual corpora. In *Proceedings of the 5th Conference of the Association for Machine Translation in the Americas: From Research to Real Users, (AMTA '02)*, pp. 135–144.

Silvia Ozdowska. 2005. Using bilingual dependencies to align words in English/French parallel corpora. In *Proceedings of the ACL Student Research Workshop*, pp. 127–132.

Manuela Sanguinetti and Cristina Bosco. 2012. Translational divergences and their alignment in a parallel treebank. In *Proceedings of the 11th Workshop on Treebanks and Linguistic Theories (TLT11)*, pp. 169 180.

Jörg Tiedemann. 2011. *Bitext alignment*. Morgan & Claypool.

Jörg Tiedemann and Gideon Kotzé. 2009. Building a large machine-aligned parallel treebank. In *Proceedings of the 8th International Workshop on Treebanks and Linguistic Theories (TLT '08)*, pp. 197-208.

John Tinsley, Ventislav Zhechev, Mary Hearne and Andy Way. 2007. Robust language pair-independent sub-tree alignment. In *Proceedings of the MT Summit XI*, pp. 467-474.

Martin Volk, Torsten Marek, Yvonne Samuelsson. 2011. Building and Querying Parallel Treebanks. In *Translation: Computation, Corpora, Cognition*, vol. 1, num. 1, http://www.t-c3.org/index.php/t-c3/article/view/8

Dekai Wu. 1997. Stochastic inversion transduction grammars and bilingual parsing of parallel corpora. In *Computational Linguistics*, volume 3, number 3, pp. 377–403.

Managing a Multilingual Treebank Project

Milan Souček **Timo Järvinen** **Adam LaMontagne**
Lionbridge
Finland
{milan.soucek,timo.jarvinen,adam.lamontagne}@lionbridge.com

Abstract

This paper describes the work process for a Multilingual Treebank Annotation Project executed for Google and coordinated by a small core team supervising the linguistic work conducted by linguists working online in various locations across the globe. The task is to review an output of a dependency-syntactic parser, including the POS types, dependency types and relations between the tokens, fix errors in output and prepare the data to a shape that can be used for further training of the parser engine. In this paper we focus on the implemented Quality Assurance processes and methodology that are used to monitor the output of the four language teams engaged in the project. On the quantitative side we monitor the throughput to spot any issues in particular language that would require intervention or improving the process. This is combined with a qualitative analysis that is performed primarily by comparing the incoming parsed data, the reviewed data after the first round and after the final cross-review using snapshots to compile and compare statistics. In addition, the possible inconsistencies in the annotations are checked and corrected automatically, where possible, in appropriate stages of the process to minimize the manual work.

1 Introduction

Multilingual dependency parsing has become an important part of dependency parsing tasks, mainly due to growing needs of the cross-language sources for supporting machine translation, search and retrieval and other natural language applications. Different approaches to processing multilingual data have been investigated in recent years and their outputs compared in a series of CoNLL shared tasks on multilingual dependency parsing (Buchholz and Marsi, 2006; Nivre et al., 2007; Surdeanu et al., 2008; Hajič et al., 2009). One of the possibilities for building multilingual parsers is training parsers from annotated data that was presented e.g. in models developed by McDonald et al. (2005) and Nivre et al. (2006). Preparing an annotated Treebank for training purposes is a resource-intensive task. For that reason, such tasks have to be planned and coordinated in such a way that the work is processed efficiently and unnecessary costs are eliminated. One manner of achieving efficiency is to prepare annotated data for multiple languages at the same time, which allows the data annotation provider to establish a consistent environment for creating and maintaining cross-language annotation guidelines and processes. In our current project, we are working with Google to review and prepare annotated data for training a multilingual parser using the Stanford typed dependencies model – a simple model represented by part of speech and dependency relation types recognizable across languages (de Marneffe and Manning, 2008).

The scope of this project covers manual review of 15 000 parsed sentences for each of four involved languages – German, French, Spanish and Brazilian Portuguese. For German, Spanish and French, a supervised training model is used for parsing the data before annotation (Zhang and Nivre, 2011). For Brazilian Portuguese, a cross-lingual parser is used (McDonald et al., 2011), where delexicalized model is trained on Spanish and French data with assistance of the part of speech tagger (Das and Petrov, 2011). Data corpus used for parsing is domain-based, the current scope of the project does not target representativeness. For German, French and Spanish, Wikipedia texts were used as the main data source, for Brazilian Portuguese, mainly news texts were included. Brazilian Portuguese also follows a different timeline and for that reason, we don´t present any results gained for this language in the current paper. Data are batched in groups of 100-500 sentences per file. The parsing system performs the tokenization of the data that separates punctuation as individual tokens. The pre-parsed data contains three levels of annotation: part-of-speech (POS) labels, binary dependencies between the tokens and dependen-

Proceedings of the Second International Conference on Dependency Linguistics (DepLing 2013), pages 292–297,
Prague, August 27–30, 2013.

cy relation labels (deprel). All these levels are reviewed and corrected in the process.
The number of dependency relations varies slightly between the languages. Some 51 to 57 labels are used. However, one of the targets of the project is to review the inventory of the relations to ensure uniform representation across the languages and some adjustments to the inventory of the dependency labels were made in the initial phase of the project.
Files are processed in PML format (Pajas and Štěpánek, 2006) using the Tree Editor TrEd 2.0 (Hajič et al., 2001) and CoNLL2009 stylesheet extension. In order to see the parser engine improvement and to be most efficient with the manual annotation, the data is processed in sprints made up of around 1500 sentences. Each sprint follows the cycle described in section 5 in this paper and its output is used for training the parser. Parser performance improves with each training and each manual annotation round requires less effort and time.

2 Initiating the project

A fundamental step for successfully running a multilingual language technology process is the planning phase. On the technical side, we concentrated on creating a consistent environment for processing the data, where all tools would be easily manageable by both the core team and the distributed linguists. A virtualized desktop environment is currently the most efficient environment for handling this kind of project. On the resourcing side, we built a multilingual team of linguists with expertise in the field of syntax. Our requirements for annotation experts emphasized candidates' target language knowledge (though, for syntax analyses, native knowledge is not strictly required) and linguistic studies background with special stress on studies in syntax and previous experience with the review and annotation work. Finally, for the actual work process, we created a model of cross-review annotation work, where two annotators work on manual annotation of the same set of data in two phases. Manual annotation is supported by automated validation tools that report statistics for evaluation of output data quality and annotators' throughput.

3 Maintaining consistency

In order to ensure technical and annotation consistency in the team that consists of several annotators per language, we developed processes that allow the team to work in a consistent environment and in a real-time online collaboration. Technical consistency is achieved by the use of a virtual machine for all project work. The possibility of instant communication allows the team to discuss actual problems related to annotation decisions and guidelines interpretation. This dynamic process is further supported by a secure online interface that contains all project data and documentation and that allows all project participants (including annotators, internal support team and product owner) to have full visibility of the production cycle and provide feedback on the tools, annotation process, output quality or any other specific aspect of the project.

3.1 Technical consistency

All work on the Multilingual Treebank Annotation Project is done in a virtual machine (Cloud), where annotators connect from their own distributed work stations via remote desktop client. This allows the core team to centrally manage the tools and support, allowing the participants to focus on the linguistic tasks. Also all project data is stored in secure data shares and is accessible at all times to the core team who can then make any necessary manipulations to the data and also easily manage the workflow progress.
In the cross-review work model, where multiple annotators are working on the same file, one of the challenges is to maintain version control. We use Tortoise SVN Version Control system to manage file versions. SVN is a powerful tool that helps to track the latest version of all files that are being worked on. It also has functions to compare different file versions and resolve conflicts between them. Finally, we use a centralized progress tracker, which is a macro-driven tool that collects statistics about processed data from annotators' individual tracking reports which are kept on the virtual server. The individual tracking reports calculate throughput and other statistics by task based on data input by the linguists. The centralized progress tracker collects the statistics from the individual reports (see example in Table 1). This data is used further for evaluation of the annotation progress for each language, as well as, with connection to quality check results, for evaluation of individual performance of each annotator.

French	All	Ann 1	Ann 2	Ann 3
Total A	1653	470	833	350
Total R	2135	150	1985	0
A Through	14,03	19,58	13,04	9,48
R Through	91,19	75	107,39	0
Total Hours	164	26	101	37

Table 1: Example of throughput statistics. The figures are the number of sentences processed by individual annotators (Ann 1, 2, 3) in the first annotation round (A) and in the review round (R). Throughput is expressed by amount of sentences processed per hour.

3.2 Annotation consistency

To ensure a high level of annotation consistency, we use a dynamic work model that includes introductory hands-on trainings for annotators, general guidelines for handling cross-language annotation scenarios, language specific annotation guidelines and a centralized team communication portal, where annotators discuss annotation problems and decisions (see also Figure 1). At the initial stage of the project, each annotator reviews language specific annotation guidelines and a sample Gold Standard annotations data. Hands-on training follows, where annotators work on actual parser output, collect questions and problematic cases and discuss them with the other team members in the discussion portal with specific reference to the language guidelines documentation. At this stage, problematic areas in dependency guidelines are reviewed and the master guidelines are updated with clarifications and annotation examples. Annotators also review each other's work and provide further feedback to the team about annotation errors observed. This annotation-review model complies with the double-review model described in section 5.

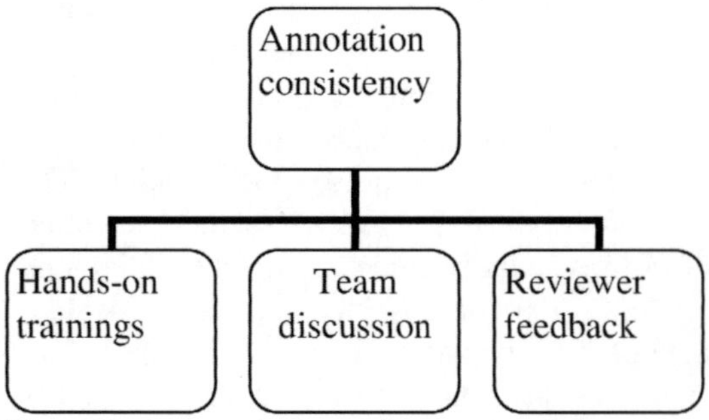

Figure1. Annotation consistency model.

During the initial project stage, usually after each annotator has processed about 500 sentences, the lead annotator for each language is identified, based on previous experience, work quality output and throughput speed. With guidance from the core team, the lead annotator is then responsible for coordinating team discussions and updating master guidelines documents. Lead annotators also review language specific guidelines for other languages and compare annotation decisions applied in their language with decisions for same or similar patterns used by other language teams. Result of this cross-language guidelines review opens up a dialog across teams and helps to further improve cross-language consistency. In the double-review work model, the lead annotator is mainly engaged in the review phase of annotation work, where data manually annotated during the first review round is reviewed for remaining consistency and human errors. This work model helps the team to achieve a consistent approach to annotating the data and minimizes inconsistency in the final output. In addition to dependency guidelines, annotators use a project-specific online discussion board, where they post questions and suggestions for preferred handling of annotation cases. Annotators can review also other languages' postings and comment on them as well as suggest general patterns handling for cross-language consistency.

4 Data validation

In addition to manual review, all files are validated using manual and automated validation tools. Automatic data validation consists of two parts – technical validation that is handled by an xml schema attached to each annotation file and linguistic validation that uses POS representation of deprel parent/child participants.

4.1 XML validation

For xml validation, we implemented lists of possible POS and deprel type labels for each language to xml schema that is attached to each pml file. POS and deprel labels appear as drop-down selections in the TrEd application, which eliminates a risk of incorrect label input, such as may occur if the labels were manually entered by the annotator. In case an invalid annotation label appears in the pml file, the TrEd application reports an error and the annotator can find and fix the label accordingly.

4.2 POS vs. deprel validation

Automated linguistic validation is based on possible combinations of POS participants in dependency relations (see Table 2 for example of validation tool settings). If the predefined POS representation for a deprel is violated in the data, the validation tool flags the item for review. The annotator can compare the validation results with annotated data to evaluate whether the error is valid and should be fixed or whether the error can be ignored for being an uncommon or exceptional combination of POS types in the particular deprel. POS representation for deprels is not absolute and we try not to over-define the representation in validation tool settings, in order not to miss obvious errors in output that might be hidden by too benevolent POS vs. deprel definitions. The validation tool results are therefore only approximate, but they can nevertheless show pattern errors or misinterpretation of deprel usage that might not be visible to annotators during manual review.

deprel	parent POS	current POS
amod	NOUN, PNOUN, ADJ	ADJ
aux	VERB	AUX

Table 2. Example of POS vs. deprel set-up for the linguistic validation tool. "parent POS" means the head of deprel for the current token, "current POS" means the POS of current token being validated.

We use linguistic validation tool results also as a source for relative statistical evaluation of data quality improvement during the annotation and review work on the data and for evaluating annotators' output quality. Assuming that the POS vs. deprel settings are consistent throughout the project, we can easily compare reported error rate between different stages of annotation work as well as between different annotators for each deprel label. For data improvement statistics, we take a snapshot upon receiving the data from the parser for a baseline reading, and then again after the manual annotation and finally after the annotation review. In addition to expected improvement in error rate between each stage, we can also compare results for each stage between different data batches to see e.g. improvement in parser output or expected error rate for the final annotated and reviewed file. Comparison of error rate for each annotator gives information about annotators' individual performance, in addition to their throughput speed. In terms of the data, this information helps to identify potential quality gaps, possible improvement areas in the guidelines and may give insight into the improvement of the parser in general. In terms of the language teams, statistical results provide insight about which annotators are good candidates for lead annotator and also give feedback about possible unwanted under-performance.

5 Data process cycle

We process the data in sprints of about 1500 sentences. Each sprint lasts about 2 weeks and all 4 languages follow the same sprint schedule, so that consistent amount of sentences can be delivered for all languages at the same time. The overall duration of the project was initially estimated for 22 weeks (11 sprints), including trainings, dependency guidelines development and manual annotation tasks. For the first three languages – French, German and Spanish, the project was also completed within the planned schedule, with the last batch of annotated data delivered at the end of 22nd week. For each project sprint, input data (natural sentences) are first parsed by the original version of the parser and converted to pml format. Parsed data is then pre-processed – the xml schema for each pml file is updated with an up-to-date list of annotation labels and systematic errors in parsed data are fixed by automated scripts. Systematic errors fixed in pre-processing are e.g. invalid and obsolete labels that were removed during the cross-language guidelines harmonization in the initial stages of the project. After automated fixes are done, the first linguistic validation snapshot is taken and statistics are reported. At this stage, pattern errors generated by the parser can be observed from validation results. The file is then assigned to an annotator for manual annotation with information about pattern errors present in the file. The annotator reviews the tree structure and syntactic labels (POS and deprel labels) and updates them, where necessary. Once manual annotation is done, a second validation snapshot is taken and statistics are reported. Validation results are shared with the reviewer, who works on their analysis and on fixing remaining errors in the input file. At this stage, quality feedback for annotator's work also is collected – both snapshot statistics and manually collected feedback from the reviewer serve as data for personal performance evaluation. After manual review of the input file, the third validation snapshot is taken and statistics are reported. Validation results are reviewed for any remaining errors, mainly for invalid annotation labels. Finally, text content of input sentences is compared between the original parsed and final reviewed file to fix any possible changes in content that are not allowed in this project. Final files are used for training the parser and another set of input data is parsed with the re-trained parser for further annotation work.

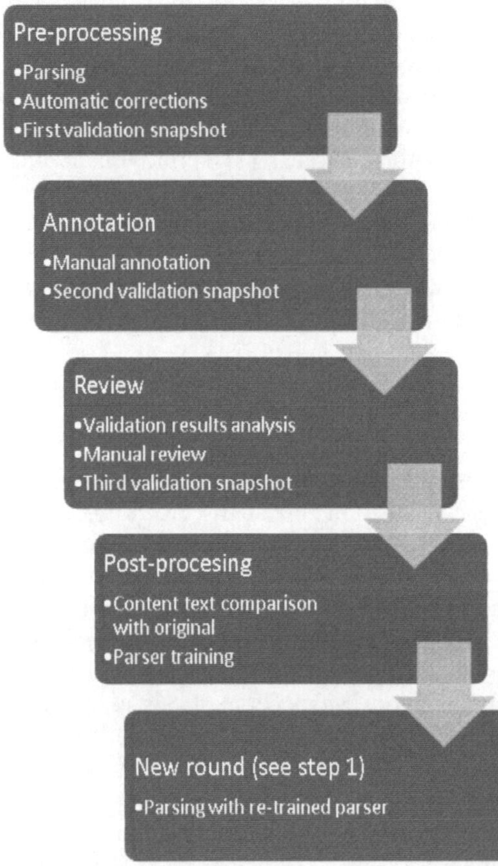

Figure 2. The parser training process cycle.

The goal of this cycle is to train the parser with batches of annotated data that improve the performance of the parser before it is used for parsing the next batch of sentences for annotation. Time, throughput and efficiency for manual annotation should improve with every new training and in every new annotation round. As a result of the training and improved parser output, a greater amount of data can be processed in the next sprint. Table 3 shows comparison of annotation throughput development for French, Spanish and German (since Brazilian Portuguese follows a different timeline in this project, comparable data was not available yet for this language). Batches represent sets of sentences received from pre-parsing. Batches marked with asterisk were pre-parsed with re-trained parser, which also reflects in throughput improvement. Other batches were pre-parsed altogether with the preceding batch and the throughput improvement reflects rather the learning curve of annotators´ individual performance. The drop in French and Spanish in Batch 6 was caused by addition of some targeted data for patterns that the parser did not treat correctly at that time (question sentences).

	French	Spanish	German
Batch1	13.00	8.91	13.94
Batch2*	23.00	14.97	23.63
Batch3*	26.50	20.88	24.05
Batch4	26.70	22.55	24.80
Batch5*	28.38	27.49	27.47
Batch6	25.52	25.56	29.37
Batch7*	30.32	27.56	43.52
Batch8	31.37	28.74	43.95

Table 3. Throughput development comparison for French, Spanish and German.

Summary

In the current paper, we presented an example of a workflow for a Multilingual Treebank Annotation Project work. We aim to provide consistency both in technical and linguistic output for the annotated data and to bring efficiency to manual processing of parsed input data. Validation and throughput tracking tools used in the project are examples of control tools for maintaining consistency, quality and efficiency in manual annotation work. As result of our initial tools and processes testing, we aim to improve our tools further by implementing e.g. lexical check tools for evaluating validity of POS annotation and more precise validation of POS vs. deprel representation. The project now continues with extended scope of languages and tasks. In our future reports, we plan to concentrate on presenting further results of the parser training process and comparison of language specific dependency guidelines.

References

Sabine Buchholz and Erwin Marsi. 2006. *CoNLL X shared task on multilingual dependency parsing*. In Proceedings of CoNLL.

Dipanjan Das and Slav Petrov. 2011. *Unsupervised Part-of-Speech Tagging with Bilingual Graph-Based Projections*. In Proceedings of ACL.

Jan Hajič, Massimiliano Ciaramita, Richard Johansson, Daisuke Kawahara, Maria Antónia Martí, Lluís Márquez, Adam Meyers, Joakim Nivre, Sebastian Padó, Jan Štěpánek, Pavel Straňák, Mihai Surdeanu, Nianwen Xue, Yi Zhang. 2009. *The CoNLL-2009 Shared Task: Syntactic and Semantic Dependencies in Multiple Languages*. In Proceedings of CoNLL.

Jan Hajič, Barbora Vidová-Hladká, and Petr Pajas. 2001. *The Prague Dependency Treebank: Annotation Structure and Support*. In Proceedings of the IRCS Workshop on Linguistic Databases, pages 105–114, Philadelphia, USA. University of Pennsylvania.

Marie-Catherine de Marneffe and Christopher D. Manning. 2008. *Stanford typed dependencies manual*.

Ryan McDonald, Koby Crammer, and Fernando Pereira. 2005. *Online large-margin training of dependency parsers*. In Proceedings. of ACL.

Ryan McDonald, Slav Petrov, and Keith Hall. 2011. *Multi-source transfer of delexicalized dependency parsers*. In Proceedings of the 2011 Conference on Empirical Methods in Natural Language Processing, pages 62–72, Edinburgh, Scotland, UK., July. Association for Computational Linguistics.

Joakim Nivre, Johan Hall, and Jens Nilsson. 2006. *Maltparser: A data-driven parser-generator for dependency parsing*. In Proceedings of LREC.

Joakim Nivre, Johan Hall, Sandra Kübler, Ryan McDonald, Jens Nilsson, Sebastian Riedel, and Deniz Yuret. 2007. *The CoNLL 2007 shared task on dependency parsing*. In Proceedings of EMNLPCoNLL.

Petr Pajas and Jan Štěpánek. 2006. *XML-based representation of multi-layered annotation in the PDT 2.0*. In Proceedings of the LREC Workshop on Merging and Layering Linguistic Information (LREC 2006).

Mihai Surdeanu, Richard Johansson, Adam Meyers, Lluís Màrquez, and Joakim Nivre. 2008. *The CoNLL-2008 shared task on joint parsing of syntactic and semantic dependencies*. In Proceedings of CoNLL.

Yue Zhang and Joakim Nivre. 2011. *Transition-based dependency parsing with rich non-local features*. In Proceedings of ACL-HLT.

An empirical study of differences between conversion schemes and annotation guidelines*

Anders Søgaard
Center for Language Technology
University of Copenhagen
DK-2300 Copenhagen S
soegaard@hum.ku.dk

Abstract

We establish quantitative methods for comparing and estimating the quality of dependency annotations or conversion schemes. We use generalized tree-edit distance to measure divergence between annotations and propose theoretical learnability, derivational perplexity and downstream performance for evaluation. We present systematic experiments with tree-to-dependency conversions of the Penn-III treebank, as well as observations from experiments using treebanks from multiple languages. Our most important observations are: (a) parser bias makes most parsers insensitive to non-local differences between annotations, but (b) choice of annotation nevertheless has significant impact on most downstream applications, and (c) while learnability does not correlate with downstream performance, learnable annotations will lead to more robust performance across domains.

1 Introduction

Syntactic structures in dependency parsing are moving targets. While intrinsic evaluations often give the impression that syntactic structures are carved in stone, in reality we have little evidence in favor of the structures we posit. While most linguists agree on how to analyze core syntactic phenomena, there is widespread disagreement about a number of cases. Do auxiliary verbs head main verbs? Do prepositions head their nominal complements? And how should we analyze punctuation?

Many dependency treebanks are created by automatic conversion from pre-existing constituency treebanks. Since there exist linguistic phenomena whose analyses linguist do not agree on, it comes as no surprise that different conversion schemes have been proposed over the years (Collins, 1999; Yamada and Matsumoto, 2003; Johansson and Nugues, 2007). The output of these schemes differ considerably in their choices concerning head status and dependency relation inventories (Schwartz et al., 2012; Johansson, 2013).

The number of languages for which we have several dependency treebanks, is limited (Johansson, 2013), but the availability of different tree-to-dependency conversion schemes raises the question of what scheme is better? So does the existence of different parsers relying on different linguistic formalisms, but whose output can be mapped to dependencies (Tsarfaty et al., 2012). But is the question of which is better really a meaningful question? Better at what?

Schwartz et al. (2012) propose to evaluate conversion schemes in terms of learnability. We argue that while learnability is relevant to assess the robustness of dependency schemes, the most important parameter when choosing conversion schemes in practice is down-stream performance. We cite Elming et al. (2013), who show that down-stream performance is very sensitive to choice of conversion scheme. We also suggest that derivational perplexity (Søgaard and Haulrich, 2010) is a less biased measure of robustness than learnability – at least the way it is measured in Schwartz et al. (2012).

The paper presents (a) an empirical analysis of distance between conversion schemes, (b) an

*Section 5 is joint work with Jakob Elming, Anders Johannsen, Sigrid Klerke, Emanuele Lapponi and Hector Martinez, published at NAACL 2013.

Proceedings of the Second International Conference on Dependency Linguistics (DepLing 2013), pages 298–307,
Prague, August 27–30, 2013. © 2013 Charles University in Prague, Matfyzpress, Prague, Czech Republic

Clear cases		Difficult cases	
Head	Dependent	?	?
Verb	Subject	Auxiliary	Main verb
Verb	Object	Complementizer	Verb
Noun	Attribute	Coordinator	Conjuncts
Verb	Adverbial	Preposition	Nominal
			Punctuation

Figure 1: Clear and difficult cases in dependency annotation.

analysis of the theoretical learnability of conversion schemes, (c) a complexity analysis of conversion schemes in terms of derivational perplexity, and (d) empirical evaluations of the downstream usefulness of conversion schemes. Section 2 introduces a few common conversion schemes and their linguistic differences. In our empirical analyses we will focus on standard conversions of the Wall Street Journal section of the Penn-III treebank of English (Marcus et al., 1993). Section 3 introduces three distance metrics defined over pairs of output dependency structures. The results presented in this section suggests that parser bias cancels out many of the differences between conversion schemes. Section 4 discusses the learnability and derivational perplexity of tree-to-dependency conversion schemes. Section 5 presents a series of experiments, evaluating the downstream performance of conversion schemes in negation scope resolution, sentence compression, statistical machine translation, semantic role labeling and author perspective classification. Section 6 concludes with a discussion of the analyses presented in the previous sections. In our experiments we will use the publicly available MATE parser (Bohnet, 2010). Obviously the downstream performance of a conversion scheme depends on the parsing model chosen and how syntactic features are incorporated in the downstream task, but we do not vary parser or syntactic feature representations in our experiments.

2 Tree-to-dependency conversion schemes

Annotation guidelines used in modern dependency treebanks and tree-to-dependency conversion schemes for converting constituent-based treebanks into dependency treebanks are typically based on a specific dependency grammar theory, such as the Prague School's Functional Generative Description, Meaning-Text Theory, or Hudson's Word Grammar. In practice most parsers constrain dependency structures to be tree-like structures such that each word has a single syntactic head, limiting diversity between annotation a bit; but while many dependency treebanks taking this format agree on how to analyze many syntactic constructions, there are still many constructions these treebanks analyze differently. See Figure 1 for a standard overview of clear and more difficult cases.

The difficult cases in Figure 1 are difficult for the following reason. In the easy cases morphosyntactic and semantic evidence cohere. Verbs govern subjects morpho-syntactically and seem semantically more important. In the difficult cases, however, morpho-syntactic evidence is *in conflict* with the semantic evidence. While auxiliary verbs have the same distribution as finite verbs in head position and share morpho-syntactic properties with them, and govern the infinite main verbs, main verbs seem semantically superior, expressing the main predicate. There may be distributional evidence that complementizers head verbs syntactically, but the verbs seem more important from a semantic point of view. Some authors have distinguished between the notion of functional (distributional) and substantive dependency heads (Ivanova et al., 2012).

Tree-to-dependency conversion schemes used to convert constituent-based treebanks into dependency-based ones also take different stands on the difficult cases. In this paper we consider four different conversion schemes: the Yamada-Matsumoto conversion scheme (Yamada) (Yamada and Matsumoto, 2003), the CoNLL (2007) format, the Stanford conversion scheme used in the English Web Treebank (Petrov and McDonald, 2012), and the LTH conversion scheme (Johansson and Nugues, 2007). The Yamada scheme can be replicated by running penn2malt.jar available at

```
http://w3.msi.vxu.se/~nivre/
research/Penn2Malt.html
```

We used Malt dependency labels (see online documentation). The Yamada scheme is an elaboration of the Collins scheme (Collins, 1999), which is not included in our experiments. The Stanford conversion scheme can be replicated using the Stanford converter available at

FORM$_1$	FORM$_2$	Yamada	CoNLL	Stanford	LTH
Auxiliary	Main verb	1	1	2	2
Complementizer	Verb	1	2	2	2
Coordinator	Conjuncts	2	1	2	2
Preposition	Nominal	1	1	1	2

Figure 2: Head decisions in conversions. Note: Yamada also differ from CoNLL in proper names.

	LTH	Stanford	Yamada
CoNLL	91.1%	89.7%	*92.7%*
LTH	-	89.7%	89.6%
Stanford	-	-	90.1%

Table 1: Unlabeled TED accuracies between conversion schemes

	LTH	Stanford	Yamada
CoNLL	6.05	5.70	*5.14*
LTH	-	6.85	7.06
Stanford	-	-	6.24

Table 2: L_1-distances between conversion schemes

`http://nlp.stanford.edu/software/stanford-dependencies.shtml`

The CoNLL 2007 conversion scheme can be obtained by running pennconverter.jar available at

`http://nlp.cs.lth.se/software/treebank_converter/`

with the 'conll07' flag set. The LTH conversion scheme can be obtained by running pennconverter.jar with the 'oldLTH' flag set.

We list the differences in Figure 2. It is clear from this list that the LTH scheme uses substantive heads more often than the other schemes. This makes sense as it was designed for downstream semantic role labeling (Johansson and Nugues, 2007). Somewhat surprisingly the scheme does not always lead to better semantic role labeling performance when relying on predicted syntactic parses, however (see Results).

3 Distance between schemes

We use three parse evaluation metrics to estimate distances between tree-to-dependency schemes.

The **NED scores** between pairs of gold annotated data using different conversion schemes give an empirical estimate of the coarser differences between the schemes. The NED scores between the Yamada scheme and the CoNLL and LTH schemes is 91.9-92.0%, for example, while the NED score between CoNLL and LTH is 93.9%. Interestingly, the NED between pairs of MATE outputs on our SMT tuning section (see Section 5.3) using different conversion schemes is 100% in all cases. This seems to indicate that differences in down-stream performance (see Table 4) should not be found in major theoretical differences, but rather small differences such as edge flippings and label granularity.

The **UA scores** (unlabeled attachment) punish edge flippings, and the fact that we observe low UA scores between conversion schemes support the above picture and also indicate that the differences are quite substantial. The overlap as measured by UA score between the Yamada and the CoNLL scheme is 78.9%, for example. These two schemes agree on the syntactic heads of about 4/5 words. The UA score between Yamada and LTH is 63.1%. Again we see that differences between gold annotated datasets using different conversion schemes are bigger than when comparing output pairs. **It seems that parser bias is canceling out differences between conversion schemes.**

We also report unlabeled **TED scores** (Tsarfaty et al., 2012) between output trees. TED is a three-step distance computation that first abstracts away from the directionality of head-dependent relations. In the second step, we separate the common and consistent parts of the two output trees, and in the third step we compute the tree-edit operations necessary to translate between the inconsistent subtrees. We use the SMT tune section again. The unlabeled TED accuracy between CoNLL and Yamada is 92.7%, and the L_1-distance is only 5.14. See tabels 1 and 2 for more results. The L_1-distances, together with the other metrics, suggest that CoNLL is more similar to the other conversion schemes than any other pair of schemes. See Figure 3.

	bl	Yamada	CoNLL	Stanford	LTH
DEPRELS	-	12	21	47	41
PTB-23 (LAS)	-	**88.99**	88.52	81.36*	87.52
PTB-23 (UAS)	-	90.21	90.12	84.22*	**90.29**
Neg: scope F_1	-	**81.27**	80.43	78.70	79.57
Neg: event F_1	-	76.19	72.90	73.15	**76.24**
Neg: full negation F_1	-	**67.94**	63.24	61.60	64.31
SentComp F_1	68.47	**72.07**	64.29	71.56	71.56
SMT-dev-Meteor	35.80	36.06	36.06	**36.16**	36.08
SMT-test-Meteor	37.25	37.48	37.50	**37.58**	37.51
SMT-dev-BLEU	13.66	**14.14**	14.09	14.04	14.06
SMT-test-BLEU	14.67	15.04	15.04	14.96	**15.11**
SRL-22-gold	-	81.35	83.22	**84.72**	84.01
SRL-23-gold	-	79.09	80.85	80.39	**82.01**
SRL-22-pred	-	74.41	76.22	**78.29**	66.32
SRL-23-pred	-	73.42	74.34	**75.80**	64.06
bitterlemons.org	96.08	**97.06**	95.58	96.08	96.57

Table 4: Results. *: Low parsing results on PTB-23 using Stanford are explained by changes between the PTB-III and the Ontonotes 4.0 release of the English Treebank.

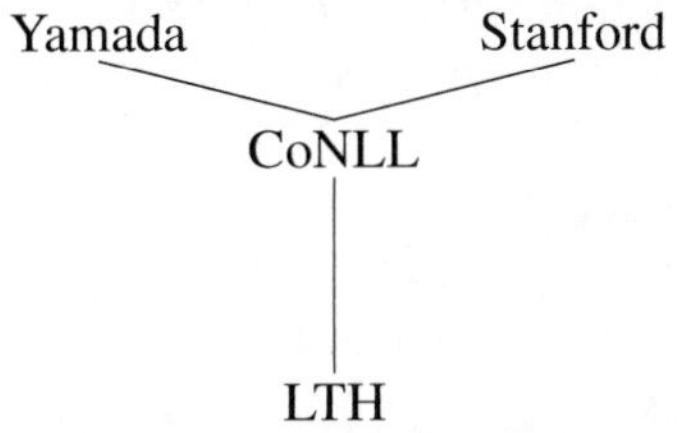

Figure 3: L_1-distances between conversion schemes

	gold		smt-tune	
	w-ppl	d-ppl	w-ppl	d-ppl
CoNLL	243.3	545.6	273.5	430.4
LTH	243.3	536.2	273.5	428.0
Stanford	243.3	541.9	273.5	425.4
Yamada	243.3	**520.8**	273.5	426.5

Table 3: Derivational perplexity of converted treebanks

4 Learnability and derivational perplexity

Schwartz et al. (2012) study the learnability of different conversion schemes, by relating choises concerning head status to parser performance. How does making prepositions head their complements affect parser performance, for example? The first two lines in Table 4 suggest, in line with Schwartz et al. (2012), that Yamada is more learnable than the other three schemes.

The derivational perplexity of a treebank T (Søgaard and Haulrich, 2010) is defined as the perplexity (per word) of the derivation language of $f(T)$, where $f(T)$ is the canonical derivation orders of the dependency trees in T: The derivation language of $f(T)$ is the set of strings $\sigma : w_1 ... w_n$ such that for any w_i, w_j $w_i \prec w_j$ in dependency structure d if w_i was attached to d in $f(T)$ prior to the attachment of w_j, according to their canonical derivation. Canonical derivations are also used to train transition-based dependency parsers, and we use the arc-eager algorithm in our experiments below (Nivre et al., 2007). We use a trigram language model with Knesser-Ney smoothing, replicating the setup in Søgaard and Haulrich (2010).

The results in Table 3 seem to indicate that the Yamada scheme is more learnable than the more recent ones, but again the differences seemed to be cancelled out by parser bias, and differences in derivational perplexity of the output (again using the tuning section of the SMT data) become insignificant. The reason for the absolute drop in numbers, as well as the drop in differences, is probably the shorter sentence length and more straight-forward syntax often associated with spoken language such as the parliament discussions in the Europarl data.

Learnability vs. derivational perplexity. Søgaard and Haulrich (2010) show that derivational perplexity correlates well with performance in multi-lingual parsing (using data from the CoNLL-X and CoNLL 2007 shared tasks), and therefore also with learnability (Schwartz et al., 2012). We think derivational perplexity is a better measure of performance robustness for two reasons: because it is a parser-independent metric, (i) derivational perplexities are not influenced by regularization, and (ii) derivational perplexities are not influenced by different parser biases. Changing a parameter in a tree-to-dependency conversion scheme may affect parser performance for several reasons: It is well known that adding features that never fire sometimes leads to improved performance with state-of-the-art parsers such as the MaltParser (Nivre et al., 2007), because regularization is sensitive to the total number of features, and it is not always clear whether a choice of head status leads to improved performance because the head choice is more learnable, or because it has an effect on regularization. Finally, annotation interacts with parser bias. Some choices of head status may be easy to learn for transition-based dependency parsers, but comparatively harder for graph-based ones. See McDonald and Nivre (2007) for an analysis of the biases of transition-based and graph-based dependency parsers. Since derivational perplexity is parser-independent we are not sensitive to regularization or parser bias, only to the choice of canonical derivation scheme.

5 Downstream performance

Dependency parsing has proven useful for a wide range of NLP applications, including statistical machine translation (Galley and Manning, 2009; Xu et al., 2009; Elming and Haulrich, 2011) and sentiment analysis (Joshi and Penstein-Rose, 2009; Johansson and Moschitti, 2010). Below we introduce five NLP applications where dependency parsing has been succesfully applied: negation resolution, semantic role labeling, statistical machine translation, sentence compression and perspective classification. We will then report on evaluations of the downstream effects of the four conversion schemes in these five applications, first published in Elming et al. (2013).

In the five applications we use syntactic features in slightly different ways. While our statistical machine translation and sentence compression systems use dependency relations as additional information about words and *on a par* with POS, our negation resolution system uses dependency paths, conditioning decisions on both dependency arcs and labels. In perspective classification, we use dependency triples (e.g. SUBJ(John, snore)) as features, while the semantic role labeling system conditions on a lot of information, including the word form of the head, the dependent and the argument candidates, the concatenation of the dependency labels of the predicate, and the labeled dependency relations between predicate and its head, its arguments, dependents or siblings.

5.1 Negation resolution

Negation resolution (NR) is the task of finding negation cues, e.g. the word *not*, and determining their *scope*, i.e. the tokens they affect. NR has recently seen considerable interest in the NLP community (Morante and Sporleder, 2012; Velldal et al., 2012) and was the topic of the 2012 *SEM shared task (Morante and Blanco, 2012).

The data set used in this work, the Conan Doyle corpus (CD),[1] was released in conjunction with the *SEM shared task. The annotations in CD extend on cues and scopes by introducing annotations for in-scope events that are negated in factual contexts. The following is an example from the corpus showing the annotations for cues (bold), scopes (underlined) and negated events (italicized):

(1) Since we have been so **un***fortunate* as to miss him [...]

CD-style scopes can be discontinuous and overlapping. Events are a portion of the scope that is semantically negated, with its truth value reversed by the negation cue.

The NR system used in this work (Lapponi et al., 2012), one of the best performing systems in the *SEM shared task, is a CRF model for scope resolution that relies heavily on features extracted from dependency graphs. The feature model contains token distance, direction, n-grams of word

[1] http://www.clips.ua.ac.be/sem2012-st-neg/data.html

REFERENCE:	Zum Glück kam ich beim Strassenbahnfahren an die richtige Stelle .
SOURCE:	Luckily , on the way to the tram , I found the right place .
Yamada:	Glücklicherweise hat auf dem Weg zur S-Bahn , stellte ich fest , dass der richtige Ort .
CoNLL:	Glücklicherweise hat auf dem Weg zur S-Bahn , stellte ich fest , dass der richtige Ort .
Stanford:	Zum Glück fand ich auf dem Weg zur S-Bahn , am richtigen Platz .
LTH:	Zum Glück fand ich auf dem Weg zur S-Bahn , am richtigen Platz .
BASELINE:	Zum Glück hat auf dem Weg zur S-Bahn , ich fand den richtigen Platz .

Figure 4: Examples of SMT output.

ORIGINAL:	* 68000 sweden ab of uppsala , sweden , introduced the teleserve , an integrated answering machine and voice-message handler that links a macintosh to touch-tone phones .
BASELINE:	68000 sweden ab introduced the teleserve an integrated answering machine and voice-message handler .
Yamada	68000 sweden ab introduced the teleserve integrated answering machine and voice-message handler .
CoNLL	68000 sweden ab **sweden** introduced the teleserve integrated answering machine and voice-message handler .
Stanford	68000 sweden ab introduced the teleserve integrated answering machine and voice-message handler .
LTH	68000 sweden ab introduced the teleserve **an** integrated answering machine and voice-message handler .
HUMAN:	68000 sweden ab introduced the teleserve integrated answering machine and voice-message handler .

Figure 5: Examples of sentence compression output.

Syntactic	constituent dependency relation parent head POS grand parent head POS word form+dependency relation POS+dependency relation
Cue-dependent	directed dependency distance bidirectional dependency distance dependency path lexicalized dependency path

Figure 6: Features used to train the conditional random field models

forms, lemmas, POS and combinations thereof, as well as the syntactic features presented in Figure 6. The results in our experiments are obtained from configurations that differ only in terms of tree-to-dependency conversions, and are trained on the training set and tested on the development set of CD. Since the negation cue classification component of the system does not rely on dependency features at all, the models are tested using gold cues.

Table 4 shows F_1 scores for scopes, events and full negations, where a true positive correctly assigns both scope tokens and events to the rightful cue. The scores are produced using the evaluation script provided by the *SEM organizers.

5.2 Semantic role labeling

Semantic role labeling (SRL) is the attempt to determine semantic predicates in running text and label their arguments with semantic roles. In our experiments we have reproduced the second best-performing system in the CoNLL 2008 shared task in syntactic and semantic parsing (Johansson and Nugues, 2008).[2]

The English training data for the CoNLL 2008 shared task were obtained from PropBank and NomBank. For licensing reasons, we used OntoNotes 4.0, which includes PropBank, but not NomBank. This means that our system is only trained to classify verbal predicates. We used the Clearparser conversion tool[3] to convert the OntoNotes 4.0 and subsequently supplied syntactic dependency trees using our different conversion schemes. We rely on gold standard argument identification and focus solely on the performance metric semantic labeled F1.

5.3 Statistical machine translation

The effect of the different conversion schemes was also evaluated on SMT. We used the *reordering by parsing* framework described by Elming and Haulrich (2011). This approach integrates a syntactically informed reordering model into a phrase-based SMT system. The model learns to predict the word order of the translation based on source sentence information such as syntactic

[2]http://nlp.cs.lth.se/software/semantic_parsing:_propbank_nombank_frames

[3]http://code.google.com/p/clearparser/

dependency relations. Syntax-informed SMT is known to be useful for translating between languages with different word orders (Galley and Manning, 2009; Xu et al., 2009), e.g. English and German.

The baseline SMT system is created as described in the guidelines from the original shared task.[4] Only modifications are that we use truecasing instead of lowercasing and recasing, and allow training sentences of up to 80 words. We used data from the English-German restricted task: $\sim$3M parallel words of news, $\sim$46M parallel words of Europarl, and $\sim$309M words of monolingual Europarl and news. We use newstest2008 for tuning, newstest2009 for development, and newstest2010 for testing. Distortion limit was set to 10, which is also where the baseline system performed best. The phrase table and the lexical reordering model is trained on the union of all parallel data with a max phrase length of 7, and the 5-gram language model is trained on the entire monolingual data set.

We test four different experimental systems that only differ with the baseline in the addition of a syntactically informed reordering model. The baseline system was one of the tied best performing system in the WMT 2011 shared task on this dataset. The four experimental systems have reordering models that are trained on the first 25,000 sentences of the parallel news data that have been parsed with each of the tree-to-dependency conversion schemes. The reordering models condition reordering on the word forms, POS, and syntactic dependency relations of the words to be reordered, as described in Elming and Haulrich (2011). The paper shows that while reordering by parsing leads to significant improvements in standard metrics such as BLEU (Papineni et al., 2002) and METEOR (Lavie and Agarwal, 2007), improvements are more spelled out with human judgements. All SMT results reported below are averages based on 5 MERT runs following Clark et al. (2011).

5.4 Sentence compression

Sentence compression is a restricted form of sentence simplification with numerous usages, including text simplification, summarization and recognizing textual entailment. The most commonly used dataset in the literature is the Ziff-Davis corpus.[5] A widely used baseline for sentence compression experiments is the two models introduced in Knight and Marcu (2002): the noisy-channel model and the decision tree-based model. Both are tree-based methods that find the most likely compressed syntactic tree and outputs the yield of this tree. McDonald et al. (2006) instead use syntactic features to directly find the most likely compressed sentence.

Here we learn a discriminative HMM model (Collins, 2002) of sentence compression using MIRA (Crammer and Singer, 2003), comparable to previously explored models of noun phrase chunking. Our model is thus neither tree-based nor sentence-based. Instead we think of sentence compression as a sequence labeling problem. We compare a model informed by word forms and predicted POS with models also informed by predicted dependency labels. The baseline feature model conditions emission probabilities on word forms and POS using a ± 2 window and combinations thereoff. The augmented syntactic feature model simply adds dependency labels within the same window.

5.5 Perspective classification

Finally, we include a document classification dataset from Lin and Hauptmann (2006).[6] The dataset consists of blog posts posted at bitterlemons.org by Israelis and Palestinians. The bitterlemons.org website is set up to "contribute to mutual understanding through the open exchange of ideas." In the dataset, each blog post is labeled as either Israeli or Palestinian. Our baseline model is just a standard bag-of-words model, and the system adds dependency triplets to the bag-of-words model in a way similar to Joshi and Penstein-Rose (2009). We do not remove stop words, since perspective classification is similar to authorship attribution, where stop words are known to be informative. We evaluate performance doing cross-validation over the official training data, setting the parameters of our learning algorithm for each fold doing cross-validation over the actual training data. We used soft-margin support vector machine learning (Cortes and Vapnik, 1995), tuning the kernel (linear or polynomial with degree 3) and $C = \{0.1, 1, 5, 10\}$.

[4] http://www.statmt.org/wmt11/translation-task.html

[5] LDC Catalog No.: LDC93T3A.

[6] https://sites.google.com/site/weihaolinatcmu/data

5.6 Results

Our results are presented in Table 4. The parsing results are obtained relying on predicted POS rather than, as often done in the dependency parsing literature, relying on gold-standard POS. Note that they comply with the result in Schwartz et al. (2012) that Yamada annotation is more easily learnable.

The **negation resolution** results are significantly better using syntactic features in Yamada annotation. It is not surprising that a syntactically oriented conversion scheme performs well in this task.

The case-sensitive BLEU evaluation of the **SMT** systems indicates that choice of conversion scheme has no significant impact on overall performance. The difference to the baseline system is significant ($p < 0.01$), showing that the reordering model leads to improvement using any of the schemes. Differences between schemes are insignificant. The reason probably is that long-distance differences between the schemes are cancelled out by parser bias. However, the conversion schemes lead to very different translations. This can be seen, for example, by the fact that the (normalized) string edit distance between translations of different syntactically informed SMT systems is 12% higher than within each system (across different MERT optimizations).

The reordering approach puts a lot of weight on the syntactic dependency relations. As a consequence, the number of relation types used in the conversion schemes proves important. Consider the example in Figure 4. German requires the verb in second position (V2), which is picked up by the Stanford and LTH systems. Interestingly, the four schemes produce virtually identical structures for the source sentence, but they differ in their labeling. Where CoNLL and Yamada use the same relation for the first two constituents (ADV and vMOD, respectively), Stanford and LTH distinguish between them (ADVMOD/PREP and ADV/LOC). This distinction may be what enables learning V2 translations, since the model may learn to move the verb after the sentence adverbial. In the other schemes, sentence adverbials are not distinguished from locational adverbials. Generally, Stanford and LTH have more than twice as many relation types as the other schemes.

The schemes Stanford and LTH lead to better **SRL** performance than CoNLL and Yamada when relying on gold-standard syntactic dependency trees. This supports the claims put forward in Johansson and Nugues (2007). These annotations also happen to use a larger set of dependency labels, however, and syntactic structures may be harder to reconstruct, as reflected by labeled attachment scores (LAS) in syntactic parsing. The biggest drop in SRL performance going from gold-standard to predicted syntactic trees is clearly for the LTH scheme, at an average 17.8% absolute loss (Yamada 5.8%; CoNLL 6.8%; Stanford 5.5%; LTH 17.8%).

The Stanford scheme resembles LTH in most respects, but in preposition-noun dependencies it marks the preposition as the head rather than the noun. This is an important difference for SRL, because semantic arguments are often nouns embedded in prepositional phrases, like agents in passive constructions. It may also be that the difference in performance is simply explained by the syntactic analysis of prepositional phrases being easier to reconstruct.

The **sentence compression** results are generally much better than the models proposed in Knight and Marcu (2002). Their noisy channel model obtains an F_1 compression score of 14.58%, whereas the decision tree-based model obtains an F_1 compression score of 31.71%. While F_1 scores should be complemented by human judgements, as there are typically many good sentence compressions of any source sentence, we believe that error reductions of more than 50% indicate that the models used here (though previously unexplored in the literature) are fully competitive with state-of-the-art models.

We also see that the models using syntactic features perform better than our baseline model, except for the model using CoNLL dependency annotation. This may be surprising to some, since distributional information is often considered important in sentence compression (Knight and Marcu, 2002). Some output examples are presented in Figure 5. Unsurprisingly, it is seen that the baseline model produces grammatically incorrect output, and that most of our syntactic models correct the error leading to ungrammaticality. The model using Stanford annotation is an exception. We also see that CoNLL introduces another error. We believe that this is due to the way the CoNLL tree-to-dependency conversion scheme handles coordination. While the word

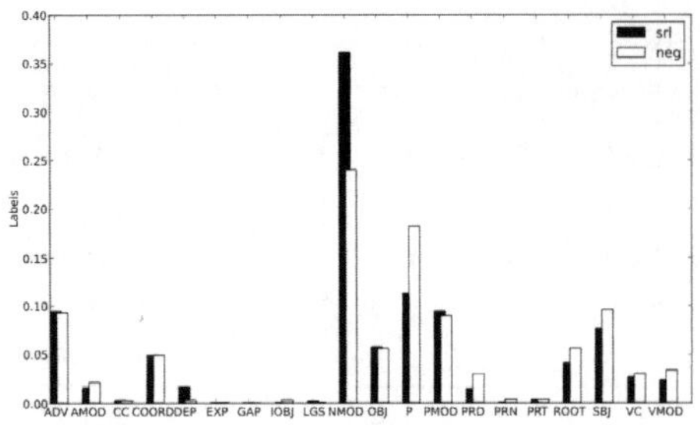

Figure 7: Distributions of dependency labels in the Yamada-Matsumoto scheme

Sweden is not coordinated, it occurs in a context, surrounded by commas, that is very similar to coordinated items.

In **perspective classification** we see that syntactic features based on Yamada and LTH annotations lead to improvements, with Yamada leading to slightly better results than LTH. The fact that a syntactically oriented conversion scheme leads to the best results may reflect that perspective classification, like authorship attribution, is less about content than stylistics.

While LTH seems to lead to the overall best results, we stress the fact that the five tasks considered here are incommensurable. What is more interesting is that, task to task, results are so different. The semantically oriented conversion schemes, Stanford and LTH, lead to the best results in SRL, but with a significant drop for LTH when relying on predicted parses, while the Yamada scheme is competitive in the other four tasks. This may be because distributional information is more important in these tasks than in SRL.

The distribution of dependency labels seems relatively stable across applications, but differences in data may of course also affect the usefulness of different annotations. Note that CoNLL leads to very good results for negation resolution, but bad results for SRL. See Figure 7 for the distribution of labels in the CoNLL conversion scheme on the SRL and negation scope resolution data. Many differences relate to differences in sentence length. The negation resolution data is literary text with shorter sentences, which therefore uses more punctuation and has more root dependencies than newspaper articles. On the other hand we do see very few predicate dependencies in the SRL data. This may affect down-stream results when classifying verbal predicates in SRL.

We also note that the number of dependency labels have less impact on results in general than we would have expected. The number of dependency labels and the lack of support for some of them may explain the drop with predicted syntactic parses in our SRL results, but generally we obtain our best results with Yamada and LTH annotations, which have 12 and 41 dependency labels, respectively.

6 Discussion and conclusion

In our experiments we made several observations. Available tree-to-dependency conversion schemes are very different. On the other hand we saw that many of the non-local differences between conversion schemes are not learned by state-of-the-art parsers, making parser output across conversion schemes less different from gold annotations. This suggests that only more local differences are important for downstream performance, which may also explain the small differences observed in our SMT experiments.

While the CoNLL scheme is very learnable (Schwartz et al., 2012), second to Yamada, downstream performance suggest that it is a suboptimal conversion scheme. The Yamada scheme is both very learnable (1st), leads to very good downstream performance (1st or 2nd in 4/5 downstream applications), and it has low derivational perplexity. We have argued that this is a better metric for performance robustness than learnability.

Note that our results extend beyond dependency parsing. Ivanova et al. (2012) show that converted dependency structures bear similarities to both Stanford dependencies and DELPH-IN syntactic derivation structures, but they are not explicit about what conversion scheme was used.

In future work we would like to combine the different methodologies discussed here to be able to learn robust annotation for given end applications that optimize end performance.

References

Bernd Bohnet. 2010. Top accuracy and fast dependency parsing is not a contradiction. In *COLING*.

Jonathan H. Clark, Chris Dyer, Alon Lavie, and Noah A. Smith. 2011. Better hypothesis testing for statistical machine translation: controlling for optimizer instability. In *ACL*.

Mike Collins. 1999. *Head-driven statistical models*

for natural language parsing. Ph.D. thesis, University of Pennsylvania.

Michael Collins. 2002. Discriminative training methods for Hidden Markov Models. In *EMNLP*.

Corinna Cortes and Vladimir Vapnik. 1995. Support-vector networks. *Machine Learning*, 20(3):273–297.

Koby Crammer and Yoram Singer. 2003. Ultraconservative algorithms for multiclass problems. In *JMLR*.

Jakob Elming and Martin Haulrich. 2011. Reordering by parsing. In *Proceedings of International Workshop on Using Linguistic Information for Hybrid Machine Translation (LIHMT-2011)*.

Jakob Elming, Anders Johannsen, Sigrid Klerke, Emanuele Lapponi, Hector Martinez Alonso, and Anders Søgaard. 2013. Down-stream effects of tree-to-dependency conversions. In *NAACL*.

Michel Galley and Christopher Manning. 2009. Quadratic-time dependency parsing for machine translation. In *ACL*.

Angelina Ivanova, Stephan Oepen, Lilja Øvrelid, and Dan Flickinger. 2012. Who did what to whom? a contrastive study of syntactico-semantic dependencies. In *LAW*.

Richard Johansson and Alessandro Moschitti. 2010. Syntactic and semantic structure for opinion expression detection. In *CoNLL*.

Richard Johansson and Pierre Nugues. 2007. Extended constituent-to-dependency conversion for English. In *NODALIDA*.

Richard Johansson and Pierre Nugues. 2008. Dependency-based syntactic-semantic analysis with propbank and nombank. In *CoNLL*.

Richard Johansson. 2013. Training parsers on incompatible treebanks. In *NAACL*.

Mahesh Joshi and Carolyn Penstein-Rose. 2009. Generalizing dependency features for opinion mining. In *ACL*.

Kevin Knight and Daniel Marcu. 2002. Summarization beyond sentence extraction: a probabilistic approach to sentence compression. *Artificial Intelligence*, 139:91–107.

Emanuele Lapponi, Erik Velldal, Lilja Øvrelid, and Jonathon Read. 2012. UiO2: Sequence-labeling negation using dependency features. In **SEM*.

Alon Lavie and Abhaya Agarwal. 2007. Meteor: an automatic metric for mt evaluation with high levels of correlation with human judgments. In *WMT*.

Wei-Hao Lin and Alexander Hauptmann. 2006. Are these documents written from different perspectives? In *COLING-ACL*.

Mitchell Marcus, Mary Marcinkiewicz, and Beatrice Santorini. 1993. Building a large annotated corpus of English: the Penn Treebank. *Computational Linguistics*, 19(2):313–330.

Ryan McDonald and Joakim Nivre. 2007. Characterizing the errors of data-driven dependency parsers. In *EMNLP-CoNLL*.

Ryan McDonald. 2006. Discriminative sentence compression with soft syntactic evidence. In *EACL*.

Roser Morante and Eduardo Blanco. 2012. *sem 2012 shared task: Resolving the scope and focus of negation. In **SEM*.

Roser Morante and Caroline Sporleder. 2012. Modality and negation: An introduction to the special issue. *Computational linguistics*, 38(2):223–260.

Joakim Nivre, Johan Hall, Sandra Kübler, Ryan McDonald, Jens Nilsson, Sebastian Riedel, and Deniz Yuret. 2007. The CoNLL 2007 Shared Task on Dependency Parsing. In *Proceedings of the CoNLL Shared Task Session of EMNLP-CoNLL 2007*, pages 915–932, Prague, Czech Republic.

Kishore Papineni, Salim Roukus, Todd Ward, and Wei-Jing Zhu. 2002. BLEU: a method for automatic evaluation of machine translation. In *Proceedings of the 40th Annual Meeting of the Association for Computational Linguistics*, pages 311–318, Philadelphia, Pennsylvania.

Slav Petrov and Ryan McDonald. 2012. Overview of the 2012 Shared Task on Parsing the Web. In *Notes of the First Workshop on Syntactic Analysis of Non-Canonical Language (SANCL)*.

Roy Schwartz, Omri Abend, and Ari Rappoport. 2012. Learnability-based syntactic annotation design. In *COLING*.

Anders Søgaard and Martin Haulrich. 2010. On the derivation perplexity of treebanks. In *TLT*.

Reut Tsarfaty, Joakim Nivre, and Evelina Andersson. 2012. Cross-framework evaluation for statistical parsing. In *EACL*.

Erik Velldal, Lilja Øvrelid, Jonathon Read, and Stephan Oepen. 2012. Speculation and negation: Rules, rankers, and the role of synta. *Computational linguistics*, 38(2):369–410.

Peng Xu, Jaeho Kang, Michael Ringgaard, and Franz Och. 2009. Using a dependency parser to improve SMT for subject-object-verb languages. In *Proceedings of the North American Chapter of the Association for Computational Linguistics - Human Language Technologies (NAACL-HLT) 2009*, pages 245–253, Boulder, Colorado.

Hiroyasu Yamada and Yuji Matsumoto. 2003. Statistical dependency analysis with support vector machines. In *Proceedings of the 8th International Workshop on Parsing Technologies*, pages 195–206, Nancy, France.

Author Index

Association for Computational Linguistics
209 N. Eighth Street
Stroudsburg, Pennsylvania 18360

CURRAN ASSOCIATES INC
proceedings.com